Burton Johnson
1/12/06
Barnes & Noble
Oceanside, CA

D1554616

Jacob L. Devers

AMERICAN WARRIORS

Throughout the nation's history, numerous men and women of all ranks and branches of the U.S. military have served their country with honor and distinction. During times of war and peace, there are individuals whose exemplary achievements embody the highest standards of the U.S. armed forces. The aim of the American Warriors series is to examine the unique historical contributions of these individuals, whose legacies serve as enduring examples for soldiers and citizens alike. The series will promote a deeper and more comprehensive understanding of the U.S. armed forces.

SERIES EDITOR: Roger Cirillo

An AUSA Book

JACOB L. DEVERS

A GENERAL'S LIFE

JAMES SCOTT WHEELER

FOREWORD BY RICK ATKINSON

UNIVERSITY PRESS OF KENTUCKY

Scholarly publisher for the Commonwealth,
serving Bellarmine University, Berea College, Centre College of Kentucky,
Eastern Kentucky University, The Filson Historical Society, Georgetown
College, Kentucky Historical Society, Kentucky State University,
Morehead State University, Murray State University, Northern Kentucky
University, Transylvania University, University of Kentucky, University of
Louisville, and Western Kentucky University.
All rights reserved.

Editorial and Sales Offices: The University Press of Kentucky
663 South Limestone Street, Lexington, Kentucky 40508-4008
www.kentuckypress.com

All maps appear courtesy of the U.S. Army, Center for Military History.

Library of Congress Cataloging-in-Publication Data

Wheeler, James Scott, author.
  Jacob L. Devers : a general's life / James Scott Wheeler ; foreword by Rick
Atkinson.
      pages cm. — (American warriors)
  Includes bibliographical references and index.
  ISBN 978-0-8131-6602-5 (hardcover : alk. paper) —
  ISBN 978-0-8131-6603-2 (pdf : alk. paper) —
  ISBN 978-0-8131-6604-9 (epub : alk. paper)
  1. Devers, Jacob L. (Jacob Loucks), 1887-1979. 2. Generals—United
States—Biography. 3. World War, 1939-1945—Biography. 4. United States.
Army—Biography. I. Title.
  E745.D48W48 2015
  355.0092—dc23
  [B]   2015028410

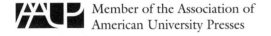

To Jane Ennis Wheeler

and

Georgie Lyon Devers,

and to all army spouses

Contents

Photographs follow page 268

Foreword

No senior American general from World War II has been forgotten more quickly or with less justice than Jacob Loucks Devers. In the final drive to liberate western Europe from Nazi occupation, he was one of only three army group commanders under Dwight D. Eisenhower (the others being the more enduringly famous Bernard Law Montgomery and Omar N. Bradley). Among top Allied commanders, no one showed a surer touch than Devers at handling recalcitrant foreign subordinates. His Sixth Army Group—an amalgam of American and French forces—swept into southern France and up the Rhône River valley, traversing the Vosges Mountains in the early winter of 1944 and standing on the west bank of the Rhine four months before Montgomery and Bradley would reach that milestone. That feat alone should have guaranteed Devers's reputation, even without his signal contributions to the Allied cause earlier in the war and in the subsequent conquest of southwestern Germany and western Austria.

James Scott Wheeler has given us the first complete portrait of Devers, from his boyhood in central Pennsylvania to West Point—where his classmates included George S. Patton—to his service as a young officer during World War I and then in the struggling, neglected interwar U.S. Army. A gifted artilleryman and administrator, Devers was among the youngest army officers to become a general. As chief of the Armored Force for two years, he helped modernize a tank arm rife with traditionalists nostalgic for the horse; under his energetic, creative supervision the force grew from two armored divisions to sixteen, plus sixty-three separate tank battalions. "I made a lot of mistakes today," he would tell subordinates during maneuvers. "So did you." In May 1943 he became commander of American forces in Europe and remained in that post until Eisenhower arrived in London from the Mediterranean to lead Operation Overlord, the invasion of Normandy. Devers then moved south, overseeing U.S. forces in Italy and the Allied juggernaut of twelve American and eleven French divisions that eventually cleared Alsace, reduced the Colmar pocket, jumped the Rhine, and crushed the last enemy diehards in the spring of 1945.

Wheeler's comprehensive account documents all this and more, including how a capable and decisive commander also had a knack for provoking the enmity of his peers. Devers and Mark W. Clark, the senior U.S.

field commander in Italy, detested each other to the point of not speaking. Former classmate Patton called Devers "a very small caliber man," while Bradley dismissed him as "egotistical, shallow, intolerant, not very smart, and much too inclined to rush off half-cocked." Eisenhower, in a private assessment for the Pentagon, ranked Devers twenty-fourth among thirty-eight senior American generals in Europe. "He has not, so far," Eisenhower wrote, "produced among the seniors of the American organization here the feeling of trust and confidence that is so necessary to continued success."

Surely such disparagement sold the man short. The top American airman in the Mediterranean, Lieutenant General Ira C. Eaker, considered Devers "the ablest commander I saw in the war." His talent for reconciling national differences and forging an effective Allied military coalition anticipated the skills needed by successful officers of a later generation. He was an innovative, forceful leader whose role in the final victory over the Third Reich was consequential if not profound.

Jake Devers lived a long, eventful life, but by the time he died in October 1979, at age ninety-two, that life was already being forgotten by the country he had served well. Now he has the biography he deserves.

Rick Atkinson

Introduction

Jacob Loucks Devers was the second highest ranking American general to serve in the European theater of operations (ETO) during the Second World War. Only General Dwight D. Eisenhower was senior to him. Devers was the commanding general of two American theaters of operations during the war—the European theater in 1943 and the Mediterranean theater in 1944. He finished his service in Europe as commanding general of Sixth Army Group, one of Ike's two American army groups in France. The other, Twelfth Army Group, was commanded by Omar Bradley. Devers was promoted to full general before Bradley was, and after the war he commanded the Army Ground Forces in the United States. He retired in 1949 after forty years of service.

Devers contributed as much as any American commander to the victory in Europe, with the exception of Eisenhower. For this reason alone he deserves a comprehensive biography. Yet in spite of his many contributions to victory in World War II, only one biography of Devers has been written. Michael Markey's *Jake: The General from West York Avenue* is a well-written summary of Devers's life and service. However, at 113 pages, it is far from an exhaustive account of the general's life. Useful as it is, it does not place Devers's service and career in the wider historiography of the U.S. Army or that of the American role in World War II. So why is Jacob Devers a forgotten general?

First, unlike Eisenhower and Bradley, Devers did not write an account of his role in the war. Consequently, two generations of American historians have looked at the war through the lens of Eisenhower's *Crusade in Europe* (1948) and Bradley's *A Soldier's Story* (1951). Second, because of the chronological manner in which the official army histories were published, Devers and his Franco-American army group were left out of the historical limelight for decades after the accounts of Bradley's army group had been published. For example, the story of Sixth Army Group's role in the liberation of France and the final defeat of Germany was untold until the publication of *Riviera to the Rhine* in 1993, whereas the actions of Bradley's and Field Marshal Bernard Law Montgomery's army groups were chronicled in official army histories published in the 1950s and early 1960s.[1]

Published memoirs and official histories are only part of the reason why

Devers and his Sixth Army Group received short shrift. For three decades after the war, Eisenhower was a nearly unassailable icon to the war generation and its immediate progeny. He and Bradley, "the soldier's general," were exemplars of the U.S. Army's successful campaigns in Europe, and detractors were discouraged from pointing out their imperfections. An account of Devers's role in the Allied campaigns in France and Germany in 1944 and 1945, however, reveals a different side to the personalities and performances of Ike and Bradley, who both disliked Devers and did all they could to marginalize him during and after the war, as this biography amply documents.

Eisenhower and Devers did not get along, and their relationship was sometimes toxic. Bradley's relationship with Devers was also less than warm. Over the years, historians have picked up on various statements made by Eisenhower, Bradley, and George Patton that portray Devers as less than competent. For example, when Eisenhower ranked his senior generals in February 1945, he placed Devers twenty-fourth out of thirty-eight. Ike noted that Devers "has not, so far, produced among the seniors of the American organization here the feeling of trust and confidence that is so necessary to continued success."[2]

Patton's diary also reflected a negative image of Devers. For example, he wrote in February 1944 that Ike considered Devers to be ".22 caliber."[3] In September 1944 Patton noted that "Ike hates him [Devers]."[4] That same month, when XV Corps was transferred from Patton's army to Sixth Army Group, Patton wrote, "as usual Devers is a liar and talked Eisenhower into giving him the corps."[5] In February 1945 he reported that Ike felt handicapped "by having to keep Devers under him, whom he distrusted. I told him I felt the same way about Devers."[6] Bradley concurred: "I was not overjoyed at the prospect of Jake Devers being elevated to high command. . . . I may have been prejudiced against Devers by Ike, who had recently had several long-distance set-tos with him."[7] Bradley described Devers as "garrulous (saying little of importance), egotistical, shallow, intolerant, not very smart, and much too inclined to rush off half-cocked."[8] Such comments by Eisenhower, Patton, and Bradley have often been quoted by historians, thus creating a picture of Devers and his wartime role that is less than flattering, unfair, and far from accurate.

In recent years, a number of historians have reassessed Devers's contributions to the campaigns in the European and Mediterranean theaters and have painted a different picture of him. Carlo D'Este's 2002 biography of

Eisenhower is a good example of the reevaluation of Devers. D'Este notes that "Devers had run afoul of Eisenhower in the summer of 1943," when he refused to transfer bomber groups from the ETO to Ike's Mediterranean theater. George Marshall and the Combined Chiefs of Staff supported Devers, further angering Ike. His ill feelings toward Devers persisted, and "Jake Devers would never become a member of Club Eisenhower nor would his advice as 6th Army Group commander ever carry the weight of [Ike's] friends like Bradley." According to D'Este, "Eisenhower's low regard for Devers was based too much on personal dislike and too little on his effective performance as 6th Army Group commander. . . . Devers never received much credit . . . despite the fact that he did a highly creditable job in a position that had no precedent."[9]

D'Este has been joined in his reappraisal of Eisenhower and Bradley and in his appreciation for Devers's contributions by historians such as Rick Atkinson, Douglas Porch, and Stephen Taaffe.[10] David Colley, in his book *Decision at Strasbourg,* also makes a strong case that Eisenhower failed to see a major strategic opportunity in November 1944 and refused to listen to Devers, who did recognize it. In Colley's view, if Ike had listened to Devers's advice when Sixth Army Group was preparing to cross the Rhine, there likely would have been no Battle of the Bulge.[11]

It is now time to explore this other point of view about the ETO's senior leaders in 1944–1945 and to explain why the relationship between Eisenhower and Devers was so dysfunctional. Although this book exposes some of Eisenhower's weaknesses and mistakes as a leader, it is important to remember that he was a brilliant coalition leader and the right man for the job of Allied supreme commander in 1944. He did a great deal to keep the Anglo-American coalition together and running smoothly. The record is clear: the Allied coalition thoroughly trounced Nazi Germany. Eisenhower was the calm figure who took care of his troops and got along with his allies. However, there was another side to Ike that his relationship with Devers reveals and this biography illustrates.

It is clear that in terms of personality and experience, Eisenhower and Bradley were considerably different from Devers. Eisenhower was a staff officer throughout his career and spent next to no time working directly with troops. He was insecure around men like Patton and Devers, who had served with soldiers for many years. He was also uncomfortable with new men on his team. Consequently, he preferred to surround himself with officers he knew from previous assignments. Devers was outside Ike's circle, even though Marshall repeatedly picked him for critical assignments. In addition, Ike may have felt that Devers was a threat to his position if he faltered, especially given Devers's seniority and Marshall's evident support. These and other ideas are explored in this biography.

Here, Jacob Devers is given the full biographical assessment he deserves. This book documents his service to the nation in peace and war and explains why Marshall placed so much trust in his abilities. Devers's performance was outstanding in every job and assignment he was given during his forty years of service. He got things done and had an uncanny ability to cut through red tape and find a solution to difficult challenges. He was loyal to his subordinates and to his commanders, including Eisenhower. This biography demonstrates these facts and sheds light on the relationships among Devers, Patton, Bradley, and Eisenhower during the Second World War.

1

From York to West Point

Jacob Loucks Devers graduated from the U.S. Military Academy on 11 June 1909. His classmates portrayed him in the *Howitzer*, the cadet year-book, as "an exceedingly earnest youth with rather Puritanical views." Lieu-tenant Devers, they went on to write, had a thorough knowledge in all subjects and was always ready to "part with knowledge to whoever is willing to listen."[1] "Jakie" Devers, as he was known at the Academy, was charac-terized as an "enthusiastic worker" and a "wonderfully clever young man" who would make his mark in the world.[2]

Forty years later the chief of staff of the U.S. Army, General Omar Brad-ley, wrote in Devers's last efficiency report that he was a "conscientious and energetic" officer who "does not hesitate to assume responsibility." In an earlier report, Bradley characterized Devers as "a fine executive" with a "very pleasing personality" who "makes friends easily."[3] These thumbnail sketches provide insights into Devers's personality at the bookends of his military career (1909–1949). During this time, he achieved the rank of full general (four stars) and was responsible for hundreds of thousands of men in both peacetime and war.

Where did such a man come from, and how did he prepare himself for a career of service to his nation? The answer can be found in his family back-ground and upbringing in York, Pennsylvania, and in his education at the U.S. Military Academy.

Family Background

Jacob Loucks Devers was born on 8 September 1887 in his parents' home at 254 West York Avenue in York, Pennsylvania.[4] The house still stands, although the street was renamed Roosevelt Avenue following the Spanish-American War. His mother, Ella Kate Loucks, was the youngest of four chil-dren of Jacob Loucks, a prosperous farmer whose land was situated a few miles west of York. Loucks was an adept businessman as well as a successful farmer. He had owned a paper mill before settling in the York area in 1863 after the death of his wife, and he was wealthy enough to afford a house in York in addition to his farm. Loucks provided his grandchildren with a role model of hard work, thriftiness, and sobriety.[5]

The paternal side of Devers's family originated in Ireland. According to family legend, Jake's great-grandfather Charles Devers eloped with an English nobleman's daughter named Catherine. She was disinherited by her father, and the couple immigrated to America and settled near Emmittsburg, Pennsylvania. Charles's son James Devers became a blacksmith; married Sophia Knoderer, a woman of French-Alsatian descent; and fathered ten children. Jake remembered his grandfather Devers as "a great man in his own right. . . . He was six feet tall, with a fine soldierly posture, and the best blacksmith and horseshoer in town." A religious man, James walked his grandson to Sunday school every week for years and "was kindly to everybody and helpful in every sense of the word."[6] When Jake was thirteen, he was confirmed as a member of St. Paul's Lutheran Church and considered himself a Lutheran for the rest of his life, although he was not overly religious.[7]

Jake's father, Philip Kissinger Devers, was James and Sophia's eighth child. Like all his siblings, Philip graduated from high school.[8] He later worked for Christian Sievers Jewelry at 17 South George Street in York, where he built and repaired watches. He proved to be so proficient and reliable that Christian Sievers brought him into the business as a partner and renamed the store Sievers and Devers Jewelry.[9] The store provided a solid living for the Devers family, allowing them to own a home with an adjacent barn, where they kept their horse and buggy. Philip was active in the Masons and was considered a "dedicated family man." He had a great deal of influence on his eldest son's development. Jake accompanied his father on his weekly visits to maintain the electric clock on top of the York County Courthouse, and each summer Philip took his sons to the Riverside Outing Club's cabin on the Susquehanna River.[10] Jake's sister, Catherine Sophia, considered her father a "man's man" who expected and got complete obedience from his children and taught them the importance of punctuality, integrity, and dependability.[11] At the same time, he and his wife Ella made certain that the children had ample time for play, creating an atmosphere that Jake remembered as a happy childhood.[12] The Devers boys considered their father a "pal" as well as a revered parent.[13]

Ella Kate Loucks and Philip Devers were married on 28 April 1886. According to Catherine, her mother "was a typical wife of her day," ensuring that her children "got to Sunday School and Church, were well clothed, and well mannered."[14] Ella may have been the source of Jake's somewhat puritanical nature noted by his classmates at West Point. She brooked no cursing from her husband or her children, looked askance at the use of alcohol, and abhorred smoking.[15] Although Jacob Devers credited both parents' "great influence" on him, he noted that his mother "kept me straight," while his father taught him how "to be meticulous and stick to the job until you finished it."[16]

The Devers and Loucks families enjoyed a friendly relationship. Jacob Devers later remarked that his was "a closely knit family. This extended to our grand-parents, uncles, [and] cousins. We met quite often for large dinners." These dinners were usually held at his grandfather Loucks's house in York "because he had more money than the rest of them and had a much larger house."[17]

Ella and Philip were blessed with four children. Jake was followed by two brothers, Frank in 1888 and Philip in 1889, and his sister Catherine in 1894. According to Catherine, "her mother often remarked that with the boys being so close together in age she felt as if she had had triplets."[18] Although Ella was assisted by a live-in maid, "her motherly duties strained her physically," as they would any mother of four children under the age of seven.[19] Nevertheless, Catherine remembered her mother as "a good housekeeper and cook," and because Philip "liked to eat, . . . we all acquired a taste for good food and generally we were endowed with excellent health."[20]

The Devers boys were close in age and close friends. According to Catherine, Frank was "a little smarter than Jake" and skipped a grade in school, making him and Jake classmates. "Though shy and over-shadowed by Jake's more aggressive personality and charm, Frank was the wit in the family." He was unselfish and loved people, "especially children."[21] Catherine fondly remembered that Frank took the time to entertain his little sister and her friends. He eventually moved to California but stayed in contact with his siblings.[22]

Catherine characterized her brother Philip as more independent; he "went his own way without paying too much attention to anyone else." His friends were younger than his brothers' crowd, and he could charm anybody.[23] Philip also skipped a grade in school and ranked second in his high school graduating class.[24] He later worked for General Electric, and the basic patent for the ultraviolet lamp was in his name, according to his sister.

Catherine later told her nephew that one of "the basic faults" of the Devers clan was that they were too modest about their accomplishments and abilities. She attributed this trait to the bad example of an uncle who "was a terrific braggart. My mother despised him and was terribly afraid that any of her children were going to be this kind of person."[25]

Catherine (also known as "Kits" or Kitts") was especially close to her eldest brother, whom she and the family called "Jamie." She never married and lived in York for most of her life, where she owned a bookstore for many years. When her father Philip died suddenly in 1930, her mother Ella sold the house on West York Avenue, and she and Catherine purchased an apartment at 152 East Philadelphia Street. According to biographer Michael Markey, they burned most of the family photographs when they moved.[26] Catherine warmly welcomed Jake's wife Georgie when they married in 1911. When Ella died, Catherine moved into Jake's home in Washington, D.C.[27]

Jacob Devers's family life and upbringing sound nearly too good to be true. One of his boyhood friends, Bill Eckenrode, wrote in 1945, "The Devers home and family life was ideal. There were no luxuries, but there was full and plenty of all things necessary."[28] According to Eckenrode, Devers and his siblings accepted their father's word as "law" and "willingly obeyed." Consequently, Devers "understood and accepted discipline from birth." At the same time, "underneath the stern exterior of the father there beat a heart of gold." Philip was proud of his children and deeply interested in their welfare. Ella was "all that the word 'mother' could imply."[29]

Although the family was not rich, the Devers children were spared the need to work to supplement the household's income.[30] Jake took a few jobs around the neighborhood to earn spending money. He ran errands for his aunt and mother and sieved ashes from the family stove every week, receiving ten cents for each of these chores. As a teenager, he worked one summer tending a loom in a silk mill for $1 a day. He also worked on his grandfather Loucks's farm, picking potatoes and harvesting hay. He thought his grandfather took advantage of him because he paid Jake half of what he paid the other boys doing the same work, but he later noted that his farm experiences reinforced the "family philosophy of hard work."[31]

Jacob Devers was a natural leader. Although small for his age, he organized his friends for games and other adventures. After his father sold the horse and buggy, Jake set up a gymnasium in the barn behind the house to serve as a storage place for all kinds of sports equipment as well as a headquarters for the neighborhood boys.[32] He fondly recalled being part of the "Park Street Gang. . . . We were a gang but we weren't a belligerent gang, but only protected our territory."[33] During the winter, the Park Street Gang engaged in snowball fights with other groups of boys for the possession of snow forts. The gang ice-skated at an abandoned quarry in winter and swam there in the summer. Another of the boys' winter highlights was riding down the Park Street and Lincoln Street hills on a ten-person coaster Philip had built for his sons. Jake often assumed responsibility for the proper loading and steering of the sled, and his friend Ira Weiser remembered him as "boss of the hill."[34] Members of the gang occasionally went with Jake to work on his grandfather's farm digging potatoes. As payment, Loucks would treat the boys to ice cream at Bierman's Ice Cream Parlor.[35] In many of these activities, Jake emerged as the planner and the leader.

According to Weiser, Jake Devers showed some interest in military matters at the age of twelve, when he organized the neighborhood boys into a cadet corps. Devers served as the captain of cadets and armed them with broomsticks to serve as rifles. Several of the boys' mothers made uniforms consisting of white slacks with blue stripes, and he drilled his troops as they chanted in cadence.[36] Eckenrode also described Devers's early penchant for leadership: "Jake assumed responsibility and leadership. It wasn't the case of bossing, or 'you do it my way or we won't play.' It was just natural leadership, without boasting or bragging. Jake seemed always to suggest the most interesting things, or he was certain to come up with the right answer on all decisions. It would be Jake who would suggest swimming in the quarry, who would advance the boyhood strategy to win baseball or football games."[37]

Devers and his friends spent a good deal of their free time playing baseball, football, and basketball, depending on the season. While in grade school, they made their own baseballs from scraps of leather, since ready-made baseballs were too expensive. Devers sometimes went to local shops, hoping to convince the woodworkers there to fashion bats for the gang.[38] His ability to find solutions to problems (such as the procurement of bats) was a characteristic that served him well throughout his life.

Some of Jake's fondest memories were of summertime visits to the "clubhouse" on the Susquehanna River. He, his brothers, and their father "would sometimes spend two weeks at a time. To get there we got on the trolley car and rode eleven miles to . . . Wrightsville, and then we walked four miles down a tow path to the cottage."[39] Philip Devers and a group of his friends had formed the Riverside Outing Club, purchased some land on the river, and built the clubhouse, which had a dormitory for sleeping as well as a kitchen and common areas.[40] When they needed supplies, the boys "would take the canoe and go a mile down the river and then walk a mile." Once they had their provisions, the boys would paddle the canoe back upriver to the camp. During these trips to the clubhouse, the Devers boys would listen to the stories of the "river men" who talked about the "progress the country was making at the time . . . and the kind of people who inhabited this area."[41] They also learned how to seine for shad and cook their own meals.

Catherine and her mother were allowed to visit the clubhouse for only one day, and they were not permitted to stay overnight. Ella was probably delighted to have some time off from cooking for and cleaning up after the Devers men. But Catherine, a tomboy, resented not being included and recalled that there were no other family trips.[42]

The childhood experiences of Jacob Devers and his siblings were as close to a Norman Rockwell painting as one could get. Their parents loved their children and allowed them to pursue a wide array of interests. Philip and Ella taught their children the importance of integrity, hard work, and self-reliance, and the children's grandparents provided good examples of sobriety and thrift. The Devers children also had a wide network of friends. Finally, the York school system instilled the academic and athletic skills that would stand Jake and his siblings in good stead all their lives.

Education and Athletics in York

Jake Devers received a good education from York's public school system. He attended Garfield Elementary School, one of York's eight public elementary schools. It was located on North Penn Street, just three blocks from the Devers home—close enough for the children to walk to and from school. He also received a solid education at York High School, which was located at the corner of West College Avenue and South Beaver Street. The high school was a nine-block walk from the Devers home, and Jake walked to and from school each day and even came home for lunch. "It is small wonder that Jake kept physically fit."[43]

York's school system served 6,052 white and 117 "colored" students in 1904–1905, according to its annual report. The elementary schools were racially segregated, but York High School was integrated.[44] There is no mention in any of the Devers family papers or letters indicating the existence of racial tension at the school. By the time the Devers children got to high school (Jake started high school in 1901), York boasted a population of about 55,000 people, and the west side of the city was a busy industrial area.

On his first day of high school, Devers and several of his friends from the Park Street Gang were ejected from school by the principal, Mr. McLaury. Years later, neither Jake nor his close friends Walter Bond and Ira Weiser could remember what their infraction was; they did, however, remember how scared they were by their predicament. The boys went to Penn Park, across the street from the school, to strategize how to avoid having to report the situation to their parents. According to Bond, Jake suggested they apologize to Mr. McLaury and ask him to let them return to school. The boys agreed and elected Devers to be their spokesman. After some swift talking and promises of good behavior, Jake convinced the principal to allow them back.[45]

The curriculum at York High School included the traditional subjects: mathematics, English, and history. Jake's favorite academic subject was mathematics, and he credited his teachers for his success, noting that they "demanded discipline in their classrooms." He was proficient enough at math to tutor his classmates. In contrast, Devers was weak in English, which he attributed to the heavily accented English spoken by the large German and Pennsylvania Dutch population in and around York. His penmanship was bad as well, prompting him to take advantage of after-school tutoring provided by the school.[46] In the middle of his junior year, the school hired a new English teacher from New England, Miss Dorothy Holland. Devers took extra lessons from her, and she taught him how to write proficiently. His love of reading certainly helped him master the English language. His favorite books tended to be action novels with heroic characters, and he especially liked books about Kit Carson and other western figures. He later concluded, "I was a good student, in that I never liked to fail in anything, and I didn't fail in high school in anything."[47]

York High School provided a variety of foreign language courses, and Jake studied Latin, German, Spanish, and French but was not proficient in any of them. French—the one language that would have benefited him the most in the future—was his worst subject.[48] Another difficult subject for Jake was music. In his junior year, the school hired its first music teacher, John Denues, who was also the choir director of the York Episcopal church.

Denues tested each student and classified him or her as soprano, tenor, alto, bass, or baritone. Denues classified Devers and his friend Walter Bond as baritones. During rehearsals, Denues would call on the different groups to sing, but he never called on the baritones. When Bond asked him why, Denues told him that being classified a baritone meant that he had no voice at all.[49]

One of Devers's extracurricular activities was debate. He was a member of the Alpha Debating Society, although he "did not really like debating because he felt it was hypocritical" to defend a position one did not strongly believe in. Even so, he must have been a pretty good debater, since the society elected him president during his junior year. In any case, his experience as a debater improved Jake's public speaking ability, an essential skill for an army officer.[50]

Devers was popular in school and served as class president for two years. He loved to dance and, according to a female classmate, was admired by the girls as a leader, although he was not considered a "ladies' man." Walter Bond noted, however, that Jake was extremely tough competition when it came to getting a date with a girl.[51]

When Devers entered York High School at the age of fourteen, he weighed about 120 pounds. He was too small to make the freshman football or baseball team, and Bill Eckenrode referred to him as a "midget." Nevertheless, Jake did play on the freshman basketball team.[52] Basketball was a relatively new sport for Devers. He had been introduced to the game at the local YMCA, where he learned the game and improved his play by observing and imitating the older boys.[53] According to his friends, basketball was his best sport because he "was as quick as a cat. He was a good shot and a hard player to guard."[54] By his senior year, Devers was team captain and played forward for the varsity basketball team. Devers noted that basketball was his favorite sport in high school, and he later played on the West Point varsity team.[55]

Devers also played on the varsity football team before he graduated from high school. He was a "defensive quarterback," a position akin to a center linebacker today. Jake was the smallest player on the team, but his intensity and effort made him a formidable opponent. He credited his success to the fact that he "listened to what people said and then went out and tried to do it."[56] In 1904 there was no forward pass in football, and the offensive team had three downs to try to move the ball five yards for a first down. Jake, as the defensive quarterback, "played close to the line unless he expected a punt." He would watch closely for a running play and often dove over his own and the opposing team's centers to tackle the offensive quarterback. This method of play worked well, and according to Eckenrode, Devers was never "caught off-side, for his timing was perfect."[57]

He had a great deal of admiration for his coach, Edison B. "Eddie" Williamson, a graduate of Dickinson College. Williamson was not much older than the players, and he seemed to have an ability to connect with them.[58] Devers later told an interviewer that although it was "not a very successful football team," it had a winning season in the fall of 1904. Eckenrode called that year's team one of the school's most outstanding and noted, "Probably the credit was due to the coach, and probably the 'will to win' of that team was due to the brainiest, 'fightenest' [sic] little package of 125 pounds that ever trod a gridiron."[59] In what became a characteristic of the mature Devers, Jake gave credit for each victory to Williamson, shouting to his teammates in the locker room: "'Who do we owe our victory to?' Without waiting for a reply, he yelled, 'You know; our coach.'" According to Eckenrode, "That was Jake Devers as a boy, generous in quick acknowledgement of a job well done."[60]

Eddie Williamson also coached the York High School baseball team. During his freshman year, Jake learned "that when a person tries really hard to perform and takes a bruising and a beating without complaint, older, bigger people help the person because it is instinctive to do so." Williamson was such a person. Observing Jake's fortitude, he encouraged Devers and coached him in the fundamentals of the game.[61] Devers eventually played every position on the York baseball team, but he most enjoyed playing shortstop. This experience gave him a firm grounding in the sport that helped him in 1915, when he coached the undefeated West Point baseball team.[62] But there was a downside to playing every position, as he later recalled: "I made a mistake one spring when our team was playing a game in cold weather and the pitcher wasn't doing good. I had a pretty good curve that I threw over my thumb and I did something to my arm which handicapped me the rest of my life in baseball."[63]

Clearly, athletics were the high point in Devers's high school career. His personality was ideal for competitive sports. His natural leadership qualities were rewarded in team sports, and his high energy level and enthusiasm were contagious. His interest in sports also led him to apply to the U.S. Military Academy. As Devers recalled, he "suddenly became interested in going to West Point" during his junior year.[64] The impetus for his interest in the Military Academy was an article in the *Philadelphia Inquirer* about

West Point football star Charlie Daley. Daley had played football at Harvard for three years before entering West Point in 1901. The article noted that "this dashing player ran through the entire Navy team in his scoring exploits."[65] Devers's interest in books about men like West Point graduate Kit Carson also drew him to the Academy and ultimately to the army. "I don't think I had a soldier's life in mind—even knew what it was all about—except, of course, those books told me all about the frontiers, the scouting, and horses."[66]

When Jake told his father about his desire to go to the Military Academy, Philip thought he could get his son an appointment to the Naval Academy at Annapolis, but he was not certain about West Point. Jake's response was that although he was probably not "a man for the water," he would go to the Naval Academy if he could not get into West Point.[67] He confidently observed, "I'm sure if I can get into West Point that I can make the grade because other people have done it with probably not as strong an idea about it—motivation."[68]

To be accepted by either the Naval Academy or the Military Academy in 1905, one first had to receive an appointment from a U.S. senator or congressman and then pass a physical examination and an academic proficiency test. Often, congressmen and senators would nominate only those with connections to their political parties. Because Philip Devers was a Democrat and the local congressman was a Republican, this lessened the chance of young Devers securing an appointment. Fortunately, however, the congressman was also Jake's Sunday school superintendent and a Mason in Philip's lodge. In addition, Congressman Daniel Lafean "was anxious to get a boy who would stay at West Point if he got the appointment."[69] Lafean's previous two appointees to the Military Academy had either failed to pass the entrance examination or failed to last a full year, so he wanted someone who could both get in and persevere. Lafean first offered the appointment to Jake's classmate Dave Young, who turned it down. Devers later concluded that Young "wasn't the type, really, to go to West Point."[70] Lafean's next appointee also refused the offer, so the congressman ordered his secretary, Samuel Lewis, to find another qualified applicant. Lewis's brother Milt lived near the Devers family and knew of Jake's solid academic and athletic records and his interest in the Academy. He passed on this information to Samuel, and as a result, Lafean offered the appointment to Devers. Jake accepted and began to prepare for the entrance exams.[71]

Jake was most worried about his academic ability in English, so his father arranged for English teacher Dorothy Holland to give him extra lessons after school, firming up his ability to pass the examination. He was far less worried about passing the math portion of the exam. In the end, Devers was spared from taking the entrance exams due to a 1902 change in the Military Academy's admission procedures, when it joined more than 200 other colleges in accepting a "valid certificate of academic achievement" from an accredited high school. The Academy's superintendent reasoned that accepting such certificates "would allow well-prepared students to continue their studies rather than making them review elementary work" for the entrance exams.[72] "As luck would have it," Devers observed, "I got in on my high school certificate."[73] The Academy stopped this practice after 1907, since many of the cadets admitted under the certificate program could not meet the Academy's rigorous academic requirements and washed out. Fortunately, this was not the case with Devers. At the end of four years of high school, he stood thirtieth in a class of seventy-six graduates. His brother Frank was eighth.[74] His studies had prepared him for the Military Academy's curriculum, with its heavy emphasis on engineering and mathematics, and his athletic accomplishments had prepared him for the physical challenges of West Point.

Jacob Loucks Devers was the first of his family to leave home. His appointment to West Point meant that his father would not have to pay for his college education, leaving enough money to fund Philip Jr.'s education (Philip later partially repaid his father). Frank decided that it would be "too much of a drain to send him to college at the same time. . . . So he went to work at the York Manufacturing Company."[75] This left Frank at home, and according to Catherine, "to the end of her days, he was the one Mother leaned on and depended on."[76]

Jake Devers had little experience of the world beyond York when he graduated from high school in early June 1905. He had visited the small towns around York, and he had been to Philadelphia to watch an Army-Navy football game and to Baltimore to play in a baseball game, but that was the extent of his travels.[77] When the time came for Jake to leave York, his family could not bear to see him off at the train station. Only his close friends Ira Weiser and Ted Shields were there to wish him luck.[78]

West Point

When eighteen-year-old Jacob L. Devers arrived at West Point as a new cadet in mid-June 1905, he stood five feet ten inches tall and weighed 120 pounds. He was one of the youngest in his class of 160 men; William Simpson was the youngest at seventeen years of age.[79] The train deposited him at the West Shore Railroad Station at the base of the bluffs where the Military Academy stands. He arrived a day early and remembered "walking up the hill with about four other people." As he did so he told himself, "Other people have done this so I think I can do it."[80]

During the next few days, he and the other new cadets, called "plebes," received their uniforms, hauled their mattresses and bedding to their rooms, and began to learn the rudiments of military drill and ceremony. In 1905 new cadets began their careers at West Point "with three weeks of segregated training in the barracks"—a period of indoctrination known as "Beast Barracks."[81] By the time Devers arrived, Beast Barracks had become a tradition that involved upperclassmen inflicting "intense psychological and physical hazing designed to drive out the weak."[82] It was characterized by "much shouting, sarcasm, condescension, embarrassment, meaningless physical demands, and many other assaults on the newcomers' dignity."[83] (Although hazing is now against the law, it has been impossible to eliminate it completely at the military academies.) In Devers's case, he believed that because he arrived a day early, he was not pushed as hard as the men who arrived the next day. All in all, he felt he "got off to a pretty good start."[84]

Three weeks after the arrival of the plebe class, the corps of cadets was united in a tent encampment on the Plain, a large open area near Trophy Point. The camp was run by the second-year cadets, known as yearlings. These men drilled the plebes and in many cases continued to haze those who needed extra training.[85] During the summer encampment, Jake met some of his classmates, including George S. Patton, John C. H. Lee, Robert Eichelberger, and William Simpson.

At the end of his first month at the Academy, Jake wrote to his friend Ira Weiser in York. After explaining that he had been too busy to write earlier, Devers described his situation: "The life of a plebe is much different from a plebe life at college. Here you have to obey all commands and can say nothing about it for you are the same as an enlisted man and most of the upperclassmen are cadet officers."[86] After promising to expand on "the beauty of West Point" in a later letter, he noted, "I am already camping and enjoy it very much." This camp was different from that shared by the two friends in Pennsylvania, however, since "ours is laid out on military principles and everything must be neat at all times or you get those beastly demerits."[87] During the summer encampment, the cadets lived in tents that had to be aligned as perfectly as possible. Each evening the entire "battalion" fell out in their gray uniforms for a full-dress parade that provided prime-time entertainment for the Academy's faculty and its numerous summertime visitors. The cadets enjoyed these parades far less than the audience did. The cadet uniform's dress coat fit "like a corset and the hat with its plume on fits so as to give you a headache. The hard part of the dress parade," according to Devers, was "doing the manual [of arms] correctly. For the 400 cadets here must do this as one man."[88]

Plebes also performed basic military functions such as close-order drill and guard duty. Devers described the latter to Ira as a tour of "24 hours with three reliefs or in other words you walk your post 8 hours and rest in those beastly guard tents 16 hours with mosquitos as big as flies eating you to death."[89] It was not long before Devers received his first "beastly demerit" for losing his gloves while on guard duty.[90] Jake also reported that there was "very little hazing done."[91]

His classmate George Patton, who had failed academically his first year, found the encampment of 1904 "hardly the ordeal he had imagined." Patton, who had attended the Virginia Military Institute for a year before entering the Academy, discovered that most of the cadets at the Military Academy were "just very respectable middle class fellows." He saw himself, in contrast, as belonging to a "different class"—a class that was, perhaps, "almost extinct."[92] Patton and Devers were not close friends, but they got along. Devers described their relationship as "congenial." Jake was academically ahead of the dyslexic Patton, but he noted that Patton "had the posture—the military posture" and was eventually appointed cadet adjutant. He further recalled that Patton was an excellent cadet adjutant who "was always right on the ball."[93]

In his first letter to Weiser, Devers concluded that in spite of "all these things I think you will find me here a year from now for I like the place but am not in love with the plebe year."[94] His sister Catherine believed "he was thrilled to be there. I think he immediately absorbed the feeling of duty, honor, country. . . . I think it was always uppermost in his mind."[95]

Two days after writing to Weiser, Devers received his second demerit for not being familiar with the standing orders for sentinels. This was followed a few days later by a demerit for "executing a movement improperly immediately after being corrected for the same offense."[96] Years later, Devers observed that the "plebe system was too severe—some of my classmates got into trouble because they carried it too far." He especially thought that having plebes do meaningless things such as carrying ants from one place to another and counting them was silly and nonproductive.[97] Nonetheless, he learned to function under the system and received no more demerits that summer.

At the end of the summer encampment, the cadets got their first real taste of military training. After a series of small-unit battle drills on the post, the battalion of cadets participated in an actual field exercise.[98] Devers described it to Weiser: "We left West Point carrying about 20 pounds and one gun on our shoulders, crossed the Hudson with 6 companies of infantry, 2 companies of cavalry & 1 detachment of artillery, also a wagon train consisting of 16 wagons & proceeded over mountains & hills into the state of New York for 25 miles. Fighting all day & camping all night was our routine. . . . We would locate the enemy perhaps on some mountain then we would try to outflank them, doing it at a run with all our equipment on our shoulders all the time firing."[99] This was the first field exercise of its kind. The commandant, Colonel Robert L. Howze, initiated the "practice march" to give cadets leadership opportunities within small units in a field environment. Howze observed that "the value of this field work cannot be overestimated."[100] "His successors agreed, and the march became a standard feature of the summer training program."[101]

The corps of cadets returned from this training exercise in late August to prepare for the academic year. The battalion was reorganized into companies. Devers was assigned to Company E and billeted in the Ninth Division, where he spent the next three years of his cadet career (in those days, the Academy did not "scramble" cadets at the end of their plebe or yearling years). His first roommates were "Dutch" Erlenkotter and Walter T. Grundy. Erlenkotter had already graduated from the Stevens Institute of Technology and did well academically. After an early fight that ended in a draw, he and Devers became good friends. Grundy was less prepared for the Academy than Devers and Erlenkotter and was turned out after his first year.[102] Jake got along well with most of his classmates, although he later admitted in an interview, "I didn't have any special friends in a way." He also revealed that he did not get along well with some of the older men in his class, although he did not mention any names.[103]

Classes were well under way on 2 September 1905 when Devers wrote to Weiser about his math class, which he attended from 0800 to 0930. There were twelve cadets in his math section, and "you get skinned for every infraction of the academic rules."[104] Devers knew this firsthand, having already received a demerit from Colonel Howze for failing to turn in a corrected paper on time. He was written up again on 4 September for failing to button up his blouse for the morning inspection.[105] He apparently shrugged off these penalties for minor infractions with little concern.

The Military Academy's curriculum was designed to produce engineers, although most West Point graduates did not serve in the Engineer Corps. In his first year, Devers was required to take algebra, geometry, trigonometry, English composition, and French. In his second year, he took geometry, calculus, French, Spanish, and drawing (which included topographical drawing and sketching). During his third year, he studied natural and experimental philosophy, chemistry, mineralogy, geology, and drawing. He spent his fourth and last year learning about civil and military engineering, science of war, law, history, and historical geography.[106] His "professional studies"—that is, courses designed to prepare him for military service—included tactics, physical education, practical military engineering, military hygiene, and military gymnastics. These courses were spread out over four years, with ordnance and gunnery training conducted in his senior year.[107] There was little free time in Jake's daily schedule, and that was filled up with athletics.

Jake did well in mathematics but was far less comfortable in his English course, which stressed composition and recitation. For each academic subject the cadets were divided into sections, based on their performance and ability. Devers was in the fifth section in math, with nine sections lower than his; in English, he was in the eleventh of eighteen sections.[108] He worried about doing well enough in English to stay at the Academy and wrote to Weiser, "The only thing that ties me up is my inability to express myself which, you know, was always my trouble."[109] Devers's concerns prompted him to work harder and persevere. His efforts paid off, and he reported to Weiser on 18 November that in English he ranked ninety-ninth out of 160 plebes. Near the end of his first term, Devers was confident he would pass all his courses and told Weiser that he was "getting along much better in everything here."[110] As the term came to a close, he summarized his academic situation: "Tonight will be the last night that I have to study for math writs this year and I am glad of it. I have been here just ½ year and it seems like 3 years but then if I get through I will be repayed [sic] for my work and that is the point."[111]

One of the hardest adjustments for most young cadets in 1905 was the fact that they were not allowed to leave the Academy except for official duties and important athletic events such as the annual Army-Navy football game. Accustomed to being with his family for the holidays, Jake anticipated that 1905 would be "the worst Xmas I ever spent and I will be very glad when it is over. The fact is I hardly realize it is Christmas for we go on with our military duties as usual."[112] But even as he lamented his homesickness, he maintained a sense of perspective and told Weiser, "This is the life I have chosen and I enjoy it in its way but do not enjoy the plebe part of it."[113]

There were distractions from the loneliness, however. For example, on 31 December the cadets decided to play a prank on the officer in charge. As Jake described it, the action began in the late afternoon:

> About 6:00 o'clock on Dec. 31 Mr. Swissballs or otherwise known as Capt. Newbold announced to the Corps that there was to be no noise in the evening and if there was the companies would be formed at the time and braced until reveille. Now this just made us roar. . . . First the drum was stolen from the guard house so they could not summon us at midnight. Then promptly at 12 o'clock about half the Corps made a rush out of the barracks giving an awful yell and immediately skipped back again so as not to be hived. Well old Swish thought he would prepare for just something like this so he had six other TACS [tactical officers] call on him. The result is about four [cadets] were hived and the joke is on the TACS for we carried out everything to perfection.[114]

Ironically, Captain "Swish" Newbold was later one of Lieutenant Devers's battery commanders in the Fourth Field Artillery.[115]

A New Year's Day tradition at West Point was to relax the rules affecting plebes. During the day, they had the same privileges as the upperclassmen, giving Jake his first opportunity to look around the mess hall. "They had quite a set out in the Mess Hall, cigars, and the like and then toasts to the different interesting things around here." He enjoyed the day and judged that the "speeches were great."[116]

There were other distractions from the monotony of cadet life as well. West Point often hosted visiting foreign dignitaries. In September 1905, for example, the Russian and Japanese delegates to the peace talks being held in New Hampshire visited the Military Academy. When such important foreigners visited, the superintendent often rolled out the red carpet, including a full dress parade in their honor. Devers described the scene to Weiser on 12 September: "It just poured and they first marched us around the large plain at quick time then the signal for double time came and we double timed around the plain and again passed in review—the plain is ¼ mile around. Talk about wet!" Each company marched in two ranks for the review, with each rank containing thirty-six men. "This large number causes it [to be] hard to have a good line."[117] There was a silver lining to the delegates' visit: they requested that all punishment tours be canceled. This tradition of allowing important visitors to ask for the remission of demerits persisted throughout the twentieth century. In 1905 Jake concluded, "This will help our football team defeat Navy."[118]

Athletics was another major distraction from the routine of the Academy. Devers tried out for the basketball team midway through his plebe year and played with the second team as a forward. This allowed him to eat at a special basketball training table, where the plebe rules were relaxed and hazing was curtailed. Jake's biggest problem with basketball was that he was not a very good shot, and he lamented, "If I could only locate these darn baskets I would do much better as that is my holdback."[119] Being on the basketball team was time consuming and affected his studies. By March, Devers was having serious trouble with French and, as a result, was removed from the basketball squad. It was disappointing, but he realized it was necessary because if he failed French, it would have been "goodbye Jacob," since failure in any course was grounds for dismissal from the Academy.[120]

French was just one of Devers's academic challenges in his second term. As he explained to Weiser, he had faced "an examination in Math every day last week. Also since I am so low in French I have to study overtime." Hard work and more study time paid off, and Devers passed all his courses in his plebe year.[121] When the term ended on 27 May 1906, Devers was elated at having survived his first year. Like most members of the Long Gray Line, he felt that "the rise from a plebe to a yearling is so great and you can do so many more things."[122]

During his second summer at West Point, Devers found life far more pleasant than it had been the previous year. "I am well fixed in [summer] camp with lots of fun before me. If any of my girlfriends visit West Point this summer they will have I think a good time, and I will have a better time. The hops [dances] are fine." Summer encampment was a lark for the upperclassmen, with dances and concerts three times a week. For the new plebes, it was different: "The poor plebes come over to camp on 6 July, and I have sort of pity for them as I only see now what I was up against last year."[123]

That summer, Devers "developed into a golf fiend and I manage to get from one hole to another but at the same time a little grass goes along" with each swing of a club.[124] He had plenty of time to practice, since he held no major leadership position during the summer encampment. Following the encampment, the corps again took part in a field exercise before returning to the barracks at the end of August. Devers remained interested in happenings in York, but his perspective about high school pranks had changed. As he told Weiser: "I used to think [pranks] were all right but now [I] think [they] are babyish so you can see I am changing my views more every day."[125]

Devers's academic schedule in the fall 1906 term was heavily loaded with math and engineering courses. This played to his advantage, and he was able to remain in the upper third of his class academically while taking a much greater part in athletics.[126] Jake described his schedule to Weiser as consisting of "football, basketball, math, French, drawing, drills and parades." Although he still found French challenging, he was confident that "I will pull through."[127] Each of the three upper classes had its own football team, and they played intramural games against one another. This allowed men who were not varsity quality to still play football. Devers made his class's football team as an "all around sub," playing quarterback, fullback, and end whenever he got into a game.[128]

The term passed quickly for Jake, and it was soon time for the Army-Navy football game in November. Army lost, but Jake "had a great time in Philadelphia with Walt [Grundy], my parents and the U[niversity] of P[ennsylvania] people I know." But he still had another Christmas away from home to endure. "I am going to make the best of it. . . . I am reading books galore now to pass the time away and will be glad when January is here as it is that much nearer to furlough for me."[129]

During his second year at the Academy, Devers met officers who mentored him and influenced his leadership style. One of the most important of these mentors was Captain Charles P. Summerall. "Honest John," as the cadets called Summerall, taught field artillery, and "the galloping horses of the field artillery fascinated Jamie [Jake]. . . . No fixed guns would do." Devers realized that he wanted to be part of a branch "with a punch, fast on its feet."[130]

Summerall arrived at West Point in the summer of 1905. An 1892 graduate of the Military Academy, he had served in combat in the Philippines (1899–1900) and China (1901). He found his assignment as the senior artillery instructor "the most difficult and disagreeable part of my service," although his relations with cadets were "all that could be desired." One of his most challenging tasks was to shape up the forty-five-man artillery detachment on the post. These men were a discontented lot who "lived in a poor building near the polo field. The detachment had no company fund," and its food was insufficient. The men had been treated as laborers rather than soldiers, and the unit suffered from low morale, poor discipline, and a high desertion rate.[131] Summerall showed a great deal of patience with the detachment as he improved its food, moved the men to new barracks at the south end of the post, and raised standards. By the time Devers's class took training from "Honest John," the superintendent considered the artillery detachment a model organization and routinely showed it off to visitors. Summerall described the instruction he provided to the cadets as "practical with the guns, horses, and instruments but theoretical in the classrooms."[132] During this training, Devers was exposed to various types of artillery weapons, including coastal defense guns, field guns, and pack artillery, and he would put this experience to good use on his first assignment.

In addition to providing technical training, Summerall interacted with the cadets during field exercises. As Summerall explained in his memoirs, "I took a battery of the first class on Friday afternoons for a practice march and a problem. Then we made camp. After the horses and guns were cared for, the cadets had supper, followed by a campfire, around which we sat and talked artillery."[133] Perhaps it was during one of these around-the-campfire discussions that Summerall advised Devers to "stay a bachelor as long as you can."[134] Summerall eventually commanded the First Infantry Division and the V Corps in World War I and became army chief of staff in the 1920s.

Devers was also coached and mentored by Lieutenant Joseph Stilwell, an infantry officer who arrived at West Point in 1906 to teach foreign languages. Stilwell was Devers's instructor in Spanish, and years later Devers recalled, "Boy did I study for him. I went up to the second section [from the last] in Spanish. Now this shows . . . I was getting values."[135] Stilwell also coached varsity basketball and baseball while Jake was a member of those teams. Devers noted that Coach Stilwell was "sarcastic but in a way that made you want to perform. I would have done anything for him."[136] Stilwell, according to biographer Barbara Tuchman, "was quick to help anyone who was really trying." He also taught infantry tactics and military history to Devers's class.[137] Stilwell, according to Jake, "could squeeze the last ounce of water out of you, and say the meanest damn things, and I liked it."[138]

Another influential instructor was Captain Guy V. Henry, a cavalryman who taught equitation. Devers recalled, "I never rode anything but a mule before I went to West Point," and "I tried like nobody's business to get a good mark in cavalry instruction because it would help my military [career]."[139] Jake described himself as "bow-legged, knock-kneed, and pigeon toed," so he had to work hard to learn to ride well.[140] His efforts paid off, and in his senior year he even learned to play polo, which became one of his passions.

From their contact with officers like Summerall and Stilwell, cadets learned that officers could and should interact with subordinates in a professional yet civil manner. Devers emulated this approach during his career.

Cadets received their first furlough, or leave, at the end of their second academic year. Long before the end of the term, Devers was counting the days. He told Weiser, "Only 103 days until June and I can tell you I am about ready to see the days fly as I am anxious to see York and her people again." In the meantime, he had been part of a group of cadets sent to serve as an honor guard for President Theodore Roosevelt at the tricentennial celebration of the founding of Jamestown, Virginia. He had also learned how to play lacrosse, a newly introduced game at the Academy.[141] His baseball career kept him busy, and he was thrilled to tell Weiser that at the Army-Navy baseball game in May, "excitement and enthusiasm reigned everywhere and hell broke loose when we pulled out of an apparent defeat [and achieved] Victory."[142] Afterward, Summerall selected Devers for "a special detail on Light Battery and I tell you it is fine for if you ever see the artillery drill you will understand why we all like it. Of all things this is the greatest for it finishes up two very strenuous years of work."[143]

Devers returned to York on furlough on 20 June 1907, after passing all his courses. He ranked somewhere in the upper third of his class and aspired to become a field artillery officer when he graduated. His leave lasted until 25 August, giving him ample time to spend with family and friends. His sister Catherine was delighted to see him and noted, "Of course, he always had a good time. The girls were awfully pleased to have this soldier come home, [although] he would never wear a uniform."[144] Devers saw his friends, went to the clubhouse on the Susquehanna with his brothers and father, and enjoyed a leisurely summer in York. In future visits, Jake would spend less time with old friends; as his sister noted, he "lost contact with most of his friends who had also gone to college and gone away from York." But he regularly returned home to be with his family and spent as much time with them as possible.[145]

When Devers returned to West Point on 25 August 1907, he faced an academic schedule that included natural and experimental philosophy (mechanics, wave motion, and astronomy), chemistry, mineralogy, geology, and drawing. In addition to tactics, his professional courses included practical engineering in bridge construction and fortifications.[146] Since he had no English or history courses, Devers felt confident that he could handle his academic load and continue his athletic interests in football, basketball, and baseball.

Devers also continued to pursue his new interest in horsemanship. He had learned to ride the previous year in the Academy's indoor riding facility and enjoyed it immensely. As he told Weiser: "I have a chance to do a lot of riding now and I certainly do. Every Saturday and Wednesday afternoon I am out on the road learning the arts of good horsemanship. Some of the nags are good but others are rather rough. It is one of the best privileges we have and I am certainly going to use it as much as possible."[147] Devers understood that horsemanship was an essential skill for an artillery officer, since all army artillery units were horse drawn in 1907. Now he went beyond the minimal requirements and set out to master this difficult and challenging pursuit.

Devers played on his class's football team in the fall, captained the varsity basketball team in the winter, and played baseball in the spring. These sports, along with horseback riding, helped keep him out of serious mischief during his West Point career, and he avoided any major infractions of the rules. He did, however, show a certain casualness about some of the Academy's minor rules. In his first two years at West Point he received fifty-four demerits; during his last two years he received thirty. Most of these were for infractions such as talking in the barracks during inspection, sleeping in his chair during call to quarters, or leaving his towel in the bath house. He was also written up for "galloping his horse at about 1030 AM."

His demerit record showed a propensity for being a few minutes late to formations of various kinds.[148]

Devers's class spent less than a full year as cows, or third-year cadets, because the War Department ordered the Academy to graduate the class of 1908 early. On 1 December Jake wrote, "We are busier than ever here now due to the fact that the 1st Class graduates February 14th instead of the 13th of June. This means that my class will have to take all the duties for the 1st Class besides our own."[149] This situation affected the morale and attitudes of Devers's class, since it was "very hard to study now . . . because . . . all you see is these 1st Classmen running around in their uniforms because of graduation and when you think of the good time in store for them it naturally diverts your mind."[150]

He continued to play shortstop on the baseball team, and during one game he dislocated a toe that "gave me such intense pain that I was unable to stand."[151] In June the West Point baseball team played Navy at Annapolis. Jake's father and sister traveled to Annapolis to watch the game and spend the evening with him. "We had a fairly good time but I had an even better time," he told Weiser, "that night at the hop and afterwards. We were certainly all in when we reached West Point and are recuperating from bad effects."[152]

In the summer of 1908 Jake and his classmates traveled to Fort G. H. Wright on Fisher's Island for a week of gunnery practice with coast artillery guns. The cadets were well prepared, since Congress had appropriated money for the installation of two six-inch naval guns on Trophy Point with "disappearing carriages and subcaliber devices that allowed realistic firing without the bulky ammunition."[153] Although he enjoyed gunnery practice, Devers found the "surf bathing, spooning, hopping, [and] receptions" more fun, as "they certainly gave us great pleasure." After this trip he reported to Weiser, "I certainly enjoy this life and will never go back to city life unless I am compelled."[154]

During his first three years at West Point, Jake maintained an interest in York politics. He generally supported the Democrats, as his father had, and he made a point of telling his Republican friend Ira Weiser, "I hope the Democrats will improve it [York] and keep it in better repair than your good old Republicans." By the beginning of his fourth year, however, Devers seems to have adopted the traditional army officer view, stating, "As to the election [of 1908], I am not giving out anything as I am an army man and wait for the man that will do the most for our little army."[155] He slipped away from this view a bit when he wrote after the 1908 election, "I see the Republicans carried everything as usual and I am for once glad to see it."[156]

As a first classman, Devers moved to Company B in the fall of 1908 to serve as quartermaster sergeant. Additionally, he was acting first sergeant of the company while the regular first sergeant was on special duty overseeing the new cadets. By then, Devers had given up any idea of playing for the Academy's varsity football squad. Instead, he considered himself "only a strong backer and rooter of a hard fighting team."[157] He played guard on the varsity basketball team and shortstop on the Academy's baseball team. He wrote to Weiser in April 1909 that he was having a "fairly unlucky season so far slipping up a few balls now and then and having hard luck hitting it." He was walked a great deal and seldom struck out. He was also challenged by another cadet for the shortstop position but observed, "If I don't get too wooden I can hold on to it."[158]

That year Devers played his first polo matches and fell in love with the sport. In fact, polo was the only sport he pursued competitively over the next thirty years. Many cavalry and artillery officers, including Patton, Lucian Truscott, Summerall, and Ernie Harmon, played polo. According to Devers, officers who played polo were "very energetic" and "competitive" men "who liked to rub shoulders with another person."[159] For an officer who lacked the independent financial means of a man like Patton, it was an affordable sport because mounted officers were entitled to two horses and received an extra monthly stipend to support the animals. It was also a dangerous and exciting sport that required participants "to obey the rules strictly." Polo players had to train their horses well, which for Devers meant that "you were up before daylight and you went to bed late at night because you were training ponies." Polo also required tremendous discipline and coordination between rider and horse.[160] Overall, polo was a sport well suited to Devers's competitive and energetic personality.

His senior year's academic courses included civil and military engineering, law, history, and historical geography; his professional courses consisted of applied tactics, practical military engineering, ordnance, and gunnery.[161] One of the highlights for Devers's class was a two-day visit in May to the Gettysburg battlefield. There, the cadets were "able to combine their knowledge of the battle with the actual terrain." During such an exercise (called a "staff ride"), men who "were willing to make the necessary leap in imagination" were able to understand the historic battle and, more importantly, think about "the eternal verities of men at war."[162] By then, Devers admitted to Weiser, "I have not much longer to stay here and I am glad of it."[163]

Devers did well enough in his final year to graduate thirty-ninth in his class of 103. He wanted to be commissioned as a field artillery officer but was worried because there were only nine such positions available. Consequently, after graduation he went to Washington, D.C., where he spent two weeks talking to the adjutant general of the army and his congressman about his prospects. In the end, Devers was commissioned in the field artillery, probably because the higher-ranking men in his class preferred commissions in the coast artillery or engineers, where promotion was faster and the assignments would take them to places such as New York City or Newport, Rhode Island.[164]

Devers then returned to York, where he spent the summer. "During that vacation leave," he recalled, "I renewed my acquaintance with my girl-friends at the high school." He spent nearly a month at the camp on the Susquehanna with his father and several friends but did not go anywhere else. "I simply rested and got ready to go West"—to his first assignment at Vancouver Barracks in Washington State. As a second lieutenant he was paid $142.50 a month, which was sufficient to support himself.[165]

Jacob Devers had met his goal of not failing in any major way during his formative years in York and the Military Academy. He had shown a clear aptitude to lead others, and he had learned that when faced with a challenge, whether academic, athletic, or personal, the best course of action was to work harder and bounce back from minor setbacks. His family, friends, and teachers in York and his officer-mentors at West Point had helped him hone his native skills and develop new strengths. He remained loyal to York and the Military Academy for the rest of his life, and his experiences there prepared him for a career of service to the army and the nation.

2

Apprenticeship

Second Lieutenant Jacob L. Devers set out for his first duty assignment as an artillery officer in September 1909. His request for duty in the West was granted when the army assigned him to the 4th Field Artillery Regiment at Vancouver Barracks, Washington (the regiment's headquarters was at Vancouver Barracks with the 1st Battalion, while the 2nd Battalion was stationed in Wyoming). This journey across the country was the first time Devers had been west of the Adirondack Mountains, let alone the Mississippi River. He took the Pennsylvania Railroad to Chicago, and from there he made his way to Walla Walla, Washington, on the Northern Pacific Railway. He traveled alone and found the trip intriguing, as only an "unsophisticated" young officer could.[1] "I learned a lot about tickets and I guarded everything faithfully and carefully. I wouldn't say that anything unusual passed on that trip. Being young, I had a chance to talk to a lot of people but I don't remember any incident out of the way, except everything interested me. I didn't have any trouble with conversation or being busy."[2]

The final leg of the trip took him along the Columbia River to Vancouver, Washington, where he arrived without his trunk, which had been lost. He then reported to his regimental commander, Colonel A. B. Dyer. Devers's assignment to the regiment's 1st Battalion, commanded by Major Leroy S. Lyon, was to be one of the greatest learning experiences of his life. For the next three years he would hone and demonstrate his leadership skills and learn all he could from the officers and enlisted men around him. He also came to know himself better and to appreciate the qualities and habits of the soldiers and officers of the regular army.

Vancouver Barracks

Vancouver Barracks was typical of many army posts across the country. A garrison of roughly 2,000 men occupied the post on the north side of the Columbia River, across from Portland, Oregon. The post commander, Colonel McDonegal, also commanded the 14th Infantry Regiment, the larg-

est unit on post. Army protocol required Devers to make courtesy calls on
the officers of the two regiments over the next several weeks. Here, Devers
became a member of what soldiers today call the "army family."

Vancouver Barracks was America's first permanent military base in
Washington State. From 1849 to 1946 it served a variety of roles for the
army, and its twenty-one sets of stately officers' quarters housed or were visited by such men as Ulysses S. Grant (1849), Omar Bradley (1915–1916),
and George Marshall (1936–1937). When Devers arrived in 1909, the post
included two sets of two-story enlisted barracks, an officers' row, bachelor living quarters, and several stables. Devers had a private second-floor
room with a separate bath and ate his meals in a mess hall on the floor
below. The post also had an officers' club. A second lieutenant's pay was
$142.50 a month, with an additional $16.50 per month for the maintenance of a horse. Most of Devers's pay was spent on food in the officers'
mess, although he tried to save $25 per month.

Devers found most of the officers friendly, although he felt that many of
them, especially the infantry officers, drank too much. But Devers adopted
a wise attitude about the issue of drinking: "I didn't know how to [drink]—
that worried me. . . . The way I decided to solve it was just don't take any
drinks." He did not object to others drinking, as long as it did not get
out of hand.[3] Fortunately, there were plenty of other activities to occupy a
young lieutenant's time.

Devers considered his battalion commander, Major Lyon, a brilliant
officer. An 1891 Academy graduate, Lyon was "small in stature, liked to
play poker, had a very straight-laced New England wife, but he had a great
sense of humor. He played polo [and] he knew his job well."[4] During his
first critical troop assignment, Devers was fortunate to have a battalion
commander he respected and who took an active interest in his junior officers' professional development. Young officers who have such initial positive mentoring tend to make the army their career.

The 1st Battalion was a "pack" artillery unit, in that all its howitzers
and equipment were carried by mules. Pack artillery units were designed to
fight in mountainous or jungle terrain. Although the area around Vancouver Barracks was relatively flat, Major Lyon's batteries often "packed out
and marched all through the countryside there, in the woods—which were
beautiful—[with] magnificent trees." One of the greatest challenges in this
field training was the heavy rain common in the Pacific Northwest. Devers
enjoyed the training but later remarked, "You never went out without your

raincoat. Your feet swelled just from the moisture. These rain clouds would come from nowhere, [and] the rain would pour down."[5] Devers recalled that when it wasn't wet, it was dusty.

The soldiers of Devers's battery were "rough and tough men. . . . The first sergeants were tough! They brought up the rear of the battery and I, being the junior second lieutenant in my battery, brought up the rear of the battery. If the battery was at the end of the battalion, I brought up the end of the battalion—in the rain." He thought the battery's first sergeant was hard on the men, sometimes too hard. Like all successful lieutenants, Devers had to learn how to approach senior noncommissioned officers: "I first had to make my good graces with him and keep out of trouble, and then said, I'll take charge of that." In this case, Devers was dealing with soldiers who were having trouble keeping up with the column due to blisters and poor physical conditioning. He tried to discourage the men from falling out without physically abusing them. The first sergeant accepted Devers's approach. "He was a good soldier," Devers noted. "His methods were just the way of the 'Old Army,' but the 'Old Army' was changing just about this time."[6]

In addition to being tough, the soldiers of Devers's unit were big men. He recalled, "The enlisted men were all over six feet, practically all of them." About their abilities he said: "This was a volunteer Army. . . . Your mechanics, some of them were reliable and married, but most of them had weaknesses; but they were very capable saddlers, blacksmiths, and horse-shoers—mule-shoers—whatever you want to call them. We had good mechanics and good service people as soon as we got over payday. They were a hard lot and they did their job well. They liked to soldier. They demanded quite a lot of you."[7]

Many of the soldiers drank too much, loafed too much, and played too much poker. The heavy drinking and gambling, however, tended to occur around payday, when the men had money in their pockets. One of Devers's duties was to go to town with the first sergeant, round up the drunk soldiers, and get them back to their barracks with the least amount of trouble. Once they had run through their cash, the men remained relatively sober for the rest of the month. Alcoholism has been a consistent problem in the army since 1776. The number of sick-call cases related to drunkenness peaked in 1876 at 72 cases per 1,000; by 1897, it had fallen to 27. In 1912 Congress passed a law that required the army to withhold the pay of men who were sick due to alcoholism. This action was in step with the Progressive Era's goal of improving society through all types of legislation, and the sick-call rate for drunkenness fell to 13 per 1,000 by 1915.[8]

Another major problem that plagued the army in the early twentieth century was venereal disease. Secretary of War Henry Stimson reported in 1912, "The high percentage of venereal disease continues to be the reproach of the American Army, and the daily average of those [soldiers] sick from that cause during the last calendar year was larger than the daily average number of those sick from all other of the more important diseases combined." Throughout the army, the hospital admission rate for venereal disease was 164 per 1,000 soldiers per year. The problem became so bad that the army resorted to court-martialing soldiers who failed to use the prophylaxis station available at every post.[9] Any officer who contracted a venereal disease could assume that his career was over.

Officers on posts such as Vancouver Barracks were part of a tight-knit group that provided many gainful social opportunities for its members. Bachelors found themselves the ready prey of officers' wives who were eager to introduce them to young unmarried women. The married ladies of Vancouver Barracks routinely invited Devers and his fellow bachelor officers to afternoon tea for expressly that purpose. There were also frequent dances. Devers tried to avoid the teas, but he did participate in the dances, noting, "We had our manners." Devers was determined to remain single for at least five years, but, he admitted, "I only lasted three years."[10]

A second lieutenant's workday in 1909 was filled with duties and activities that kept him busy and prepared him for future duties. The primary task was to learn how to serve as part of a combat unit. Devers worked with his soldiers to master the skills of the field artillery in general and pack artillery in particular. One of his greatest challenges was loading mules. Although he had been a good athlete at West Point, Devers (who stood only five feet ten inches) found it difficult to hoist heavy cargo such as hay or beef onto the packing frames and properly tie it down. However, he eventually became proficient at loading mules and later learned many of the fundamentals of a mule skinner.[11]

Army officers had to study for and pass examinations before they were eligible for promotion. The army expected units or posts to operate schools where the lieutenants studied military law, field engineering, topography, and international law. These schools were part of an educational system designed and implemented by Secretary of War Elihu Root from 1901 to 1903. This system comprised a hierarchy of schools, beginning with the post schools and including (from the base up) branch schools such as Infantry or Field Artillery Schools, the School of the Line, the Staff School, and the War College. All but the last two schools required a tremendous amount of rote learning and frequent examinations and grading, the results of which were placed in the officer's personnel file.[12] Thus, Devers's afternoons were spent studying for his examinations.

As a leader, Lieutenant Devers had some advantages due to his athleticism. Since soldiers must be in good physical condition to perform their duties properly, the army of the twentieth century stressed athletics and physical conditioning, and Devers set the standard for his troops. Baseball and football were the two most popular sports among the enlisted men, and officers were expected to participate as both players and coaches. Infantrymen often used calisthenics, road marches, and bayonet drills for physical conditioning. Artillerymen and cavalrymen got their workouts from riding and training horses. The army paid for the upkeep of two horses for each officer and encouraged them to play polo for its physical conditioning and competiveness.

Devers had played some polo at West Point, and when he arrived at Vancouver Barracks, he immediately took up the sport again. He acquired his first horse for $150 and played polo with the other officers on a field next to the Columbia River. His horse "was a white Arabian, [a] very small pony. . . . That little pony stayed with me and came all the way to West Point and got to be my wife's—some years later—riding horse. He was a good polo pony . . . because he had been broken in to work with cattle. This gave me a much better chance to play polo and made a better player out of me." He paid a soldier, called a striker, $5 a month to take care of his horses in the post's stables. Polo provided good exercise, but equally important, it allowed Devers to get to know his fellow officers.[13] In addition, playing polo can teach lessons that are directly applicable to leadership in the army: "What got me interested in this sport was the horse and also the intelligence of the horse," Devers observed. "Also, I learned what a light hand meant and what relaxation meant. . . . There's nothing more interesting than trying to train a green polo pony. You try all the incentives. . . . This effort helped me a lot, not only in dealing with horses, but with men, because the same principles apply when you're dealing with a difficult person."[14] For the next thirty years, Devers continued to play polo, often with West Point classmates such as George Patton.

As it turned out, Devers was a better polo player and athlete-coach than he was a student of military subjects. He failed the military hygiene and military topography examinations in the garrison school at Fort D. A. Russell in mid-1910. This displeased his regimental commander, who ordered him confined to the post for twenty-one days so he could study for and pass these exams.[15] He evidently succeeded, since his rating officer, Captain Henry L. Newbold, wrote in his efficiency report for January–June 1910: "[he] is qualified for his position and should be intrusted with important duties."[16]

As in today's army, special assignments or duties were thrust upon junior lieutenants to give them experience dealing with challenging situations. Within a week of his arrival at Vancouver Barracks, Devers was detailed to serve as an aide to President Taft during his visit to the Rose Festival in Vancouver. "So I dressed up in my new uniform and my saber and I had a horse that pranced too dang much!" Devers rode behind the president's car in the parade, and he "didn't know whether or not that horse was going to stand up or fall down, or what, and I didn't know whether that saber was going to get mixed up with me and the people alongside [the parade route]." Overall, he concluded, "it was a very broadening experience, but it all went off very well. We had breakfast and met the President. Then he departed and we went back to business."[17]

The 1st Battalion and the 4th Field Artillery's regimental headquarters left Vancouver Barracks just three months after Devers joined the unit. The post was too small to allow the artillerymen to fire their howitzers, and the regiment's 2nd Battalion was returning from the Philippines. The regiment's new post was Fort D. A. Russell, on the outskirts of Cheyenne, Wyoming.

Fort D. A. Russell

Fort Russell (later renamed Fort Warren) was a much larger post than Vancouver Barracks, with plenty of room for three regiments with two battalions each. The 4th Artillery joined the 9th Cavalry and 11th Infantry Regiments and a signal battalion at the brigade-sized post. This consolidation was part of the army's effort to bring the three major combat arms together where they could train with one another. The ultimate purpose was to better prepare for the type of warfare envisioned by reformers such as Root. The regiments at Fort Russell formed the 2nd Division's 6th Brigade on the Mexican border in 1913.[18]

The train carrying Devers and his battalion arrived at Fort Russell in December 1909 during a blinding snowstorm. The change from the rainy but temperate climate of the Northwest to winter on the Great Plains was profound. Devers later remarked that it seemed to snow eleven months of the year in Wyoming, and "the wind was terrific. . . . In the blizzards the cattle and horses crowded in there over the fences, [and] came in to get up against the buildings to keep warm." The artillerymen often had to break trails through the snowdrifts with their mules, and the temperature regularly dropped as low as twenty degrees below zero.[19] Just surviving in such an environment was difficult, although it was a valuable experience for Devers, who would eventually command two armies fighting in the Vosges Mountains of France in the winter of 1944–1945.

Fort Russell was a relatively new post, and although it was somewhat isolated, both the post and nearby Cheyenne were on the main line of the Union Pacific Railroad, ensuring year-round communications to anywhere in the nation. Cheyenne in 1909 was "a real Western town" with a theater, a fairground, and a red-light district. The post commander, Brigadier General Clarence Edwards, made a point of introducing his officers to community leaders and took them to visit state legislators and the governor. Devers noted that the local population worked well with the post.[20]

Shortly after his arrival at Fort Russell, Devers was reassigned to Battery C, commanded by Captain Henry "Swish" Newbold, who had been a tactical officer at the Military Academy when Devers was there. Devers recalled that Newbold "was sort of a social leader there. He was unmarried and demanded all the proper social graces of his officers." Shortly thereafter, First Lieutenant Lesley J. McNair (West Point class of 1904) assumed command of the unit. "He and his good wife added much to the post." Devers considered him a "brilliant officer. . . . He was very serious minded and we worked hard." McNair was an important role model for young Devers, reinforcing his work ethic and his understanding of how to get things done. "He used to go over and work in the blacksmith shop and I was his helper with the blacksmith. In that way I picked up a great deal of information about how you got things done as you go along. I admired McNair greatly and this proved to be a good judgment because he, as you know, became, really, the head trainer of the Army that fought the Second World War."[21]

Fort Russell was a large post with plenty of room for artillery practice and other types of training for infantry, artillery, and cavalry units. Battery C did a lot of howitzer training, and Devers learned "an awful lot about firing because you didn't have many aiming points, [since] the ground was more or less flat. You had to go a distance to get into the hills where you learned something about clearing the crest. . . . We had a lot of trouble judging overs and shorts because of the nature of the terrain."[22]

While at Fort Russell, Devers's assignments included assistant to the post adjutant, post engineer, and post signal officer. He was responsible for a great deal of property and for mundane but important matters such as the efficient operation of the furnaces in the men's quarters. As signal officer, he was in charge of the post switchboard. His handling of this duty shows that he understood the need for a hands-on approach to leadership: "I always had a problem with that switchboard. . . . So I went up and ran the switchboard for a week myself, at peak loads, and found out what the problem was. I found that it required a lot of concentration and that we didn't have enough people. I got that corrected. . . . While you can't be as skillful as the people that are doing it, it gives you the information which you need to make a just decision."[23] Devers admitted that although these additional duties were difficult, they were also challenging and interesting and kept him alert. "There wasn't any chance to be dull at Cheyenne, certainly not for a second lieutenant of Field Artillery."[24]

One of the most instructive experiences for Devers was a 1,000-mile march across seven passes in the Rocky Mountains over a two-month period. Like most army units, the 4th Field Artillery was well below its authorized war strength. For this exercise, all regimental personnel were consolidated into one battalion consisting of a headquarters battery, three firing batteries of four guns each, and three quartermaster trains of fifty mules each. This reorganization allowed the officers to experience wartime conditions.[25] The field exercise allowed the battalion to train as realistically as possible for its wartime mission as a mountain artillery unit; the firing batteries were able to fire their howitzers in the mountains, and the support units practiced their missions under arduous conditions. In addition, the officers and men were hardened by weeks of cross-country movement over difficult mountain terrain. The battalion also experimented with several types of pack saddles and frames for the mules.

Devers was assigned to McNair's Battery C, where he helped conduct artillery practice. He was also put in charge of the battalion's seven pack trains—four from the battalion and three quartermaster trains led by hired civilians. Each train had about thirty-five mules that were led and cared for by a pack master, a cargodor, two cooks, a farrier, and seven mule handlers (one for every five mules). The work was hard from the outset. "In the first five to ten days of this march—when we were covering twenty miles a day—we lost a lot of civilians in the Quartermaster trains," he recalled. Devers was forced to replace these civilians with soldiers. About 13 soldiers deserted from each of the 200-man batteries during the expedition.[26]

Desertion was a major problem for the U.S. Army during the first thirty years of the twentieth century. In 1907 more than 7.4 percent of enlisted soldiers deserted. This rate fluctuated each year, partially in response to the civilian job market. From 1926 through 1929, more than 22 percent of the garrison at Fort Hamilton, New York, deserted. This was probably representative of the army's overall rate. In the early 1930s desertion rates remained high, even in units such as the 1st Infantry Division.[27] Reports by the inspector general indicate that low pay was the primary cause of desertion, especially when army pay was less than civilian pay. In 1909 privates received $13 per month, or $156 per year, whereas the annual civilian wage averaged $524; agricultural workers earned an average of $319 annually. Even during the Great Depression, the army paid its privates only $18.75 a month, while members of the Civilian Conservation Corps (CCC) received $30. Both soldiers and the CCC men received housing, food, medical care, and clothing. Whenever the training was arduous, as it was for the 4th Field Artillery during its two months of mountain training, the desertion rate rose. One month, 6.5 percent of the men deserted, forcing the unit to send for additional soldiers from Fort Russell to fill the ranks.[28]

Nonetheless, the battalion continued its journey while Devers's pack trains moved supplies of food, ammunition, and forage from various railheads to the batteries. "We carried three days' rations, two days' forage, and I used to come into the camp—sometimes passing the batteries . . . drop my loads where the batteries were to camp, pick up my mantas and ropes and start out for a railhead which might be another twenty miles away. Frequently I would arrive at midnight at the railhead; then I'd get water and clean up my equipment, get ready to load up early the next morning and join the batteries at the next camp."[29] Such hard and important work gave Devers a superb understanding of the most important task in the army: logistical support. He learned to plan for future operations and to adjust to conditions. For example, the average load carried by a mule was 250 pounds, but due to a shortage of mules, he had to figure out how to transport more than 300 pounds per mule without breaking the animals. He and his men did this by rotating the loads so that each mule got a break from the overload periodically.[30] Since the army, with a seemingly perverse sense of humor, often expects officers to do more than they have the resources for, this type of experience was good preparation for Devers's later service.

The soldiers and animals of the 4th Artillery marched twenty miles a day for the first five days. In retrospect, this was too much, given the physical condition of the men and the mules. A number of soldiers suffered blisters and other injuries. Devers and the other officers inspected their soldiers' feet every day and helped the battalion's medical officer treat blisters. Soldiers who were too injured to walk or were suffering from other ailments were carried in travois suspended from mules. Devers and his men also had to treat sore spots on the backs of the mules with a purple fluid, and they shifted the animals' loads to prevent further injury. On the evening of the fifth day they arrived at Denver, Colorado, where they stopped for several days to reorganize and bring replacements from Fort Russell.[31]

The lessons learned during that first week were applied, and the unit continued its trek for another seven weeks, moving through the Rockies to Canyon City, Colorado, then on to Fort Collins and eventually back to Cheyenne and Fort Russell. According to Devers, "those were long marches, men leading mules. . . . Each train had a bell mare—a mare with a bell around its neck—and the mules were trained to follow the bell mare in their particular pack train." The weather was cooling down as fall approached, and the men often found ice on their water buckets in the morning. Bedrolls got wet from the nightly dew, forcing the column to stop and readjust the loads and knots in the late morning as the ropes dried out. Perhaps the most difficult part of the journey was crossing the narrow mountain passes. Mules sometimes fell from the trail and plunged into the valley below. Then Devers and his men had to climb down to retrieve the animal's load and the mule itself if it was not killed.[32] Even if all the animals made it to the top of the pass, "we frequently ran into a swamp of accumulated water, dried and broken wood, trees, and leaves. Not once or twice, but about ten times in order to get the mules across such a place we had to build roads of saplings we cut down." If a mule got bogged down, Devers learned that the best way to get it moving again was to climb onto its back "and bite his ear."[33]

The officers and men learned to cope with the elements, difficult terrain, and stubborn animals. Devers learned a great deal about soldiers and how to care for them. He and McNair also became closely acquainted. McNair found that his subordinate got things done and never failed to throw himself into his duties completely. This undoubtedly accounts for their smooth working relationship in 1941–1943, when McNair was Army Ground Forces commander and Devers commanded the Armored Force. McNair remarked in Devers's 1911 efficiency report that he was "excellent" in "attention to duty, professional zeal, general bearing and military appearance and intelligence and judgment shown in instructing, drilling and handling enlisted men."[34]

Devers's years at Fort Russell gave him the professional grounding essential for an officer's successful service to the nation. They also gave him the opportunity to meet his future wife.

Major Leroy S. Lyon remained in command of the 1st Battalion, 4th Field Artillery, during Devers's service at Fort Russell. Devers greatly respected Lyon and enjoyed his "keen sense of humor." By early 1911, Major and Mrs. Lyon had taken Jake's measure and considered him to be a promising young officer—promising enough to introduce him to their nineteen-year-old niece, Miss Georgie Lyon, when she visited Fort Russell in January or February. As Devers remembered, it was, "of course, one of my responsibilities" to escort the major's niece to various functions. "She was going to stay one month but she stayed three."[35]

When Georgie arrived, Devers was not the only bachelor at Fort Russell. In fact, two of his closest friends in the battalion, Lieutenants McBride and Erlenkotter, were single. And at the time, Devers was a confirmed bachelor. While at West Point, he had listened to the advice of Major Charles Summerall, a popular artillery officer on the faculty, and resolved to stay single for at least five years. Nonetheless, he clearly fell in love with the petite young lady, and she soon reciprocated his affection.

Georgie was from Arlington, Virginia, where her father, Frank Lyon, was a prominent attorney. Being new to the West, she threw herself into the social activities at the isolated army post. With Jake's help she learned to ride Major Lyon's horse. She proved to be a natural and accomplished horsewoman and continued to ride for pleasure and exercise for most of her life. There was a theater in Cheyenne, and officers and their families frequented it regularly. There was a streetcar line connecting the fort to downtown Cheyenne, and Devers remembered, "I used to ride with her considerably and we had a lot of fun together. Pretty soon—it took quite a while—I was engaged."[36]

When Georgie returned home in early April, she and Jake were engaged, and they planned to marry in Arlington in the fall. By then, Devers's friends McBride and Erlenkotter were also engaged to girls from back east. The young officers hoped to get leave at the same time so they could attend one another's weddings. Unfortunately, their commander would not allow all three lieutenants to be gone at the same time. As it worked out, Devers and McBride had leaves that overlapped, so McBride was able to be Devers's best man.

Devers first met Georgie's father in early October. He found that Frank Lyon "was a different man from Major Leroy S. Lyon. He was very serious minded, very active and a very brilliant mind, as his brother was, but he didn't have the sense of humor, and he didn't play poker. He didn't do a lot of things like that." Frank proved to be a good influence on the young couple and was very supportive of their marriage, despite his daughter's youth. In addition to being a successful attorney, he owned a lot of real estate in the Washington, D.C., area. Lyon served on the Interstate Commerce Commission and introduced his son-in-law to politics.[37]

McBride and Devers headed east in late September. McBride married first, and then he traveled to Virginia for Georgie and Jake's wedding, which took place in the Lyons' home in Arlington. As Jake recalled, "The wedding went off all right but I had a problem because Georgie wanted lilies-of-the-valley and it seems lilies-of-the-valley aren't in existence in October, so I had a hard time getting the florist to go to some house and get me a bunch."[38] McBride and Devers stayed at the Army and Navy Club in Washington, and on the day of the wedding they got lost on their way to the Lyons' home. With flowers in hand, they finally made it, and the wedding proceeded.

While in Arlington, Devers drove an electric car for the first (and probably the last) time. Frank Lyon owned "one of these electric automobiles. I didn't have a driver's license, but I could drive, so I used to drive that electric automobile to take Georgie downtown to do some shopping." On one of these trips, Devers turned the wrong way onto a one-way street, right in front of a policeman. "The policeman held up his hand, and, of course, I was young and pretty niftily dressed, I guess, and scared to death. He gave me a ticket and told me I'd have to appear at the police court the next morning. . . . This was my first experience with the law. I told the judge my story and he sort of smiled and said, 'Well, we'll give you a year's grace.'"[39]

After this adventure, the newlyweds traveled to Niagara Falls for a brief honeymoon before returning by train to Fort Russell. There, they settled into an apartment in a new fourplex. The building was on the edge of the prairie, and there was a large lake about half a mile away. The lake provided ice for the post, and Devers often had to take a detail up to the lake to cut ice and store it in the nearby icehouse. "That lake froze over solid! We had great cakes of ice to handle and we didn't have too good equipment in those days. . . . Every now and then one of these men would be thrown into the water. Boy when he came out he was a cake of ice! We never stopped— we just threw him in that wagon" and headed for the hospital to thaw him out.[40] The lake was also a great place to ice-skate, and skating parties helped break the monotony of winter on the plains.

Georgie and Jake attended the weekly post dance. "Each regiment prepared the punch for one month so we alternated. . . . Each of those regiments had their special punch. Believe me, ours in the 4th Mountain Artillery was something!" These dances gave the officers and the ladies an event to look forward to and a chance to socialize with people from the other regiments. Dinner parties were a routine part of these evenings. After dinner, the couples would ride together to the post's dance hall in a four-wheeled wagon pulled by four mules. "There we'd all congregate and that is the way we got to know each other."[41]

At the theater in Cheyenne, road shows traveling from New York or Chicago to San Francisco often made a one-night stand. Unmarried officers usually sat in the front row. During musical comedies, "some of the brave souls would go up on the stage and dance with the girls. . . . Sometimes the train was held up for an hour or so because we didn't get the girls back in time for them to leave about two o'clock in the morning."[42]

The Deverses remained at Fort Russell until December 1912, when Jake was reassigned to West Point. Their time together at Fort Russell, away from their families, allowed the young couple to develop their relationship and establish their own routine. It also introduced Georgie to army life. For the rest of their lives, the Deverses would cherish many of the friends they made in Wyoming.

West Point

In November 1912 Lieutenant Devers received orders to return to the Military Academy as a mathematics instructor. The assignment was somewhat unexpected, and Jake and Georgie had only about a week to pack before they were to leave for New York. The hardest part of the trip was getting across the western plains in early December. As Devers recalled:

> I was to report there by the 15th of December. So we planned and packed up to go East. We had our reservations on the Union Pacific Railroad and we got into one of the worst storms the country has ever known. So that train didn't appear in Cheyenne for three days. But I could see that, with field glasses, top of the mountain where it was to come over in that cold weather. So I watched for it! . . . I had a driver and four mules and a wagon standing by and, of course, along about three o'clock one morning I got the call, "the train's coming over the mountain."[43]

Quickly, they roused the wagon driver and headed for the train station in Cheyenne, three miles away. Jake rode on the box seat with the driver, and Georgie was bundled up inside with their luggage. "Well the first thing that happened was the mules started to run away with us." With some effort, the driver got the team under control and stopped the wagon. In the process, a trace loosened, forcing Devers to "jump off into the snow—in all my finery, and get that fixed." They quickly resumed their race to the station, arriving barely in time to board the train. After that hectic start they had a comparatively calm journey to Washington, D.C., where they enjoyed a brief visit with the Lyons before going on to West Point.[44]

When Jake and Georgie arrived at the Military Academy in December 1912, they were assigned quarters at 16 Kingsley Row—a three-story wooden house that remains in use today. Their apartment was on the middle level, with a beautiful view over the Hudson River toward Garrison, New York. They had a kitchen, a living room, and a bedroom. The other apartment in the house was on the first floor and was occupied by a civilian who worked in the paymaster's office on post.

Devers recalled that "one of the first things I did, of course, after I arrived there was to call on the Superintendent, General Townsley. General and Mrs. Townsley returned the call." When they arrived, Mrs. Townsley observed to her husband that the Deverses ought to have a porch on the front of the house, overlooking the river. "So within a couple of weeks I had a porch and an awning. You could sit out there in great comfort and have the greatest scenic view in the world."[45] That view can still be enjoyed from that porch today.

Devers arrived in the middle of the academic year, with no teaching experience. "I was thrown into the middle of Plebe Math, Convergency and Divergency of Series, Probability and Chance, and I hadn't been too good in those subjects when I was a cadet." Fortunately, the head of the Mathematics Department, Colonel Charles P. Echols, had developed a method of preparing newly assigned instructors for their classroom duties. He "required all his new instructors to recite on the subjects two or three days ahead of the lessons." Colonel Echols personally supervised these sessions and "handled us just as though we were cadets—and we were cadets, really—although we were young officers."[46] This type of training for new instructors remains a tradition at the Military Academy, ensuring that the cadets receive the finest technical education possible while exposing them to young officers recently returned from field duty.

Devers taught two classes a day, six days a week. Each class section had about twelve cadets, ensuring a great deal of individual attention. In 1912 the officers wore their blue uniforms in the classroom, and Devers observed that "they're expensive, and chalk gets on them. They are hard to maintain, but we were immaculate in that sense." The most tedious part of teaching at West Point was the grading. Cadets recited daily and were graded on their work. Examinations were frequent, and instructors spent hours scoring them. In the Math Department, Devers and his peers marked exams in teams of two. If they disagreed on the marking of a paper, they met with Colonel Echols and explained their rationales for their scores. Echols would then decide on the final grade. However, according to Devers, "I never knew him to give the cadet the lower mark. He always gave him the higher mark of the two."[47]

Cadets were assigned to sections based on their previous grades. The lowest section in math was called the Goat Section. Devers taught the second to lowest section. His cadets faced expulsion from the Academy if they failed the course, so Devers considered it his duty to save as many of his students as possible by providing them with good instruction and frequent tutoring. "I was able to save more than 50% of the people, particularly in the Plebe Year, which was quite a good record. I got terribly interested in why they were having trouble with Math. . . . Well, you know, that taught me a good lesson because in all the rest of my career I found out that you must look very carefully at both sides of the question to get the facts before you get rid of a man you don't like or you don't think is any good."[48]

Devers's teaching experience at West Point demonstrates a facet of the

Military Academy's history that is sometimes overlooked. There are actually two graduation classes each year: the first is the cadets, who are commissioned as officers; the second is the group of young officers who were brought back to the Academy to teach and then return to the field army with greatly enhanced intellectual capabilities and more finely honed leadership skills. In 1912 most of the instructors were West Point graduates. Today, about half of them are graduates of other colleges or universities.

Georgie and Jake found social life at the Academy to be both challenging and enjoyable. They often invited cadets to their home for dinner. These dinners were expensive, and the young couple received no additional funds to pay for such gatherings. Jake also ate with the cadets in the mess hall, where he could assess their attitudes and habits. Such personal mentorship is an important part of the West Point experience and is a terrific way to introduce cadets to army traditions and values. Devers himself had received this kind of mentoring from Joe Stilwell and Charles Summerall, both of whom became four-star generals.[49] In addition, there were numerous officers' functions such as dances and dinners. Social life at the Academy in 1912 centered around the academic department to which an officer was assigned. These officers and their wives often established lasting friendships.

Devers studied hard for his teaching duties; in addition, he coached the basketball team and worked with the artillery detachment on post. "I was the only one there that knew anything about pack artillery. So after my academic obligations were filled, I had to go to work there. This kept me very busy." Devers also helped coach the baseball team, on which Omar Bradley played. "Were the hours long? I would say they were long but they didn't bother me very much."[50] One of his fellow instructors noted that Devers seemed to be "in perpetual motion."[51] Devers left no record of his relationship with Bradley during this time, and it is possible he did not even remember him. Bradley and Devers would serve together at the Academy in the early 1920s.

We do not know what Georgie thought about her husband's work schedule or the responsibilities of entertaining cadets and other officers and their wives. She certainly worked hard to be the proper hostess for the athletic coaches from visiting schools such as the Naval Academy and Cornell. Sometime during their first tour of duty at the Academy, Georgie gave birth to a baby boy who was either stillborn or died shortly after birth.

During his years in the Math Department at West Point, Devers clearly impressed Echols, the department head. Echols noted repeatedly that Devers did an excellent job teaching and interacting with the cadets. He recommended that Devers be given increasing responsibilities and deemed him "fitted for promotion." In his final efficiency report, Echols wrote, "[Devers] cooperates loyally with others, [and is] a fine young officer, of most agreeable personality, enthusiastic in his work and thoroughly efficient."[52]

After teaching at the Military Academy for more than three years, Devers was assigned to the 9th Field Artillery at Schofield Barracks, Hawaii. The newly established regiment was one of the army's first motorized field artillery units. This assignment would expand Devers's professional horizons significantly.[53]

Schofield Barracks

The post known as Schofield Barracks was established in late 1908 to provide housing and training areas for regiments of the Hawaiian Division. The mission of the Hawaiian Division was to provide mobile forces to defend the naval base at Pearl Harbor from landward attack. Schofield Barracks and Pearl Harbor were part of the American Pacific empire that stretched from Alaska to the Philippines and from Wake Island to the Hawaiian Islands. Schofield Barracks remains a critical installation for American forces in the Pacific. Devers asked to be assigned to the newly organized 9th Field Artillery Regiment because it was one of the first units in the U.S. Army equipped with motorized vehicles.[54]

During the summer of 1916 Jake was able to take several months' leave, and the couple visited Georgie's parents in Arlington—a time he described as "a most enjoyable summer."[55] To reach Hawaii, Georgie and Jake endured a four-day train ride from New York to San Francisco and then an ocean voyage from there to the island of Oahu. At Pearl Harbor they were met by their sponsor and driven to Schofield Barracks. Their quarters were primitive, since the post was less than a decade old. As Devers remembered, "We lived on post, up near the [Kolekole] pass, and many of the quarters had been built from the crates which had been used to ship the furniture over there." Their home was a one-story house with a bathroom, kitchen, bedroom, and living room. They were able to afford domestic help, so they hired servants from among the "Chinese (who inhabited the valleys around the post) for a reasonable amount of money."[56] Since the area was more than 1,000 feet above sea level, the climate was pleasant, except when it rained.

The Deverses' social life revolved around the two artillery regiments on post. Officers' families were close, and "if somebody gave a dinner party on the post, the servants found out who the guests were to be. If you were one of them and you went to that house, you were liable to see your own silver or your china on the table. This was common and you'd also see some of your servants working there. In other words, the service family was also well organized and very efficient." It is clear that Devers found Hawaii a very pleasant place to be assigned:

> We weren't very well paid in those days. . . . We did go down to the beaches in the afternoon, and on weekends, to bathe and picnic. Oahu has lots of good beaches. . . . We sometimes went down to visit friends at other posts on the island to enjoy their beaches, but we stuck strictly to our business because our money ran out too fast if we didn't. . . . We lived close together in the areas of the post. We intermingled at the club and if we had a party, we returned our party invitations at the proper time and in the proper way, generally on dance night, which was Saturday night always. Our social life was very normal and very interesting.[57]

By late fall 1916, Georgie was pregnant. Her parents came for a visit in November or December, and the young couple showed them around Oahu. Devers had given them a preview, describing the island in a letter to the Lyons in October: "It is small for you can see across the island from the divide upon which we live and it is one of the most beautiful sights one can see. . . . We live right up against the mountains and the weather is ideal."[58]

One of Devers's duties was serving as judge advocate of the General Court. This was in the era before the establishment of the Judge Advocate Corps, and Devers was surprised by the assignment "because I'd never been a Judge Advocate in my life. . . . However, I had been well educated, both at the Military Academy and in my short experience at D. A. Russell—and later at West Point—in the duties of the Judge Advocate." The job required Devers to travel all over the island to deal with about a dozen military justice cases. Because there was no public transit system, the Deverses had to buy their first car, taking out an $800 loan for a new 1916 Buick. He also had to find a stenographer to serve as the court recorder. He located a competent civilian stenographer on the post, but the man tended to drink too much. On several occasions Devers had to sober him up after a four-day binge. To do so, he used "the water cure—I got his clothes off him and with the help of a couple of sergeants I gave him a cold water bath and sobered him up." Devers managed to resolve the cases assigned to him and was able to return to his regular duties with his battery.[59]

First Lieutenant Devers was assigned to Captain Pratt's Battery C of the newly established 9th Field Artillery Regiment.[60] The technical aspects of this job were different from his experience as a pack artilleryman. The battery was equipped with caterpillar-type tractors to pull its 4.7-inch guns and 155mm howitzers. Four-wheel-drive trucks carried the ammunition and the gun crews, and a number of motorcycles were used by messengers and officers. One of his main tasks "was to teach everybody how to ride a motorcycle because that was our mode of transportation. . . . As a result we had a good many accidents. You might call them minor, but there were broken legs and broken arms, and I learned to dislike the motorcycle extremely." Soldiers with broken bones had to spend time in the post hospital, and Devers lost their services until they healed.[61]

Devers and the newly established unit had to learn to move and fire its heavy guns. An even greater challenge was maintaining the artillery pieces, tractors, and trucks, "which meant training a lot of mechanics." The soldiers had to learn how to drive the tractors and trucks on the highways, as well as how to maneuver the vehicles and guns over rough terrain. According to Devers, he "had no problem of reacting to the adjustment from pack to horse-drawn artillery. . . . However, I had had nothing to do with tractor-drawn artillery. This presented quite a problem because we found that with a heavy gun behind the tractor if you didn't handle it just right going down a steep incline, the weight behind the tractor had a tendency to push it around and overturn it." This happened several times before the men figured out how to put ropes on the wheels of the guns to keep them behind the tractors.[62]

Devers also faced the normal personnel problems encountered in a newly organized army unit. The cadre for the new regiment had come from the 1st Field Artillery Regiment, which was also assigned to Schofield Barracks. It is quite likely that the 1st Artillery had not sent its best noncommissioned officers and soldiers to the newly formed 9th Artillery. Within four months of his arrival, Devers was ordered to take command of the problematic Battery F and straighten it out. Colonel McMahon advised him that the unit had had a "sort of mutiny," and Devers would be the sole officer in the battery. Further, he advised Devers to "look at your noncommissioned officers and see what the problem is. Whatever you decide to do, go ahead and do it. If you need any advice, come to me; and if you need any help, come to me; and I'll back you up."[63]

First, Devers observed the unit during and after duty hours and identified the main problem: the battery's low morale, poor discipline, and inadequate training stemmed from weak leadership by several key noncommissioned officers (NCOs). The first sergeant was a competent artilleryman but a young and inexperienced NCO. He was too close to the men and regularly played blackjack with them at night. The mess sergeant was incompetent; therefore, meals were distasteful and often cold. Then Devers took action: "I called the First Sergeant in and told him I was going to reduce him from First Sergeant to sergeant and that Sergeant Jones [the battery's junior section sergeant] . . . was going to be the First Sergeant. . . . Then I assembled the battery and told them of the changes I was going to make and what we had to do, [and] that I would start to improve the Mess. Well I had to get a new Mess Sergeant, which I did. I took the senior cook and I made him Mess Sergeant."[64] Devers backed the new first sergeant to the hilt and spent a great deal of time helping the new mess sergeant improve the chow. The process of building unit morale and enhancing training and discipline took time and a great deal of energy. However, once the food got better and the men saw a firm but fair leader at their head, the battery improved. Devers demonstrated a good understanding of his men when he decided to put the former first sergeant in charge of a gun section, keeping an experienced individual in a critical position. From that time on, the sergeant's gun section was always the best one in the unit. "I suppose," Devers reflected, "this was because he knew we meant business."[65]

Devers's approach to training was innovative. He followed the battalion's training guidance but did things his own way. For example, if he had too few soldiers to man the battery's four guns, he combined the men into one or two gun sections and took them to the ranges. When the soldiers completed their training missions with proficiency, he would organize a baseball game as a reward. He varied the drills and organized "short difficult marches through the ravines where they had to manhandle the guns and tractors. This took a lot of skill." He also willingly listened to ideas from his NCOs and his men. It was a noteworthy performance, especially considering that Devers was the only officer in the battery, even though five were authorized.[66] His new battalion commander, Major Raymond Pratt, noted that Devers showed "remarkable zeal and efficiency as an organizational commander, and has obtained remarkable results from his battery."[67] This was high praise indeed!

The 9th Field Artillery was one of the first regiments in the army to become motorized. It was the beginning of a dramatic transformation that would take more than twenty years. There was a lot of support for the continued use of horses in the 1916 army. However, the war in Europe was demonstrating the need for howitzers and guns that were too heavy for teams of horses to move across torn-up and muddy battlefields. In Devers's view, motorization was inevitable because "mobility is very important to artillery and it was the coming thing. . . . I was glad to get this assignment." Officers like Devers who could readily adjust to tactical and technical innovations and lead others in the process of modernization were well positioned for future success in the military. Devers "wasn't sorry to lose the horses," even though he loved to ride and to play polo. From his perspective, the gradual transition from a horse-equipped army to a mechanized and motorized force was necessary.[68]

One additional duty illuminates an element of Devers's personality that was important to his later career success and explains why he irritated certain other senior officers, such as Bradley and Eisenhower. Colonel William Snow made Devers responsible for the officers' club, which was experiencing serious financial problems because some of the officers failed to pay their bills promptly. Devers found an effective solution that shamed them into meeting their obligations. As he recalled:

> I had to notify them and post their names on the bulletin board. This had never been done before and involved one of the highest ranking men in one of the regiments. I warned him and then I posted his name on the bulletin board. The officer sent his Adjutant to get the name removed. . . . I told him there was only one way this could be done properly and that was by paying his bill promptly. As each bill was settled, I reprinted the bulletin board list.[69]

This got results, but it did not make Devers any friends. Fortunately, Colonel Snow appreciated Devers's initiative and his success in getting the club's finances on a better footing. In his future service, Devers would often take whatever action he deemed best, regardless of the political consequences.

Self-confident superiors like Colonel Snow valued this dedication to duty and mission accomplishment.

Amazingly, the officers at Schofield Barracks seemed to give little thought to the war raging in Europe and the possible consequences for them and the American army. This is somewhat understandable, since U.S. policy at the time was to remain neutral. Also, as Devers observed, "We had our family problems, [and] our local problems, which kept us plenty busy. We studied the war a little bit but not as we would do today. We never spoke about the coming U.S. involvement in World War I until it actually happened."[70]

On 6 April 1917 Congress declared war against Imperial Germany. Devers recalled that "when the war finally came, we got orders in a hurry to move the regiments from Schofield Barracks to Fort Sill, Oklahoma, which was being built and expanded into a great artillery school. . . . So I packed up my family, which then consisted of a six-month old daughter [Frances] and my wife. We took the first transport." They had just two days to pack up their personal household effects.[71] By that time, Devers had been promoted to the rank of major. Colonel Snow, who would be commandant of the artillery school, preceded Devers to Fort Sill. Together, they would cope with the largest and fastest expansion of the U.S. Army in its history to that date.

Jacob Devers's first eight years in the army gave him a variety of experiences. He made the transition from mule-carried pack artillery to motorized artillery. He learned to deal with soldiers effectively and demonstrated an ability to learn from his men, his peers, and his superiors. Georgie and Jake found a comfortable place in the army family. During his assignments at Fort Russell, West Point, and Schofield Barracks, they grew together as a couple and were mentored by people such as the McNairs and the Snows. By 1917, they were ready for greater challenges in difficult times.

3

World War I and the Roaring Twenties

When the United States declared war on Germany in 1917, the nation was totally unprepared to wage modern warfare. The regular army was small, with just 127,588 soldiers, while European armies numbered in the millions. Roughly 30 percent of these American troops were stationed overseas. The U.S. Army had no permanent combat organization larger than a regiment, and little training of large units had taken place. There were fewer than 6,000 officers in the regular army, making rapid expansion of the force difficult. Fortunately, 180,000 National Guardsmen were available for federal service, thanks to the National Defense Act of 1916, but these men were not well trained.[1] Nonetheless, President Woodrow Wilson and Secretary of War Newton Baker acquiesced to British and French pleas to send a large expeditionary force to France to help the Western powers stave off the German army.

It was one thing to raise an army of several million men; it was another thing to arm and train such a large force. The personnel issues were daunting: where would the army find sufficient officers and noncommissioned officers to train the new soldiers? Severely aggravating the training challenge was the fact that the American industrial base could not produce enough machine guns, rifles, artillery pieces, airplanes, ammunition, or ships to arm the expeditionary forces going to France. The burden of solving these problems fell heavily on the officers of the regular army and the nation's political leaders.

In spite of these difficulties, President Wilson knew that if the United States wanted to earn a meaningful place at the negotiating table at the war's end, the nation would have to expand its armed forces dramatically to influence the fighting on the western front. The army was not totally unprepared for this daunting task. In less than eighteen months, it expanded to over 4 million men and deployed 2 million soldiers in forty-two divisions to France. The entry of the American Expeditionary Forces (AEF) into France in 1917–1918 tipped the military balance in favor of the Western powers and ensured the defeat of the Central powers. This phenomenal achievement by the regular army and the National Guard was possible in large part because of a series of military reforms that had taken place in the United States since 1900. These reforms profoundly affected the lives and careers of officers who were on active duty when the war began, including John J. Pershing, George Marshall, Dwight Eisenhower, and Jacob Devers.

The Root Reforms

During the first two decades of the twentieth century, the U.S. Army underwent a dramatic transformation. Professor Mac Coffman has correctly called this a "managerial revolution." The reforms implemented by Elihu Root, secretary of war from 1899 to 1904, initiated this revolution; they were a direct response to the need to transform the army from a frontier constabulary dealing primarily with American Indians to an expeditionary force able to conquer and garrison the Philippines, Puerto Rico, and Hawaii. The Root reforms focused on the development of educational institutions to prepare American army officers to manage and direct modern warfare.[2]

Root believed that "the real object of having an army is to provide for war." Consequently, he convinced Congress to approve the creation of a General Staff to plan for potential wars and to oversee the army's preparation for its wartime missions. He rationalized and expanded the army school system with post schools for lieutenants, the School of the Line for captains, and the Staff School and War College for midcareer and senior officers. This educational system prepared officers to run the General Staff in Washington and to command the staffs of brigades, divisions, and armies in the field. The army also made significant efforts to concentrate infantry, cavalry, and artillery regiments at larger posts so they could train together. By 1912, efforts were under way to create new combined-arms organizations known as divisions. The army also adopted new weapons and equipment such as the 1903 Springfield rifle, airplanes, telephones, machine guns, trucks, tractors, and motorcycles. Although limited funds precluded rapid changes in equipment and practices, these steps proved valuable when the army was called on to mobilize a massive expeditionary force.[3]

Most of the initial inspiration for the Root reforms and subsequent military modernization was provided by two factors. The first was public reaction to the miserable administrative performance of the U.S. Army in the

Spanish-American War of 1898. During that struggle, it became clear that army officers lacked the training necessary to manage the logistical aspects of overseas warfare; in addition, there was no military institution designed to plan major campaigns against modern armies. The second factor was the need to conquer and hold an American empire as the army fought to subdue Filipino and Puerto Rican nationalists from 1899 to 1905.[4] By 1916, however, American leaders perceived an even greater military challenge to the nation's security: the war that had engulfed Europe, the Middle East, and parts of Africa and Asia. Although the United States tried to remain neutral and stay out of that conflict, the global nature of the industrial economies involved in the war made such a position increasingly untenable.

When the European war broke out in 1914, American defense policy was based on the belief that the U.S. Navy could prevent an invasion of the homeland. Therefore, Congress authorized a significant expansion of the navy and smaller increases in the army. By 1916, however, the German submarine threat to American commerce led Congress to authorize a rapid increase in the navy's battle fleet to deter war. At the same time, the National Defense Act of 1916 increased the regular army from 100,000 to 175,000 men and authorized an expansion of the National Guard to 400,000 soldiers, providing a ready reserve of manpower in case of war. But the army's role was uncertain in the face of the German submarine threat.[5]

When the German government unleashed unrestricted submarine warfare against all ships in European waters in February 1917, the expansion of the U.S. Army was barely under way. The creation of the 9th Field Artillery Regiment in Hawaii in 1916 was part of that process. Shortly after the American declaration of war, President Wilson and Secretary of War Baker agreed to send a large army to France. To raise the millions of men needed for this force, Congress authorized conscription and allocated funds to equip and train these men. The first million were selected during the summer of 1917. The regular army's mission was to train these conscripts and organize the divisions in which they would fight. Fortunately, the Root reforms had provided a cadre of trained officers and the General Staff to accomplish these tasks. By December 1917, the army had created thirty-two training camps, and Jake Devers was on his way to Fort Sill, Oklahoma, to help train artillerymen. In the meantime, the first American combat division sailed for France in June 1917, signaling to the war-weary French and British that the Yanks were coming.[6]

Fort Sill

Army officers scrambled to meet the challenges of rapid expansion. Devers immediately felt the effects of this effort: he was promoted to captain in June 1917 and then to major in the fall. As he later remembered, "We got orders in a hurry to move the [1st and 9th Field Artillery] regiments from Schofield Barracks to Fort Sill, Oklahoma. . . . I was one of the first officers to be ordered to Fort Sill."[7]

The artillery school at Fort Sill was part of the army's effort to modernize training in the first decade of the twentieth century. The impetus to adopt state-of-the-art artillery practices involving fire direction and control came from observations made during the Russo-Japanese War of 1904–1905. During that conflict, indirect fire by guns using smokeless powder proved to be the best way to strike the enemy without exposing the guns to counterbattery fire. However, new techniques were needed to allow artillery observers to relay target information to the firing batteries and to allow battery commanders to coordinate the firing of the guns. As a result, "the battery became a firing unit and not just a tactical element." The new theory of artillery employment was clear, but the process of training the officers of the newly created field artillery branch was more difficult. As Boyd Dastrup concluded in his history of that branch, "Americans still made provision for direct fire as late as 1916 and were reluctant to make a clean break because indirect fire was more complicated."[8]

The army's School of Fire was established at Fort Sill in 1908, the year after the field artillery branch was separated from the coastal artillery. However, effective organization of the training base took several more years. Captain Dan Moore was selected as commandant of the School of Fire for Field Artillery in 1911; he was replaced in 1914 by Lieutenant Colonel E. F. McGlachin. The initial class enrolled in the four-month-long course of instruction included about twenty-five officers. At that rate, it would have taken at least four years to train the 408 field artillery officers in the new techniques. There were few adequate buildings to house the course, and students were forced to live in tents until temporary quarters could be constructed on the 55,000-acre post.[9] This halting progress toward establishing an artillery training base was interrupted in 1916, when the school was closed and its instructors and students were sent to join the artillery regiments deployed along the Mexican border. A contemporary observer noted, "It is a serious commentary upon our military policy, or lack of the same, that whenever an emergency arose, such as the Mexican border troubles, the first act to meet the emergency was to suspend our schools."[10]

In 1917, as in 1912, the American army was "so far behind the Europeans in the quality of their artillerymen 'that it really makes one shudder.'" This observation echoed that of Brigadier General John Story, chief of artillery, who noted in 1904, "There is no first-class power which has so systematically neglected its field artillery as the United States."[11]

The reopening of the artillery school and the transfer of the 1st and 9th Field Artillery Regiments to Fort Sill were major steps forward. The 1st Field Artillery Regiment was a horse-drawn light artillery unit, and the 9th was equipped with tractors to pull its medium artillery pieces (155mm howitzers and guns). These two regiments reflected the mix of light and medium artillery that the AEF would be equipped with in France. Regular army officers and men played a major role in the successful expansion of American artillery from 6 regiments in 1917 to 234 regiments two years later.

Devers's mission at Fort Sill was to help create an artillery school where artillerymen could be trained and new artillery regiments created. He, like Dwight D. Eisenhower and Omar Bradley, remained in the United States throughout the war, as did nearly a third of regular army officers, who were needed to turn raw conscripts into soldiers. Initially, it was thought that the war would last for several years and that officers such as Devers and Eisenhower would eventually go to Europe to fight. Certainly, these ambitious professional soldiers looked forward to combat, since that is how regulars achieve rapid promotions. But their training missions were essential to the ultimate success of the army. When asked years later whether he regretted missing the experience of combat, Devers answered: "This never bothered me. I've always felt if you had a job to do, you did it, and if you did it well, the Lord took care of you—and he certainly did in this case. I was never discouraged. I knew that if the war continued—and I expected it would—they were going to need me."[12]

His reaction at the time, however, was quite different, One of his former colleagues, Colonel H. C. Jackson, reminded him of this in 1949: "I have a clear recollection of sitting at my desk in the Topography Section, School of Fire when you came in from firing. . . . Your face was red from the cold wind: you were in heavy uniform. . . . You commented bitterly that your Army career was ruined because you had not gone to France; that any officer who had not been to France during the war was done for."[13] Devers wrote back to Jackson: "You are right—I didn't think I had much of a chance after the First World War and, as a matter of fact, I did miss some of the better experiences of that time. However, when one loves his job, he has no trouble working at it, and I have always loved the Army and what it stood for."[14] But that was written with the benefit of hindsight. In 1917 Devers was looking forward to his new assignment at Fort Sill.

Devers had only about forty-eight hours to pack up his family and leave Schofield Barracks after receiving his orders in November 1917. He barely had time to clean out his desk. A fellow officer agreed to sell his Buick and to pay off the car loan with the proceeds. Jake, Georgie, and baby Frances occupied a small cabin on an army transport that had stopped in Hawaii on its way from the Philippines to San Francisco. Devers recalled the trip: "I had a very bad cold. . . . [I was worried] about that new baby and a young wife—we were still ignorant about a baby. When we got on the transport, of course, the first thing that happened was that my wife got very sick and this young daughter had to be fed. She had a special formula which had to be made up with condensed milk. . . . I got rid of my cold pretty fast."[15]

Once in San Francisco, Jake and Georgie decided that she and the baby would stay with her parents in Virginia while he went to Fort Sill and set up their quarters. He accompanied them only as far as Albuquerque, New Mexico, on the Southern Pacific Railroad. "This was in December and the weather was miserable—snow storms were everywhere," he recalled. Fortunately, Mrs. Arnold, the wife of a fellow artillery officer and the daughter of General Treat, was traveling on the same train and agreed to help Georgie and Frances on their journey east. The trip was anything but routine, as Georgie lost her tickets. When they arrived in Atlanta, General Treat's aide straightened out the ticket situation, and Georgie and the baby completed their journey to Virginia.[16]

Meanwhile, Major Devers traveled from Albuquerque to Oklahoma City on the Rock Island Line and then south to Fort Sill. "That was some ride! The Rock Island was all right, but when I had to get off and catch my train for Fort Sill, I had a room which was full of Indians—and everything else—so I had a miserable trip." When he arrived, he found that "the weather had been freezing and the set of quarters was all frozen up. I spent Christmas day under those temporary quarters with a blow torch trying to thaw out the pipes." His quarters were in a fourplex located on a new part of the post. Each unit had its own coal stove for heat, "so we had an awful fire hazard. We had problems with the fire too but we managed to survive that."[17]

Fort Sill, located six miles north of Lawton, Oklahoma, was established in 1869 to serve as a base for troops overseeing the Kiowa and Comanche reservations. In August 1917 the base was expanded so that the 35th Division could train there until it went overseas in May 1918. A field artillery firing center was also organized in 1917, and the Field Artillery School of Fire was formally reestablished in July.[18] In the fall of 1917 the artillery school was expanded to accommodate 1,200 students and a detachment of 250 enlisted men and 150 officer-instructors. A field artillery officer candidate school was opened in June 1918, with 160 instructors and 3,800 candidates. This school trained the officers for the artillery branch, which grew from 408 officers before the war to 17,529 officers by November 1918. More than 9,000 of these officers served in France.[19] Future president Harry Truman was one of the battery commanders who trained at Fort Sill.

During the rapid expansion of the army in late 1917, a crisis developed: an insufficient number of artillery officers and gunners had been trained to serve in the forty-two artillery brigades then being formed. There were only 8,253 enlisted men in the field artillery branch in April 1917. In February 1918 the War Department appointed a chief of field artillery to oversee the training of a force that would total more than 400,000 artillerymen by November 1918. The chief of artillery ordered the reorganization and enlargement of the School of Fire at Fort Sill and established several replacement depots at other posts. A twelve-week course of instruction for artillery officers was established and operated by regular army officers such as Devers and combat veterans returned from France. Fifty-four classes graduated during the war, providing 3,200 new officers. Standards were high, and 2,481 men failed the course.[20]

Devers's selection to serve as an instructor and then assistant director at the artillery school made sense. Given his experience with pack artillery, horse-drawn artillery, and motorized artillery, he had a comprehensive understanding of field artillery. He had been in the army for eight years and had the know-how and maturity to direct a group of instructors. His regiment, the 9th Artillery, had moved from Hawaii to Fort Sill to serve as school troops, making his assignment even more logical. In addition, he and the commandant of the artillery school, Colonel William J. Snow, had served together in Hawaii. Over the next year, Devers was promoted to lieutenant colonel and then to colonel as the army continued to expand to over 4 million men. He concluded that he was "the highest ranking man with any real knowledge of the problems we had to work with and I became what you might call 'the trouble shooter' there, as I seemed to be all during my life."[21]

Georgie and Frances joined Jake in early 1918. Although he found their quarters comfortable enough, in spite of the hazardous coal stove, Georgie had less than pleasant memories of the isolated post on the southern plains. Devers recalled, "We had a young daughter there and it was a real rough time, and my wife didn't particularly like Sill. There wasn't any idea why she didn't like it, she had a sad experience down there trying to raise a child."[22] While he was immersed in the challenging but satisfying work of training new instructors and young artillery officers, Georgie found herself in a hostile climate (compared with Oahu) a long way from home; she had a young child, few friends, and a husband who worked twelve-hour days, six days a week. Georgie eased her loneliness by spending the three summer months in Virginia and Pennsylvania with the Lyon and Devers families—a practice she and Frances continued every year until 1940.[23]

A move to different quarters may have helped raise Georgie's spirits. As Devers recalled, "One day, after I had been there about two months and had been living in this firetrap with a wife and a young baby—just about seven months old—I came home about eight o'clock, after dark, to find my family gone from the apartment, with a note there saying I had been assigned to new quarters which had been a major's set in the new post." The new apartment was significantly better than the old one. Devers believed that Colonel Adrian Fleming, with whom he had served in the 4th Artillery at Fort Russell, had arranged for the move and had been instrumental in getting him assigned to the artillery school in the first place.[24]

American field artillery units in the First World War were equipped with three different types of artillery pieces. Light artillery units used the French-designed 75mm gun, and medium artillery regiments were equipped with either the 155mm howitzer or the 155mm gun, both of which were also French designed. Because American industry could not gear up quickly enough to manufacture these weapons, the AEF received more than 3,000 of its total 3,500 artillery pieces from the French. Consequently, the artillery school at Fort Sill centered its instruction on these three guns. Initially, all of them were horse drawn, but by mid-1918, the 155mm guns and howitzers were pulled by tractors, and the ammunition trains had been equipped with trucks. Devers's experience with tractors and trucks in

Hawaii was valuable in his role as an instructor. His positive attitude toward problem solving and his habit of working himself as hard as he worked his subordinates proved to be important factors in his quick advancement to colonel in 1918.[25]

The army's efforts to create a modern artillery arm paid off on the battlefields of France. In the Meuse-Argonne offensive in the fall of 1918, more than 3,900 artillery pieces fired in support of the U.S. First Army. Each day, fourteen railroad trains carried a total of more than 4 million artillery rounds to the front. The AEF equipped most of its heavy and medium artillery units with caterpillar-type tractors, and roughly half of its light (75mm) artillery units were motorized with trucks. By the end of the war, the American army deployed eleven tractor-drawn artillery regiments.[26] Devers and his colleagues had every reason to be proud of their achievements in the training centers.

By late 1918, Devers was the artillery school's assistant director of training and commander of the 1st Field Artillery Regiment, which provided instructors and demonstration units for the school. Devers later admitted feeling that he had "simply [been] thrown into command because it wasn't going right and I guess they needed somebody to pass the buck to. . . . The school troops were overburdened because they had to handle different guns and they had to train a lot of green men; however, they were very bright."[27]

Although the quality of the conscripts in 1918 was higher than that of the prewar enlistees, there were few experienced NCOs in the units being organized for service in Europe. Devers worked with junior officers who learned their jobs quickly and willingly spent long hours preparing for instruction. They often worked seven days a week, twelve to fourteen hours a day. Colonel Devers and the school's new commandant, Brigadier General Lauren L. Lawson, established the courses needed to train soldiers in the operation of the new weapons; they also organized a faculty of officers and NCOs to teach the courses. A great deal had to be accomplished in a limited amount of time. General Lawson later wrote that Devers was "an officer of exceptional energy, willing to undertake any task and perform it to the best of his ability."[28]

For the first time in his career, Devers worked with African American officers at the artillery school. One of the provisions of the 1917 Conscription Act was that Americans of all races would be equally liable for the draft.

Blacks served in roughly the same proportion as their share of the total population during the war. About 400,000 African Americans joined the U.S. Army in World War I; of these soldiers, 200,000 served in France. Seventy-five percent of these men were in service units, but roughly 50,000 fought in infantry and artillery regiments.[29]

When America entered the war, about 10,000 African Americans were serving in the regular army in four regiments—two infantry and two cavalry. At that time, only three African Americans had graduated from the U.S. Military Academy. Of these men, only Lieutenant Colonel Charles Young was on active duty in 1917. Young was quickly retired on medical grounds to prevent him from commanding one of the African American infantry regiments being formed. The situation was different in the National Guard, where most of the officers in the African American regiments were black and all the officers in the 8th Illinois Infantry Regiment, from colonel to lieutenant, were African American.

African American leaders saw the war as an opportunity for blacks to demonstrate through military service that they were loyal Americans deserving of equal treatment with whites. The NAACP encouraged blacks to enlist and pressured the Wilson administration to create African American combat units for service in the front lines. In response, four African American National Guard infantry regiments were accepted into service: the 369th, 370th, 371st, and 372nd. These regiments were notionally part of the 93rd Division, but that division was never organized in France. Instead, these regiments served separately in French divisions, where they performed magnificently. As Coffman concluded, "In France, the Negroes found a white people who would accept them as social equals." The French trained and equipped these units and treated them like their own. Most of the officers were African American. They did so well that the French asked for eight more black regiments, a request that John J. Pershing, commander of the AEF, refused. The British, in contrast, refused to accept black combat units for training or service, even though Pershing offered to send an African American division to their sector.[30]

The army organized, trained, and equipped one African American division for combat duty in France. The 92nd Division included four infantry regiments, an artillery brigade consisting of three regiments, and division service troops such as military police, medical personnel, and signalmen. Although 82 percent of the division's officers were black, all the field-grade and general officers were white. Nonetheless, for the first time in American history, African Americans served in artillery units, and the officers of these units trained at Fort Sill. Devers seemed to be relatively open-minded about these men. He later stated, "Colored officers were coming in there and had to be trained in basic subjects and worked in with white officers who were much ahead of them. The racial question was no problem in respect to living conditions, but there was quite a gap between the knowledge of some of these officers. They were all enthusiastic, always willing, and always put out."[31] Sadly, the rest of the officer corps and the nation as a whole were less open-minded about racial integration or racial equality. Apparently, the minds of white officers "were closed to the effect of racial prejudice" and decades of discrimination in American educational institutions.[32]

White southern politicians opposed plans to organize and train African American combat units. The four African American regiments in existence when the war began were not sent to France. Most blacks served in service units and performed difficult, labor-intensive tasks as stevedores and construction troops. The army was careful to scatter its black units across the country to prevent a large concentration of armed blacks at any one training camp. When there were shortages of stoves, blankets, or coats during the winter of 1917–1918, African Americans often received less than their fair share of equipment. When there were not enough wooden barracks, blacks lived in tents while whites lived in the buildings.[33]

White officers of African American units usually encouraged their men to obey the Jim Crow segregation laws of local communities. When the black soldiers of the 24th Infantry Regiment refused to do so in Houston, a major racial conflict broke out. The army reacted by court-martialing 118 black soldiers involved; 19 of them were executed.[34]

African American officers of the 92nd Division routinely experienced discrimination and disrespect from white enlisted men and from their own superiors, and they often received inadequate training for their combat duties. The 92nd Division's regiments were scattered across seven posts for their training in the United States; they were not united for division-level training until they arrived in France in July 1918. The division commander, Major General Charles Ballou, seemed to believe that African Americans could perform well as combat soldiers. However, his division chief of staff, Lieutenant Colonel Allen Greer, had no use for African Americans and told the division's black officers that "white men made the Division, and they can break it just as easily if it becomes a trouble maker." It is not surprising that in the division's first offensive operation in the Meuse-Argonne campaign, one of the regiments performed very poorly.[35] A postwar investigation of the 368th Infantry Regiment's actions found that it had failed because of inexperience, lack of proper equipment, and poor artillery support. Despite these conclusions, most of the army's white officers probably would have agreed with Lieutenant General Robert Lee Bullard, Second Army commander, who later wrote: "Poor Negroes! They were hopelessly inferior. . . . Altogether, my memories of the 92nd Negro Division are a nightmare. . . . If you need combat soldiers, and especially if you need them in a hurry, don't put your time upon Negroes."[36]

The dismal record of African Americans' treatment during the First World War is a sad chapter in the history of the nation and the army. Little was learned from the experience, and it would take three more decades before segregation in the armed forces officially ended. It would take another thirty years for the army to accept full responsibility and to treat all soldiers equally. Devers would play a role in the process of integration in the 1940s.

One of Devers's additional duties was running the general officers' mess. He was allotted just $1.25 per day per officer to operate the dining facility and provide meals of sufficient quality and variety to satisfy four generals and their wives. He solved this problem by finding a very able woman to run the kitchen, and he instructed her to plan meals based on the specialties of the senior officers' wives: "on Monday with Mrs. Wright, on Tuesday with Mrs. Ennis, and so on down the line."[37]

Colonel Devers's opportunity to serve in France came in September, when he was assigned to command the 60th Field Artillery Regiment. By the fall of 1918, the U.S. Army had grown to nearly 4 million men; there were forty-two divisions in France, and plans were in the works for another twenty divisions to be formed and sent overseas. The 60th Regiment was training at Fort Bragg and was scheduled to move to New York in November, where Devers would join it. However, as Devers told the story, "I simply never got to that command because the Armistice [on 11 November 1918] came before it ever got to New York and I was immediately assigned to a group of Company Officers, Senior Colonels and young, new Brigadier Generals, to go to France to school at Treves [Trier, Germany]. Since I was free at the time, about to join a regiment, I was free to go to Europe; so I got off a month ahead of time and this gave me quite a chance to see what the problem was in France."[38]

Devers was one of several regular army officers who had missed the chance to serve in the front lines. Consequently, the army sent many of these men to Europe in 1919 so they could study the war and walk the battlefields. The army also carefully collected the historical records of the units that had fought in France and compiled extensive histories of the war and of the army's expansion. The War Department and the army used the lessons learned about training, mobilization, and leadership to shape the National Defense Act of 1920.[39]

Over There: Europe, 1919

Devers arrived in France in late May, a month before his course started. This gave him and his fellow officers a chance to tour the most important battlefields of the Franco-Prussian War of 1870. Their travels around Sedan and Metz "gave us a chance to see France before we had to go to school and gave us a fine chance to visit with some of the troops who were still in the field." This was possible because part of the AEF remained in Europe until after the German government accepted the Treaty of Versailles in late June 1919.

On 1 June Devers's formal course began with a tour of the American battlefields of the war. The course also included classroom instruction, mainly by American officers. As Devers remembered:

> The instructors were excellent; they were men who had been in battle and had experience, and they were supplemented by French instructors. We debated the problems and our discussions were thorough and I was well equipped. In fact, I think I was as well-equipped as any officer in that school not only because of what I'd read in textbooks and other sources, but because I knew the practical side as a result of the experiences I had had. After talking about what their problems were with the officers on the battle front, I came to realize where I'd been wrong and how I could improve myself.[40]

The classroom instruction was supplemented by field trips to the battlefields in an exercise known in the U.S. Army as staff rides. "We were taken to critical points of the battle. The whole situation was explained to us on the ground. This was invaluable." Senior officers who had commanded divisions in the Meuse-Argonne campaign joined Devers's group on the battlefield and gave the younger officers their impressions and thoughts about what could be learned from that experience. "A lot of this rubs off on you," Devers observed. The course also included discussions with foreign officers, giving Devers a perspective of national differences. He later commented:

> I wasn't too impressed with the British Officers, although their methods of generalship in battle were adequate. It seemed to me (I got my information from the British soldiers, who were real tough) that their non-commissioned officers were good, and they had discipline. As for the French, the French Officers seemed to be better equipped, certainly in technical matters, from my view point. I didn't form any bad impressions. I didn't find the French lazy or anything like that. I found them very industrious and this stood me in good stead when I came back [to France during World War II] because I was in the same wave length with the French. I understood them better.[41]

Devers's negative view of the British was not unusual for American officers in the first half of the twentieth century. These first experiences with British and French officers helped shape his later perceptions of those allies in World War II and may have affected the way he dealt with them.

During his brief trip to the battlefields of France, Devers drew some conclusions that served him well as commander of an army group in Alsace in 1944: "I never believed in Trench warfare and I never permitted it to be practiced where I could help it from that time on. . . . This was very much in my mind and I knew that in the future we were going to have to move faster. . . . I could never see anything but change to a fast pace, strike them where they least expect it with your main force, get a hole and drive through it. And this is the policy and philosophy of the tanks. You can't stop. If you stop, you're going to get fired upon and killed. You've got to pull back or go forward."[42]

Demobilization and the National Defense Act of 1920

When the First World War ended, the U.S. Army numbered over 4 million soldiers, with about 200,000 officers. Although this was supposed to be the war to end all wars, it was not. Most officers, such as army chief of staff Peyton March and AEF commander John J. Pershing, believed that the army would be called on again to fight against a major military power and that its prewar structure and size would be inadequate.[43] Many in Congress also believed that the regular army had to be enlarged, and after much debate, Congress passed the National Defense Act of 1920. The act authorized a regular army of 280,000 enlisted men and 13,000 officers. It also recognized the value of citizen-soldiers by authorizing a National Guard of up to 435,000 soldiers. Reserve Officers' Training Corps (ROTC) programs were set up at state universities across the nation. By 1925, there were 325 ROTC programs, and an average of 6,000 reserve officers were commissioned each year.[44]

Many Americans and their elected representatives saw no need, however, for such a large army. They reasoned that the navy was still the nation's first line of defense, and in the 1920s, the other two major navies in the world, the British and the Japanese, seemed to pose little threat to American security. The army paid the price for this perception of American defense. By 1923, Congress had reduced the authorized strength of the regular army to 137,000 enlisted men and 12,000 officers. It remained at this level until 1936, when Congress authorized a total of 189,000 men and officers. The National Guard also remained well below its authorized strength, with about 180,000 soldiers. One of the few bright spots was the ROTC program, which provided a pool of more than 80,000 reserve officers by 1940.[45]

The regular army's officer corps remained at about 12,000 officers from 1920 through 1939. More than half these officers had entered the army between 1917 and 1920. Since officers were promoted based on seniority, and since promotions occurred only when there was a vacancy (due to retirement or death), a lieutenant in 1920 would have to wait twenty-three years to be promoted to major. Although Devers and the other officers who had entered active service before 1917 were ahead of this "hump" in the officer promotion system, they still had to wait for vacancies to occur (mandatory retirement age was sixty-four). Until 1939, there was no way for the army to promote promising officers, such as George C. Marshall, ahead of less talented officers who were higher on the seniority list.[46]

A significant number of officers considered leaving the service in the early 1920s. Many had been reduced in rank after the war, and salaries in the civilian economy exceeded those in the military. Devers, however, maintained a very positive attitude about the army: "I had everything ahead of me. Though I hadn't been in the war—neither had a lot of my contemporaries and I had everything before me. I had good health. I had had a wide experience. I was at a place that gave me every opportunity—as I've just said—to improve myself and I believe that Georgie and I improved our outlook on life and made the most of it." He recognized that the reduction from wartime ranks caused resentment, and he felt that "a little more consideration should have been given to the sacrifices which officers had made during the war."[47]

Back to West Point

Before going to Europe, Devers had been told that his next assignment would be teaching mathematics at West Point for a second time. Consequently, the Devers family cleared their quarters at Fort Sill in early May and traveled to Washington, D.C., where Georgie and Frances stayed while Jake was overseas. In late July 1919, while in Germany, he received orders to return to the United States and proceed to the Military Academy.

Devers was still a colonel at the time and was therefore assigned a stateroom on his return journey across the Atlantic. Traveling with him on the ship were Lieutenant Colonels Robert M. Danford and Bill Bryden. Both men had been brigadier generals a month earlier and were five years senior to Devers on the officer promotion list. Devers knew that when he got to West Point he would return to his permanent rank of captain, and he knew that Lieutenant Colonel Danford would be the commandant of cadets there. Sensing a possible predicament, Devers consulted his cabinmate, a classmate by the name of Miner, and they decided that since the stateroom slept four, they would invite "the two [former] generals to room with us. This caused a lot of amusement, but it went fine because we had a chance to talk about our problems. Danford was coming back as Commandant of Cadets. When he found out I was coming back to teach math, he said, 'I'd like to have you be my senior artillery instructor.' I said, 'believe me, that's the finest detail in the whole United States Army and I would certainly like to have it.'"[48] For an artillery officer, this was a superb assignment because it allowed him to command an artillery unit while working directly for the commandant as the senior artillery instructor.

Colonel Devers reverted to Captain Devers when he stepped off the train at the West Point station on 20 August 1919. "But that didn't bother me," he said. "I was going back to a wonderful environment and a great experience. As it turned out, General MacArthur, whom I had never met, had just been assigned Superintendent." Over the next few years, the Military Academy would undergo a major transformation as the young superintendent worked to reform the nineteenth-century curriculum and reestablish the corps of cadets. At the same time, the U.S. Army went through the pains of demobilization and reorganization and a serious debate in Congress about how to organize the armed forces. Congress and the nation were anxious to put the war behind them, and their neglect of the regular army resumed. Devers was fortunate to be promoted to major on 20 August 1920.

The sacrifices of soldiers and their families in the interwar period included trying to survive on inadequate pay. For much of the twentieth century, officers' pay was insufficient to support a middle-class lifestyle, and it was well below the salaries and wages of civilians with similar experience and responsibilities. The saving grace for Devers and his fellow officers was that "we were living in an atmosphere where everybody else had about the same pay I had, and most of them were dedicated to the job they were doing." At West Point, Devers did not feel like he was in competition with his fellow officers. Instead, he focused on encouraging the cadets to achieve their full potential in both their studies and athletics, and he shared his experiences as an officer with them. "This was always rewarding in more ways than one and still pays off to this very day."[49] However, this was also one of the most trying periods in West Point's history.

The U.S. Military Academy's purpose has always been to train and educate officers of character to serve in the regular army. When the United States entered the First World War, the army faced a critical shortage of trained officers. As a result, the Academy graduated both its senior and junior classes in June 1917. Then, as the demand for officers increased in November 1918, the next two classes of cadets were commissioned early. Consequently, by December 1918, only the plebe class remained at the Academy. This was disastrous for the Academy's cadet development system because the upperclassmen traditionally trained each new class of young men and helped shape them as future officers. William Ganoe, who served in the superintendent's office as adjutant during this period, concluded, "Never in its precise production of officers through the previous hundred and sixteen years had the U.S. Military Academy been so battered and broken as in 1918. It wasn't a single violence, leaving debris and destruction in its wake, but a succession of tempests which persistently kept people within the gates looking dazed. . . . The Corps was not the unit of the past. In fact it was not a corps. There were three odd lots moving separately and clad differently."[50]

To ameliorate this situation, the army decided in early 1919 that the former yearling class that had graduated and been commissioned in November 1918 must return to the Academy to serve as the upper class. This would add to their academic education and allow them to help train the new cadets. In June 1919 a new class of plebes entered the Academy. This meant that there were three classes in the corps of cadets for the 1919–1920 academic year. Ganoe noted, "Such was the state of affairs and feelings when it was announced that Brigadier General Douglas MacArthur was to be the new Superintendent."[51] The cadet education and training system was still in disarray when Devers arrived.

Due to the breakdown of the Academy's four-class system, Devers noted, "We had no cadets with any experience. . . . We had to set up a new honor system, so I was at West Point at a very difficult time; but a very progressive time. General MacArthur was young and aggressive and he knew how to solve the academic situation and how to tie it in with tactics—and he did it in a big way."[52]

MacArthur was thirty-nine years old and an Academy graduate, but he had never served on the faculty of any educational institution. As Devers wrote years later, "He inherited an old institution with a great heritage of success and tradition, but now reduced to a pitiable state as a result of the actions of the War Department. . . . There was no written code of procedure. The physical plant was in great need of repair. The morale of the student body, the faculty, and staff was at low ebb."[53]

West Point was at an academic and military crossroads in 1919. Throughout the nineteenth century the Military Academy had been one of the leading engineering schools in the nation. As such, the curriculum was designed for engineers, with a strong core of mathematics and physics courses but few courses in foreign languages, history, and English. In the twenty years preceding MacArthur's arrival as superintendent, the world had undergone a technological revolution that included airplanes, telephones, wireless radios, machine guns, smokeless powder, and chemical weapons. The United States had also acquired an empire that encompassed peoples who spoke several foreign languages, and it had become a world power that regularly dealt with foreign armies. These developments prompted General Peyton March, the army chief of staff, to tell MacArthur, "West Point is forty years behind the times."[54] MacArthur's tasks were to rebuild the cadet honor code and training system and to modernize the curriculum to prepare officers for service in the twentieth century.

As commander of the artillery detachment and senior field artillery instructor in the Department of Tactics, Devers was in a good position to observe MacArthur's attempts to reform the Academy. MacArthur left a lasting impression on him:

> I had never met MacArthur. . . . One of the first things I had to do was go to see him in his office, by direction. I had never been in a Superintendent's office, really, even as a cadet, and when I went in at this time I guess I was a cadet. I was very rigid, I saluted, I did everything that I had been taught, and General MacArthur very quietly said, "Sit down." Then he came over and offered me a cigarette. I said, "General, I don't care to smoke." He said, "Take a cigarette." So I took the damn cigarette. Then he lit it for me. Then he paced the floor . . . but the conversation was terrific. I just don't remember what he was saying—but he was thinking out loud. . . . When he got through, he simply went to his desk and picked up a two-inch report from the Inspector General on my detachment. And if anything was wrong with that detachment—everything was wrong with that detachment! All he did was say, "Here, I give you ten days to clean this up. I'll be down to inspect you ten days from today." I said, "Yes Sir," saluted, and left.[55]

Assignment to West Point promised the Devers family a somewhat less hectic pace than they had experienced for the past three years. At the very least, they would not have to move so often. Georgie, Frances, and Jake settled into "a very fine set of quarters" overlooking what is now called Buffalo Soldiers' Field at the south end of the main post. The quarters were close to the new stables and garages where the artillery detachment kept its horses, motorized vehicles, and artillery pieces. Georgie hired a maid from Highland Falls to help take care of the large house; she was "the wife of a colored man," Devers recalled, "and we had no problems there." Devers had an enlisted soldier who served as an orderly, and he could always call on his detachment for help with entertaining and home maintenance.[56]

Many officers' families had live-in servants as well. While at Fort Sill, Jake and Georgie had employed a sergeant's wife named Allie, and when they moved to West Point, they asked Allie (who was part Cherokee) and her three daughters to join them there. Evidently, Allie and her husband had divorced by then. For four years, Allie and her girls lived on the third floor of the Deverses' large quarters. When they left in 1924, Allie married a sergeant and raised her daughters at West Point. The girls eventually married West Point graduates, according to Frances.[57]

The Deverses' social life revolved around Friday-night dances and get-togethers with other members of the tactics department and officers who had graduated from the Academy around the same time as Devers. Since his duties occupied twelve or more hours a day, Jake spent little time with his wife and infant daughter during the week. He seldom took Georgie to New York City for anything except Army football games and sometimes a baseball game at Yankee Stadium. They visited Georgie's family "once in a while," but her life must have been fairly lonely most of the time. She maintained a large garden with vegetables and flowers and kept busy caring for Frances and running the household. This pattern—with Jake often being absent from his family—continued through the 1920s and 1930s.[58]

Part of Devers's responsibility was to ensure that his soldiers and their families were properly fed, so the detachment maintained a working farm. Devers recalled:

> I had a good farm—and I ran a pig farm—and I ran a chicken farm—and I used the produce from this to enrich my Mess. When I butchered the pigs, instead of selling them on the market and using the money in the Battery Fund, I always did both. I used to cut them up—the pigs—and used the money to take care of my married enlisted men because they thought they weren't getting a fair deal. So every time I used a lot of pork in the Mess I had a drawing—a lottery—in which they drew to see what package they were going to get of the pigs we cut up for them.[59]

His hands-on approach to such important family concerns remained a characteristic of his leadership style.

Devers served with a remarkable group of officers during this tour at West Point. Future generals such as Leslie McNair, Bill Bryden, Willis Crittenberger, and Omar Bradley were on the faculty. McNair and Devers were well acquainted from their days together at Fort Russell in the 4th Field Artillery. They would serve together again in 1941, when McNair was commanding general of the Army Ground Forces and Devers was appointed the Armored Force commander. Bryden would be deputy chief of staff for operations in the War Department in 1940, when Marshall selected Devers to command the Provisional Brigade in Washington, D.C. It is possible that Bryden and McNair influenced Marshall's decision to make Devers his troubleshooter and appoint him to represent the War Department on a board that selected air and naval bases in the Atlantic and Caribbean that year.[60]

The relationship between Crittenberger and Devers lasted throughout their careers. After interviewing Crittenberger, Colonel Tom Griess related the following: "The first time there was a meaningful association was when Crittenberger and Devers were at West Point together as instructors. . . . Crittenberger remembers this as a time when the Devers and Crittenberger families got to know each other quite well socially and did much together. He particularly remembers the great fun they had tobogganing on the slopes of nearby Bear Mountain. They played polo together on the West Point team and participated in the many horse shows given at West Point in those years."[61] According to Crittenberger, Devers was "already noted for being aggressive, a doer, and very interested in professional matters (preparedness, development of weaponry, tactics, etc.). He also had a great interest in the activities of the cadets, particularly their athletic contests."[62] Crittenberger would introduce Devers to Henry Cabot Lodge Jr. in 1941 and bring Lodge to Italy in 1944.[63]

Bradley served in the Math Department during Devers's second tour of duty at the Academy. Neither officer commented about any personal or professional association during their four years together on the faculty. They may have known each other socially, but they were in different departments, and Devers was four years senior to Bradley. Bradley was an avid golfer, and Devers was a polo player. Whereas Devers was a supporter of MacArthur's reforms, Bradley was less enthusiastic about them due to MacArthur's emphasis on intercollegiate athletics.[64]

Younger officers remembered Devers fondly. General Williston Palmer, then a junior instructor in the English Department, noted that "General Devers was very highly regarded at West Point. The job [of commander of the artillery detachment] was a job of real prestige in the Army, although for a low ranking officer. . . . Devers' qualities, which have followed him all his life, of leadership, enthusiasm, and anxiety to have his outfit always doing well, was just as marked there as it always has been every place else."[65]

Brigadier General Eugene L. Harrison remembered meeting Major Devers near the enlisted men's post exchange when Harrison was a plebe. The exchange was off-limits to cadets, and Devers, "with a very nice smile on his face," asked Harrison and a fellow cadet if they realized they were off-limits. Devers told them to report back to their quarters, and Harrison expected to be reported for a serious infraction of the rules. "However, he never did report us. Since this was a rather compassionate attitude for a tactical officer towards a cadet, and particularly a Plebe, we from then on had a very good opinion of General Devers."[66]

Devers's command of the 200-man, 5-officer artillery detachment and his assignment as the Tactics Department's senior artillery instructor consumed the majority of his time. The detachment included a horse battery of 75mm guns, a motorized battery of tractor-drawn 155mm howitzers, and a headquarters section. During the cadets' summer training, the artillerymen demonstrated artillery techniques and trained the cadets to fire the guns and howitzers. During the academic year, the artillery detachment provided demonstration units to assist Devers and the other tactics instructors. In these tasks, the detachment worked for Colonel Danford, the commandant of cadets, but Devers was also responsible to MacArthur for the command of the detachment.[67]

Since the artillery detachment was one of the largest nonacademic organizations on the post, it was regularly tasked to perform maintenance chores such as cutting ice for the icehouse in the winter or raking the leaves that fell from the thousands of beautiful trees in the autumn. When Devers took over the unit, he found that it was being assigned several such details daily; this piecemeal use of the soldiers diverted them from their primary duties, weakened the detachment, and made training very difficult. Taking advantage of his direct subordination to the superintendent, Major Devers proposed a solution that would be mutually beneficial to his unit and the post: "I went to General MacArthur and requested that I be given the job of cutting the ice, filling the ice house, and relieved of all other details; and on the spring and fall cleanup that I be assigned certain sections of the post, with instructions to clean them up and that the inspection could then be made by the Quartermaster to satisfy him. In this way I could take the whole battery to perform that job in two days. I'd have every man working. . . . And the job would be much better done."[68] MacArthur approved the arrangement, which allowed the artillery detachment to train as a unit and to care for its trucks, horses, guns, and tractors in a concentrated effort.

Devers remembered that "it was a great help and a great inspiration to my men that we always did a better job than anybody else."[69]

The artillery detachment's performance set a high standard for the Academy. When the inspector general of the army addressed the cadet captains on the subject of soldierly standards in 1922, he stated: "I have recommended to the Superintendent that every cadet of the present 1st Class be given the opportunity to visit the barracks, stables, gun sheds, store room, and mess of the Detachment of Artillery. Such a visit will give you a very good idea of what we expect of an efficient army organization. . . . The organization is as near a model as any I have inspected in the army and it represents a very high soldierly standard."[70]

With remarks like this from the inspector general, it comes as no surprise that Colonel Danford was very pleased with Devers's work. In a 1923 efficiency report, Danford summed up Devers's service at West Point with these comments: "The all around efficiency of this officer is exceptional. Has made the U.S.M.A. Detachment of Field Artillery a model organization. Is full of enthusiasm and initiative. Would feel fortunate to have this officer as my subordinate at any time."[71]

These examples of Devers's imagination, initiative, and leadership, and of the respect others had for him, explain why, when given the opportunity to rise to prominence in 1940, Devers did so. His understanding of soldiers and his desire to find a better way to accomplish the mission were essential attributes in his later superb performance of duty.

Devers was not a major participant in MacArthur's attempts to modernize the Academy's curriculum. He spent some time defending MacArthur's changes, but his duties in the Tactics Department and with the artillery detachment were not greatly affected by the academic turmoil.[72] The one innovation that did affect him was the superintendent's decision to end the summer encampment that had always taken place on the open area near Fort Clinton known as the Plain. Although this traditional activity had been considered "military training," it was largely a social season that gave officers and their wives the opportunity to parade unmarried young women before the cadets at the weekend dances.

MacArthur substituted tactical training at Fort Dix for the summer encampment. Cadets and tactical officers moved to Fort Dix during the summer, where they trained with the officers and NCOs of regular army units such as the 1st Infantry Division. Fort Dix was large enough for the cadets to actually drive tanks, fire light and medium artillery, and learn the rudiments of infantry maneuver in a realistic environment. Devers described the training at Fort Dix as "one of the greatest experiences I ever had—moving over the road with a group of cadets who had had very little coordinated training. We put the team together, really, when we put them on driving those draft horses and riding those cavalry horses, commanding their own units and going into camp, and going into traffic."[73] When MacArthur left the Academy in 1922, the summer encampment was reinstituted. The Academy finally ended the summer encampment and resumed cadet tactical training when mobilization for the Second World War commenced in 1940.

One of MacArthur's reforms that survived his tenure was the creation of an intramural system that required every cadet to participate in a sport each athletic season. The officers took an active interest in the intramural program. Jake and Georgie often entertained the athletes in their home, and he "consider[ed] my hosting them as part of the education of a cadet."[74] Because Devers coached the Academy's baseball team, he was a member of the Athletic Board, which gave him insights into the operation of intercollegiate athletics. This experience helped prepare him for a stint as the Academy's athletic director in the 1930s.

MacArthur's attempt to change the Academy's venerable curriculum caused the greatest resistance among the faculty. He sought to decrease the amount of math in the core curriculum while increasing the number of foreign language, history, and philosophy courses required for graduation. According to Devers, MacArthur's methods and changes "were good ones—and I was with him all the time. The professors did balk but he seemed to be able to handle his academic board meetings."[75] In reality, Colonel Charles P. Echols, head of the Math Department and a man Devers knew and respected from his first tour as a math instructor, fought MacArthur's academic changes tooth and nail.

It was probably inevitable that the department heads would resist MacArthur's efforts to dramatically revamp the curriculum.[76] All but two of the professors had graduated from the Academy between 1875 and 1895. The exceptions were Colonel Frederick Reynolds, professor of military hygiene and an 1890 graduate of the University of Pennsylvania, and Colonel Lucius Holt, head of the English Department. Holt, the only senior faculty member with a PhD, supported most of MacArthur's efforts, while Reynolds opposed them. D. Clayton James correctly identified the attitude of most members of the Academic Board: "Possessing tenure and, in most cases, long experience as academy professors, the department heads viewed the superintendents as passing phenomena. . . . They were not favorably impressed by a reform-minded superintendent who wanted to turn the system upside down and then depart in a few years, leaving them with the shambles."[77] The consequence was a collision between an ambitious superintendent and a powerful and well-entrenched senior faculty.

In spite of this resistance, MacArthur managed to make some changes that lasted. He got history and social science courses added to the curriculum and reinforced language instruction. The Academic Board agreed to eliminate required courses in geology and mineralogy and to increase instruction in subjects such as electricity, aerodynamics, and optics. The board agreed to modifications in Echols's math program, but this reform did not survive past MacArthur's time at the Academy.[78] MacArthur also successfully defended the four-year academic curriculum and the use of a military faculty when the War Department attempted to change both practices.

Perhaps one of MacArthur's greatest contributions to the Academy was the institutionalization of the cadet honor system. He created the Honor Committee, composed solely of cadets, to serve as watchdog of the honor code, which required cadets to "foreswear acts of dishonesty" and to report violations by themselves or other cadets. The West Point honor code remains in effect today, and the Honor Committee continues to enforce it. MacArthur's work with the honor system was key to ensuring that the Academy's motto of "Duty, Honor, Country" still has real meaning today.[79]

MacArthur left West Point in 1922 to serve as military governor of Manila, in the Philippines. Many of his academic and military reforms were revoked by the Academic Board or the next superintendent. Nonetheless, most of his ideas are still alive and well at the U.S. Military Academy.

Devers remained at West Point until 1924. He continued to play a great deal of polo and was good enough to participate on the Academy's traveling team. This activity brought him into contact with Averell Harriman, who "was then a young player . . . and he was just learning, really to ride; but he owned the big estate . . . over in Central Valley." The weekend matches at the Harriman estate introduced Devers to a number of important people. He would meet Harriman again in London in 1943, when Devers was the commanding general of the European theater of operations.[80]

Devers's second tour of duty at the Military Academy furthered his professional development. He observed firsthand General MacArthur's vigorous and fearless attempts to rapidly modernize a venerable institution while preserving its core values. Devers commanded the largest troop unit on post for five years while also serving as the senior artillery instructor in the Tactics Department. He worked closely with a number of talented peers with whom he would serve again in the future. As a result, he honed his skills as a leader and a trainer.

After five years at West Point, Major Devers was selected for further military schooling and received orders to attend the Command and General Staff Course at Fort Leavenworth, Kansas. Completion of the course was an essential step in an officer's progression to senior field-grade rank and to positions of increased responsibility on the War Department General Staff and division and corps staffs.

4

Professional Growth

Major Jacob Devers had been on active duty for fifteen years when he was selected to attend the Command and General Staff School at Fort Leavenworth, Kansas, in 1924. Later known as the U.S. Army Command and General Staff College, the year-long course is a central element in the army's officer education system and a prerequisite for assignments of greater responsibility. For Devers, it was his first formal military schooling since the month-long course of instruction at Trier, Germany, in 1919.

Fort Leavenworth

Various military schools have existed at Fort Leavenworth since 1881. By 1907, there were two advanced schools there: the Army School of the Line and the Army Staff School. Officers who graduated in the top half of their class at the School of the Line stayed a second year and attended the Staff School. During the First World War, the graduates of the staff officers' course proved invaluable to General John J. Pershing and the American Expeditionary Forces (AEF) in France. Officers such as George Marshall and Hugh Drum organized staffs for divisions, corps, and armies and directed the operations of a force that exceeded 2 million soldiers.[1] Staff School graduates proved equally essential to the working of the War Department. During the war, however, the army closed its schools due to a shortage of qualified officers for staff duty with active units. When the war ended, the army quickly reopened the Staff School and reaffirmed its role in preparing officers for service in future large-scale wars. The importance of the army officer education system in the interwar period (1919–1940) has been well summarized by Peter Schifferle in his superb book *America's School for War:* "After World War I, the army officer corps understood that competency in the craft [of war] was largely a matter of skill in handling large formations in both stable defensive and mobile offensive operations. They also appreciated a sense of obligation for preparedness and for basic competence, especially in a society where the desire to avoid another major war rapidly deteriorated to an article of faith: 'Never again!' This officer competence in handling large formations, and in the organization and effective performance of large-unit staffs, occurred primarily within the education system."[2]

In 1918–1919 army leaders discussed the proper way to reestablish the officer education system, which would include basic branch courses for new officers, advanced branch courses for captains, a Command and General Staff officer course for majors, and a war college for colonels. In 1919 the War Department appointed commandants for the latter two elements and, after careful study, gave the Command and General Staff School the mission to teach the skills needed by field-grade officers to serve in divisions and corps and assigned the War College the mission of teaching the skills needed at the army level and above.[3]

Initially, the School of the Line and the General Staff officer course at Fort Leavenworth were each supposed to be a full year. However, by 1924, the School of the Line and the Staff School had been combined into a single one-year course due to the army's need to graduate more staff officers each year without increasing the faculty. The combined course included instruction in leadership and command as well as in staff work at division and corps levels. The Command and General Staff School remained a one-year course until 1929, when it reverted to being a two-year course. It was reduced again to a one-year course from 1935 to 1940, when the army perceived the need to graduate more General Staff officers.[4]

Selection to attend the staff officers' course was highly competitive, and advancement in the officer corps depended on its successful completion. As a biography of Dwight D. Eisenhower notes, the "one-year course at Leavenworth was taken very seriously by those fortunate enough to be selected. Careers were made and broken—as were more than a few marriages. Nervous breakdowns were unexceptional; depression and insomnia were as common as colds and there was even the occasional suicide by officers who failed to make the grade."[5]

In preparation for the staff course, Devers took extension courses from the infantry school so that "he could hold his own."[6] Nonetheless, he felt challenged intellectually during his year at Leavenworth: "I went directly from West Point to Leavenworth. . . . My competitors at Leavenworth were all graduates, with few exceptions, from the basic schools of Infantry, Cavalry, and Field Artillery; and Signal Corps and Ordnance, and so forth. So I was in competition and these fellows were top men that were selected."[7]

Although Devers had served as a math and tactics instructor at the Military Academy, he valued hands-on experience as much as or more than formal military education: "What counts is experience. You don't get experience by just going to school." Nonetheless, he found the faculty at Leavenworth to be competent, and the instruction was useful in his later service. "I followed everything they taught me at Leavenworth about forming a staff, how to form it, what each element of that staff meant; not to have it too large—totally different—and handle it with some leadership and with the experience of the people that you're putting in the spots that are going to count."[8]

The staff course's curriculum provided officers with a professional vocabulary and standardized organizational and tactical concepts that made planning for and executing large-scale operations possible. Perhaps even more important, officers learned to approach problems systematically. George Marshall, the 1908 Honor Graduate, said later, "My habits of thought were being trained. While . . . I learned little I could use [directly] . . . I learned how to learn."[9] As Coffman notes, "the common tie of Leavenworth training bound together a professional elite."[10] It is difficult to imagine how Pershing could have organized a modern army in less than two years without trained staff officers. General Hunter Liggett, the commander of I Corps and then First Army, commented: "The more mechanical and complex war grows the greater the importance the staff must take on. It is the nervous stem and the brain center of the army."[11]

During the interwar years, Fort Leavenworth provided a "vibrant intellectual" atmosphere for officers. Army doctrine was studied, discussed, and questioned. The Field Service Regulations of 1923 and Field Manual 100–5 provided a distillation of the lessons learned in World War I and "were guides for officers working on any problem above individual branch and below 'large units.' Focusing on the division, and encompassing the lowest echelon of combined arms, these were the critical doctrinal documents for division commanders and general staff officers. From 1923 through 1944, the fundamentals of combat at division level . . . did not change significantly."[12] Devers's first opportunity to study doctrine outside the artillery branch occurred at the Command and General Staff School. He would have only one other opportunity to study large-unit operations before becoming a division commander in 1941.

When Devers attended the Leavenworth course, the curriculum included a fair amount of rote memorization of the principles of war. He "never tried to outguess the instructor." Instead, he recalled, "I just took the problem based on the principles that they lectured about and I thought I remembered. I worked hard because this takes a lot of concentration." He especially favored principles or lessons of war that emphasized offensive over defensive tactics and operations, later noting, "I always was an offensive guy because I'm an athlete."[13] This habit of viewing war through the eyes of an athlete was typical of his generation of West Point graduates and reflected his lifetime devotion to athletics.

Devers's greatest challenge at Leavenworth seems to have been overcoming his insecurity as a writer and speaker. "Some of them [officers] are better using the English language than others and others that play polo or are in the athletic field are better than those that are good with the English language. But I've always felt that my great drawback was that I didn't have a good control of the English language. At least I didn't feel I could write or speak it the way I would like to have spoken it."[14] Nonetheless, he did well enough to be a "Distinguished Graduate" in June 1925, ranked in the top fifth of his class.

Attendance at the Command and General Staff course gave officers like Devers their first chance to interact with officers from other branches. For example, Devers got to know army aviators Frank Andrews and George C. Kenney there. They and Devers shared common interests in airpower and mobility, although Devers was thinking primarily about artillery forward observers in airplanes, while Andrews and Kenney were thinking about bombers and fighters.[15]

Polo remained an important physical outlet for Jake, and it provided a chance for him and Georgie to socialize with the other players and their families. By this time, Devers was a first-rate player, and he earned a place on the Fort Leavenworth polo team. He enjoyed the camaraderie and excitement of the game, and he later remarked that polo was good for the army because it developed character, stamina, and the aggressive nature needed in offensive military operations. Playing polo also introduced him to members of the Leavenworth faculty, since many of the cavalry and artillery officers participated in the sport. During polo matches between Forts Leavenworth and Riley, Devers also got to know Lucian Truscott, a member of the cavalry team and one of the best polo players in the army.[16]

According to Devers, he began to think strategically at Fort Leavenworth. As he later told Tom Griess: "I was thoroughly familiar with strategy and tactics. Eisenhower always, I'm told, said I was a good administrator but he intimated I didn't know anything about strategy. Well, I knew more than any of those fellows because if they [Eisenhower and Bradley] had followed my plan we wouldn't have had all the problems we had in Europe."[17]

The class of 1924–1925 graduated 258 officers. Devers ranked forty-second, with an 88.15 percent academic average.[18] Almost all these men had been commissioned before the First World War, and roughly 90 percent of them were majors. Their commissions were evenly divided among three sources: West Point, direct commission from the enlisted ranks, and commission by competitive examination of college graduates. Through use of the "applicatory method," the faculty (which included some of the army's finest officers) had instilled in these men "competence in handling large formations, mastery of problem-solving and decision-making skills."[19] For Devers, these skills would prove highly valuable when he moved to Fort Sill, Oklahoma, to serve his second tour of duty with the field artillery school.

Fort Sill

Near the end of Devers's year at Fort Leavenworth, Major General William S. Snow, chief of field artillery branch, met with each field artillery officer attending the course to discuss his career and preferences for his next duty assignment. As Devers remembered, "I was the first one called in and I had some very definite ideas. I told him I had been an instructor but I had never served with either the Guard or the ROTC, or any Reserve, and I thought I ought to have some service in that field to balance up my professional confidence; I, of course, preferred an assignment in the east. . . . I did say to him, 'There's just one place I don't want to go and that's Fort Sill, Oklahoma.'"[20]

Devers's desire to serve with the National Guard or the Army Reserve made a lot of sense professionally. Such assignments gave regular army officers a chance to work with citizen-soldiers. The National Defense Act of 1920 had made it clear that the United States would count on guardsmen and reservists to provide the majority of army personnel in a large-scale conflict. Thus, Devers believed that professional soldiers would be better prepared if they first served with citizen-soldiers in peacetime. However, he did not get such an opportunity; instead, General Snow assigned him to the artillery school, where he would serve as director of the Department of Gunnery. Snow knew Devers well, having worked with him at Schofield Barracks and at the artillery school at Fort Sill during the war. Snow believed the artillery school needed fresh thinking about gunnery training, and he thought Devers could deliver such a boost.

Brigadier General Bill Ennis was the commandant of the artillery school. He had worked with Devers before, and it is possible that he asked the field artillery branch to assign Jake to Fort Sill. Although Devers was only a major, he and his family were assigned a large house next door to General Ennis's quarters on the "Old Post." Georgie had plenty of room for her dogs, which she loved, and the Devers and Ennis families also shared common interests in horses and gardening.[21] These quarters did a great deal to improve Georgie's attitude toward living at Fort Sill for a second time. However, she was still a long way from her parents, and she continued to travel to Virginia each summer to be with them.

For the next four years, Devers played a part in the transformation of field artillery practices. These important changes included the refinement of techniques for indirect fire, for the massing of fires of multiple batteries against one target, and for the use of artillery against moving targets. Major (later Major General) Carlos Brewer, director of the Gunnery Department after Devers left Fort Sill in 1929, has received much of the credit for these improvements in field artillery firing techniques.[22] He and his officers certainly did a lot to modernize artillery practices, but Brewer built on the work of Devers, Ennis, and many other officers who served at the artillery school in the 1920s. In the early 1930s Brewer and his successor, Orlando Ward, developed fire direction centers and surveyed battery positions, which enabled American artillery to "mass battalion fire accurately after registering one battery on a target without all forward observers being able to see the target."[23]

Devers later recounted how he and his officers helped conduct "experimental work in how to put down mass fire on an area 200 × 200, 400 × 400. . . . We were doing a lot of research work, really, in the Gunnery Department to get it [artillery] to fire off quick, get it done before the enemy can get out of an area, and things of that sort."[24] They also put pressure on the Signal Corps to provide better telephones and wire. Devers's later assessment of these contributions indicates the importance of this transformation of American field artillery practices: "Over a period of years this is what developed so the artillery in World War II was probably the finest artillery the world has ever known. It started with General Ennis putting the needle into us and the fine group of instructors, who later became staff officers and commanders . . . ; young students coming up with new ideas. . . . So we did a lot. I figure about two hundred officers—between the time I went down there and left in 1929—gave the Field Artillery the tools to do the job that was done in that war."[25]

Ennis knew how to get the most out of Devers and the other senior department directors. Devers noted, "General Ennis was a great man. He had a lot of influence on me. He always knew how to needle you to get more out of you and I reacted to this. . . . This always got the best out of me." Devers and his team of instructors were "determined . . . to improve gunnery, make it what General Ennis wanted it to be, only to outdo him. I think we did this."[26]

Ennis held Devers in equally high regard. In an efficiency report for the period ending June 1928, the general stated that Major Devers was fully qualified to serve as a colonel in peace or in war and that he was "well fitted for duty with any field artillery component of the army." The following year, Ennis concluded that Devers was capable of serving successfully "as a brigadier general in peace or war."[27]

Devers's main responsibility, however, was to teach gunnery to two types of officers. One was "the advanced class which was the older officers of the service; above the grade of major. . . . The other was young officers coming in for the first time to learn to fire." Devers found the instructional methods in use at the time "very rigid and unsatisfactory." For example, when a student made an error, the instructor would humiliate him by blowing a whistle to stop action, but he would not explain what the student had done wrong. "This was very disconcerting and wasn't always fair to the officer. It certainly lowered his morale, so he wasn't much use."[28] Believing that most of the students were dedicated officers who were doing their best, Devers eliminated grading in the senior officers' course and relaxed the methods of instruction in both courses. "We simply checked up to see why somebody wasn't doing well and then worked on him individually until we brought him up to standard." This approach seemed to achieve positive results most of the time.[29]

Devers took advantage of the lessons learned about the training of new artillerymen during the First World War. He remembered, "We tried all kinds of schemes" to help the students learn. "We took the whistle away, for one." And when a student made a mistake, Devers would try to determine whether "he picked up his mistake or if it was one of those mistakes that come out instinctively and, if he knew it immediately and went on, we didn't count it against him." He also discovered that a number of students had poor eyesight. "So I had every student examined for eyesight and you'd be surprised how many had to wear glasses."[30]

Although Devers believed that his leadership of the Gunnery Department made an important contribution to the army, he also gave a great deal of credit to the dozen or so officer-instructors who worked with him. They taught classes of ten to twelve students, with classroom work in the morning and firing practice in the afternoon. He and his instructors met during their free time on Saturday mornings to work through the various problems they would pose to the students over the next week. "We developed in this way the techniques of firing so we could get into action in a hurry. We finally got into firing at moving targets."[31]

A number of fine young officers worked with Devers at Fort Sill. Several, such as Edward "Ted" Brooks, would serve with Devers in the Armored Force and in Sixth Army Group during World War II; Garner Helmick would succeed Devers as chief of artillery in 1929. The officers who came to his attention "had quick minds" and accomplished their jobs swiftly and efficiently. In later years, Devers wished he "had kept better track by written memoranda of these associates because when you get into war you certainly are at the hands [or mercy] of the personnel [types]."[32]

The interwar army was forced to choose carefully when it came to spending the limited funds allocated by Congress. The army could not modernize and also retain its personnel strength and a robust officer education system. It prioritized the maintenance of skeleton formations and its schools over the modernization of equipment well into the 1930s. It was not until 1931 that Chief of Staff Douglas MacArthur directed the army to begin full motorization. This process of replacing horses with trucks, tractors, and tanks took nearly a decade even in the field artillery branch, which was a leader in motorization during and after the First World War.[33] Field artillery units continued to use 75mm and 155mm guns as their primary weapons until the 1940s, when the 105mm howitzer replaced the 75mm gun. During Devers's time at Fort Sill, all the units equipped with 155mm weapons used tractors to move their guns; units with 75mm guns were also motorized, with four-wheel-drive trucks replacing horses. The phasing out of horses in light artillery units had met stiff resistance in the early 1920s from the chief of field artillery, Major General Ernest Hind. When Snow replaced Hind in 1927, he supported the findings of two boards of review that had recommended motorization and other reforms.[34]

Lessons learned at Fort Sill in the 1920s stood Devers in good stead during the army's buildup for the Second World War. He learned how to get things done quickly without browbeating subordinates. When faced with the challenge of how to improve artillery practice without new weapons, he sought the input of both subordinates and superiors. As in all his previous assignments, Devers worked long hours and expected his officers and men to do the same, but he still found time to pursue his passion for polo. His workload increased when, in April 1929, he was given command of the 1st Artillery Regiment for about three months while still retaining his responsibilities in the Gunnery Department. His successful command experience in the 1st Artillery, like his command of the West Point artillery detachment, developed his leadership skills and prepared him for greater responsibilities. As he remembered, "My tour at Fort Sill was very profitable to me in dealing with officers of all ages and of all branches of the service."[35]

It is hard to know how Jake's intense dedication to his job affected his family, but it certainly forced Georgie to fend for herself and Frances much of the time. Fortunately, she was able to hire people to help with the household chores. As Devers remarked, "We did have servants because there were always colored troops around. They wanted extra money and this was good because it kept us in touch with the family life of our soldiers."[36]

The whole Devers family took an interest in horses, polo, and horseback riding. Frances began to learn to ride at West Point at about age three. She and her parents rode regularly on weekends at Fort Sill, although she was not enthusiastic about it. A cousin of Georgie's, Georgie Hays Craig, stayed with the Deverses for several months while they lived at Fort Sill. She later recalled:

> The general [Jake] taught me to ride polo ponies. At that time he had five polo ponies. I had never ridden before, but wanted to. So he took me out one afternoon . . . on the equitation course, which at Fort Sill was quite famous—it was a very stiff course—but he took me first on a very quiet sort of ride. . . . So the next day Mrs. Devers and I set out and she was telling me that the five ponies must be exercised every day. Of course, the officers who were stationed there were teaching and so they were busy during the week and the weekend was their time for polo and festivities.[37]

Georgie and her younger cousin exercised the five ponies daily—three in the morning and two in the afternoon. "During the months I was there,"

Craig remembered, "I just loved it and at the end I think he [Jake] was proud of the way I could 'sit the horse.'"[38]

Frances, however, never cared much for horses. When she agreed to marry Alexander Graham in 1935, she made him promise that she "would never have to put my hand on or turn my head over another horse."[39] While at Fort Sill, Jake took Frances and her friends on outings to Mount Scott, where they "went in and out of all the rock caves and everything and Dad would tell us how the Indians used to live in them. We found out later that a lot of rattlesnakes would come and go in those caves we'd just been in and out of—had our picnic lunch in."[40]

Devers was expected to entertain and to mix with civilian leaders in the surrounding communities. Entertaining was expensive, however, and Jake and Georgie had to budget their resources carefully. "If we didn't have enough [money], we didn't serve any liquor; if we did, we served a little. We were very careful about this." It probably helped that Prohibition was still the law of the land. One of the main social venues at Fort Sill was the officers' club, where they held dinner parties and dances on Friday nights. The Deverses often visited Lawton and Oklahoma City and were quite familiar with the mayors and local bankers there.[41]

Polo tournaments were a big part of Devers's social life. His polo games took him as far afield as Colorado Springs, Colorado, where, for several summers, the Deverses and four other families shared a rented house while the polo-playing officers participated in tournaments sponsored by the Broadmore Hotel. Devers had fond memories of these summer trips to Colorado: "That's a great—oh that was a healthy climate—and we met all the prominent people, we thought, in the United States passing through there because it was a summer resort. . . . We visited all the famous [places]—Pike's Peak, Valley of the Gods, things of that sort in that vicinity. Of course we motored up there with our motor cars."[42] Such exposure to prominent civilians gave officers like Devers a wider perspective on American society.

Family life was not always bliss, however. For example, Georgie was suspicious of vaccinations, even for Frances, who was eight when the family arrived at Fort Sill. Jake tried—unsuccessfully—to convince Georgie to have herself and Frances vaccinated against smallpox. He recalled, "Frances was going to school on a bus down in Lawton and I told Georgie that I was going to take Frances—and her—by their necks and have them vaccinated. We were going to see about this! Well, Frances came home about four o'clock and when she got out, she said, 'mother, a little girl on my right got sick yesterday and the one on my left got sick today, and I think they had smallpox.' I didn't have any more problems and we were vaccinated within the hour."[43]

Georgie coped with Fort Sill, and Frances found friends her own age in the neighborhood. Jake remembered the post as a healthy place to live and raise a family, even though it could be dry and dusty. On balance, their posting to Fort Sill seemed to strengthen their marriage, and it gave them four years together as a family.

Office of the Chief of Artillery

In December 1928 Major General Fred Austin, chief of field artillery, offered Devers an assignment at his office in Washington. Austin told Devers that he was high on the list for selection to attend the War College, which he could do after completing a three-year tour in the field artillery office.[44] Major Devers accepted the assignment, and in the summer of 1929 he moved his family from Fort Sill to Washington, D.C.

Military families move a great deal from one post to another, and these journeys often include an opportunity to see the country. Jake and Georgie took some time between postings to do a bit of traveling. They visited the north side of the Grand Canyon by way of Amarillo, Texas, and Santa Fe, New Mexico. They also stopped at Bryce Canyon before driving through Salt Lake City and on to Teton and Yellowstone National Parks. The trip took nearly two months, and the family (including a niece who was Frances's age) stayed in motels along the way. "It took quite a little doing, however, because the roads weren't too good."[45] Their route took them through the heart of the Dust Bowl and the states hit hardest by the ten years of drought and agricultural depression that devastated small family farms in the 1920s. Devers did not mention seeing any of this misery on the journey, but the army felt the results of the Great Depression that would soon hit the nation. In his new job, Devers would have to deal with a number of major artillery modernization initiatives that were stymied by the lack of financial support from Congress.

When the Deverses arrived in Washington, they rented a house on N Street, where they would live for the next four years. Their landlord was a marine general who charged them $100 a month for rent; when army salaries were later cut, he reduced their rent by the same percentage. The house was easy walking distance from the War Department and was just one block north of the Army War College at Washington Barracks. This assignment brought the family close to Georgie's parents in Arlington, Virginia, allowing the Lyons to see Frances and Georgie throughout the year and not just during their annual summer visits.

Being stationed in Washington was expensive, and there were insufficient officers' quarters to house all the military families assigned to the area. This became a more serious problem when the Great Depression hit the nation in 1929. In 1933, in an effort to save taxpayers' money, President Roosevelt reduced the pay of federal employees, including soldiers, by 15 percent. These cuts were hard on officers, but they were especially hard on enlisted men, who lost reenlistment bonuses and incentives such as marksmanship pay. As a result, privates received only $18.75 per month, significantly less than the $30 paid to members of the Civilian Conservation Corps in 1933.[46]

Congress had established the Office of the Chief of Field Artillery in the National Defense Act of 1920. It created branches to represent and manage the personnel and doctrinal affairs of the major professional elements of the officer corps and the army. Field artillery, coast artillery, infantry, and cavalry were the traditional branches of the tactical army. Congress also created new branches to represent advances in military practice that had been critical in the First World War. As a result, air service, chemical warfare service, and finance became permanent branches as well. Congress missed the opportunity to retain the Tank and Motor Transportation Corps, which had been an important part of the American war effort in France.[47]

Major Devers worked in the war plans division of the artillery office during his first year in Washington and in the training section for the next two years.[48] He referred to himself as "the third pencil pusher." His duties included finalizing Field Manual 430–85, which he described as an effective tool that "helped the new artillerymen and the old artillerymen because it was very well written and very simple." He noted, "In that text we pointed out that we had to have forward observers, we had to have more ladders, we had to see over those crests; if we didn't, we had to get way out in front. It started us thinking about the airplane and so we began to get light airplanes [for forward observers]."[49]

It is unclear what his other duties entailed, since he rarely mentioned his service in the artillery branch office in later interviews. Nonetheless, his earlier experience prepared him to deal with two major issues facing the field artillery branch in the interwar period: What type and caliber of artillery pieces should field artillery units be equipped with? And how far should motorization be carried out in the artillery units of the infantry division? The terms *motorization* and *mechanization* were used interchangeably in the 1920s, creating some confusion. In 1932 a War College student committee, chaired by Major George Patton, defined these terms: "A mechanized force 'not only [is] transported in motor vehicles, but also fights from some or all of its vehicles . . . having armament and protective armor.' A motorized force, in contrast, is transported, in whole or in part, in vehicles to the scene of action; the troops dismounting from their vehicles to fight."[50]

Devers's previous work with motorized artillery units in Hawaii and at West Point and Fort Sill gave him a "hands-on" appreciation of the challenges involved. That may have been why General Austin asked him to work in the field artillery office. By 1929, these issues affected the entire army, and in fact, Patton was working on the same problems in the Office of the Chief of Cavalry.[51] Devers was far more enthusiastic about motorization than was his former West Point classmate. The way the field artillery branch dealt with motorization in the 1920s and 1930s illustrates the efforts made by the interwar army to prepare for future conflict. These efforts would pay off when the nation mobilized for another war in 1940.

The army conducted a number of investigations after the First World War to help it prepare for another major conflict. From December 1918 to March 1919 a board chaired by Brigadier General Andrew Hero evaluated the training and equipping of the artillery. The Hero Board concluded that a mix of light, medium, and heavy artillery pieces was required in divisions and that medium and heavy artillery was needed in corps. The board endorsed the retention of 75mm guns and 155mm howitzers in divisional artillery brigades, and it recommended continuing the practice of hauling the heavy 155mm howitzers with tractors. However, the Hero Board concluded that the lighter 75mm-equipped units should rely on horses for transportation because of the lack of reliable trucks and the perceived cross-country advantages of horse-drawn light artillery.[52]

During the same period, Major General William Lassiter chaired a Third Army board that evaluated the motorization of all types of artillery units. The Lassiter Board agreed with the Hero Board that heavy artillery had to be motorized because horses could not move the guns adequately in all conditions. The Lassiter Board concluded, "Motor vehicles gave the field artillery speed, power, and the ability to take long marches." It recommended that tractors be used to pull the 155mm guns and that the 75mm batteries be fully motorized with light trucks.[53]

Conservative senior army officers such as Major General Ernest Hinds, chief of artillery of the AEF, and Major General William J. Snow, chief of field artillery from 1920 to 1927, cautioned against the total motorization of artillery units. Although they understood that motorization was inevitable, they believed the technology was not yet reliable enough to provide cross-country transportation and horses could still play a critical role in places such as Mexico and the Philippines, where there were few good roads. The army also faced severe budget restrictions from 1920 through 1939 that made it difficult to pay for vehicle testing and for motorization.[54]

In 1930 Major General Harry G. Bishop became the chief of field artillery. Bishop was an advocate of the total motorization of field artillery and "openly criticized the War Department's reluctance to adopt motorized guns and howitzers for the division." Under Bishop's direction, Devers and other officers studied two- and four-wheel-drive trucks produced by General Motors, International Harvester Company, and Ford Motor Company to determine whether they were reliable and powerful enough to pull light and medium artillery. They also investigated tractors produced by Caterpillar Tractor, Allis Chalmers Company, and other manufacturers to see whether they could pull medium howitzers over rough terrain. These investigations confirmed that American technology had advanced significantly since World War I and that American vehicles were dependable and suitable for on-road and cross-country hauling of artillery pieces. "Only the scarcity of money stood in the way of motorizing all of the division's artillery" in 1931.[55] This work gave Major Devers his first experiences with American manufacturing companies.

Army studies also indicated the need for greater firepower on the battlefield. The army seriously considered replacing the 75mm gun with a 105mm howitzer and experimented with captured German 105mm weapons to work out problems of mobility and operation. Perhaps the greatest obstacles to upgrading the firepower of division artillery brigades were the large inventory of 75mm guns and ammunition on hand and Congress's unwillingness to authorize sufficient funds to field a modern 105mm howitzer. The army developed 105mm howitzers during the 1930s, but it could not afford to start replacing the 75mm guns until 1940. Some divisions were still equipped with 75mm guns as late as 1943.[56]

The Office of the Chief of Artillery also helped manage artillery officers' careers. When called on to do so, Major Devers would counsel younger officers on critical career choices. For example, Lieutenant Anthony McAuliffe (later of Bastogne fame) informed the office that he was planning to transfer to the infantry. As McAuliffe remembered, "I was a lieutenant for seventeen years and I was very much fed up with giving gunners' examinations." He met with Devers, who was on the duty desk, and explained his plans. Devers "told me that he thought it would be a mistake for me to leave the Field Artillery, that I had made many contacts and knew many people, [and] that if I went to the Infantry I'd have to start all over again and make . . . a new reputation for myself. So he persuaded me to stay with the Field Artillery. I know it was a fine decision. That's what I did and I've always been grateful to him for his advice."[57]

Devers's service in the Office of the Chief of Field Artillery taught him how to deal with the General Staff and the other army branches. His performance continued to impress his superiors, and their high regard for him can best be summed up by remarks from his 1930 and 1931 efficiency reports: "An energetic, aggressive and active officer; robust and of strong personality. He carries through well whatever he undertakes; possessed of great common sense and of a keen desire to be thoroughly posted on all subjects pertaining to his profession. A natural leader. . . . Well fitted for duty with civilian components, but will not tolerate lax or slipshod performance. . . . Possessed of a happy, cheerful disposition and innate qualities of leadership; robust and courageous mentally and morally, as well as physically."[58]

The Army War College

In 1932, after serving three years in the Office of the Chief of Artillery, Major Jacob Devers was selected to attend the Army War College. Established in 1901 by executive order, the War College was the apex of the officer education system. In 1907 the college moved from its original home across the street from the White House in Lafayette Square to Washington Barracks, along the east bank of the Potomac. Today, the War College is located at Carlisle Barracks, Pennsylvania.

Devers's year at the War College was his last opportunity for formal schooling that would prepare him to serve as a general officer. The course of instruction included lectures by prominent military and civilian leaders, map exercises, and war games. In the Conduct of War course, Devers and his classmates listened to analytical lectures by leaders such as Peyton

March and James Harbord. March had played an important role in mobilizing more than 4 million men in 1917–1918, and Harbord had directed the largest overseas logistics effort in U.S. Army history to that date. Devers's generation would build on the work of such experienced war leaders in 1940–1945.

During these exercises and war games, the students were expected to act like generals commanding large wartime units. This program of study gave Devers and his classmates an opportunity to think systematically about commanding divisions and corps before a number of them would actually be called on to do so in the 1940s. During the interwar period, 3,677 officers graduated from the Army War College, providing the nation with a cadre of leaders who could successfully oversee the army's expansion to nearly 8 million men and women.

The students received no grades. Special emphasis was placed on collaborative work in small seminars consisting of roughly ten officers plus an instructor. Devers and his group studied the "organization, control, and operation of motor transport in the theater of operations" for their logistics topic; their operations topic was the "comparison of the march of the First German Army, 12–24 August 1914, with the march of an American force of present organization of equal strength." In the first study, Devers's subcommittee concluded that the Ordnance Corps should be charged with all procurement and maintenance of automotive equipment. The second study allowed the students to envision an army of 150,000 soldiers moving across northern France, an experience that would have been physically impossible for the tiny American army of 1932.[59] In 1941 Devers put this work to good use when he recommended that the Ordnance Corps oversee the development and procurement of tanks and automotive equipment for the army.

Major Devers also served as chairman of a seminar that studied expeditionary forces. This study had been commissioned by the War Department to determine what sort of expeditionary force could be formed with the regular army's current resources. The active-duty army totaled roughly 132,000 enlisted soldiers and officers in 1932–1933. Of this number, 33,400 officers and enlisted men were stationed in overseas garrisons, leaving 97,000 soldiers in the United States to form an expeditionary force. The study group concluded that an expeditionary corps would have to be a balanced force of one cavalry and three infantry divisions totaling at least 45,000 men, including support troops. If the army were to form and deploy such a force overseas, there would be few officers and men left to train additional forces for deployment.[60]

The committee determined that the twenty-four infantry regiments in the country were scattered over forty-five posts, making the training of brigades and divisions nearly impossible. "The dispersion of the regular army in the continental limits of the United States . . . makes it impracticable to have immediately available an adequate, properly balanced and efficient force of regular troops to meet an emergency."[61] The chief of staff, General Douglas MacArthur, asked that the regular army be increased from 118,000 to 165,000 enlisted soldiers, partially in response to this study. This recommendation, if adopted, would have provided sufficient troops to field an expeditionary corps while also garrisoning the American empire and providing a cadre of officers and men for training purposes at home. Congress refused to act on MacArthur's recommendation.[62]

For his intelligence seminar, Devers and his fellow students conducted "a strategic study of the British Empire for use in the preparation of war plan red." Devers and another officer prepared a supplemental report consisting of a "psychological appraisal of the British people":

> Broadly speaking, the British people may be said to be ambitious, industrious, and egotistical. . . . [Their] best characteristics [are] good humor, give and take, fair play, intuition and universal willingness to give every man a fair chance and just rights. They are not quarrelsome, not oversensitive, not unduly pugnacious, but they have unbounded tenacity and persistency, linked with the general stability which goes with cold common sense. They know how to take care of themselves as do no other people, and maintain a deep rooted belief in their own superiority. . . . The British lack dash and impetuosity but their bull dog tenacity that never knows when it is beaten and consistently refuses to admit defeat, has brought them victory on many a hard fought battlefield. The British soldier never shows to better advantage than when in desperate straits and fighting with his back to the wall. Their racial characteristics will persist and must always be taken into account when making estimates or plans in regard to the British army.[63]

Devers and his collaborators may have just read Winston Churchill's *The World Crisis,* published in 1931. In any case, their work provided insight into the people who would become America's closest ally in the Second World War.

During the 1920s and 1930s, many Americans came to believe that World War I had been unnecessary and that militarists were partially to blame for America's entry into the war. These feelings led to an aversion to soldiers in general and to officers in particular. Such antimilitary feelings were exacerbated by the fact that the regular army was called on to suppress labor strikes and other protests on a number of occasions. One of the most famous was the suppression of the "Bonus Army" in July 1932. In that action, General MacArthur personally supervised tanks, saber-wielding cavalrymen, and bayonet-carrying infantrymen in an assault against the Anacostia encampment of destitute war veterans seeking a bonus payment from Congress.[64]

Because of these antimilitary sentiments, army officers serving in the District of Columbia generally avoided wearing their uniforms in public or when testifying before Congress. George Marshall, chief of staff from 1939 to 1945, did not wear his uniform when testifying until after the attack on Pearl Harbor and the declaration of war in 1941. Devers and the other War College students wore civilian clothes both on and off duty and led an active social life, intermingling with politicians, military officers, and senior civilian leaders of the War and Navy Departments.

Polo continued to be Devers's favorite athletic activity during his seven years in and around the capital. When commanding a battalion, Devers taught his young officers to play, and he competed at every opportunity. Reputed to be one of the best polo players in the army, Devers was rated as a three-goal player by the National Polo Association, while Patton was at the four-goal level and Lucian Truscott was a three-goal player as well. Two-thirds of all rated polo players in the army were rated at two or less, to put these ratings in perspective. Patton and Devers competed against each other on the cavalry and artillery teams, respectively. They also played on the War Department's team, which traveled to a number of tournaments in the eastern United States. Patton's family still displays the silver cups engraved with their names in the Patton home in Massachusetts.[65]

The army supported polo as a competitive sport for officers until 1940. Mounted officers in the cavalry and field artillery were entitled to two horses purchased at government expense and were allowed to maintain two additional horses if they played polo. Devers believed the sport attracted "a very energetic, competitive officer" and was good publicity for the army, since its teams competed with those fielded by elite academic institutions and leading citizens such as Averell Harriman. He also believed that competitive sports developed character and stamina.[66]

Troop Command at Forts Hoyle and Myer

During the interwar period, many officers, including Eisenhower and Bradley, had few opportunities to serve with troops and to command companies or battalions for any length of time. Devers was an exception. During the first fifteen years of his career, he spent more than nine years with troops at the battery and battalion levels. In 1933 he returned to troop duty for another three years at Fort Hoyle, Maryland, and Fort Myer, Virginia.

In July 1933 Devers was assigned to Fort Hoyle, where he served initially as the executive officer of the 1st Field Artillery Brigade under the command of Colonel C. D. Scott. Fort Hoyle was located on Edgewood Arsenal, about twenty miles east of Baltimore. There, the Devers family moved into a nice set of quarters on the Patuxent River, which runs into Chesapeake Bay. Devers was promoted to lieutenant colonel on 26 February 1934, after fourteen years as a major.[67]

Colonel Lawson, commander of the 6th Field Artillery Regiment at Fort Hoyle, asked Colonel Scott to assign Devers to command the motorized 2nd Battalion of the 6th Field Artillery. Lawson, who had served with Devers in the 4th Field Artillery in 1911 and again at Fort Sill in 1918, believed that Jake's experience with motorized artillery units in Hawaii, Oklahoma, and West Point made him an ideal choice to lead the battalion as it tested new gun mounts with rubber tires and worked to determine the best trucks to pull the 75mm guns and 105mm howitzers.[68] Devers later described these tests: "Now we had two methods of towing the artillery. One of them was developed by a firm in my hometown of York, Pennsylvania . . . on the French guns; and then the American[-built] 75mm guns had an Ordnance [Department] method. We towed these with 2 and ½ ton trucks. I spent quite a little time working out on the reservation and my small board came to the conclusion that the civilian approach to this, rather than the Ordnance was the one we wanted."[69] After testing the two designs at Fort Hoyle, Devers organized a march through eastern Maryland and Pennsylvania to test the rubber tire–equipped gun mounts on paved and unpaved roads. The forty-five-mile route he selected took the batteries through York, where the artillerymen consulted with the civilian mechanics who had made the York-built carriages. When the artillery batteries returned to Fort Hoyle, Devers made his recommendation, and "this [civilian-designed] method of towed artillery was adopted and used for quite a while."[70]

Although Devers was evidently very pleased with his assignment to the 6th Field Artillery, his daughter Frances had less pleasant memories of this period. Fort Hoyle was an isolated post with no accredited high school, so sixteen-year-old Frances was enrolled in St. Mary's Seminary in St. Mary's City, Maryland. It was the first (and only) private school she attended, and she "despised it." Part of the problem may have been that she boarded at the school, living away from her family for the first time. She also missed the social life she had grown accustomed to in the Washington area. According to Frances, she felt she "had outgrown the kind of things girls do in girls' schools because I'd been in the public high school for two years; . . . and I'd been going to the Naval Academy to dances at least—well whenever I had a date. . . . So I had nothing in common" with the girls at St. Mary's. Her father promised she wouldn't have to return for a second year "if I behaved myself and [did] not get thrown out."[71]

As the 1st Brigade's executive officer, Devers was responsible for coordinating artillery practice for units that came to Fort Hoyle to take advantage of its firing ranges. One of the units that came in the summer of 1933 was the 1st Battalion, 16th Artillery, from Fort Myer, Virginia. Second Lieutenant Alexander Graham, who was assigned to that battalion and would later become Jake's son-in-law, was impressed with Devers's ability to get "a whole bunch of ammunition over there at Hoyle so that young lieutenants could shoot." For Graham and most of his peers from the West Point class of 1932, this was the first time they fired their 75mm guns. He later remarked that Devers "really taught us all how to handle the guns."[72] To do this, Devers organized a firing range on Edgewood Arsenal, where the 6th and 16th Artillery could fire their guns without "doing any harm. . . . Also, the motorized people were always in competition with the horse outfits and we learned a lot from each other."[73] Throughout his service, Devers enjoyed working with young officers, cadets, and students. He shared his experiences with them and taught them how to interact professionally with enlisted soldiers. As Graham remembered, Jake "was interested in the leadership of everybody right down the line, especially the second lieutenants. I think he always had a love for the young people."[74]

While Lieutenant Graham's unit was at Fort Hoyle in 1933, he met sixteen-year-old Frances Devers at a "duty hop." One of Graham's friends, Lieutenant Harry King, talked him into dancing with the colonel's daughter. Apparently, Graham was not overly impressed, because when they met again at Fort Myer a year later, he did not remember Frances. But he quickly asked to escort her to the hop at the officers' club the following weekend. She accepted.

During the year Devers served with the 6th Artillery at Fort Hoyle, he practiced his administrative and leadership skills and learned to cope with a scarcity of resources in line units. On 15 June 1934 he assumed command of the 1st Battalion, 16th Field Artillery, stationed at Fort Myer, Virginia. This assignment once again allowed the Devers family to live near Georgie's parents.

We have a good idea of Devers's qualities as a commander from the oral history provided by Alexander Graham, who served in the battalion during Jake's tenure: "Devers came to Fort Myer on the heels of [Lieutenant Colonel John George]. The only time we ever saw John George was at an officers' call, and very infrequently then, or at a horse show. The Captains were the big thing then. They ran the batteries without any help at all. The whole front office [of the battalion] was run by the Adjutant. Then all of a sudden General Devers came and the first thing you know—I was a Second Lieutenant—here he was appearing on a horse right in the crowd."[75] Lieutenant Colonel Devers imposed his personality on the battalion during his two years of command. Graham recalled that when Devers took over, the battalion was "just a plain parade outfit" that suddenly became a field outfit as well. At every opportunity, the battalion moved to a training area where the batteries could learn how to deploy and maneuver. In addition to its annual firing practice at Fort Hoyle, the battalion—or "16th Corps," as Graham called it—trained at Tobyhanna, Pennsylvania, and Camp Hill, Virginia. Devers focused his energy on training his lieutenants, hoping to mold them into the kind of officers he wanted, "which is what he did."[76]

The 1st Battalion, 16th Artillery, was well understrength in 1934–1936, even though it was a demonstration unit and was often called on to participate in public ceremonies. Most of the captains and many of the noncommissioned officers were on detached service with the Civilian Conservation Corps (CCC), leaving the batteries under the command of lieutenants like Graham. At the time, many army officers thought the CCC was a major distraction from training; they were correct. However, the CCC provided the army with some rare opportunities to deal with the American people in a positive manner—in sharp contrast to the use of regular army troops to suppress bonus marchers or union strikers. The CCC allowed the army to call 5,000 reserve officers to active duty and gave 2.5 million American men a chance to earn a living and keep their families afloat. Many of these men would serve in the military during World War II. The cavalry squadron at Fort Myer, commanded by George Patton, was likewise stripped of officers and NCOs to serve with the CCC.[77]

The army's mission to house, feed, clothe, and lead the men of the CCC gave it a chance to "do in peacetime something of what it was trained to do in war—to mobilize, organize, and administer a civilian force." The program also protected the army from further slashes in its appropriations during the 1930s, allowing the army to maintain its education system and to keep its officer corps intact. In addition, officers like Colonel George C. Marshall learned how to manage the problems associated with a massive and rapid mobilization of civilians. By 1934, more than 275,000 Americans were enrolled in 1,330 companies across the nation. Each enrollee was required to send $25 of his monthly pay of $30 home to his parents or family.[78] Marshall noted in 1938 that the CCC gave officers the opportunity to work with other federal agencies and local communities on a routine basis. He called his duty with "the CCC the most instructive I have ever had, and the most interesting."[79]

Although many of his key leaders were involved with the CCC, Devers did his best to make his battalion a well-trained and highly motivated unit. He took an interest in every aspect of the battalion, from the mess halls to the stables (the battalion was still horse drawn at the time). Each of the understrength batteries had fewer than thirty soldiers to care for their ninety horses, so Devers and his lieutenants took an active part in exercising the horses for at least two hours a day, seven days a week. As Graham remembered, "We used to ride up the hill—there was a long drive, horrible going—up behind Fort Myer, it was narrow and just full of holes. . . . We used to take a big loop up in there and came back, groom those horses; get on another set, take them out, bring them back and groom them; and now it's about lunch time. Right after lunch then we took them down and we did cannoneers for an hour or so, or cleaned the leather, or polished up the guns. . . . We were in wonderful physical condition."[80]

One of the biggest challenges in the interwar army was the lack of a personnel system that retired older enlisted men and officers who were unfit for duty. Devers found that many of his senior NCOs were "retired on active duty," or, as Graham labeled them, "old, old men." Such soldiers were deadweight and did not set the right example for the younger men and new officers. Devers found it easier to just ignore these older men and deal directly with his lieutenants and younger soldiers. As a result, according to Graham, the battalion went "from just a parade outfit, you know, to go on funerals and parades downtown, suddenly it became a field outfit."[81]

During his two years of battalion command, Devers thoroughly trained his lieutenants in the fundamentals of field artillery. Because of this thorough grounding in the basics of artillery, Lieutenant Graham found that when he later attended the artillery course at Fort Sill, he was "over-harnessed"—that is, "I had all the background from him."[82] Devers demonstrated a clear understanding of how to train soldiers and units. He knew how to work through or around the limitations of worn-out NCOs and a lack of soldiers in the batteries. He showed his subordinates how to get things done and how to cut through red tape. His battalion S3, Captain (later Colonel) Erskine, worked very closely with Devers at Fort Myer and later noted: "Devers was very effective as a battalion commander. His professional knowledge was of the highest. . . . He was recognized by his compatriots as being an individual well versed in Field Artillery. His handling of personnel was such that individuals were given a task and permitted to carry out the task and/or instructions in their own way; but the General required excellence in the execution and was there to see, from first knowledge, that those instructions were carried out. The General was a man of the highest integrity and also a most energetic person."[83] Erskine summed up Devers's command style by noting, "It seemed that he was always present whenever trouble occurred in a unit under his command; not to criticize and castigate, but to see that proper action was being taken and if suggestions were needed he was there to give them."[84]

Georgie and Frances were pleased to be back in the Washington area after a year at Fort Hoyle. Frances was able to finish high school while living at home, in quarters at Fort Myer. She once again enjoyed an active social life, including weekly hops, parades, and polo matches. On Fridays, President or Mrs. Roosevelt often came over from Washington to watch exhibitions of cavalry and artillery horsemanship. Cavalrymen, commanded by Patton, would ride into the parade field "at a gallop through a close-order drill—trying to shoot out balloons with blank pistols." The artillery crews wheeled their horses, caissons, and guns onto the field and performed firing drills in front of the crowd. Devers took an active interest in ensuring that these demonstrations went well. A tea dance, open to the public, was held afterward at the officers' club. Such activities allowed officers and their families to meet many congressmen and cabinet officials.[85]

Frances loved the excitement and showed an independent streak (not unusual in a teenager). She had no ambition to go to college, nor did her parents feel it necessary to push her in that direction. They did, however, expect her to finish high school. It appears that Frances was a bit of a handful for her parents, and they no doubt looked forward to her maturity. Much of the daily burden of dealing with her fell to Georgie, due to Jake's long workdays and his weekend polo matches.[86] Then, in her senior year of high school, Frances's life changed forever.

During Christmas season 1934, Frances was accompanying her father through the mess halls, admiring their decorations. Along the way, she recognized Lieutenant Alexander Graham from their dance at Fort Hoyle more than a year earlier. Graham did not recognize Frances and asked her "why I'd not been to any of their hops." She replied that she "hadn't been to any of the hops because no one asked me." Graham responded by saying, "Consider yourself asked for one next Friday." Over the next few months, Alex was a frequent visitor to the colonel's quarters, and the young couple soon fell in love. He often helped Frances with her English assignments, for he was "determined she was going to graduate for that's the only way we were going to get married."[87]

In the late spring of 1935 Graham was ordered to France to study French in preparation to teach at the Military Academy. He wanted to marry Frances and take her with him, but when Frances told her parents their plans, her father said, "Don't be ridiculous. He's a smart second lieutenant and he's too damn smart to ever marry you." Devers was wrong. In late June Graham announced to Frances that he wanted to get married the following Friday. Jake was away at a polo match in White Sulfur Springs, and Georgie was at her parents' house, but she told Frances over the phone that "of course" she could get married. The two women then discussed how to break the news to Jake. As Frances remembered the event: "Well we had quite an argument about that. She [Georgie] said, 'you call him. I'm not going to call him and break up his polo game.' . . . Well finally we called him . . . and she told him that Alex and I wanted to get married the next Friday night, could he come home and give me away? Dad said he guessed that could be arranged and hung up." In the end, Jake and Georgie insisted that the couple wait until Frances turned eighteen on 20 July 1935. Ten days later Alex and Frances were married, and they left for France on 5 August.[88] The Grahams spent a year in Paris before moving to West Point, where Alex taught French until 1939. The Deverses were pleased to have Alex in the family and hoped he would help his young bride mature.

After two productive and enjoyable years at Fort Myer with the 1st Battalion, 16th Field Artillery, Devers received orders to return to the Military Academy to serve as the graduate manager of athletics and the post's executive officer. He had long hoped for such an assignment, and in 1936 this looked like a great place to live and work in the small peacetime army.

During his first twenty-seven years of army service, Lieutenant Colonel Devers had demonstrated his ability to lead, train, and motivate soldiers. He had become technically competent in his branch of the service and was well versed in the challenges faced by an army badly in need of modernization. He had also completed the staff officer course and attended the War College. If the nation were to go to war, he was prepared to assume a position of responsibility. However, in 1936 that seemed unlikely.

5

The Approach of War

Lieutenant Colonel Devers relinquished command of the 1st Battalion, 16th Artillery, at Fort Myer in April 1936. This immensely satisfying two-year tour of duty was his fifth assignment with troop units, a record that was relatively rare in the interwar army.[1] During his twenty-seven years of service, Devers had led troops as a lieutenant, captain, major, and lieutenant colonel. The closest he had come to a staff assignment was at the Office of the Chief of Field Artillery, which was not considered General Staff duty. Thus, his perspectives about leadership and the army had been shaped by his extensive experience as a commander, not as a staff officer. However, as a senior lieutenant colonel, his chances of commanding a brigade were slim, since there were only three active artillery brigades in the regular army. His next assignment was anyone's guess, but he hoped to return to the Military Academy.

The State of the Army, 1936

As the members of the Military Academy class of 1909 approached thirty years of service, their prospects for promotion beyond colonel looked dim. Mandatory retirement at age sixty-two was still thirteen years off, but promotion was based strictly on seniority, and advancement was slow. Although some insightful observers saw the danger of military aggression by Hitler's Germany and Imperial Japan, the vast majority of Americans believed there was no threat to the United States and no reason to get involved in some other country's war. Similar antiwar views prevailed in Britain. However, Hitler renounced the disarmament provisions of the Treaty of Versailles in 1935; in March 1936 he ordered his army to reoccupy the Rhineland and sent troops and bombers to Spain to support Franco's fascists. In Asia, Japanese troops continued a relentless effort to conquer China. Still, "most Americans looked on with an air of detached indifference. . . . No people came to believe more emphatically than the Americans that the Great War was an unalloyed tragedy, an unpardonably costly mistake never to be repeated."[2]

The United States was withdrawing from parts of its empire in the mid-1930s. In 1934 American troops left Haiti and Congress passed the Tydings-McDuffie Act, which guaranteed the Philippines independence from the United States within ten years. "Beginning in early 1935, American isolationism hardened from mere indifference to the outside world into studied, active repudiation of anything that smacked of international political or military engagement." Congress passed the first Neutrality Act, reflecting and enforcing the nation's isolationist mood, and nearly 200,000 college students marched against the ROTC. The United States turned its back on the world as Hitler renounced the Versailles settlement and disarmament.[3]

Given the nation's mood in 1936, the army did not seem like a growth industry. Congress allocated the lion's share of military appropriations to the navy, which was still considered the first line of national defense. Any increases in the army's budget tended to go to the Army Air Corps, which was then in the process of developing the B-17 bomber; however, little was done to develop aircraft for ground-support missions. Only three army divisions were anywhere near authorized strength, and a major portion of the army was committed to the management of the Civilian Conservation Corps.

There is no evidence that Devers foresaw American participation in another major war. He and Georgie were, according to their daughter Frances, reasonably well informed about current events, but Jake was mostly interested in sports news. The Deverses did not vote in state or national elections before 1952, mostly because they moved around so much and absentee voting was not an option.[4] Unlike many senior army officers, Devers did not seem to be anti-Roosevelt.

Third Tour of Duty at West Point

As his tour as battalion commander at Fort Myer neared its end in late 1935, Devers was approached by former classmate Thurston Hughes about the possibility of returning to the U.S. Military Academy as the graduate manager of athletics.[5] From Devers's perspective, this seemed to be a very interesting and personally fulfilling prospect in an army that offered few other promising alternatives.

Lieutenant Colonel Hughes was the adjutant at the Military Academy and worked for the superintendent, Major General William D. Connor. Devers expressed interest in the assignment and told Hughes that his prior tours of duty at the Academy had prepared him well for it. Hughes took this answer back to his boss, and in the early spring of 1936 General Connor traveled to Washington and met with Devers at the Army-Navy Club. The meeting apparently went well, because the general said, "All right, I've talked to the people and I'm going to select you to be the Graduate Manager of Athletics."[6]

Taking this assignment did not preclude future service in field artillery, since Devers and his classmates did not face mandatory retirement until their fortieth year of service, in 1949. So for the third time in his career, Devers returned to his alma mater. The graduate manager of athletics was an important officer at the Military Academy, and he enjoyed a fair amount of autonomy. He ran the meetings of the Athletic Board; directed the maintenance, repair, and construction of most athletic facilities; scheduled the intercollegiate competitions of varsity-level sports; oversaw the work of the coaches of the intercollegiate teams; and supervised the Army Athletic Association (AAA). There were eighteen varsity sports (also known as corps squad sports) in 1936, compared with only six during Devers's years as a cadet. The most important sport at West Point was football; the other major intercollegiate sports included baseball, basketball, fencing, hockey, lacrosse, polo, soccer, tennis, and wrestling.[7] Consequently, a great deal of work had to be done to build or improve the facilities required for these sports. Devers tackled all challenges of his new job with the same vigor and initiative he had demonstrated in his previous assignments. He was to be helped in his work by several bright and innovative assistants.

The Athletic Board met about every four weeks, and all its decisions had to be approved by the Academy's superintendent. Among other things, the Athletic Board was in charge of hiring and supervising the coaches of the corps squad sports.[8] Most of the funds for the construction and maintenance of the intercollegiate sports facilities came from AAA members' dues and profits from the sale of football tickets. The AAA's financial situation was solid when Devers assumed his new responsibilities, in spite of the Great Depression. A report by the Athletic Board to the superintendent in February 1936 noted that the association was in "sound financial condition and does not need to schedule games with undesirable rivals solely for revenue." Annual receipts of about $450,000 provided a net income of $300,000. This money was used to supplement government appropriations for athletic facilities and activities.[9] A large cash reserve of roughly $5 million had been accumulated as well.[10]

Devers turned over command of the 1st Battalion, 16th Artillery, on 30 April 1936. His commanding officer, Colonel Kenyon Joyce, noted in Devers's last efficiency report as a battalion commander, "This officer is one of the best soldiers I have come in contact with during my active service. He is energetic, resourceful, loyal and a fine leader of men."[11] The cavalryman was clearly impressed by his talented subordinate, who had repeatedly shown that he could work with officers from any branch in a professional and loyal manner.

Devers arrived at West Point on 1 May 1936 and attended his first Athletic Board meeting as a nonvoting observer on 15 May. Major L. D. Worsham continued to serve as graduate manager of athletics until June, giving Devers time to assess his challenges and opportunities. The major agenda item for the April board meeting was the indoor polo schedule for 1937 and Yale's request to play two polo games at West Point. The board recommended approval of both, and General Connor concurred. On 19 June Devers signed his first document as graduate manager.[12]

This posting to West Point was Devers's eleventh permanent change of station and the tenth time he had moved his family to a new post in twenty-five years of married life. Georgie must have had mixed feelings about her husband's new assignment. On the one hand, she had fond memories of their earlier years at West Point; on the other hand, the couple would be required to do a great deal of entertaining. In addition, Georgie had enjoyed living in the Washington area, close to her parents, and Virginia was a long day's train trip from West Point. But on the plus side, Frances would also be moving to the Academy when her husband, First Lieutenant Alex Graham, began his teaching assignment in the Foreign Language Department. Whatever her feelings, Georgie knew from long experience that her husband would devote nearly all his time to his work and most of his leisure time to polo.

The Deverses were assigned Quarters 29, near the center of the campus, since Jake was one of the more senior officers on the post. This location made it easy for him to walk to his office and to visit the athletic facilities nearby. The graduate manager of athletics was expected to use his quarters to entertain athletic directors and their families when they came to the Academy for athletic events. Over the next three years, Georgie and Jake hosted a steady stream of visitors and cadets. There is nothing to suggest that Georgie did not enjoy this active social life at the Academy. She was certainly kept busy entertaining, and she accompanied Jake to football and baseball games played away from West Point. Frances, who was at West Point from 1936 to 1939, described the pre–World War II army as a society in which officers and their wives "had big dinner parties, battalion parties, battery parties, and they always had a Saturday night dance, which the family always attended."[13]

When Devers took over intercollegiate sports at the Academy, all the major team schedules were in place for the next three years. Cadet participation in corps squad sports was high, with between 20 and 30 percent of cadets active in the eighteen intercollegiate sports, depending on the season. The Athletic Board had a clear vision of the purpose of sports at the Academy: to "develop [in each cadet] 'a will to win,' a quality essential in a military man," and to teach a cadet to "be careful of his conduct to avoid special punishment which would remove him from the squad." The board also believed that "the varsity squad sets an ideal" for all cadet competition.[14]

Devers set out to shake up an organization that he considered "too conservative." He concluded that the Athletic Department "had operated in the big [football] games with full houses—in the Navy and Notre Dame games particularly—and they had a surplus of something like half a million dollars. They weren't spending it and that was the first thing I looked at. They had wonderful office personnel. They had been there a long time and all we had to do was give them some new tools to work with."[15] During the next two years, the athletic facilities would undergo major renovations and additions.

Two construction projects were already in the works when Devers assumed his duties. A new bathhouse was being built at Delafield Pond to support recreational swimming, and there were plans to expand the intramural sports fields on the north end of the post. The bathhouse project was well in hand, but the project to expand the sports fields presented a more complex problem. West Point is geographically constricted by the Hudson River to the east and rugged mountains to the west and north. Most of the open ground was taken up by the parade field on the Plain and the academic buildings and barracks. Devers's challenge was to find space for the new athletic fields even though there seemed to be no more space available. When he examined the ground north of the railroad tunnel of the West Shore Railroad, he came up with an idea: he would get the railroad to move its line to the east by creating a roadbed where the Hudson River flowed. He presented his idea to the railroad engineers, who told him, "all you have to do—[with] all this rock you're getting—is build us a right-of-way up there. We've already got the easement. We can just drag those tracks out and straighten it up. We save all kinds of money in having a straight track with those freight trains."[16] So the Academy provided the rock fill for the new roadbed, and the railroad moved its line east. This gave Devers space between the new tracks and the hills to the west, which he had filled in and leveled. The new athletic fields were completed in December 1936.[17]

Devers delegated a great deal of this work to three talented subordinates. "They handled all the details and the athletic fields. . . . They did the leg work and got the job done." He brought Captain Dave Erskine to West Point to manage the financial aspects of the department, and another officer named Harrison managed the athletic facilities. Captain Alvin G. Viney, a 1929 Academy graduate, joined the team as the engineer in charge of construction operations. Viney's tasks included determining how to improve existing facilities, overseeing the construction of a new field house, and working to expand the gymnasium.[18]

Devers presented his first budget to the Athletic Board on 30 June 1936. His planned expenditures for the 1936–1937 academic year totaled $677,109.09—a large increase from the $381,841.19 spent in 1935–1936. More than $300,000 was for improvements to the armory and the field house and to furnish the new gymnasium. The board, consisting of Colonel R. G. Alexander and Lieutenant Colonels Fenton, McCunniff, and Devers, voted unanimously to recommend that the superintendent approve the budget, which he did.[19]

The gymnasium project is a good example of how the Military Academy mingled funds appropriated by Congress with money raised by the Army Athletic Association in the 1930s. The federal government paid for the basic structure, including the outer walls and the internal partitions. The AAA provided $137,700 for the football team's weight room, the squash courts, and the handball courts. When spending the AAA funds, Devers could hire the best contractors and buy the best-quality equipment, whereas he was required to accept the lowest bid when using government funds.[20]

Devers worked with Lieutenant Colonel Robert L. Littlejohn, the post quartermaster, to get additional materials. Pointing out their common interests in maintaining an attractive and functional facility, Devers convinced Littlejohn to support the renovations with lumber, nails, and paint paid for with government funds. In return, Devers convinced the Athletic Board to make a $6,000 no-interest loan to the Association of Graduates to redecorate the superintendent's quarters. In addition, the AAA paid for improvements to make the swimming pool deep enough for Olympic-level competition. Devers's ability to solve problems in innovative ways was evident in a number of situations. For example, when Littlejohn's maintenance crews could not get rid of dandelions on the parade ground, Devers organized a detail of kids to pull the weeds and paid them with Athletic Department funds. He then got Littlejohn to support his idea of having the Athletic Department buy modern mowing equipment and tractors to cut the grass on the sports fields, the golf course, and the parade grounds, replacing the old mule-pulled mowers and hand tools. With Littlejohn's support, Devers convinced the Athletic Board and the superintendent to approve the purchase of the new mowers.[21]

The most important sport at West Point was football, and Devers believed the football team represented not only the Academy but also the army. When he assumed his duties, Captain Garrison Davidson, a 1927 graduate of the Academy, was the head coach. Davidson, who later served as the Seventh Army engineer in 1944–1945, was one of the more successful football coaches in West Point history. He had played on the varsity football team as a cadet, and when he graduated he accepted an offer to stay and coach the plebe team. After three years as the plebe coach and two as the junior varsity coach, "Gar" Davidson became the head coach of the varsity squad in 1933. During the next five seasons, Army won thirty-five games, with eleven losses and one tie. After his first winning season in 1933, Chief of Staff Douglas MacArthur summoned Davidson to Washington and offered to give him any officer he needed for his coaching staff. As Colonel Lance Betros notes in his history of the Academy, "Additionally, he required Davidson, during future seasons, to prepare an after-action report on each game for MacArthur; if time did not permit a written report, Davidson was to render it telephonically to Eisenhower."[22] Eisenhower was MacArthur's aide, and one would have thought he had better things to do.

Football was the only sport for which the Academy recruited players. As Betros explains:

West Point had big advantages in recruiting athletes. Most significant was the Academy's refusal to observe the NCAA's three-year varsity eligibility rule, to which most colleges adhered. As a result, a three-year letterman at a civilian college could have a second playing career by entering West Point prior to his twenty-second birthday—the maximum permissible age of entry. In contrast, the maximum entry age at Annapolis was only twenty years, which made West Point the destination of choice for athletes wishing to extend their collegiate playing careers by attending a service academy. . . . Enough collegiate athletes matriculated to allow the West Point football team to continue its unbroken string of winning seasons through 1938. In that year, the Academy finally adopted the three-year eligibility rule and thus lost its recruiting advantage. Not coincidentally, West Point amassed two consecutive losing seasons in 1939 and 1940. It was quite a shock, as the last time the football team had suffered a losing season was in 1906.[23]

Devers was forced to deal with the issue of three-year eligibility. The Naval Academy was pressuring West Point to adopt the three-year rule. According to Devers, President Roosevelt, who considered himself a navy man since he had served as assistant secretary of the navy in the First World War, lent subtle support to the navy's position. But even greater pressure came from the Ivy League universities and Notre Dame, against which West Point played the majority of its games in the 1930s. Devers, as athletic director, represented the Academy at meetings with the Ivy League schools, and he concluded that it was in the Academy's best interests to adopt the same eligibility and recruiting rules as its chief competitors. In exchange, schedules would be modified to enable Army to play more home games against schools such as Yale, Harvard, and Penn.

At first, the Athletic Board and General Connor did not agree with Devers about adopting three-year eligibility, probably because they recognized the advantage the Academy would be losing. However, Devers convinced the superintendent that it was important to show other schools and the nation that West Point was not taking unfair advantage of its competitors, nor was the Academy lowering its academic standards for its star athletes.[24] This latter point was a major source of contention. The Academy did in fact lower academic standards for certain key athletes in the 1930s, especially for the "stars," as Devers called them, who were recruited to play for West Point after losing their eligibility at other colleges.[25]

Like many Academy graduates, Devers placed a great deal of emphasis on winning, and he deserves credit for getting the Academy to join the rest of the collegiate world in its recruiting rules. However, he refused to join the Ivy League in banning spring football practice. He justified this position by noting that West Point cadets participated in a rigorous military training program in the summer that did not allow the football team sufficient time to practice. "We had to have spring practice," he claimed, "because of the shortage of time that we had to practice football. We stood out for that and so did navy. And that's the reason we've never been able to schedule the games with the Ivy League."[26]

Devers loved football and attended as many games as possible. The two biggest games of the season were the annual ones against Navy and Notre Dame. These contests were also the biggest moneymakers for the Army Athletic Association and were very popular with the public, senior army officers, and congressmen. Getting tickets for these events could be difficult, as they were usually sold out. Devers and his office regularly received requests from congressmen and senior officers looking for blocks of tickets in the most desirable seating areas and for complimentary tickets. He recalled:

> I had problems but we had a definite system up there that every Senator and Congressman got two complimentary tickets [to the Army-Navy game] and the Heads of the Military Affairs Committee—and this agreement was with the Navy, the Navy did the same—got four. . . . Well, now, this didn't always satisfy people because the constituents, particularly the New York ones, went to their Congressman to get extra tickets. Then they'd call up and ask for tickets and I'd say, "We don't have tickets, complimentary tickets, and we haven't any to sell because we're sold out." In one case, a Congressman threatened me. He said he'd send an inspector up there [to see if the tickets were really gone]. . . . Well, I said, "have me investigated! I'd welcome it because you've just attacked my integrity and I don't take that lightly."[27]

A more serious issue arose when the secretary of the army, Harry Woodring, and the assistant secretary, Louis Johnson, each wanted large blocks of tickets for the Army-Navy game. Devers told the superintendent this was impossible for two reasons: first, the tickets had to be paid for, and second, there were not enough tickets available to meet the demands of the two civilian heads of the War Department. Devers stood on solid ground, noting, "They've got to be paid for because we are not operating with government funds. We're paying for everything we do here [in the Athletic

Department]." General Connor agreed and sent Devers to Washington to explain these facts to the chief of staff, General Malin Craig. Craig agreed with Devers and supported him when he informed the secretary and the undersecretary that they would have to take what was available and pay for the tickets. According to Devers, they paid, and it "only happened once!"[28]

Another major challenge facing the Athletic Board was ticket scalpers or speculators. Members of the AAA and the West Point community of cadets, staff, and faculty could buy football tickets for seventy-five cents each, including tickets for the popular Navy and Notre Dame games. Members of the football team were allocated additional tickets, and traditionally they sold these extra tickets for personal profit. Other people bought tickets in the name of deceased members of the AAA and sold them for a profit. This practice was widespread, and when the Athletic Board looked into the matter in December 1936, it found that the ticket scalpers included AAA members who were colonels and lieutenant colonels, as well as cadets. After a long deliberation, the board decided in January 1938 to warn all legitimate ticket holders that if their tickets ended up in the hands of speculators, they would lose their AAA ticket privileges.[29]

Membership in the Army Athletic Association was considered highly desirable in the 1930s. When active-duty army officers who were not Academy graduates asked to join in 1938, the Athletic Board decided to restrict membership to West Point graduates, reasoning that "if all officers of the Army were permitted" to join, the AAA would get too large "to take care of its members for certain games such as the Army-Navy and Notre Dame games." Besides, any officer could purchase tickets to any game "without prejudice." There also was a shift away from the idea that the Academy's football team belonged to the army when the Athletic Board concluded that the "institutional side should be emphasized, that is, West Point rather than the Army."[30]

The duties of the graduate manager of athletics were complex and varied. Eugene L. Harrison, who was Devers's assistant, observed his boss in action at the New York meeting of the Intercollegiate Athletic Association and later told Colonel Griess, "General Devers appeared to be quite friendly with the other directors and quite respected by them." Harrison observed Devers's leadership style firsthand: "General Devers endeared himself to me, and almost to everyone else, because he gave you a job—gave you the means to do it—and did not interfere. And, so far as I know, he did not interfere with any of the coaches. . . . And he also said, 'I do not want you to be sitting around this office just because you think you should be here. At times when you have nothing to do, I want you to go out and play polo, or golf, or anything else. Do your work, but when you get it done, don't sit in this office.'" Harrison concluded, "It is very seldom that you find a person with this attitude, particularly in the military service at that time."[31]

When one evaluates the reasons for Devers's success in his later assignments, one must bear in mind his experience dealing with the varied challenges of major construction projects, civilian leaders, large-scale financial management, and internal army politics. He continued his practice of finding talented officers to work for and around him, and he delegated power effectively without losing control of the organization. Finally, his leadership style was hands-on, personable, and friendly. Major General Connor was impressed enough with Devers's accomplishments by 1937 to expand his assignment to include the duties of "Executive Officer for Construction, Maintenance, and Fiscal Affairs."[32]

Devers was promoted to colonel on 1 July 1938, and with his increased rank came increased responsibilities. The new superintendent, Brigadier General Jay Benedict, asked Devers to fill the newly created position of executive officer for the Academy. Benedict explained the reasons for establishing the new position and expanding the superintendent's staff:

> My observations led me to conclude that correlation of activities and staff development had not kept pace with the growth of the Academy. Studies were initiated to bring about better coordination, decentralization and delineation of functions pertaining to administration. Requests were made upon the War Department for the few additional officers deemed necessary. . . . The few additional officers authorized have improved administration. They have made it possible to assign officers to full time duty as Executive, Graduate Manager of Athletics, Recreation and Welfare Officer, and Post Inspector, all of which duties are extensive and important to the efficiency of the Academy.[33]

The superintendent's observations about the dramatically increased complexity of the Academy and the need for a larger staff were true. In 1909 Devers's class had graduated 103 cadets, and the entire corps had consisted of 396 men. The class of 1939 graduated 456 men, and the corps had increased to 1,842 cadets. The staff and faculty had increased from

111 in 1909 to 299 in 1939, and the number of enlisted men on post had increased to over 1,200.[34] Clearly, it made sense to increase the number of staff officers and to create the position of executive officer.

Devers relinquished his position as graduate manager of athletics to Lieutenant Colonel Louis E. Hibbs in the fall of 1938. Devers had recruited Hibbs, an artilleryman, as his assistant in 1937, when General Connor had expanded his job to include executive officer for construction. After Devers was promoted to colonel and General Benedict arrived in 1938, the reorganization of the staff allowed Devers to concentrate on running the post and Hibbs to take over management of the athletic program.[35]

One of his first challenges as executive officer was to deal with problems in the budgeting process. The Academy disbursed funds to each separate agency and department in one lump sum at the beginning of the fiscal year, and the money had to be spent before the end of the fiscal year, which was 30 June. Many of these organizations did not manage their funds well, and as Devers told the superintendent, "They all wait until April to spend all this money and then they buy pencils! They've got so damned many pencils over there in the Academic Board that they don't know where to store them now. . . . I want them to make these plans ahead of time." He proposed giving the departments and agencies their funds in four quarterly allocations. "It will be spread over the year, which is the way it ought to be spent." The superintendent agreed, and the new procedure seemed to lessen the problem of "end-of-year" excess funds.[36]

Devers also played a role in establishing Stewart Army Airfield. By the late 1930s, the Army Air Corps was growing, and many army aviators claimed that a large force of heavy bombers would allow the army to protect America's coasts from a possible threat by the Japanese navy. They also believed that heavy bombers could defeat any potential enemy through aerial bombardment of the enemy's homeland. This second belief was popular with many Americans because, if true, it meant a large ground force of infantry and artillery would not be needed in the event of a major land war. Army aviators such as Hap Arnold, Ira Eaker, and Carl "Tooey" Spaatz actually believed that the Army Air Corps could meet such expectations. In any case, the Army Air Corps required more officers and expected its "fair share" of Military Academy graduates. As a result, cadets were allowed to take aeronautics courses and undergo flight training, but there was no airfield near the Academy until the late 1930s.

In 1935 the Academy had acquired land west of Newburgh, New York, on which to build an airfield for cadet flight training. The Academy applied for and received $400,000 in Works Progress Administration money to begin construction in 1936 and to acquire more land. As Devers remembered, "They gave us Stewart Field and the Quartermaster was going to do the building. . . . I went up there with Littlejohn [the post quartermaster] and he said . . . , 'No, I can't handle this.'" So Devers volunteered to oversee the initial construction as part of his job as executive officer for construction. Fortunately, two young officers, Captains Elvin Heiberg and John Weikert, took over detailed planning for the airfield in 1937. Heiberg was an officer in the engineer detachment, and Weikert was a philosophy instructor and the officer in charge of the Academy's air corps detachment.[37]

Devers studied their plans and pointed out that a 1,500-foot-long runway was too short. This would have been adequate for single-engine aircraft, but not for modern aircraft such as the B-17 bomber or the P-40 fighter. He suggested that a much longer runway could be built if it were reoriented to avoid a mountain on the site. Weikert and Heiberg agreed and laid plans for an airfield that has 10,000-foot-long runways today. When construction got under way, the engineers had to overcome drainage problems resulting from the clay soil in the area, and they had to deal with power lines that ran across the proposed runway. For the first problem, Devers encouraged Heiberg to seek advice from the army engineers involved with the building of La Guardia Airport. In the end, the contractors dug a big trench for drainage and buried the power lines under the runway, as Devers had suggested. The construction of Stewart Airfield took about five years and was not completed until the Army Air Corps put more resources into the project. Devers recalled that when Hap Arnold took an interest in the project, the army acquired additional land, "cut the mountain down," and built a concrete runway and taxiways.[38]

During his last six months at West Point, Devers was busy with official social events and planning for the 1939 graduation ceremony, at which Franklin Roosevelt was scheduled to be the speaker. However, as Georgie described in an April letter to Catherine "Kitts" Devers, Jake's sister, the Academy and its executive officer had other challenges to face:

The Swedish Crown Prince and Princess are coming the 19th of April, the Danes in May and their British Majesties will be at Hyde Park in June, the 10th and 11th. So far as they know here that ends their stay in the States, but with the Mayflower in the river and graduation parade to be seen on Sunday afternoon [11 June], I believe no one would be surprised at having a last minute call to have seats reserved for them. It would be very difficult to arrange to have adequate police protection, but they very probably would have a large supply of that on hand [since Roosevelt was speaking at the 12 June graduation ceremony] so that West Point would not be responsible, but I can assure you that Jamie [Jake's nickname] hopes that they decide in favor of a nap that afternoon. The responsibility of having the President here on Monday is all the headache he needs.[39]

Traditionally, the Academy held its graduation ceremonies on Trophy Point. However, Devers and General Benedict had decided to hold the 1939 ceremony in the field house so they would not have to worry about the president being rained on. Devers arranged to have the floor of the field house planted with grass to make it look green and pastoral. He also had the engineers install a ramp so the president could drive in his car to the speaker's platform. The ceremony went off smoothly, with 456 cadets receiving commissions.[40] President Roosevelt appreciated the consideration shown by Academy personnel, and in a thank-you note to the superintendent he wrote, "My information and observation leads me to request you to commend, in addition to the above personnel, the services rendered by Colonel Jacob L. Devers."[41]

That month, Jake and Georgie were also the unofficial hosts of his class reunion. As Georgie told Kitts:

Time is growing short till June and the 30th reunion. Some ten sons of 1909 are in the Corps and each one will have more family than he remembers. . . . Some eighty people have decided to come to the reunion, counting wives and daughters. This will of necessity be headquarters since Jamie is the only member of the class here. Hot water, ice water, towels, cigarettes, drinks, all sorts of food at all hours of the day and night, rafts of strange people rushing in to phone, change clothes, use my lipstick, ask for hankys, stockings, umbrellas, change, and that's not a beginning![42]

On a more upbeat note, Georgie told Kitts, "It will end however and if I survive, we will go, immediately after graduation, aboard Stanley Rumbough's boat, and go to Great Neck, L.I. From there we will go to the [World's] Fair. . . . I will sure need a rest after that, for they will sing all night or at least try to and there will be no sleep." As many an army spouse has wondered, "Why do these things happen to us after the years when we could enjoy them? This would be fun for Frances and Alex and they aren't doing it, I am! I'll feel much more like a room in a hospital."[43]

At about the same time they were preparing for visiting dignitaries, the graduation ceremony, and the class reunion, Devers received word that he had been selected to serve as chief of staff for the army garrison in the Panama Canal Zone; he and Georgie would depart for that assignment in late June. As Georgie told Kitts, "Orders to Panama mean a little head work for a soldier's wife if anyone should stop to think of her. We go to the big house next to the General's at Quarry Heights. It sounds immense, larger than this. That means taking almost everything we own to fill it, and it indicates to me that I will have lots of company or we would be assigned a smaller house." Georgie was excited about "seeing the palms and hibiscus and pepper trees again," as she had in Hawaii, and living "that easy lazy life again. . . . And there is so much activity at the Zone that Jamie will be happy. In fact . . . it's a recognition of his ability to get things done, going as chief of staff of the Zone."[44]

General Benedict summed up his feelings about Devers's performance at the Academy in a farewell note to Jake: "Upon the occasion of your relief from duty under my command I wish to convey my sincere appreciation of your loyal, invaluable and conspicuously efficient service. . . . You have handled with vision, tact, energy, sound judgment and leadership all of the difficult duties that devolved upon you."[45]

On 27 June 1939 Jake and Georgie left the Academy. They visited Jake's family in York and Georgie's in Virginia before boarding an army transport, the *Leonard Wood*, in early August for the voyage to Panama. At the time, Devers did not seem to anticipate the possibility that war would break out in Europe or that the United States would once again be drawn into the struggle.

Panama Canal Zone

During his last three years at West Point, Devers had come to the attention of the most important American military leader of the mid-twentieth century, George C. Marshall. President Roosevelt selected Marshall to succeed Craig as army chief of staff on 23 April 1939, but until 1 September, Marshall served as acting chief of staff. During this time he began the task of identifying capable and energetic officers who could enlarge, reshape, and prepare the army for the major war that Marshall thought was nearly unavoidable.[46] Russell Weigley has concluded that Marshall "filled the office [of chief of staff] with a consistency and fullness of success unmatched by any other commander of the American Army in any previous war. . . . He was an excellent judge of the capacities of soldiers, and he selected his subordinates with a wisdom that permitted the Army to go through a long war with fewer important command upheavals than ever before."[47]

Devers owed his chance to be one of "Marshall's men" to his own successful performance as a leader and manager and to Lesley McNair, who had been his battery commander in 1910–1911. McNair had served with Marshall in World War I and was a close friend and confidant of the new chief of staff. In 1939 Marshall called on McNair to take over and reform the Command and General Staff School at Fort Leavenworth. McNair later served as chief of staff of the General Headquarters and then as commanding general of the Army Ground Forces in 1942. McNair helped Marshall create the American army of World War II, and Marshall relied on McNair to keep him "informed of those promising officers to whose leadership divisions and corps could be entrusted in case of war."[48] One such man was Jacob L. Devers.

The condition of the U.S. Army when war broke out in Europe in 1939 was lamentable. "The total strength, officers and men, was approaching 190,000. More than a quarter of that strength, however, was dispersed through the outlying possessions. The 140,000 soldiers within the United States were still scattered in a fashion remarkably reminiscent of the days of the Indian wars, across 130 posts chiefly of battalion size." The troops were equipped with weapons from the First World War, and aviation units had no aircraft comparable to those of Germany and Japan. The National Guard had about 200,000 men, but most of its units were woefully ill prepared for war.[49] It was clear to Marshall that the army would have to face its current threats with inadequate forces while laying the foundation for a major expansion to meet various overseas contingencies.

One of the more pressing concerns in September 1939 was the security of the Western Hemisphere in the face of Germany's increasing interest in Latin America. It quickly came to Marshall's attention that he needed a more energetic team of senior leaders in the Panama Canal Department, which was in charge of land defense of the canal. In a letter written to Major General Daniel Van Voorhis on 2 September, Marshall expressed the following concerns: "The Secretary of War is disturbed over the situation in Panama. He has just returned from an inspection there and is of the opinion that conditions are not what they should be. . . . He feels that General [David L.] Stone has made every effort to cooperate [with the governor of the Canal Zone], but he is also strongly of the opinion that General Stone has not the force to command the situation, and does not visualize the more important aspects of the requirements."[50]

The security of the Panama Canal was critical to U.S. defense plans. Any damage to the canal would make it very difficult to move parts of the navy's Atlantic Fleet to the Pacific Ocean, where the potential for Japanese aggression was growing. The canal was also critical to the flow of commerce from the Pacific to the Atlantic. Concerns about the canal's security increased dramatically on 1 September 1939, when Germany invaded Poland. When the British and French declared war on Germany, the Panama Canal became a major defense concern. In response to these heightened tensions, President Roosevelt declared a limited national emergency and ordered the expansion of the regular army to 227,000 men. This small increase gave the War Department sufficient manpower to activate two corps headquarters and to reinforce Panama.[51]

As Marshall told Van Voorhis (who would soon take command of army forces in the Canal Zone), "during the next few months, at least, the Canal Zone will probably be the point at which most of the critical international incidents will develop, concerning this country. For some time past, six British cruisers have been lying off the Canal; we have the question of German submarines to consider; air fields in nearby Colombia have German reserve pilots operating planes, who have already excited the suspicions of our Embassy." To ensure that an officer with "the force, leadership, and good judgment to meet the situation" was in charge in Panama, Marshall selected Van Voorhis to replace Stone.[52] On 5 September 1939 plans were also under way to send the 5th and 13th Infantry Regiments and 6,000 antiaircraft crewmen to Panama, requiring major construction to accommodate these men and their weapons.

The United States had gained control of the Panama Canal Zone with the Hay-Bunau-Varilla Treaty of 1903. For $10 million the United States obtained control of territory extending six miles on either side of the canal and agreed to pay the new Republic of Panama an annual rent of $250,000.

In 1911 the first army troops arrived to protect the engineers building the canal under the command of George Goethals. After the canal was completed in 1914, army coast artillery troops established defenses on both the Pacific and Atlantic sides. By 1917, the army had created the Panama Canal Department; its headquarters was located at Quarry Heights, overlooking the Atlantic entrance to the canal. The U.S. Army provided garrisons for the Canal Zone, Hawaii, and the Philippines. During the interwar years, roughly a quarter of the army was overseas at any one time, and the soldiers in these garrisons rotated back to the continental United States every two to three years. To get the men to and from these overseas possessions, the army maintained and manned a fleet of troop ships. Jake and Georgie traveled to Panama on one of these ships, and she found the voyage quite pleasant. In a letter to Kitts she wrote: "We are having a Caribbean cruise in the Presidential suite [aboard the *Leonard Wood*]. . . . I don't know many people—but that's an advantage in a way. . . . Stopped in Charleston [on the way south]. . . . I wish I had married a sea captain and lived on a ship."[53]

The Deverses arrived in Panama in late August 1939, just in time for Jake to take part in the rapid expansion of the garrison and defenses. His first impressions of his new responsibilities reflected concern about the job's complexity and a realization that the command needed reorganization. He had to deal with five army generals and two navy admirals to coordinate policy and carry out the necessary expansion of facilities on a number of small posts in the zone. He also found that a steady stream of dignitaries from Washington liked to visit the Canal Zone and, of course, give advice. For example, the day after he arrived, Secretary of War Harry H. Woodring showed up to help celebrate the canal's twenty-fifth anniversary. As Devers told General Benedict in a letter, his new job required plenty of tact and ingenuity to avoid friction and secure results.[54]

The Canal Zone's limited facilities made it difficult to find space for troop billets and defense installations, and it was impossible to build quarters to house the families of the officers and men being sent to the zone. This was a major problem. Because the United States was not at war, many military families chose to accompany their service members overseas. As Devers told Brigadier General J. Cummins, commander of the 18th Infantry Brigade (which would soon be on its way to Panama), "For your information there are now on duty officers of the 14th and 33rd Infantry who have not been able to bring their families to this department, as there are no quarters of any kind available."[55]

Devers threw himself into the task of building facilities for the in-bound units. By 13 September 1939, a million dollars' worth of construction was under way, with plans to have the basic facilities, consisting of "cover, food, and shower baths," operational within forty days. He sought advice from Major John Gilman, the quartermaster at West Point, and told Gilman there were not enough hours in the day to get the job done. To add to his challenges, the War Department ordered the Panama Canal Department to go to a "war footing."[56]

Georgie, meanwhile, was thrilled to be in Panama, as she indicated to her sister-in-law: "Quarry Heights has completely won my heart. . . . I have the cook, Maud, the maid, Ethel, and the laundress, Irene—and a striker—and all for less than Annie May and Eddie cost me [at West Point]. . . . We swim almost every day at Fort Amadon. I have found some old friends here and am making some new ones. The Governor is an acquaintance from Leavenworth days—so we are meeting the Canal people as well as the Army."[57] The Deverses lived at 176 Quarry Heights, in a large house next to General Stone's quarters. Georgie had a real need for a household staff, since she and Jake were expected to entertain local dignitaries and commanders and visitors from Washington. Georgie was in charge of entertaining, although Jake invited the guests. She told Jake's mother, "It's a great life, and there's no time to weaken, but sometimes I feel as if my knees were made of water. Thank goodness for cocktails at such a time for they do break down the timidities and relax the reserves."[58]

Living overseas had its attractions for officers and their families. Servants were very affordable, even on an army salary, and the climate was pleasant in places like Panama. As Georgie wrote to her mother-in-law, there was "a languor about the tropics that makes one so worthless. . . . I get up at 6:30, the only effort of my day, as the ordering must be done by 7:30. . . . Then I have papaya—and coffee—read the wretched excuse for a paper—and am ready to set out upon the daily prowl of the PX's and commissaries. . . . I get back for a late lunch . . . and then if Jamie can get a few minutes off, we have a visit together."[59] However, as the news from Europe darkened with the collapse of Poland and the Russians' enslavement of the Baltic nations, it was impossible for Georgie and Jake to ignore the increasingly dangerous international situation. They realized in the fall of 1939 that American involvement in another major war was becoming more likely.

Georgie had a lot of time to think about the future, and her prognosis in late 1939 was not optimistic: "I feel I must enjoy each day—get all I can out of it as they may be the last time we'll live on a regular army post—under conditions I know and love. The whole army in the states will go into intensive training in the south and in Texas this winter and spring in camps and cantonments like those of 1917–18. There will be an end of garrison life, and the families will either be lonely or camp followers. . . . It seems to me that the war is closing in—slowly—but inexorably."[60]

During their leisure time, Jake and Georgie read a great deal. Kitts Devers sent them a bundle of books from her bookstore in York, and Georgie reported that "we fell on your books like ravening wolves."[61] Many officers, such as Dwight Eisenhower and Omar Bradley, played bridge for relaxation, but the Deverses apparently did not enjoy the game. Jake was unable to play polo in Panama, even if he had been able to find the time, and his life was only going to get busier.

Meanwhile, Georgie had a bird's-eye view of the harbor from her house in Quarry Heights. She watched ships arrive daily from around the world and soon realized that some of the cargo was human. When Hitler launched his assault against German Jews in November 1938 and then annexed the remainder of Czechoslovakia in March 1939, many European Jews fled to safety in the Western Hemisphere. To the shame of the United States, they were not welcomed and were not allowed to stay. Georgie wrote:

> I sit up here in my eyre watching ships come and go. . . . Panama City has more refugees—and when their sixty days are up, the Zone gets them put aboard some ship. The Germans won't take Jews aboard. . . . They have no passports anywhere else. The Zone can intern them or feed them to the sharks—or let them starve on the roads. The Unions won't let them be employed, even temporarily. 3,000 of them are here, more every day. The [army] doctors can't buy them medicines, even if they attend to them. They can't use the hospital stores for them unless they want to do a turn in [the army prison in] Leavenworth. A large no. are interned in some condemned buildings [and] the rain comes through. They infect one another with every kind of illness. . . . I don't see what can be the end—for us or for them. Their presence here begins to brutalize us. . . . It's a crazy world.[62]

National policy and xenophobia in the United States made it difficult for military officers to take the initiative and help those who were fleeing

Nazi tyranny and lacked the proper entrance visas. There is no evidence that Devers or Stone tried to provide the refugees in Panama with adequate shelter or medical care during their internment before deportation. Devers was typical of many Americans in terms of his less-than-favorable view of Jews in 1939–1940. He wrote home in June 1940, "We are becoming very closed mouthed and watching for the 5th column. It is a very active organization and needs checking. Apparently a German, a crook, a Russian, and of course the same goes for a Jew. Trust none of them."[63] His view of Jews would change dramatically in the next five years, as it did for many Americans.

In October 1939 the secretary of war decided that the military construction being carried out in Panama was to be done "upon a cost-plus-a-fixed-fee basis," hoping to accelerate the availability of facilities for the additional forces moving to Panama. Marshall cautioned Stone that "even under this plan careful supervision by the Government is essential."[64] This task fell largely to Devers, as chief of staff of the department. Additionally, the army and navy created a joint command for the naval and ground forces in the Panama Canal Zone, and the senior army officer was in charge of the new structure. One major problem, in addition to interservice rivalry and parochialism, was the fact that the army commander was a two-star general, whereas the senior navy officers held a three-star rank. The establishment of a truly "joint" command would take some time to work out under the command of Major General Van Voorhis.

Although Marshall chose Van Voorhis to replace Stone in September, the change of command would not occur until December. Devers thus had the additional challenge of organizing the new command structure and staff while preparing for Stone's departure and Van Voorhis's arrival. The timing was bad when Devers had to undergo an emergency tonsillectomy in November. As he wrote to his sister, "I lost three pounds of tonsils, but I am going strong." Georgie stepped up to the task of making General and Mrs. Van Voorhis feel welcome and comfortable. As she wrote to Jake's mother: "The day after tomorrow, the 26th [of December], the new general and Mrs. Van Voorhis and Miss. Betty Van V arrive—they will have dinner with us but sleep in their own house. I've had beds put in and cooking utensils and china and silver and engaged servants, and ordered the first day's food and menus. I hope I've done everything I should. . . . Well Merry Christmas to all at your house and with all our love, we are, your devoted children."[65]

For his part, General Marshall worked to get Congress to approve the promotion of army officers who ran large organizations like Panama to the rank of lieutenant general. However, it took him until July 1940 to get this accomplished. Van Voorhis was one of the first men selected for such a promotion, which gave him the same rank as the admirals in the Canal Zone. This made his task of coordinating a joint army-navy command somewhat easier. Van Voorhis also had to deal with senior army officers who could not work amicably with their navy counterparts. In particular, Marshall felt it necessary to write to Van Voorhis in April 1940 to tell him to rein in Brigadier General Herbert Dargue, commander of the 19th Air Corps Wing. Marshall wanted Van Voorhis to tactfully order Dargue to direct all his energy to doing army business and leave relations with the navy to the chief of staff.[66] Devers, in contrast, worked well with the navy and would be promoted again. Dargue would not.

In spite of the challenges, Devers was making real progress in reorganizing the department's staff and getting construction projects under way. In a letter to Lieutenant Colonel Robert Crawford of the General Staff's War Plans Division, Devers explained that initially, the department's staff had not functioned well as a cohesive group, with the biggest problem being a lack of coordination among the infantry, antiaircraft artillery, air corps, and navy units. By October, however, he had the staff "working along proper lines" and believed he would get a lot more out of them. Devers reported in mid-October that permanent construction was proceeding well and that planning for the future expansion of facilities was much improved. He hoped the contractors selected for the work would be good ones, and he believed that the biggest problem would be getting supplies delivered and finding quarters for the workers. Devers also provided his vision of how the Canal Zone could best be defended, noting that the command needed plenty of long-range heavy bombers with experienced pilots who could fly far out to sea and intercept enemy naval forces.[67] Devers learned a great deal about the air corps during his service as chief of staff in Panama, and he demonstrated to Van Voorhis and Marshall that he could work well with its officers.

Devers continued his practice of seeking talented officers to solve problems. He convinced Red Reeder, a captain stationed in the Canal Zone in 1939, that his military future lay with the infantry rather than as a football coach at West Point. Reeder accepted Devers's advice and later told Colonel Griess, "[I] worked under him for about 10 months and found him honest, alert, direct, abrupt—a man who explored a question and was not hasty, as I had heard. He could get the job done. He listened to you. If you were thin-skinned, his briskness could irritate you."[68]

During the winter of 1939–1940, the War Department was very concerned about the troop strength in the Canal Zone. Van Voorhis and Devers recommended that a total of four infantry regiments be assigned to the garrison, in addition to the increase in antiaircraft and coastal artillery units. The lack of adequate troop billets for an enlarged garrison was being addressed, but there were still few quarters for soldiers' families. Van Voorhis saw this as a problem that "ties in with that of morale. . . . The lack of quarters to accommodate dependents is a serious one." A major problem was the rapidly increasing costs of construction and the shortage of officers to oversee it. The estimates provided by Devers and his staff for new barracks and family quarters in Panama exceeded those of the quartermaster general's office in Washington, so Van Voorhis invited Quartermaster General Edmund Gregory to visit the Canal Zone to discuss these issues.[69] When Major General Gregory arrived in late March 1940, Devers and his staff briefed him on the costs associated with new construction and how the new units fit into the department's defense plans. Gregory saw the challenges involved in building so many new installations in such a small area. He recognized the need for additional personnel to supervise the contractors, and the quartermaster general assumed the burden of providing qualified personnel to oversee construction.

Relations between the Panama Canal Department and the local government were generally good during Devers's tenure as chief of staff. On the night of 13–14 April 1940 about one-third of the town of Colon, at the Caribbean end of the canal, was destroyed by a fire. The army moved quickly to help the displaced population and protect property. The department provided troops to patrol the city and tents and field kitchens to house and feed about 10,000 homeless people. The American Red Cross also sent $15,000 to finance rebuilding. Marshall wrote to Van Voorhis on 15 April, "Your prompt action to assist and succor the people of Colon is to be commended. The War Department feels confident in trusting to your good judgment as to the further requirements of this situation."[70] Devers was intimately involved in the swift action taken to deal with this major crisis. His staff orchestrated the relief efforts efficiently, indicating that his reorganization had paid off.

In April 1940 Colonel Jacob Devers was selected for promotion to brigadier general, five months ahead of his classmate and friend George Patton. His outstanding performance as chief of staff of the Panama Canal Department earned him his first star. He had proved to Van Voorhis and Marshall that he had the leadership qualities necessary for higher command. When Devers's tour of duty in Panama ended, Van Voorhis wrote in his efficiency report, "I consider him the most promising general officer in the Army."[71] Marshall visited the Canal Zone in February 1940 and told Van Voorhis, "As far as the Panama Canal Department is concerned, I want you to know that I was greatly impressed with how much you had done in the brief period of your leadership, you have given me a feeling of complete confidence regarding matters in the Canal Zone."[72]

Georgie and Jake were thrilled with his promotion. Georgie wrote to his mother and asked, "How does it feel to have Jamie one of the top 50 brigadier generals in the army, and on April 30th he becomes one. . . . I stand by in my role of tail to the kite, and wear that smile that can't come off."[73] Omar Bradley was one of the officers who wrote to congratulate Devers. Devers had been his baseball coach in 1915, and they had both worked at West Point in 1938. Bradley's note said the following: "Dear Georgie and Jake, I can't tell you how pleased Mary and I are to know of your selection to be a general. . . . It is nice to get it so young."[74] Devers and many others who considered themselves "Marshall's men," such as Terry de la Mesa Allen, Teddy Roosevelt Jr., Alexander Patch, and George Patton, would provide the energy and leadership needed to turn raw conscripts into soldiers and build a force that would eventually reach 8 million men.

On 15 June 1940 Devers wrote to his son-in-law, "I have been ordered to Washington for duty. I have no idea what this duty will be or whether I will stay there any length of time." Georgie wrote to Jake's mother on 6 July, "I simply can't believe the Panama detail is behind us—and that we are almost home, and will see you all again soon."[75] Their journey was just beginning, and it would take them in a direction that was sharply different from the one they had envisioned in 1939. In this, they were representative of the army and the nation.

6

Marshall's Fireman and Division Command

In early 1940 the U.S. Army began an expansion that would increase its strength nearly tenfold by November 1941. The impetus for this rapid growth in both strength and congressional appropriations was the increasingly bad news from Europe and East Asia. In April, Hitler's forces overran Denmark and Norway. In May, the German army shattered the cohesion of the French army in six days. By late June, the Germans had conquered France, Belgium, and the Netherlands and had driven the British army off the Continent. The Japanese took advantage of this situation by demanding free access to the French and Dutch colonies in Southeast Asia.

In early 1940, before these German and Japanese victories, President Roosevelt submitted a military budget of $853 million to Congress, twice the size of the 1939 request. Congress initially cut this sum by about 9.5 percent, but by June, the legislature had approved a military budget of $3 billion and authorized the expansion of the regular army to 375,000 officers and men. The General Staff, meanwhile, was working on plans to equip a force of 1.1 million men. Conscription was the only way such a large force could be raised.[1]

The secretary of war and the army staff agreed with Roosevelt that implementing conscription would create a major political backlash. However, as Russell Weigley concludes in his history of the army, "In the summer of 1940 public and Congressional sentiment so outran the President and the Army that conscription was enacted without their leadership."[2] The army faced the daunting task of absorbing 600,000 conscripts while expanding the regular army from roughly 250,000 to 375,000 men. George Marshall's quest for quality senior officers to command the divisions and corps that would be formed was an essential part of this expansion.

Provisional Brigade

Brigadier General and Mrs. Devers returned to Washington from Panama just as major changes were taking place in the War Department's leadership. The collapse of France and Belgium and the defeat of the British army by Nazi Germany transformed the American political scene. The isolationists could no longer claim that the United States was safe behind the protection of the French army and the Royal Navy. The pendulum of political discourse now swung toward those Americans who had been calling for greater military preparedness. In response to this swing, President Roosevelt finally removed the extreme isolationist Harry Woodring from his post as secretary of war, ending a bitter internal feud between Woodring and Louis Johnson, the assistant secretary. Johnson, a former head of the American Legion, was a strong advocate of increased military preparedness, while Woodring had opposed and hindered the administration's efforts to expand the armed forces. The German conquest of western Europe was the catalyst for change in the army's civilian leadership, and Chief of Staff Marshall no longer found himself caught between his civilian bosses as he laid the foundation for army expansion.[3]

Roosevelt selected Henry L. Stimson as the new secretary of war on 19 June 1940. The seventy-two-year-old Stimson was an attorney, a lifelong Republican, and a strong advocate of increased military preparedness and greater American involvement in international affairs. He was noted for his probity and commitment to public service, having served as secretary of war in the Taft administration, governor-general of the Philippines under Coolidge, and secretary of state for Hoover. On the eve of his appointment, Stimson delivered a radio address urging Congress to repeal the Neutrality Acts and to give all possible aid short of war to Great Britain. He agreed with prominent members of the preparedness movement that Congress should institute conscription to obtain the manpower needed for a greatly expanded military. The president assured the new secretary that Stimson's strong support for aid to Britain, compulsory national military service, and a rapid increase in the armed forces were compatible with FDR's views and goals.[4]

In these rapidly changing circumstances, the army needed senior officers who could get things done quickly and efficiently, without constant supervision from the chief of staff. Marshall judged Devers to be such a soldier. Devers had initially been slated to work in some capacity for Woodring, but as he told his classmate Colonel Thurston Hughes, "The job I was ordered to Washington for disappeared with the former Secretary of War and General Marshall, having started me on my way, decided to bring me in any case [to the War Department]."[5] General Marshall assigned the new brigadier general to command the Washington Provisional Brigade, an organization created in 1921 to oversee army units in the DC area, such as the 3rd Cavalry Regiment at Fort Myer. As the tempo of operations dramatically increased in 1939–1940, Marshall shifted a number of administrative tasks to the Provisional Brigade.[6]

By the time Devers took command in July 1940, responsibility for routine matters such as ceremonial events, personnel leave, and vehicle registration had been transferred from the army's general and special staff sections to the headquarters of the Provisional Brigade. According to Marshall, "The troops involved are those stationed at Fort Myer, the Arlington Cantonment, and the Headquarters Company located near the Munitions Building. The District Commander has a competent staff to coordinate military plans concerning the District [of Columbia]. . . . The Commander himself has a great many obligations of a semi-official nature—social and otherwise."[7]

In a letter to his former boss, General Van Voorhis, Devers explained the organization of the Provisional Brigade and admitted feeling somewhat underemployed in his new position:

> I miss Panama, particularly you, for as work is concerned there has been a considerable let-down, while I try to read myself into some of the background of my present work and try to guess what may happen, if and when. I have just come from inspecting the entraining of the 16th Field Artillery for the First Army maneuvers. My command will consist of all of the 3rd Cavalry, all of the 12th Infantry, and a battalion of the 16th Field Artillery after September 1st. There are many "ifs" and "ands" but I suppose all of this will straighten out, in another month.[8]

It is not clear what Devers meant by "ifs" and "ands," but he was certainly hoping to see the army expand. Two critical questions directly related to that expansion were under congressional consideration in the summer of 1940: conscription and federalization of the National Guard. Congress was debating the Burke-Wadsworth bill, which called for the induction of selected men for one year of active military service. The initial intake of draftees would be as high as 600,000 men. The War Department realized that the regular army was too small to accommodate and train that many men, so Secretary of War Stimson recommended the federalization of the

National Guard's eighteen infantry divisions and the call-up of thousands of reserve officers to fill out the regular army's nine infantry, two armored, and two cavalry divisions. Such an expansion would require significantly more senior officers to command these formations.

Like many officers in 1940, Devers felt that Congress was moving too slowly, as he indicated in a letter to Van Voorhis: "Congress, as you have read, is bickering over the draft bill and the bill to call the National Guard into active service and this has taken almost all of the time of the Secretary and the Chief of Staff because nothing can be done until these two bills, and the money [bill] for five billions, are passed."[9] Despite this perception of slowness, the speed with which Congress enacted the first peacetime draft in American history was in fact remarkable.

On 27 August Congress authorized the president to call up the National Guard and reserves to active duty for one year. Less than a month later, on 16 September, Congress passed the Burke-Wadsworth Act, implementing a selective service system for one year. More than 16 million Americans aged twenty-one to thirty-five registered with their local draft boards in the next month.[10] The first draftees would join army units beginning in January 1941.

This was an exciting and hectic time to be a senior army officer in Washington, D.C. As commander of the Provisional Brigade, Devers came into contact with a number of key military leaders just as the nation was beginning to mobilize. One of these men was Lesley McNair, Devers's friend and former battery commander. McNair arrived in July to set up the General Headquarters (GHQ), which was designed to provide a staff for an expeditionary force, similar to the GHQ of the American Expeditionary Forces in World War I. Marshall was the designated commanding general of the Field Forces, and the GHQ would be his expeditionary headquarters if the United States went to war and an army was sent overseas. As chief of staff of the GHQ, McNair also oversaw the training of the rapidly expanding army. "During 1940 and 1941 McNair and his staff worked out the details of this course to frame a [training] program that could be retained through the war and which gave the soldier of World War II a much better preparation for combat, especially in proportion to training time consumed, than any of his predecessors."[11]

General Marshall assigned Devers "many odd jobs as representative for both the Chief of Staff and Mr. Stimson, Secretary of War," in addition to his duties as Provisional Brigade commander. For example, Devers wrote to a friend, "Last week I sat with governors and attorney generals at the Department of Justice for a two-day session on what can the states do to assist national defense. This covered plant protection, sabotage, espionage, mob violence, etc. I was particularly impressed with the seriousness with which the governors and attorney generals approached the whole subject of national defense." He also spent a week observing First Army maneuvers, where he hoped to "get in touch with some of the field soldiers' problems."[12]

Devers needed to surround himself with men he could trust, and Major Eugene L. Harrison was such a person. They had met at West Point, when Devers was the Academy's executive officer. Harrison later recalled that when Devers got to Washington, he "phoned and asked if I wished to come as his aide. Well of course I wanted to come as his aide, but I had another motive because I could see that war was coming on. . . . So I was very glad to get out of West Point." Harrison organized Devers's personal staff and helped organize his command, "because at that time the district was not as well organized as it is now."[13] Harrison remained Devers's aide until Marshall selected him to serve as Secretary Stimson's military assistant in late 1941.

Devers's tenure as Provisional Brigade commander lasted only two months. At that time, Marshall gave Devers a higher-priority mission that allowed him to prove he could work well with the navy and air corps and get things done efficiently. It also gave him the opportunity to deal with Marshall and Stimson personally.

Presidential Base-Selection Committee

In July 1940 many Americans (including Joseph Kennedy, the Anglophobic ambassador to Great Britain) believed the British would cave in to Hitler rather than face an aerial blitz by the Luftwaffe and an invasion by the Wehrmacht. Winston Churchill, the British prime minister since 10 May, had other ideas. Churchill used his oratorical skills to come to the defense of Britain as he spoke to the British people and, indirectly, to Americans. He also cultivated a close relationship with Franklin Roosevelt that was designed to nudge the president and the U.S. government closer to war over the next year.

First, however, Churchill had to prove to the Americans that the British were going to stay in the war and fight with every tool available. His greatest fear after the surrender of France was that the French battle fleet would fall into German hands, permitting the enemy to protect an invasion force crossing the English Channel. To forestall this eventuality, Churchill and his War Cabinet ordered the British navy to seize all French ships in English ports and to strike at French warships in Mers el-Kebir, near the city of Oran, Algeria. On 3 July the Royal Navy launched an attack against the French fleet, after offering it the option of surrendering or being interned. Churchill reported to the House of Commons the next day that three French battleships, eight cruisers, and a large number of smaller vessels had been seized in British ports, with little loss of life, and that four French battleships had been disabled or sunk in Mers el-Kebir.[14] Churchill later said that these naval actions "made the world realize that we were in earnest in our intentions to carry on."[15]

On 10 July the Germans opened the aerial assault known as the Battle of Britain. Over the next two months, the Royal Air Force (RAF) succeeded in fighting off the Luftwaffe's bombers and fighters by a narrow margin. Churchill, realizing the importance of civilian morale and hope, renewed his request that Roosevelt transfer fifty obsolete American destroyers to the Royal Navy. The ships were marginally serviceable, as Churchill and FDR realized, but their transfer would be a powerful symbol to the British people that they were not alone. As Churchill wrote in a letter to Roosevelt, "The moral value of this fresh aid from your Government and people at this critical time will be very great and widely felt."[16] However, this request posed a political problem for the president, who had just been nominated for an unprecedented third term. How could he convince a seemingly isolationist Congress to give the destroyers to the British? Roosevelt's answer was to issue an executive order on 2 September announcing the transfer of the vessels. In exchange, the British agreed to give the United States ninety-nine-year leases to naval and air bases in the western Atlantic and the Caribbean that would greatly strengthen the U.S. ability to defend the sea approaches to the East Coast and the Panama Canal. Wendell Willkie, the Republican presidential candidate, criticized the use of an executive order to circumvent Congress, but he did not attack the president for helping the British. Churchill later concluded that the destroyers-for-bases deal "marked the passage of the United States from being neutral to being non-belligerent."[17]

Moving swiftly to cement the deal, the president ordered the armed services to create a joint committee to select base sites. Each service was asked to provide a senior officer to cochair the committee. Initially, Marshall wanted to appoint Brigadier General Edmund Daly, commanding general of the Puerto Rican Department, to the committee, but as he told Daly, "Things moved too rapidly and I had only a few hours in which to get together the Army representation; so Devers was selected."[18] Marshall told Devers, "You're temporarily appointed to this board until we can find a man for it. In the meantime, you go up to the Fifth Section and . . . report to Admiral Greenslade and then come back and report to me." When Devers arrived, he found that the planners were thinking of stationing two army divisions on Bermuda, even though no one on the board's staff had ever been to the island. Devers had just read an article in *Reader's Digest* about Bermuda, and as the saying goes, "in the land of the blind, the one-eyed man is king." Devers pointed out that Bermuda was only twenty miles long and not much more than half a mile wide, making it too small for 40,000 troops to train properly. Worse, the only source of water was rain that was collected and stored in cisterns. He concluded there was no way two divisions could be stationed on the island.[19]

Devers informed Admiral Greenslade that he was only a temporary member of the base-selection committee. Greenslade, however, wanted Devers assigned to the committee permanently, so he took him to see the chief of naval operations, Admiral Stark. Stark, who had already been impressed by Devers's concise and thoughtful memorandum about joint army-navy command arrangements in Panama, instructed Devers to go back and tell Marshall that the navy wanted him assigned permanently to Greenslade's board. When he arrived at Marshall's office, the chief of staff told Devers, "It's the President's board of experts. You go tell the President."[20] So Devers had to figure out how to arrange a meeting with the president. Then he remembered that a friend from West Point, Brigadier General Edwin "Pa" Watson, class of 1908, was FDR's military aide. He called Watson and soon found himself in Watson's office. Watson listened to his friend's predicament and said, "I'll fix that." As Devers later recalled, "So he opens the door [to the Oval Office], he walks in, and I know damn well he walked around the desk and came out. The president wasn't in there. He says, 'the president has appointed you.'" Armed with this authority, Devers returned to the War Department and recruited an air corps officer and an engineer to advise him about potential base sites.[21]

This entire charade that Marshall put Devers through may have been a test of his ability to operate at higher levels of authority and get things done without making unnecessary waves. Evidently, he passed the test. On

28 September 1940 the adjutant general of the army notified Devers that he had been nominated for promotion to major general. At the same time, Marshall nominated Devers's classmates George Patton, J. C. H. Lee, and William H. Simpson for promotion to brigadier general.[22]

Meanwhile, the base-selection committee worked fast, as Devers wrote in a letter to a friend on 29 September: "I have just finished a reconnaissance of Bermuda and Newfoundland, and leave next week for the Bahamas, Jamaica, Trinidad, and British Guiana. I am traveling by Navy cruiser, patrol planes, and Army bombers. [I] expect to be gone about a month. This is interesting but exacting work, since the Board [of] which I am a member must come back with answers."[23]

While Devers was traveling with the base-selection committee in early October, Georgie remained at home worrying about his next assignment. In a letter to Jake's sister Kitts, Georgie wrote, "I am watching the papers to learn where and when we go, or if we go. Jamie expects to have orders almost at once, but nothing yet, and plans change so rapidly that I can't guess where I will be when the smoke clears. 'They' told Jamie that he was to go to Bragg to command the 9th Division, but I am not believing anything but orders and even that may never happen. . . . It has been such a lot of promotions . . . but I love it!"[24]

While the committee was finishing its base-selection work, General Marshall received disturbing news from Fort Bragg, North Carolina. Evidently, money was disappearing from the officers' club. Anthony McAuliffe, then a major on the General Staff, remembered riding in a carpool with Walter Bedell Smith, who was one of Marshall's key assistants by this time. When the problems at Fort Bragg came up, Smith told McAuliffe, "General Marshall told me that the thing to do was to get a hold of General Devers and have him ordered to Fort Bragg, put him in command, tell him what the situation is and tell him to straighten it out."[25] Marshall called Devers personally and informed him, "I am going to send you down to Bragg. . . . I am going to give you command of the 9th Division and the Post of Fort Bragg. Things down there are about nine months behind schedule. I want you to go there immediately—take over—and see what you can do to step up that situation."[26]

After hanging up the telephone, Devers told his aide, Gene Harrison, to go to Fort Bragg immediately and prepare quarters for him and Georgie. He also wrote a quick note to Brigadier General DeRussy Hoyle, the 9th Division's artillery commander, informing him that he and Georgie would arrive late in the day and requesting that "no honors or other ceremony be given upon my arrival."[27]

Fort Bragg

Two days later, on 30 October, Jake and Georgie arrived at Fort Bragg at five o'clock in the afternoon, just as the civilian workforce was leaving post for the day. The Deverses were held up by the heavy traffic coming out of the post for two hours. Devers remembered years later, "I knew immediately what I had to do." The next day, Major General Devers "had the Constructing Quartermaster, the officer in charge of the building operations, and the builders in my office where they briefed me on . . . the problem" with the construction of the main roads into and out of the post. "They had a definite plan of what they wanted to do and how they wanted to do it, [but] they couldn't get a go-ahead on it. So I gave them a go-ahead within half an hour, and told them to work Sundays—to open up a single road—that entrance road into Fort Bragg—to use everything and everybody they had to clean up that road so we could operate. Furthermore, I wanted all roads into the building areas put in condition so we could really move with speed."[28]

The process of getting approval for the entire road system for Fort Bragg was more complex than finishing the entrance road. First of all, the army engineers needed state approval for the road network, and they had to find a construction company that could build the roads and buildings fast. Colonel Norman Peace from Charlotte, North Carolina, took charge of the overall planning for the post; the civilian building contractor was Loving and Company, from Goldsboro (Devers called them the "Peace-Loving Machine"). Their task was enormous: they had to expand Fort Bragg, which had a capacity of 5,400 men in 1940, to a post capable of housing and training more than 67,000 by early 1941.

Devers contacted the head of the Construction Division of the Quartermaster General Corps, Brigadier General Brehon Somervell, for help. Somervell had run the Works Progress Administration in New York in the 1930s (which included the construction of LaGuardia Airport), and Devers had sought his advice for some of the construction projects at West Point. As the new chief of the Construction Division, Somervell oversaw the construction of hundreds of installations needed in 1940–1941 to accommodate the rapidly expanding force. Devers got through to Somervell on a

Saturday afternoon and told him, "We need help." Somervell was responsible for more than 375 major projects costing $100 million, but he was more than willing to help a local commander. As Devers told him, "We aren't going to get this job done unless you send somebody down here. And I don't want a pencil-pusher. I want a man who can come down here and make decisions. . . . And I'd like him to be here in the morning—Monday at the latest." Somervell came through: "He sent in the roads man from North Carolina and a man from his office. Plans were gone over thoroughly and, within the next forty-eight hours, we laid out a complete road system for Fort Bragg. And we built them the proper widths. . . . This was during the fall and winter months."[29] The result, as Gene Harrison remembered, was impressive: "Almost overnight you'd see a new group of barracks go up. We spent days out inspecting the construction and pushing the contractors along until finally they were building barracks so fast that you didn't even know where you were when you got out in these areas."[30]

Before Devers took command, relations between the army and the local community near Fort Bragg were not positive. Understandably, local farmers resented being forced to give up cropland to enlarge the base to 257 square miles. Many of the construction workers were outsiders, and many of the supplies purchased by the fort's quartermaster were shipped in from distant locations. Devers could not assuage the farmers who had lost land, but he prodded the quartermaster to buy as much local produce as possible for the mess halls.[31] The post engineers also hired more farmers to work on the post, especially in the late fall and winter after their crops had been harvested. They appreciated the work, and this local labor helped Devers deal with a problem that developed with the unions. When the union bosses threatened to stop work, the construction engineers and contractors turned to the farmers, who arrived in force, ready to work.[32]

Marshall visited Fort Bragg in the fall, at which time he appraised the progress and assessed Devers's leadership. He wrote to Van Voorhis: "Devers has gone a long way since he left your place. He is now a division commander, and making a fine job of it. We want more men of the same type, and I am willing to go down the list quite a way to get them."[33]

The rapid mobilization of 1940–1941 placed a great strain on the officer corps and the General Staff. The nation, which had once been convinced that war could be avoided, now recognized the growing dangers posed by Germany and Japan. In response, Congress had passed conscription and appropriated unprecedented funds for the armed services. In return, Congress, the press, and the public expected the army to train hundreds of thousands of new soldiers. Devers's work at Fort Bragg was just one example of how those challenges were met.

George Marshall found himself in a difficult position: he had to tell Congress and the American people about the challenges of mobilization while at the same time reassuring them that the army was doing a good job in organizing the rapidly expanding force. By November 1940, Marshall was able to report to the American people in a radio address that the army was making substantial progress:

> A year ago last summer our active Army consisted of about 170,000 soldiers. . . . Today there are 500,000 men in the field and within a few weeks this total will approach 800,000. . . . One of our most difficult problems has been the hurried erection of the temporary shelter at cantonments. . . . A contract to build something within a period of a year is not to be compared in difficulty with the contract which must be completed in three months' time, involving the construction of complete utilities, and roads, hospitals, offices, and barracks for twenty to fifty thousand men. . . . With time the dominant factor, this phase of the task has been a very trying one, but we are proceeding more rapidly than we at first thought would be possible. Literally, nothing has been allowed to interfere with the accomplishment of this task at the earliest possible date.[34]

One of the leading critics of the army's performance was syndicated columnist Westbrook Pegler. He traveled from post to post reporting the army's missteps and problems as it tried to cope with a massive building program and an influx of new soldiers. Devers was not spared Pegler's attention, as he recalled years later: "Westbrook Pegler was quite popular in those days. He wrote devastating articles about everything we were doing in the war effort. General Marshall called me up and said that Pegler was going to arrive on my Post and was going to stay about ten days. [He] just wanted to warn me about it. I asked him if he had any instructions, and he said, 'No, it's your problem.'"[35]

When Pegler arrived, Devers took him out in the woods, where General Hoyle "was giving a party . . . for a lot of officers." Devers and Hoyle figured that if Pegler "arrived while our party was on, he could come out here and see how we operated. Well, he did. He came out and it was a good time [for him] to meet all the officers when they were at play."[36] The next day Devers gave Pegler a short briefing about the ongoing construction and handed him a map of the current projects. He also sent a lieutenant to accompany Pegler as a guide, assuring the journalist that the young officer was not a spy. Before turning Pegler loose, Devers asked him for one thing: "If you unearth anything that is bad about this Post, write your article and send it in. But I would appreciate it if you would call me on the phone, or come in and see me, and tell me about it so I can clean it up. . . . And he did this. He was around there almost three weeks."[37]

Pegler drove to Fayetteville, North Carolina, several times a day to file his stories, and he often gave two or three soldiers a lift into town. He told Devers that during these rides, he "asked them all the questions and I dig at them for all the news I can get. You know, there was only one of them who ever said anything that wasn't good about this camp and the training they were getting. . . . [That soldier] said he represented the *Chicago Tribune,* and he's no damn good and that paper's no damn good anyhow."[38] Whether or not Pegler's story was accurate, the bottom line is that he got a very favorable impression of how Fort Bragg and the 9th Infantry Division were being run.

Within two weeks of Pegler's arrival at Fort Bragg, Jake's brother Frank wrote and asked, "What have you done to Westbrook Pegler? The articles he is writing out of Fort Bragg are something new in his line and are very helpful to you." As if to punctuate this thought, Marshall wrote to Devers in March 1941, "I note in the morning's papers that Westbrook Pegler is searching for words to properly appraise what is being done at Fort Bragg. This reversal of form is almost revolutionary. The greater part of the reason is your capable management and leadership."[39]

One of the great things about American democracy is that elected representatives are responsive to their constituents' complaints. The men drafted in 1940–1941 had the right to appeal to their congressmen if they thought they were being mistreated by the army. Devers found this out firsthand when he had to deal with congressional inquiries about conditions at Fort Bragg. For example, New York congressman Hamilton Fish announced in the *Congressional Record* that Fort Bragg was not providing its soldiers with enough fresh vegetables and milk. The congressman from North Carolina responded to this allegation on the House floor, saying that Devers was doing all he could to purchase fresh produce and milk locally. But that was not the end of the story. According to Devers:

Later on, an ironic turn of fate resulted in Colonel [Hamilton] Fish's being assigned to Fort Bragg for training. At the time there was on post an engineer regiment under a very fine officer, Wood. . . . It was a magnificent regiment. . . . When Fish arrived, I had him assigned to that regiment, and my orders were that he be put in charge of that [regiment's] mess: [I thought,] "Just let him do the battling around here to get milk and vegetables, and he'll find that, everything considered, the soldiers are well taken care of." That was exactly what happened—and we had another friend in Ham Fish.[40]

Devers concluded, "In the Army, as in every walk of life, if your attitude is positive and good, if you know how to play on a team—when to take it and when to give it—if you carry out orders to the best of your ability, you soon draw together a lot of people who will cooperate with you. This was very necessary at Fort Bragg because of the immense job to be done there."[41]

One of the nation's major challenges during the mobilization of 1940 was determining how to properly use African American soldiers in the racially segregated army. In 1940 there were only about 4,000 black soldiers in the regular army and another 3,000 in the National Guard. "Established by law and tradition and reinforced by the Army staff's conviction that Negro troops had not performed well in combat [in World War I], segregation" flourished in the army of the 1920s and 1930s. Although there were four African American regiments in the regular army, blacks were excluded from the air corps until 1940.[42]

Many southern congressmen did all they could to prevent the draft from opening the door to racial integration. However, after a great deal of lobbying by African American leaders, the Selective Service Act stipulated, "in the selection and training of men under this act, and in the interpretation and execution of the provisions of this act, there shall be no discrimination against any person on account of race or color." The president also approved a War Department policy in October 1940 that stated, "the services of Negroes will be utilized on a fair and equitable basis. In line with this policy provision will be made as follows: 1. The strength of the Negro personnel will be maintained on the general basis of the proportion of the population of the country." This meant that about 9 percent of draftees would be African American. Further, blacks were specifically allowed to serve in all branches of the service, including the air corps.[43]

Army policy regarding the use of African American troops was spelled out by General Marshall in a letter to Senator Henry Cabot Lodge Jr.: "It is the policy of the War Department not to intermingle colored and white enlisted personnel in the same regimental organization. The condition which has made this policy necessary is not the responsibility of the Department, but to ignore it would be to produce situations destructive of morale and therefore definitely detrimental to the preparations for national defense in this emergency."[44] Ironically, the national emergency required the use of all American manpower, but it was also the pretext for maintaining racially segregated units. The principle of separate but equal became the army policy.

In January 1941 Devers faced a deluge of new soldiers and new units at Fort Bragg. One National Guard unit from Newark, New Jersey, forced Devers to address the difficulties involved in the army's segregation policy. A "whole brigade of anti-aircraft [troops arrived]—all colored; [with] twenty-five colored doctors, and no colored nurses." This was a major problem because white nurses were not allowed to care for black men, and many of these soldiers "were sick when they came off the train." Devers and his medical officer dealt with this crisis. Their short-term solution was to find local African American nurses to care for the ill men and to request additional hospital wards on post to serve black soldiers.[45]

Other problems arose as well. For example, there were too few recreational facilities for the black population at Fort Bragg. The army's answer was to request extra funds from Congress to build segregated facilities for African American soldiers and, specifically, to provide Fort Bragg with a 1,000-seat motion picture theater, a Negro service club, and a separate guesthouse. The army also provided eight wards in the post hospital for "colored" patients and quarters for twenty-two black medical officers and twenty-eight black nurses who were assigned to Fort Bragg.[46] Although Devers did not create the challenges caused by racial segregation, he dealt with them effectively. As the inspector general of the army reported after a visit to Fort Bragg in the summer of 1941: "I visited three colored units and found that they were well housed and well cared for. I was informed that no colored problems were arising at this time that caused the post commander or unit commanders any concern."[47]

Georgie was justifiably proud of her husband's accomplishments, but she paid a personal price, being forced to move with little notice whenever Jake was reassigned. In 1940 alone she moved from Panama to Washington and then to Fort Bragg, which was excessive even for the army (in peacetime, officers normally stayed in one place for three years). Nonetheless, she faced her challenges in a positive manner, as a letter to her sister-in-law indicates:

> I am beginning to be better settled; perhaps it's partly mental. . . . I am putting up what curtains I have and can hang up some of my pet pictures. That's like daring Fate, but I haven't had some of them up since Fort Myer days, and what a long time ago that seems. . . . When all of this is over I doubt that such a thing as a private cook will be left. We will all be working in munitions factories or in farmettes. This looks like the end of an era, of our way of life. . . . But the sun shines as bright as ever and the birds are singing in the early morning light. . . . The old world seems to be able to take it and I guess I will be taking it too years from now.[48]

The Deverses were part of an army that was moving into high gear as it prepared for a major war. Georgie could see through her own experiences that the "old army" way of life was ending.

Frances and her husband, Lieutenant Alexander Graham, were also part of the changing army. Graham had served in the Language Department at the Military Academy from 1937 to the summer of 1939, when he was sent to the field artillery advanced course at Fort Sill. He was then assigned temporarily to the 17th Field Artillery Battalion at Fort Bragg, before joining the 8th Infantry Division at Fort Jackson, South Carolina. Frances accompanied her husband on all these moves.[49] Shortly after Alex joined the 8th Division, it deployed for field training, which presented the young couple with some significant challenges. As Georgie wrote in a letter to Kitts: "Frances and Alex are trying to decide what to do with their rugs and furniture—how to pack it—or protect it while they are away. They have no idea how long the training will last, no one has. The first period is for four months. . . . She says they leave, drive to Washington Feb. 1st and Alex goes on to Bragg. . . . You know this is their first separation."[50] Georgie also kept Jake's mother apprised of Frances's whereabouts and activities: "On July 15th [1940] Alex goes on maneuvers which I pray will not be the final preparations for war. Surely we can keep out of it this time. . . . Frances and Alex are not good about writing, are they? I hear of them but not often from them. However, we all hear when they need us, and always will I expect."[51]

Following maneuvers in South Carolina in December 1940, Alex Graham was assigned briefly to Fort Bragg, shortly after his father-in-law had been sent there. He and other soldiers from the 8th Division were in the cadre of officers and men who provided the nucleus for the 9th Division. However, Alex requested a transfer, and by April 1941 he was in an armored field artillery battalion in the 4th Armored Division at Camp Pine, New York. Graham was soon promoted to captain and assigned to command an artillery battery in the division. For the remainder of the war, Graham served in the 4th Armored Division, where he commanded the 94th Armored Field Artillery Battalion before being promoted to colonel in 1945.[52]

Georgie was relieved when she could write to her sister-in-law in January 1941 that "Frances is here [at Fort Bragg]. She has Mrs. Hughes with her. I was so upset by the way she drove all over creation last year alone that I made Alex uneasy. He insists now that she not go [traveling] alone."[53] From April through October the 4th Armored Division remained stationed at Fort Pine, but it deployed several times to the South, where most maneuver training was conducted. In November 1941 the 4th Armored Division moved to a desert training center in California. While Georgie worried about Frances, Jake had his hands full building Fort Bragg and commanding an infantry division.

On 17 March 1941 Jake's mother died. Ella was fortunate, in that she had been able to continue living in her own home at 152 East Philadelphia Street in York until the age of eighty-one. She died of heart failure after being bedridden for about a month. It is unclear from the family records whether Jake, Georgie, and the rest of the family were able to attend the funeral.[54]

Then in June, Jake contracted pneumonia. Georgie told Kitts that she was "keeping Jamie comfortable and cool as possible. . . . I have never seen any illness so absolutely devastating to energy—mental and physical—as this has been." A visit from Frances seemed to amuse him and helped him recover. As Georgie noted, "she cheered him up a lot."[55]

9th Infantry Division

When Marshall selected Devers to assume command of Fort Bragg, he also placed him in command of the 9th Infantry Division, one of nine regular army divisions maintained in some form of active service from

1919 to 1939. When expansion began in 1939, the army started to fill its regular divisions with men who had enlisted voluntarily. By the fall of 1940, the 9th Infantry Division had been reorganized as a triangular division of three infantry regiments and four artillery battalions and consisted of about 9,000 men. The division's authorized strength was 14,000 soldiers; the remaining 5,000 would be draftees, who began arriving in January 1941.

Before he arrived at Fort Bragg, Devers had received a letter from his close friend Colonel Carlos Brewer containing an appraisal of the 9th Division: "I think you will find the Ninth Division going along reasonably well when you take over. . . . Our greatest handicap is that our company officers are nearly all reserve officers and not the best of that class either, but you will have to make the best of them. Our regulars as a whole are considerably above average, most of them from ROTCs, so we are fortunate in this respect."[56]

The U.S. Army's mobilization of 1940–1941 would have been much harder, if not impossible, without the reserve officers commissioned from ROTC programs at more than 300 colleges across America. As Weigley notes, "The quality of these men proved to be remarkably high; the Army soon concluded that they were already sufficiently disciplined and trained that they only needed conditioning in the increasingly rigorous training camps before they stepped promptly into instructional roles themselves."[57] Brewer's favorable appraisal of the ROTC graduates who joined the regular army confirms this view. These young officers trained the draftees who joined the 9th Division.

The first review of the entire division took place on 16 November 1940. This was also the first time Devers saw all his soldiers at one spot. The division history, *Eight Stars to Victory,* describes the event and reveals a great deal about the leadership qualities of the new division commander:

When the commanding general arrived upon the field he found an extremely cold day: A 30-mile-an-hour wind whipped across the clearing. The *old man* was mighty glad to be wearing his overcoat. But as he looked down the lines of GIs he saw old uniforms. Some were made for the CCC; others were model 1917's; few fit their wearers. Most of the soldiers were in their shirtsleeves, as blouses (coats) and overcoats were unavailable. When General Devers saw the Division wearing such inadequate clothing he was amazed. Off went his overcoat, he flung it to one side. If the men could make the parade in their shirtsleeves so could their general. For one hour and a half he stood in the cold, reviewing the troops.[58]

Knowing that his soldiers had been living in tents and had inadequate shower facilities, Devers concentrated on getting the new barracks constructed. He used the occasion of the division review to announce to the men that there would be heaters in their bathhouses by Saturday and that their new barracks would be completed within a month. Devers's engineers found steam engines to provide hot water for the bathhouses, as promised. On 15 December the troops moved from their tent encampments to their newly built barracks. The *Raleigh News and Observer* reported that the 9th Division was the first in the army to move into permanent barracks. For the soldiers, hot showers, glass windows, and indoor mess halls seemed almost too good to be true.[59]

Initially, the army had hoped to induct 75,000 men in October, 115,000 in November, 115,000 in December, and 95,000 in January. The plan was to spread these men across regular army and National Guard divisions, allowing each division time to conduct basic training for a few hundred men at a time.[60] Because the construction of posts was behind schedule in the fall of 1940, this plan was abandoned. Only after sufficient barracks had been constructed at Fort Bragg did the 9th Infantry Division receive its first 500 draftees on 16 January 1941; another 500 arrived the next day. The division's cadre of regular army soldiers immediately began training these men. In a span of 109 days, Devers had overseen the construction of 586 buildings, including 253 sixty-man barracks and 80 mess halls. The 9th Division's area included eleven infirmaries, ten post exchanges, three theaters, and five recreation buildings. The division's cantonment alone cost $4.4 million and housed more than 14,000 men.[61]

In January 1941 Devers placed Fort Bragg and the 9th Division on a forty-four-hour-a-week training schedule to carry out the thirteen-week-long basic training program. This basic training was part of a program created by General McNair's GHQ for use throughout the army, since all divisions were receiving thousands of new soldiers. The GHQ program was designed to prepare these divisions for combat in just one year. The first thirteen weeks focused on basic skills and physical conditioning, and the second thirteen weeks focused on the training of small units. For the remainder of the year, the division conducted "combined training, that is, training in the coordination of the various weapons of the regiment and the division; and large-unit maneuvers."[62]

The GHQ training program assumed that once a soldier had joined a division, he would complete the full year's program. In the case of the divisions trained in 1940–1941, many of the men remained with their units for at least a year. However, with the creation of specialized forces, such as airborne units, the army recruited some of these partially trained men from the 9th Division and others. The 9th Infantry Division lost 172 trained soldiers in July to airborne units, forcing the army to replace them. This came just as the division was beginning its first divisional war game. The army also took soldiers from trained divisions in 1942 to form new divisions. The resulting turmoil adversely affected unit training and cohesion for those divisions that remained in the United States in 1942 and 1943. The 9th Division, however, deployed to North Africa, where it acquitted itself well under the command of Major General Manton Eddy in 1943.[63]

Based on staff's visits to divisions during the winter of 1940–1941, McNair determined that the army needed centralized replacement training centers to provide basic training to men drafted after the divisions were full. Consequently, the army created a replacement training system to provide the soldiers needed to maintain the strength of divisions deployed overseas. Unfortunately, there were major problems with the replacement system that Devers and other commanders would have to deal with in 1943–1945.

By the spring of 1941, the 9th Infantry Division was at full strength and in the midst of a well-planned training program. In March the division conducted a major command post exercise under the supervision of Lieutenant General Hugh Drum, the First Army commander. The division "reacted well in its first big test," and when Drum left he commented, "The Ninth was one of the best divisions in the First Army." In June the 60th Infantry Regimental Combat Team, which included the 3,700 men of the infantry regiment and the 34th and 60th Field Artillery Battalions, road-marched with its 741 motor vehicles to Bowling Green, Virginia. There, the combat team took part in a two-day war game against the 44th Infantry Division. The *New York Times* reported about these maneuvers in glowing terms: "Few regiments in peacetime have been through such a campaign in one week as have the troops of the Sixtieth Combat team which went 276 miles to Virginia last week, met and confused the entire Forty-fourth Division, came home without denting a fender of their 741 vehicles, and that night went out on the reservation here, on schedule, to take part in more maneuvers."[64]

The division made special provisions to ensure that its soldiers received four-day furloughs. This allowed them enough time to visit home, since most of the draftees were from New Jersey and New York. Around Washington's birthday, for example, 500 men rode chartered buses to New York, "with state police escorts meeting the buses at each state boundary and convoying the soldiers to the next one [to speed them on their way]."[65]

General Marshall closely monitored the expansion of the army and the performance of his senior officers. He traveled around the country visiting units and posts to see how things were going. These visits were usually unannounced, giving the chief of staff a candid view of the progress being made. His visit to Fort Bragg on 14 March 1941 gave him an opportunity to evaluate Devers as a commander, as the *Raleigh News and Observer* reported: "With no more warning than a brief telephone message that he had taken off from Washington, Gen. George C. Marshall . . . took this post unawares but not surprised today, looked at every corner of it, [and] praised it bluntly and hoped that he would find another like it."[66] Marshall drove around Fort Bragg for four hours, "look[ing] at the great 2,500 bed hospital, and completed regimental areas." He visited the new artillery replacement center and the mile-long rifle range, "where the Ninth Division was firing today. He went down in the butts and talked for some time with enlisted men." After meeting the division staff, Marshall talked informally to 500 NCOs in the post theater, telling them they were the backbone of the army. Before leaving that afternoon, he talked to all of the 9th Division's officers in the theater and spoke with as many soldiers as possible. He summed up his impressions as follows: "The post had been ideally laid out, its engineering was as near perfect as he could imagine it, and . . . the pace of construction here had set an example for the world to look at—and to follow if it could."[67]

When historians discuss Marshall's selection of senior officers during World War II, they must remember that Marshall kept close tabs on the men he chose for high command. Further advancement depended on continued outstanding performance. Jacob Devers met the chief's high expectations. By July 1941, he had come to national attention, as indicated by an article in the *Washington Post*: "[The] Army['s] new leaders are of varying qualifications: . . . Major General Jacob L. Devers . . . is both a scholar and a mixer. He enjoys people and likes to make speeches. A human dynamo, full of restless energy, he will go far his colleagues predict. Scorning red tape, he cuts corners and gets a job done in spite of all obstacles. . . . [At Bragg] he is given most of the credit for the speedy, efficient development of that large post."[68]

At the end of June, the 9th Infantry Division was ready for division-level training. Despite the summer heat, the infantry and artillery units practiced how to work as combined-arms combat teams. The training was rigorous, with long foot marches and artillery practice. This hard work would pay off in the Carolina maneuvers of November, when the division performed well as part of the First Army under Hugh Drum. Devers, however, did not have the pleasure of commanding the division in its final phases of training. As the division history observed, in early July, "a mixed feeling of sadness and surprise hit the Division next. The Army announced that General Devers was to command its entire Armored Force."[69] Devers remained with the 9th Infantry Division until its first reactivation ceremony on 1 August. The next day, as the men of the division lined the curbs, Jake and Georgie Devers left for Fort Knox, Kentucky. Brigadier General Hoyle took command of the division, and Colonel Leroy Irwin took over the division's artillery.[70]

During his year at Fort Bragg, Devers had learned how to build a major army post, cultivate good relations with the local population, impress the press with the army's efficiency, and train an infantry division. It had been a remarkably busy year and a successful one for Devers. He had met General Marshall's high standards and vindicated General McNair's trust in his longtime friend. As a result, McNair and Marshall selected him to command the Armored Force at a critical juncture of its development, even though he had never served with tanks or armor.

7

Forging the Thunderbolt

For many officers, commanding a unit in combat represents the fulfillment of their service to the nation. Devers was no exception. He would have loved to command the 9th Division in combat, especially after he had done such a good job of organizing and training it. His work paid off, and the 9th Division went on to be one of the best infantry divisions in the European theater of operations in World War II. Major General Devers, however, did not command it or any other division in combat. Instead, as Devers remembered, "Early one morning in July 1941 the telephone rang." On the line was General Marshall, who said, "I want you to get in a plane, go to Fort Knox, Kentucky, look over the situation down there, and then report back to me here in Washington. General [Adna] Chaffee is sick and has left the post, and probably will never return."[1] This brief phone call meant that Marshall had selected Devers to command the Armored Force. This assignment would be one of Devers's toughest challenges, as well as one of his greatest contributions to the war effort.

Creation of the Armored Force

The First World War brought about a series of technical innovations that dramatically changed tactics, operations, and the face of battle. Chemical weapons, combat aircraft, heavy artillery, advanced machine guns, submarines, wireless communications, and tanks played a major role in the war. By the end of the conflict, it was clear to many military thinkers and observers that future battlefields would be significantly altered by such modern weapons and communications systems. For twenty years after the First World War, the armies of the major powers wrestled with the challenge of adapting to these new technologies and transforming their military forces to take advantage of them. For the U.S. Army, the application of modern communications, airpower, and mechanization was among the most visible aspects of warfare's transformation in the 1920s and 1930s.[2]

Transitioning the horse-drawn U.S. Army of the nineteenth century into a modern mechanized force was a slow process for many reasons. After World War I, the American people and Congress had no desire to spend large sums of money on new technologies and equipment for the armed services. Even with the rise of dangerous dictators in Japan, Germany, and Italy, the United States spent little on its military until the mid-1930s, when growing threats from both East and West pushed Congress to lay the foundation for the modern armed forces. The history of the army's mechanization and the replacement of horse-mounted forces with armored forces illustrates the difficulties encountered as the army sought to modernize.

Armored warfare was created in the crucible of war, as the army's *History of the Armored Force* points out: "The tanks of World War I were a product of military necessity. Trench warfare, the defensive power of machine guns, and a defensive spirit had sapped the offensive power of the Allied Armies. The British and French studied the problem; and with great secrecy, the British produced a number of lumbering armored vehicles, which they led many people to believe were water carriers. Hence the name tanks!"[3]

The U.S. Tank Corps was created in January 1918, under the command of Colonel Samuel Rockenbach. Well-known future leaders such as George S. Patton and Dwight D. Eisenhower helped train and lead American tankers during the First World War, and tanks proved to be of significant value in the American victories at Saint-Mihiel and in the Meuse-Argonne campaign. By the end of the war, there was general agreement that tanks had a future in the U.S. Army, but the exact nature of that future was up for grabs. Many army leaders favored maintaining a separate tank or armored force branch equal to the cavalry, infantry, and engineer branches. Others believed the tank was a supporting weapon that was best used as part of the infantry or cavalry branch. A bitter dispute over how to develop and use tanks took place in 1919–1920.[4]

As the debate about tanks swirled, Patton gave a lecture titled "The Effects of Tanks in Future Wars." He postulated, "The tank is new and for the fulfillment of its destiny, it must remain independent. Not desiring or attempting to supplant infantry, cavalry, or artillery, it has no appetite to be absorbed by any of them. . . . Absorbed . . . we become the stepchild of that arm and the incompetent assistant of either of the others."[5] In the end, however, the National Defense Act of 1920 assigned the development of tanks to the infantry branch. The Tank Corps of World War I was disbanded, and Patton and Eisenhower returned to their respective branches (cavalry and infantry). The few tank battalions in the army were divided into separate companies and spread out among the nine infantry divisions in the regular army. Although a tank school was established at Fort Meade, Maryland, few resources were committed to develop modern vehicles or doctrines. In the eyes of the infantry, the tank was a support vehicle that only needed to advance at the speed of foot soldiers. In 1932 the tank school was moved to Fort Benning, Georgia, the "home of infantry."[6]

The cavalry branch did not lose interest in armored vehicles. Because tanks were under the exclusive purview of the infantry branch, the cavalry developed mechanized cavalry vehicles called "combat cars" in the 1920s and 1930s. These vehicles were designed to exploit the mobility gained by motorization, but they were not armored sufficiently to serve as part of an infantry tank team. Thus, two views of armored fighting vehicles coexisted in the army until 1940. The vehicles envisioned by the infantry required little speed but more armor and heavier firepower. The cavalry envisioned armored vehicles that were fast, light, and not heavily armed so that their speed could be used to exploit success. Not everyone was a fan of mechanization, however. For instance, the chief of cavalry testified in 1938: "It [mechanized cavalry] has not yet reached a position in which it can be relied upon to displace horse cavalry. . . . We must not be misled to our own detriment to assume that the untried machine can displace the proved and tried horse."[7]

Despite such conservative views, army chief of staff Douglas MacArthur and the War Department decided in 1931 that every part of the army would motorize or mechanize. Although a shortage of funds during the depths of the Great Depression greatly slowed the process, new vehicles were tested, and infantry, cavalry, and artillery units slowly transitioned from horse power to machine power.[8] However, the conflicting views about tanks were not reconciled.

Experiments in armored force organization began in the 1930s. The first was a mechanized force under the command of Colonel (later Lieutenant General) Daniel Van Voorhis at Fort Eustis, Virginia, in 1930. Although pitifully equipped with surplus equipment from the First World War, the unit enabled the army to test various mixes of equipment and different organizational configurations. Van Voorhis, nicknamed the "grandfather of the Armored Force," advocated an independent force that combined infantry, tank, and artillery units under a single command. Twelve years later, Van Voorhis noted, "I pointed out to the then Chief of Staff . . . that to assign the mechanized mission of the Army to one particular branch would be a great mistake; that mechanization was a problem which concerned all branches of the service."⁹ The army's answer was to disband the mechanized force in 1931 and allow the infantry and cavalry branches to continue to develop their own visions of what tanks and armor should be. The cavalry moved the 1st and 13th Cavalry Regiments to Camp (soon Fort) Knox in the mid-1930s, where they experimented with various types of combat cars and developed techniques for the employment of mechanized units. Colonels Bruce Palmer and Charles Scott directed these efforts. In 1938 the regiments were combined to form the 7th Cavalry Brigade (Mechanized), under the command of Colonel Adna Chaffee. During the same period, the infantry branch developed the tank as an infantry support vehicle at Fort Benning, an effort that would culminate in the organization of a provisional tank brigade.[10]

The First Army maneuvers of 1939 tested the 7th Cavalry Brigade in a variety of scenarios that included infantry, artillery, and mechanized cavalry. Although both the cavalry and the infantry balked at the idea of converting more units to a mechanized format, the First Army's commander, Lieutenant General Hugh Drum, concluded, "The Mechanized Cavalry Brigade had taught us many lessons. It is a powerful arm and a great asset."[11] Van Voorhis and Chaffee used the results of the maneuvers to advocate expanding the mechanized brigade into a division-sized organization. However, both the infantry and the cavalry vetoed the idea. By the fall of 1939, the army had made little progress toward the development of modern tanks or larger armored units.

While debates about tanks and mechanized units continued in the United States, the German army unleashed its armored offensive against Poland. Seven German armored, or panzer, divisions made short work of the Polish army, including its horse-mounted cavalry. Using a combination of close air support aircraft and armored divisions, the Germans defeated Poland in less than two months. George C. Marshall had just become army chief of staff. Although this action by the Germans marked the beginning of the Second World War, it would be two years before the United States became fully involved. During the winter of 1939–1940, the army staff and senior leaders continued to discuss the best way to create armored forces that could match the German panzers, but little action was taken.

On 10 May 1940 the German army launched its offensive in the west against the British, French, Dutch, and Belgian armies. The Germans massed three armored corps consisting of several panzer divisions each and executed a deep thrust through Luxembourg and southern Belgium and into the plains of northern France. By 18 May, the French front had been pierced at Sedan, allowing the panzer corps to drive to the North Sea. This maneuver isolated the Allied forces in Belgium. By early June, the British army had been driven from the Continent, and Belgium and the Netherlands had surrendered; France surrendered before the end of the month. These panzer divisions were combined-arms formations composed of infantry, artillery, and tanks, and they had proved their worth as both breakthrough and exploitation forces.[12] These battlefield results forced the U.S. Army to abruptly change its approach to armored forces and doctrine. General Marshall ordered the creation of a new organization to unite the cavalry and infantry concepts of armored warfare and to develop modern armored divisions.

The U.S. Army's Armored Force was established on 10 July 1940. Since the National Defense Act of 1920 had limited tank development to the infantry, the Armored Force was "provisional" at first. The new organization's headquarters was at Fort Knox, Kentucky, making it independent of the cavalry center at Fort Riley, Kansas, and the infantry center at Fort Benning, Georgia. The Armored Force obtained control of all tank units then with the cavalry and the infantry, as well as certain artillery and service units. Major General Adna Chaffee was the first chief of the Armored Force and the commanding general of I Armored Corps. The existing armored units were combined into the 1st and 2nd Armored Divisions, stationed at Fort Knox and Fort Benning, respectively. The Armored Force also exercised authority over all nontank elements in the two armored divisions, including infantry, artillery, signal, and service units.[13]

Even after the official announcement of the creation of the Armored Force, the cavalry and infantry branch chiefs continued to hold on to their visions of tanks and armored warfare. Finally, at a meeting of all those involved in the debate, Chaffee, with Marshall's full support, announced, "Speed is . . . essential. . . . We must not stop and haggle over a lot of detail."[14]

The Armored Force was responsible for the organization and training of all armored units, the development of tanks and other specialized armored vehicles, and the training of men assigned to the new armored divisions. Over the next year, the 3rd and 4th Armored Divisions were organized around cadres from the first two armored divisions. Debate still lingered about the optimal mix of light and medium tanks and how the new armored divisions should be employed. "As one G-3 officer stated, it was a case of the cavalry 'raised pistols and charge' versus the infantry 'look before you leap' [mentalities]."[15] Because General Chaffee was a cavalryman, much of the Armored Force's combat doctrine was based on the cavalry viewpoint. Light tanks were favored, and the divisions were expected to serve as exploitation forces in the manner formerly envisioned for horse-mounted cavalry. Another cavalryman, Major General Charles L. Scott, commanded the 2nd Armored Division at Fort Benning and ensured that the former infantry tank units and personnel adopted the cavalry view.

The Armored Force was semiautonomous during the first two years of its existence. General Lesley McNair's GHQ had limited authority over the Armored Force's organization, doctrinal development, schools, and replacement system. However, GHQ exercised direct supervision over the training of the army's field forces, which included I Armored Corps, the armored divisions, and the separate tank battalions. GHQ also directed the deployment of the armored field units in the 1941 army maneuvers. Only after the reorganization of the army in March 1942 did GHQ, renamed the Army Ground Forces, assume control over the Armored Force.[16]

During the first year of the Armored Force's existence, it faced numerous challenges. For example:

Training had to be sacrificed to expansion. Hardly were the 1st and 2nd Armored Divisions organized when they were required to produce cadres for the 3rd and 4th. From February to May, 1941, the 2nd Armored Division was needed for air-ground tactical tests. In November 1940 the GHQ tank officers reported that basic training was being neglected, but the Armored Force authorities were aware of the problem; in January 1941, . . . training within divisions suffered from the creation of new units and . . . the Armored Force was expanding before any of its existing units were properly trained; in March, that expansion was still proceeding, but was handicapped by the failure of the War Department to activate new division headquarters in advance.

General McNair also discovered that the training certification tests of armored battalions were being carried out by the units themselves, rather than by higher headquarters.[17]

By the spring of 1941, the Armored Force faced a crisis in leadership.

Chaffee was dying of cancer and was increasingly unable to lead the new organization as it tried to surmount the many challenges related to training, supervision, equipment, and organization. Consequently, Marshall and McNair sought a senior officer who had proved himself capable of training troops and exerting effective control over large organizations. They chose Major General Jacob Devers.

Devers's Introduction to the Armored Force

Marshall and McNair were well aware of the internal disputes in the Armored Force over doctrinal and equipment issues. Many of these could be traced to the parochial views of the cavalry and infantry officers who made up the initial cadre. What Marshall and McNair wanted was a man who could lead an independent Armored Force through its growing pains. The 1946 *History of the Armored Force* summarized some of the traits Devers brought to his new command: "The new chief was as bold and aggressive as the tactics of armor. He had no patience with purely administrative delay. The answer to red tape, he once advised a private, was to 'keep going and the tape soon breaks.' He had a clear vision of long-range objectives. He believed the best way to promote the combat efficiency of the Armored Force was to concentrate topnotch personnel and equipment into armored units, and to centralize authority at Fort Knox."[18]

Devers was selected to lead the Armored Force over several noted armor leaders, such as Major Generals George S. Patton and Charles Scott. Scott was the senior officer in the Armored Force and the commander of I Armored Corps when Devers arrived. Patton commanded the 2nd Armored Division and was a veteran of the Tank Corps of the First World War. Scott was disappointed that he was passed over, but he was part of the parochialism that Marshall and McNair were trying to eliminate. Patton was disappointed too, since he believed he would have been promoted to command I Armored Corps if Scott had been elevated to Armored Force commander.[19] But if Marshall had settled matters that way, the bickering between cavalrymen and infantrymen probably would have continued.

Devers bridged the gap between the cavalry and infantry views of armor development due to his extensive artillery experience. He told his staff, "In this air-gun-tank war, the tank, like the battleship and the airplane, was nothing more than a mechanism to carry fire power to the enemy position, utilizing the mobility of the tank for tactical and strategic surprise."[20]

Devers had followed the developments in the mechanized brigade while he was working in the Office of the Chief of Artillery in 1930–1931. Although he had no experience with tanks in the First World War, he knew an awful lot about their development and "had attended—as the representative from the Chief of Field Artillery's office—all the tests at Aberdeen Proving Grounds. . . . So I was equipped as well as anybody that I knew of except [Sereno] Brett—and possibly George Patton [to command the Armored Force]."[21]

Devers visited Fort Knox in July 1941. He later recalled his initial impressions:

> We arrived there in good shape and were met by General Scott, who was the senior officer in the Armored Force at that time. . . . I found that Chaffee had been sick for about a year with cancer; that he hadn't operated too much—only at certain periods—that his staff had been running the job more or less in secret. . . . I found no staff whatsoever. The Chief of Staff was probably the greatest tanker in existence—Colonel Sereno Brett. He had done a fairly good job. I knew he drank too much, but I didn't pick it up on that particular day. . . . I found one man on the staff, Colonel David Barr, who had the Logistics Section, G-4, an excellent officer. . . . There were four [armored] divisions, the 1st Division, commanded by Major General Bruce Magruder, an Infantryman, was at Fort Knox. . . . The 2nd Division, commanded by Major General George Patton, a Cavalryman, was at Fort Benning. . . . This seemed to be the way General Marshall was trying to break down the competition between the Infantry and Cavalry and make a team of the Armored Force.[22]

He found that the infantry and cavalry branches had transferred a number of poorly performing officers to the Armored Force. There was no personnel officer (G-1) for the Armored Force, and the Fort Knox adjutant general was trying to do that job plus his assigned work simultaneously. Devers concluded that a tremendous amount of staff work would be required to weed out the "discards in officers throughout the organization." To accomplish this, he would need to recruit a new staff, keeping the few competent officers such as Colonels Barr and Brett.[23]

There were some bright spots in the Armored Force, according to

Devers. Colonel Steve Henry was doing a good job running the officers' training school, and Brigadier General Jack W. Heard had the training center in "fair shape; but too much showmanship and not enough imagination as to how to improve instruction."[24] Because of his extensive experience with the artillery school at Fort Sill during World War I, Devers knew how to solve problems associated with a rapidly growing force and training program. Over the next two years, the thousands of officers, noncommissioned officers, and tank specialists needed to man fourteen armored divisions would be trained at Fort Knox.

Devers's first decision in terms of building a staff to operate the Armored Force was to keep Brett as his chief of staff for the first few months. He discussed Brett's drinking problem with Marshall, who told him "to tell Brett that he knew what he was doing and if he didn't change his ways, he would have to go." Devers thought "Brett really knew the armored problem better than anybody in any of the services," so he kept him. It proved to be a good choice: "he served me faithfully and was very helpful in developing the organization." When Devers found a suitable replacement in the fall, he sent Brett to command an armored regiment in the 5th Armored Division. As Brett's replacement, Brigadier General Ernest Harmon did a good job reorganizing the headquarters and staff, and Devers recommended him for promotion to major general and assignment as an armored division commander. Harmon went to North Africa in 1942 and became one of the best armored division commanders of the war.[25]

Colonel John B. Murphy accompanied Devers from Fort Bragg to serve as the Armored Force G-1 (personnel officer). Colonel David Barr continued to serve as the G-4 (logistics officer). Barr did such a good job that Devers promoted him to chief of staff when Harmon left. Marshall had given Devers permission to recruit the right officers to build his staff, and he told Marshall, "The first man I want is a good live artilleryman with some imagination who can help me develop the artillery part of this because it's on dead center at the moment." When Marshall asked who he had in mind, Devers replied, "I'd like to have Colonel Edward H. Brooks," who was working in the General Staff's G-3 (operations) office. Marshall agreed, and before he could change his mind, Devers had Brooks clear out his desk and head to Fort Knox as swiftly as possible.[26]

In terms of building a staff, Brooks "was a terrific help," according to Devers. "We talked over the personnel he needed. He spotted [Brigadier General] Willie Palmer commanding some kind of unit at Fort Bragg. We flew in there and got Williston Palmer to assist him and then we picked up some other very smart young artillerymen. Then Ted [Brooks] went to work on getting self-propelled artillery." Devers built his team at the Armored Force by retaining the solid officers he had inherited, like Barr and Brett, and recruiting talented officers from other parts of the army. He followed the recommendations of men he knew and trusted, like Brooks.[27] Brooks also got the ball rolling for the army to develop and field the self-propelled 105mm howitzer, or M7; it was known as the Priest due to the high, tower-like mount for its 50-caliber antiaircraft machine gun. He and Devers coordinated the M7's development with the American Locomotive Company, which began producing the self-propelled howitzer in 1942. This weapons system was one of the greatest success stories of the Second World War.[28] Brooks would later successfully command a division and a corps in combat.

Devers also had to deal with Major General George Patton. Patton was correct in his belief that Devers had little direct experience with armored units or vehicles. Patton, in contrast, had enhanced his World War I reputation with the Tank Corps by his very solid performance with the 2nd Armored Division. "He knew more than any other American how to run, maintain, repair tanks, organize and train tank units, and employ them in combat." He had also studied the ideas developed in the 1920s and 1930s by British and German military thinkers about tanks and their employment.[29] Patton exuded self-confidence, and he made a real name for himself in the army maneuvers held in early 1941.

Devers was well acquainted with Patton. They had been West Point classmates. They were both polo players and had played against each other on the cavalry and artillery teams; they had also played as teammates on the army's polo team. They had commanded battalion-level units together at Fort Myer in the mid-1930s and thus had socialized a great deal. The Devers family considered George and Beatrice Patton to be friends. Frances remembered the families playing lunchtime baseball games at Fort Myer to stay in shape.[30] Devers recalled, "Patton was my next door neighbor at Fort Myer for quite a period. We worked very closely together on things that had to do with the Post. We played polo together on the same team. He was the '3' and I was the 'back' and captain of this team." They won several major international polo matches as part of the army team, and the Patton family still has the silver cups to prove it.[31] Devers, however, had been promoted to brigadier and then major general ahead of Patton, which may have caused some jealousy.[32] This might explain why Patton said some less-than-flattering things about Devers during the next two years.

Patton's views of armor and horse cavalry were complex. Although he was dedicated to his armored division, he wrote to a friend: "I am convinced that the day of the horse is far from over and that under many circumstances horse cavalry and horse drawn artillery are more important than ever." However, during major war-game exercises in June 1941 Patton demonstrated to General McNair and Secretary of War Stimson that his unorthodox training and operational methods were effective. The 2nd Armored Division adopted the nickname "Hell on Wheels" after its successful maneuvers, and it was clear to Marshall that Patton had the qualities needed to lead American soldiers in wartime.[33]

When it was announced that Devers would take over the Armored Force, Patton immediately wrote him a letter of congratulations. After meeting with his new boss in early August, Patton told his wife Beatrice, "I was very much impressed with Devers, he has developed a lot and is a very fine leader." Though disappointed about Devers's elevation over General Scott, he went on to say, "It is easy to see how any one comparing him to Scotty would be inclined toward Devers unless he knew how realy [sic] smart Scotty is in spite of his chipmunk expression." As usual, Patton assessed Devers's promotion in terms of his own prospects for further advancement and concluded, "as I am concerned, I think the change will not be to my disadvantage." In the final analysis, Patton seemed to be unaware of the real reasons Marshall had selected Devers over Scott. He told Beatrice, "Devers is so sure of himself that I am certain he has drag with the President and Pa Wat[son] both, but the final decision of the high man in the Army will be the result of war and not friendship."[34]

General Scott was easier to deal with than Patton. Scott led I Armored Corps in the Louisiana maneuvers in September and the Carolina maneuvers in November 1941. Overall, the two armored divisions put on a credible performance. In the Louisiana maneuvers, however, "unfavorable terrain, inclement weather, and underutilization by higher headquarters hobbled the armored forces."[35] The brightest spot came in the second phase of the maneuvers, when Patton's 2nd Armored Division made an impressive flanking movement around the opposing forces. When McNair ended the operation, the defending army was under pressure from three sides, and armor enthusiasts pointed to Patton's actions as proof of the superiority of the armored division concept.[36]

Scott, however, did not impress either Marshall or McNair. At the conclusion of the maneuvers he disagreed strongly with McNair about the efficacy of truck-towed antitank guns. In spite of contradictory evidence in the Louisiana maneuvers, McNair believed that towed antitank guns were the best weapon to stop and destroy tanks. As the history of the maneuvers noted, "The source of McNair's confidence is not clear, for the Louisiana maneuvers revealed that virtually nobody but McNair believed in or practiced the aggressive antitank concept. General McNair's own son, who served as a GHQ director's headquarters liaison officer at the maneuvers, noted as much in his written report: 'still have seen no indication of offensive action for the three [antitank] groups.'"[37]

Scott was not the only general who openly disagreed with McNair about the best way to defeat enemy tanks. Devers concluded that the tank, not the towed antitank gun, was superior and that tanks would be able to break through antitank gun defenses. He made his views clear in a letter to McNair in December 1941:

Dear Lesley:

Fire power concentrated at a point will dominate the fight if followed through with proper mobility. I hope you and your staff have not been misled by the maneuvers. To date all successful advances—German, Russian, British, Italian, and now Japs—have been led by armored vehicles (tanks principally) and only bridges and weather have stopped them. Only guns slow them up, but properly led tank units will always win. . . . Yours, Jake[38]

Devers may have irritated McNair when he publicly expressed his doubts about the entire antitank concept, but their friendship was close enough and strong enough to survive such a disagreement. Marshall and McNair, however, remained convinced that using towed antitank guns en masse was the best way to defeat an armored onslaught.[39] The debate would continue for much of the war.

Devers concluded from the maneuvers that the armored divisions had to be reorganized, and they needed more infantry to allow the commanders to maneuver the combined-arms team most effectively.[40] During his tenure at the Armored Force, Devers reorganized the division structure twice and ensured that the equipment, especially the medium tank and the self-propelled 105mm howitzer, was good enough to defeat German armored forces.

On a positive note, the army maneuvers of 1941 taught staffs and commanders a lot about moving and maneuvering large forces. For example, Scott, Patton, and Magruder found that it was hard to deploy an armored division from just one or two main roads. One of the most important results of the 1941 maneuvers was that they gave Marshall and McNair a chance to assess the leadership abilities of army, corps, and division commanders. Although they thought the exercises were valuable for the troops, they found serious deficiencies that needed correction. As McNair told journalist Hanson Baldwin, "lack of discipline and effective command" were the two major faults revealed by the maneuvers. McNair went on to say, "I feel emphatically that leadership and command can and must be improved." He noted, "So far as I know no drastic purge of weak leaders is contemplated," though "it seems reasonable and probable that leadership will be improved by removal of weak officers as developments warrant."[41]

Important tactical lessons were learned as well. Devers wrote to General Marshall about his impressions and some of the conclusions he had drawn: "The exercises in Louisiana were an education to me and the other commanders of the Force. I was particularly impressed with the lack of careful planning, such as permitting long columns of fast, powerful forces on roads to be stopped by bridges which were out, causing these troops to be dissipated into small forces seeking a crossing. There was little or no effective traffic control. All could have been corrected by proper reconnaissance well ahead of time and some careful planning. The Armored Force will do better in the Carolinas."[42]

Scott was reassigned shortly after the Carolina maneuvers ended in November, but he was just one of the senior commanders found wanting. "Most of the forty-two division, corps, and army commanders who took part in the GHQ maneuvers were either relieved or reassigned to new commands during 1942 (including twenty of the twenty-seven participating division commanders). Only eleven of the forty-two went on to significant combat commands during World War II."[43] On the eve of the Japanese attack on Pearl Harbor, Marshall was still looking for more senior officers like Devers and Patton to lead the army. This search became crucial after 7 December 1941.

Scott was let down easy on 8 December 1941 when Marshall selected him to be the senior American observer with the British in Egypt. This assignment made sense, as it seemed likely that American armored forces would fight alongside the British against Erwin Rommel's Afrika Korps, and having an experienced armor commander in place to observe operations would be useful. Scott's departure left an opening in I Armored Corps, and Devers wrote to Marshall requesting that "Major General George S. Patton be assigned to command the I Armored Corps with station at Fort Benning, Georgia, and that Brigadier General Willis D. Crittenberger be assigned to command the 2nd Armored Division."[44] Marshall accepted those recommendations.

Fort Knox and the Training Center

Georgie and Jake Devers moved to Fort Knox in August 1941. Initially they lived in temporary quarters because Adna Chaffee's wife was still occupying the commander's house. As Georgie wrote to Kitts, they were lucky to have any quarters at all: "The houses here are very handsome—the few that there are in the old post. But 2,200 officers can't all get into 200 sets of quarters and are living all over the country—as far as 50 miles [from post]." She was very proud of her husband's promotion and loved "to see Jamie happy and well and doing his heart's desire—commanding all these thousands of men and tanks. He is one of the top three or four top drawer generals."[45] Jake also stayed in touch with his sister, telling her in a letter, "This job is a big one and I have gotten off to a fine start but there is much disagreeable work to be done. Adna Chaffee, who preceded me, died Friday, he has been sick for a ½ year and as a result it makes my work hard at the start."[46]

In addition to recruiting a talented staff of officers such as Barr and Harmon, Devers identified sharp younger officers to command the brigades and divisions of the expanding Armored Force. One of these was Brigadier General Willis Crittenberger, who succeeded Patton as commander of the 2nd Armored Division at Fort Benning. A cavalryman, Crittenberger was a 1913 graduate of the Military Academy and Devers's classmate at Fort Leavenworth in 1924–1925. Crittenberger later assessed General Devers's command style:

> It was a very wise decision on the part of Marshall to appoint a Field Artilleryman to organize the Armored Force and overcome the parochial tendencies which cavalrymen and infantrymen had

with regard to the newly building force. . . . Devers was extremely considerate of people—all his life—[and] he knew what he wanted done. He spent a great deal of time on the road, visiting his people, his units, and inspecting activities. . . . Devers seemed to have the knack of identifying those people who could lead and do the best job under difficult conditions.[47]

After Crittenberger's successful command of the 2nd Armored Division, Devers recommended him to command III Armored Corps. Crittenberger organized the corps, which was redesignated XIX Corps in 1943, and led it to England in 1944. Eisenhower and Bradley, however, did not know Crittenberger, and they wanted only combat-experienced commanders to participate in Operation Overlord. According to Stephen Taaffe's *Marshall and His Generals,* "It is also likely that Eisenhower's antipathy was motivated somewhat by his knowledge of Devers's partiality toward Crittenberger." Consequently, Crittenberger moved to the Mediterranean, where he assumed command of IV Corps and led it successfully during the remainder of the Italian campaign.[48] Tellingly, despite his insistence on having only combat-experienced corps commanders for D-day, Eisenhower selected Leonard Gerow to lead V Corps on Omaha Beach, even though Gerow had no prior combat experience as a general officer.

During the two years that Devers commanded the Armored Force, ten new armored divisions and dozens of independent tank battalions were formed. As he remembered, "We organized a good many divisions with cadres from the ones we had trained. I set up an armored division at Fort Knox—the 8th—as a training division for the purpose of training cadres for new divisions. The cadres were made up of a fixed number of men with certain specialties." As these men were transferred from existing divisions, replacements had to be trained and assigned to fill those vacancies. Consequently, a training center had been established at Fort Knox in 1940 to teach the special skills needed in a fully mechanized force. Devers took an active interest in the training center and applied some of the lessons he had learned at Fort Sill to its operations. For example, the courses ran on a weekly schedule. "If a man failed or got sick in the middle of the week, or failed at the end of the course and we thought he had potential, we simply started him off at the [same course starting] at the beginning of the [next] week. We didn't fire him or release him, or send him away—we gave him another chance. If he made the grade he went on. I would say 99%-plus did make the grade. In that way we saved some very good men who were slow starters."[49]

For the training center, Devers set up a special board that included experienced educators from the University of Louisville. The board administered aptitude tests to all new trainees to determine which of them were officer material. The existing divisions also selected promising men to attend officer candidate school, and this opportunity "helped morale no end" in the armored units. Likewise, the board of educators identified men with aptitudes for technical positions such as mechanics, tank drivers, and clerks.[50]

Soon after Devers arrived at Fort Knox, he received a message from Marshall questioning the administration of the officer candidate school. The chief of staff was concerned about the objectivity of the selection process and the age of the candidates admitted to the program.[51] Devers looked into the matter and quickly responded to Marshall's concerns:

> Your letter reference Officer Candidates was on my desk when I arrived from Louisiana Saturday afternoon. I have thoroughly investigated the points raised in your letter. The report of the Inspector General has just been received.
>
> The candidates graduated yesterday and were the cleanest finest group of second lieutenants that I have seen anywhere. . . . Colonel Motts, the inspector, stated in the presence of the instructors of the school: "You have the best run school, the highest morale and your instruction is sound, but the quality of your candidates is the lowest." . . . Fifty (percent) of the graduates were older than I would like them to be. . . . I recommend that the age be set at 26 years [by the War Department] not 29 or 37 years in special cases as it is now. . . . There is no evidence that the local boards or the final board showed any partiality [when picking candidates].[52]

Devers further reported cases of inefficient administration, largely due to inexperience, poor record keeping, and misunderstandings. He traced these problems to "too many changes of unit commanders and the rapid expansion of the force. Corrective action has been taken." The school carefully screened applicants for the October class, and commanders reviewed their recommendations based on soldiers' performance in the recent maneuvers.[53] Such challenges were common due to the rapid mobilization in

1940–1941, but the key point is that Devers and others faced these problems squarely and worked to correct them as quickly as possible.

Personnel and training issues were not the only ones faced by the army in 1941. All kinds of new equipment had to be developed and fielded. For the Armored Force, a tank that could face German armor in battle was a critical requirement. Devers played an important role in the development of the medium tank that would be the mainstay of American, British, and French forces in World War II.

Equipping the Armored Force

The U.S. Army developed few armored vehicles before 1940. The tanks used by the American forces in World War I were of French and British design and construction. During the interwar years the army used surplus tanks, and only a few new designs were tested. By 1940, the army was using a light tank, known as the M2, and was working on a medium tank, designated the M3. The light tank weighed about eleven tons and was reasonably fast; it was lightly armored and had mounted machine guns. A later version, confusedly called the M3 light tank, had a 37mm gun mounted in a small turret, but it was obsolete before it came off the production lines owing to the Germans' development of the Panzer (PZ) III light tank. A replacement, the M5 Stuart light tank, was developed and fielded in 1942, and by 1944, more than 6,000 M5s had been produced. Although fast and mechanically reliable, the M5 had less than two inches of armor in the front and still mounted the increasingly ineffective 37mm gun. The light tank concept never made sense, given that light tanks were too easy to kill and lacked sufficient firepower to destroy the Germans' medium tanks. The army needed to develop a medium tank that could rectify these deficiencies.

Recognizing the need for a more powerful tank, the Armored Force developed the M3 medium tank. The M3 weighed about twenty-five tons and was armed with a 37mm gun in a small turret and a 75mm cannon in the right sponson of the hull. Development of the M3 (also called the Lee or the Grant tank) commenced at Rock Island Arsenal in July 1940, but it took a full year for a significant number to be produced. The M3 had several design problems: The 75mm gun in the hull could only be deflected across an arc of fifteen degrees, which meant that the entire vehicle had to be turned to shoot at targets off to the sides. The small turret mounting the 37mm gun was on top of the riveted hull, giving the tank a high silhouette. The M3 tank was given to the British as part of the Lend-Lease program in late 1941. Though mechanically reliable, it proved to be inferior to the German PZ IV medium tanks in the desert battlefields of North Africa, mainly because of its poor armor protection and high silhouette and the difficulty of aiming its hull-mounted gun quickly in combat.[54]

After using the M3 in North Africa, the British reported a number of shortcomings to the American liaison team in Egypt, and these observations were sent to Devers and the chief of ordnance. In a meeting with the senior officers of I Armored Corps in November 1941, Devers summarized the British and American experience with the M3 Grant: "The tank's engine, the Wright W-975 has given excessive trouble due to defects in the engine and its installation. 10% of the engines in the M3 have been replaced after fewer than 100 hours of operation. The M3 is underpowered and cannot march fast enough on road marches. The track life is too short and the 75mm gun needs to be turret mounted." In conclusion, Devers told his senior subordinates and the chief of ordnance, Major General C. M. Wesson, that he preferred the design of the next-generation medium tank, known as the M4, and was "willing to let the M3's go to foreign armies and wait for the M4's."[55]

General Wesson reported to the group that efforts had been under way for months to correct the defects in the Wright engines, which were caused by faulty carburetors and high oil consumption. He also announced that those problems had been fixed in the newly manufactured M3 tanks. Wesson went on to report that the M4 medium tank (known as the Sherman tank) would go into production in January 1942. Though pleased with this news, Devers pointed out that the M3 and the new M4 medium tanks needed more powerful engines. Wesson replied that a number of engines were being tested to find the most reliable one that could deliver the power needed.[56]

Devers realized that the development of equipment was an army problem, and he recommended to General Brehon "Bill" Somervell, chief of the Army Services of Supply, that "the first thing you have to do is put all this motor equipment and responsibility [for development] in one hand, either in the Ordnance or the Quartermaster [Corps]." Devers suggested, "I'd put it in . . . Ordnance and I'd move the head office to Detroit. . . . They have some pretty good men . . . but they need some better leadership."[57] Somervell accepted this recommendation, concentrating the development of army vehicles in an ordnance corps office in Detroit.

The Armored Force worked closely with the ordnance office and the auto manufacturers in Detroit to come up with the right solutions for the Sherman tank's engine, armor, and main gun. Problems arose, but they were faced directly and efficiently. As Devers noted, "I haven't made this too clear—but these were some of the problems, and the way we solved them was by direct contact, telephone, and what not." Devers set up a battalion at Fort Knox to test tank engines and other components. He "set aside a part of the reservation which was dusty and hilly, and sometimes very muddy," where three shifts of soldiers could test tanks day and night in a variety of conditions. These tests revealed that the Ford engine needed components with tougher steel, and "some of the steel from one producer wasn't as good as from another one." According to Devers, "all these developments took place with the magnificent cooperation of the motor industry in Detroit."[58]

The relationship between the Armored Force and auto company executives paid dividends. Devers met in Washington with "Wilson of General Motors"; "Sorenson, who represented Ford"; and "K. T. Keller, who represented Chrysler." There, they asked Devers to make a basic decision about the medium tank, which he was able to do not "because of my great knowledge, but it is the fact that I had thoroughly drained and picked the brains of the experts who had been on this job within the Ordnance department and in industry." Devers recalled, "We accomplished these things because when we ran into these 'bugs'—as we called them—we were immediately able to get a man on the job and it's surprising what the motor industry can do when they work together. I want to state here and now there was never better teamwork than in the City of Detroit with the motor industry and the Armored Force than when I was in command of it. . . . Out of it we got the power plants and developed the M4 tank."[59]

The Sherman tank was significantly better than the Grant. The 75mm gun was mounted in a turret, and the turret and hull were protected with better and thicker armor. The Armored Force worked closely with manufacturers and the Ordnance Department to find the best available engine, testing four types of engines in the process. Devers personally visited the executives of manufacturing companies to explain the urgency of this search. By April 1942, he was able to report to Major General James H. Burns, "We in the Armored Force know what we want. At the moment it is a rugged gasoline engine that has the horsepower, with some to spare, to drive a tank. We believe that this is the new Ford engine."[60]

In the summer of 1942 the new tank was tested by the Armored Force for durability and reliability with the Ford GAA-V-8 engine. "From the standpoint of performance, necessary maintenance, and the failure of component parts," the tests indicated that the hull and transmission were satisfactory, but the engine required modification. After two more iterations of modifications and tests, the Ford engine was selected to power the Sherman tank. After reviewing the early test results for the M4, Devers recommended to McNair that "no Medium Tanks, M3, be manufactured after July 1, 1942, other than as necessary to consume available M3 parts now on hand." McNair agreed, but the head of Army Services of Supply pointed out, "It is impracticable, from a production standpoint, to stop the manufacture of Medium Tanks M3 and at the same time meet our requirements under Lend-Lease." However, "further assignment of this type of tank to our troops is not contemplated."[61]

In the fall of 1942 the Grant tank was phased out as production of the Sherman tank increased. By the end of the war, about 50,000 Sherman tanks had been manufactured. With its heavier gun and more powerful engine, the Sherman proved to be a match for the German medium tank (PZ IV), but its main armament and armor protection were inferior to the German Panther and Tiger tanks (PZ V and VI), which entered battle in late 1942.

During the 1941–1942 debates about tanks, Devers fielded some questions from Secretary of War Henry Stimson. It seems that Patton, Stimson's former military aide, had been providing the secretary with his views about the appropriate type of tank for the armored divisions. Patton wanted a light, fast tank with multiple mounted machine guns to execute the sorts of exploitation missions envisioned by the cavalry. Stimson then raised these issues with Devers as decisions regarding the M4 were being made. As Devers explained later, "George (Patton) was always trying to put on more machine guns and to weaken the tank." Devers "had to do something about Patton's recommendations [to Stimson]," both to ensure that he got the heavier and better-gunned tank he wanted and to sort out the issue of who was the boss of the Armored Force—him or Patton. The points of disagreement between them included the weight of the tank, the type of engine, and the kinds of weapons mounted on the vehicle. They also disagreed on the proper mix of light and medium tanks in the tank companies, with Patton favoring more light tanks and Devers opting for more medium tanks in each company, battalion, and regiment. Based on the reports of liaison officers with the British and the studies and tests conducted by the Armored Force, Devers concluded that the medium tank should have its main gun (75mm) mounted in a turret, and there should be three machine guns as well. The tank would weigh about twenty-nine tons, and the Ford V-8 would power the vehicle. Initially, he had hoped to equip the Sherman tank with a 105mm howitzer, but this idea was scrapped in favor of the 75mm gun.[62]

Once Devers had made these decisions, he decided it was time to deal with Patton. "So I had to go down to see Patton [at Fort Benning]. . . . I stayed with him and he [and his wife] entertained us at dinner and after dinner . . . I said, 'Well George, you and I have half a night's work here because I came down to straighten out this Armored Force and I thought I ought to talk to you personally.'" When Beatrice Patton got up to leave, Devers said, "No Bea, you better stay in here because George and I are going to have a fight and I'd like to have a referee." So she stayed and listened. Devers briefed Patton on the current state of the Sherman tank's development and then said, "Now, George, you don't agree with all this. . . . We're not going to put any more holes in the armor of that turret because it just weakens it for some extra machine guns. . . . It makes it too complicated and we have to get horsepower to run these tanks. . . . These are my decisions. . . . Now, are you going to fall in line and be on the team and work with me on this or are you going [to continue] to send these notes up to Mr. Stimson?" Patton, according to Devers, "got up and saluted me, just like a good soldier would, and said, 'Jake, you're the boss and I'm one of your commanders, and I'll play ball.' That was it! This is the way I always worked with George."[63] Patton kept his word and was a loyal subordinate to Devers and later to Bradley and Eisenhower. In the meantime, Devers would need to call on Patton's leadership abilities.

The Desert Training Center

The Armored Force headquarters was responsible for selecting new camps or stations where armored divisions could be organized and trained. For example, Devers oversaw the establishment of Camps Campbell and Hood and the desert training center near Indio, California. The impetus for the creation of a desert training center was the German victory against the British Eighth Army in the Libyan desert in late January 1942. Since the British and Americans had agreed on a global strategy that envisioned defeating

Germany first, before dealing with Japan, it was logical that some American forces might be needed to face Rommel in North Africa.[64] Devers believed that the armored divisions would greatly benefit from desert warfare training, so he set out to sell the idea to Marshall and McNair.

General Lesley McNair was not easily convinced. He believed that specialty training for desert warfare was unnecessary. When McNair balked, Devers told his longtime friend, "Well, Les, I'm on my way to see General Marshall. I'm quite sure he'll approve this because I talked to him—I gave him my ideas on this about a month ago—and he encouraged me. He gave me some good advice and I have followed that advice. I think I'm going to get a real quick approval on this and I just want to let you know that I'm not trying to work against you, but just trying to be helpful."[65] Devers was right: Marshall agreed, and the decision was made to set up a training camp in the desert Southwest. Devers assigned Patton the mission of establishing the desert training center, using his I Armored Corps and the 2nd and 3rd Armored Divisions as the initial force. Patton was not enamored with the mission at first and asked Devers, "What are you trying to do? Can me?" Devers replied, "George, I'm not trying to can you—I'm giving you the greatest opportunity of your life. . . . Now I'm sending you out there because I think you are the most capable commander for that job."[66] He then told Patton: "George, let's get one thing straight again. I'm not in competition with you for anything. I think that the only place the tanks are fighting right now is in the desert. . . . This is your chance to make it go and I'm sure you're the man that can do it."[67]

Patton moved with alacrity. On 4 March he flew to Riverside, California, to conduct an aerial reconnaissance of the area where Arizona, California, and Nevada meet. He found the region well suited for an armored training center, with three major railroads serving the area and enough water to sustain three division-sized base camps. He reported to Devers, "The area possesses tremendous advantages for all forms of training, because, in addition to its climatic and geographical similitude to Libya, it is the only place I know where the artificial restrictions are almost wholly non-existing, and where there is room to burn."[68] By April, Patton's corps was established in tent camps in the desert and was ready to commence training.

At about the same time, in February 1942, Marshall reorganized the army and established three major subordinate commands. The Army Air Forces under General Hap Arnold was given charge of all air-related matters. The Services of Supply, later renamed the Army Service Forces, under

General Brehon Somervell, was responsible for most supply and services matters. The Army Ground Forces (AGF), under Lesley McNair, took charge of the training of all combat forces in the continental United States. The Armored Force was placed directly under the AGF, and the offices of the chiefs of infantry, cavalry, and artillery were abolished. With this reorganization, Marshall rationalized and reduced his personal workload and span of control, thus ensuring greater coordination among the various functions in each of the three major commands. However, there was some confusion about who was in charge of what. For instance, Patton was unclear whether the new desert training center fell under the AGF or the Armored Force. To cover all his bases, Patton "remain[ed] in close contact with both McNair and Devers, as well as with members of their headquarters, striving always to satisfy them, giving his utmost, working hard to justify his selection for combat overseas."[69] Although the Armored Force (and Patton's training center) was now part of the AGF, it retained a great deal of effective autonomy due to Devers's personal relationship with McNair.

The decision to place the Armored Force directly under the AGF ended any discussion of the creation of a separate Armored Force similar to the Army Air Forces. Major Generals Scott and Chaffee had made this proposal in 1941, before Devers took command. Devers had favored the creation of a separate tank army composed of additional armored corps and the inclusion of a motorized infantry division in each armored corps. Generals Marshall and McNair, however, decided that armored divisions would serve in infantry corps alongside infantry divisions and that all corps and army commanders needed to know how to employ armored formations as part of a combined-arms team. By the end of 1943, the three armored corps in existence were redesignated army corps.[70]

McNair and Devers had somewhat different views about the training of tank destroyer and mechanized cavalry units. Devers proposed that the Armored Force assume responsibility for their training, since he envisioned them operating together in combat. McNair disagreed and settled the issue in a May 1942 letter:

> You want to merge the Tank Destroyer Command with the Armored Force. . . . As I got the picture, the predominant thought was that the tank destroyers should free the Armored Force as much as possible so that it can strike the hostile force as a whole in decisive fashion, while the hostile armored force is taken care

of as much as possible by the destroyers. . . . Tanks and destroyers should be rivals, not partners, although they are associated closely in operations. For these general reasons, I am against merging the two forces. . . . As to your taking over mechanized cavalry, I do not question that you could do so effectively; but on the other hand, the Cavalry School already is organized to teach reconnaissance and there seems to be insufficient reason to make the change. . . . Speaking in general, the general picture seems to me sound—that is, the Armored Force for armored units properly speaking, Riley for mechanized reconnaissance, and Temple for tank destroyers.[71]

The "Old Army" Ends

When Devers took command of the Armored Force in mid-1941, the nation was at peace and there was serious talk about releasing the National Guard divisions from active service. At that time, Georgie felt that life was going along as it always had. She wrote to Kitts in October 1941, "This is such a nice house and I am so comfortable—but six bathrooms to myself are a little lonely." Georgie continued to worry about Frances, who had been "in an auto accident two months ago—fractured her ankle and is still in a cast and on crutches. . . . Thank fortune it was no worse."[72]

Although Jake was very busy, he and Georgie still planned to visit York for Christmas. After Pearl Harbor, however, the tempo of their lives increased dramatically, as did their concern for Frances, who was following her husband from post to post. Georgie wrote to Kitts in April 1942, "Alex spent a few days with Frances and now Frances is here. . . . She knows lots of people here and keeps on the go as always. Jamie came home today—[he] has been gone most of the time for weeks."[73]

During the Second World War, many army wives and families lived as Frances did. They followed their soldiers from camp to camp, spending as much time as possible with them before their units were sent overseas. In most cases there was no on-post housing available, so it was a real hardship for them. Georgie made the following observations about the wives and children involved:

My fish pond is a source of pleasure. It's alive with all the gold fish the departing children have brought to put in it. Army young ones are having to find homes for all their pets, and many of their dear possessions, these days. Past life is past, families are getting settled in towns or at home for the duration and those who are still brave enough to try to follow the army, are arriving with suit cases or a trunk at most, in the back of the car—and few pets. The houses are becoming furnished with things abandoned by their owners and people get along with what there is there or with what neighbors can spare.[74]

Georgie did not wallow in self-pity. As the casualty lists from the Philippines arrived, she remarked to Kitts, "I am among the blessed. My friends are being widowed, and with every dispatch, and there are hundreds, I know who await news of any kind—good or bad—and wait day after weary day."[75] A couple months later she wrote: "I have such a nice grey horse—Peanuts—who helps me get out in the sun and wind, and keeps the cobwebs wiped out of my brain."[76]

Georgie continually worried about Frances. In October she was living in a hotel in Nashville so she could be near her husband, who was with the 4th Armored Division on maneuvers. Alex's unit was slated to go to the desert training area next. The 4th Armored Division had been stationed at Pine Camp, near Watertown, New York, so Frances faced a long journey north, alone, to pack up the things they had left there. This gypsy-like life was not unusual for army wives during the war, and Georgie noted, "It's war, and the future is going to be tough on us gals."[77]

The Deverses' relationship was certainly strained by the increasing separations and fast-paced tempo of Jake's work by the summer of 1942. Georgie was feeling the pangs of loneliness, but her letters to Kitts also showed real love and concern for her husband:

I shall watch Jamie to see that he doesn't follow too closely the family pattern of leaving his wife flat! Poor man, he scarcely knows he has a wife anyway these days. He is out in the California desert at the moment. . . . I can't bring myself to leave here. I am miserable when I am far away, for fear Jamie will come back and need me before I can get here, and these months are just so much velvet for me, more than nine tenths of my friends have [left]. So many troops are overseas and so many women left to wait the outcome of this dreadful war before it has really begun. . . . I am tempted to sell out if Jamie leaves here. What can I do with all these things? . . .

The army is going to move belongings only once more for any of us, a new rule. That is right of course, but that changes our way of life I can tell you.[78]

When Jake was at Fort Knox, he and Georgie managed to get away for an occasional pleasant evening alone. But even then, Georgie saw the signs of war and its effect on the nation: "We went to a place called Arden on the Ohio. . . . The entertainment was a quartet of darkies unaccompanied who sang the spirituals and Stephen Foster songs. . . . There are so many such places and people here to whom the wars and depressions seem to be only opportunities to grasp—to be successful."[79] Georgie's mention of "darkies" indicates that the Deverses and the army found themselves in much more intimate contact with African Americans than before the draft was initiated in 1940. National policy was that blacks would be drafted in a proportion that matched their representation in the total population (about 9 percent). Although the army remained segregated, as in the First World War, change was clearly coming. The U.S. Army would be at the center of this change in race relations over the next six years.

Race Relations at Fort Knox

Once conscription was in place, the NAACP and other organizations, with support from the White House, called for an increase in black combat units, including fighter squadrons and tank battalions. During the initial expansion of the armed forces in 1940–1941, black field artillery and antiaircraft units were formed, and existing African American National Guard infantry regiments were mustered into service. However, because many senior army officers believed that blacks were not suited for direct combat, these infantry regiments were converted to artillery and antiaircraft organizations.[80]

When the Armored Force was established, the army staff pushed for the creation of black tank units. In December 1940 the Armored Force staff tried to argue that its proportion of black servicemen was provided by two service units stationed at Fort Knox, so there was no need to establish any black tank units. The army staff rejected this position, and Marshall ordered the Armored Force to organize African American tank battalions. Although Major General Scott continued to argue against this move, the War Department, with General McNair's strong support, persisted. The 78th Light Tank Battalion, organized on 1 June 1941, became the first black tank unit.

"Despite strong objections from the Armored Force, two additional [black] tank battalions were scheduled. The 761st was activated on 1 April 1942 and the 784th Tank Battalion a year later."[81]

This pace was too slow for Secretary of War Stimson, who became personally involved in the issue when he rejected efforts by the Armored Force to reduce the number of African Americans assigned to Fort Knox. In January 1942 he noted, "Activation of the 767th Tank Battalion, a colored unit, will result in but two colored units in the total of ten Armored Divisions and twenty-five separate Battalions planned for the Armored Force. This disproportionately low percentage of colored personnel requires that other branches of the service absorb more than their share of Negroes." He then directed that "an additional allotment of colored personnel will be made to the Armored Force to activate the 767th Tank Battalion, and this personnel must be absorbed either in the new battalion or in the Armored Force School overhead."[82] The 767th Tank Battalion was activated in July 1942.

The newly formed African American battalions created a need for black officers, especially lieutenants. The 78th Tank Battalion initially had thirty-two white officers, but this was a temporary expedient until black officers could be trained. The commanders of the tank and tank destroyer battalions, however, would be white, since there were no black majors or lieutenant colonels in the Armored Force. The army needed tens of thousands of lieutenants in 1941, and that number would grow exponentially after Pearl Harbor. Consequently, Marshall and McNair pushed their staffs to expand the number of officer candidate schools.

The officer candidate schools were racially integrated, although there was a distinct bias against blacks because of the tests used to select candidates. The army's "mental" tests measured academic achievement rather than intelligence, and in 1941 an individual's academic achievement depended more on social class and geographic location than on race. The majority of black soldiers came from parts of the country where segregated schools were inferior to white schools. Consequently, the majority of African Americans scored in the lower three quintiles of inductees and thus were not eligible for officer candidate school or other specialized training. Segregation was a moral illness that hindered the nation's ability to take full advantage of its manpower in time of war.[83]

By the spring of 1942, a number of African American officers and soldiers had been assigned to Fort Knox. Since there was insufficient on-post housing, most officers, regardless of race, lived in hotels until they were assigned to units. As Devers recalled, "We had problems there because we were getting colored officers and the hotels in Louisville—as it is in all those kinds of states—had no proper place where they could stay before they reported to duty at Fort Knox." At the time, Devers believed there was nothing he could do about this situation, but he was offered a solution by Mrs. Margaret Collier. Collier "happened to be the daughter of a Sergeant of the 25th Infantry—which was black—[and had been] brought up in the traditions of the Army. She was the hostess of the colored club and in the training section." Devers continued:

> She heard about this [situation] and so she came to my back door and got in, and I happened to be home—or she waited for me. I took her into the reception room and sat down and talked to her. . . . Now, this was really the first direct communication that I had had on this subject. I had been putting it off all the time. . . . She said, "General, if you'll set a barracks aside out there for me—one of those that has single rooms in it—and let me use it for colored officers that come into this post instead of going to the hotels downtown, that will remove the embarrassment there."

Mrs. Collier thus convinced Devers to approve the establishment of on-post quarters for black officers. She became a regular adviser to Devers, but he recalled, "I never could get her to come to the front door. She always came to the back door when she visited me—and never at my office—always at my home." And she never left by the front door either.[84]

There were other racial problems at Fort Knox, as there were at many other army bases. Segregation was the rule in the army, and this included seating in on-post theaters. At Fort Knox, African American soldiers were required to sit in the gallery, away from the white patrons on the main floor. Devers saw no problem with this rule, and when it was challenged by two African American sergeants, he concluded that black newspapermen from Pittsburgh or Chicago had probably instigated the incident. When the NCOs sat in seats on the main floor, they were arrested by white military policemen. The sergeants "didn't make much of a fuss, just enough to cause trouble," so they were put in the guardhouse. Devers then reacted:

> Now this was brought to my attention early the next morning. I called up the Post Commander and told him that he had two peo-

ple down there and he said he was going to try them. I said, "No you're not! I want you to release those two men and have them report to me in my office right now. . . . This is a set game and I think I can handle it." So those two sergeants did come to my office. I had them come in and close the doors and I talked to them alone. I said to them, "You're two of the finest sergeants we have in the training section out here and I know that those two newspapermen—who've been in here interviewing me—must have motivated you to do what you did. . . . Why don't you tell those people the good things that you men are doing for your race; not the bad things, and not create other bad things for me?"[85]

Devers made a deal with the sergeants to buy their silence and cooperation. He reduced their rank to private but promised that if they soldiered faithfully for one month, he would restore their rank. The men accepted the offer, and according to Devers, a month later they were both sergeants again.

Devers was clearly worried about the possibility of protests or riots. In fact, there were numerous racial incidents across the South. In August 1941, shortly after Devers left Fort Bragg, there was a major confrontation between military police and black soldiers in Fayetteville, North Carolina. One white military policeman and one black soldier were killed and five soldiers were wounded. Fort Bragg's provost marshal reacted by arresting all African American soldiers on the post who were not in their barracks at the time of the incident. A more serious incident occurred during the Second Army's maneuvers in August, when men of the 94th Engineer Battalion, made up of African Americans from Michigan, were attacked by the Arkansas state police in their bivouac. When the soldiers left their camp, the state police reported to the military police that there was a group of unruly soldiers proceeding down the highway. "The provost marshal, accepting the report as fact, requested the state authorities to take charge until the military police arrived. Fully armed state police and deputies started for the scene of disorder. . . . State troopers, using insulting epithets to both the troops and their officers, ordered the marching unit off the road and into a ditch lately filled with rain. . . . When one of the officers protested the police actions and epithets, a state policeman removed his glasses and struck the 'Yankee nigger lover' in the face."[86] The military police, who had arrived by that time, did nothing until the white officer was struck. Then they took charge of the unit. Word of this incident spread among the troops, under-cutting morale and discipline among African American soldiers.

Devers believed that his handling of the situation with the two black sergeants was humane and effective at preventing further racial trouble. He dealt with the "infraction" of the army's segregation policy outside the for-mal military justice system and took steps to keep the theater incident out of the newspapers. However, Mrs. Collier's intelligent leadership probably did more to keep race relations at Fort Knox under control by ensuring that blacks were treated with the dignity due them as citizens and soldiers. On her advice, the post eased off on the theater seating rules. Reflecting a tradi-tional and widespread view among army officers in 1941, Devers observed that blacks "were always good soldiers. They never were bad soldiers. . . . We got the town to ease up . . . and finally we broke the barriers there to some extent . . . through our close contact with the mayor of the town and the newspapers."[87]

African American tank units performed well in the war. For example, the 761st Tank Battalion—known as the "Black Panthers"—landed in France in October 1944 and fought its way into Germany with the Third Army. Simi-lar success was achieved by the 767th Tank Battalion and a number of African American tank destroyer battalions. But too many Americans ignored these units' achievements and looked for their fellow citizens of color to fail.

Promotion and Greater Challenges

Devers and his staff worked on many fronts to get new armored units orga-nized, to select training sites, and to get the best possible equipment into the hands of the troops. By the summer of 1942, the 1st and 2nd Armored Divisions were ready for combat, and twelve other armored divisions were in the process of activating and training. The M4 Sherman tank and the M7 Priest self-propelled howitzer were in full production. Although there were severe shortages of equipment for the training of new divisions, great strides had been made to eliminate bottlenecks and to curtail the produc-tion of obsolete equipment such as the M3 light and medium tanks. The Armored Force was well organized, and it was testing tank engines and working to develop a heavy tank (an effort that would not come to fruition until 1945). In less than a year, Devers had energized the Armored Force and coordinated weapons development with industry, the ordnance branch, and the War Department.

The inspector general of the army, Major General Virgil Peterson, visited Fort Knox in early September 1942 to assess the condition of the command. In a report to General Marshall, Peterson concluded that there had been "a marked improvement . . . in the general appearance of the post, sanitary conditions and the discipline of the command as particularly indicated in saluting. I participated in a command show-down inspection of the entire 8th Armored Division, and was very much impressed. . . . It was my first visit to General Devers' headquarters since he assumed command of the Armored Force." Based on this visit, Peterson concluded that Devers "is one of our most outstanding general officers and is doing a wonderful job in the organization and training of the Armored Force."[88]

Marshall, who had followed Devers's work closely, had already come to the same conclusion. In August he had recommended that Devers be promoted to lieutenant general; Stimson and the president concurred. The Senate confirmed the appointment, and on 6 September 1942 Jacob L. Devers became a lieutenant general in the U.S. Army. In his letter of congratulations, Major General A. D. Bruce, commanding general of the Tank Destroyer Command, remarked, "Not only have you done an outstanding job at Knox, but you have found time to help the other fellow along."[89] General McNair, who was Devers's immediate superior and rating officer, ranked him as one of the top five lieutenant generals in the Army Ground Forces for the period 9 March to 31 December 1942.[90] With such a rating, it seemed clear that Devers was headed for big things in the future.

The tempo of the war, meantime, continued to increase. In July, President Roosevelt ordered the American chiefs of staff to prepare to join the British in an invasion of French North Africa. The 1st and 2nd Armored Divisions were slated to participate in what became Operation Torch. Those divisions had received the best possible training at Patton's desert training center, and it was no surprise when Patton was selected to command the American forces assaulting the Moroccan coast. On 8 November American and British forces under the overall command of Lieutenant General Dwight D. Eisenhower landed in Algeria and Morocco. After a short period of hard fighting against the Vichy French garrisons at Casablanca, Algiers, and Oran, the Allies secured the two French colonies and pushed east toward Tunisia.

These developments set in motion a chain of events that would lead Devers from the Armored Force to the United Kingdom and increased responsibilities. In December, however, all this was unknown. Marshall's Christmas message to Devers read: "My best wishes for the Holiday Season and my appreciation for the outstanding job you have done during the past year. . . . I congratulate you on your ability to get things done and I send my personal thanks for your highly efficient manner of doing them. Only the vast importance of the Armored Force program has barred you, for the present, from employment in active operations."[91]

8

On to the War

By the end of his first year as commanding general of the Armored Force, Devers had reorganized the command, expanded the training center for armored crewmen and specialists, and played a personal role in the development of equipment such as the Sherman tank and the Priest self-propelled howitzer. He had a flair for working with men from a wide range of professions, and he knew how to get things done. As a result, by December 1942, the Sherman tank was rolling off assembly lines in increasing numbers to equip the fourteen armored divisions and twenty-five separate tank battalions created by the Armored Force. After being promoted to lieutenant general in September 1942, Devers was summoned to Washington in early December to meet with General Marshall to discuss a special assignment. This assignment would include traveling 23,000 miles and visiting Allied forces in North Africa and the United Kingdom. It would also put Devers in contact with Eisenhower and Patton, with major implications for their future relationships.

Operation Torch

Operation Torch, the Anglo-American invasion of French Northwest Africa in November 1942, opened a new front in the war. However, for the first half of 1942, General Marshall had vigorously opposed the Allies' decision to invade North Africa. He believed that diverting American divisions to the Mediterranean theater would be a setback to the buildup of forces in the United Kingdom for the Allied invasion of western Europe. He was convinced that the cross-Channel invasion should be launched in 1942 or early 1943 and that it was an essential component of the "Germany first" strategy. The British, in contrast, correctly believed that the American and British armies were not ready to face the enemy in France. They reasoned that the American generals and their ground forces had little experience of modern warfare; in addition, the German naval and air forces had not been defeated, the Wehrmacht continued to advance in Russia, and German forces in North Africa threatened the Suez Canal.[1]

After one last trip to London in June 1942 to try to convince British leaders to stay focused on the cross-Channel invasion, Marshall had to admit failure. In July, President Roosevelt ordered the American chiefs of staff to take part in an Anglo-American invasion of French North Africa in the fall. This decision, though unwelcome to Marshall, gave the U.S. Army an opportunity to "blood" some of its commanders and soldiers and to fix some glaring doctrinal and equipment shortcomings.[2]

Since a majority of the soldiers in the initial landings were to be Americans, the Combined Chiefs of Staff and Churchill asked Roosevelt to appoint an American to be the Allied supreme commander of what became known as Allied Forces Headquarters (AFHQ). Roosevelt followed Marshall's recommendation and, on 13 August 1942, appointed Lieutenant General Dwight D. Eisenhower to command Torch. Eisenhower, then the commander of the European theater of operations in London, had barely settled in when he was ordered to plan and execute Operation Torch.[3]

Eisenhower would become one of the great coalition commanders in Western history. A 1915 West Point graduate, the infantryman had trained tank units in the United States during World War I and had served in a variety of staff positions in the interwar period. While a cadet, Eisenhower probably at least knew of Devers, who was the baseball coach and a math instructor at the time. His classmate Omar Bradley certainly knew Devers, having played on the championship baseball team Devers coached in 1915. Devers and Bradley had also served together on the staff and faculty of the Military Academy from 1920 to 1924.[4]

Operation Torch commenced on 8 November 1942 with amphibious assaults by American forces in Morocco and Algeria. After three days of bitter fighting between the defending French and the invading Americans, the French army accepted a cease-fire. Over the next several months, French North African forces transitioned from foes to allies. The next phase of the Allied campaign in North Africa was less clear-cut. As Rick Atkinson aptly notes, "Proverbially, no military plan survives contact with the enemy," but in the case of Torch, there was "no plan to begin with. No scheme existed for integrating U.S. units into British organizations, or for provisioning them, or for getting them to the front in the first place."[5] The operation did call for British forces to land in Algiers so they could swiftly push east and seize Tunisia before the Germans could respond. For a variety of reasons, this plan quickly collapsed.

Eisenhower's major subordinate in charge of the drive toward Tunisia was Lieutenant General Kenneth Anderson, commander of the British First Army. Anderson's army was hardly bigger than a three-division corps during the first month of the operation. Due to a shortage of support units, insufficient transport, and poor roads from Algeria to Tunisia, Anderson's Eastern Task Force moved slowly. This gave the Germans time to pour men and equipment into Tunisia and to establish strong defensive positions protecting the plains and the key ports of Tunis and Bizerte. In addition, the Anglo-American forces had given little thought to how to integrate the French army into the coalition force.[6]

The Allies soon suffered costly defeats by land, air, and sea. By early December, the Germans had sufficient forces on the ground to counterattack the British and American columns in northern Tunisia. The Luftwaffe controlled the airspace over the battlefield, allowing its bombers to sink a number of British ships and to attack American and British land forces nearly at will. The first major encounters between American and German armored forces also demonstrated the serious deficiencies of American tanks and tactical doctrine. On 28 November American M3 medium tanks encountered German Mark IV panzers at Tebourba, Tunisia. The M3, also known as the Grant, had distinct weaknesses, as Devers and the Armored Force had already recognized. It was ten feet tall, prompting one American to note that "it looked like a damned cathedral coming down the road." The German tanks, equipped with long-barreled 75mm guns, quickly destroyed more than half a battalion of American tanks and then went on to slaughter the British infantrymen accompanying the American tankers. "This Sunday [fight]—precisely three weeks after the Torch landings began—marked the apogee of the Allied offensive for the next six months."[7]

Similar encounters between American and German armored units in the first ten days of December further demonstrated that Devers had been right to question the ability of antitank guns to stop enemy tanks. As Atkinson observes, "To Eisenhower's surprise, American tanks and armored tactics also seemed wanting. U.S. Army doctrine held that tanks ought not fight other tanks, but should leave that job to specialized tank destroyers while armored formations tore through defenses and ripped up the enemy rear." American antitank guns, however, were too light to destroy German medium tanks from the front. In addition, the Germans introduced the sixty-ton Tiger tank in Tunisia. With its 88mm gun and thick armor, the Tiger Mark VI could not be stopped by the Americans' guns.[8]

The fighting of November and December 1942 was disastrous for

American and British forces, which suffered a number of defeats in Tunisia. Eisenhower, as supreme Allied commander, was responsible. For the first two weeks of the campaign, he tried to command British and American forces in Algeria and Tunisia from an underground office in Gibraltar. The results were not good. Finally, on 23 November, Eisenhower moved his headquarters to Algiers, which was still nearly 600 miles from the front. Communications between the supreme commander and his British field commander were poor, and Eisenhower did not visit Anderson's command post in eastern Algeria until the end of November. Even then, Eisenhower was still 120 miles from the front-line units, and he had no grasp of what was happening at the front.[9]

Eisenhower's initial performance as a combat theater commander left doubts in many people's minds about his ability to command such a large operation. Field Marshal Alan Brooke, chief of the British Imperial General Staff, thought that "Eisenhower was far too busy with political matters. . . . Not paying enough attention to the Germans." He seemed "unable to grasp the urgency of pushing on to Tunis before the Germans built up their resistance there."[10] Brooke later noted in his memoirs, "It must be remembered that Eisenhower had never even commanded a battalion in action. . . . I had little confidence in his having the ability to handle the military situation confronting him."[11]

This was fair criticism: Eisenhower had spent very little time commanding soldiers during the first twenty-seven years of his career. He had made his reputation as a superb staff officer and planner. Ike's lack of troop-leading experience was in sharp contrast to Devers's eleven-plus years with the troops. Eisenhower and Devers had distinctly different experiences, and as a result, their approaches to dealing with problems and people were remarkably dissimilar.

Winston Churchill was also worried, and he prodded Ike with messages encouraging a rapid advance. Unfortunately, there was little Eisenhower could do to turn the situation around, given the faulty initial plans drafted by General Mark Clark. Ike felt the political pressure from afar and was frustrated by the Byzantine political intrigue among the French generals in Algeria. As the debacle in northern Tunisia unfolded, even President Roosevelt privately expressed doubts about Eisenhower's suitability for his post.[12]

George Marshall seemed concerned about the supreme commander as well. Knowing that Eisenhower was still operating from his Algiers headquarters in late December, the chief of staff sent him the following message: "I think you should delegate your international diplomatic problems to your subordinates and give your complete attention to the battle in Tunisia and the protection of the Straits of Gibraltar. . . . You are doing a magnificent job and I want you to feel free to give your exclusive attention to the battle particularly as the German intentions against your right flank seem evident."[13] Marshall reemphasized his concerns on 30 December, when he told Eisenhower to "clear your skirts of all that interferes with your complete concentration on the fighting and let subordinates or us carry these other burdens."[14] Marshall also offered to promote George Patton to lieutenant general so that Ike would have a competent senior American commander who could take charge of the American and French forces along the central Tunisian front (the promotion would have been necessary because the commander of the French XIX Corps was a three-star general). Eisenhower turned down Marshall's offer and found a French major general to command the French forces at the front. This allowed him to assign Major General Lloyd Fredendall to coordinate the Allied forces in the center and south, which included the U.S. II Corps and the French XIX Corps.

The first six weeks of the North African campaign were miserable for the inexperienced Eisenhower. He was ill suited for the rigors and challenges of combat command or for the daunting tasks of the supreme commander of an Allied theater of operations. To make matters worse, he was suffering from high blood pressure and an upper respiratory infection, both aggravated by chain smoking. Any suggestion by aide Harry Butcher that he take better care of himself set the general off.[15] In addition to his health problems, Eisenhower possessed a fiery temper. As biographer Carlo D'Este notes, "When Eisenhower erupted in public his tantrums were fearsome to behold, although he would usually later regret his lack of self-control."[16]

Devers's Trip to North Africa

As the North African campaign unfolded, the poor performance of American tanks and the failure of armored warfare doctrine in Tunisia prompted General Marshall to send the chief of the Armored Force to North Africa to assess the army's equipment, tactics, and training. Devers organized a team that included himself, Major General E. H. Brooks, and Brigadier Generals G. M. Barnes and W. B. Palmer. After a short visit with the army chief of staff, the team boarded a plane for Africa on 14 December 1942. Jake told Georgie in a letter, "General Marshall was wonderful this morning. He really seems to think a lot of me."[17]

The Armored Force team had been dispatched by Marshall to look into problems reported to him after the first encounters between the German and American armies. It made sense that he wanted to analyze these first battles and correct any deficiencies noted. Eisenhower probably saw the purpose of Devers's visit differently. Eisenhower had been sent by Marshall on a similar inspection trip to England in early 1942 to assess the American command under Major General James E. Chaney. Ike reported that the U.S. command was "befuddled and unclear about its mission," and he told Marshall, "It is necessary to get a punch behind the job [of a cross-Channel invasion] or we'll never be ready by spring [of 1943] to attack. We must get going!" Eisenhower suggested that Major General Joseph T. McNarney replace Chaney, but Marshall selected Eisenhower instead.[18] It is quite possible that Eisenhower saw Devers's visit similarly—as a preliminary move to replacing him with Devers. Clearly, this was not Marshall's intent, but Eisenhower felt extremely vulnerable, even going so far as to tell his aide that anyone who wanted his job could have it.[19]

The Armored Force team flew more than 11,000 miles to Cairo, Egypt, stopping along the way to refuel in British Guiana; Natal, Brazil; the Ascension Islands; Kano, Nigeria; and Khartoum, Sudan. The team prepared brief reports about the facilities at each stop, noting, for example, that "Natal has a splendid airport suitable for night operations. Command is also faced with problem of feeding large numbers of transients. This base also handles a sizeable amount of air freight. . . . Apparently relations with the Brazilians were excellent. A regiment of Brazilians was guarding the base."[20]

The Devers team visited British bases and armored units in Egypt and Libya from 19 through 26 December. Devers met with senior British generals Bernard Montgomery and Harold Alexander and with Air Marshal Cunningham to discuss how the British operated and commanded their tactical forces and to ascertain their views of the American equipment sent to them as part of the Lend-Lease program. General Alexander, commander in chief of the Middle East, told Devers, "You must have first, leadership, second, material and third, training." In addition to this somewhat condescending observation, Alexander assessed the German strategy in Libya to be one of slow, strategic withdrawal to delay the advance of Montgomery's Eighth Army toward Tunisia.[21]

On 24–25 December the team spent time with the British 22nd

Armored Brigade near Marble Arch, Libya. The 22nd Brigade had been heavily involved in the Battle of El Alamein and the pursuit of Rommel's forces to the west. Brigadier Roberts, the brigade commander, told Devers, "Tank tactics in the desert involved extreme caution and thorough reconnaissance, with a complete avoidance of tank charges." The British had learned this lesson through hard fighting and heavy tank losses in 1941–1942, and the American forces in Tunisia were having the same experience.[22] In fact, the 1st Armored Regiment of U.S. Combat Command B, 1st Armored Division, had lost many of its tanks in "tank charges," and by mid-December it had been withdrawn from the front lines to await replacement tanks and crews.[23]

While in Cairo, Devers and his team met with Lieutenant General R. L. McCreery and other British officers to discuss American equipment. McCreery told them that "the M4 [Sherman] tank is the best tank in this war. He also held that the American M3 light tank, which the British call the 'Honey,' has been of outstanding value and has remarkable speed and reliability." McCreery suggested that a certain number of Sherman tanks be equipped with 76mm guns to give them greater killing power than that provided by 75mm short-barreled guns. The British had a much lower opinion of the M3 Grant, especially because its sponson-mounted gun made it impossible to use the tank in a "hull-down" position, "which is the tactical method of tank employment used by the British."[24]

The British found the Sherman tank to be mechanically reliable, and their tank crews "were confident they could easily defeat any German tank." They claimed that "General Rommel came into the battle [of El Alamein] apparently expecting to defeat the British with his tanks of superior gun power. When he came into contact with the M4 tanks in hull-down positions the German tanks were knocked out and destroyed in great numbers, thus insuring Rommel's defeat." The British also reported that the rubber tracks of the Sherman tanks and the American half-tracks were reliable and could operate for more than 1,500 miles without a change of track.[25]

These British views about the Sherman tank were based on combat experiences before the Germans introduced the Panther and Tiger tanks to battle. In Tunisia the Allied armored forces were already discovering that the newly introduced Tiger tank could outgun the M4, and the Tiger's armor could not be penetrated from the front by the Sherman's gun. The British suggested some improvements to the Sherman tank, including better sights and relocation of the fifty-caliber machine gun to the rear of the turret for antiaircraft protection. The British also impressed the Devers team with their tank recovery organization, which was responsible for preparing tanks for delivery to front-line units and retrieving and repairing damaged tanks from the battlefield. This organization had recovered more than 1,200 tanks in November from the El Alamein battlefield, 1,000 of which were later put back into service.[26]

General McCreery also praised the performance of the 105mm howitzer on the medium tank chassis, which the British called the Priest. The Priest was used to destroy German tanks at ranges of 2,000 to 6,000 yards and proved superior to the British twenty-five-pounder. None of the Priests in the Battle of El Alamein broke down or were permanently disabled. All in all, the British experience with the Sherman tank and the self-propelled 105mm howitzer confirmed that the Armored Force's efforts to develop and test equipment had paid off.

On 26 December Devers and his team visited several American Army Air Forces units in Gambut, Libya, including the 93rd Bombardment Group (Heavy). They noted that "Gambut is located in a dusty part of the desert, and the troops showed evidences of the usual shortage of water. Appearance and morale did not appear as high as in the [57th] Fighter Group at Agedabia, [Algeria]."[27] The next day they flew in a B-24 bomber to Algiers to visit Eisenhower's headquarters and American forces in Tunisia. They "left Algiers at 8:00 AM the following morning in two automobiles followed by a truck carrying bedding rolls and rations." After crossing a mountain range into Tunisia, they arrived at First British Army headquarters, where Devers met with General Anderson and received permission to visit Brigadier General Oliver's Combat Command B of the American 1st Armored Division at Teboursek. This "trip involved the crossing of another mountain range reaching an altitude of 10,000 feet."[28]

During their visits to American armored units, Devers and his team received a great deal of both positive and negative feedback about equipment. The tankers liked the M2 half-track's reliability and armor protection. They were also pleased with the 75mm antitank guns mounted on half-tracks. The commanders and troops were less satisfied with the towed 37mm antitank guns, which could not penetrate enemy tanks at ranges over 300 meters. American artillery commanders were very happy with the 155mm gun's 24,000-yard range and recommended that a self-propelled version be produced. Overall, the final report mentioned nothing derogatory about the units visited or the men interviewed.[29]

On 2 January 1943 the team returned to Algiers, where Devers conferred with Eisenhower for two days. He could not have come at a worse time for Ike, who was seriously ill. According to his aide, navy captain Harry Butcher, Eisenhower had come down with the flu on 30 December but was unable to stay in bed because of his duties. The strain of the first six weeks of the North African campaign had taken a toll. In addition to dealing with the various French factions in Algeria, Eisenhower was under pressure from Roosevelt, Churchill, and Marshall to get the drive to Tunis going again.

Devers spent the evening of 3 January talking with Eisenhower. The next day Butcher wrote in his diary, "The succession of political difficulties [with the French], the setbacks in Tunis, the bombing of Bone, where the cruiser *Ajax* took a dive bomb down her funnel and got her guts strewn around sufficiently to require four or five months for repair, the loss of four supply ships in one day, the apparent ability of German air to hit us effectively and our air's apparent inability to hit commensurately hard with its proportionately larger forces—all these, plus the repetition of monotony of office to house and vice versa, contributed to Ike's foul frame of mind last evening."[30] Three days later Butcher noted, "After a solid month of colds, sniffles, and general below-par physical condition, Ike laid up in bed until lunch, then got up and sat by the fire. . . . He feels punk and looks the same."[31]

One can picture the enthusiastic and cheerful Devers telling Eisenhower about all he had seen, including the comments about poor discipline and morale in some air force units. Devers probably discussed his views about the inadequacy of American antitank guns and poor tactical doctrine for the employment of tanks. Brigadier General Williston Palmer, who accompanied Devers on the trip, later told Eugene Harrison, "Devers was rather critical of the way they were handling the 1st Armored Division there," especially the way the division was scattered across the front rather than concentrated for effective action.[32] Harrison, who worked for Devers throughout the Second World War, concluded that "this criticism might have turned General Eisenhower against General Devers."[33]

It seems reasonable to conclude that Eisenhower took Devers's observations as criticism, especially given his belief that Marshall might have sent Devers to eventually replace him. Devers was not sensitive to how his "honest" comments were received by the harried Allied commander, nor could he know how Eisenhower viewed his mission in the first place. He certainly was not obsequious toward Ike. Eisenhower was convinced that the final report of the Devers team would be critical of himself. In reality, the report contained nothing derogatory about the Allied supreme commander.[34]

After visiting Eisenhower, Devers moved on to Oran, where he and the team met with Brigadier General Thomas Larkin. Larkin was the commanding general of the Mediterranean Base Section, the logistics organization that supported American forces in North Africa. In February 1943 Larkin would organize and command the Services of Supply for the North African theater of operations. He and Devers hit it off immediately, and Larkin would eventually command the southern lines of communications in France under Devers in 1944.[35]

The Armored Force team also visited Major General Orlando Ward and a number of 1st Armored Division leaders at a desert bivouac twenty miles outside of Oran. Ward was frustrated that his division had been deployed to the front piecemeal, instead of as a concentrated unit. He blamed Anderson, commander of the British First Army, for the misuse of his troops, although the real problem was that there were insufficient truck units in the theater to move and supply additional forces in Tunisia. The 1st Armored Division's situation was similar to that of Major General Terry Allen's 1st Infantry Division, whose units had been spread throughout Tunisia on a 300-mile front. Only after battalions from both these divisions suffered some serious setbacks were the two division headquarters sent to southern Tunisia to command the troops.[36]

Leaders of the 1st Armored Division who had been involved in the November assault on Oran told the Devers team that antiaircraft and antitank protection had to be fully integrated in the tactical units. This was a common recommendation by American troops that had felt the full force of the Luftwaffe and the German armored units in battle.[37] The way American antitank and antiaircraft units were trained and assigned to army divisions had been one of Devers's concerns during the 1941 maneuvers. Now more than ever, Devers believed that the separate antitank, antiaircraft, and tank battalions should be permanently assigned to infantry divisions. This would facilitate their combined-arms training and strengthen the cohesion of the combat team. General McNair, however, continued to believe that the army should have a pool of tank, antitank, and antiaircraft battalions that could be attached to infantry divisions based on the tactical mission at hand. Devers was right, as time would tell.

Major General Orlando Ward and Devers had established a close working relationship while the 1st Armored Division was training in Britain in

1942. In a September letter, Devers acknowledged receiving three letters from "Pinkie" Ward expressing concerns about equipment. Devers replied, "The matters which you have spoken about in your letters . . . insofar as equipment is concerned, have been taken care of. We are standardizing equipment, reducing types, and securing better and bigger guns. . . . The modern equipment which is now coming off the line is first class. It has been worked out with the British to meet all the sound criticisms. Our big problem is now to get fully equipped and then properly trained."[38]

Unfortunately, Ward's armor battalions were still equipped with M3 Grant tanks, and they performed poorly in the December battles. In November, just before the Torch invasion, Ward wrote to Devers, "I have two battalions of the new tanks and am very much pleased with them. . . . Your training material is A-1. We have gotten a lot of model terrains and small model tanks which might be a good thing to put into universal use in the Armored Force."[39] The provision of training materials was an important function of the Armored Force.

In another letter written in December, three weeks before Devers visited North Africa, Ward gave him direct feedback from "some of the men who participated in the battle of Oran." They found "that dust accumulated on the external lens of the main gun sight in the M3 light tank so badly that it precluded aiming the gun after a short time. They removed the sight and aimed at close range through the aperture. One man developed a method of taking a handkerchief and putting it through the aperture thereby covering the sight from the dust, then removing it just before firing and replacing it immediately thereafter." Ward concluded by noting, "The possibility of having a rubber tube which will blow the dust off or some other means of clearing the sight is indicated. I think you should know this as it is good battlefield experience."[40]

This exchange of letters is a good example of how the Armored Force not only organized and trained armored units but also provided training materials for use in the field and solicited feedback on equipment. They show that Devers was personally involved in the whole process of his command. Devers's trip to North Africa was just one way the U.S. Army worked to improve the equipment and training of its forces in World War II.

The team's last stop was Casablanca, where they interviewed Major General Patton, his staff, and leaders of the 2nd Armored, 3rd Infantry, and 9th Infantry Divisions. The report reflected very favorably on Patton and his subordinate commanders:

Visited rear elements of the 2nd Armored Division . . . and por-
tions of the 9th Infantry Division, also bivouacked in the vicinity of
Casablanca. The appearance of the camps and apparent discipline
of the soldiers, particularly with regard to saluting was outstanding
in comparison with other units visited. In the afternoon proceeded
by plane to Rabat, 60 miles distant, and visited the bivouac of the
3rd Infantry Division and 2nd Armored Division; both of which
were encamped in cork forests. The appearance of the camps and
the individual soldiers of these units continued on the same high
standard as previously witnessed in the area around Casablanca. . . .
It was the consensus of the party that of all commands visited, General Patton's was the finest.[41]

Devers spent the evening with Patton, discussing the North African campaign and Devers's observations. Patton quickly tired of Devers's propensity to offer advice and opinions about tactical matters and noted in his
diary, "Jake, who has at last heard a gun go off in anger, talked in a big way
till [late]. . . . He has now become a great strategical expert, but he believes
everything he is told [by the British] until someone tells him different."[42]
A few days later Patton wrote to his wife Beatrice about his impressions of
Devers:

Jake has been with both the First and Eighth British Armies and is
much impressed with them. It amuses me how our country boys
fall for tea and titles. . . . Jake is now—in his own opinion—a master of strategy. He orated until 0100 the night he was here. I often
wonder what people who have seen war the easy way and for the
first time think of us few professionals—they must believe we are
fools not to have learned all they think they know. However, he was
much impressed with the discipline and order he saw here and compared it most favorably to conditions elsewhere which are bad—in
my opinion very bad.[43]

Patton and Devers had gotten along well when they were peers at Fort
Myer in the mid-1930s. Although Patton was clearly disappointed that
Devers had been promoted to general officer and been given command
of a division before him, he regularly ingratiated himself to his boss in the
Armored Force and was more than willing to let Devers recommend him

for promotion to command a corps in 1942. All of Patton's comments about Devers, Eisenhower, and Bradley during the war in Europe need to be taken with a grain of salt, but his observations that Devers had never heard a shot fired in anger nor commanded a unit in combat were correct. It was irritating to Patton, and probably to Eisenhower as well, that they had to listen to the views of a man they considered a rear-area soldier. And Devers was not as attuned as he might have been to the way his observations and ideas came across to busy commanders in a combat zone.

In contrast to Patton's observations in his diary and in his letter to Beatrice, he wrote the following to Devers in August 1942: "Should you be in Washington, I would like very much to see you . . . first, because you are one of my dearest friends; second, because I think you would be interested in hearing orally what I cannot put on paper; and third, because I would like to have the opportunity of personally thanking you for all the good turns you have done for me during the thirty odd years of our service together."[44] He wrote to Devers in October, "I want to thank you from the bottom of my heart for the many good turns and magnificent backing you have given me during my entire career, and particularly since I have been serving under you. With affectionate regards to Georgie, I am your devoted friend and admirer."[45]

On to Britain

On 7 January 1943 the members of the Armored Force team began their journey to England, where they planned to visit the American forces in training. They stopped at Gibraltar to refuel but, due to bad weather, were forced to stay for seven days. When the weather cleared on 14 January, they headed north. The pilot of the bomber they were flying in followed a course well out over the ocean to avoid German aircraft; however, due to the thick cloud cover, he and his navigator missed several critical navigational points and got lost. The next morning, as they were running low on fuel, the pilot sighted land and decided to set down in a farm field. "The size of the field was such that after hitting the ground, the plane crashed through a stone wall at approximately 70 miles per hour. Although the plane was wrecked, the members of the party were uninjured. The plane was immediately surrounded by Irish civilians and members of the Home Guard. The local inhabitants were very friendly, offered food and any medical assistance necessary."[46]

The plane had crash-landed in the Irish Republic. Because Ireland was neutral, international law required that the American soldiers be arrested and placed in an internment camp for the duration of the war. Fortunately, a captain from the Irish regular army arrived, "took charge of the situation," and transported the Americans to a hotel in the nearby town of Athenry, where Devers was able to call the U.S. embassy in Dublin. Whatever he said to the embassy, the result was that, "at approximately 8:30 p.m. that night, the entire party departed by car to the border of North Ireland, crossing the border near Sligo at 2:00 a.m."[47]

After a brief halt at the base of the 8th Composite Group in Ulster, Devers and his officers traveled by boat and train to Haysham, England, arriving on 17 January. They reached London that afternoon and experienced their first German air raid that same evening. "A tremendous anti-aircraft barrage was put up and out of 20 planes in the first German wave, 9 were shot down. The danger of anti-aircraft fire to local inhabitants was indicated by a number of casualties during this raid [caused by antiaircraft artillery shell fragments falling to earth]."[48]

The next morning Devers met with General Weeks, deputy chief of the Imperial General Staff, to discuss the needs of the British and American armored forces in North Africa. In the afternoon, after inspecting the damage from the air raid, Devers and his team were briefed about Bolero-Roundup, the plan for the buildup of Allied forces in Britain and the cross-Channel invasion, originally scheduled for the fall of 1942. The plan was based on the assumption by Marshall and his planners that "we must actually prepare to fight Germany by actually coming to grips with and defeating her ground forces and definitely breaking her will to combat. . . . They assumed that the way would have to be paved by achieving overwhelming air superiority in Europe."[49] Thus, a concentration of heavy bomber units in England for an Anglo-American combined bomber offensive against Germany was an essential part of the plan. For the Americans, this meant that more than 100 airfields had to be built in England for the Eighth Air Force before a sustainable air campaign could be maintained against the enemy's heavily defended heartland.[50] As noted earlier, Bolero-Roundup had been postponed after the British suffered a number of defeats in North Africa, and American ground forces had been diverted to Operation Torch. Thus, by January 1943, the Allies were busy trying to conquer Tunisia, and the timetable for the buildup of air and ground forces in Britain was in shambles.[51]

While Devers was visiting Britain, Roosevelt, Churchill, and the Combined Chiefs of Staff were meeting in Casablanca to determine the war's strategic direction after completion of the North African campaign. The British, represented by General Alan Brooke, chief of the Imperial General Staff, took the position that a cross-Channel invasion of northern France could not be launched until German U-boat forces in the Atlantic were defeated and the German army and air force were sufficiently weakened to at least give the invading force parity. Since the German army and air force remained strong in the Mediterranean theater and on the Russian front, the British were convinced that a successful invasion of France could not be carried out in 1943. Thus, they recommended that the forces deployed in the Mediterranean operate against the Axis powers' most vulnerable member, Italy, while the buildup of bomber forces in Britain continued.[52]

Marshall and the other American chiefs of staff argued that the campaign in the Mediterranean should be scaled back dramatically once North Africa was cleared and that those forces should be moved to Britain for a 1943 Bolero. After days of argument, Roosevelt accepted the British position. The forces in the Mediterranean would operate against Italy, invading Sicily and possibly the Italian mainland after expelling the enemy from Tunisia. General Eisenhower was officially designated the supreme Allied commander for these operations, with British general Harold Alexander acting as his deputy commander in chief and commanding the Allied ground forces operating in Tunisia. In exchange, the British accepted the possibility of a 1943 cross-Channel operation if the Germans suddenly collapsed, as well as the creation of a combined command and planning staff to plan the invasion of France in 1944.[53]

The Anglo-American Allies agreed that an essential part of their global strategy was the combined bomber offensive against Germany to destroy the enemy's ability to sustain the war effort. The American Eighth Air Force and the British RAF Bomber Command were to conduct around-the-clock bombing against the German industrial base and transportation system, with the Americans attacking in daylight and the RAF striking at night. In January 1943, however, the Eighth Air Force was incapable of carrying out a sustained air offensive against the strong German air defenses. A delay in the cross-Channel invasion gave General Henry "Hap" Arnold, chief of the Army Air Forces, time to build the infrastructure needed to support thousands of heavy bombers (B-17s and B-24s) and get the bombers and aircrews over to Britain.[54] All these events and decisions were very important to Devers, although he did not know it at the time. His visit to England in January introduced him to the problems he would be asked to solve beginning in May.

Meanwhile, Devers and his team visited the 29th Infantry Division in Tidworth. The division commander, Major General Leonard Gerow, had instituted a vigorous training program that included athletics to keep the men fit and entertained while they waited for the invasion of France. The team's report noted that "one of the greatest defects of the 29th Division has been its replacements. It appeared that it had been assigned a number of men available for limited service only, and these men could not keep [up] with [a] rigorous training schedule . . . [and] many replacements had long guardhouse records." In contrast, it reported that "the discipline of the division appeared to be excellent and General Gerow has done a credible job."[55] This report confirmed Marshall's high regard for Gerow, who would be the commander of V Corps on D-day. The 29th Infantry Division would be the second division ashore on Omaha Beach.

Some of what the team saw was not so impressive. During a demonstration of antitank training, the guns' sights were 400 yards off target, and during an air-ground fire exercise, the ground team could not communicate by radio with the airplanes. A great deal needed to be done if American ground forces in Britain were to be successful against the German army in France.

Given the importance of the combined bomber offensive to Allied strategy, Devers's impressions of the Army Air Forces units in England were depressing. Team members remarked that since they had traveled mainly by air, they had extensive experience with air force personnel, materiel, and operations on three continents. They offered the following observations and conclusions, which they thought might be of assistance to the chief of the Army Air Forces:

There is a noticeable lack of fundamental discipline in Air Force personnel, principally among junior officers and enlisted men. It is felt that correction of this will only increase the effectiveness of combat missions. . . . The following points may be of interest:
1. A casual attitude towards important matters indicates a lack of a sense of responsibility. This is evidenced by a habitual failure to observe punctuality as to time of departure, or careful checking of equipment, such as maps, required for a particular flight.
2. Lack of leadership on the part of officers, particularly with respect

to the discipline of enlisted crews. This is evidenced by dirty airplanes, failure to stow equipment efficiently, filthy personal appearance, failure to observe fire precaution regulations, and lack of training in military courtesy among enlisted men. Also noticeable was the failure of the commanding officer of a plane to exercise supervision over the crew in matters which pertain to the plane in general.

3. Utilization of personnel on flying missions whose technical proficiency is not adequate to meet a particular requirement. This applies particularly to navigators and radio operators and invariably results in unnecessary loss of lives and airplanes.

4. The failure to establish a command arrangement whereby authorized members of the Air Transport Command, for instance, can institute corrective measures where obviously necessary in tactical units which utilize their facilities and vice versa.[56]

The "Air Force Annex" was the most negative part of the report sent to Generals McNair and Marshall. It is likely that Major General Carl "Tooey" Spaatz, commander of the Twelfth Air Force in North Africa, heard from Marshall and Arnold about the shortcomings in his command. He certainly did not appreciate the negative attention, and he quite likely talked to his close friend Eisenhower about it. They had worked together in England in 1942, when Spaatz had been commander of the Eighth Air Force. When Ike got the call to command in North Africa, he took Spaatz with him. When he became the supreme Allied commander, he nominated Spaatz to command the Allied Northwest Africa Air Force. This part of the report may have added to Eisenhower's dislike of Devers.

On 26 January the Armored Force team began its journey home via Scotland, Marrakech, Dakar, Georgetown, and Trinidad.[57] After leaving Marrakech, they were forced to turn back for repairs when one of the engines on their plane failed. But they completed the trip without further incident, arriving in Washington on 28 January.

Results of the Armored Force Team's Report

Some of the conclusions of the Devers team were hardly earth-shattering. For instance: "The present war is definitely one of guns. The attack is built around air, tanks, and artillery. Defense is built around air, concealed anti-tank guns, and artillery. . . . Hostile aircraft must be rendered ineffective."

Other conclusions were more controversial. For example, the report noted: "To achieve success all combat units must be able to repel tanks and low flying aircraft with their own weapons. They must have 75mm antitank guns and .50 caliber antiaircraft weapons organically assigned. . . . A higher standard of discipline of American troops must be attained."[58]

Several of Devers's conclusions irritated his boss, mentor, and Army Ground Forces commander Lesley McNair. For example, Devers stated, "The separate tank destroyer arm is not a practical concept on the battlefield. Defensive antitank weapons are essentially artillery. Offensively the weapon to beat a tank is a better tank. Sooner or later the issue between ground forces is settled in an armored battle—tank against tank. The concept of tank destroyer groups and brigades attempting to overcome equal numbers of hostile tanks is faulty unless the tank destroyers are actually better tanks than those of the enemy."[59] These observations contradicted McNair's belief that tank destroyer units alone could defeat enemy armored attacks.

The report recommended that each infantry battalion be assigned eight self-propelled 75mm antitank guns and that all battalions include four antiaircraft vehicles, each with four mounted fifty-caliber machine guns. It also proposed that all tank destroyer battalions be renamed antitank artillery battalions and that the Tank Destroyer Center at Fort Hood should train the soldiers and units equipped with 75mm antitank guns.[60] These recommendations reopened a debate about the employment of antitank and antiaircraft battalions that Devers and McNair had carried out in late 1941. Devers was convinced that antitank and antiaircraft battalions should be organically assigned to each infantry division and that each armored division should have a tank destroyer and an antiaircraft battalion permanently assigned as well.[61] McNair received a copy of Devers's report from the army staff, and one of his staff officers wrote on an attached note, "Looks as if we have a fight on our hands!"[62]

There was also considerable debate within McNair's AGF headquarters about whether to deploy antitank (also known as tank destroyer) and antiaircraft units as permanent parts of divisions. McNair's G-3, Brigadier General John M. Lentz, told his boss, "I have come to believe that TD [tank destroyer] and AA [antiaircraft] equipment should be organic in the divisions. The concept of attachment is sounder, but its effect has been absence of combined training."[63] Devers had seen the effects of weak combined-arms training in North Africa, and most of the American commanders in the European and Mediterranean theaters agreed with Devers that anti-tank and antiaircraft battalions should be organic elements of infantry and armored divisions. "General McNair would have none of it, declining to add to 'the monstrous array of transportation already encumbering' the armored division."[64]

Marshall responded to Devers's report after he returned from the Casablanca conference, although it is not clear exactly when he received it. After meeting with Stimson, Marshall sent a memorandum to McNair and informed him, "The Secretary of War is deeply concerned regarding the anti-aircraft gun complement of divisions under present organization. He was much impressed by Devers report on this subject. . . . He will undoubtedly wish to discuss with you the question of the anti-aircraft complement in divisions. . . . Please be prepared for this call and for the discussions."[65]

McNair responded to Secretary Stimson's query by pointing out that "Devers raises the issue of the number and organic set-up of (1) AA guns (2) AT guns. Equally logically and pertinently he might have raised similar questions with reference to (1) GHQ tank battalions, (2) Air Base defense units, (3) Command post and train defense units. All these items involve the basic question of whether we are building an offensive or defensive army—whether we are going to invest our military substance in security to the last detail or in elements which can be used to defeat the enemy's armed force." McNair concluded by telling Stimson, "Our limited manpower and production facilities can be utilized to better advantage by deploying such units in mobile masses which can be concentrated at the decisive point under the principle of the economy of force. Devers and his group are obviously dispersionists [sic] of the first water."[66] Marshall and Stimson supported McNair's point of view.

McNair remained convinced that he was right and that tank, antiaircraft, and tank destroyer battalions should not become organic parts of divisions. He made this clear to Major General A. D. Bruce, commanding general of the Tank Destroyer Center at Fort Hood:

I imagine that you have heard or will hear of General Devers' report. . . . Here is a copy of his conclusions and recommendations. I am writing in the possibility that this report may start rumors of an upheaval in our tank destroyer organization. I was called today by the Secretary of War. . . . When I reported to the Secretary, he said he did not have the Devers report on his mind, being content to leave such complicated and controversial questions to the Staff. . . . However, the matter of tank destroyers came up incidentally, and I remarked that Devers seemed not to care much about tank destroyers. The Secretary bounced back that he was one of the original backers of the tank destroyers, and that he would have Devers in for a talk on the question. . . . I feel confident that the track we are on at present—in both tank destroyers and antiaircraft—is sound and is not in jeopardy.[67]

McNair reacted in a constructive manner to Devers's observations about poor discipline in the army units in North Africa. In a response to Marshall's comments about the need for better discipline, McNair told the chief of staff, "I have taken the liberty of transmitting your comments to the several high commanders of the Ground Forces. . . . Of course, much emphasis already has been placed on discipline and leadership, but your observations mean that there must be still greater pressure in this direction, and steps to that end have been taken." McNair added that "the superiority of divisional units is understandable in view of the more extensive and immediate supervision" received by smaller units in a division commanded by a major general. His response to the need for better supervision of independent battalions was to create group headquarters to supervise three or more independent tank, tank destroyer, or antiaircraft battalions.[68]

McNair also made an interesting observation to Marshall about the nature of the young officers available to lead the ground forces in the Second World War:

While nothing can excuse a lack of discipline, I do feel it is becoming harder this war than the last one—perhaps for two reasons: a. Our experienced officers are spread very thin indeed. A division this year is entitled to a quota of Regular officers of little more than 20. We have headquarters all over the world, and I allege that most of them are grossly over-staffed; b. The quality of our manpower declined visibly toward the end of 1942. In 1917 our officers were largely college men. This time, the college graduates in candidate schools run from 15 to 20%. The Air Forces have made tremendous inroads on the leadership of the Ground Forces—unavoidably, but nevertheless with telling effect.[69]

In the end, McNair noted, "While I hardly expect to send perfect units overseas, I do feel confident that the present quality can be improved greatly."[70]

The War Department sent copies of the Devers report to the commanding generals of the Army Ground Forces, the Army Service Forces, and the Army Air Forces. Their responses to the specific deficiencies noted were collated in a short report by the army G-4 and sent to General Marshall on 9 April 1943. McNair reported that "all facts presented in the Report are known to his headquarters." Arnold replied that "corrective action has been taken on all Air Force items. Regular officers in the grades of Colonel and Lieutenant Colonel have recently been placed in command of Air Transport Command bases for the specific purpose of correcting the reported deficiencies in discipline, military courtesy, training, and maintenance." Somervell responded that his command "has taken appropriate action on the applicable recommendations," with the exception of those related to assigning self-propelled 75mm antitank guns and 37mm antitank guns to various units.[71]

Many of the recommendations of the Armored Force report were ignored in 1943. Infantry divisions continued to be assigned separate tank and tank destroyer battalions only on a temporary, "mission-needs" basis. As a consequence, American infantry and armor units did not habitually train together, and when they went into combat for the first time, they were often unable to execute combined-arms tactics effectively. This was demonstrated repeatedly in Normandy in the summer of 1944. Eventually, field commanders established relationships between the infantry divisions and the separate tank and tank destroyer battalions attached to them, greatly facilitating combined-arms training. McNair won the bureaucratic battle, but combat experience proved that Devers was right about training for the proper use of tank-infantry teams.

Reorganization of the Armored Divisions

McNair had been concerned about the "costs" of armored divisions since their inception in 1940. They required significantly more support troops and equipment than infantry divisions, and the initial organization developed by General Chaffee and Armored Force headquarters was very cumbersome. When Devers assumed command of the Armored Force in 1941, he worked with McNair and Army Ground Forces headquarters to improve the organizational design of the armored divisions, even as they were being created.

When army leaders organized the first two armored divisions in 1940, they followed a German panzer division model with a high ratio of tanks to infantry. Three tank regiments of three battalions each and one infantry regiment with three battalions were assigned to each of the new divisions. Two of the three tank regiments were equipped with light tanks, reflecting the cavalry's influence among the first leaders of the Armored Force. The organization had a division headquarters, an armored brigade headquarters, and three regimental headquarters to oversee the seventeen battalions of all types in the division. The armored brigade, with nearly 400 tanks, was the division's main offensive striking power.[72]

During the training maneuvers of 1941, the armored divisions proved to be difficult to maneuver and command, and they occupied too much road space when marching. Christopher Gabel, historian of the 1941 maneuvers, noted, "In Louisiana, the armored division had operated as if it were a collection of single-arm regiments rather than a combined-arms team. With the exception of the division commander himself, there existed no command link joining the armored brigade with the infantry regiment or the reconnaissance battalion."[73] Devers observed these maneuvers and set in motion a redesign of the cumbersome armored division. McNair, never an advocate of the armored division concept, supported this effort by stating, "In the matter of size, cost and complication, as compared with the number of tanks which can be used against the enemy, the armored division presents an amazing picture of extravagance."[74]

Devers approved a new organization for armored divisions in March 1942. The number of armored regiments was reduced to two, and the percentage of medium tanks was increased. The armored brigade headquarters and the headquarters of the armored and infantry regiments were eliminated, removing unnecessary and cumbersome levels of command. In addition, the number of soldiers in the division was reduced by more than 2,000, to 14,620. Three combat command headquarters replaced the two levels of command that were removed, and the tank and infantry battalions worked together on a mission-needs basis under these combat commands. Of the 3,630 vehicles in the division, 390 were light and medium tanks. The division artillery component was increased to three battalions each, with eighteen self-propelled 105mm howitzers.[75] This was the structure used by the 1st and 2nd Armored Divisions in North Africa and Sicily in 1942–1943.

As the fighting progressed in the Mediterranean theater in 1943, it became clear to Devers and McNair that the armored division was still too big and cumbersome. Between January and August, numerous conferences were held to discuss the best way to organize the armored divisions. Devers helped set that process in motion, but he did not see it through to the end because he was reassigned to command the European theater of operations in May. McNair and Devers's successor, Major General Alvan C. Gillem Jr., agreed on another reorganization that cut the number of tank battalions from six to three and reduced the strength of the division to 10,937 soldiers. The 1943 armored division consisted of three infantry, three tank, and three artillery battalions that could be task-organized into three combat commands as the mission required. The 2nd and 3rd Armored Divisions retained the 1942 structure, since it was deemed too difficult to reorganize them in England. Another factor in this decision may have been that these divisions were in Devers's theater of operations in the fall of 1943.

Following his trip to Africa and the United Kingdom, Devers continued his work of organizing and training armored units. Using the 8th Armored Division at Fort Knox as a training base, the last of the sixteen armored divisions of World War II were established, and efforts to improve equipment continued. One of Devers's critical tasks was to recommend officers to command the new armored divisions. For example, he recommended Ernie Harmon to command the 2nd Armored Division, "P" Wood to command the 4th, Jack Heard to lead the 5th, Bill Surles to command the 6th, and John Leonard to lead the 9th.[76] Devers, like McNair, was an important extension of Marshall's famous "black book," especially for artillery and engineer officers.

Devers's ability to cut through red tape is perhaps best documented by his role in the fielding of an amphibious 2.5-ton truck known as the DUKW (pronounced "Duck"). The DUKW became a logistical workhorse beginning with Operation Husky, the amphibious invasion of Sicily in July 1943. DUKWs carried artillery and supplies from the transports to the beaches at Licata, Gela, and Scoglitti. Without these supplies, the forces that went ashore could not have repulsed Axis counterattacks or moved inland as quickly as they did.[77] The DUKW also played a crucial role in the amphibious operations in Italy (Salerno and Anzio) and later in Operation Overlord.

General Eisenhower was so pleased with the work of the DUKWs during the Sicilian campaign in July 1943 that he wrote to Marshall: "Amphibious truck . . . commonly called DUKW, has been invaluable. . . . We would be delighted to get more of them." Marshall subsequently investigated the origins of the DUKW and found that the Office of Scientific Research and Development was "in large measure responsible for the development of this truck." When he wrote to congratulate the head of that organization, Dr. Vannevar Bush, Bush replied: "You mention three men who may have had a large part in the matter, and this gives me the opportunity to pay tribute to two men in particular. The first of these is General Devers himself. In the very early stages of this matter he was the only man in the Army who fully saw the possibilities and his encouragement was much needed."[78]

In a note to Devers, Marshall expressed his thanks "for the part you played in the development of this vehicle." By the time he sent this letter, Devers had already assumed command of the European theater of operations, with headquarters in London.

Marshall's Next Call

"Suddenly, in early May 1943, again the telephone rang—General Marshall on the phone, 'Anybody listening?' I replied: 'If they were, they aren't now.'" The chief of staff told Devers that he was sending his personal plane to Fort Knox to pick him up and fly him to Washington. "You report in here tomorrow morning," Marshall instructed. "I'm going to send you to England to replace Andrews who, as you know, was killed by flying into a mountain in Iceland. Keep this quiet until announcement is made."[79]

Devers left the Armored Force in good shape, with smoothly functioning training and administrative systems in place. McNair certainly thought Devers had done a superb job, ranking him one of the "first five of seventeen lieutenant generals" in the army and describing him as "a magnetic, vigorous, and forceful leader of the highest caliber."[80]

9

European Theater Commander

Jacob Devers's chance to serve overseas in a combat zone came unexpectedly in May 1943. At that time he was deeply engaged in the affairs of the Armored Force and did not anticipate a new assignment. But as so often happens, unforeseen events reshape the best-laid plans. In this case, the death of Lieutenant General Frank M. Andrews in an airplane crash in Iceland left the U.S. Army's European theater of operations (ETO) without a commander. Andrews's death was a great loss. As General Harold "Hap" Arnold, commanding general of the Army Air Forces, noted, "All Air Corps officers saw in him the leader among air force generals who might become one of the outstanding combat commanders in the war."[1]

Marshall's unexpected call also dramatically changed Georgie's life—a situation faced by tens of thousands of spouses when their soldiers were sent overseas during World War II. In a letter to Kitts, Georgie showed both her disorientation and her spunk: "Jamie had a phone call Wed—about 2:30—and thought he would leave here on Saturday—or maybe even Monday—but a plane was sent down for him on Thursday and he was off at 10 AM. I packed up all his clothes—summer and winter—and made lists of things to do—how to move etc—all night. And I am afraid I have not had much sleep since. There is so much to do—that I have never had to do alone before: However—everyone helps—it is on decisions I have to make alone."[2]

Marshall selected Devers to replace Andrews as commander of the ETO on 3 May. Devers reported to Washington on 6 May and boarded a flight for England on 8 May. Accompanying him were Colonel Tristram Tupper, his public relations officer in the Armored Force, and his personal aides Lieutenant Colonel Earle Hormell and Major Edward Shumaker.[3] This assignment to command American forces in the United Kingdom placed Devers center stage in the war against Germany.

Early History of the European Theater of Operations

The ETO was at the heart of Marshall's plan to get the cross-Channel invasion of Europe under way. As early as January 1942, Marshall hoped to build up massive air and ground forces in the United Kingdom in an operation code-named Bolero. The air forces would soften up Hitler's "Fortress Europe" with a bomber offensive conducted by the U.S. Eighth Air Force and the British Bomber Command. The goals of this combined bomber offensive were to defeat the German air force and sap German morale and economic capability through the bombardment of German cities and industries. Once the German military had been severely weakened by the air campaign, the invasion of France, code-named Roundup, could be launched. Marshall hoped to carry out Roundup in early 1943.[4]

An organization known as the U.S. Armed Forces, British Isles (USAFBI), was created in January 1942 to receive, house, and train the American ground, service, and air forces needed for these operations. Major General James E. Chaney, an air corps officer, initially commanded USAFBI, which had three major components: an air component of heavy bombers for the bomber offensive, a Services of Supply organization to sustain American forces in the United Kingdom, and a ground forces component to train units for the invasion of France.[5]

In April 1942 General Marshall and a small planning staff visited the United Kingdom to meet with the British chiefs of staff and Prime Minister Winston Churchill. After eight days of discussions and negotiations, Marshall believed the British had agreed to the Bolero and Roundup operations, with a planning date of 1943 for the cross-Channel invasion.[6] Based on this understanding, Marshall and the War Department made Bolero their top priority for resources. Eighth Air Force headquarters was alerted to prepare for a move to the United Kingdom, and Somervell's Services of Supply began to organize a sustainment command for deployment as well.

Eighth Air Force elements had already begun to arrive in the United Kingdom in February 1942, led by Brigadier General Ira Eaker, commander of VIII Bomber Command. Major General Carl Spaatz arrived in May to take command of the Eighth Air Force. The first B-17 bombers arrived in England in July, having been flown via a ferry route from Maine through Labrador, Greenland, Iceland, and Scotland. Although Marshall hoped the American aircraft could soon play an active role in the bombing of Germany, it would be months before VIII Bomber Command had enough heavy bombers and crews to fly missions over German-controlled territory. The first U.S. bombing mission in Europe was launched against the French rail junction of Rouen-Sotteville on 17 August 1942.[7]

The first major ground combat units arrived in Northern Ireland in May and were put under the command of V Corps. The 34th Infantry and 1st Armored Divisions would train for the invasion and help defend the United Kingdom if necessary. Their arrival freed British divisions for deployment to Egypt, where the British were in a deadly struggle with the German Afrika Korps.[8]

The Services of Supply (SOS) for the American forces in Britain was established on 14 May under the command of Major General John C. H. Lee. Lee, a classmate of Devers, had served as chief of staff of the 89th Division in World War I and commanded an infantry division in 1942. Lee was difficult to work for or with, but he commanded the ETO's logistics system for the remainder of the war.

Major General Chaney was not consulted by the War Department concerning the structure of either the Eighth Air Force or the SOS. Instead, Spaatz and Lee, respectively, organized their staffs in Washington in March and April and then deployed them to England. Chaney repeatedly argued with Marshall, Arnold, and Somervell about the structure of these organizations, and they came to believe that Chaney was "poorly oriented on the entire concept under which the War Department had recently reorganized itself."[9]

Chaney clearly irritated Marshall, who concluded during his trip to England in April 1942 that Chaney had failed to demonstrate the aggressive leadership and energy needed to organize and command the expanding USAFBI (soon renamed the ETO). In late May, Marshall sent Eisenhower to England to assess Chaney's command. Arnold, commander of the Army Air Forces, also made the trip to London and concluded that the United States needed a theater commander "who could meet the British senior officers on even terms." He and Eisenhower agreed that the theater commander "must be a man who had the experience and knowledge of our ways of doing things, and was fully acquainted with our War Department plans."[10] Eisenhower reported back to Marshall that Chaney's organization was a "muddle" and that Bolero was not progressing as it should. Marshall agreed with this assessment and selected Eisenhower to replace Chaney in London.[11]

Eisenhower arrived in London in late June to assume command of the ETO. He operated under a directive that gave him the "tactical, strategical, territorial, and administrative duties of a theater commander." All his forces were to cooperate with the British, but American forces would "be maintained as a distinct and separate component of the combined forces."

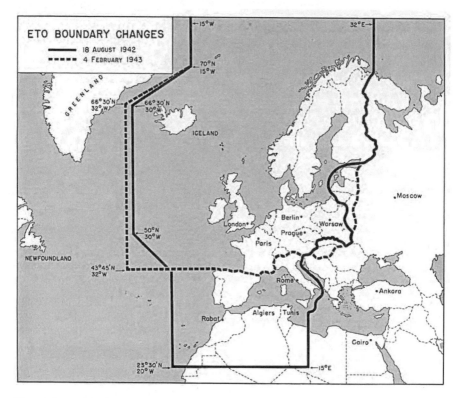

Figure 9.1. ETO boundary changes

He also had authority over all administrative and logistical matters and was instructed "to prepare for and carry-on military operations in the European Theater against the Axis Powers and their allies under the strategical direction of the combined U.S.-British Chiefs of Staff."[12]

Eisenhower had been in command for less than two months when President Roosevelt ordered the U.S. military to plan for and execute an invasion of North Africa (code-named Torch) to help the British drive the Axis forces out of Africa and secure sea-lanes through the Mediterranean. The American chiefs of staff fought hard against this decision because it meant there would be no cross-Channel invasion in 1942 and probably not in 1943 either. After weeks of transatlantic discussions and visits by the American and British chiefs of staff, Roosevelt "stated very definitely that he as Commander in Chief had made the decision that TORCH would be undertaken at the earliest possible date."[13] General Arnold later wrote, "My own top priority was knocked on the head. Our plan for the rapid buildup of an American heavy bomber force in Britain, striking at Germany itself with a thousand Flying Fortresses and Liberators by April, must wait."[14]

Torch's Impact on Bolero

By the time Eisenhower reached London to command the ETO and the buildup for Bolero, the War Department had developed a plan to move more than 1 million American airmen and soldiers to the United Kingdom. The logisticians had determined that the infrastructure required would include 98 airfields for more than 5,000 aircraft, storage for 245,000 tons of ammunition, hospitals with 90,000 beds, and thousands of new troop billets. By the end of July 1942, 81,273 American troops were in the United Kingdom, and VIII Bomber Command was training heavy bomber groups for the air offensive against the Luftwaffe. The buildup of ground forces included the arrival of the 1st Infantry and 82nd Airborne Divisions.[15]

Just as Bolero was getting under way, the strategic direction of the war changed when Roosevelt and Churchill decided to have Anglo-American forces invade French North Africa. Eisenhower was selected to be the Allied commander for Torch, and Spaatz became chief of the Allied air forces for the operation. From July through October, Eisenhower's ETO scrambled to prepare forces for the assaults against Algeria. On 8 November American forces landed at Oran and Algiers in Algeria and at Casablanca in Morocco. After three days of fighting, the French accepted an armistice that was their first step toward rejoining the Western powers.

Eisenhower moved to Gibraltar just before Torch commenced, bringing most of his key staff from London with him. In January 1943 he also took over a new combined headquarters, known as Allied Force Headquarters (AFHQ), created by the Combined Chiefs of Staff to control Allied forces in northwestern Africa. This gave Eisenhower and Spaatz unhindered access to the ETO's air and ground resources for operations in Algeria and Tunisia.[16] As a result, efforts to execute Marshall's preferred Operation Bolero nearly came to a halt.

From November 1942 through February 1943, most of the air and ground forces that had arrived in the United Kingdom for Bolero were siphoned off for operations in North Africa. By February, more than 150,000 American ground troops had been sent from England to North Africa, and the 29th Infantry Division was the only American division remaining in the

United Kingdom. More than 570,000 tons of supplies originally meant for Bolero were shipped south, and the staffs of the ETO and the SOS in England were largely ignored by Eisenhower and his AFHQ staff.[17]

The Eighth Air Force was drastically reduced as the majority of its aircraft and personnel were transferred to North Africa. The official air force history summarized the situation as follows: "On 5 January 1943 . . . General Spaatz was placed in command of the newly created Allied Air Force in North Africa. In addition to his duties in that connection he held responsibility under Eisenhower for coordinating air operations between the Eighth Air Force and the Allied Air Force and for allocating, when necessary, replacement aircraft and crews among the Eighth Air Force, the Twelfth Air Force, and the Eastern Air Command. The arrangement was weighted heavily in favor of the North African campaign."[18]

In late January 1943, as the fortunes and resources of the ETO and Bolero reached a low point, Roosevelt and Churchill met with the Combined Chiefs of Staff (CCS) in Casablanca to develop a strategic blueprint for the rest of the year. On 21 January the CCS issued the "Casablanca Directive," calling for a powerful "combined bomber offensive" to be launched from the United Kingdom against the Nazi war machine. The priority targets, in order, were the German submarine program, aircraft industry, transportation system, oil facilities, and other war industries. On 5 February the CCS promoted Eisenhower to supreme commander of the Allied forces in the Mediterranean theater, with British general Harold Alexander as his deputy. At the same time, the War Department split the European theater from the North African theater and made Eisenhower the commander of the latter.[19]

Marshall picked Lieutenant General Frank M. Andrews to succeed Eisenhower as ETO commander in London. Andrews, the first air corps officer to serve on the army staff in Washington (as G-3), was a perfect choice, since the Casablanca agreement had "reaffirmed the plans [Bolero] on the basis of which a combined bomber offensive had originally been conceived." The agreement called for the "heaviest possible bomber offensive against the German war effort."[20] Andrews had been an early advocate of the B-17 heavy bomber. He believed, along with Arnold, that strategic attacks with heavy bombers against Germany would destroy the enemy's air force and industrial infrastructure and break the morale of the German people, forcing German leaders to sue for peace. A strong Eighth Air Force was essential to this strategy.

The ETO and the Eighth Air Force

When Marshall selected Andrews to command the ETO, Spaatz remained the Allied and U.S. air commander in the Mediterranean under Eisenhower. Consequently, Marshall and Arnold selected Major General Ira Eaker, then commander of VIII Bomber Command, to succeed Spaatz as commanding general of the Eighth Air Force. Eaker was charged with rebuilding the Eighth Air Force and executing the American portion of what officially became known in June 1943 as the combined bomber offensive. Before being assigned to VIII Bomber Command in January 1942, Eaker's background was in fighter aircraft. He was the pilot of the bomber named the *Question Mark* when he, Spaatz, and other crew members set a world aircraft endurance record in 1929.

Eaker was charged with conducting a daylight precision bombing campaign against enemy targets in northern Europe. He, Arnold, Spaatz, and most air force leaders believed that heavily armed bombers like the B-17 and B-24 could fly over France and Germany in large formations and defend themselves against German fighters without undue losses. Arnold also believed that large flights of heavy bombers would force the German air force to send its fighters up against the bombers, allowing the bombers to shoot down enough enemy fighters to defeat the Luftwaffe and achieve air superiority.[21] To do so without the support of long-range fighter escorts, the Eighth Air Force had to mass large numbers of bombers over the Continent.

Because of the heavy commitment of ground and air forces to the North African campaign, the buildup of American forces in the United Kingdom remained slow for three months after Andrews's and Eaker's appointments. Not until May did the Eighth Air Force begin to receive replacements for the 1,100 aircraft and 27,000 airmen it had sent to North Africa. Supplies, aircraft, and replacements from the United States were a "mere trickle" during the winter months.[22] Finally, the Allies defeated the Axis forces in Tunisia in May, and the drain on the Eighth Air Force ceased. Forces remained concentrated in the Mediterranean, however, as the Allies prepared for the invasion of Sicily.

During a long winter of discontent for Andrews and Eaker, "the Eighth Air Force continued to fight a battle of critical importance with too few bombers for economic operation. . . . It was not until March that a force of more than 100 bombers could be put into the air with some consistency."[23] The demands for Torch also diverted replacement aircrews and aircraft from the bomber groups that remained in England. By late February, "attrition was beginning to wear down the operating groups to an alarming extent. This was especially noticeable in combat crews where total effective strength suffered not only from actual combat losses but from war weariness."[24] Andrews, the perfect advocate for the Eighth Air Force, urged the War Department to accelerate the buildup of bomber forces in England. He and Eaker argued that it was "essential that the Eighth Air Force be increased at once to permit the simultaneous dispatch of at least 300 heavy bombers, an objective that would require an estimated 600 to be on hand in the theater."[25]

On 1 May 1943, with these problems in mind, Andrews submitted a troop list for the ground, air, and supply forces needed in the British Isles for Bolero and for a buildup of forces for a cross-Channel invasion in the spring of 1944. Andrews recommended that 887,935 men be stationed in the United Kingdom by December, with priority given to the air forces.[26] This was feasible for several reasons: First, the Allies had won a decisive battle against the U-boat campaign in the North Atlantic in the spring of 1943, securing the sea-lanes from America to Britain. Second, Allied shipbuilding capacity exceeded the losses incurred in combat around the globe, providing the means to transport the forces and supplies needed for Bolero and Roundup. Third, American aircraft production and the creation of bomber and fighter groups had reached a point where the Eighth Air Force could be built up more rapidly.

With victory in Tunisia secured, Marshall agreed with Andrews that the combined bomber offensive was the top priority in the European and North African theaters, as he noted in a memorandum to Arnold: "There is no doubt in my mind as to the over-all importance of heavy bomber operations out of the United Kingdom, the more so as the likelihood of cross-channel ground operations appears less probable in 1943. . . . We have given Eisenhower practically everything he has asked for within the capabilities of ocean shipping. We are now to consider to what extent, as regards Air, we do the same for Andrews. Our problem is complicated by the fact that we have been unable to carry out our general conception as to the concentration of force in the United Kingdom."[27]

Two days after Andrews submitted his estimates to the War Department, he died in an airplane crash in Iceland. His place was hard to fill, given his special expertise as an aviator and a senior War Department staff officer. Marshall quickly decided, however, that Jacob Devers had the experience and the qualities needed to continue Andrews's work. Secretary of War Stimson noted in a press release that Devers has shown "an immense capacity for organization and administration" and is "thoroughly cognizant of present and future plans."[28] Before his departure for England, Devers spent a day with Marshall and Stimson at the War Department and was briefed about his new command and its missions. He ate dinner with General and Mrs. Marshall, where the chief of staff expressed his concern that too many resources, especially aircraft, had been diverted from the European theater to support operations in the Mediterranean.[29]

As Jake left for England, Georgie faced challenges of her own. Fortunately, the Deverses owned a house in Georgetown, so she had somewhere to live when she moved from Fort Knox. Georgie wrote to her sister-in-law with evident relief, "I am absorbed for the moment with my old house. It will take all summer [to remodel], but Dad is doing everything—3 new baths and two lavatories, a complete new kitchen except walls and ceiling, 9 closets where there were two, new wiring, mostly new plaster, paint and paper, all 5 fire places relined, a new furnace flue, and a few hundred other changes. I had not expected any of it, but am certainly pleased. . . . I have all my belongings here too."[30]

Devers did not have to worry about his wife's living arrangements, but he continued to worry about Frances. He did not hear from his daughter during his first five months in London, and he complained to Georgie, "That kid has written me twice in two years, but I have yet to receive a line from her since I left Fort Knox. I thought she might overcome her lack of writing which she inherited from me if I fell back into my old habits of not writing myself."[31] By November, he still had not received a letter from Frances.

Georgie and Jake wrote to each other fairly often. Georgie also sent packages of items that were not easily obtainable in wartime Britain. Jake expressed his appreciation and let Georgie know that she was in his thoughts: "The box of oranges and candy arrived and was joyfully received. . . . Don't worry about me. . . . Buy yourself an anniversary present. I shall be thinking of you as always with love and admiration."[32] Devers also took the time to write to his mother-in-law and his sister, giving them a bright view of his situation. To Mrs. Lyon he wrote, "You are always a help and an inspiration. Here we are busy. . . . Last night I attended the Royal Albert

Theater to hear one of the finest choruses. They were superb in every way. . . . Sunday I again attended St. Paul's Cathedral where I saw all the British and foreign celebrities. . . . About 4,000 attended and we about froze to death for it is cold here in England and there are few fires."[33]

Relations with the British

One of Devers's most important tasks was to establish and maintain good relations with the British people in general and their military leaders in particular. In one of his first meetings with his senior subordinates, Devers noted that standards of dress and military courtesy were too low; he stressed that American soldiers needed to exhibit better discipline, especially during their time in London. This was in response to British complaints about the poor deportment of American soldiers. He also made it clear that any racial problems were a "command responsibility," and he admonished his officers to avoid off-the-cuff remarks to reporters and "careless, impromptu interviews."[34]

After five months in command, Devers felt that the Americans in the United Kingdom were making real friends with the British. Still, incidents of poor discipline by American troops were a major concern because of the effects on relations with the host nation. In the year before the Overlord invasion, more than a million American ground troops and another half a million airmen had to be accommodated in the British Isles. Given such numbers, there were bound to be some soldiers who stepped out of line in some fashion, and the British expected the American commanders to take appropriate action. Devers noted that serious problems were "far and few between and we pounce on them quickly and deal cold hard justice in a hurry."[35] Williston Palmer remembered that disciplinary problems were "routine" and that Devers normally did not have "any great concern about them."[36] Instead, Generals Lee and Eaker and their chains of command in the SOS and Eighth Air Force, respectively, dealt with most disciplinary issues. Their ability to do so was made possible by Parliament's passage of the Visiting Forces Act in 1942. This was the first time in British history that another nation was allowed to deal with its own citizens who violated British law while on British soil.[37] An ETO study concluded that "much of the trouble in which American soldiers found themselves was the result of liquor, women or racial problems which had been transplanted from the United States and aggravated by the lack of a 'color line' in Britain." Drunkenness and absence without leave were the two most common offenses, and "almost all serious crimes were linked with either or both of these common offenses."[38]

Devers was concerned about the overall impression being made by African American troops in the United Kingdom, since a significant percentage of the disciplinary problems seemed to come from the relatively small number of black soldiers in the command. "The color problem," as one study termed it, "stemmed from the treatment of Negroes by the [British] civilian whites and the reaction of the Negroes and white Americans to this treatment."[39] This study illustrates the presence of racism in the army, even as it provides insight into race relations in the ETO: "The average British civilian, especially girls of doubtful morals, welcomed the American Negro as a complete equal. His reaction to this treatment was sometimes to parade the equality and 'rub it in' to the white Americans. . . . The white Americans, Southerners especially, were puzzled by, and resentful of, the British attitude and frequently attempted to impose the restrictions which were traditional in their home states."[40]

One of the tragedies of American history is that we fought to make the world safe for democracy in World War I and for the Four Freedoms in World War II, but we failed to uphold these noble principles when it came to race relations at home. In 1941 Jim Crow laws were accompanied by deep racial prejudice among a majority of white Americans. The military reflected that racial prejudice. The official policy of the War Department called for segregation of the races, with African Americans serving in separate combat and noncombat organizations, including air force units.[41] Although Secretary Stimson and General Marshall defended the policy of segregation, the army did far more than the other services to employ black soldiers. For example, the Marine Corps rejected all African American enlistees until the president intervened, and the U.S. Navy and Marine Corps had no black officers during the war. In contrast, 755,000 African Americans were serving in the U.S. Army by January 1944, with about 4,500 black officers.[42] Nonetheless, all senior army officers defended segregation as the will of the people and rejected calls for the army to serve as a "social experiment" in integration.

Devers had dealt with segregation and racial tensions at Fort Bragg and in the Armored Force at Fort Knox. As a theater commander he had to deal with American prejudice and its effects on Anglo-American relations. On 11 March 1943, before his arrival in London, African American soldiers in

Burton-on-Trent mutinied because of the unfair treatment of a black soldier. The white commander was reassigned.

The records of the theater's provost marshal indicate that African Americans were charged with eleven of the twelve serious crimes committed by Americans in March 1943. They also indicate that officers were punished less severely than enlisted men and noncommissioned officers.[43] In most areas of the command, the military police units were white, making it hard to ensure that all soldiers received fair treatment and due process of the law. To alleviate this problem, Devers accepted the assignment of African American military police battalions to his command—something that some other theater commanders rejected.[44]

As the buildup of American ground forces accelerated in the fall, Devers confided to Georgie, "One of my real jobs is to be sure our American contingent sees the British people as they are, learn to know them for what they are in order that they may better assist in the solution of World problems when they are returned to normal and are running the country [after the war]."[45] This was not as easy as some had hoped, and Devers admitted, "It is a tough job to keep real friendly relations when we have much different standards of thought and living even though all [of us] make a real effort. The living wage, class distinctions, color, all are live questions [in the United Kingdom]."[46]

Pressure to encourage "fraternization between American troops and British troops in the United Kingdom" came from the highest levels of government. During the Quebec conference in August 1943, British foreign secretary Anthony Eden spoke with Roosevelt about relations between the two nations. The president encouraged him to bring the subject up with General Marshall. Instead, Eden wrote to Field Marshal John Dill to complain about the lack of Anglo-American fraternization. Eden believed the ETO had done very little to foster good relations and claimed the American Red Cross excluded British civilians and soldiers from its clubs. Eden asked Dill to raise the issue with Marshall, since Dill was the British representative to the American Joint Chiefs of Staff. Eden told Dill, "I am inclined to believe that the attitude of the military authorities (which, I should add, is not in the least unfriendly) could be changed very easily by a suitable directive." He suggested that Marshall telegraph Devers, "asking him to give his attention to this question. . . . I need hardly say that this request implies no reflexion on General Devers himself, who has been consistently helpful and friendly."[47]

Dill forwarded Eden's letter to Marshall, who in turn sent a message to Devers containing the gist of Eden's observations. Marshall reported back to Dill that "the reaction from London was quite violent," and he provided Dill with excerpts from Devers's 3 September reply: "The statements referred to are completely without foundation and contrary to the practices and policies of this theater. Steps have already been taken to commence at port of embarkation the indoctrination of officers and enlisted men coming to this theater on the necessity for cultivating the closest relationships with our British Allies. Long established procedure for such indoctrination is followed upon their arrival in this theater. All commands have been instructed to encourage fraternization."[48] Devers assured Marshall that joint attendance at sporting events, motion picture shows, church services, and unit dinners and dances was routine. In addition, American units were sponsoring orphans of deceased British military personnel, and Churchill Clubs had been established to encourage British civilians to socialize with American soldiers and airmen. He also informed Marshall that British civilians and military personnel were allowed in American Red Cross clubs as long as they were the guests of American personnel. After a meeting between the head of the American Red Cross in Britain and the adjutant general of the British army, it was clear that the British "had been misled and misinformed as to the policy of the Red Cross. . . . They were surprised to learn that any member or members of the Allied Forces are cordially welcomed to any American Red Cross Service Club when accompanied by a member of our forces."[49] Marshall closed the communication with Dill by forwarding Devers's assessment of the reasons for these misunderstandings between the Allies.

Eisenhower had done a good job establishing warm relationships with Churchill and senior British military leaders during his first tenure as commanding general of the European theater in 1942. One of his greatest contributions to victory in World War II was his ability to hold the Anglo-American coalition together and maintain positive personal relationships with the British. Among senior American military leaders, no one could have done this as successfully as Eisenhower did. Although he certainly had difficulty warming to Bernard Montgomery and Alan Brooke, he got along well with most of the important British leaders and found ways to work with the rest. As a consequence, Churchill and most British leaders liked Ike and accepted his role as supreme commander of the combined Allied forces, first in the Mediterranean and then in the European theater.

Andrews and Devers, in contrast, never established close relationships with British leaders; nor, for that matter, did Marshall. Several staff officers observed that Devers did not get along well with the British. Brigadier General Eugene Harrison attributed this to the fact that Devers "would not kowtow and agree to everything Mr. Churchill wanted."[50] Because Devers's mission was to get Bolero on track and to prevent forces from being diverted from the European to the Mediterranean theater, Churchill and the British chiefs of staff saw little to be gained from dealing with him. Harrison may have assessed the situation correctly when he noted, "I had a feeling that Mr. Churchill wanted Eisenhower back there because he could handle Eisenhower and he didn't think he could handle Devers."[51]

Williston Palmer, who worked for Devers in the Armored Force and in the ETO, got the impression, "from various things that were said," that Devers's "relations with the British were not perfect. Of course the British were hard people to have perfect relations with, I guess, unless you just yessed them. I imagine a man as outspoken and full of his own ideas as General Devers could not have had perfect relations with the British at that [time] when they considered us beginners."[52]

The American ambassador to the United Kingdom, John G. Winant, was very supportive of Devers and felt he needed some help from Washington to get the British chiefs of staff to fully accept him. In a June 1943 message to President Roosevelt, Winant stated, "It would greatly help General Devers' standing here if our Chiefs of Staff made known to the British Staff that we wanted him to be informed in total global strategy rather than having his information limited to plans in the European Theater only." The president shared Winant's observations with Marshall.[53] In response, Marshall told the president and the ambassador that Devers was aware of American global strategy and that Marshall was "very glad that Mr. Winant is so interested in building up Devers' prestige, because this is a matter of great importance to us as it was in the case of Eisenhower."[54] Marshall had "previously requested the British Chiefs of Staff to call in Devers in relation to all matters of the Combined Chiefs of Staff that relate to his theater," but Winant's message indicates this was not happening. Marshall now suggested to the president that "in some message of yours to the Prime Minister you express the hope that he has met Devers and that he will give him the fine support he gave General Eisenhower and General Andrews."[55]

Devers dealt personally with Churchill on various matters and was an infrequent visitor to the prime minister's country retreat Chequers.[56] He met with Alan Brooke on at least six occasions from May through December 1943, and Brooke and the British chiefs of staff supported Devers and Eaker in their tussle with Eisenhower over the transfer of bombers in the summer. Devers learned to work through Ambassador Winant and his assistant Wally Carroll to save "many hours in obtaining needed decisions" from the British. He also found that Averell Harriman, a friend from his polo-playing days at West Point, was in charge of American Lend-Lease to Britain.[57] The evidence shows that Devers had sufficient contacts with the British government and military to get the job done. It also seems that his blunt style of saying what he thought rubbed Churchill and Brooke the wrong way at times. This was unavoidable, since Devers represented the American position in the debate over concentrating on Bolero and the cross-Channel invasion rather than continuing to pour forces into the Mediterranean theater.

Buildup of the Eighth Air Force

Devers's command had three major tasks to accomplish when he arrived in the United Kingdom in early May 1943. The Eighth Air Force had to be expanded to carry out the daylight bombing program the Americans believed was essential to defeating Germany. Air and ground force bases had to be built in the United Kingdom to house more than a million American troops and to provide logistical support facilities for the combined bomber offensive and the cross-Channel invasion. Finally, the operational planning process had to be initiated for the invasion of northern France.

The buildup of the Eighth Air Force was the European theater's first priority in the summer of 1943. Marshall, recognizing that Devers needed an experienced chief of staff who thoroughly understood air force matters, suggested Major General Idwal Edwards for that position. Edwards was an air corps officer and the current G-3 of the War Department staff. Devers readily accepted Marshall's suggestion, even though he did not know Edwards very well. Nor had he met Ira Eaker before his arrival in London. Devers later had this to say about Eaker:

> I knew my work was cut out for me. Edwards proved to be a very fine Chief of Staff. He worked well with Ira Eaker—and Ira Eaker and I were on the same wave length from the first hour we met. We are to this day. We had our differences but we always came up

with the answers when the chips were down—and this accounted for a great many successes such as the beginning of the daylight bombing raids out of England—and on the civic side, cleaning up the troubles in London and in many English towns caused by the arrival of hundreds of young air force officers. We had the job of building airfields—lengthening some—about 120 in all—given us by the British. We had a myriad of complex problems to solve.[58]

Once in London, Devers assessed his key leaders and the condition of the command. He reported to Marshall on 18 May, "We are improving the organization of the Theater. The staff is weak in spots, particularly in G-2 matters and in public relations. Apparently all has not been smooth with British intelligence. Colonel Tupper [Devers's public relations officer] is fast cleaning up the public relations set-up with its many ramifications. . . . Edwards is doing a splendid job. . . . Eaker is an ideal commander for the air effort."[59] About two weeks later, Devers informed Marshall, "Since the Eighth Air Force is already heavily engaged with the enemy, I consider it my primary and immediate responsibility to support its efforts with all the means available in the theater."[60] He also recommended that Eaker be promoted to lieutenant general, a rank commensurate with his responsibilities as commander of the Eighth Air Force.

The flow of new bomber groups (each with about sixty bombers) and support units accelerated in May, and by the end of June, there were twelve heavy bomber groups and five groups of medium bombers and fighters in the United Kingdom. In June the Eighth Air Force reached a strength of over 100,000 men, more than half of all American soldiers in the country. By July, the Eighth had twenty-six groups of all types, with a goal of twenty-five heavy and seven medium bomber groups by September and thirty-eight heavy and nine medium groups by the end of December 1943.[61] Unfortunately, the buildup of Eighth Air Force combat units was accomplished at the expense of maintenance and service units. The official air force history notes, "Faulty planning, reflecting a general tendency in the AAF to emphasis [sic] its combat program at the expense of service organizations, had produced a serious lack of balance between combat and service units by the summer of 1943."[62]

By early June, General Arnold was deeply concerned about the poor bomber maintenance situation in the Eighth Air Force. As a result, he asked Eaker and Devers to let him know "whether this situation is due to shortage of material, inexperienced maintenance personnel, shops and repair facilities and other causes which can be remedied by assistance from this country."[63] Devers and Eaker saw the situation somewhat differently, but they too were concerned about the maintenance and availability of aircraft. As Eaker noted, "The records show that we have been able to keep in commission a larger percentage of aircraft than the British"; however, "many of our depots and maintenance establishments have not yet been completely equipped or manned." In spite of this, "the records show we have generally been able to keep in commission as many tactical bombers as we have crews to operate. Our status of maintenance, therefore, has not resulted in a lowered rate of operation or in less pressure on the enemy."[64]

The Eighth Air Force's major problem with bomber availability was caused by shortages of aircrews and aircraft repairmen, incomplete maintenance organizations, and heavy damage inflicted by the Luftwaffe's fighters during bombing missions. It was not unusual for a bomber group to suffer damage to twenty-seven of its twenty-eight aircraft during a single mission. "All this damage had to be repaired before the planes were again ready for combat. Some of it, approximately one-half," according to Eaker, "could be repaired over-night; all of it could have been repaired in two or three days if we had enough mobile repair units." The situation was exacerbated because new bomber groups were arriving in England without organizational support and maintenance equipment, forcing the support crews of other groups to maintain the new groups' aircraft.[65]

Arnold was not convinced that the right men were serving as wing and squadron commanders, as he pointed out in a message to Devers: "Recent events, as you know, have caused me some concern as to our operations, administration, and maintenance in the 8th Air Force. . . . It looks to me as if what you need more than anything else is a guy who is a driver, one who knows how to take care of problems by utilizing to the maximum the facilities, materials, and equipment of any kind which may be available. Personally I don't think this is being done." This could be interpreted as criticism of Eaker, even though Arnold understood that "many of your best personnel were taken by Spaatz and Eisenhower when they went to North Africa." He encouraged Devers to consider battle-experienced younger men for higher commands in the Eighth Air Force. Arnold "talked these things over with Eaker" as well, but Eaker had not yet made any major changes in senior air commanders and staff officers.[66]

Devers rose to the defense of his air force commander in his response to

Arnold: "Eaker is doing a splendid job. As I wrote you, he needs help. . . . Spaatz picked his head men [from VIII Bomber command]; Kenny picked his head men [from the fighter command]; Eaker tried to do something with what was left, and he is succeeding. . . . We are taking the best man in the command and giving him the bombers, namely, [Brigadier General Frederick] Anderson. . . . I concur fully with your reference to maintenance. . . . We are doing this and competing well with the British who have the same troubles as we do, namely, not enough trained personnel nor enough facilities, material, or equipment."[67]

During his entire career, Devers demonstrated an ability to work with and support the subordinates on hand when he took over a unit or organization. For example, he kept Brett in the Armored Force and readily accepted men like Edwards when they were offered. Unlike Eisenhower, he did not need to surround himself with men he was used to working with. Devers had inherited Eaker, and he stood by him. With this in mind, he wrote to Arnold: "The 8th Air Force will deliver. Have no fear. . . . I have carefully studied with Eaker his many and varied problems" and concluded that "the officers and enlisted men of the 8th Air Force are doing a good job, but it is not good enough."[68] In his and Eaker's view, the leaders, pilots, and crews of the Eighth Air Force "have the fighting spirit and they drive into the target; they are pretty good on the bombing end; they need lots of practice on the shooting end. Then they get careless. This is where the real leadership takes place, and it must take place in each plane. All these things Eaker is taking care of. And finally, there must be no empty places at breakfast any morning. This latter means trained replacements."[69]

Secretary of War Henry Stimson was also concerned about the condition of the Eighth Air Force. To get a better understanding of Eaker's and Devers's challenges, he sent the assistant secretary of war for air, Robert A. Lovett, to England in early June. Lovett got a thorough update from Eaker and toured many of the Eighth's facilities. Upon Lovett's return to Washington, he sent a long message to Eaker, outlining his observations and what he and General Arnold had concluded from them:

There is a substantial misunderstanding between headquarters here and 8th Air Force headquarters as to the problems you face, their cause, their cure and the loss of operational time involved as a result of the necessity for modifications [of bombers], combat crew training, etc. The fundamental reason for this misunderstanding is, in my opinion, the inadequacy of the reports and the methods of accounting for aircraft received. Next in importance is the lack of full realization on this side of the extraordinarily high percentage of battle damage incurred by the operating units. . . . There has not been a complete meeting of the minds.[70]

Lovett informed Eaker that he had told the chief of the Army Air Forces about the need for more replacement aircrews, better training of gunners and pilots in high-altitude gunnery and formation flying, and accelerated delivery of ground support equipment. Arnold had agreed to put pressure on the air staff to resolve these problems. It had also been decided to provide at least two aircrews for each heavy and medium bomber deployed in the European and North African theaters and to delay the overseas deployment of several bomber groups to provide additional aircrews for the groups already overseas.[71] Lovett assured Eaker that "the handling of the transportation for ground echelons and operational equipment will hereafter be handled more expeditiously because, for the first time, we have the dope cold on the Services of Supply shipments which caused the 94th, 95th, 96th, 351st and 379th Groups to arrive in your theater without maintenance personnel or working tools." Lovett and Arnold made it clear to Eaker that he needed to fire senior leaders who were not getting their jobs done and replace them with men who could do so.[72]

After his discussions with Lovett, Arnold wrote to Devers, "I have always had faith in Eaker and I realize that probably we have few like him who can carry a heavy burden successfully and at the same time maintain a clear mind and a determined attitude towards the fight."[73] Devers reported to Arnold that he and Eaker were recommending Colonels Curtis Le May and Edward Timberlake for promotion to brigadier general and were culling the weaker leaders from the group and wing commander positions.[74] This process has been well dramatized in the movie *Twelve O'Clock High*.

With Lovett's and Arnold's personal interest, the Eighth Air Force became a more balanced force. Devers's faith in Eaker and his defense of the air chief to Arnold allowed Eaker to get on with the job of finding the right leaders and fixing the maintenance and repair systems. However, there were still threats to the Eighth Air Force's ability to carry out its part of the combined bomber offensive.

The combined bomber offensive was central to Marshall's strategy for defeating the Luftwaffe and, ultimately, Germany. The plan was to force

German fighter aircraft to defend the homeland and then shoot them down during engagements with the heavily armed bombers of the Eighth Air Force and their fighter escorts. Operation Torch had delayed the buildup of bombers in England until the late spring of 1943. Once the buildup resumed, Eisenhower's Mediterranean headquarters exerted pressure to divert the heavy bomber groups to the Mediterranean. Eaker warned Arnold, "I am greatly disturbed about the diversions which have come up to the Combined Bomber Offensive. The Combined Chiefs of Staff have approved it, but there is evidence that the force will be dispersed."[75]

Arnold agreed with Eaker: the diversion of resources to the Mediterranean had to stop. In a memo to Marshall in early May, Arnold noted, "We have given Eisenhower and Spaatz complete support. We must now turn to an equally complete support of Andrews and Eaker. The task which we have given them is of paramount importance to the successful conclusion of this war at an early date." In addition, he told Marshall that sending bomber groups to the Mediterranean on a temporary basis was not a good idea because their effectiveness deteriorated when they were deployed without their normal base support, which was in England.[76]

Eaker's concern in June was related to the retention of a B-24 bomber group in North Africa by the Twelfth Air Force. His long-term concern was that Spaatz and Eisenhower would try to pull additional heavy bomber resources south. This fear was well founded. He told Arnold that he had "talked with General Devers and General Edwards along this line and we see the problem exactly the same. In this connection I wish to say now that I never have had, and never expect to have, better relations with my Commander than now prevail with General Devers and his staff. He has greatly strengthened the Theater Staff and he is as strong a supporter of true air force operations as I have ever seen."[77]

On 28 July Eisenhower and Spaatz requested the transfer of four heavy bomber groups from the Eighth Air Force to the Mediterranean theater on a temporary basis, until 15 September. Eisenhower and Spaatz believed they needed four groups of B-17s to "paralyze the German air effort in all southern Italy and almost immobilize his ground units." In his message to the Combined Chiefs of Staff requesting the additional bombers, Eisenhower suggested that Eaker "should, if possible, lead his formations here in person in order that there may be no misapprehension as to the temporary and specific nature of this reinforcement."[78] Such a suggestion indicates that he had very little understanding of Eaker's heavy responsibilities in England.

Eaker and Devers realized that diverting about one-third of the Eighth Air Force's heavy bombers from the combined bomber offensive would significantly affect its ability to carry out its mission. They reacted immediately. Devers rejected Eisenhower's request, stating that he had to consider "the overall war effort" and "must be guided by the greatest damage to the German enemy and I must never lose sight of the imminence of Overlord."[79] Devers and Eaker also met with the British chiefs of staff on 30 July to ask for their help in fending off the request. The British chiefs agreed with them and notified their American counterparts of their decision.[80]

When Devers turned down his request, Eisenhower appealed to the CCS and to Generals Marshall and Arnold. On 1 August the two generals agreed that diverting these bomber groups was not in the best strategic interest of the Allies.[81] Such a disagreement was not unusual, given that there were too few air force resources to meet the needs of the many theaters of operations around the world. Eisenhower had done what any good commander would do: he asked for more resources for his organization. Devers had responded in the same way: he defended his command's ability to execute its main mission. In this case, Devers demonstrated a better understanding of the overall Allied strategy than Eisenhower; therefore, he had the support of the American and British chiefs of staff.

Unfortunately, Eisenhower was deeply offended and blamed Devers for the decisions of the American and British chiefs of staff, with long-term implications for their relationship. Harry Butcher, Eisenhower's aide, wrote in his diary, "Ike is furious. He feels that the much flaunted mobility of our Air Force has been exposed as talk rather than action."[82] Matters got worse in mid-August when Eisenhower asked to be allowed to keep three groups of B-24 bombers that had been sent to the Mediterranean theater on a temporary basis. Devers again recommended that his request be denied, and Marshall and Arnold agreed with him.[83]

This second episode further soured Eisenhower's view of Devers. He had not been impressed with Devers's report about the situation in North Africa in January 1943 (see chapter 8). Eisenhower also seemed to fear that Marshall had interpreted his request for the four bomber groups as "empire-building," so he assured the chief of staff that his "suggestions for additional air strength here are made from a purely impersonal estimate of the results to be attained and their probable effect on the general situation."[84] One historian notes, "From that point on Eisenhower denigrated Devers as a lightweight in over his head," and "many of Eisenhower's staffers and subordinates were quick to embrace this evaluation of Devers."[85]

In his second memoir of the war, Omar Bradley notes, "I may have been initially prejudiced against Devers by Ike, who had recently several long-distance set-tos with him over airpower."[86] Although Bradley's book is unreliable on many facts, in this case it reflects the impact of Eisenhower's temper on his judgment. He seemed unable to see the bigger strategic picture when his requests were overruled by Marshall and the CCS. Even Devers's classmate and onetime close friend George Patton wrote in his diary on 12 February 1944 that Eisenhower characterized Devers's intellect as ".22 caliber."[87]

In September, when U.S. Fifth Army's badly planned and poorly executed invasion of Italy at Salerno was nearly defeated by German counterattacks, Eisenhower asked for the return of three B-24 bomber groups. Devers, Marshall, and the CCS agreed to this request, and the bombers arrived in North Africa on 17 September.[88] When the Salerno crisis receded, the bombers returned to England to continue their participation in the bomber offensive. By then, according to the air force official history, "So severe were the demands imposed [on the Luftwaffe] by the activities of the Red Air Force and by the Combined Bomber Offensive, indeed, that the GAF [German air force] was forced to withdraw aircraft from the Mediterranean—an act which helps explain the decline of the GAF there toward the end of August from about 1,100 to less than 600 serviceable planes." The German air forces in Eisenhower's theater could no longer seriously challenge the Allied air forces, which by then numbered 3,619 American aircraft in the Mediterranean theater alone.[89]

Devers and Eaker continued to focus on the challenges of getting the Eighth Air Force up to speed in the bomber offensive. By mid-August, Devers was confident that it had turned a corner, as he told Marshall:

Shortly after you assigned me to the command of this Theater the combined bomber offensive was launched. It was the first matter about which I informed myself and I have followed its progress closely since its initiation. As you know, the first phase, which was concluded on July 1st, was largely directed against the German submarine effort. . . . The second phase of this air offensive which has as its main objective the destruction of the German Air Force is now under way. I remain convinced that the strategic conception of the plan is sound. . . . The destruction of the critical systems of German industry can be accomplished *provided the force as calculated is furnished*. The continuation of this air offensive is of overriding importance as a preliminary to OVERLORD.[90]

Of course, Devers was preaching to the choir. He and Marshall saw eye to eye on the combined bomber offensive's relationship to Overlord and the defeat of Germany. When Devers refused to send bombers to the Mediterranean in July and August, he was doing exactly what Marshall and Arnold expected him to do. His mission was to stop the diversion of American resources from the European theater to the secondary effort, which in their view was the Mediterranean theater. For this, Devers would later pay a heavy price in terms of his relationship with Eisenhower.

But Devers had more important things to worry about than Eisenhower's pique. He and Eaker had to make room for the Ninth Air Force, which was moving to the United Kingdom to provide tactical air support to the ground forces in Overlord. Initially, Eaker commanded both the Eighth and the Ninth Air Forces, but as Devers told Arnold in a 17 August letter, "as we go along and get our many difficult problems solved, the two air forces would naturally be separated. There are many really complicated problems of supply, maintenance and control when flying from such a small country as the South and East of England. Therefore, it takes a wise head like Eaker's to keep things running smoothly." In the same letter, Devers encouraged Arnold to visit England to see the progress being made in training, maintenance, construction, and combat effectiveness. Though proud of the theater's achievements, Devers did not minimize the costs associated with the bomber missions over Germany. "When we lose more than our proportion of planes, it is because of somebody's judgment under pressure, or the weather. The Germans are smart. They are deathly afraid of closing with the large formations [of heavily armed bombers]; they simply lie back and pick off the weak ones as they drop out of formation due to engine trouble or wounds."[91]

Arnold, who had recovered from a heart attack suffered in the spring, visited England in September, after the Quebec conference of Anglo-American leaders. During his three-day visit, the Eighth Air Force sent 337 B-17s to attack a German ball-bearing factory near Stuttgart. Forty-five of those planes were lost, each with a ten-man crew. Many more bombers were badly damaged by German fighters and antiaircraft fire. Not one bomber hit the assigned target with its bombs. This news did not cheer Arnold up, but his visit to the air force service depot at Burtonwood, near Liverpool, did. As he later wrote in his memoir, "Thousands of disabled planes and engines were returned to combat. . . . We had some 10,000 Americans in that one plant. Disabled engines were brought all the way from North Africa for Burtonwood to fix."[92]

Arnold left England convinced that the Eighth Air Force was on the right track and that the problems of maintenance, training, and crew availability were well on their way to being solved. The heavy losses by the bombers did not obscure the fact that the Eighth Air Force's primary mission from April 1943 to the spring of 1944 was to defeat the Luftwaffe. To do that, Arnold later noted, "We had to come to grips with it, not defensively, as the RAF had done in the Battle of Britain, but on our own initiative." The bombers had to force the German fighters to take to the air to defend their aircraft facilities, and since Allied fighters lacked the range to reach Germany in 1943, the bombers had to attack the German fighters themselves. The "German fighters came up savagely every time," Arnold observed. "These bombs on German aircraft factories, the German fighters shot down by our gunners in the air battles, were the beginning of the end for the *Luftwaffe*."[93] By early 1944, once the American P-47 and P-51 fighter planes were equipped with external fuel tanks, the bombers were able to focus on their bombardment mission while the American fighters beat the living daylights out of the German fighter forces. By May 1944, the Allied air forces had defeated the Luftwaffe, driven its fighters out of France, and severely damaged the German industrial heartland of the Ruhr.

Devers and Eaker overcame many serious obstacles to the buildup of the Eighth and Ninth Air Forces. They oversaw the construction or expansion of more than 100 airfields, the organization of effective aircraft maintenance and repair systems, and the establishment of dozens of depots for munitions and equipment. Devers stood by Eaker and recognized his talents, and he effectively communicated the needs of his air force component to Generals Marshall, Arnold, and Somervell. As he had done in Panama and at Fort Knox, Devers worked well with air corps officers and supported his subordinates as they sought to accomplish the mission at hand. At the same time, he played an important role in the development of the plan for Overlord.

Planning for Overlord

The central tenet of the Allied strategy was that the quickest way to defeat the Nazi regime was to invade northern Europe with British and American forces, defeat the German forces, and drive into the heart of Germany to destroy Hitler's Reich. From the spring of 1942 on, George Marshall had advocated a cross-Channel invasion. Nonetheless, the Anglo-American Allies did not attempt to invade France in 1942 or 1943; instead, they pursued the British preference for operations in the Mediterranean theater.

It was, in hindsight, fortunate that the Allies did not invade France before 1944. Combat in North Africa and Sicily proved that the U.S. Army lacked the training and experience to match the veteran German formations in France. By the summer and fall of 1943, however, American soldiers and their leaders had been blooded in battle, and their combat capabilities were steadily improving. At the same time, the German armed forces had suffered a series of disastrous blows in Russia, in North Africa, and in the air over northern Europe. The time had come to plan for and execute the invasion of northern Europe.

Planning tentatively began in January 1943, when the Combined Chiefs of Staff at the Casablanca conference agreed to create a combined planning staff for the operation. In March, British lieutenant general Frederick Morgan was appointed chief of staff for the as yet unnamed supreme Allied commander. By May, Morgan and his planning staff—known as COSSAC (the acronym for Chief of Staff to the Supreme Allied Commander)—were evaluating options for what became known as Operation Overlord.[94] The CCS also agreed that the commanding general of the ETO would be the direct representative of the U.S. Joint Chiefs of Staff to COSSAC, and he would "be consulted on all plans with respect to the employment of United States forces."[95]

When Devers assumed command of the European theater in May, Morgan had already organized a combined staff to coordinate planning for Overlord. Morgan intended the COSSAC staff to focus on major decisions, such as the operation's location and size; detailed tactical planning would be left to the commanders of the army groups and the appropriate air and naval organizations assigned to carry out the plan. All sections of the COSSAC staff, except for the solely British G-2 (intelligence) section, were composed of both British and American officers. Devers assigned his operations officer (G-3), Major General Raymond Barker, to serve as Morgan's deputy chief of staff, further strengthening the Allied nature of the organization.[96] Morgan presented the initial outline for Overlord to the American chiefs of staff in July; after receiving their concurrence, he presented the plan to the CCS for approval at the Quadrant conference in Quebec in August. The CCS approved the plan but ordered Morgan to increase the projected size of the force.[97]

The Overlord plan of 1943 called for an invasion of France along the coast of Normandy, north of the city of Caen. The main objective of the British and American forces that landed on D-day would be the establishment of a "lodgment" where the Allies could build the logistical base and airfields needed to sustain up to 100 Allied divisions in northern Europe. Once the base was established, the Allied armies planned to defeat the German forces in France and drive into the heart of Germany.[98] In this scenario, both American and British groups of armies would take part, requiring each of the partners to initiate planning for the tactical aspects of the operation.

To ensure that most of the initial assault divisions in Overlord were battle tested, the CCS agreed in May that seven veteran divisions (four American and three British) would be transferred from the Mediterranean to the United Kingdom after the conclusion of the Sicily campaign. However, in August the Allied forces headquarters in the Mediterranean asked that the four combat-tested American divisions remain in the Mediterranean and be replaced in Overlord by four untested divisions from the United States. The War Department asked General Barker, who was in Washington at the time, if the ETO would accept this substitution. Barker called Devers and Morgan, and Devers was "most emphatic" that this was unacceptable; he instructed Barker to demand that the four divisions from the Mediterranean be transferred, as earlier agreed.[99] This request to retain the four divisions may well have come from Eisenhower, the supreme commander in the Mediterranean; if so, Devers's negative response did nothing to improve their relationship.

The British wasted little time in providing navy, army, and air headquarters to plan the tactical elements of Overlord. By the end of July, the British Twenty-First Army Group, commanded by General Sir Bernard Paget, was ordered to develop tactical plans for the invasion, and the Canadian First and British Second Armies were assigned to the Twenty-First Army Group.[100] Ironically, the Americans did not respond as quickly, even though they had been the biggest champions of an early cross-Channel invasion. Marshall and the American chiefs of staff did not establish comparable headquarters until October. Consequently, V Corps was the senior U.S. headquarters directly involved in tactical planning.

Devers was concerned about the lack of senior American officers and higher-level tactical headquarters in Britain well before the Overlord plan emerged. In May he recommended to Marshall that Bradley be moved from North Africa to the United Kingdom to command V Corps because, "with plans now in the making it is believed that a man of Bradley's experience and judgment is indicated."[101] He also informed Marshall that Morgan, "who heads the group [COSSAC], is a lieutenant general and the heads of his sections are major generals," but the American planners are "officers ranking from captain to colonel." He recommended that an army commander be sent to London "for the purpose of initiating actual planning for the 1944 operation . . . with at least a skeleton staff, sometime in July."[102] The War Department was slow to heed his advice, primarily because there were too few qualified commanders available. Major General Omar Bradley, for example, was one of the few combat-vetted senior commanders in the army, and he was slated to command II Corps in the invasion of Sicily. Eisenhower did not feel he could release Bradley until September, and it was October before Bradley arrived in England to organize and command, simultaneously, First Army and First Army Group.[103] Bradley wanted to bring most of his key staff officers from II Corps to England to fill the First Army staff positions, but Eisenhower (who six months later would insist on bringing most of his senior staff officers with him to the ETO) allowed only a few key officers to accompany Bradley.[104]

Combined planning was new ground for Devers, since this was his first time serving on a combined Allied staff. He did not always work well with the British, as shown in a memorandum written for the War Department by Lieutenant Colonel Cary, an American officer on temporary detail with the British joint planners:

A bad situation is arising re command and control in OVERLORD. COSSAC stated a few "principles" in OVERLORD Plan (Pars. 40–41) which Americans believed were designated with malice aforethought to insure British command. A detailed paper on same lines was prepared by British half of COSSAC, and violently vetoed by Devers. Unfortunately, General Devers handed his comments to Morgan in draft form, personally, unsigned, and the British are making much of the informality and saying the paper represents solely General Devers' personal views. Americans have advanced a different proposal. . . . No final conclusion yet. Incidentally, Morgan's plan makes Anderson, of Tunisia fame, solely responsible for planning and directing all operations.[105]

In this case, Devers was reacting to a September proposal that the Allied forces participating in the initial assault be under the command of a British general and remain under a British army group commander until the Brest peninsula had been taken or an American army group had been established on the Continent. Devers believed that such a command arrangement would place American "units smaller than a corps under direct British command and deprive the Supreme Commander of operational control in the early stages of the assault."[106] Ultimately, it was decided that the commander of the British Twenty-First Army Group would plan the operation and command two armies, one British and one American, that would carry out the initial invasion. Then, once a large enough lodgment had been established and sufficient U.S. forces were ashore, the U.S. First Army Group would assume command of the American forces in France.[107]

During the summer of 1943 it became clear to all involved with Allied strategy that the majority of the forces participating in the campaign in northwestern Europe would be American. This realization changed a long-standing assumption that the supreme commander would be British. The question then became, who would he be?

When Secretary of War Stimson visited England, he and Devers discussed the British attitude toward Overlord, and Devers bluntly told Stimson that he did not believe the British would push hard to execute it.[108] Stimson concluded, after discussions with Churchill and Brooke, that the British were not enthusiastic about Overlord. He told President Roosevelt, "We cannot now rationally [expect to] be able to cross the Channel and come to grips with our German enemy under a British commander. His Prime Minister and his Chief of the Imperial Staff are frankly at variance with such a proposal. The shadows of Passchendaele and Dunkerque still hang too heavily over the imagination of these leaders of his government. Though they have rendered lip service to the operation, their hearts are not in it. . . . The difference between us is a viral difference of faith." Stimson went on to advise Roosevelt that the time had come for the U.S. government to take responsibility for the command of Overlord and to put "our most commanding soldier in charge of this critical operation at this critical time." Stimson had General George Marshall in mind, given his "towering eminence of reputation as a tried soldier and as a broadminded and skillful administrator."[109]

Roosevelt agreed in part and announced to the American chiefs of staff on 10 August his decision that an American should command Overlord. Churchill had come to the same conclusion and had, in fact, raised this point even before FDR announced his decision. The two leaders formally agreed on the appointment of an American commander while Churchill was visiting Hyde Park in mid-August.[110] It was assumed, but not announced, that Marshall would be the supreme commander.

Devers had assumed since at least July that Marshall would be selected to command Overlord. Therefore, he had worked to shape the Overlord command structure in a way that would best serve Marshall. It would have been totally out of character for Devers to fail to get to the heart of a problem and seek a straightforward solution. He had never been reluctant to recommend to his superiors how to address the business at hand. Now he wrote to Marshall, "I am concerned that we direct our thinking and planning along lines you may have in mind and avoid any commitments or even apparent acquiescence in matters that may prove contrary to your purposes." He went on to present his thoughts on the command organization for Overlord:

- The senior United States Commander should command the field forces and should continue in the capacity of Commanding General, ETOUSA.
- There should be a direct line of communication between the senior United States Commander and the United States Chief of Staff.
- The senior United States Commander should be the representative in this Theater of the United States Joint Chiefs of Staff on a level with the British Chiefs of Staff.
- While the Supreme Commander [in Overlord] may initially be British, the eventual commander may be an American.[111]

He followed this letter with another recommending a group of officers to staff an American army group. Marshall did not answer immediately, but in August he told General Barker that he was ready to select the army commander (Bradley). Barker, however, informed Devers that, "as to the Army Group, I have a distinct impression that he will not name a commander as such, until perhaps this fall, leaving you to carry the load, meantime."[112] In another discussion, Marshall told Barker that he expected to name an army group commander by about 1 November.[113]

In spite of Marshall's comments to Barker, Devers recognized the need to form an army group headquarters as soon as possible. In fact, he was under pressure from General Morgan to get one established.[114] So he pushed Marshall to act with the following message on 13 September: "I recommend the organization here at once of an Army Group Headquarters, to be known as United States General Headquarters European Theater of Operations, since it will have responsibilities of supply and communications and other functions beyond those normally visualized for a field headquarters of a group of armies. . . . This USGHQ should be organized and activated along the lines of T/O [table of organization] 300–1, with an initial strength of 156 officers and 355 enlisted men."[115]

Marshall responded five days later, telling Devers, "At this time, designating the Field Headquarters of American Forces in your Theater as a general headquarters does not appear to be advisable. The organization in the UK of an Army Group Headquarters to be known as the US Army Group Headquarters, does however, appear to be sound. This would give us a Field Headquarters under the Supreme Allied Commander capable of directing the operation of the American Armies." The ETO would continue to handle administrative matters from England until after the invasion. Marshall further directed that the development of the army group headquarters would be gradual, with only a nucleus of capable staff officers to initiate tactical and logistical planning. For the time being, Marshall decided that Devers would exercise overall control of First Army and First Army Group, with Bradley in direct control of planning for both organizations.[116]

Devers notified Marshall that the army group headquarters would be established on 1 October, "along the lines suggested in your R-3267." The staff would remain small, and special staff sections such as engineer, medical, and so forth would not be added to the headquarters. Instead, a small liaison planning group from J. C. H. Lee's Services of Supply would be located at the army group headquarters to coordinate logistical planning. The army group headquarters would focus on "high level planning," leaving the detailed tactical planning to Bradley's First Army. Devers, however, questioned the wisdom of merging the planning activities of First Army Group and First Army, believing that the "command channels should be separate and distinct from the beginning."[117] This last suggestion was vetoed by the

War Department's assistant chief of staff, Major General Thomas Handy. Handy instead recommended to Marshall that the army group and First Army both be controlled by Bradley and colocated.[118]

Marshall spent considerable time in September thinking about the organization of Allied supreme headquarters, which he assumed he would command. On 24 September he provided guidance for Devers to use in "discussions with British authorities leading to decisions on the command organization under the Supreme Allied Commander": "Under the Supreme Commander, there should be initially the American Army Group Commander, British Army Group Commander, Allied Naval Commander, Allied Tactical Air Commander, and Allied Strategic Air Commander. The Combined Chiefs of Staff in their 113th meeting agreed upon the appointment, for OVERLORD, of Admiral Sir Charles Little as Naval Commander and Air Marshal Sir Trafford Leigh-Mallory as Allied Expeditionary Air Force Commander." Marshall told Devers it was not a good time to introduce the idea of an Allied ground force commander or to bring up the question of a deputy supreme commander. He made it clear that the staffs in the various sections should reflect equal representation by British and American officers. He agreed with Devers that the staffs of the Allied air and naval commanders "should be only of a size necessary to effect coordinated direction" of the forces under their command. Finally, Marshall commented on the status of the ETO. He advised that all American forces in the theater should be administered by one U.S. headquarters under one commander, and "the Field Force Commanders should be relieved of as many administrative responsibilities as possible."[119]

Marshall instructed Devers to give Morgan his full support and to ensure that the best officers available were provided to staff the new headquarters. Devers, in turn, told Morgan that he would direct his staff sections to maintain close touch with the COSSAC staff and that Bradley would organize the First Army and First Army Group staffs "under my supervision." In addition, the ETO headquarters "will be charged with all administrative features of the American Forces, thus relieving the field forces of as many of their burdens of administration as possible."[120]

The transatlantic correspondence about Overlord command and organizational issues between Devers and Marshall took place after it was widely assumed that Marshall would be Roosevelt's pick for supreme commander, as Stimson had strongly recommended. In Devers's mind, if Marshall became supreme commander, then Devers had a strong chance of being selected to command the American army group. Years later, Williston Palmer, who worked for Devers in the fall of 1943, stated as much, remarking that it was believed that Marshall would come over and that Devers "hoped to get the Army Group."[121] Devers believed that "if General Marshall . . . had been the overall commander that I would have remained in England because I still feel I did a pretty good job there and was very helpful."[122]

Jake's letters to Georgie at the time indicate that he had high hopes about playing an important role in Overlord. On 9 October he wrote that he wished "General Marshall could arrive here to head up the combined command. We would go places and once started nothing could stop us." A few weeks later, however, some doubts had crept in and he wrote, "Lots going on and too much politics. So far I am holding my own and we are getting plans."[123]

Clearly, Devers wanted to command First Army Group. His correspondence with Marshall can be construed in such a way that he seemed to be trying to put himself in that position. But there is no direct evidence that Marshall saw things that way, and his later decisions concerning Devers's abilities indicate that he did not. However, one comment Marshall allegedly made to historian Forrest Pogue indicates that Marshall saw Devers as self-serving. According to Pogue, Marshall said in a 1956 interview that Devers was "pretty much embittered. Did good work in Europe at first. Got the personal ambition thing in too much. He was on a board which listed generals in order they should be promoted. Moved his own name up. Two generals wanted me to change it back. I didn't touch it, but it changed my view toward him. He got in the ambition class."[124] In fact, Devers never sat on a general officer promotion board, and he never put his own name at the top of a promotion list.[125]

Devers was certainly no shrinking violet, as his December report to Marshall indicates. However, this message was a fair summary of the tremendously important work he had been deeply involved in since May:

> As the year ends I desire to report to you that we in this Theater feel we have made considerable progress.
>
> The Air Forces have steadily improved. They are carrying the war to Germany. . . . Eaker is the ablest air commander I know.
>
> The S.O.S. has accomplished much. It has been able to keep ahead of the peak loads, has worked well with the British, has a fine

organization and is well-disciplined. . . . Lee has been particularly aggressive and efficient and is responsible for the fine condition of his organization.

The Ground Troops are moving into this Theater in an orderly manner. All seem to need jacking up as to standards, this being particularly true for units below division. However, they quickly take hold and make their abode into a small part of America.

General Bradley has done an exceptionally fine job since he has arrived here, but with new duties assigned to him by COSSAC I strongly recommend that an Army Group Commander be appointed immediately. I desire this command if it is possible to give it to me.[126]

When this letter was written, the president had already announced his selection of Eisenhower to serve as the supreme Allied commander. Devers concluded the letter by asking Marshall to give him "any guidance and help as to what you are thinking about with reference to the command in this complicated set-up."[127] Before too long, he would receive guidance related to the command arrangements for Overlord.

10

Mediterranean Theater of Operations

Throughout the fall of 1943, Devers, Marshall, and many others thought that Marshall would command the Allied forces for the invasion of northern Europe, including the army chief of staff himself. Devers worked on the command setup for Overlord based on that assumption. Unfortunately, once word of Marshall's probable command leaked out, a political firestorm erupted. Some anti-Roosevelt politicians believed that Marshall was being forced out of Washington so the administration could appoint a compliant army chief of staff who would grant contracts to help Roosevelt's reelection bid in 1944. Congressional leaders of both parties made it clear they did not want Marshall to leave his current post; they trusted him to lead the Joint Chiefs of Staff and the global war effort. Finally, his fellow service chiefs, Admiral Ernest King and General Hap Arnold, told Stimson they did not want to lose Marshall.[1]

In spite of this furor, Stimson and Marshall continued to believe that the latter would command Overlord. Marshall was so certain that he expended a great deal of effort and time ensuring that the COSSAC chief of staff, Lieutenant General Frederick Morgan, got to know America and American soldiers. Toward this end, Morgan spent six weeks in the United States in October. Marshall's correspondence with Devers also indicates that he expected to get the command. This is confirmed by his deliberations over commanders for the army group and the armies participating in the operation. His short list for senior commanders included Devers, Eisenhower, Mark Clark, Bradley, and Patton.[2]

The president, however, had not announced a decision about the commander for Overlord when he left for the Allied conferences in Tehran and Cairo in November. By then, FDR had witnessed the furor around a Marshall appointment, including a letter from General John J. Pershing stating that he was "deeply disturbed by the repeated newspaper reports that General Marshall is to be transferred to a tactical command in England." The former commander of the AEF felt that Marshall was the best officer to provide "the wise and strategic guidance" needed for a global war.[3] This letter did not close Roosevelt's mind to Marshall's appointment, but it cast doubt on its wisdom. In response, FDR told Pershing, "I want George to be the Pershing of the Second World War."[4]

Roosevelt looked for a way to give Marshall the command and at the same time quiet his critics who claimed he wanted to get rid of the army chief of staff. One solution was for Marshall to assume command of all Allied operations in the European and Mediterranean theaters, accompanied by a promotion to five-star general. When the British received this proposal, Churchill and Brooke vehemently rejected it, knowing that Marshall opposed their desire to extend major operations in Italy and the eastern Mediterranean. The British wanted a British supreme commander in the Mediterranean and an American one in the European theater.[5]

Roosevelt, Churchill, and their military advisers met in Cairo in late November, where they agreed to disagree about the Mediterranean strategy.[6] They then proceeded to Tehran to meet with Soviet dictator Joseph Stalin. When the subjects of the cross-Channel invasion and the Mediterranean strategy came up, Stalin strongly supported Overlord and a concurrent invasion of southern France (code-named Anvil). He compared this to the great pincer attack his armies had used against the Germans at Stalingrad. He also told the Western leaders that he would not consider them serious about Overlord until they selected a commander. Churchill informed Stalin that it had been agreed that the supreme commander would be an American, and Roosevelt would announce his name within a fortnight.[7]

Before they adjourned on 30 November, the Western Allies endorsed Stalin's suggestion for an invasion of southern France in conjunction with Overlord. The overall concept was that two divisions would invade from Corsica and Sardinia and be reinforced by eight additional divisions.[8] Roosevelt again promised that he and Churchill would make a decision about the commander for Overlord. On 2 December the British and Americans returned to Cairo to finish their discussions about how to proceed in the wars against Germany and Japan. By the time the conference ended on 6 December, they had agreed that "nothing was to be undertaken in any part of the world to jeopardize" the success of Overlord and Anvil.[9] As the conference neared an end, Roosevelt told Marshall and Churchill that he had selected General Eisenhower to command Overlord.[10]

This was a shock to Marshall. As late as 2 December, he had still thought he was the designee. Marshall accepted FDR's decision gracefully and drafted the message to Stalin announcing the appointment. He also thoughtfully sent the handwritten original, signed by Roosevelt, to Eisenhower, saying, "I thought you might like to have this as a memento."[11] Marshall then departed on a long-planned trip to the Pacific to visit MacArthur.

Trading Places: Eisenhower and Devers

The announcement that Eisenhower would be the supreme commander for Overlord ended the suspense and set in motion a number of personnel changes that would affect Devers and Eaker, among others. When Devers heard the news, he sent a congratulatory message to Eisenhower on 12 December, which Ike acknowledged the next day. Eisenhower did not mention his thoughts on key leaders, and Devers still believed that he would be staying in England to work for Eisenhower.[12]

On 18 December Devers shared his thoughts and concerns with Georgie: "Feel a little deflated this morning. The fortunes of war certainly exist and I believe my luck has deserted me for a time. . . . I want to get into a fight and from these shores. I do not believe Gen. M. will come here. This is in a way not so good. He has the drive and the force to do the job. Others may have but I do not know who they are. . . . [I] understand George Patton will be saved. He is really lucky. I am glad."[13] Devers hoped to stay in the European theater and take part in Overlord. Eisenhower had other plans.

On 17 December Eisenhower sent Marshall a message outlining his personnel plans for the European theater. He would take Major General Bedell Smith with him from Africa to serve as his chief of staff in Supreme Headquarters, Allied Expeditionary Force (SHAEF). The British air chief, Marshal Arthur Tedder, was his choice as chief Allied air officer, and Spaatz would command the American Strategic Air Forces. He recommended that Patton go to England to command the next American army established for Overlord (Third Army) and that Devers serve as the American theater commander in the Mediterranean, as "it would appear that he will be superfluous in [the] U.K." Ike came to this conclusion because he intended to have Bradley command the First Army Group once there were two American armies in France.[14] Eisenhower's aide, Butcher, noted in his diary, "This disposes of Devers, but more importantly, retains Clark as Field Commander, leaves Patton for Army command in England, and keeps Lucas as commander in Italy or of ANVIL."[15]

Eisenhower's message did not reach Marshall until 22 December, when he returned to Washington from the Pacific. Marshall was surprised to learn that Eisenhower would be taking most of his senior leaders with him to London. The next day he responded, questioning Eisenhower's "tendency" to gut the Mediterranean theater of key leaders and adding, "what makes it more questionable in my opinion is the business of transferring from England to the Mediterranean those that you do not see clearly in place in the UK setup. I am referring to Eaker and Devers." Eaker's transfer was at the request of Tedder and Spaatz, and Marshall noted, "I am forced to the conclusion that their attitude is selfish and not purely objective."[16]

In an earlier message, the chief of staff had suggested that Devers or McNair be given command of the First Army Group, with Bradley and Patton as army commanders.[17] However, Eisenhower ignored this advice and defended his decisions to Marshall, noting that he had "nothing whatsoever against Devers, and thought I was recommending him for an important post, particularly as I know he would be acceptable to the British." He also claimed to have nothing against Eaker.[18] Marshall accepted Eisenhower's decisions, believing that local commanders should pick their key subordinates. Eisenhower seemed to be reconsidering his decision about Devers when he told Marshall on 27 December that if Devers stayed in England, he would be acceptable as an army commander, along with Patton; they would both serve under Bradley, Ike's pick for army group commander. He then pressed Marshall to select his replacement in the Mediterranean as quickly as possible.[19] Marshall saw this as the ploy that it was, and he acquiesced in Devers's move to the Mediterranean.

No one, however, had told Devers of Eisenhower's plans. On 27 December Devers sent a message to his new boss, telling Eisenhower, "I will be looking forward with real pleasure to your arrival. I have kept the Command System here flexible." He also noted that "personalities are good. Morgan fine personality, the best British officer I deal with. Barker weak. You will need Bedell Smith. For myself, I am delighted to serve under you and believe I can be of most use as the commander of the First Army Group."[20]

Jake wrote to Georgie on 27 December, telling her, "I am indeed glad that Eisenhower has been chosen to lead this effort." He also noted that Eaker was going to the Mediterranean theater. The next day, as he perused the *London Times*, he read that he was being transferred to the Mediterranean to serve as deputy supreme Allied commander under British general

Sir Henry Maitland Wilson and as the commanding general of American forces in the Mediterranean theater. As he told Georgie on 29 December, "imagine my surprise when I learned of my new job. The first word was out of a clear blue sky and the last of my thoughts. . . . Now I feel as I did on three previous occasions a big letdown, another job to clean up and a most difficult one."[21]

On 27 December the president approved a War Department memorandum informing the British of Devers's assignment as the American commander in the Mediterranean and as the deputy supreme commander of Allied forces in the theater. Lieutenant General Eaker was to be the Allied air commander, Mediterranean theater, and the American air component commander in charge of the U.S. Twelfth and Fifteenth Air Forces.[22] Devers received official news of his transfer from Marshall. In a letter sent on 28 December, the chief tried to let him down gently:

> As the year draws to a close, I send you my congratulations and thanks for the fine job you have done in England. During this period of preparations, you have carried on splendidly. . . . Your initiative and sound judgment in handling the many complicated matters has been, as usual, on a high level. Now that decision has been taken that Eisenhower will command OVERLORD, I believe that many matters will clarify. . . . All of the command problems in connection with OVERLORD are not yet determined. I have been in correspondence with Eisenhower in order to obtain his views as to the various assignments involved. You will probably be assigned as the American Commander in the Mediterranean under Wilson and as his Deputy Commander. Your experience in dealing with the British and other Allied Headquarters qualifies you for this assignment. . . . Your assignment there leaves [Mark] Clark in command of an Army.[23]

What was Devers thinking about as he moved to North Africa? He certainly looked with pride on his time in Britain, and in a message to the ETO historian, Colonel W. A. Ganoe, he listed his major accomplishments. Upon taking command he had "found a weak staff organization and a dissatisfied command due to the fact that there seemed no objective outlined." During his tenure he concentrated on building a staff and a proper command setup to prepare for the cross-Channel invasion. He was also proud of his work assisting Eaker in the rebuilding of the Eighth Air Force "in every way possible to increase the tempo of their bombing of Germany." He could have mentioned that he was instrumental in ensuring Eaker's well-earned promotion to lieutenant general. And he had overseen the efforts of Lee's SOS to house and support forces that grew to more than 1 million men by the end of 1943.[24]

Why did Eisenhower abruptly eject Devers from the European theater? He certainly knew that Marshall thought highly of Devers, even suggesting him for a senior command in Overlord. Clearly, Eisenhower was motivated partly by revenge, dating from his encounters with Devers in January and during the summer of 1943. Eisenhower was also happiest when surrounded by his own loyal followers and uncomfortable with someone as outspoken as Devers. As his biographer wrote, "Eisenhower was ruthless in accepting only men he knew and trusted in the ETO. Those who crossed him also paid, among them Lt. Gen. Jacob L. Devers." D'Este went on to say that "Jake Devers would never become a member of Club Eisenhower."[25] Ike's personality was in stark contrast to Jake's, who "invariably looked for the good in people and took it for granted that others acted in a similar manner."[26] Getting rid of Devers also eliminated someone Marshall thought highly of and might pose a threat to Ike's position.

Assuming Command in the Mediterranean Theater

As he prepared to leave London, Devers wrote to Georgie: "Gen. Marshall wrote me a grand letter today. He is sincere and the letter is helpful but some of our men in high places are feeling their oats and are most obnoxious to me."[27] It is unclear who he was talking about here. It could have been Major General Bedell Smith, Eisenhower's chief of staff and hatchet man, who had arrived in London to begin organizing SHAEF on 28 December. Or he may have been talking about Omar Bradley, Eisenhower's close friend. In any case, Devers was lucky from a professional point of view: he was getting out of the European theater, where Eisenhower and Bradley disliked him intensely.[28]

Four days later Devers flew to North Africa. Since Eisenhower was changing the entire staff of the European theater, Brigadier General Tristram Tupper, Devers's public affairs officer, and Major General David Barr, his chief of staff, accompanied him and filled their respective positions in the North African theater. When Devers arrived in Algiers, the Allied and

American headquarters were in chaos due to the transfer of senior staff officers to London. He met his new boss, General Wilson, and wrote to Georgie, "He is a grand man. We will soon have a great fighting loyal team with Eaker as the other member."[29]

He was not so pleased with some of his other colleagues. He told Georgie, "[I wish] I could re-arrange some of the command set up in commanders. [Lieutenant General Mark] Clark is not a good commander. I have known this for some time but now it drifts in to me from many sources. Also I have the Patton problem. George should go home. I hope Washington handles this one as I am devoted to George. . . . Omar Bradley is a top commander. Wish I had him in Africa."[30] Clark and the Fifth Army would be major concerns over the next ten months. As for Patton, Eisenhower told Marshall that Patton and Devers were not "congenial," but he admitted having "nothing but impression on which to make the above statement."[31] Eisenhower took Patton, removing a potential source of trouble for Devers and saving a fine army commander for the European theater.

While Wilson and Eaker welcomed him, Devers was not comfortable with Bedell Smith's treatment of him and the theater headquarters. When the decision was made to move Eisenhower to the European theater and Devers to the Mediterranean, Churchill asked that Smith stay at Allied Forces Headquarters (AFHQ) for a while to ensure a smooth transition for Generals Wilson and Devers. So, after a brief stay in London, Smith returned to Africa on 5 January. A few days after he arrived in Algiers, Jake wrote to Georgie: "The C of S to Ike is a very important person and rather difficult at times. He is very aggressive and efficient but does know that others are also."[32]

Smith rubbed Devers the wrong way, but he could still see "Beetle's" talents. Smith certainly did not hesitate to assert himself to more senior officers. While in London in December, Smith had demanded that the chief of the Imperial General Staff, Alan Brooke, transfer three British generals from AFHQ to SHAEF. Brooke did not appreciate the aggressive manner in which Smith made these demands, writing in his diary on 31 December that Smith and "Eisenhower are anxious to take all the heads of Staff departments out of the Mediterranean!! This will want watching!" He wrote that "Bedell Smith had gone off a lot and was suffering from a swollen head." Brooke found it necessary "to put Smith in his place. . . . I told him I would have no string pulling."[33] Brooke later told Eisenhower that he did not appreciate Smith's rude approach, a remark that "amazed" Ike.

Nonetheless, Brooke allowed Generals R. N. Gale and J. F. M. Whiteley to be transferred from the Mediterranean to serve on the SHAEF staff.[34]

Smith and Devers quickly clashed over the issue of personnel transfers. Smith and Eisenhower wanted Lucian Truscott, probably the best division commander in the Mediterranean theater, and other senior staff, including Major General George Strong, the G-2, and Major General Thomas Larkin, commander of the theater's logistical system, moved to England. Devers refused to release them and several other officers.[35] Outraged, Smith charged into Devers's office insisting that they go over the list of requested officers one by one. In what turned into an "acrimonious free-for-all," Devers "proved a tough nut to crack," which irritated Smith. Smith, who "had once considered Devers 'a good friend,'" now described him as a "light weight."[36] Devers wrote to Georgie: "[I] had quite a session with Bedell Smith and brought him around to a sane man again. It is very difficult to have to tell a Chief of Staff of another commander what he will have to do. . . . Bedell and I have been friends for a long time and it would have been a big mistake for him to have gone from here with a very bad odor behind him. He was in the wrong all the way and it was scandalous what they were proposing to do."[37] Devers still considered Smith a friend. Unfortunately, he was wrong.

The AFHQ staff said farewell to Smith on 17 January, and he departed the next day for London. The internecine struggle between the European and Mediterranean commands for key officers continued into February. Eisenhower was frustrated with Devers's slowness in picking which corps commander he wanted transferred from England to the Mediterranean, and he complained to Marshall about Devers's deliberateness and his refusal to release Truscott.[38] Eisenhower also wrote to Devers on 1 February, stating that he could have any corps commander except Leonard Gerow. Devers asked for Willis Crittenberger and his IV Corps staff and released Major General Everett Hughes to serve on Eisenhower's staff.[39]

The tussle over officers did not improve Eisenhower's view of Devers. Devers, however, had much bigger issues to deal with than badgering from London about personnel assignments. He faced significant challenges in his new job, which had been sprung on him with no warning. To make matters worse, he became seriously ill with pneumonia and was forced to stay in bed for nearly a week in mid-January.[40]

Devers had two major responsibilities in the Mediterranean theater. First, in his role as deputy supreme Allied commander, he worked closely with British general Henry Maitland Wilson, who had replaced Eisenhower. Known as "Jumbo" due to his height (six feet, seven inches) and girth, Wilson was one of the more successful senior British officers in the war. A veteran of the Boer War (1899–1902) and the First World War, Wilson had done a solid job extricating British troops from Greece in 1941. He then served in the eastern Mediterranean, where he showed considerable political skill in dealing with the French. Wilson was self-confident and understood that he worked for the Combined Chiefs of Staff, not just for Churchill.[41] Devers and Wilson worked well together over the next year. Devers called Wilson an "exceedingly fine officer" and observed that his chief of staff "has a marvelous personality. I feel sure that this Headquarters, which at this moment seems to be disorganized, will soon straighten out and become an efficient, cooperative organization."[42]

The AFHQ was a combined British and American organization with responsibility for strategic operations in the Mediterranean. Wilson was in charge because the majority of forces in the theater were British. His and Devers's major concerns were the Italian campaign, planning for the invasion of southern France (Operation Anvil), and the Allied air campaigns against German strategic targets in the Balkans and tactical targets in Italy.

Devers's second major responsibility was serving as commanding general of the North African theater of operations, U.S. Army (NATOUSA). As theater commander, Devers was responsible for the logistical and administrative support of all American forces in the Mediterranean region. The Fifth Army in Italy, commanded by Lieutenant General Mark Clark, and the Twelfth and Fifteenth Air Forces, under Lieutenant General Ira Eaker, were the largest American contingents in the theater. The two American air forces were commanded by Major Generals John Cannon (Twelfth) and Nathan Twining (Fifteenth). Eaker's Allied command included the British air forces in the theater as well.

Devers was not responsible for the tactical employment of American ground forces in Italy. British general Harold Alexander was in charge of the Italian campaign; Clark's Fifth Army and Lieutenant General Oliver Leese's British Eighth Army served under him in the Fifteenth Army Group. Alexander had been a good tactical commander at the division level and below. Sadly, he was in over his head as an army group commander. "Intellectually he was unimpressive, although whether this stemmed from genuine stupidity or an Edwardian desire not to appear too keen is open to doubt," wrote the editors of Brooke's war diaries.[43] Brooke, after a visit to Alexander's headquarters, wrote, "To my mind it is quite clear that Alex is not gripping this show."[44] Amazingly, Eisenhower had preferred Alexander over Montgomery as the British army group commander for Overlord, but Brooke had overruled him. Brooke knew Alexander lacked imagination and wrote, "I am afraid that Winston is beginning to see some of Alex's shortcomings! It was bound to come some time or other, but means difficult times ahead. I wonder how I have succeeded in keeping him covered up to now."[45] Devers would have to deal with Alexander on a number of major issues, and they would clash over strategic priorities in the Mediterranean theater.

Major Generals Everett Hughes and Thomas Larkin handled American logistical and administrative details in the Mediterranean. Hughes commanded the NATOUSA Communications Zone (COMZ), and Larkin ran the American Services of Supply (SOS). Hughes soon followed Smith and Eisenhower to London, and Larkin became the essential logistical operator in the theater and later in the Southern Lines of Communication in France. Larkin proved to be one of the most effective logisticians of the war, and Devers warmed to him immediately.

In addition to all his other responsibilities, Devers found himself involved with the Free French Forces under Charles de Gaulle and the French Committee of National Liberation. In mid-1943 the Combined Chiefs of Staff had decided to arm a French army of about ten divisions in North Africa, and they gave the American NATOUSA commander responsibility for this task.[46] Devers inherited the program, which was about two-thirds complete in January 1944. Two of these French divisions were serving in Italy in the French Expeditionary Corps, and Fifth Army was responsible for their logistical support. The remaining French divisions were in the process of being armed and trained. Devers would face major challenges working with the French for the rest of the war. These responsibilities prompted him to write to Georgie, "No job that I have had to do has been as difficult as this one. The theater is as large as the U.S. and even larger. British influence predominates. I get along fine with the British for we have a fine group of real men here. . . . Of course I miss you always, but most when these changes come which require so much thought and planning."[47]

The Stalemate in Italy

The stalemated campaign in Italy immediately got Devers's and Wilson's attention. Eisenhower, as supreme Allied commander until January 1944, had created the strategic situation they faced. Historian Douglas Porch concluded, "Eisenhower's strategy, based on wishful thinking and best-case scenarios, had drawn the allies into a campaign without clear strategic objectives beyond a vague desire to capture Rome and tie down German divisions."[48] By early 1944, it seemed impossible to end the campaign in Italy and equally hard to push the Germans out of their positions south of Rome.

The Allied armies had invaded the Italian mainland in September 1943. The Germans, after stiff fighting at Salerno against U.S. Fifth Army, executed a fighting withdrawal to a line anchored in the center of Italy at the town of Cassino. Throughout the fall, German troops fought to slow the Allied advance, while German engineers and Italian laborers fortified what they called the Gustav Line. There, they stopped Clark's Fifth Army and Leese's British Eighth Army. Field Marshal Albert Kesselring, the senior German commander, believed that he could hold most of Italy well into 1944 with minimal forces, while inflicting heavy casualties on the Allies.[49] The Allies, conversely, hoped to tie down German divisions in Italy by continuing to attack, thus denying those forces to the Russian front or France. In trying to achieve these limited goals, the Allies found that combat in Italy was "continuous, casualty-heavy, and physically and psychologically exhausting."[50]

The British had high hopes for operations in Italy and looked for a way to break the stalemate on the Gustav Line. Churchill, who remained in North Africa after the Allied conferences in Cairo and Tehran, pushed hard for amphibious operations to land forces behind the German defenses. To make this possible, he convinced Roosevelt to leave landing craft, especially landing ship, tanks (LSTs), in the Mediterranean until January. These naval resources would allow the Allies to execute an amphibious end run around the Gustav Line. Planning for the amphibious operation (code-named Shingle) was the responsibility of Fifteenth Army Group in Italy.[51]

In November 1943, well before he was selected for the Overlord command, Eisenhower had ordered General Alexander to plan Shingle, with an initial target date of 15 December. Alexander delegated the mission to Clark's Fifth Army, since the majority of the troops involved would be American. Clark selected the seaport of Anzio and the beaches nearby as the invasion area because they were within range of Allied fighter aircraft, just thirty-five miles southeast of Rome and twenty miles from the Alban Hills and Italian Highways 6 and 7. If the landing force could cut those highways, the Germans would be unable to sustain their divisions farther south. For this operation to succeed, the Allied armies along the Gustav Line needed to tie down the German reserves, break through the German defenses, and link up with the Shingle forces. Fifth Army planned to accomplish this by launching a major offensive in the two weeks before the Anzio operation was to take place. British Tenth Corps was to attack across the Garigliano River near the Italian west coast, and U.S. II Corps was to launch an assault across the Rapido River at Sant'Angelo, in the mouth of the Liri valley. Clark and Alexander believed that attacking the Gustav Line would tie down the German reserves, preventing their use against the Anzio landing. Clark further hoped that once his II Corps broke through the German lines near Cassino, the American 1st Armored Division would be able to drive up the Liri River valley to Frosinone and link up with the Shingle forces.[52]

Before Eisenhower left, the operation was delayed while Churchill tried to convince Roosevelt to leave landing craft in the region. Clark then canceled Shingle on 18 December; a stalemate was developing along the Gustav Line, and he thought there was insufficient time to prepare the invasion force and launch the assault before the landing craft had to sail to England. However, even before the British were firmly in charge of the Mediterranean theater, Shingle was resurrected and forcibly advocated by Churchill, who felt that "stagnation of the whole campaign on the Italian Front is becoming scandalous."[53] From 18 to 25 December, Churchill badgered Eisenhower and Alexander with ideas and arguments for undertaking the amphibious end run. Eisenhower, who now knew that he would be leaving the Mediterranean, "refrained from active participation in the discussions," and Wilson was too new to make an impact. Clark warmed to the plan again when he realized that it might allow his army to be the first to capture an enemy capital. He prepared a plan for VI Corps, under the command of Major General John Lucas, to land with one American and one British infantry division at Anzio. Clark submitted the plan to Generals Wilson and Alexander shortly after Christmas.[54]

Clark nonetheless remained ambivalent about Shingle. On the one hand, he had no other ideas about how to break the stalemate at the Gustav Line; on the other hand, he was worried about the logistical elements of the amphibious operation. As he told Alexander and wrote in his diary, "None of those [in AFHQ] who thus lightheartedly decided on the SHINGLE operation understood the details of shipping and of loading necessary to put ashore the requisite force and maintain it when once ashore."[55] He also remembered the nearly disastrous Allied assault at Salerno in September, when German forces nearly drove the Allies back into the sea. Clark insisted, therefore, that Alexander and Churchill guarantee the retention of sufficient LSTs to sustain the landing force. Alexander agreed, and Churchill was able to convince Roosevelt to delay the departure of the landing craft until February.[56]

Due to this sequence of events, Devers found himself at a meeting in Marrakech on 7 January with Churchill, Wilson, Bedell Smith, and Alexander, discussing whether to undertake Shingle. The group decided to launch the operation with a target date of 20 January.[57] At the time, Devers "wondered why the conference was necessary, for what to him seemed to be a simple military decision [that] could have been reached, he believed, without the eloquent and lengthy discussion that went on."[58] Devers noted that "the answers that came out of [the conference] were correct."[59] The eloquence in this case came from Churchill, who was working hard to impose his vision of Mediterranean operations and opportunities on Wilson and Devers.

Wilson, Devers, and Alexander should have paid more attention to the assessment of the AFHQ intelligence officer, Major General Kenneth Strong. Strong believed that the Allied leadership had underestimated the strength of the Gustav Line, and it was wishful thinking that Kesselring would abandon his fortified line when two Allied divisions landed at Anzio.[60] To the officers at the Marrakech meeting who pointed out the grave risks in the Shingle plan, Churchill answered: "Of course there is risk. But without risk there is no honour, no glory, no adventure."[61]

After the conference, Churchill informed Roosevelt that "unanimous agreement for action" had been reached. "Everyone is in good heart."[62] In an earlier message to Clark, he had reminded the Fifth Army commander "of the importance of this battle, without which the campaign in Italy will be regarded as having petered out ingloriously. . . . I know you will do everything in human power."[63] Clark was less than confident about the amphibious operation and felt that "a pistol was being aimed at [my] head" by Churchill.[64]

The Preliminaries to Shingle

In the first half of January, while VI Corps was preparing to launch the assault at Anzio, Fifth Army fought its way across the last eight miles of rugged Italian terrain to close with the Gustav Line. Clark's army included three corps. On the left (west), British Tenth Corps, commanded by Lieutenant General R. L. McCreery, fought its way to the Garigliano River with three British divisions. In the center of Fifth Army, facing the mouth of the Liri valley, Major General Geoffrey Keyes's U.S. II Corps' three divisions clawed their way over the mountains south of the Gari-Rapido-Garigliano line near Cassino. On Clark's right, the French Expeditionary Corps, under General Alphonse Juin, closed to the Gari River with two divisions.[65]

Under heavy Allied attacks, the Germans finally began to withdraw into their well-prepared positions on the Gustav Line on 7 January, and by the middle of the month, Fifth Army had reached the main German defenses. The Germans had spent three months preparing their fortifications. Concrete bunkers, well-protected weapons pits, and steel-turreted machine gun emplacements made the defenders nearly immune from Allied air attack and artillery fire. Italian workers, supervised by German army engineers, had cleared the brush along the front to obtain better fields of fire. German engineers had installed mines along obvious avenues of approach, and German artillery observers overlooked the Liri valley and the front lines from high ground such as Monte Cassino. Ninety thousand Germans manned the defenses in front of Fifth Army, and I Parachute Corps, with two panzer grenadier divisions, was in reserve near Rome; from there, it could reinforce the Gustav Line or counterattack amphibious operations near Rome.[66]

Clark realized that the initial Anzio assault would succeed only if the German reserves near Rome were drawn south to help defend the Gustav Line. Therefore, he planned for Fifth Army to attack the Gustav Line across the entire front in the two weeks before Shingle was scheduled to begin on 22 January. British Tenth Corps would attack across the Garigliano River on the west coast, near the towns of Minturno and Castel Forte; Keyes's II Corps would attack across the Rapido River in the Liri valley; and the French Expeditionary Corps would assault the German positions north of Cassino, with the objective of capturing Monte Cassino.[67]

Juin's French Expeditionary Corps attacked north of Cassino on 12 January. During the next three days, the French fought their way across four miles of mountainous terrain before being stopped by German reserves. McCreery's Tenth Corps launched its assault across the Garigliano River on the night of 17 January, with the British 5th Division on the left, next to the coast, and the 56th Division in the center. Thanks to the element of surprise, the British advanced three miles in the next two days against the

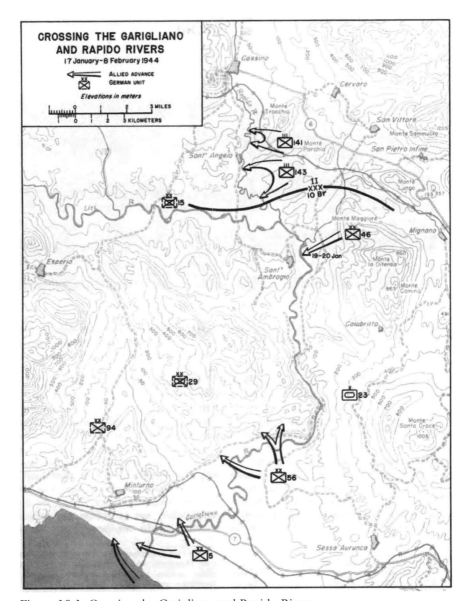

Figure 10.1. Crossing the Garigliano and Rapido Rivers

German 94th Infantry Division. After the British captured the high ground around Minturno, Kesselring concluded, "This is the greatest crisis that we have so far experienced," and he feared that Tenth Corps' attack was an attempt to outflank the Liri valley defenses from the south. In response, he ordered I Parachute Corps and its two divisions to move from near Rome to reinforce the Gustav Line and stop the British drive.[68]

Kesselring's decision to move his reserves south played into Clark's plan for Shingle. The German commander and the German intelligence agencies had completely missed preparations for the Anzio operation. Admiral Wilhelm Canaris, chief of German intelligence in Berlin, told Kesselring on 15 January, "There is not the slightest possibility of an imminent Allied amphibious operation," and "there is not the slightest sign that a new landing will be undertaken in the near future."[69]

Thanks to Ultra, Alexander and Clark knew that the German reserves around Rome had moved south.[70] Consequently, it was not necessary for Keyes to launch II Corps against the Germans' heavily fortified positions in the mouth of the Liri River valley. Instead, he could have shifted American divisions from his center to reinforce the successes on his flanks.[71] Such a move would have allowed the British and French corps to continue their efforts to outflank Kesselring's heavily fortified Liri valley positions. Unfortunately, Clark stuck to his plan to attack the Gustav Line near Sant'Angelo.

Battle of the Rapido

Clark's plan called for a phased assault against the Gustav Line by his three corps: first the French, followed by the British Tenth Corps on 17 January, and then Keyes's II Corps on 20 January, two days before Shingle. II Corps' goal was to breach the German defenses along the Rapido River near Sant'Angelo and open a hole for the 1st Armored Division to send its armor toward Frosinone. Keyes gave Major General Fred Walker's 36th Infantry Division the mission to assault across the Rapido.[72]

Sant'Angelo was heavily fortified by the Germans and defended by their 15th Panzer Grenadier Division, one of the strongest German formations in Italy. The Rapido River was about fifty feet wide and at flood stage. The ground on the American side of the river was marshy and had been mined by the Germans; their artillery observers and machine gunners had clear views and fields of fire on both sides of the river. The Germans controlled the high ground overlooking the Liri valley, and the British 46th Division had failed to cross the Garigliano River and capture the town of Sant'Ambrogio, to the left of the 36th Infantry Division. Neither Keyes nor Walker believed the 36th could cross the Rapido. Keyes informed Clark that the river assault was "unsound" due to the Germans' defenses and their control of the high ground overlooking the valley.[73]

Walker evaluated the terrain along the Rapido and recognized that the chance of his division being cut to pieces was high. As Rick Atkinson observed, "By early January he [Walker] had persuaded himself that the Rapido resembled the Marne, where in July of 1918, as a thirty-one-year-old battalion commander, he had earned the Distinguished Service Cross for repelling an attack across the river by ten thousand Germans. He had never forgotten the sodden enemy corpses lining the muddy banks and drifting on the current."[74] Walker wrote in his diary on 8 January, "I do not see how we, or any other division, can possibly succeed in crossing the Rapido River."[75]

Nonetheless, on the night of 20 January, two regiments of the 36th Infantry Division attempted to cross the fast-flowing Rapido in rubber and wooden assault boats. Everything went wrong from the outset. American engineers and infantrymen were cut down by German artillery and machine guns as they tried to move the boats across the open marsh on the near side of the river. The engineers had marked clear lanes through the minefields, but these were soon obscured by the churning of the earth, and many men set off mines as they wandered around in the dark. The few men who got across the river were pinned down by German fire. By dawn, hundreds of men had been hit by gunfire, drowned in the river, or blown up by mines. Yet Clark ordered Keyes and Walker to launch another effort to cross.[76]

On the afternoon and evening of 21 January, the soldiers of the 36th Infantry Division tried again. Atkinson described the second assault: "Off they went, trudging like men sent to the scaffold. A soldier stumping down a sunken road toward the Rapido observed, 'There was a dead man every ten yards, just like they were in formation.'"[77] The second effort brought some gains, as five battalions of infantry got across at two bridgeheads. Then disaster struck again. South of Sant'Angelo, three battalions of the 143rd Infantry Regiment moved less than 500 yards from the far bank before German fire pinned them down. To the north, two battalions of the 141st Infantry Regiment got across but were hemmed in by German fire and counterattacks. German artillery and machine gun fire prevented the engineers from installing heavy bridges for tanks, leaving the infantrymen on the far shore at the mercy of German armor. Without support, both regiments were decimated by fire. Casualties mounted, and in the 141st Regiment, every commander save one was killed or wounded. Reluctantly,

Walker ordered the survivors to pull back across the river.[78] Far too few made it.

The 36th Infantry Division suffered heavy casualties in the disastrous Rapido operation. In forty-eight hours, 1,681 men were killed, wounded, or captured out of the roughly 6,000 soldiers in the two regiments. These losses were on top of the 23,000 casualties Fifth Army had suffered since the middle of December. German losses were negligible at the Rapido, and only after they had counted the American dead and prisoners on their side of the river did the Germans realize the magnitude of the 36th Division's effort to cross.[79]

Many of the soldiers who fell or were captured at the Rapido during those two miserable nights were replacements who had never even met their leaders. They had joined the 36th to fill the ranks thinned in the fighting to get to the Gustav Line.[80] The division had insufficient time to integrate and train these new men because there were too few divisions in the theater, and in the U.S. Army, to allow divisions to periodically rotate out of the line. Devers would work hard to remedy this problem over the next five months in the Mediterranean theater.

The Personnel Crisis and Fifth Army

Devers had not been privy to Fifth Army's plans due to his short time in the Mediterranean and his illness. But once he grasped the situation in Fifth Army, he set to work to correct some of the personnel problems highlighted by the Rapido disaster.

One of the most difficult problems faced by the U.S. Army in the Second World War involved manpower. Although nearly 8 million soldiers were serving in the U.S. Army (including the Army Air Forces) in January 1944, there was a serious shortage of replacements for combat units. The first message Devers received from Marshall in his new command concerned the proper use of manpower in the Mediterranean theater. Marshall wrote, "The present manpower situation is critical. There is a shortage of planned strength by several hundred thousand men. The situation has been aggravated by a tendency to discharge men who could render further service, and the excessive use of physically qualified personnel in limited service positions. . . . The Army must be maintained with the personnel at hand, and it rests with the commander to do so. A commander who permits the discharge of an enlisted man, in preference to making the necessary effort to properly place and train him, fails to meet his responsibilities." Marshall was also concerned that commanders placed too little emphasis on soldiers' hygiene, sanitation, and preventive medicine, as indicated by high sick rates, high rates of discharge, and transfers for mental or physical reasons. He closed his message by telling Devers and the other theater commanders around the world to give such matters their "prompt personal and continuing attention."[81]

Devers promptly investigated the personnel situation and found that of the roughly 17,000 "limited assignment" men who had accumulated in the Mediterranean theater over the past two years, 12,000 had been placed in service units, freeing "Class A" men for assignment to combat units. He also found that a significant number of these men were "neuro-psychiatric" cases and that a screening process was in place to return as many of them as possible to duty. He reported to the chief of staff that "this type of casualty is first scrutinized by Regimental Surgeons and all those suspected of malingering are returned to their units after a brief period of observation. A similar screening is continued in the case of those who are sent back to hospitals." After this process, "there are very few who are not out-and-out psychiatric cases." Once such a soldier reached the replacement depot in Oran, a final evaluation board determined whether to send him home for discharge or place him on limited duty in the theater.[82]

Devers further discovered that the sick rate in Clark's Fifth Army was "abnormally high." He directed all commanders to increase training in mental and physical hygiene, sanitation, and other preventive measures. These steps, however, would not eliminate what Devers concluded to be the root cause of high casualty rates: "A great deal of this . . . is due to exhaustion which is a result of the necessity of continuing the same units in combat month after month, and the very severe conditions of rain, mud, cold, and mountain warfare" in Italy.[83]

The strain on the American infantry divisions in Italy was the result of a decision made in 1943 by Secretary of War Stimson and Marshall. They elected to limit the number of army divisions to 90 or fewer because there appeared to be insufficient American manpower to fill more divisions and still have enough workers to meet the needs of industry. When the United States entered the war, the War Department staff planned to field an army of 215 divisions, based on the assumption that the U.S. and British armies would have to face the Germans without help from the Soviet army. By the summer of 1942, Marshall had reduced the planned number of divisions to

111, due to the shortage of manpower and the survival of the Red Army. In the spring of 1943, as the American industrial base rapidly expanded, the War Department recognized the need to further reduce the number of divisions to 100. Marshall and Stimson decided to field no more than 88 divisions that year, and the remaining 12 divisions would be organized in 1944. Ultimately, as manpower remained constrained, the army created only 90 divisions.[84]

This decision caused a major shortage of divisions in the combat theaters. Consequently, commanders such as Clark had to leave their divisions in the front lines for long periods because they had no divisions in reserve to rotate in and out of the line. In the words of historian Peter Mansoor, "a decision based on the erroneous belief that American industry could not give up more manpower to the military without incurring shortfalls" led to a severe shortage of divisions in the European and Mediterranean theaters.[85] In addition, the Fifth Army in Italy was hit hard in 1943 by the withdrawal of four divisions for Overlord (1st and 9th Infantry, 2nd Armored, and 82nd Airborne), leaving Clark with just four infantry divisions and one armored division in early 1944. Devers's response to Marshall confirmed Mansoor's view that this situation forced Clark to keep his few divisions "engaged more or less continuously" during the 1943–1944 campaign in Italy. Mansoor concluded, "The provision of more combat divisions to the overseas theaters would have resulted in fewer casualties over the course of the war."[86]

Having been in the Mediterranean theater for less than three weeks, and having just recovered from a serious bout of pneumonia, Devers responded to the message from Marshall by visiting Fifth Army to assess the situation. As he wrote to Georgie on 18 January, "I am on my way to the front tomorrow."[87] When he arrived at Fifth Army headquarters on 19 January, Devers was impressed with the staff but concerned about the personnel situation in the infantry divisions. He concluded:

> The big turnover in manpower in the 5th Army is due fundamentally to the fact that the divisions are left in the line too long; in the case of the 45th, as long as 90 days; in the case of other divisions, longer than 50 days. It is my fixed opinion that no division should be kept in the line longer than 21 days, when it should be withdrawn to refit. Men get tired; colds, trench feet, and so forth tend to debilitate them, slow them up, bring lack of enthusiasm,

make them careless, causing the hospitalization of large numbers. It is like the plague—once it starts, it is hard to stop. Also there is an epidemic of neurosis, brought on, in my opinion, by the Patton incident [Patton had slapped a patient suffering from post-traumatic stress disorder]. This needs firm handling in order that the men may be put back to do the job they can do.[88]

The medical system was a crucial part of the personnel system. If more soldiers who were sick or wounded could be returned to their units fit for combat, the shortage of trained replacements would be less severe. After his investigation of the system, Devers concluded, "Our hospitals and doctors are working hard and effectively in taking care of the wounded. They are entirely too soft on the sick, or non-battle casualties. This is something that has grown up in this theater before my arrival and should have been solved many months ago. The mental side of it was given considerable publicity and propaganda due to the Patton incident which was very unfortunate. This has not affected the fighting of the troops in the front lines, but has demoralized the return of non-battle casualties to the front."[89]

While in Italy, Devers shared some of his thoughts with General Edwin Sibert in London. "We are making some progress here with a very difficult situation. The theater is tremendous. The organization must have been good to have functioned at all but seems terribly complicated to me. I have put Barr to work . . . to determine what the organization should be. . . . Finally I have been to the front, have seen the French Corps, actually fighting, have been bracketed by the German artillery and have seen our artillery reply fivefold." He concluded the letter to his friend with this observation: "I am particularly pleased with General Clark and the 5th Army. They are doing a magnificent job, using imagination," but "troubles are the same— lack of trained replacements—too many men in the [replacement] pipeline via hospitals—too much overhead."[90]

Devers remained in Italy for two weeks, during which time he noted, "I have seen all our army and division commanders. . . . There is much to be done and it will be a slow process for we are slugging it out with the enemy in a way I do not like. The enemy is getting a beating but we are paying more than I like."[91] When he visited Juin's French troops north of Monte Cassino, he remarked on the incredibly difficult terrain along the Gustav Line: "What mountains, just like the back roads in the Rockies with switchbacks, very narrow." On 22 January he was in Clark's headquarters in Caserta, near Naples, when VI Corps launched the amphibious operation at Anzio.[92]

Even before he returned to AFHQ in Algiers, Devers initiated an effort to convince key army leaders to provide more divisions for the theater. He first wrote to General Thomas Handy, Marshall's key staff officer in the War Department, offering his observations and implying a solution:

> There is one point that I wish to leave with you, one which it will take time to correct, and that is the fact that divisions cannot stay in the line more than 40 days without being pulled out for a rest, to be reequipped and brought up to strength. In fact, 21 days was a long time in the last war. The result in this theater of not doing so is that every division, including the French, British and American, is having a hard time maintaining their replacements and their morale. It is the old story of playing a man too long at one time. He gets tired, and then he becomes careless and becomes a casualty.[93]

He ended the letter by telling Handy that it was essential to have good senior commanders who knew how to organize and use a staff. "We are making some adjustments in this line," he stated, "and I have started reorganizing my command so we can be more effective."[94]

In a similar letter to Lesley McNair, Army Ground Forces commander, Devers told his friend and former boss that when troops were in the line too long, "everybody gets tired, then they get careless, and there are tremendous sick rates and casualty rates. Everybody should know this. The result is that you feed replacements into a machine in the line, and it is like throwing good money after bad."[95] In a letter to Marshall he stressed that because the divisions were in the line too long, "our replacement system is breaking down as we have an unusually large number of non-battle casualties. . . . The shortage of divisions makes the solution of this problem difficult, but we are going after it energetically."[96]

Back in the fall, Generals Clark and Eisenhower had recognized that there were too few infantry divisions in Fifth Army and had asked for at least one new division to be assigned to the Mediterranean theater. Marshall acceded to this request, promising that the 88th Infantry Division would arrive in February or March and that the 85th Infantry Division would follow shortly thereafter.[97] But with the theater planning for a two-division invasion of southern France, there would be little relief.

The eventual arrival of the 85th and 88th Infantry Divisions in the spring enabled Fifth Army to rotate weary divisions out of the line, but in January and February the situation remained critical. When the 34th and 36th Infantry Divisions tried to fight their way into Cassino and cross the Rapido River, their units suffered severe setbacks, due in large part to poorly trained replacements in exhausted infantry units. Devers remained deeply concerned about this situation and directed his staff to comb the rear-area units for men who were fit for combat and to ensure that the personnel system was operating as efficiently as possible.

In an effort to solve the army-wide problems of manpower and replacements, the War Department created a Manpower Board whose mission was to visit all army theaters and assess their efforts to improve the personnel system and make the best use of the available manpower. Major General Jack Heard was in charge of the team that investigated the Mediterranean theater from January to March 1944. His report to the Manpower Board in Washington was not flattering to Devers. For his part, Devers wrote to Georgie, "The War Dept. sent Jack Heard and a group over here to work on manpower. What an insult to one's intelligence."[98]

After spending two months in the Mediterranean theater, Heard observed that although Devers had initially intended to clean house, "the influence of an empire building atmosphere was too much for him. He now seems to be of the opinion that the 'tail cannot at this time be curled up.' And no reductions can be made until after future operations have been mounted." Heard believed that the theater was overstrength and was not using native manpower resources to the extent possible. Heard reported to the War Department that General Larkin was traveling to Washington to emphasize to the staff "the requirements of service units to mount future operations" and that he would attempt to get authorization for even more personnel.[99]

What the Manpower Board's team did not understand was that, since his arrival, Devers had become fully aware of the immense operational difficulties faced by his Services of Supply, commanded by Major General Thomas Larkin. The SOS was responsible for the logistical support of two air forces, two field armies, and the Air Transport Command. Its units and responsibilities were spread throughout a huge geographic area, with bases in Corsica and Sardinia and extending from Morocco to Tunisia, from Sicily to Italy. Devers's command was also in charge of rearming the French army and providing ongoing logistical support, planning for Operation Anvil, and reconstructing the rail, port, and road infrastructure of Italy.

Larkin visited Washington, made his case, and sent a response to the Manpower Board. He opened by stating, "The data provided by these documents are incomplete, inaccurate, misleading and, although represented as factual, are not founded on facts." He explained that there was not an excess of personnel in the SOS, nor were there too many hospital units in the theater. In fact, he noted, there was a shortage of hospital beds, sometimes making it necessary "to turn patients out of hospitals prior to completion of treatment." He went on to note that the recommendation to cut 57 percent of the ground service units in the base sections of the SOS could not be taken seriously, since there were only 140,580 U.S. personnel in those organizations.[100]

However, Devers and Larkin did try to reduce the size of the headquarters and improve the replacement system. When Marshall directed that Eisenhower and Devers appoint a single senior officer to control the personnel systems in their respective theaters,[101] Devers responded with a defense of his handling of the manpower challenges:

> The system now is tremendously improved [since January] and functioning, since for the first time, at least since I have been in the theater, the fighting troops are up to strength and are happy with the support being given to them from the rear. There are two ways of handling replacements and personnel in a theater: the one which I established in England under a centralized command, and which I have now adopted in Italy by your direction; the other is to decentralize under base sections. I favor the first method. However, because Larkin favored the second method and because he was to have the responsibility, I desired to give him a fair chance to improve the situation. He had no control before. He has greatly improved the situation since then. I am sure, however, that we will have no more trouble along these lines.[102]

This message highlights how Devers empowered and trusted key subordinates like Larkin and how he dealt with Marshall in such a situation.

Devers also used this opportunity to educate Marshall about the unique characteristics of the Mediterranean theater: "Because of the numerous elements in the British and American armies in this theater, the supply and replacement problems are extremely difficult. When you move an Indian Division it is necessary to move its hospitals, its food establishments, its dumps. The same goes for the Poles and the French. There is little flexibility under these conditions. I am sure that the changes that have been made in the regrouping are in the direction of the greatest possible flexibility."[103] Devers had explained his approach to these difficult issues in an earlier letter to Marshall: "We are making strenuous efforts to use our troops to the best advantage in the battle now in progress in Italy with a view that sometime in the future, if ANVIL should be successful, we can close out completely in Africa and Italy. . . . We are concentrating the entire air force, except the Air Transport Command, in Italy." He further told Marshall that he could not consolidate headquarters and move logistical installations out of Africa until the Germans had been forced north of Rome and the scope of Anvil was clear. Even then, he observed, "we will have to support the French army to some extent. . . . To summarize, we are trying in every way to roll up our tail as soon as possible."[104]

While he dealt with such issues in his own theater, Devers followed closely the fighting in Italy, and especially Operation Shingle, which began on 22 January at Anzio.

Operation Shingle, or the "Stranded Whale"

The decision reached at Marrakech on 8 January 1944 set in motion Operation Shingle, the amphibious assault at Anzio set to begin on 22 January. While Fifth Army hammered at the Gustav Line, Major General John Lucas's VI Corps prepared for the assault. From the beginning, there were diverging views about its immediate purpose. On 2 January the commander of Fifteenth Army Group, Harold Alexander, ordered Fifth Army to "prepare an amphibious operation of two divisions plus to carry out an assault landing on the beaches in the vicinity of Rome with the object of cutting the enemy lines of communication and threatening the rear of the German 14 Corps." Alexander supplemented this mission on 12 January with instructions to land a strong follow-on force to strike quickly from the beachhead to cut the "enemy's main communications in the Colli Laziali [Alban Hills] area southeast of Rome."[105]

General Clark ordered VI Corps "to seize and secure a beachhead in the vicinity of Anzio" and "advance on Colli Laziali." There was no mention in Clark's order of striking north to cut German communications.[106] Clark wanted to avoid a repeat of the near-disaster at Salerno, where the German counterattack nearly drove the Allied amphibious forces back into the sea. To ensure that Lucas clearly understood that he should not take any risks, Clark sent his operations officer, Brigadier General Donald Brann, to reiterate to Lucas that his "primary mission was to seize and secure a beachhead. This was the extent of General Clark's expectations."[107] Lucas was very concerned about a potential German counterattack and wrote in his diary, "This whole affair had a strong odor of Gallipoli [the mishandled British assault on the Dardanelles in 1916] and apparently the same amateur [Churchill] was still on the coaches' bench."[108]

The rehearsal for the landing on 18 January deepened the foreboding of Clark and Lucas. The U.S. Navy mismanaged the operation and lost forty-three DUKWs carrying twenty-eight guns and their crews. There was no time for another rehearsal, since the troops and equipment had to load the ships on 19 and 20 January. According to the army's official history, Lucas was increasingly "out of sympathy and out of touch with the thinking at higher levels." His mental state was made clear when he wrote in his diary: "Army has gone nuts again. . . . They will end up by putting me ashore with inadequate forces and get me in a serious jam."[109]

In spite of Clark's and Lucas's misgivings, VI Corps' assault went off flawlessly on 22 January. The Germans were completely surprised and had fewer than two battalions along the coast from the mouth of the Tiber to Terracina, sixty miles to the southeast. The 3rd Infantry Division landed east of Anzio without resistance and drove three miles inland by noon, with no opposition. Colonel William Darby's three ranger battalions landed in the port of Anzio and secured the town in less than an hour. The British 1st Division's only difficulty was sandbars offshore, but since the port was secure, the division was able to land most of its men and equipment in Anzio. By evening, VI Corps had more than 36,000 men and 3,200 vehicles ashore and had established a beachhead about five miles deep. Thirteen Allied soldiers were killed and ninety-seven wounded, mostly by mines.[110]

Devers, who was visiting Fifth Army headquarters at Caserta, wrote to Georgie: "It was the best plan I have seen anywhere and at this moment it worked for the Germans were completely fooled."[111] It looked as if the road to Rome, or certainly the Alban Hills, was open. Lucas, however, did not unleash an exploitation force, as Alexander had ordered. Instead, he organized a strong defensive perimeter around the beachhead, and for

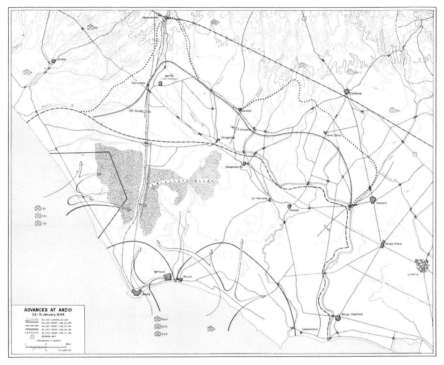

Figure 10.2. Advances at Anzio, 22–31 January 1944

the first four days he concentrated on establishing air defenses around the port. Clark and Alexander, who visited Lucas in Anzio on D-day, were pleased with the initial results. Over the next two days, Clark ordered the 1st Armored and 45th Infantry Divisions to move units to Anzio, but he did not order Lucas to push aggressively toward either Rome or the German communication lines to the north.[112]

Devers later commented in an interview, "Once you get the jump on the Germans, don't stop, keep moving, and keep them moving because if you stop and give them twelve hours, they'll regroup. They did it at Anzio and it was a mistake."[113] This was a lesson he tried to use in the Alsatian campaign of November 1944.

The German reaction to the Anzio landings was swift. On 22 January Kesselring ordered six divisions to start moving to the Anzio area, with the first two arriving by 23 January. By the end of the month, Kesselring had moved two corps headquarters and twelve divisions into the line and placed Generaloberst Eberhard von Mackensen's 14th Army in charge of the defenses. Hitler cooperated by sending divisions from Germany, France, and the Balkans. Kesselring planned to launch a counteroffensive by early February.[114]

There had been little offensive action by Lucas when Devers wrote to Georgie on 27 January, "We have our ups and downs. . . . My trouble—everyone acts so slowly, decisions are so slow to be made and then it trickles down."[115] Finally, on 29 January, Lucas ordered the 3rd Infantry Division and the British 1st Division to launch attacks the next day to capture Cisterna and Campoleone Station, respectively. The British nearly reached their objective, pushing a bulge three miles into the German lines. Major General Lucian Truscott's 3rd Infantry was stopped well short of Cisterna; in the process, Darby's three ranger battalions were mauled, with more than 700 men captured by the Germans.[116]

Lucas resumed his defensive stance—a move Clark approved, since he and Alexander knew from Ultra intercepts that the Germans were ready to launch a major assault against the beachhead. Over the next two weeks, the Germans crushed the British salient near Campoleone and drove the 1st Division back four miles to Carroceto. Lucas was forced to commit the newly arrived American 45th Infantry Division to plug the gap between the British and the Americans. The Germans continued their attacks until 19 February, when the front stabilized. A stalemate then developed as the Germans failed to push VI Corps back further, and the Allies could not drive the Germans back either.[117]

Operation Shingle failed to accomplish the goals set by Alexander. Instead, he and Clark were forced to reinforce VI Corps with the British 56th Division from the Garigliano front and the 1st Armored and 45th Infantry Divisions from II Corps. Casualties in the Anzio bridgehead and along the Gustav Line were heavy on both sides, aggravating the manpower situation. Churchill, who had such high hopes for Shingle, told the South African leader Jan Smuts that "instead of hurling a wild cat on to the shore all we got was a stranded whale and a Sulva Bay over again."[118] Brooke assessed the situation on 31 January by noting in his diary, "News from Italy bad and the landing south of Rome is making little progress, mainly due to the lack of initiative in the early stages."[119]

Victory has a thousand fathers, but defeat only one. The scapegoat in the case of Shingle was Major General John Lucas. As the German counterattack reached its crescendo in mid-February, General Alexander visited the beachhead and was displeased with the lack of initiative and drive on

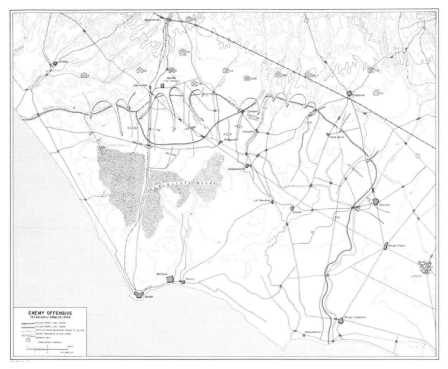

Figure 10.3. Enemy offensive at Anzio, 16 February–3 March 1944

Lucas's part. He returned to his headquarters determined to get Clark to fire Lucas.[120] Devers visited the beachhead on 16 February and was impressed with the logistical arrangements in place but was not pleased with the stalemate. According to Lucas, Devers implied that he had not driven his forces far enough in the first few days, but Lucas believed, "had I done so, I would have lost my Corps."[121]

Devers, Alexander, and Clark met at Clark's headquarters on 17 February and agreed that Lucas should be removed from command, but only after the current German attacks had been defeated. In the interim, they appointed two deputy corps commanders, intending for one of them, Major General Truscott, to take over VI Corps. On 22 February Clark replaced Lucas with Truscott. He explained to Lucas that he had done so because he thought Lucas was worn out, Alexander thought him defeated, and Devers thought him tired.[122]

Lucas paid the price, but his and Clark's decision not to drive to the Alban Hills on D-day was correct. Kesselring's swift reaction showed that if VI Corps had extended itself with its two or three divisions, it most likely would have been cut to pieces. Nonetheless, Wilson, Devers, Alexander, and Clark found themselves with two stalemates in Italy: one at Anzio, and the other along the Gustav Line. This situation made it harder for Devers to solve the manpower problems in the Mediterranean theater, and it jeopardized the operation to invade southern France.

Devers and his mother at West Point, ca. 1905–1906. (From the collection of the York County Heritage Trust, York, PA)

C Battery, 4th Field Artillery, Texas, ca. 1910. Lesley McNair (second from left, seated) was their commanding officer. Devers is third from left. (From the collection of the York County Heritage Trust, York, PA)

Devers and Douglas MacArthur at a baseball practice at West Point, 1920. (From the collection of the York County Heritage Trust, York, PA)

Devers on his pony, Glendale, hitting the polo ball in full stride. (From the collection of the York County Heritage Trust, York, PA)

Devers and the War Department polo team receiving a trophy, 1932. (From the collection of the York County Heritage Trust, York, PA)

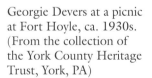

Georgie Devers at a picnic at Fort Hoyle, ca. 1930s. (From the collection of the York County Heritage Trust, York, PA)

Devers, Omar Bradley, and Major General Benedict inspecting Academy cadets, 1939. (From the collection of the York County Heritage Trust, York, PA)

Devers with contractors and his jeep at Fort Bragg, fall 1941. (From the collection of the York County Heritage Trust, York, PA)

Devers and Georgie on horses at Fort Bragg, ca. 1940–1941. (From the collection of the York County Heritage Trust, York, PA)

Devers, ca. 1942. (From the collection of the York County Heritage Trust, York, PA)

Devers with three stars as commander of the Armored Force, 1942. (From the collection of the York County Heritage Trust, York, PA)

Various dignitaries posing with a prototype of the T6 medium tank on "presentation day." Devers was head of the Armored Force, and Colonel William Hardigg was director of the Proving Center, which oversaw the T6 project. General J. B. Rose was commandant of Aberdeen Proving Ground at the time. Note that the protectoscope (1), taken from the M3 medium, was installed a little forward of center on the right side of the turret but toward the rear on the left. The grab bars (2) were eliminated with the side doors. The round object (3) that protected the antenna mount was replaced with a ventilator. (National Archives)

Colonel Leon W. Johnson points to the scoreboard of the B-24 Liberator "Victory Ship" as Devers and Ira Eaker look on, Norfolk, England, 22 November 1943. The horizontal bomb represents the low-level attack on Ploesti, 1 August 1943. (National Archives)

From left to right: General Alexander Patch, Air Marshal Sir John C. Slessor, Devers, General Sir Henry Maitland Wilson (with map), and Major General Lowell W. Rooks, 1944. (U.S. Army)

During his tour of Fifth Army's front, General George Marshall talks with soldiers of the 142nd Infantry Regiment, 36th Division, in the Grosseto area of Italy, 18 June 1944. Left to right: Devers, Major General David G. Barr, Marshall, and Lieutenant General Mark W. Clark. (National Archives)

Left to right: Patch, Eisenhower, Patton, unknown, and Devers (pointing down). (National Archives)

Left to right: Truscott, Patch, and Devers in late 1944. (National Archives)

Devers (right) with Jean de Lattre de Tassigny, Alphonse de Monsabert, and George Marshall, October 1944. (From the collection of the York County Heritage Trust, York, PA)

Lieutenant General Alexander M. Patch Jr., commander of U.S. Seventh Army in southern France, and his son, Captain Alexander M. "Mac" Patch III, shortly before the young officer's death. (U.S. Military Academy)

Allied generals at the "Lion of Belfort" monument near Belfort, France, 1944.
(From the collection of the York County Heritage Trust, York, PA)

Major General Frank Millburn, commanding
general of XXI Corps, and Devers, commander
of Sixth Army Group, during World War II.
(National Archives)

Left to right: Marshall, General Jean de Lattre de Tassigny of the French army, and Devers, 1944. (National Archives)

Devers and his personal staff at the Brenner Pass, May–June 1945. (From the collection of the York County Heritage Trust, York, PA)

Left to right: Kitts, Jake, Frances, and Georgie at a reception at Glatfelters, York, PA, 1945. (From the collection of the York County Heritage Trust, York, PA)

Devers and six army commanders in 1946. (From the collection of the York County Heritage Trust, York, PA)

Devers, Colonel Alexander Graham, and Frances Graham, Fort Knox, 1948. (From the collection of the York County Heritage Trust, York, PA)

Devers with Dorothy and Bonnie Benn at Captain Benn's interment at Fort Knox, 1957. (From the collection of the York County Heritage Trust, York, PA)

11

Stalemate in Italy and the Invasion of Southern France

Devers's first month in the Mediterranean was incredibly busy as he set out to reshape the U.S. Army's North African command and grasp the complexity and magnitude of his duties as the Allied deputy supreme commander and commanding general of all American forces in the Mediterranean. He was fortunate that Lieutenant General Ira Eaker had also been transferred to the Mediterranean, replacing Spaatz as air component commander. Eaker and Devers had worked well together in England, preparing the Eighth and Ninth Air Forces to carry out the combined bomber offensive. Eaker was now the commander of the Mediterranean Allied Air Forces (MAAF), which included the U.S. Twelfth and Fifteenth Air Forces.

American Air Forces in the Mediterranean

When Devers and Eaker arrived, the MAAF was in the process of moving its squadrons from bases in North Africa to airdromes in Italy. MAAF headquarters also needed to be reorganized and relocated closer to the front. As Eaker explained to the assistant secretary of war, Robert Lovett, "Both General Spaatz and Air Chief Marshal Tedder apologized to me for what they termed 'the loose control and organization in effect here.'" Tedder and Spaatz had begun the process of "washing out the N.W. African Air Force and consolidating the Mediterranean Air Command into one organization," but when they learned that they would be going to England, they decided to "leave for me as the new commander the job of working out the new organization the way Generals Wilson and Devers thought it should be."[1]

Eaker met with Wilson and Devers in Algiers the day after he arrived in North Africa and recommended that MAAF headquarters be transferred to Italy, where it could operate closer to its forward units and be near Wilson's AFHQ in Caserta, just north of Naples. Wilson and Devers agreed. Within a week, Eaker and a small staff arrived in Caserta, and on 20 January

"MAAF Headquarters officially opened at Caserta, communications having been completed to all Air Force subordinate commands."[2] The administrative headquarters remained in Tunis until suitable accommodations could be built in Italy.

Eaker also visited his two American air forces during his first week in the theater. In Bari, Italy, he met with Major General Nathan Twining, commander of the Fifteenth Air Force. Twining commanded the strategic bombers in the Mediterranean theater of operations (MTO), with most of their targets located north of the Alps. The Fifteenth Air Force was part of a unified American strategic bombardment organization that Spaatz commanded from England. Twining, in Eaker's words, "is faced with a difficult task somewhat similar to what I had with the Eighth Air Force in that he is rapidly quadrupling the size of his force. He is faced with the conduct of daily operations, training and initiating into combat of new groups [of bombers] at the rate of two or three a month." New bomber groups were trained in North Africa, where they could take advantage of generally good flying weather and well-established airfields.[3] When their training was completed, they moved to airfields in Italy.

After evaluating his American air forces, Eaker concluded that "the tactical situation here is in excellent hands and good control. . . . Twining and Cannon are able officers and their Air Forces are doing excellent work."[4] However, he found that the "logistical situation—airdromes, supplies and administration—is not in as good shape as the tactical and strategic situation." This, Eaker believed, was due to the command's "wide dispersion over a vast area" and the tight shipping situation, which gave priority to supporting the ground forces of Fifth Army.[5]

Devers was responsible for supporting Eaker's units, and his efforts to improve the replacement situation affected the air forces as well as the ground units. Eaker was extremely well qualified for his responsibilities, allowing Devers to focus on other challenges in the AFHQ and the MTO. Eaker kept Devers informed of the situation, however, and candidly told Lovett that things were not all that rosy in the air units:

> The brief visits I have made to the tactical units to date and the talks I have had with the Tactical Commanders lead me to believe that the morale is not as high here as it was in England and as I would like to see it. Here again the fault does not lie with the Commanders but is due to such circumstances as the following. They are

on temporary airdromes, many of them very poor; they are widely scattered over a vast area and not in [a] compact little bundle such as we had in England; they have not had prompt action on their promotions and decorations due to their distance from Allied Air Force Headquarters at Algiers and to the attitude of some of the Staff Sections there.[6]

Eaker also reported that his airmen felt they were not receiving a fair share of the press coverage back home. For example, of the sixty-five news-papermen covering Shingle, only two were assigned to report about air force units. But, Eaker noted, "I expect to get this . . . situation straightened out with the great help of General Devers and his P.R.O. [public relations officer] he has brought with him, with whom we have worked so well in England."[7] Eaker was referring to Brigadier General Tristram Tupper, who had served as the public relations officer in the Armored Force and in the European the-ater and was now working for Devers in Algiers. Tupper, coincidentally, was Marshall's brother-in-law, and Devers had had to persuade Marshall that Tupper was the right man for the job at a senior-level headquarters.

Eaker assessed the command climate in the AFHQ by noting, "We have a very happy official family. It starts with the person of General Wilson and with his Chief of Staff, General Gammell, who we knew and got along with so well in England. It is most fortunate that General Devers and I are here together because we worked with the greatest harmony for nearly a year in [the] U.K." On the "debit side," they had too many jobs to accomplish and not enough forces to do them all. "In addition to that, I went through the period in England when our bones were being picked to support the Afri-can operation. Now I find myself in Africa with my bones being picked to support operations out of U.K."[8]

During the next six months, Eaker and his team improved living condi-tions at the air force installations in Italy. He also helped make it possible for the 99th Fighter Squadron, the Tuskegee Airmen, to take an active front-line role against the enemy in the skies over the Anzio beachhead. Eaker, in short, lived up to Devers's high expectations.

The Home Front: Georgie and Frances

In spite of his busy schedule, Devers did his best to stay in touch with Georgie. She, in turn, kept him informed and shared news with his sister in

York, Pennsylvania. In a letter to Kitts, Georgie let her pride in Jake's success shine through: "To begin with what means so much to us, Jamie has the 2nd ranking command in Europe for an American, and is the ranking American in the Mediterranean Theater."[9] She also updated Jake's family about Frances and her husband, Lieutenant Colonel Alex Graham, and shared gossip obtained from other senior officers' wives in Washington: "Frances wired that she would be here late tonight. Alex was on the move. I do not know where he is, only that he is finally gone. . . . The 4th Armored Division moved out on the 22nd! It's been a long time, since last November a year, that Frances has seen her clothes. . . . Bea Patton is in town. I see her and always enjoy it. She is a real person. . . . Had lunch today at the White House—Some sixty wives of Senators, top executives, and admirals and generals. They were pretty good looking for a decrepit lot of old girls."[10]

Devers wrote a short note to Georgie after his trip to the Fifth Army's front in Italy, where he had visited all the American and French division and corps commanders. He told her, "Having returned to Algiers, I found plenty to keep me busy. Our hours are long. . . . My staff is too large and I will send some of them on or place them on a staff somewhere. At the moment we are trying to reorganize."[11] He also informed her of Marshall's decision to move Patton to England to command an army in Overlord and about the arrival of Major General Willis Crittenberger. Eisenhower did not want Crittenberger as a corps commander, "so I have asked for him," Devers wrote.[12]

Georgie also received a long letter from Jake's secretary, Mary Alice Jaqua, telling her about his personal staff and living conditions in Algiers:

> I have often thought I would write you and tell you some of the details about the way the General and Aides live. . . . Most of the villas, any kind of an old house is called a "villa" here—are on a long road which winds up along the hillside above the harbor. . . . The General's house used to be an old Arab house, though it is completely re-done and modernized. . . . I think the General finds it lonely living there alone. . . . The General has a good staff, though very heterogeneous. Sergeant Nutter runs his household. . . . Then there is Ali, the Arab houseboy, who makes the beds, does the serving, and arranges flowers beautifully. Juliette . . . is the maid. . . . She is an excellent maid; does all the valeting for the Gen-

eral, plus for the Aides, and all the personal laundry on the side. She also helps in the pantry and dining room, makes salads and so forth. Of course, John Turnipseed you know. . . . Then there are the drivers: Paul Miller and Mike and Corporal Gunning. . . . It must be very lonely being a lieutenant general—he can't say one word to a soul here except in an official or semi-official capacity. . . . He has no one to blow off to. . . . I thought I would tell you I am not a WAC, but a civilian. I had gone to England before Pearl Harbor with a Harvard medical unit, and I went to town to work for General Eisenhower.[13]

Georgie summed up Jake's activities in a letter to Kitts: "Jamie seems to be busier in Algiers than he was in England. He has been at Cassino lying in a ditch, under shell fire, and at the landing at Nettuno—looking over the German gun batteries from an unarmored observation plane on the beach head."[14] Georgie was right about her husband being far busier in the MTO than he had been in the ETO. One of his major challenges for the next six months would be to ensure that the invasion of southern France was well planned and executed. This endeavor would bring him into direct conflict with senior British leaders and into intimate contact with the French forces then fighting in Italy and training in North Africa.

The Allies' Mediterranean Strategy

The stalemate that had developed in Italy by February 1944 had serious implications for Allied strategy. The American Joint Chiefs of Staff saw the Mediterranean as a secondary theater that threatened to suck in the resources of divisions, ships, and aircraft, diverting them from the main Allied effort: Overlord. Marshall expected Devers to prevent the expansion of U.S. operations in Italy and to plan for an invasion of southern France, known as Operation Anvil, which had been agreed on at the Allied conferences in November and December. Anvil would directly support Overlord by forcing the Germans to face two Allied invasions in France. Devers assured Marshall, "We are making strenuous efforts to use our troops to the best advantage in the battle now in progress in Italy with a view that sometime in the future, if ANVIL should be successful, we can close out completely in Africa and Italy. . . . It looks at the moment as if the fight in Italy will be with a French army, an American army, and a British army."[15]

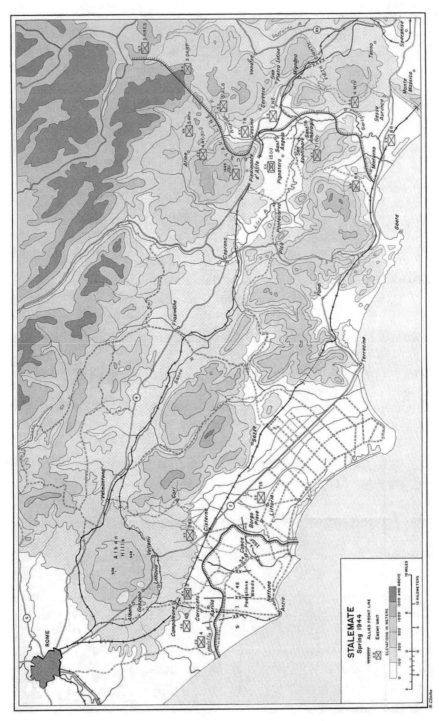

Figure 11.1. Stalemate in Italy, spring 1944

Whether to launch Anvil would be a major bone of contention between the Anglo-American Allies in 1944. The British were opposed; they saw it as a diversion of resources and divisions from the Italian campaign and further operations in the Balkans. The Americans, especially Marshall, Eisenhower, and Devers, were in favor; they saw it as an important element in the main effort against the Germans in France. The British believed that if Anvil were launched, the United States might move Fifth Army from Italy to southern France, along with all the French troops in the theater and most of the American service troops. They were right to fear such a development. So, for the next six months, Churchill, Alexander, and Brooke worked to derail Anvil and thus keep American resources committed to the slugging match in Italy. Meanwhile, the American chiefs pushed for Anvil's execution. Devers inherited this situation, and he quickly became a firm advocate of the American position about Anvil and the course of future Mediterranean operations.

The Origins of Anvil

An invasion of southern France had first been proposed at the Trident conference in Washington, D.C., in May 1943. The American Joint Chiefs of Staff believed it would be an effective use of Allied divisions in the Mediterranean after the conquest of Sicily, which was scheduled for July, and as an alternative to the British-favored invasion of Italy. British and American planners, however, believed it would be too risky to invade southern France in 1943. The Anglo-American Combined Chiefs of Staff agreed and gave Eisenhower, supreme commander in the Mediterranean, the option of invading Italy or the islands of Corsica and Sardinia after completion of the Sicilian campaign. As a result, the idea of invading southern France was tabled, although the British agreed to a May 1944 date for Overlord.[16]

The debates at the Trident conference illustrated the fundamentally different strategic views of British and American leaders. As Douglas Porch summarized the situation, "Marshall led a chorus that argued that the Allies must stick to their game plan to move rapidly to pierce the heart of the Axis. Churchill, on the other hand, favored a flexible strategy to exploit opportunity in the Mediterranean."[17] At their conference in Quebec City in August 1943, the Combined Chiefs of Staff agreed to an invasion of Italy, the objectives being to keep pressure on the Germans and to establish air bases near Foggia. The Americans saw no reason to push much farther north than

Rome, whereas Churchill and the British military leaders saw an opportunity to drive into the Balkans across the Adriatic Sea or north through the Ljubljana Gap and into central Europe. The debates continued for another year.[18]

Anvil had seemingly fallen through the crack between the direct approach favored by the Americans and the peripheral strategy preferred by the British. Then, at the conference with the Russians in Tehran in November 1943, the idea of an invasion of southern France in conjunction with Overlord received a powerful push by Stalin. When asked whether he favored an Anglo-American drive into the Balkans or a reinforced Overlord, Stalin told the Western Allies that he preferred Overlord, along with a strong concurrent invasion of southern France. Churchill and Roosevelt promised Stalin they would follow that course of action: Anvil was back on.[19]

Following the meetings with Stalin, the Combined Chiefs of Staff met in Cairo and agreed that Overlord and Anvil were the "supreme operations for 1944." They ordered Eisenhower, as Allied Mediterranean commander, to plan for an invasion of southern France to coincide with Overlord. They also agreed that the campaign in Italy would be pushed no farther than the Pisa-Rimini line. "Mediterranean operations were to be limited—in timing, extent of advance, resources, roles."[20]

When General "Jumbo" Wilson became the supreme Allied commander in the MTO, he assumed the task of planning Anvil. However, as the supreme commander for Overlord, Eisenhower was authorized by the Combined Chiefs of Staff to determine the timing of Anvil to support the cross-Channel invasion. When Eisenhower, Montgomery, and Bedell Smith got to Britain and calculated the requirements of landing the force necessary for a successful Overlord, they concluded there were not enough LSTs and other landing craft available to execute an enlarged Overlord. Montgomery and Smith recommended "a serious reduction in ANVIL." Eisenhower disagreed, telling Marshall, "This seems to me to be justified only as a last resort."[21]

Senior American military leaders understood the situation. As Eisenhower wrote, the "British and American staffs at Tehran definitely assured the Russians that ANVIL would take place. Secondly, we have put into the French Army a very considerable investment" by equipping and training eight French divisions in North Africa. Eisenhower and Marshall believed that the French divisions "cannot profitably be used in decisive fashion in Italy." Anvil, Eisenhower reasoned, would "open a gateway for them into France" so as not to waste the American investment in the French.[22] Although there was concern about the lack of sufficient landing craft to execute Overlord and Anvil simultaneously, the Combined Chiefs of Staff agreed that the AFHQ should continue to plan for Anvil.

On 31 December 1943 General Wilson gave Lieutenant General Mark Clark the task of overseeing the planning for Anvil, in addition to his responsibilities for Shingle and the Fifth Army's offensive against the Gustav Line. Seventh Army headquarters, sitting idle in Sicily, was also assigned to the mission. The initial thinking by Wilson and Devers was that Clark would move from command of Fifth Army to command of Seventh Army once the Germans were driven north of Rome by the ongoing offensives. But when Shingle and the Fifth Army's offensive failed to force the Germans north in January, the ensuing stalemate forced a change in plans. Wilson, Clark, and Devers agreed in February that Clark would remain in command of Fifth Army and that someone else would command Seventh Army for Anvil.[23]

George Patton had relinquished command of Seventh Army in January, in anticipation of moving to England to serve as an army commander in Overlord. When he left, Devers allowed Patton and his chief of staff, Brigadier General Hobart Gay, to take most of their key staff officers with them to Third Army.[24] Devers did not, however, allow Patton to take Brigadier General Garrison Davidson, Seventh Army's engineer officer. Patton appealed to Eisenhower, who in turn sent a message to Marshall, stating, "This officer has been with Patton since the landing at Casablanca and is not only widely experienced in the technical requirements of engineers on the battlefield but has become a mainspring in his staff organization." Eisenhower claimed that practically all the battlefield-experienced American senior officers "are now in the Mediterranean Theater," and he felt strongly that "our senior commanders are clearly entitled to a few individuals in this category."[25] When asked by Marshall if he would release Davidson, Devers informed the chief of staff that Davidson was in charge of the staff that was developing the Anvil plan and that his loss would hurt the planning process.[26] Marshall supported Devers and told Eisenhower that Davidson could not be transferred. Eisenhower was probably displeased, but Patton took the news well. He wrote to his wife, "[I'm] glad you have been nice to Georgie D. as he [Devers] has been pretty fair about letting me have my old men back although he is at sword points with every one else."[27] Patton also observed, "Jake is . . . messing things up and at the same time running counter to Destiny [Patton's name for Eisenhower], which is foolish."[28]

Brigadier General Garrison "Gar" Davidson was well known to Devers. Davidson had served as a football coach at the Military Academy from 1927 to 1937, compiling one of the best win-loss records in Academy football history. He served as Patton's chief engineer from the invasion of Morocco in November 1942 through the successful invasion and conquest of Sicily in July–August 1943. Davidson led Seventh Army's Anvil planning cell from Sicily to its new headquarters in Algiers, where it was christened Force 163 on 12 January (the name came from the room number of the group's first office in an Algiers hotel). It quickly became a joint and combined planning headquarters when navy captain Robert English, from Admiral Hewitt's U.S. Eighth Fleet, and British group captain R. B. Lees, of the Mediterranean Allied tactical air force headquarters, joined the team. In early March a small contingent of French officers joined Force 163, since the operation was to include two French corps and seven French divisions.[29]

Force 163 had a tight schedule, with a proposed D-day in early May. Davidson and his planners picked the beaches east of Toulon for the initial assaults and developed a concept that called for three U.S. divisions to land on D-day, followed as quickly as possible by the French troops. The Anvil forces would then liberate Toulon and Marseille, allowing those ports to support the Allied force as it drove north along the Rhône valley to link up with Eisenhower's armies coming from Normandy.[30]

Wilson and Devers still needed to find a combat-tested officer to command Seventh Army and Anvil. On 21 February Devers received word from General Handy that Major General Alexander Patch and his IV Corps staff would arrive in the Mediterranean theater in early March to serve wherever they were needed most. Handy further informed Devers that Patch and a few key officers would arrive by air immediately, "as you may need him now."[31] Devers quickly decided that Patch was the right man to command Seventh Army and to plan and execute Anvil. Marshall approved this decision on 28 February.[32] General Wilson announced Patch's assignment to command the Anvil ground forces on 2 March, allowing Patch to take control of Force 163.[33] On 5 March Patch officially assumed command of Seventh Army. Davidson remained the army engineer, and Colonel John Guthrie became the operations officer.[34]

Alexander Patch was a superb choice for the command of Anvil. A 1913 graduate of the Military Academy, Patch had served with distinction as a machine gun officer in World War I. Marshall had worked closely with Patch in the 1st Division and had noted his capabilities.[35] When war began in 1941, Marshall sent him to New Caledonia to command an American pickup force of three infantry regiments. Patch organized these units into the "Americal" Division and led it into combat on Guadalcanal. Patch and his division relieved the exhausted 1st Marine Division and were soon joined by the 25th Infantry Division under the command of Major General J. Lawton Collins. Patch assumed command of XIV Corps in January 1943 and led the Americal and 25th Infantry Divisions through a tough but successful campaign to expel the Japanese.[36]

Devers had known Patch from before the war and had tried to get him assigned to command a division in the Armored Force in 1942.[37] After Guadalcanal, Patch was in hot water with Marshall for letting it slip to reporters that American cryptologists had broken the secret Japanese radio code and used that information to intercept and shoot down the plane of Japanese admiral Yamamoto. Patch was relegated to a training command with IV Corps at Fort Lewis, Washington, as a result. Marshall relented, however, when the need for successful, combat-experienced officers became evident. Hence, Patch was assigned to the Mediterranean theater, just as two other combat veterans of the Pacific campaigns, Major Generals Joe Collins and Peter Corlett, were sent to serve with Eisenhower.[38] Devers's choice of Patch was well received in the War Department.[39]

Major General Willis Crittenberger, whom Eisenhower had rejected for a corps command in the ETO, replaced Patch in IV Corps. He brought with him Major Henry Cabot Lodge Jr., who had recently resigned his seat in the Senate to serve in the army, where he had been a reserve officer for nearly twenty years.[40] In addition to his patriotism and sense of service, Lodge spoke fluent French, having attended school in France for a number of years. He had also honed his ability to work well with difficult people during his years as a senator. Lodge would eventually become a key member of Devers's staff because these skills made him the ideal choice to command the American liaison section that would work with the French forces involved in Anvil and later with Devers's Sixth Army Group. In the meantime, the British continued to try to cancel the invasion of southern France.

The Italian Campaign's Effects on Anvil

In January the Anzio landing failed to force the Germans to evacuate the Gustav Line. Fifth Army was unable to break through the Gustav Line in the Liri valley at the Rapido. In turn, the German counteroffensive at Anzio failed to drive VI Corps and its British and American divisions into the sea. Clark also tried to break through the German defenses near Cassino; he threw the 34th Infantry Division against the town and sent Juin's French divisions into the mountains north of Monte Cassino. Although the 34th got a toehold across the Rapido River near Cassino and the French drove a wedge into the mountains five miles deep, there were insufficient reserves to break through the German defenses. By 11 February, the French had suffered 10,000 casualties, and the 34th Infantry Division had lost another 3,000.[41]

Fifth Army was exhausted, yet Wilson wanted the offensive around Cassino to continue. For this effort, General Alexander, Fifteenth Army Group commander, assigned the three fresh divisions of the provisional New Zealand Corps, under Lieutenant General Bernard Freyberg, to Fifth Army. Freyberg planned to have the 4th Indian Division attack north of Cassino, between that town and Monte Cassino, where a fifth-century Benedictine monastery overlooked the Liri valley from a 1,700-foot-high perch. The 2nd New Zealand Division was to attack south of Cassino into the Liri valley. Freyberg and Major General F. S. Tucker, commander of the 4th Indian Division, concluded that the Germans were using the monastery on Monte Cassino as an observation post and that it must be destroyed before the Indian and Kiwi troops could break through the enemy defenses around Cassino. They also decided that the town of Cassino had to be bombed into oblivion before the attack, so the New Zealand infantry could just walk through the strong defenses.[42]

In reality, the Germans had no troops in the historic monastery, although they had observation posts and gun positions on the slopes of the massif below. The monks remained in the monastery, giving sanctuary (but little else) to several thousand Italian civilians who had fled the fighting in Cassino. Kesselring had given the Vatican his word that the Germans would not put troops in the monastery, and he had provided trucks to move the priceless religious documents and artifacts to safety in Rome. Furthermore, the Allies had strict rules that such historically important sites were to be spared if at all possible. Thus, when Freyberg requested that Fifth Army order bombers to destroy the monastery, the army's chief of staff, Major General Alfred Gruenther, refused, noting that the ancient building was on a list of protected sites. He did, however, forward the request to Fifteenth Army Group headquarters, along with a message stating Clark's views on the matter. According to Gruenther, Clark believed "that no military necessity [existed] for its destruction," and "it is unnecessary to bomb the Monastery."[43]

Freyberg was insistent about the need to bomb the monastery before his troops attacked. He and the 4th Indian Division commander believed there were Germans inside the building. Their view was reinforced by reports from a German prisoner of war and an Italian civilian who claimed the Germans were using the building as a command post. Clark was still not convinced, but he was unwilling to take the blame if the New Zealand Corps' attack failed. General Alexander agreed that the monastery needed to be bombed, but he asked General Wilson for permission to do so. Devers got involved in the debate at this point. He and Eaker flew over the monastery in a Piper Cub on 13 February to ascertain whether the reports about the Germans were true. They flew over the building at less than 200 feet, and "both officers believed they saw at least one military radio aerial inside the monastery and enemy soldiers moving in and out of the building."[44]

Wilson approved Freyberg's request the next day, saying later that he had "irrefutable evidence" that the Germans were using the monastery as part of their defenses. The heavy bomber advocates, who included Eaker and Fifteenth Air Force commander Nathan Twining, saw an opportunity to show that heavy bombers could blow a hole through enemy defenses at Cassino and obliterate the enemy in the abbey above the town. On 15 February Twining sent 250 bombers over the target area to drop 600 tons of high explosives. Hundreds of artillery pieces added their fire to the aerial bombardment. The monks and the refugees had been warned by leaflets dropped the day before that they should evacuate, but the bombing began before the abbot could obtain assurances of safe passage from the Germans.[45]

After the dust settled, the monastery was in ruins, and the town was reduced to rubble. Although Alexander's headquarters claimed that hundreds of Germans had been seen fleeing the abbey when the bombing started, there were no Germans in the building. The commander of the 36th Infantry Division, Major General Fred Walker, observed the bombardment and wrote in his diary, "The Germans were not using it and I can see no advantage in destroying it. No tactical advantage will result since the Germans can make as much use of the rubble for observation posts and gun positions as of the building itself."[46] In fact, after the bombardment the Germans occupied and fortified the ruins.

The Indians and Kiwis attacked Monte Cassino and the town of Cassino on the evening of 15 February. In assaults against the dug-in Germans over the next week, the divisions made little progress. The rubble in the streets of Cassino prevented tanks from supporting the infantry, and the rubble of the monastery gave the Germans a very defensible position. Heavy losses and bad weather finally halted Freyberg's efforts, and the stalemate along the Gustav Line continued.[47]

Devers summarized the situation to Georgie: "Have been to Italy. . . . Saw many soldiers and quite a lot of fighting. Italy is still dirty." Having seen the assault at Cassino, he wrote, "I learned a lot and received a real shock that we were not able to go faster. . . . This is a tough job. The problems are many and varied as I have said before and sometimes I feel quite helpless."[48]

In late February both sides temporarily ceased offensive operations and licked their wounds. The German commander Kesselring saw no reason to retreat as long as his two armies could hold their strong positions facing the Anzio beachhead and Fifth Army's front. This situation thoroughly irritated Churchill, and he pressured Wilson to get the forces moving in Italy. Since the British were the lead Allied partner in the Mediterranean, his demands had a major effect.

In response, Alexander decided to realign his two armies along the Gustav Line, in preparation for another offensive. He ordered U.S. Fifth Army to reinforce the Anzio beachhead with a British division from Tenth Corps and to send that corps and its two other divisions to Eighth Army. Fifth Army shifted U.S. II Corps and the French Expeditionary Corps to the west and sent another American division to reinforce Truscott's VI Corps at Anzio. The British Eighth Army shifted two British corps into the area facing the Liri valley and Monte Cassino and received the mission of breaking through the Gustav Line. The Americans and French would play a supporting role along the line of the Garigliano River to the west.[49]

As the bulk of Eighth Army began to shift positions, Alexander ordered Clark to have the New Zealand Corps try to break through at Cassino again. The attack called for the British 78th Infantry Division, the 2nd New Zealand Division, and the 4th Indian Division to attack the town of Cassino from three directions, each on a narrow front. Once the town was secured, the British 78th Infantry Division and a combat command of tanks from the U.S. 1st Armored Division would drive around Cassino on the west and charge up the Liri valley toward Rome. At the same time, the Indians and Kiwis would have another go at capturing the Monte Cassino monastery.[50]

For this attack, Freyberg demanded that the air forces drop 750 tons of bombs on Cassino to level the town and allow Allied infantry and tanks "to walk through." Fifth Army's air support officer, Colonel Stephen B. Mack, told Freyberg that the bombers could drop the tonnage he asked for over a period of three hours, but the bombardment would not open the roads through the town. In fact, Mack warned Freyberg that the tanks would be unable to negotiate the rubble-clogged streets, and the infantry would find it very difficult to do so as well. Freyberg brushed Mack's comments aside.[51]

Freyberg's high hopes for the aerial bombardment were echoed in Washington by Hap Arnold. When he heard of the plan, Arnold wrote to Eaker in early March and encouraged him to push for a massive attack by all available heavy and medium bombers in the MAAF, "which for one day, could really make air history."[52] Eaker was skeptical and tried to explain the situation to Arnold: "It is apparently difficult for anyone not here to understand the full effect of the combination of the terrain and rainfall on the battlefield. The streams are swollen; there are no bridges, these have all been destroyed; the land is a complete quagmire—it will not support foot troops let alone heavy equipment. . . . The picture with respect to the future is this and you can rely on it. . . . We shall go forward and capture Rome when the weather permits . . . and not before."[53]

Eaker, in spite of his misgivings, directed the Twelfth and Fifteenth Air Forces to plan a four-hour bombardment by 560 medium and heavy bombers, followed by fighter-bomber attacks against selected targets. The weather finally cooperated on 15 March, and the bombers struck in waves, dropping 1,000-pound bombs for maximum effect against enemy positions. Eaker and Devers were in the area to watch as the bombers dropped a total of 1,000 tons of high explosives, with about 80 percent of the bombs hitting their targets. Cassino was demolished. Once the bombers departed, 746 artillery pieces opened fire, throwing an additional 1,500 tons of explosives against the target area.[54]

Freyberg expected most of the German defenders to be killed and the survivors to be completely demoralized. As things turned out, the veteran soldiers of the German 1st Parachute Division suffered few casualties and were still full of fight. The toppled walls of the stone houses in Cassino formed effective bulwarks to stop Allied tanks. When the Kiwi and Indian infantry attacked, they ran into heavy machine gun, mortar, and artillery fire.[55] Without armor support, they made little progress. General Clark wrote in his diary, "I have repeatedly told Freyberg from his inception of this plan that aerial bombardment alone never has and never will drive a determined enemy from his position. Cassino has again proven this theory."[56]

Devers described the results of the operation in a letter to Marshall:

> We are struggling here. On March 15th I thought we were going to lick it, for the attack on Cassino and advance up the Liri Valley planned to use air, artillery and tanks, followed closely by infantry, got off to a start with excellent weather. I witnessed this attack from across the valley. The bombing was excellent and severe, and the artillery barrage . . . was even more severe and accurate. . . . In spite of all this and with excellent support all afternoon with dive bombers and artillery fire, neither the 4th Indian nor the 2nd New Zealand has yet attained its first objective. Consequently, the tanks . . . could not get started. These results were a sobering shock to me.[57]

The New Zealand Corps tried to bull its way through the German paratroopers for another week, but Devers told Marshall, "All we will gain will be the town of Cassino and possibly a bridgehead over the Rapido in the vicinity; . . . General Alexander will then stop and regroup his forces" and prepare for an offensive all across the front in late April or early May.[58]

Finally, on 23 March, Freyberg admitted that his divisions were exhausted and were not going to break the German resistance. Having suffered more than 2,000 casualties, they were badly in need of rest and refitting. They were withdrawn from the line, and General Alexander disbanded the New Zealand Corps.[59] The stalemate in Italy continued, as Devers had predicted. Devers was also worried that, "with a small force of 7 or 8 divisions and the use of mines and demolitions the Germans could contain our forces."[60]

The first three months of 1944 had been bleak for the Allies, as the official history aptly summarized: "Three times the Allied forces had tried to break the Gustav Line and get into the Liri valley, and three times they had failed—in January the frontal attack across the Rapido, in February the attempt to outflank the Cassino spur, and in March the effort to drive between the abbey and the town. They would try again, but only after the weather cleared and the ground was firm, after the troops had rested."[61]

As Alexander shuffled the Eighth and Fifth Armies west, the British pushed even harder for the cancellation of Anvil and the diversion of all resources in the MTO to the campaign in Italy. The stalemate in Italy meant that Anvil was unlikely to take place in conjunction with Overlord in June, the new target month for the main event. Devers told Marshall that, according to his planners, 1 August was the earliest date that troops and shipping could be readied for the invasion of southern France.[62]

Devers was frustrated by his inability to directly affect the tactical situation in Italy, since Alexander was in command. Nonetheless, he contributed to the American forces' capabilities by tackling the replacement problems he had observed in the infantry divisions. He found that new soldiers were thrown into battle directly from the replacement depots, resulting in high casualty rates. To fix this problem, Devers authorized divisions to maintain about 600 infantrymen over their authorized strength, even though the War Department did not endorse this action. These men would then fill losses in the combat units. By April, each American infantry division in the theater was overstrength and was able to train its replacements before they saw combat. For the next offensive in Italy, the division commanders were able to advance "rapidly and continuously only because their infantry units were always up to strength."[63]

His discussions with division and corps commanders during his many trips to the Anzio beachhead and the Gustav Line gave Devers clear insight into the problems they faced. As a result, he convinced Clark to permanently assign a separate tank battalion to each of the infantry divisions, allowing tank crews and infantry units to train together and ensuring that the armor troops identified themselves as part of the division.[64] As commander of the Armored Force, he had tried to get McNair to make this move across the army. Devers wrote to McNair again in February 1944, stating, "I am also convinced that separate tank battalions and separate battalions of all kinds should be organized into something of the division caliber with a major general to look out for them."[65]

Devers encouraged his senior commanders to write to him about their problems and recommend ways to fix them. Truscott, commander of the 3rd Infantry Division and then VI Corps, emphasized that infantry divisions needed to train replacements before sending them into the line. Ernie Harmon, commander of the 1st Armored Division, told Devers that his division needed two infantry regiments to perform the type of missions it was routinely given in Italy. Harmon also shared his personal frustrations: "Today was my 50th birthday and while I do not feel any older than yesterday I realize that I am rapidly joining the ranks of the old birds. . . . I have been a little bit unhappy recently; first because the high command when relieving Lucas placed Truscott in command of the Corps instead of me, Truscott being much junior to me and I felt had no better record than I. . . . I have given and will continue to give Truscott my fullest all-out efforts on every occasion."[66]

Devers responded to Harmon within a week, congratulating him on his birthday and on a successful counterattack against the Germans. He told Harmon, "I know how you feel with reference to command. This cannot be helped. You profited, as I have, at the expense of others who feel exactly as you do. Truscott has done an outstanding piece of work as commander of the 3rd Infantry Division, which is probably our best fighting infantry division. He was selected on his record. . . . You are a good fighting commander and everybody knows it. . . . So keep up the fine morale which I found when I visited the troops in the beachhead."[67]

Harmon was one of the most outstanding armor commanders in the war. He continued to offer Devers his candid opinions and gave him a feel for the pulse of the American troops on the line. For example, on 28 March Harmon told Devers, "I feel that the morale of the troops in the beachhead is remarkably good considering the tedious times, lack of ability to be free from harassing fire and the noise of battle."[68]

Devers spent a great deal of his time with forward units—air, ground, and service. In this, he was quite different from Eisenhower. Devers understood the strengths and weaknesses of the senior American commanders in the theater, and he mentored newly arrived leaders such as Major General Willis Crittenberger, IV Corps commander. Crittenberger wrote to Devers, "I feel greatly benefited by having been in contact with your thoughts, both on the general situation and on the tactical doctrines. . . . May other commanders have an equal opportunity, also, to benefit from your thoughts along these lines!"[69] Devers fought to keep great leaders like Truscott, Larkin, and Crittenberger. He earned their trust, and he relied on them to carry out their jobs without his constant supervision.

Anvil: Off Again, on Again

During February 1944 the British pushed the American chiefs to cancel Anvil; they argued that there was a shortage of landing craft for an enlarged Overlord, and an invasion of southern France would draw resources away from the Italian campaign. Eisenhower had the authority to cancel Anvil, but despite pressure from Generals Montgomery and Bedell Smith, he chose to keep it as part of the overall strategy. Ike was bolstered in this decision by agreement from President Roosevelt and the American Joint Chiefs of Staff. On 24 February Eisenhower and the British chiefs of staff agreed that the Italian campaign would remain the priority in the Mediterranean until the Germans had been driven north of Rome. Meanwhile, the supreme Allied commander in the MTO, General Wilson, would continue to plan for an amphibious operation in France to support Overlord. The Allies agreed to review the situation on 20 March.[70]

In late March Wilson reported heavy losses in Italy to the Combined Chiefs of Staff and recommended that Anvil be canceled. SHAEF planners recognized that Anvil could not be undertaken until after the Italian stalemate was broken, but they thought it should remain on the planning books. The CCS finally agreed that Anvil might take place after Overlord if Eisenhower agreed that it would help Allied progress in France.[71]

The failure to break through the Gustav Line in March made it necessary to postpone Anvil until after Fifteenth Army Group launched its May offensive, when the ground would be dry and better weather would allow close air support. The American chiefs agreed that the Italian campaign would have priority until Alexander's forces linked up with VI Corps and drove the Germans north of Rome. After that, the British wanted to put all the MTO's resources into a drive toward the Po valley, in northern Italy.[72] The Joint Chiefs agreed to a postponement of Anvil but not to its cancellation.[73]

Wilson directed Alexander to push ahead with his plans for the May offensive, but he also warned him that, according to Devers, the "U.S. Chiefs of Staff intend to bring off ANVIL in spite of objections on the British side." This, Wilson felt, was causing some of the American staff in AFHQ to "take their eye off your campaign which has absolute priority." However, Wilson also believed that "the landing craft situation before Anzio is joined up will be such that there will be nothing like enough available to carry out the Operations they have in mind" much earlier than winter.[74] Devers agreed with Wilson that Anvil could not be launched until the Anzio beachhead was no longer reliant on LSTs and landing craft, tanks (LCTs) for its sustainment. He told Wilson that although Anvil could not be launched before 1 August, which might "be . . . so late that it might be unwise to attempt it," he believed "that we should continue to plan and prepare for ANVIL, to the extent that that can be done without prejudice to [the] Italian battle, until our main forces have joined hands with the bridgehead." Once that was accomplished, Anvil should be executed if it would help Overlord.[75] With this in mind, Devers directed Larkin, the SOS chief, to keep cargo ships that had arrived with material for Anvil in the Mediterranean as a floating theater reserve. Thus, the supplies would be available if Anvil were executed in July or August.[76]

Major General J. E. Hull, the War Department G-3, summarized the American position on Anvil in a 14 March memorandum for Marshall, after Hull had visited both Wilson and Devers:

> The present Italian situation has greatly increased the difficulties of preparing for ANVIL. We must, however, continue to make the most strenuous efforts to keep that operation alive. . . . OVER-LORD may have an acute need for ANVIL. . . . If we commit all our forces to Italy where there are no further important strategic objectives, we will lose the use in France of the French divisions we have equipped and trained. . . . Since this operation is to be almost entirely American and French, it is particularly a U.S. responsibility to press the preparations. . . . General Patch's previous experience in operations with limited resources should be a help.[77]

Marshall ordered a copy of Hull's memorandum sent to Devers. The chief of staff was convinced that Hull was right: If the Allies canceled Anvil and pursued the Italian campaign with all the American and French forces in the Mediterranean, the Germans would be able to bottle up the Allied armies with a handful of divisions in Italy. The enemy could then move ten to fifteen divisions from Italy, the Balkans, and southern France to oppose Eisenhower's invasion forces in Normandy. Marshall concluded, "I am in little doubt as to whether Hull's memorandum, as now written, will make a sufficiently clear picture to Devers to justify sending it, because to a certain degree, it is bound to irritate him to read a statement by a visitor with which he does not entirely agree."[78] Devers got the message.

Marshall also wrote to Eisenhower to share his concerns about the Mediterranean strategy and its effects on Overlord. He seemingly left it up to Eisenhower to decide the fate of Anvil.[79] However, when Eisenhower recommended the cancellation of Anvil, Marshall informed him that, in the Joint Chiefs' opinion, "once the beachhead and the 5th Army front have joined, the major concern in the Mediterranean is to prepare for a later

ANVIL, July 10th as the target date, and that Rome would not be considered a primary effort to the disadvantage of the proposed ANVIL. Dill indicated the British would view this with concern because of the political importance of Rome."[80] The debate persisted through April and May and into June. Meanwhile, planning for Anvil continued, and the forces to carry it out were tentatively identified. The majority of them would be French, which meant that Devers would be intimately involved in military and political relations with the Free French leaders.

Dealing with the French

Devers assumed the mission of arming the Free French forces when he took over the NATOUSA. He worked with French commanders and forces for the remainder of the war, demonstrating an unparalleled ability to work effectively with the sometimes difficult ally. He was successful in part because he understood recent French history.

The German conquest of France in 1940 had shattered the self-confidence of the French military and people. Not since 1870–1871 had France suffered such a humiliating defeat. The Germans occupied Paris and northern France and set up an Axis-friendly regime under Marshal Henri Petain in the spa town of Vichy, in southern France. Petain's government cooperated with the Nazis in many ways, including the surrender of French Jews for transportation to the German death camps. The French army was limited by the terms of the surrender agreement to roughly 100,000 soldiers in metropolitan France and another 130,000 or so in France's North African colonies.[81]

The United States maintained relations with the Vichy regime until the Allied invasion of North Africa in November 1942. The British, in contrast, had poor relations with the French because of British naval attacks against the French fleet in 1940. Therefore, when the invasion of Algeria and Morocco was planned, American troops were placed in the first wave of each assault, in the hope that the French would refuse to fight the Americans. Unfortunately, when the landings came on 8 November, the French forces resisted for several days before a cease-fire was arranged. The French joined the Allies shortly thereafter, and by December, French units were in the Allied lines fighting the Germans in Tunisia.[82]

When the French aligned with the Anglo-American Allies, Roosevelt extended the Lend-Lease program to them. This was fortunate, because the

40,000 French soldiers fighting in Tunisia were woefully ill equipped and lacked modern armored vehicles, artillery, and antitank weapons. Eisenhower moved to remedy these shortcomings by giving the French whatever small arms and other equipment were available; however, he soon realized that he could significantly increase the size of the Allied forces in Africa if the French army were rearmed. The French army commander in North Africa, General Henri Giraud, estimated that the French could mobilize 197,000 men immediately from the colonial and French populations in Africa, and another 68,000 could be conscripted within six months.[83] The French saw an opportunity to rebuild their army and play a significant role in the liberation of France if the Allies would provide the weapons, supplies, vehicles, and training needed for a modern army. In January 1943 Giraud approached President Roosevelt and the Allied military leaders at the Casablanca conference and formally asked the Allies to equip eleven divisions. In exchange, Giraud would give the Allies control of 160,000 tons of French shipping, with the proviso that a portion of that tonnage be made available to carry equipment to the French forces in North Africa.[84]

The British chiefs of staff were not impressed with Giraud's request, believing that the French army was only good for garrison duty and rear-area police functions. In addition, French rearmament would mean less U.S. material available for British forces. General Marshall, however, supported the request; he believed that with U.S. equipment, training, and organization, the French could become reliable combat troops, allowing the U.S. Army to field fewer divisions of its own. President Roosevelt agreed with Marshall, and on 23 January he initialed a letter of agreement with Giraud to arm French divisions.[85]

Meanwhile, in historian Douglas Porch's view, the French commanders and largely Muslim forces fighting in Tunisia under General Alphonse Juin, "despite being poorly armed, displayed a tough resilience utterly lacking in barely blooded British First Army and American Second Corps troops." Juin displayed an understanding of his mostly illiterate African troops and provided steady professional leadership.[86] He and his men began the process of rebuilding the French army and its reputation.

Over the next six months, the Combined Chiefs of Staff and the French negotiated the exact meaning of the Roosevelt-Giraud agreement and established the level of support to be provided. By May, they had agreed that eleven divisions would be armed and employed in combat under the direction of Allied commanders. The first three French divisions under the rearmament plan received equipment and training by May, and in December they were deployed to Italy under the command of General Juin. Juin's force, known as the French Expeditionary Corps, established a superb reputation as fighters in the mountains north of Monte Cassino in January. French troops also liberated Corsica in September, giving the Allies advanced air bases and allowing the French to get combat experience.[87]

When Devers arrived in Africa, the rearmament of the French army was well under way. He had already met the future commander of the French First Army in London. General Jean de Lattre de Tassigny remembered that Devers "showed me the most friendly confidence from our first meeting."[88] In November 1942 de Lattre had tried (unsuccessfully) to rally his French troops at Montpellier to resist the German occupation of southern France, leading to his arrest by the Vichy collaborators. He was tried as a traitor and sentenced to ten years' incarceration, but he escaped from prison in September 1943 and fled to Britain. De Lattre immediately pledged his loyalty to General Charles de Gaulle, the de facto head of the French government in exile.[89] De Lattre flew to Algiers to meet with de Gaulle and Giraud on 20 December, and in early January he was appointed the commander of French Second Army, later known as Army Detachment B, and placed in charge of the French forces training in North Africa. When de Gaulle forced Giraud out of his position as French army commander in chief, de Lattre remained loyal to de Gaulle and was selected to command the French forces slated to take part in Anvil.[90]

Because of the importance of the French contribution to the war effort, Wilson and Devers officially called on Generals de Gaulle and Giraud shortly after assuming command of the Mediterranean theater. Protocol was extremely important, and the AFHQ's liaison officer with the French, Colonel L. Higgins, prepared a synopsis of de Gaulle's career as background material. The fifty-four-year-old de Gaulle was the president of the French Committee of National Liberation. He had distinguished himself in the First World War, and during the 1940 campaign in France he had commanded an armored division. When France fell, he was in England on a mission for the French premier. He remained in London, established the Free French organization, and encouraged all Frenchmen to fight with the British. The Vichy authorities considered him a traitor, and he had a rocky relationship with President Roosevelt, who feared de Gaulle might make himself dictator of France. Churchill, in contrast, welcomed him to the alliance and tried repeatedly to get the Americans to accept de Gaulle as de jure head of the French government in exile.[91]

Shortly after his first visit with de Gaulle, Devers received a message from Marshall about "a possible lack of cordiality and understanding" shown by the Americans toward the French. Marshall observed that this "may well militate against the most successful combined operations with the French" and directed Devers to perform an independent evaluation of the relationship.[92]

Marshall also sent Devers a report concerning Franco-American relations that was based on the views of French officers who had worked in North Africa before being transferred to Washington. The report described a number of problems, such as impatience with the French for their failure to understand English, intolerance of French desires to have arbitrary decisions explained, and unnecessary curtness and severity in refusing small French requests. It also alleged that the Americans seemed to doubt the veracity of French officers, often did not exchange salutes, and referred to the French in "uncomplimentary terms, in their hearing." The report noted that "the French are everlastingly astonished that their relations are so much more cordial with the British," since the French "consider themselves temperamentally more like us and instinctively expect to get along with us more easily than with the British." Relations had apparently deteriorated to the point where French and American officers tried to avoid each other "to prevent embarrassment."[93]

One of the root causes of misunderstandings between the French and the Americans was the language barrier. Most Americans could not speak any language other than English. Devers recognized this problem and was working with his houseboy, an Algerian named Ali, to polish his own imperfect French. He reported to Georgie that in spite of Ali's efforts, "I am so tired [at the end of the day that] I have no reserve to help him much."[94] Nonetheless, he made the effort. He also looked for an officer to serve as his interpreter and as a liaison with the French.

Devers looked into the complaints about Franco-American relations and concluded in a message to Marshall that "misunderstanding does exist," resulting in administrative difficulties. "Under the set-up I found in the Theater, the procedure through which requests from the French for supplies had to pass was very complex." He resolved this problem by authorizing the French to deal directly with Larkin "in all matters pertaining to French Rearmament upon which an overall policy has been established." As

to reports of discourtesy and rudeness, Devers found that these were isolated instances, not widespread, and "of course, will not be tolerated." He
went on to identify problems that stemmed from things beyond his immediate control. For example, the rearmament agreement did not provide
for the equipping of French units that remained in North Africa to support their expeditionary forces. Also, the French felt that promises made in
Washington were not being fulfilled in North Africa. In both cases, Devers
explained to the French that he had to follow the policies of the Combined
Chiefs of Staff, but "in the application of those policies we will be as liberal
as possible."[95]

During his visits to the French troops fighting in Italy, Devers identified
another problem that he could easily correct. The American supply system
was giving French soldiers a smaller food ration than that given to American troops. He immediately ordered General Larkin to ensure that the
French received the same rations as Americans.[96] This had a positive effect
on French perceptions of Devers and of Americans in general.

Devers also informed Marshall of a problem that would be more difficult to correct:

> There is still, however, a bar to the closest confidential relations
> with the French, and that is our inability to discuss freely and frankly
> with them future operations. Generals de Gaulle and Giraud, of
> course, have been advised in general terms of the plan under con-
> sideration. However, the details cannot be discussed with members
> of the French Planning Staff until the higher French commanders
> have been designated, and that cannot be done until the directive
> for the [Anvil] operation has been received from CCS. During this
> time the French resent the idea that American and British members
> of AFHQ must be discussing the employment of French Forces
> without the French being brought into these discussions.[97]

General Wilson was the only person who could authorize French access to
the planning process for Anvil. Devers told Marshall, "I will make sure that
General Wilson fully considers the importance of amicable French-Ameri-
can relations in arriving at his decisions in these matters."[98]

Devers got Wilson to agree to add a French liaison and planning team
to Force 163. On 20 March French colonel Jean Petit and five other
French officers joined Patch's planning headquarters. In April de Gaulle

announced that General de Lattre would command Army Detachment B in the invasion of southern France. De Lattre established contact with Lieutenant General Patch and his chief of staff, Colonel White, and Patch and his team briefed Wilson, Devers, Eaker, and de Lattre about the assault plan on 28 April. De Lattre initially wanted to command the entire Allied force, since he outranked Patch. But after some serious negotiations, de Gaulle and de Lattre agreed that Patch would command the invasion and that an American would command Seventh Army and the French army during the campaign.[99]

Devers was surprised to learn that some of the French leaders were virtually powerless. He told Marshall, "Giraud can make few if any, decisions which are final. He is very hard to talk to, or to convince with reference to Service Troops, or any other matter in which he is not interested." In contrast, when Giraud and de Gaulle were consulted together, "things seemed to go more easily." He found other French leaders "difficult personalities to deal with,—one, the Commissioner for War and Air, M. le Trocquer, and the other General de Lattre de Tassigny. Both of them seem to have the inside track, and both of them are in my opinion and that of my advisors, dangerous men. They are brilliant men, and General de Lattre de Tassigny particularly, make a favorable impression on first meeting with most people."[100] Devers made strenuous efforts to establish and maintain good working relations with the French. Early on, he visited the French divisions accompanying Fifth Army and gave "them justly high praise for the fine work they are doing." He assured Marshall that "proper calls have been made on all French officials" and "special attention given French troops and commanders, which has been greatly appreciated."[101]

Devers was disposed to like the French, and he reported to Georgie in March, "I am having a liberal education with the French. They are all trying to get together and do the correct thing. De Gaulle is a very intelligent man and I like to talk to him. He's a worker and a thinker and is getting over his early mistakes. God forbid that I should ever see my country beaten and occupied. It is a horrible thing to behold. The French are sensitive and easily hurt and I understand their suffering."[102]

The May Offensive in Italy

The Allied armies in Italy spent the second half of March and all of April repositioning and resting their forces for a major offensive. General Alexander believed that British troops should spearhead the main attack, which he planned to launch in the Liri valley near Cassino. For this effort he shifted two corps of Eighth Army into positions formerly held by the French and by U.S. II Corps. Alexander shifted Clark's Fifth Army to the west and assigned it a secondary role in the upcoming offensive known as Diadem. On 19 April the CCS ordered General Wilson to launch an offensive in Italy as soon as the weather improved and the ground had dried out sufficiently to allow armored vehicles to move cross-country.[103]

Devers had worked hard to improve the morale and capability of Fifth Army's infantry divisions by revamping the replacement system and getting new divisions into the front line so tired units could rest and train. By March, after the New Zealand Corps' defeat at Cassino, he saw little progress. He wrote to Georgie: "It is a struggle and we are getting nowhere. . . . Well the trouble is it takes too long to succeed. I must have patience. I am certainly getting hard-boiled."[104] Less than a month later, he sensed a significant improvement, as he told General McNair: "There is a total change in the attitude here for we have succeeded in relieving our divisions, giving them a little rest, getting excellent replacements and giving them a chance to train for their next battle. The 88th and 85th Divisions, recently arrived in this theater, are excellently commanded and have made quite an impression on our allies because of their appearance and discipline." There still were major problems that needed to be addressed, but as he told McNair: "The big problem is infantry replacements. Also, it is not the battle casualties that cause us trouble; it is the non-battle casualties" such as those resulting from trench foot and malaria, which were epidemic in Fifth Army. Devers believed that "the answer is leadership, simple things, patrolling [and] discipline." He also complained that "our officers, particularly our higher ranking officers, are too much impressed by the Germans." The remedy he prescribed was to "impress our soldiers that they must kill the Germans, not capture them, kill them."[105]

In mid-April Devers informed Marshall that, "for the first time, at least since I have been in this theater, the fighting troops are up to strength and are happy with the support being given them from the rear." He also noted that "the Air Force under Eaker is improving steadily." Malaria, however, continued to be a major problem, and he told the chief of staff, "We have instituted energetic measures to combat malaria in all its forms." Overall, Devers felt that things were headed in the right direction and proudly informed Marshall, "We are working now on improving the fighting attitude of the soldiers."[106]

By late April, the Allied forces were poised to launch coordinated assaults against the German armies at Anzio and on the Gustav Line. Devers assured Georgie, "We are going out against a foolish foe and this time mountains and rivers shall not stop us."[107] He told General Handy, "We are well prepared for our next push. . . . The American forces in this Theater are gradually improving and becoming stern, determined soldiers." Devers attributed this development to sound organization and a considerable improvement in leadership, and he noted that the "impetus is from the rear to the front rather than from the front to the rear as I found it when I came here."[108]

Although Alexander had relegated Fifth Army to a secondary role, Clark had other ideas. At the Anzio beachhead, Truscott's VI Corps had two British and five American divisions ready to attack north to capture the Alban Hills and cut the German lines of communication at Valmontane. Along the Garigliano sector, Keyes's II Corps was poised to attack northwest along Highway 7 with the 85th and 88th Infantry Divisions. On Fifth Army's right flank, the French Expeditionary Corps' four divisions faced the most difficult mountainous terrain in the Allied line. For this reason, Alexander expected little from Fifth Army's attack.[109]

Juin, the French commander, had a very different opinion of his corps' chances of penetrating the German lines. He believed that, owing to the difficult terrain, the Germans had only one major defensive line facing him. He convinced Clark that his Moroccan and Algerian troops should attack on a narrow front over the Aurunci Mountains, thus outflanking the Liri valley from the south. Once they penetrated the single line of defense, he planned to commit all his forces at the breaking point before German reserves could be shifted to close the gap.[110] Devers agreed with Juin and considered him "one of the best, if not the best, general on this front. . . . He is small, smart, quick, and a real fighter with quite a balanced force."[111]

By 11 May, conditions were right for the Allied offensive. The British Eighth Army struck the strongest German defenses around Cassino, while the American Fifth Army attacked into the mountains along the Garigliano valley. For the first few days, little progress was made. Then, Juin's Moroccans broke the enemy line, and he committed his reserves through the breach. By 15 May, the French had driven twelve miles into the German defenses on a front that was sixteen miles wide.[112] This move unhinged the

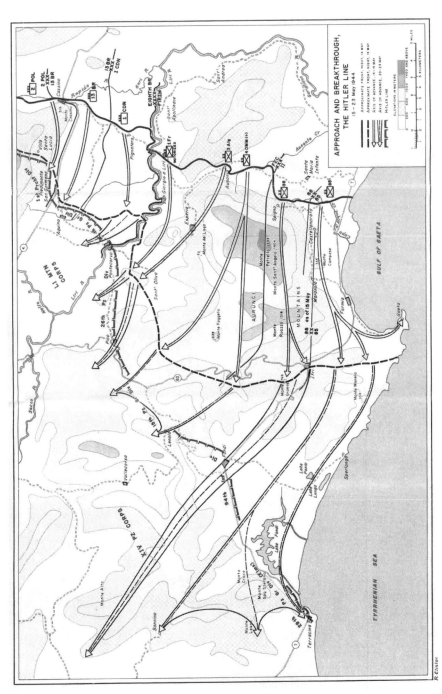

Figure 11.2. Approach and breakthrough of the Hitler Line, 15–23 May 1944

German defenses to the west and east, allowing U.S. II Corps to crack the German defenses it faced and allowing the British to move up the Liri valley. A Polish corps captured the monastery on Monte Cassino on 18 May, clearing the way for the British push.[113] On the western flank, II Corps' two divisions were able to continue offensive actions despite their losses because of the replacements already in the divisions.[114]

As the Gustav Line crumbled, it was time for VI Corps to launch its offensive from the Anzio beachhead. According to Alexander's plan, Truscott's main effort was a drive to the northeast to cut Highway 6 at Valmontane, thus trapping part of the German Tenth Army. Clark moved his headquarters to Anzio on 22 May and ordered Truscott to attack on 23 May. By 25 May, the German lines had been breached, and few Germans stood between VI Corps and Valmontane. But then Clark changed Truscott's direction of advance from the northeast to the northwest, leaving only two divisions driving toward Fifth Army's assigned objective of Valmontane. Clark was going for the glory of capturing Rome rather than cutting off the retreating German forces.[115]

The German defenses along the Alban Hills proved to be stronger than anticipated, and VI Corps advanced slowly during the next few days.[116] Then, in a daring nighttime operation, the 34th Infantry Division found a breach in the German defenses near Velletri and infiltrated its infantry regiments through the gap. By the next day, the 34th Division had outflanked the defenders, opening the way for the rest of VI Corps to move toward Rome. Although the German commander Kesselring extracted most of his troops from the trap, which did not close, he was forced to retreat north of Rome, allowing Fifth Army to enter the city unopposed on 4 June. The Germans lost more than 25,000 men and nearly 600 tanks and guns during the fighting from 11 May to 4 June.[117]

The Germans probably would have lost a much larger part of their Tenth Army had Clark followed Alexander's orders and focused his attack on Valmontane. As Rick Atkinson wrote, "Mark Clark would spend the rest of his long life defending an indefensible impertinence that for more than sixty years has remained among the most controversial episodes in World War II."[118] Alexander took no action against Clark and put a good face on the successes achieved. Devers was pleased to have the stalemate broken and reported the progress to Marshall, pointing out that the infantry divisions' success had been aided by changes in the replacement policy:

Thank you for the letter informing me of the decision to authorize us to drop combat personnel when they go to the hospital. It will result in the effective strength of the combat units being the same as the assigned strength. . . . The effectiveness of infantry in combat is increased greatly by authorizing them an advance on replacement requirements. . . . The effect is prolonging the effective period of the assault. I authorized a 15% advance on replacements prior to the recent offensive. . . . Talking to [the division commanders, John E.] Sloan and [John] Coulter the other day, they emphasized the point that they were able to advance rapidly and continuously only because the infantry units were always up to strength.[119]

After spending several days with Crittenberger's IV Corps near Rome, Devers wrote to Georgie, "We have done it and how. . . . Clark did well, he was my problem child. . . . Truscott, Keyes, Critt[enberger] and Harmon all were outstanding in a big way. . . . The French led by that great little soldier Juin and by far the outstanding Frenchman I have met fought a great battle."[120] He also wrote to Hap Arnold to praise Juin, Eaker, Keyes, and Truscott for their "leadership and unselfishness." He concluded, "It is a fine feeling to have a great team who play to win no matter what the cost to themselves."[121] Devers did not single out Clark for such praise.

Eaker wrote to Arnold on 6 June, telling him that Devers's personal leadership "has had a more important effect than any other one thing on the current successes in the air and on the ground in this theater." He singled out Devers's "boundless energy and drive, which made it possible for him to visit practically every combat unit in this theater, air and ground." Eaker had accompanied Devers on many of his inspection trips and concluded that his positive effect on the soldiers and airmen, "particularly his encouragement to commanders," had "been a large factor in the fine showing that our American units have made during the past two weeks." Arnold passed Eaker's letter on to Marshall, who forwarded it to President Roosevelt.[122]

On 13 June Devers recommended to Marshall that Patch, Truscott, Keyes, and Crittenberger be promoted to lieutenant general. He informed the chief of staff, "I suggested to General Clark that he recommend [the last three of] these officers for promotion but he has taken no action. I am accordingly taking it upon myself to recommend their promotion." In addition, he noted that Truscott, Keyes, and Crittenberger had not "received due credit for the success of Fifth Army in the operations in Italy and that it is time that appropriate recognition was given." In Patch's case, Devers stated that "his capacity for command was amply demonstrated in the South Pacific"; therefore, he felt "strongly that he should be a lieutenant general now since he is commanding French troops who are in turn commanded by a [French] full general."[123] Marshall agreed to promote Patch and Truscott, but deferred on the other two. Devers's action showed his ability to reward successful officers and indicated the limit of Clark's professionalism.

Anvil Resurrected

On 22 May, in response to the Allied armies' successes along the Gustav Line, General Wilson instructed General Alexander to prepare to pull from the front an experienced American corps headquarters, three veteran American divisions, and all the French forces fighting in Italy for an amphibious operation. These actions were to be taken only after the fall of Rome. Wilson made it clear that there would be insufficient landing craft to execute any amphibious operations on the Italian mainland. Fifteenth Army Group headquarters passed these instructions on to Fifth Army.[124]

Immediately after Fifth Army captured Rome, Wilson ordered Alexander to pull VI Corps out of the line by 10 June and send it and Truscott to Naples to prepare for Anvil.[125] Wilson was now committed to Anvil, in spite of the opposition by Churchill, Alexander, and the British chiefs of staff. He correctly believed that he should take his strategic direction from the Combined Chiefs of Staff, rather than from the British chiefs or Churchill. This was not the first time Wilson had irritated Churchill. In March Churchill had raked Wilson over the coals:

> Since you have taken over in the Mediterranean, I have been much embarrassed to find you sending a number of telegrams to Combined Chiefs of Staff about military politics, which are quite contrary to policy reached on highest level with the President. A further set of difficulties have arisen about L.S.T. puzzle in its relation to ANVIL. Our Chiefs of Staff reached an agreement through General Eisenhower to effect that though ANVIL would not be cancelled, the battle in Italy had supreme priority over it, and that fighting in Italy was not to be hampered for the sake of preparing for ANVIL. . . . However, you apparently misunderstood the relationship of para. 2 (about ANVIL) to para. 1 (about the bat-

tle in Italy) and instead of asking us to clear up any point about which you may be in doubt, you proceeded to give a much greater emphasis on ANVIL preparation than is compatible with safety and success of Allied Armies so heavily engaged. Unfortunately, under the "shadow of ANVIL" you put forward detailed proposals with which we do not agree and which are far less favorable to the Battle in Italy than those we had agreed with General Eisenhower.[126]

Observing the pressure that Wilson was under, Devers noted in a letter to Handy that Wilson "is an exceptionally fine and courageous officer who serves two masters loyally and well. He is anxious that he serve us, and particularly General Marshall, well."[127]

With the Germans in retreat north of Rome, Churchill crowed to Alexander, "How lucky it was that we stood up to our USA Chiefs of Staff friends and refused to deny you the full exploitation of this battle. . . . I am sure the American Chiefs of Staff would now feel this was a bad moment to pull out of battle or in any way to weaken its forces for the sake of other operations of an amphibious character which might very soon take their place in the van of our idea."[128] The prime minister could not have been more mistaken.

Overlord commenced on 6 June, stealing Clark's headlines. Four days later, the American chiefs of staff arrived in London to meet with their British counterparts and determine the future of Mediterranean strategy. During the next week, Eisenhower weighed in on their discussions and told the CCS that Anvil would provide substantial aid to his efforts in Normandy by keeping the German divisions tied down in southern France and by securing Marseille, one of the largest ports in Europe. Marshall added that the Allies needed a large port that was not already choked with cargo, as the British ports were, through which forty to fifty American divisions could reach the battle in France. The destruction of the artificial port at Omaha Beach in late June made it even more important logistically to seize Marseille.[129]

As the Combined Chiefs of Staff deliberated, Alexander tried to push his views into the debate by telling Brooke that he was "seriously perturbed at the probability that my present successful operations are going to be hamstrung again. I am being pressed to release an American corps H.Q. for planning other operations and I foresee quite clearly that in a short time I shall be told to release some of my American and French Formations."[130]

Alexander clearly overstepped his authority as an Allied army group commander when he questioned orders issued by the supreme Allied commander in the Mediterranean. When Wilson saw a copy of this message, he sent the following reprimand to Alexander: "I must ask you to refrain from sending or repeating anything except purely operational reports direct to the Chief of the Imperial General Staff. Any reference in your telegrams puts me in an impossible position with the Americans. You must remember that I am the servant of the Combined Chiefs of Staff and that the Americans are sticklers for correct channels. Further, they regard direct communications between you and London with the gravest suspicion as an attempt to influence the British Chiefs of Staff by a British as opposed to an Allied expression of opinion."[131]

The renewed Anvil debate swirled for several more weeks before the British finally accepted the American position. On 2 July the Combined Chiefs of Staff ordered Wilson to carry out Anvil with ten divisions. As supreme Allied commander in the European theater, Eisenhower gave Wilson the goals for the operation: contain and destroy German divisions, secure a major port, advance north along the Rhône to threaten the German forces in northern France, and develop lines of communications to support the Allied armies in France.[132] Churchill grudgingly acceded to the decision to invade southern France, but he insisted that the operation's name be changed to Dragoon, since he felt "dragooned" into accepting it.

Final Preparations for Anvil-Dragoon

Patch and the Seventh Army staff, along with the navy, air, and French planning groups, moved to Naples, where they finalized plans and oversaw preparations for Anvil-Dragoon. Admiral H. K. Hewitt was the commander of the Western Task Force, which included the French and American assault troops as well as the naval units that would carry Truscott's VI Corps and the follow-on French divisions to France. In accordance with American doctrine, Hewitt would be in command of the operation until the ground forces were securely established ashore.

Wilson gave Alexander a timeline for releasing the three American and four French divisions from the front lines so that they could receive replacements and train. The French Committee of National Liberation had decided to allow General de Lattre to serve under Lieutenant General Patch's command in the initial invasion, thus clearing the way for full French participation in the final planning and preparation. Devers had agreed that de Lattre would command the French First Army once the Franco-American Allies were firmly established in France, reassuring de Gaulle that an independent French army would take part in the liberation of France.[133]

Because there were two armies involved in the invasion of southern France and the advance up the Rhône valley, they had to be coordinated. Devers addressed this issue in a letter to Marshall on 1 July:

> It is believed that, as soon as we get the Seventh Army ashore, the French will want to organize their divisions into an army; that we will send in one or more additional corps to build up Patch's Seventh Army, followed by the Fifth Army, plus all remaining U.S. troops in this theater. This will require an army group headquarters, and I believe such a staff should be authorized now and quietly formed in order that it may have experience and be able to operate when the time comes. It is realized that at some point after the landing the overall command of these troops going into southern France will pass to Eisenhower. If you could see fit, I would greatly appreciate it if you would give me command of this army group.[134]

From this message, it is clear that Devers, and probably Marshall, hoped to shut down American operations in Italy. In the end, this did not happen, for the sake of Anglo-American harmony. Fifth Army remained in Italy and received reinforcements, including the 91st and 92nd Infantry Divisions and the 10th Mountain Division. II and IV Corps remained in Italy and fought another grueling winter campaign through the mountains south of the Po River valley.

Devers's recommendation to activate an army group headquarters made sense. His request to command it was also appropriate, given that he was the senior American general in the Mediterranean and had amply demonstrated his ability to command a large organization. Devers's fine performance in the MTO was known to Marshall, thanks to Eaker's letter to Arnold. Equally important, Wilson supported the creation of an army group and told Marshall that he wanted Devers to command it.[135] The question remained, however, would Eisenhower accept Devers as a major subordinate ground commander in the European theater?

Marshall sent a message to Eisenhower on 13 July, briefing him on the details of Anvil-Dragoon and Wilson's and Devers's recommendation to establish an army group for the operation.[136] Ike had already heard that Devers wanted to command the army group, and he was aware of Devers's concern that, "looking forward to the time those forces come under my jurisdiction, he might not be acceptable to me." Eisenhower told Marshall on 12 July, "I well know that such things are not my business, but I do want to make it clear that I have nothing in the world against General Devers." He told the chief of staff he had heard that Devers was doing "a very fine job," which had eliminated "the uneasy feeling I once held with respect to him." Eisenhower based his current view in large part on reports that Devers "had been on the battle front a lot and that he had demonstrated a happy faculty of inspiring troops. That is enough for me."[137]

That was enough for Marshall as well. On 16 July he notified Devers that, "after considering all factors, I agree that we should set up an Army group for ANVIL and am glad General Wilson wants you to command it. Eisenhower agrees with this. . . . It should probably be primarily an American headquarters, with a carefully chosen French representation." Marshall emphasized that "we must push ANVIL to the utmost," while at the same time supporting General Wilson in "the two battles he has to fight in southern France and Italy."[138] The good news for Devers was that he was getting into the fight as the commander of Sixth Army Group.

12

Sixth Army Group

The Riviera to the Vosges

Devers finally realized his dream of commanding American forces in battle when he was selected to lead Sixth Army Group into France. The capture of Rome made it possible to launch an invasion of southern France because it freed up the American and French divisions and the amphibious resources needed for the endeavor. Although there would be some final bickering between the Anglo-American Allies, the course was set for Operation Anvil.

The final decision by the Combined Chiefs of Staff to conduct Anvil (renamed Dragoon on 1 August) was strongly influenced by the situation in Normandy. By mid-June, Eisenhower's American forces were finding it difficult to advance against the Germans in the hedgerow country known as the Bocage and in the difficult terrain of the Cotentin Peninsula. On the left flank, Montgomery's British troops had been stopped short of the city of Caen, barely fifteen miles inland from the English Channel. The only major port in the invasion area, Cherbourg, had not yet been captured, and it was sure to be heavily damaged by the Germans before it fell. When the CCS met with Eisenhower in mid-June, he told them he needed Anvil to prevent a possible stalemate in France, and the capture of Marseille and Toulon would greatly ease his logistical difficulties.[1]

Despite steady pressure from Churchill to cancel Anvil, Eisenhower did not change his mind. Eisenhower's aide, Harry Butcher, reported one such encounter: "Ike said no, continued saying no all afternoon, and ended saying no in every form of the English language at his command. . . . Ike's position was that sound strategy called for making the Germans fight on as many fronts as possible."[2] When Churchill and Brooke made their final appeals to Roosevelt to cancel Anvil-Dragoon, Eisenhower told Marshall, "I will not, repeat not under any conditions agree at this moment to a cancellation of DRAGOON. . . . There is nothing that justifies a recasting of plans in the Mediterranean but rather that DRAGOON should be pushed energetically and speedily."[3] The president and the American chiefs of staff were equally adamant that Dragoon must take place on 15 August.

Planning for Invasion

The plans for Anvil-Dragoon were completed before the fall of Rome. Patch and his staff briefed Marshall on 17 June, and Wilson approved the plan on 28 June. The strategy was to land VI Corps' three infantry divisions on a number of small beaches from Cape Cavalaire, thirty miles east of Toulon, to a beach thirty miles east of Cape Cavalaire, near St. Raphael. The initial objective was to drive west to capture Toulon and then Marseille. VI Corps would establish the beachhead and push inland. On D-day, a provisional airborne division composed of American and British troops would jump into a drop zone around Le Muy, inland from Frejus, to prevent the Germans from counterattacking the beachhead in the early hours of the assault. French forces would begin landing on D+1. The planners hoped the French could capture Toulon by D+20 and Marseille twenty-five days later. French and American special operations forces would land west and east of the invasion area to secure the flanks and eliminate long-range German artillery.[4]

Patch sent the plan to Truscott, the ground force commander, on 25 June, asking for his input.[5] Truscott responded two days later, telling Patch that he agreed with the idea to land his three infantry divisions on the nine beaches selected, but he recommended that his most experienced division, the 3rd Infantry, land on the left-hand beaches, closest to Toulon, and his weakest division, the 36th Infantry, land on the right flank, giving it a primarily defensive role. He asked that each of his divisions land two of its regiments using assault landing craft, ensuring their ability to quickly mass combat forces ashore. Patch adopted these suggestions, and Admiral Hewitt assigned his navy sub–task force commanders accordingly.[6]

Truscott was concerned that the navy did not have a planning staff at the corps level. Instead, Hewitt and his staff dealt with Patch and his Seventh Army staff, while the navy sub–task force commanders dealt directly with the three army divisions in the assault force. This arrangement left Truscott out of the picture. In written appeals to Patch and Devers, Truscott pointed out the similarities with the invasion at Salerno in September 1943, when the Germans nearly drove the Allied forces back into the sea. In that assault, the VI Corps commander had not been involved in plan-

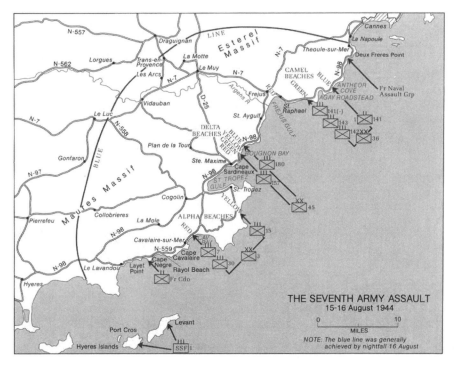

Figure 12.1. Seventh Army's assault, 15–16 August 1944

ning and landed on the beachhead without proper communications. Truscott believed "that much of the difficulty that attended the Salerno landing was due to the confused command organization during the assault phase." He suggested that he work directly with the senior naval commander, since the "planning and command of the assault troops should be vested in the assault force commander. . . . It is, in my opinion, absolutely essential that the Army and Navy assault force commanders be aboard the same ship during the actual operations. . . . Since the detailed planning must be done on Corps level, it seems perfectly obvious to me that there should be a naval component to coordinate all matters involving this assault which, in its early stages, is largely of naval concern." In his view, a naval planning staff should be moved to Naples as soon as possible to work with the VI Corps staff and commander.[7]

Patch and Hewitt refused to send a naval planning staff to Naples; instead, they assured Truscott that he would be aboard Hewitt's flagship with Patch and that he would be fully involved in commanding the assault forces. Hewitt, as senior naval commander, would remain in charge of all land, sea, and air forces until the three assault divisions reached the designated beachhead line. At that time, Truscott's corps would assume control of the ground forces, including the French and the airborne divisions, until Seventh Army's advance headquarters could set up operations ashore. Devers supported this decision.[8]

All available French combat forces in the Mediterranean theater were committed to the operation, with the first 40,000 French soldiers scheduled to land on 16 August. De Lattre's Army Detachment B would remain subordinate to Patch's Seventh Army until the linkup with Allied forces in northern France. At that time, de Lattre's command would be renamed the French First Army, and Sixth Army Group would be activated and placed in charge of the two armies. De Lattre could be difficult to work with, but he had a good relationship with Patch. He wrote of the American: "At Naples I frequently saw General Patch. From the first I entered into friendly and confident relations with him. . . . Quiet, somewhat taciturn, his ascetic features above a violet scarf, General Patch impressed one with the clearness of his affecting bright blue eyes. Deeply religious, of mystic turn of mind, he had a charming manner. . . . But this sensitive man, who spoke tenderly of his wife and dearly loved son . . . was also a resolute commander, of high and clean intellect, and exceptional steadfastness. The plans upon which he resolved were conceived with perfect wisdom."[9]

Logistical planning for Anvil-Dragoon was conducted by Major General Thomas Larkin's Services of Supply (SOS), the logistical headquarters for the NATOUSA. Supplies and material for the operation had started arriving in the Mediterranean in January, and by April, there were sixty-five large ships loaded with supplies. When Anvil was canceled in April, Devers decided to keep those ships in the theater and to earmark and protect the supplies in dumps in North Africa, just in case the CCS changed its mind about the operation.[10] When Anvil was resuscitated in June, Larkin's SOS and the Army Service Forces requisitioned and shipped the balance of the materials and ammunition needed for a ninety-day operation in southern France. The official history notes, "There is no doubt that this goal was attained on such short notice largely because of Devers' generally successful efforts to freeze ANVIL supplies after the CCS had cancelled the operation in April."[11] Devers was pleased with the responsiveness of the Army Service Forces in filling requisitions for the operation and with the SOS in preparing Sixth Army Group's logistical system. However, he and Larkin were concerned about the supply of artillery ammunition and the need for additional army railroad units to rebuild and operate the French rail lines from Marseille to the north. The chief of staff of the Army Service Forces suggested obtaining additional railway units from either Italy or England, but there was no quick fix for this potential problem.[12]

One of the biggest logistical challenges in the invasion of southern France and subsequent operations by Sixth Army Group was the French army's weak support and service organizations. From the beginning of the French army's rearmament, French leaders wanted to focus on creating combat units and were reluctant to provide sufficient manpower for service, supply, and maintenance units. After a great deal of debate, the French bowed to pressure from Wilson and Devers to convert several combat divisions into support and maintenance units.[13] However, this failed to produce enough literate and mechanically skilled Frenchmen. AFHQ had estimated that 112,000 support troops would be needed, but in the end, only 39,000 Frenchmen were available for the French service and maintenance forces. Only 30 percent of the 133 French service units had more than 30 percent of their equipment and personnel by the end of July. By Seventh Army standards, French Army B was "not ready for battle."[14]

American doctrine was for the army-level headquarters to be the main logistical operator in support of the corps and divisions assigned to it. Seventh Army played that role for VI Corps and the other corps assigned later. When Devers realized in March that the French were not going to field enough service and support units for an army of over 250,000 men, he requested permission from the War Department to provide American service units to support the French. Marshall rejected this request, but in June, when it was clear that the Americans would have to provide most of the logistical support to both armies, he relented.[15] This decision stretched Seventh Army's resources thin; at the time, the Americans themselves were short 10,000 service personnel in the Mediterranean theater.[16] This was an imperfect solution that would cause problems in the future, but in August it was sufficient to allow Dragoon to begin. To help coordinate the supply of French troops, Colonel Jean Gross, commander of French Base 901 (the French logistical unit), became the deputy commander of the American Coastal Base Section (COBASE), and each of the American staff sections had a French deputy chief. COBASE would assume responsibility for the logistical support of the two armies of Sixth Army Group at about D+30.[17]

The final staging of forces for the operation took place in July and

August, as the French divisions in Italy were withdrawn from active combat and VI Corps rested and trained its three assault divisions. Hewitt commanded 885 ships and landing craft sailing under their own power, with 1,375 smaller craft carried by the assault ships. His armada consisted of 151,000 men, excluding ships' crews, and 21,400 vehicles of all types.[18] When the fleet sailed for France on 13 August, ships came from ports in North Africa, Corsica, and Sardinia, and the main force sailed from Naples. As the ships carrying VI Corps steamed out of Naples harbor, a smiling Churchill waved at them from a launch. The soldiers responded with waves and cheers for the great British leader who, ironically, had tried to derail the operation right up to the last moment.[19]

Devers followed the preparations for Dragoon closely. On 9 August he gave General Marshall an appraisal of the preparations:

> Everything seems set for DRAGOON. Patch has done a remarkably fine piece of work in coordinating the activities of the Americans, the French, and the British, the Navy, and the Air. He is well liked by all and his problems have been numerous and difficult. I have set up a small headquarters at Bastia which is now functioning and ready to develop into a small, but, I hope, aggressive army group staff at a moment's notice. General Wilson has now taken the lead and imbued everybody with the idea of exploiting any success which we may have. Patch will be a willing pupil to this doctrine. We have just completed dry runs by every unit concerned in the operation. The troops look fine and are keyed up to go. The Navy is alert that they will have a very difficult and complicated problem. I have just returned from the exercise with the Special Service Force . . . whose mission is to capture two islands off the coast. . . . It is a most hazardous and daring undertaking. Needless to say, I saw plenty of the Mediterranean and wandered around the coast in a Navy boat with both engines out most of the night.[20]

Devers's message included references to some of his other responsibilities at the time. As the senior American commander in the Mediterranean, he decorated General Anders, whose Polish troops had captured the Monte Cassino monastery. As deputy supreme Allied commander, he was still dealing with Clark and Alexander and the campaign in Italy. As the Sixth Army Group commander-designee, he was preparing to assume command of the

U.S. Seventh and French First Armies. He would continue to hold all these positions and responsibilities until October, when a new American commander would replace him.

Devers spent a great deal of time with his soldiers and senior combat leaders. Marshall never had to tell him to move forward and acquaint himself with the front-line situation (as he had urged Eisenhower to do in 1942–1943 during the North African and Sicilian campaigns). Devers regularly gave credit to Patch and Wilson and to the air and naval forces for their accomplishments. Devers let people know when he thought they were doing a good job (unlike Ike, who was very reluctant to compliment subordinates). Devers and Eisenhower could not have been more different. Devers's command style was based on many years of duty with the troops and the confidence to make difficult decisions.

The Dragoon Invasion

On the evening of 14 August, the Allied fleet reached the invasion area. Hewitt had not planned for a long naval gunfire bombardment, believing that the element of surprise was more important. German Army Group G, led by General Johannes Blaskowitz, commanded the enemy forces defending southern France. By August, Lieutenant General Frederich Wiese's Nineteenth Army was in charge of the three corps defending the Spanish and Italian borders. Wiese had seven understrength infantry divisions available, and only three of them were in the area from Marseille to Nice. The only German panzer division in Army Group G, the 11th, was in reserve to the west of the Rhône River. Only one German infantry division was defending the beaches where VI Corps planned to attack.[21]

The Mediterranean Allied Air Forces began air operations designed to isolate the invasion area in early August. To avoid tipping the enemy off as to the actual location of the planned invasion, Eaker and his air staff struck targets from well west of Marseille all the way to Nice, paying special attention to bridges over the Rhône River. These strikes were effective. By 15 August, every bridge south of Avignon had been destroyed or severely damaged.[22]

French partisans, known as the French Forces of the Interior (FFI), also carried out hundreds of attacks against German communications and transportation lines, overwhelming the Germans' ability to repair them. The FFI cut the main rail lines in southern France more than forty times in August and destroyed or damaged thirty-two bridges, most of them east of the Rhône. Blaskowitz and Wiese were forced to rely on radio communications, allowing the Allies to intercept their messages and use Ultra to unscramble their codes.[23]

On D-day Eaker's medium and heavy bombers began their bombardment of the actual invasion beaches at 0610 and ceased their attacks at 0730, to allow the dust to settle. Naval gunfire then hit selected targets such as bunkers and command posts. After that, fighter aircraft from carriers and from Corsica flew patrols over the battle area to support the ground forces, and Hewitt's warships stood by to support them as well.

German air and naval units were negligible in the western Mediterranean and were unable to threaten the invasion force. Hewitt was convinced that the enemy had not emplaced underwater obstacles in the landing areas. Consequently, he refused Truscott's request to have divers clear the beaches, believing that such activity might alert the Germans that an invasion was imminent.[24] Hewitt's judgment proved sound. The initial air and seaborne assaults took the defenders by surprise, as the Allies' airborne deception operations commenced at 2330 on 14 August.

The landing of airborne pathfinders began at 0330, and the 1st Airborne Task Force commenced its drops at 0430. The British and American airborne troops met limited resistance in Le Muy, and by the end of the day, more than 9,000 soldiers had arrived by air. Casualties were relatively light. Major General Robert Frederick's forces accomplished their mission of isolating the beachhead and blocking German reinforcements from counterattacking on D-day.[25]

Soldiers from VI Corps' assault divisions began to land just before 0800. On most of the beaches the landings went smoothly, and the Germans offered little opposition. The entire 3rd Infantry Division was ashore by 1030 and had secured the left flank of the invasion area. Major General Mike O'Daniel established his headquarters ashore at about 1045. In the center, Major General William Eagles's 45th Infantry Division secured all its D-day objectives with minimal losses against weak resistance. The air and naval bombardments had subdued most of the defenders, and Eagles did not have to commit his reserve regiment to combat.[26]

The landing of the 36th Infantry Division on the right flank of the invasion area did not go as smoothly. Admiral Hewitt and General Patch had estimated, correctly, that the Germans would fortify and mine the approaches to the Gulf of Frejus. The only coastal airstrip and seaplane base in the entire invasion area were near the town of St. Raphael, close to the mouth of the Argens River. The coastal railroad ran through the area as well. Both the Allies and the Germans recognized the area's tactical and logistical importance. As a result, the Germans had planted extensive minefields across the beach near Frejus, where the 36th Infantry Division's 142nd Infantry Regiment was to land. They had also built an antitank wall and a three-foot-deep antitank ditch across the exits from the beach. Machine gun positions and bunkers with antitank guns covered the wall and the ditch, and a double apron fence of barbed wire completed the defenses. St. Raphael was occupied by a German infantry battalion.[27]

The original commander of the naval task force assigned to land the 36th Infantry Division was Rear Admiral Don P. Moon. Moon had commanded the task force that successfully landed VII Corps on Utah Beach in Normandy in June. Apparently, after studying the intelligence about enemy defenses in his sector, Moon had "begged Hewitt to postpone the invasion," convinced that there had been too little preparation and assault training and that the "Germans would butcher the landing teams."[28] Hewitt agreed to consider Moon's plea, but he did not believe the situation was so dangerous. The next morning, Moon was found dead in his cabin, having blown his brains out with a pistol. Hewitt later discovered that Moon had been treated for acute depression and that the fleet medical officer had "interviewed Moon about his mental balance."[29] Moon's tragic end reminds us of the pressure on senior commanders in wartime. As Major General Joe Collins wrote later, Moon "was a casualty of this war just as much as if he had been killed in action."[30]

Based on intelligence reports, Hewitt and Patch had planned to delay the landing of the 142nd Regiment until the 36th's other two regiments had landed west and east of the Gulf of Frejus and cleared the German positions there. The 142nd Infantry Regiment was to land at 1400 hours on the beach near St. Raphael, after the other regiments had encircled the town. The 141st and 143rd Regiments assaulted their beaches at 0800 and moved inland against stubborn German resistance. Neither regiment reached Frejus or St. Raphael as planned, leaving the German defenses intact. Air and naval bombardment failed to subdue the defenders, even though four destroyers, two cruisers, and a battleship pounded the area for forty-five minutes. When minesweepers attempted to clear the approaches to the beach, they were driven back by heavy German artillery fire. When the time came to land the 142nd, Rear Admiral Spencer Lewis, commander of Task Force 87, decided that the beach, known as Camel Red, could not be assaulted head-on without incurring serious casualties. Therefore, he shifted the landing of the 142nd to an already secured beach to the west.[31]

The 142nd Infantry Regiment landed on Beach Green at 1515 hours and moved toward Frejus. The regiment's only casualties were five men wounded. Nonetheless, Admiral Lewis's decision to shift the 142nd to another beach displeased Truscott, who had not been consulted. As it turned out, Lewis had tried repeatedly to get in touch with the division commander, Major General John Dahlquist, who had gone ashore in the morning. Unable to establish contact, Lewis made one of the best decisions of the entire operation. As Dahlquist told him, "[I] appreciate your prompt action in changing plans when obstacles could not be breached."[32] Lewis saved many lives and still accomplished the mission. It took two more days for the 36th Infantry Division to overcome the strong resistance in and near St. Raphael and for naval forces to clear the sea mines from the area.[33]

On the left flank, Truscott sensed an opportunity to push his divisions inland more quickly than planned. On D+1 he ordered the 3rd and 45th Infantry Divisions to drive to the west and northwest, while the 36th Infantry Division cleared the beachhead of any further resistance. The success of the 3rd and 45th Infantry Divisions led Hewitt and Patch to accelerate the landing of French forces. On 16 August two French divisions landed behind the 3rd Infantry Division, and ships returned to Corsica to pick up the next wave of French troops. Over the next two days, de Lattre landed and then pushed four divisions toward Toulon and Marseille. This advance was initiated six days earlier than planned.[34]

As the Allied armies began their drive inland, Devers and Eaker landed on 18 August and spent two days with Patch, Truscott, and de Lattre. Devers wrote to Marshall that he was "delighted with what I saw." He noted, however, that there were major challenges to overcome, including securing airfields and solving supply problems.[35] The logistical problems were the result of pre-invasion estimates based on a strong German defense of the invasion area, as had been the case in all previous amphibious operations. Consequently, the plan called for landing combat troops and ammunition in the initial assault phase and delaying the landing of logistical units, trucks, fuel, and food until the beachhead was secure. Thus, when Truscott and de Lattre ordered their divisions inland in the face of weak resistance, shortages of transportation, fuel, and food became critical.[36]

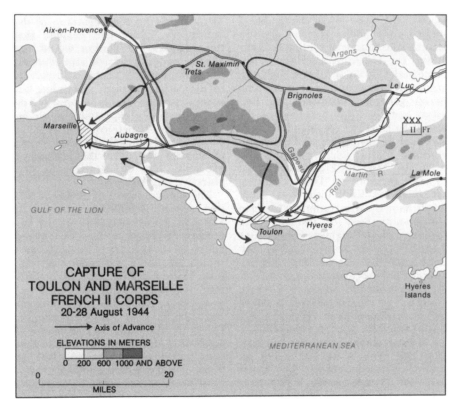

Figure 12.2. Capture of Toulon and Marseille, 20–28 August 1944

With French II Corps ashore and the remaining French divisions on their way to southern France, de Lattre wanted to push his forces toward Toulon and Marseille immediately, hoping to catch the German garrisons unprepared. His bold concept went against the original plan, which was to drive west only after all the French forces and artillery were ashore. De Lattre believed the Seventh Army staff would balk at his plan, so he first convinced Wilson and Devers that it was a risk worth taking. He then went to Patch's headquarters to get the army commander's approval. As de Lattre recalled, "By sheer insistence, I succeeded in overcoming the opposition of the cautious. General Patch gave me a free hand, the munitions, and my [armored command]."[37]

French troops, aided by the partisan FFI forces in the area, assaulted the outer defenses of Toulon and, at the same time, began a drive into the heart of Marseille, the second largest city in France. The fighting for both ports was vicious, as de Lattre described: "Attacks and counter-attacks followed one another without respite in the torrid heat of the Mediterranean summer and the acrid white dust raised by shots which cut the tops off walls and ploughed up the chalky soil of this region of lime-kilns, quarries, and cement-works. The Germans defended themselves with desperate fury. Infiltrating into the alley-ways, they watched all our movements and punished the least carelessness."[38]

Although ordered by Hitler to fight to the last man, the garrisons of both cities surrendered, with the last die-hard defenders in Marseille giving up on 28 August. Thirty-seven thousand Germans were taken prisoner, at a cost of 4,000 French casualties. According to de Lattre, "On the 29th August, when the smoke of battle had scarcely dispersed, a ceremony of thanksgiving took place at Notre Dame de la Garde."[39] Although both ports had been heavily damaged by the defenders, American army and navy engineers quickly cleared the mines and major obstacles, allowing the first Liberty ships to discharge cargo in Marseille on 15 September—a full month earlier than planned.[40]

De Lattre's forces had pulled off a seeming miracle with their swift capture of the two ports. In just twelve days, the French had accomplished the single most important mission of Dragoon. De Lattre's audacity and persistence made it possible, although Patch found it somewhat vexing to deal with the mercurial French warrior. De Lattre was an inspirational leader who pushed his staff, his troops, and himself hard. He was conscious of his role in the revival of France's military reputation and its return to the front ranks of European powers. He also had to deal with the FFI in his area, ensuring that the de Gaulle–led government was recognized in all parts of France and preventing communist elements in the Resistance from taking over regions in the liberated zones.

Since Devers did not speak or understand French well, it was essential that he find a man to serve as his personal translator and his key liaison with de Lattre. Fortunately, Devers knew an officer who spoke fluent French: Henry Cabot Lodge Jr. Lodge, the grandson of Senator Henry Cabot Lodge of Massachusetts, had lived in France as a boy. Since the late 1920s, the younger Lodge had served as a reserve officer in the cavalry, and during his annual training periods he often worked for Willis Crittenberger. Devers was first introduced to Lodge in 1941 and immediately recognized his leadership potential. Devers wrote in a 12 December 1941 letter to Lodge: "I hope that when the [Armored Force] gets into active campaign you will be a member in command of one of our units, for I am sure that you have the qualities which secure successful results quickly."[41]

When America entered the war, Lodge was a U.S. senator from Massachusetts. He came on active duty as a major and was assigned to the 2nd Armored Division. He donated his senatorial salary—$833 a month—to the U.S. Treasury. He served as an observer with the British Eighth Army in May 1942 and saw combat in June with several American tank crews that were temporarily assigned to the British 4th Armored Brigade. When he returned to the States, he wrote a report for the Armored Force that reinforced Devers's favorable opinion of him. Crittenberger wrote to Lodge, "General Devers, on the phone, was so enthusiastic about your report to him, [and] said you are one of the outstanding observers so far developed in this war."[42]

The Roosevelt administration, however, decided in 1942 that members of Congress could not serve on active military duty. Those who were reserve or National Guard officers had to choose one or the other: military service or Congress. Lodge's friend, Secretary of War Henry Stimson, wrote to him, "I cannot but feel, therefore, that you will render more service to the American people by performing the important duties of a United States Senator rather than to devote your energies solely to the purely military phase of the war as a junior officer."[43] Initially, Lodge stayed in Congress, but in late 1943 he resigned his Senate seat and rejoined the military.

Once he was back on active duty, Lodge was assigned to the staff of Crittenberger's IV Corps in Italy. Devers, anticipating his need to communicate with the French on a regular basis, asked Crittenberger for Major Lodge's services, but only if "Lodge is willing to come and you are willing to release him."[44] It was a wise move by Devers, and Lodge accepted the offer. Lodge became Devers's voice with General de Lattre and his French army staff for the rest of the war.

On 14 August 1944 Lodge wrote a memorandum describing his duties: "To liaison with the French Army and Corps commanders; To Liaison with the CG and Chief of Staff, 6th Army Group with the French high command; To serve as an interpreter for the CG and Chief of Staff, 6th Army Group; Prepare summaries of proceedings or matters when acting as interpreter; Translate correspondence to the CG and Chief of Staff from the French command; Work directly for the CG and the Chief of Staff, 6th Army Group."[45] The success of the Allied forces in southern France was due in part to the relatively smooth functioning of the French and Americans in

Devers's army group. Lodge played a critical role, and Devers never regretted entrusting him with so much responsibility.

The "Champagne" Campaign

As de Lattre's forces closed in on Toulon and Marseille, VI Corps moved north to protect the French right flank and secure a bridgehead over the Durance River at Aix en Provence. While the 3rd Infantry Division secured Aix, Task Force Butler, an ad hoc organization of tank, infantry, and mechanized field artillery units, drove north through the mountains east of the Rhône. Through improvisation and hard work, Truscott found ways to supply his three divisions as they advanced more than 160 miles from the coast in five days. Thanks to Ultra, Devers and Patch knew by 17 August that Hitler had ordered the German forces in France to retreat. Patch shared his Ultra intelligence with Truscott, the man who could put it to best use.[46]

Knowing that the Germans were retreating, Truscott tried to cut them off at a constricted part of the Rhône valley north of the town of Montelimar. From 22 through 30 August, VI Corps units attempted to establish a firm blocking position while the German 11th Panzer Division fought to keep the escape route open. In an eight-day battle north and east of Montelimar, the Germans succeeded in preventing Task Force Butler and the 36th Infantry Division from closing the escape route. Although the enemy was able to extract many of its units, VI Corps captured 5,800 Germans and inflicted roughly 7,000 German casualties. VI Corps lost 1,575 soldiers killed, wounded, and missing.[47]

Truscott was disappointed that a large part of the German Nineteenth Army had escaped, but his spirits were raised when he observed the results of the battle: "For fifteen miles along the river, the detritus of eight days' fighting stretched like a black mourning ribbon: two thousand charred vehicles; at least a thousand dead horses, many still harnessed to caissons and gun carriages; and 'fire-blackened' Germans said to be 'an affront to the nose' that this grisly segment of highway became known as the Avenue of Stenches."[48] By the end of August, VI Corps had captured 17,134 Germans and destroyed roughly half the armored vehicles in the 11th Panzer Division. The French captured another 32,656 prisoners.[49]

As Truscott fought to cut off the German retreat, de Lattre began to push his forces north. Logistical difficulties plagued French and American units alike as they raced to get ahead of the retreating Germans. There was also disagreement within the Allied command about the best way to deploy the French forces in the pursuit. This was a major issue because, by this time, French Army B contained seven divisions and constituted more than two-thirds of Patch's Seventh Army. This dispute led to a confrontation between de Lattre and Patch, with Devers and Lodge playing the role of conciliator.

Patch had focused on the activities of Truscott's VI Corps during the last two weeks of August, which was understandable, as this was the main effort. What Patch did not comprehend was the power and élan of the French formations and de Lattre's determination to ensure that they played a prominent role in the liberation of France. Consequently, Patch and his staff assigned the French the mission of protecting VI Corps' right flank along the Alps, putting them to the right and rear of the main effort. As Lodge remembered later, "de Lattre was unhappy about being given the job of covering the Franco-Italian front, which was completely dead."[50] Instead of being relegated to the east side of the Rhône, behind VI Corps, de Lattre wanted to deploy his two corps abreast of VI Corps, giving them room to maneuver against the retreating Germans. To make this possible, he had already ordered General Alphonse de Monsabert's II Corps to advance from Marseille northwest to the Rhône and seize crossings in the vicinity of Avignon. De Monsabert would then cross the Rhône with the French 1st Armored and 1st Infantry Divisions and push as fast and as hard as possible toward Lyon. De Lattre ordered French I Corps, with two divisions, to advance on the east side of VI Corps to cover its eastern flank and advance along the Swiss border toward the Belfort Gap.[51]

A major crisis might have ensued, but Lodge informed Devers that de Lattre was "strongly dissatisfied" with Seventh Army's plan for his forces.[52] Judging the situation correctly, Devers intervened and suggested that Patch "send the II French Corps up the west bank of the Rhône to clear out any Germans who might be there and to attack Lyon from the west." This would preserve Allied unity and Patch's theoretical authority.[53] Lodge later remembered that Patch's chief of staff, Brigadier General White, "didn't want to change the prior arrangement, but General Patch did. He grasped the thing right away. General Patch was extremely open-minded and welcomed new ideas. He wasn't at all hidebound."[54] Patch ordered French II Corps to advance along the Rhône's west bank.

With this orientation of forces, the Franco-American army pushed north. Truscott, with his VI Corps in the center, sensed another opportu-

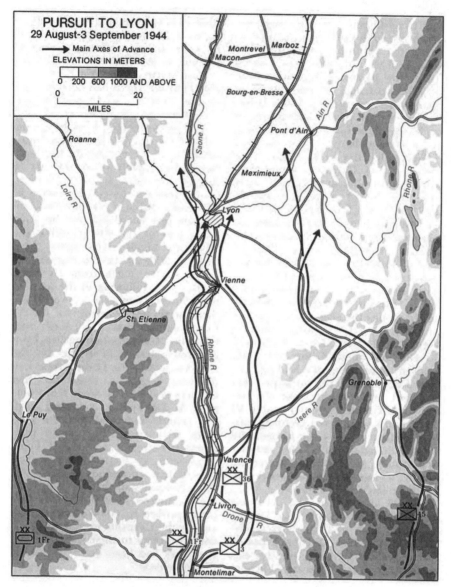

Figure 12.3. Pursuit to Lyon, 29 August–3 September 1944

nity to cut off the German escape route north of Lyon. On 2 September
he sent the 36th Infantry Division north along the east bank of the Rhône
while his 45th Infantry Division moved along roads well east of the river,
intending to get ahead of the Germans and cut off Route N-75 northeast
of Lyon. Truscott came close to cutting the Germans off, but in two days

of fierce fighting, the 11th Panzer Division was able to keep the route open long enough for most of the German forces to escape.[55]

French II Corps, west of the Rhône, was equally active. On 3 September the French 1st Infantry Division seized Lyon with help from the FFI; meanwhile, the 1st Armored Division overran the rear guard of the IV Luftwaffe Field Corps twenty miles north of Lyon, capturing 2,000 prisoners.[56] At this point, Patch planned to move French II Corps over to the east side of VI Corps, putting de Lattre's two corps next to each other. This would allow the French to fight as a united army as they tried to enter Alsace through the gap between the Vosges Mountains in the north and the Jura Mountains in the south.

On 2 September, however, after failing to cut the German escape route north of Lyon, Truscott proposed a different plan to Patch. Truscott wanted to turn VI Corps northeast to attack into Alsace through the Belfort Gap, while de Monsabert's corps continued north to seize Dijon and link up with Third Army. Patch agreed, without discussing the new plan with de Lattre. When the Frenchman learned of the scheme that would put his two corps on divergent axes, he was incensed. A serious argument ensued, but de Lattre ultimately agreed to the plan, with the following modifications: Bethouart's I Corps would attack on the right of VI Corps and seize Montbeliard in the southern half of the Belfort Gap, and Patch promised to unite the French corps once the Belfort Gap had been seized.[57]

From 4 to 8 September, Seventh Army's three corps advanced against light and disorganized opposition. French II Corps drove the Germans out of Dijon and continued to push north. Truscott and Bethouart coordinated their attacks as VI Corps seized Besançon and French I Corps pushed across the Doubs River, about twelve miles south of Montbeliard.[58] As the Franco-American forces approached Belfort, German resistance stiffened. On 10 September the 11th Panzer Division stopped the French drive ten miles south of Montbeliard, and the forces facing VI Corps slowed Truscott's divisions to a crawl. Believing he could still push through the German defenses at Belfort Gap, Truscott planned a coordinated attack. But as he was in the process of doing so, Patch ordered him to halt his eastward advance and reorient his forces to the northeast, into the highest mountains of the Vosges. These orders reflected guidance from Eisenhower, who had advised Devers to have Seventh Army advance alongside Patton's Third Army and protect its right flank. The French forces would be united on the right of Sixth Army Group, facing the Belfort Gap.[59]

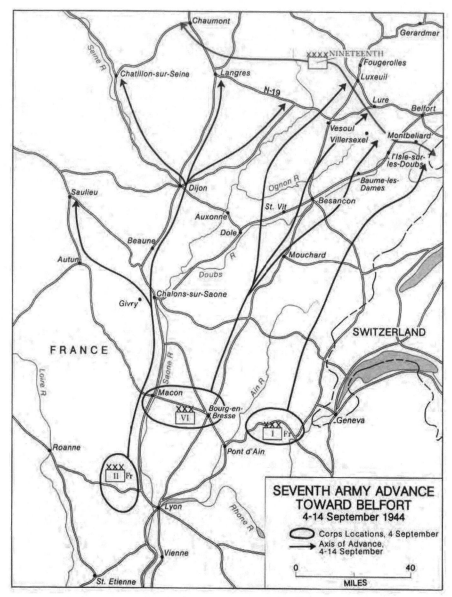

Figure 12.4. Seventh Army's advance toward Belfort, 4–14 September 1944

Truscott vigorously disputed Patch's order to change direction, but to no avail. The time it took to reorient the French and American corps gave the Germans a badly needed respite, and it allowed them to prepare defenses along the western Vosges and reinforce defenses in the Belfort

Gap. The Champagne campaign came to an end in the face of increasing German resistance and the overextension of Allied lines of communication. Devers's armies were not the only Allied forces facing serious logistical difficulties. All across the Western Front the Allied armies ground to a halt owing to a lack of fuel and replacement equipment.

Devers's Relations with AFHQ and Fifth Army

As the successful campaign unfolded in Provence, American service and air units began a steady buildup in southern France. Generals Alexander and Clark watched nervously as Devers and Larkin moved service units and supplies from Italy and North Africa to France. The British also feared that Devers intended to pull additional combat units from Clark's Fifth Army. In a letter to Marshall, Devers reported in August that he "had much evidence of British opposition to the withdrawal of American troops from Italy. It appears quite certain that Alexander pressed for their retention. . . . Further, there have been increasing signs of irritation at each new proposal for the withdrawal of units from Fifth Army required by Seventh Army or 6th Army Group."[60]

The Anglo-American debate over Mediterranean strategy in 1944 had caused a major rift in Allied ranks. Churchill, in the words of Rick Atkinson, "raged with the ineffectual petulance of a declining power" and denounced "the sheer folly of his 'strong and dominating partner.'"[61] Devers observed firsthand the frustrations of the British and reported to Marshall: "Important conferences on the British side are now in progress here involving the Prime Minister. . . . [The] Agenda, I am informed, covers the entire organization and strategy in the Mediterranean." The British, he claimed, were irked that the Americans were unwilling to underwrite their policy in the Balkans, and there "was a question if the Mediterranean should not become a British show." Devers also told Marshall that he was doing everything he could to help Fifth Army prepare for the Allied offensive in Italy slated to begin on 25 August. "This offensive, of course, is being inspired by the Prime Minister and his assistants. With the forces available it should be successful. I do not see what it can accomplish. All the Army in Italy can hope for is to eventually arrive in the Po after hard fighting now that they have wasted six weeks in permitting the Germans to build up their troops." Devers "strongly" recommended that the U.S. combat forces in Italy be transferred to southern France, where the 1st Armored Division in particular was "badly needed." Devers characteristically ended his letter by paying "high tribute" to the work of Kent Hewitt and Ira Eaker in Operation Dragoon.[62]

When Devers met with Mark Clark on 21 August, the Fifth Army commander expressed little faith in the upcoming Allied offensive in Italy. He told Devers that "he did not think the British would fight, that the [American] 2nd and 4th Corps would have to drag them along." Devers thought Clark was depressed, and he noted the presence of "considerable antiBritish feeling" in Fifth Army headquarters, caused in part by BBC radio reports that "always mention British units and seldom mention American units."[63] In a letter to Georgie, Jake expressed his feelings about the British:

> I have been to France several times and am well pleased with Sandy and his boys who know how to play ball. On the other side of the fence [in Italy] we are at the moment bogged down, resting, wondering, etc., but it must change. I have my trouble fostering AngloAmerican relations for it takes two to make it work and the British are always doing something [like] claiming credit or what not that belongs to our American boys. Result, a growing feeling of AntiBritish [sentiment]. . . . It is hell being a Deputy. You must not expect me to be either an Ike or a Mark. I am just different and get results in my own way.[64]

Devers also encountered tensions at Allied headquarters in Caserta, where he visited General Wilson. "I was greatly disturbed by the jitteriness I found at AFHQ, particularly among junior officers on the British side. They greatly feared that the U.S. will pull out of Italy and leave them to carry on, and they are confident they cannot do it, although they do not say so."[65] In the long run, Clark's Fifth Army remained in Italy, where its presence maintained Allied unity. In the short run, the British encouraged Devers to ask Marshall to relieve him of his responsibilities as American theater commander, fearing that he would use that position to move more American troops and resources to France. Larkin, his logistics commander, encouraged Devers not to give up either post as U.S. theater commander or deputy supreme Allied commander. Devers retained these positions for the time being, although he did "not like the idea of occupying two positions where I might be accused of favoring my own command."[66]

Marshall retained Devers as Mediterranean theater commander into late October, when he selected Lieutenant General Joseph T. McNarney to replace him. During Devers's last two months as theater commander, he continued to deal with Clark, whom he considered a poor army commander. Devers's biggest concern was Fifth Army's high losses, including casualties related to combat fatigue. In a letter to Wilson he wrote, "I have just noted Clark's casualty rates, which on the surface seem excessive to me and which will break any replacement system. It is my opinion that Clark should rest divisions or regiments within divisions . . . in order to provide better fighting units. Clark made the same mistake in handling his troops last January and February, and as you remember we then forced him to rest divisions and re-equip them out of the line. Up to the time I was in the theater he was throwing replacements into divisions without resting them."[67]

Devers could not order Clark to do anything, since Fifth Army was part of Alexander's Fifteenth Army Group. Devers did, however, encourage Clark to follow his advice, but Clark did not respond positively to this prodding. In September Devers's frustration increased when Clark sent him two cables that, in Devers's view, showed "quite well his lack of judgment and tact, and indicate[d] definitely that he is not a team player, nor has he the instincts of a fighting soldier and gentleman." Devers noted in his diary, "I shall take no action at this time but my judgment is that I should reprimand him. Both his telegrams are inaccurate and stupid."[68] When McNarney took over the theater, Devers no longer had to deal with the British or with Clark.

Even with his multiple responsibilities, Devers increasingly focused on his role as an army group commander. In this assignment, he was fortunate to have such reliable subordinates as Patch, de Lattre, and Truscott. He recognized that Seventh Army's drive up the Rhône was "Patch's show," as he told Georgie in a letter. "I am in a way the coach and maybe might be said to be in operational control to all intents and purposes, but it is certainly my team and Patch and Truscott have done wonders."[69]

The Drive North to Join SHAEF

August 1944 was one of the worst months of the war for the Germans. Bradley's bold July breakout in the Bocage (known as Operation Cobra) and his defeat of German counterattacks at Mortain broke the stalemate in Normandy. The successful invasion of southern France came two days before Hitler ordered all German forces, with the exception of the garrisons of major ports, to retreat. The race across France would not end until the Germans got to defensible terrain and moved new forces to the Western Front.

By 20 August, Devers knew that Seventh Army was going to link up with Bradley's Twelfth Army Group in the near future. He asked Wilson for permission to visit General Eisenhower, "with a view of learning at first hand just how he proposed to use this force, the 6th Army Group."[70] This request made good sense, since Eisenhower had not given Devers any guidance. In fact, beyond his desire to capture Toulon and Marseille, Ike had not given much thought to using Sixth Army Group in his theater strategy. This was understandable, given how quickly the strategic situation changed in August.

On 29 and 30 August Wilson and Devers met with Patch at Seventh Army's headquarters to discuss the linkup of MTO and ETO forces and Patch's plans. Wilson was convinced that Sixth Army Group headquarters needed to be activated soon because of the size of the zone, the long lines of communication from the ports to the armies, and the Allies' growing civil affairs responsibilities as they liberated France. He agreed with Devers that once the advance reached Dijon, it would be appropriate to formally turn over control of operations to the army group.[71]

With Wilson's blessing, Devers requested permission from Eisenhower to visit SHAEF. On 3 September Devers, Eaker, and Larkin flew to Granville, in Normandy, where SHAEF headquarters had been established in early September. Devers and Eisenhower had not met face-to-face since January 1943, and that meeting had left a bad taste in Eisenhower's mouth. In fact, Eisenhower had little knowledge of Devers's role in Dragoon, as indicated when he asked Marshall on 30 August, "Is Devers in operational command of Dragoon or is Patch in command?" This was a strange question, possibly intended to sow doubt in Marshall's mind about Devers's ability to command an army group. In the same message, Eisenhower mentioned that he was in communication with General Maitland Wilson to coordinate the Dragoon forces' operations. He knew that Devers was Wilson's deputy and that Wilson had given Devers the mission of overseeing Patch's operations.[72]

On 4 and 5 September Devers, Eisenhower, Spaatz, and Eaker met with the SHAEF staff and worked out the details of uniting the southern group of armies with SHAEF's main force. Eisenhower decided that once Seventh Army had linked up with Patton's Third Army, Sixth Army Group and

French First Army would officially be activated. At that time, command and control of the southern forces would shift from Wilson's AFHQ to Eisenhower's SHAEF. AFHQ would continue to provide logistical and administrative support to Sixth Army Group.[73]

Eisenhower had already determined that he had to leave Seventh Army in Sixth Army Group so that Devers's command would not be primarily a French force. As he told Bradley, "Except for political reasons, I would prefer to throw Patch's Army of that group under your control but I must preserve an American complexion to the Southern Group for reasons you will understand."[74] So while he was telling Montgomery that the front was too big for one ground commander to control, he was telling Bradley that he wished he could give him control of another army, in addition to the three that were already in his Twelfth Army Group.

Marshall sensed that the relationship between the supreme commander and Devers was not a warm one. Therefore, he gave Eisenhower some pointed advice on how to bring Sixth Army Group into the Allied command:

> Your proposal for assuming command of ground forces advancing from the Mediterranean appears satisfactory. I think you should get Devers into group control as quickly as possible for several reasons related to French ambitions and Mediterranean complications. I doubt if you are proposing sufficient tactical air support for Devers' command. The DRAGOON forces have already merged into the main effort of OVERLORD and are now the right wing of the great attack on Germany. There should be no improvisation in their support so long as needed resources are available. . . . Somervell is examining, as a matter of urgency, your problem concerning the diversion of divisions through Marseilles to strengthen the right wing of your effort. I think this very important if only for the purpose of giving Patch a U.S. Army to match the French.[75]

After his 5 September meeting with Eisenhower, Devers flew to Bradley's Twelfth Army Group headquarters near Paris. He noted that "the atmosphere around this headquarters is superb. General Bradley himself is in excellent condition and spirits. He gave me the lowdown on the situation."[76] In a 9 September letter to Georgie he wrote: "I have been all over France the past few days, saw Ike, Omar and my many friends in the Northern Army. . . . I leave General Wilson with regret. He is a great man, a fine British General, the best they have and a square shooter. . . . Monty is a flash in the pan, he does not compare with Wilson."[77]

At the echelons of command above "reality," as some people called higher headquarters, Eisenhower faced daunting tasks. He had just moved SHAEF headquarters to the Continent in August. He had to integrate Devers's Sixth Army Group into the Allied front in September and take over as Allied ground forces commander. He had to deal with personalities such as Charles de Gaulle and the newly promoted Field Marshal Bernard Montgomery. His army group commanders were new to their roles, and there was steady disagreement among them about how to complete the destruction of the German army and the Nazi state. Given the challenges of dealing with Montgomery, it is likely that Eisenhower would be less than pleased if his two American army group commanders openly disagreed with his strategic guidance.

Many of Eisenhower's immediate problems were logistical in nature, as Bradley's and Montgomery's armies outran their supply lines in their headlong pursuit of the Germans. Captain Butcher noted in mid-August, "Ike is thanking his stars that he held out for the forthcoming invasion through southern France because of our great need of the port of Marseille."[78] The success of Dragoon vindicated Ike's strategic judgment.

The incredible collapse of the German forces throughout France in August 1944 led many Allied leaders to think that the war in Europe would end in victory before Christmas. On 31 August Eisenhower reported to Marshall that the German army is "no longer a cohesive force but a number of fugitive battle groups, disorganized, even demoralized, short of equipment and arms."[79] His decision to drive east and north with all available forces was fraught with risk due to the weak logistical base of his armies, but the rewards would have been immense if the German armed forces had disintegrated further. In a memorandum written on 5 September Ike noted that "resistance has largely melted all along the front."[80]

Devers also believed that the German army might collapse. On 22 August he wrote to AFHQ, "The situation as it now looks in southern France indicates to me that there is a good chance that *Army Group G* and *19th Army* will cease to exist in the next week or so; at least I hope that Patch can bag it. His moves have been brilliant and rapid." Devers believed "that with another corps, or possibly two corps . . . we should be able to march right straight on Berlin."[81]

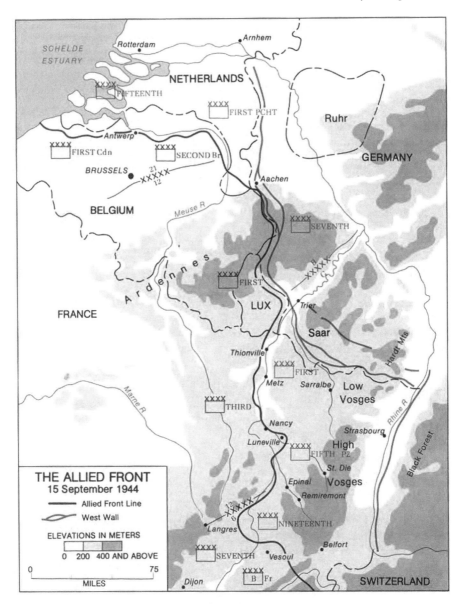

Figure 12.5. Allied front, 15 September 1944

Allied successes supported these optimistic assessments. The rapid drive of French and American forces from the Riviera to the foothills of the Vosges by mid-September allowed Eisenhower to establish a continuous front line from Switzerland to the North Sea. On 11 September 1944 French reconnaissance troops from Patch's Seventh Army met units from Patton's Third Army.[82] On 15 September Devers activated Sixth Army Group, and on 19 September de Lattre's Army B became French First Army.

The Allies' heady advance came to an end for two major reasons: first, the Germans reestablished a continuous front from the North Sea to Switzerland and were able to regenerate remarkably potent combat power along the Western Front by mid-September; second, the iron hand of logistics intervened against the Allies. The British, American, French, and Russian armies outran their supply lines; ran short of fuel, ammunition, and equipment; and were forced to halt most major offensive operations by the end of September. With hindsight, we can see that it was a miracle the Wehrmacht survived the hammer blows delivered by the Russians in the Bagration offensive in the east and the strikes delivered by the Western Allies in Normandy and southern France.[83] As a result of the enemy's resurgence, months of vicious fighting remained before the war would end for Devers and Sixth Army Group.

Activation of Sixth Army Group

Although Sixth Army Group was not officially activated until 15 September, its headquarters had been established in late July in Bastia, on the island of Corsica. In August advance elements landed in France and followed Seventh Army north. In preparation for its activation, Devers and his staff had done a fair amount of thinking about how an army group ought to operate. A study concerning the roles and functions of the headquarters, prepared in July, provided the army group staff with guidance for its work. Since none of the members of Sixth Army Group's staff had ever served in an army group, this was a useful document. It stated: "The Army Group Headquarters is the headquarters of a tactical unit and has no strategic functions except the execution of strategic directives received from the Theater Commander. . . . Territorial jurisdiction is left to the armies except that the Group Headquarters will ensure compliance with the policies of the Theater Commander. A Group Headquarters should have few supply or administrative functions. . . . G-3 should rarely, if ever, need to prepare detailed field orders. The rule should be brief orders of the mission type, including objectives, boundaries, timing, air-ground coordination, main axes of advance and allocation of means."[84]

Devers approved the study, and his staff prepared a table of organization for the headquarters. The table called for 198 officers, 20 warrant officers, and 338 enlisted men to carry out staff functions.[85] For the remainder of the war, Devers and his chief of staff, Major General David Barr, worked to keep the headquarters as small as possible. In October, as the forces assigned to the army group increased, the army group headquarters grew to 918 personnel, including 223 officers and warrant officers.[86] Roughly half as large as Bradley's Twelfth Army Group headquarters, Devers's headquarters remained near that size for the rest of the war.

Seventh Army and French First Army were the main components of Sixth Army Group. Immediately after it was activated, Devers assured Patch that he "would interfere as little as possible with Seventh Army tactical operations and would cooperate in every way possible."[87] Devers also met with de Lattre to discuss the operations of his two corps. They agreed that French First Army would be concentrated on the right of Sixth Army Group, with its right flank on the Swiss border and its left linked with Seventh Army in the Vosges Mountains northwest of Belfort. De Lattre was to drive through the Belfort Gap, his objective being Mulhouse, on the Alsatian plain. This orientation required Truscott's VI Corps to shift north and for de Monsabert's II Corps to swing from the army group's left flank to the French army's left flank, northwest of Belfort.[88] Once this shift was completed, Seventh Army was oriented toward Saverne and Strasbourg, and the French army was aimed generally at Belfort and Mulhouse.

Lodge remained invaluable to the effective working relationship between Sixth Army Group and French First Army. He often received the full force of de Lattre's sometimes irrational blasts. For example, in September the French general felt that his army was being treated like a poor relation by the Seventh Army staff, which was responsible for its logistical support until Sixth Army Group was activated on 15 September. After having lunch with de Lattre on 8 September, Lodge prepared a memorandum for Devers and Patch, informing them of the French leader's mood. He quoted de Lattre as saying, "I am through with the 7th Army. There are on the staff of the 7th Army idiots who hate France. Poor Patch is not up to the rapid change of events. I want to be under Devers, as soon as possible. . . . I have had enough of this miserable General Tupper [the public affairs officer of Sixth Army Group]. Do I speak plainly? Do you understand?"[89]

Lodge certainly understood de Lattre's plain speaking, but he was also able to reason with him and smoothe relations just by listening to de Lattre and assuring him that Devers and Patch would get his message. In fact, much of what de Lattre wanted was also desired by Devers and Patch. For example, he told Lodge, "I want a special zone for the French Army and I want to start re-grouping right away. I want a separate zone with separate objectives and dependable line of supply." Lodge reported, "I assured him of my agreement with his desire to control his own publicity. . . . I said I would seek to obtain for him a separate zone [on the] right of the line which could be supplied from Marseille."[90] This promise accurately reflected Devers's plans for the realignment of his two armies. Lodge could give such assurances because Devers kept him well informed; Devers also empowered Lodge to speak for him in such situations, knowing that Lodge would not exceed his authority. As Devers told Georgie, "Lodge is my French part. He is quick as lightning and most helpful and since I have a large French Army under command, he comes in very useful."[91]

Devers responded to de Lattre's concerns about the lack of publicity given to the French forces. As he wrote to Eisenhower, "It is the belief of Patch, de Lattre and other well informed officers, supported by my observations, that continuing emphasis on the FFI in French press and radio to the detriment of French regular [army] troops is bringing about a situation which, if allowed to develop, may make necessary diversion of fighting troops to maintain order and due process of law [in France]."[92] Within Sixth Army Group, Devers instructed Tupper to regularly brief reporters about the successes of the French army. All announcements were to refer explicitly to "French First Army," and Tupper was to give special attention to the French forces' quick liberation of Marseille and Toulon.[93] Though relations with de Lattre would never be easy, Devers managed to cooperate effectively with the French commander and got him to conform to Eisenhower's strategic vision. Eisenhower's relations with Field Marshal Montgomery were much more difficult than Devers's relations with de Lattre.

Eisenhower's Strategic Vision and Guidance

After personal meetings in early September with his three army group commanders—Montgomery (Twenty-First), Bradley (Twelfth), and Devers (Sixth)—Eisenhower held several conferences to discuss options and his strategic vision with them. On 14 September the supreme Allied commander summarized his plans in a message to General Marshall: "The only profitable plan is to hustle all our forces up against the Rhine, including Devers' forces, build up our maintenance facilities and our reserves as rapidly as possible and then put one sustained and unremitting advance against the heart of the enemy country."[94]

This was a good description of Eisenhower's "broad front" strategy that so irked Montgomery. In Ike's words, Montgomery had become "obsessed with the idea that his Army Group could rush right on into Berlin provided we give him all the maintenance that was in the theater—that is, immobilize all other divisions and give their transport and supplies to his Army Group, with some to Hodges." The SHAEF staff studied this proposal and declared it impossible.[95] From a political standpoint alone, the American people would not have accepted the British being given the resources and the glory of the main effort while the U.S. Army supplied most of the forces in France. This was especially true in 1944—an election year. Eisenhower rejected Montgomery's view, although the field marshal apparently did not get the message.

With the union of Sixth Army Group and SHAEF, Eisenhower made his strategic goals and objectives clear to his senior ground commanders. Based on the premise that Twenty-First Army Group's Operation Market Garden would be successful and that the Germans would fall back across the Rhine and "try to check our advance on the remaining important objectives in Germany," Ike determined that "Berlin is the main prize. . . . There is no doubt whatsoever, in my mind, that we should concentrate all our energies and resources on a rapid thrust to Berlin." There were two possible ways to do this: "To direct forces of both [northern] Army Groups on Berlin astride the axes Hanover-Berlin *or* Frankfurt-Leipzig-Berlin, *or* both." In any event, Devers's army group was to seize Augsburg-Munich and perhaps the Nurnberg-Regensburg area.[96] SHAEF directed Sixth Army Group to orient its armies to advance on the lines of Dijon-Besançon on the left and Epinal-Belfort on the right.[97]

Devers, after meeting with Eisenhower, Bradley, and other senior commanders on 22 September, described his understanding of Ike's strategy in his diary:

The strategy apparently [is] to be to capture the area called the Ruhr. To do this, and because of the terrific maintenance problem, requires the shifting of considerable troops to the north; a left hook to be undertaken by the 21st Army Group, and a right hook by the 1st Army of the 12th Army Group; the 3rd Army to go on the defensive; the 6th Army Group to be reinforced as soon as possible by at least two divisions and possibly three, to drive across the Rhine and through the Vosges Mountains in order to hold as many troops as possible in the south of Germany.[98]

In reality, the SHAEF staff and Eisenhower failed to consider how to maneuver Sixth Army Group to unhinge the Germans' southern flank along the west bank of the Rhine, let alone cross the river. They thought the best use of the southern group of armies was to protect Twelfth Army Group's right flank. Basically, SHAEF planners had not envisioned how to use a major force coming through the south of France.[99]

Because he expected little of Sixth Army Group (and perhaps because of his personal antipathy as well), Eisenhower gave Devers a fair amount of autonomy. Although he talked with Bradley nearly every day, he seldom communicated with Devers. For his part, Devers soon expressed doubts about Eisenhower's strategy. For example, on 5 October, after being part of Ike's command for less than a month, Devers noted in his diary, "I believe we emphasize too much the capture of terrain. There is no question in my mind but that the capture of Antwerp and making it a sure port for supply was the essential necessary to permit the army groups of the north and center to advance. Considerable time has been lost which may delay the end of this war until next year."[100]

In addition to the personality issues in the European theater, another major problem was caused by Eisenhower's failure to plan for operations beyond the Normandy landings and the consolidation of the Overlord lodgment. This failure helps explain SHAEF's less-than-smooth dealings with Devers and Sixth Army Group. In the year before D-day, SHAEF had prepared only one plan for post-Normandy operations, which Eisenhower approved on 27 May 1944. In essence, it called for a broad-front advance by the Allied armies after the establishment of a logistical base in Normandy. Apparently, the plan was never shown to Montgomery or Bradley.[101]

By the end of September, the Western Front had solidified along the eastern border of Belgium and along the western edge of the Ardennes and the western foothills of the Vosges Mountains. For the next six weeks, most Allied forces paused to bring up additional supplies and troops while the logisticians and engineers repaired French railroads and bridges. Sixth Army Group, however, was authorized by Eisenhower to continue offensive operations because its armies had their own lines of communication to Marseille.[102]

13

The Vosges and Alsace Campaigns

The Dragoon forces accomplished a great deal from the time they landed in southern France to their linkup with Third Army on 12 September. They liberated Toulon and Marseille, advanced more than 480 miles from the coast to Besançon and Belfort, captured approximately 96,000 prisoners, and inflicted an additional 35,000 casualties on the retreating German armies. Seventh Army and French Army B lost approximately 4,500 battle casualties each.[1] Both pursuer and pursued were tired from a month of continuous combat operations; Allied supply lines were stretched to the limit, and the German lines of communication became shorter as they neared the Rhine. For the Franco-American Allies, it was time to reorganize the command structure, rebuild the ports and railroads, and bring up reinforcements.

Sixth Army Group Takes Over

Sixth Army Group headquarters became officially operational on 15 September 1944, although it had been functioning as a command post for Devers since 1 August. Before the invasion of southern France, the headquarters' advance section was in Bastia, a small port on the northeast coast of Corsica. There, it served as the advance headquarters of both AFHQ and the army group.[2] Although the advance section moved to St. Tropez on 31 August, most of the staff and support personnel remained in Italy until early September. Once communications were established with Seventh Army, AFHQ, and SHAEF, Devers and his operations and intelligence officers were able to work effectively from St. Tropez.[3]

Devers traveled a great deal in the first week of September, meeting with Eisenhower in Granville, Bradley in Versailles, and Patch and de Lattre in Lyon. He returned to St. Tropez on 9 September to brief his staff on Eisenhower's strategy and the army group's role in it. He also met with Admiral Hewitt, who was in charge of getting the ports of Marseille and Toulon back into operation. Hewitt acquainted him with the difficulties involved

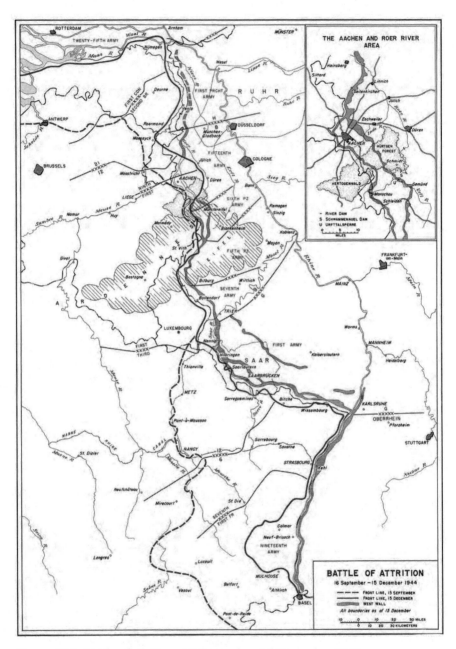

Figure 13.1. Battle of attrition, 16 September–15 December 1944

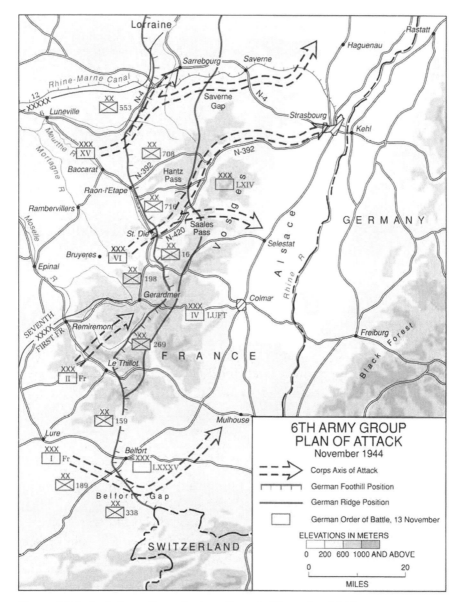

Figure 13.2. Sixth Army Group's plan of attack, November 1944

in clearing mines and removing underwater obstacles, but he promised that Marseille would be open for ships within a week.[4] By the time Devers's headquarters moved to Lyon on 15 September, the first Liberty ships were docking in Marseille.

As Sixth Army Group set up operations in Lyon, the enemy, who "had been reeling drunkenly backwards, was beginning to stabilize his defenses." The army group intelligence officer (G-2), Brigadier General Frank Allen, estimated that the "Germans would attempt to hold a line running generally west of Belfort and tying into the easily defended Vosges mountains to the north."[5] Evidence soon corroborated this assessment, as the Germans stopped the French short of Belfort and fought stubbornly to slow Seventh Army's crossing of the Moselle, west of the Vosges.

General Allen believed the enemy was done withdrawing and seemed determined to hold the current front: "Defensive works, terrain, a large number of second rate troops and the possible arrival of reinforcements seem to satisfy him as to his ability to hold this area. The Vosges Mountains offer natural positions for defense which the enemy has built up considerably to form the center of his line. The build-up of armored strength which is continuing along the German First and Nineteenth Army boundary (Luneville-Sarrebourg area) shows that the enemy is obviously aware of the danger to his forces should any penetration in the Luneville area open the road net to Strasbourg and the Rhine."[6]

Once the French First Army had consolidated its two corps on the right flank, the army group's front faced north-northeast from the Swiss border near Belfort and ran west to the Moselle River. The French held the eastern two-thirds of the line, and Seventh Army's single corps held the western third. Seventh Army's junction with Third Army was at Chaumont, on the Moselle, where XV Corps anchored the right of Patton's army. The provisional airborne force, commanded by Major General Robert Frederick, protected the long eastern flank of the army group from the Mediterranean to near Geneva, Switzerland.[7] Faced with stiffening opposition and a very long front, Sixth Army Group needed additional combat forces to continue offensive operations. During a 22 September meeting with Eisenhower and Bradley, Devers asked that a corps with two divisions be transferred from Twelfth to Sixth Army Group.

Seventh Army Is Reinforced

Marshall, meanwhile, was pressuring Eisenhower to build up Seventh Army by transferring a corps with two or three divisions from Bradley's army group. Ike agreed, mainly because the southern lines of communication, based on the ports of Marseille and Toulon, were capable of supporting additional forces in Sixth Army Group, whereas Twelfth Army Group's lines of communication back to Normandy were badly overstretched.

In response to the logistical situation and to Marshall's prodding, Eisenhower and Bradley decided to transfer XV Corps, commanded by Major General Wade Hampton Haislip, to Sixth Army Group. "Ham" Haislip was a talented and hard-driving corps commander. A 1912 graduate of the Military Academy and a combat veteran of the First World War, he had handled his corps, composed of the 79th Infantry Division, the 5th Armored Division, and the 2nd French Armored Division, in an exemplary fashion during the drive east from Normandy. Haislip and Devers had been classmates at the Command and General Staff College, and Haislip had served on the West Point faculty at the same time Devers commanded the artillery detachment (1921–1924). Haislip spoke fluent French, had attended the French Ecole Superieure de Guerre (1925–1927), and had mastered the difficult art of commanding Leclerc, the mercurial and aggressive leader of the French 2nd Armored Division—in French, the Division Blindee (DB). He was also one of Eisenhower's oldest army friends and had introduced Ike to his wife Mamie.[8]

Initially, Haislip brought only the 79th Infantry Division and the French 2nd DB to Sixth Army Group. Eisenhower promised Devers an additional infantry division from Twelfth Army Group and three more infantry divisions that were en route from the United States and were scheduled to land in Marseille in October and November.[9] Bradley and Patton resented the transfer of XV Corps to Sixth Army Group, although they were forced to admit the logistical and tactical logic of it. When Devers saw Patton on 22 September, he noticed that Patton "was subdued and I got the impression, rather hostile."[10] Patton wrote in his diary on 21 September, "If Jake Devers gets the XV Corps, I hope his plan goes sour."[11] After being told on 25 September that he had to give up XV Corps, Patton wrote in his diary: "May God rot his guts. . . . As usual, Devers is a liar and, by his glibness, talked Eisenhower into giving him the Corps."[12] This unprofessional attitude was typical of Patton.

Bradley kept his feelings to himself, leading Devers to believe that at least Bradley was not antagonistic toward him. He wrote to Georgie: "I am very happy about Omar. He is an excellent commander in a difficult place at the moment but will come out on tops as always."[13] Eisenhower's biographer identified a different side of Bradley, noting that "behind his mild-mannered façade," Bradley "bore grudges longer and with far more vehemence than Patton."[14] After his visits to SHAEF, Twelfth Army Group, and Third Army, Devers realized he was "going to need all my old luck to keep abreast of the undercutting that goes on." Still, he felt that "Eisenhower and Smith who are my bosses were exceptionally friendly in their way."[15] Clearly, his relationship with SHAEF was not a warm one.

Eisenhower's decision to move XV Corps to Sixth Army Group gave Devers the forces he needed to make Seventh Army a balanced combat force. Devers noted in his diary, "Patch and I are in complete agreement and accord, and I believe that when we once get 7th Army on a proper basis of two corps of two divisions each, that this army, which has been a great fighting army, will be even greater."[16] Haislip's XV Corps joined Sixth Army Group and Seventh Army on 29 September, and the boundary between the Seventh and Third Armies was moved north to include the existing XV Corps zone. By that date, VI Corps had captured Epinal and three bridge-heads over the Moselle.[17]

After his conference with Eisenhower on 22 September, Devers believed that Sixth Army Group's mission was to drive through the Vosges Mountains and the Belfort Gap, destroy the enemy forces in Alsace, and then establish bridgeheads across the Rhine.[18] This view accurately reflected SHAEF's 26 September order to Sixth Army Group, which instructed it to protect Twelfth Army Group's right flank by securing the Luneville area. In turn, Sixth Army Group issued "Letter of Instruction Number One" to its armies, directing them to continue offensive actions "to destroy the enemy in zone west of the Rhine, secure crossings over the Rhine, and breach the Siegfried line."[19] Seventh Army was to direct its offensive toward Luneville and then Strasbourg, while de Lattre was to aim his forces through the Belfort Gap toward Mulhouse and Colmar. Both armies were "to take advantage of any opportunity to seize [a] bridgehead and exploit across the Rhine without instructions from Sixth Army Group."[20]

Seventh Army's Field Order 6, issued on 29 September, stated the missions of XV and VI Corps: to continue the offensive and "prepare to cross the Rhine and breach the Siegfried Line."[21] Patch, anticipating that his army would have to launch an assault across the Rhine somewhere near Strasbourg, ordered his army's engineer, Brigadier General Garrison Davidson, to establish river-crossing schools to train engineers and infantrymen for this type of assault. Davidson had already anticipated the need for such training and, "independent of any directive or suggestion from above, made an engineering plan for an assault crossing of the Rhine" and "started assembling the necessary equipment and supplies."[22] Davidson assigned two engineer regiments the mission of establishing schools on the Rhône and Doubs Rivers. Army and corps engineers rotated through these schools, attending courses that lasted ten days. The instruction included the operation of DUKWs, the construction of pontoon bridges, and the use of infantry assault boats. Sixth Army Group still had two battalions of DUKWs under its control and made one, with about 250 DUKWs, available to Seventh Army for river-crossing operations.[23] Davidson and the Seventh Army chief of staff also organized a planning board to prepare for the crossings. Davidson assured Patch that, "given 72 hours-notice the army engineers are prepared to cross a corps on a two division front in accordance with loading plans already prepared."[24]

Devers was briefed about these plans on 30 September, and Patch suggested that when Seventh Army crossed the Rhine, it should advance in the general direction of Saarburg-Stuttgart-Nurnberg.[25] Patch also told his boss that the army would not be ready to cross before 1 November because it needed to accumulate ammunition and supplies and rest several divisions. The Seventh Army staff thought the crossing should be made somewhere near Rastatt.[26]

Logistical Support of Sixth Army Group

Devers and his commanders believed they could accomplish their missions. One of the key conditions for success was adequate logistical support for the two armies operating nearly 500 miles from Marseille. Further offensive operations depended on the engineers' ability to repair the French railways and bridges, allowing the armies to be supplied by rail. Fortunately, the railway system in southern France was in reasonably good shape, as Sixth Army Group's history described:

> Southeastern France was served by a rail net adequate for normal requirements in peace. The German retreat was so precipitate that time and means were lacking for the complete destruction of railways as was brought to a fine art in Italy. The many railway bridges, however, were practically all destroyed and there were numerous blocks caused by the strafing and destruction of enemy trains. One such block, eighteen miles long, included in its wreckage guns and other items so heavy that no available wrecking equipment could

clear them from the tracks and it was necessary to lay a new track
to by-pass the block.[27]

Seventh Army initiated limited traffic on a small coastal railway east of
Toulon on 18 August. Over the next month, railway traffic was extended
and expanded into the Rhône valley through the combined efforts of the
U.S. Military Railway Service and French railway organizations. Efforts
were focused on rebuilding key bridges and segments of line that produced
the quickest increase in tonnage hauled. Few railway and engineer personnel had been assigned to the early landing phases of Dragoon, so Devers
ordered the accelerated arrival of units of the 1st Military Railway Service
from Italy. Consequently, a number of railway and engineer units arrived a
month earlier than planned, thanks to Devers's decision and the availability
of additional air and sea transportation. On 14 September Brigadier General Carl Gray moved the 1st Military Railway Service's headquarters from
Rome to Lyon.[28]

By 2 October, rail lines were operating from Marseille to Dijon and
Besançon. Rail operations were facilitated by the fact that far more rolling
stock and locomotives had survived Allied bombing and FFI demolitions
than had been anticipated by the planners.[29] By 10 October, the Seventh
and French First Armies "could shift from a hand-to-mouth consumption of artillery ammunition and begin the slow accumulation of forward
reserves" for major offensive operations. During October, a daily average
of 5,690 tons of supplies was hauled to the forward supply dumps by rail.[30]

Although the accomplishments of the logisticians were impressive,
major problems remained in the army group's supply systems. During the
first month of operations in France, Seventh Army had been responsible
for the supply and maintenance of its own and the French forces. After
French First Army was activated on 19 September, Seventh Army logisticians believed that French logistical organizations should take care of de
Lattre's forces. As a result, in late September Seventh Army directed the
lion's share of gasoline and ammunition to its own forces and gave a much
smaller allocation to the French, even though the French army was bigger. Devers became aware of this situation on 26 September, when Patch
told him the French had reported a shortage of gasoline. Thinking that
the problem stemmed from a waste of available fuel, Devers encouraged
de Lattre to conserve the scarce gasoline supplies. In his view, the causes of
fuel "wastage" were fast driving, unnecessary trips, and diversion of gaso-

line from military to civilian purposes.[31] In reality, the cause of the gasoline shortage was more complicated.

On 28 September Devers visited de Lattre and de Monsabert and expressed his admiration for the French troops' determination and the French commanders' skill. Devers noted that de Lattre seemed optimistic: "He feels he will be able to punch through as soon as we can get enough ammunition up to him." Devers assured de Lattre that this was a major priority and told him, "We should solve it in the next 3–4 days."[32] He also arranged for the shipment of weapons, clothing, and equipment from American depots in North Africa to equip 12,000 recruits from the FFI who had joined de Lattre's ranks.[33]

When Devers next met with Patch and his staff on 30 September, he pointed out that de Lattre had expressed concern about supply shortages. Seventh Army's chief of staff replied that investigations had revealed that these shortages "were due to slow handling of supplies by the French, even though those supplies had been turned over to them for delivering to proper destinations."[34] The same day, de Lattre talked with Patch about "his urgent need for supplies and requested assistance" from American logistical units. After looking into the matter, Patch's G-4 phoned de Lattre and told him, "What little supplies could be spared by VI U.S. Corps had to be given to XV Corps, recently placed under Seventh Army control."[35]

De Lattre also sent Devers two messages on 30 September. In the first, he pointed out that the northward shift of Seventh Army's right boundary would force his II Corps to stretch its forces across a wider front, making offensive operations difficult. In the second message, he told Devers that in the last week, Seventh Army had received 2,102 tons of supplies by rail each day, while the larger French army had received just 968 tons a day. Devers responded by postponing the movement of the army's boundary and by ordering that supplies to the French "be more normally assured."[36]

The following day the French army's chief logistician visited Sixth Army Group headquarters and briefed Devers on the serious French supply problems. Devers thought the situation was due in large part "to the French themselves in not building up surpluses" and to Seventh Army's failure to "properly supervise the supply arrangements" of the French army. That evening Devers wrote in his diary, "I have taken energetic steps to correct the shortages of ammunition and gasoline in order that this army may pick up its momentum."[37] As a result, Seventh Army provided 65,000 gallons of gasoline, 53,000 rations, and 279 tons of ammunition to the French on 1

October and promised another 60,000 gallons of fuel the next day. Seventh Army also agreed to provide additional fuel and rations until the revised rail delivery schedules had time to take effect.[38] With these measures taken, Devers believed that "everything is now buttoned up in this line and that from now on supply will work smoothly and build up."[39]

During this period, Devers understood that the French people were suffering the effects of five years of war. In a letter to Georgie he noted that France "is a land of barter. Money does not mean much. You will see these dregs of the world trading their canned goods sent to them by relatives for eggs, chickens, and what not." But there was little he could do for the civilians, since "we outran our supplies and have to catch up."[40] In this same letter, Jake gave Georgie some news about their son-in-law and shared his feelings about the Italian campaign:

> Almost caught up with Alex a few days ago. They tell me he is Division Artillery Officer of the 4th AD [Armored Division] and that he is doing a splendid piece of work. . . . Sandy Patch's big fine boy, graduated from the Point in 42, has been wounded twice but is in fine form again and anxious to get going. . . . I am certainly glad to get out of Italy. I never believed in that campaign and I was right. . . . Now the going is tough for they rested for no reason at all [in June] and gave the Germans a chance to rest and get set and that always hurts.[41]

On 4 October Devers and his chief of staff, Major General David Barr, flew to Versailles for a meeting with Eisenhower and the other army group commanders. SHAEF staff briefed them on the current situation: the British Operation Market Garden had failed to establish a bridgehead over the Rhine, the Canadian army had failed to clear the sea approaches to Antwerp, and Twelfth Army Group was beginning a limited offensive to capture Aachen. SHAEF also announced its decision to transfer the 44th Infantry Division from Twelfth to Sixth Army Group and to land the 100th and 103rd Infantry Divisions and the 14th Armored Division in Marseille and assign them to Devers.[42]

Eisenhower did not make any changes in his strategy. Devers concluded that the mission of his and Bradley's army groups remained to "destroy the German army west of the Rhine River"; after that, "the advance across the Rhine and on to Berlin should be easy." He continued to believe that "we emphasize too much the capture of terrain," and he thought Montgomery's failure to open the approaches of Antwerp "may delay the end of this war until next year."[43] Eisenhower also informed Devers and Bradley that Marshall would arrive in France on 6 October and planned to visit Twelfth and Sixth Army Groups. Eisenhower and Bedell Smith met Marshall at Orly Airport on 6 October, and Eisenhower accompanied him to Bradley's headquarters in Verdun the next day.[44] Ike remained with Marshall and Bradley throughout the day before returning to Paris that evening.

On the morning of 8 October Marshall flew to Eindhoven, in the Netherlands, to visit Field Marshal Montgomery. This visit was less than pleasant, as Montgomery regaled Marshall with criticism of Eisenhower. Montgomery later recalled telling Marshall that "since Eisenhower had himself taken personal command of the land battle . . . the armies had become separated nationally and not geographically. There was a lack of grip, and operational direction and control was lacking."[45] For the sake of Allied unity, and in an effort to stay out of Ike's business, Marshall refrained from responding to Montgomery's observations. He later recalled, "It was very hard for me to restrain myself because I didn't think there was any logic in what he said, but overwhelming egotism."[46]

Marshall's next stop was Sixth Army Group. He arrived at the headquarters of French II Corps in Luxiel, where he met Devers, de Lattre, and de Monsabert. Up to this point, Marshall's visit had gone smoothly, but de Lattre soon changed that. As Devers described in his diary: "On his [Marshall's] visit to the French Army General de Lattre staged a show with the idea of impressing General Marshall that the French Army had not received proper logistical support in its advance up from the beaches and went into a lot of anti-Patch talk, all of which was very unfair and untrue. Later, de Lattre promised me that he would hereafter forget the past and start with the future. He goes into these tirades at least twice a week, at which times he seems to lose his balance."[47]

According to de Lattre, Marshall seemed surprised but recognized that the complaint about supply shortages was "well-founded and promised me that he would put the matter right."[48] Marshall, however, had a different memory of his reaction to the Frenchman's complaints. In 1956 Marshall recalled that he had been "outraged" and had set de Lattre straight by telling him, "The truth was there were no supplies to get. A division was supposed to have nine hundred tons a day, I think, and they were cut down. Patton was getting only three hundred tons. . . . And on top of that de Lattre was making this a triumphant march and they were delaying in villages after villages and cities [to celebrate]."⁴⁹

De Lattre was totally out of line to discuss supply issues and his views of his American colleagues with Marshall. His criticism of Patch (and possibly Truscott and Devers) in front of reporters was politically stupid and remarkably wrong. Marshall was certainly outraged, but his response was likely more measured than he later recalled. In his 1973 biography of Marshall, Forrest Pogue wrote, "Marshall's temper flared, but he decided to avoid a scene by terminating the discussion." He went on to say that the chief of staff got even with de Lattre several years later when the Frenchman wanted to be named ground forces commander in the NATO theater. In that case, according to Pogue, Marshall told de Lattre, "That was the most outrageous business of yours. I restrained myself, very, very carefully from tearing you down to the ground."⁵⁰

After their meeting with de Lattre, Marshall and Devers flew to Sixth Army Group headquarters in Vittel, where they spent the night. The next morning Marshall traveled with Devers and his G-3, Brigadier General Reuben Jenkins, to Seventh Army headquarters in Epinal, where they were met by Patch. After a short briefing, the group visited the headquarters of XV and VI Corps and all six divisions in Seventh Army. Marshall talked with a number of soldiers and traveled to division and regimental headquarters very close to the front.⁵¹

That afternoon Marshall went on to visit Patton's Third Army. On the way, the chief of staff took the time to write a note to Devers, telling him, "You arranged my program in such a way that I was able to see a maximum of activity in a minimum of time. I was particularly glad to be able to work in a visit to the French. Thank you for your thoughtfulness and hospitality. I noticed especially the high state of discipline and morale in your command, and along with this expression of appreciation, I send my congratulations."⁵² Clearly, de Lattre's tirade had not soured Marshall's visit to Sixth Army Group. However, it must have embarrassed and irritated Devers. After talking with his boss, Barr wrote a note to Henry Cabot Lodge Jr. that reflected Devers's feelings:

It is quite apparent from the visit of General George C. Marshall, Lieutenant General Jacob L. Devers and party to the First French Army on 8 October 1944, that much spade work of an educational nature must be accomplished by you and your staff, particularly along supply lines, in order that unwarranted criticism by General de Lattre and his assistants, including Major Bullitt, shall cease. The French must be made to realize (it is believed that Lieutenant Colonel Gazounand, their G-4 is familiar with the facts) that the method of supply and maintenance under the Joint Rearmament Program and subsequent War Department instructions has not changed in the slightest since the arrival of the French in Metropolitan France.[53]

Sixth Army Group formally established a liaison section commanded by Lodge on 17 October to work with and monitor the French army.[54]

For his part, Devers learned several things from the latest incident with de Lattre. First, he realized that the French "do not know how to support themselves logistically, and I believe I will have to give them every possible assistance."[55] This response to the situation was far more productive than anger or frustration. Devers ordered Sixth Army Group's G-4 to play a greater role in the support of the French, who, as Devers had realized as early as June, did not have sufficient service units of their own and did not have enough experienced and trained administrative personnel. Devers also noted that he had "to give more definite instructions to the two armies in order that their attacks may bring the greatest good to the common cause. At the moment there seems to be some misunderstanding which I shall straighten out."[56] This insight was remarkably important to Devers's development as an army group commander. Throughout his career he had tried to empower subordinates to run their own organizations, with guidance, ideas, and counsel from him as needed. Now he had to learn how to coordinate two armies of different nationalities so that their efforts were mutually supporting.

One of the most important aspects of making Sixth Army Group more tactically effective was to reorient the staff to their current situation and responsibilities. On 11 October Devers assembled his staff officers "and gave them a short orientation talk, stressing the fact that the Sixth Army Group headquarters was small and going to be kept small." He emphasized that he wanted the atmosphere of his headquarters "to be one of aggressiveness and helpfulness." He warned that anything else would not be tolerated. Finally, he "particularly wanted them to be helpful to the French Army and to be sure that they understood the French methods and that the French understood what we are trying to do, in order that we may make a most successful team."[57] Characteristically, after giving these stern instructions, Devers presented three staff officers with service awards.

Devers also thought about his role as the commander of a multinational force. He wrote to Georgie: "I am using all my personality and psychology on the French. They are a great people but one must understand them and their problems. Lodge is most helpful for he speaks and writes fluent French and is smart and wise."[58] Just as Eisenhower and Marshall realized they needed to deal with Montgomery in a diplomatic fashion, Devers learned how to work with de Lattre and his countrymen in ways that were conducive to getting the most out of their army. For example, on 16 October Devers traveled with de Lattre to Besançon, where he presented the thorny Frenchman with the Legion of Merit in a public ceremony. As a result of such actions, Franco-American relations in Sixth Army Group improved, and ways were found to sustain French First Army in the coming offensive.

The October Battles

October 1944 was a frustrating month for the Allied armies in the west. With the stabilization of the front by the Germans, Eisenhower realized that an "operational pause" was required; however, this did not mean the cessation of all offensive action. In the north, Twenty-First Army Group finally concentrated its forces and resources in an operation to clear the water approaches from the North Sea to Antwerp. By 7 November, Montgomery's two armies had cleared the Germans from the banks and islands of the Scheldt estuary, allowing the Royal Navy to remove the extensive minefields there. Bradley's Twelfth Army Group hammered away at the German defenses in Aachen and began to penetrate the Huertgen Forest, hoping to establish a good jumping-off point for the next big Allied offensive.[59]

Since it had its own lines of communication and supply, Sixth Army Group was able to continue its push through the Vosges Mountains and the Belfort Gap to reach the Alsatian plain and the west bank of the Rhine. Haislip's XV Corps and Truscott's VI Corps reached and crossed the Mortagne River and aimed at Baccarat and the town of St. Die, respectively. They found the fighting in the forests costly and time-consuming as the Germans took advantage of the mountainous terrain. Consistently bad weather prevented close air support, and the narrow roads in the area made supply and armor operations difficult. By the end of the month, it was clear that Seventh Army needed a pause in order to bring up the 44th, 100th, and 103rd Infantry Divisions and to rotate tired divisions out of the line to recuperate and absorb replacements.[60]

To ensure close liaison with Third Army on his army group's left flank, Devers visited Patton on a number of occasions. During a visit in mid-October, Patton sent for Lieutenant Colonel Alexander Graham, allowing Devers to see his son-in-law. In a letter to Georgie a few days later, Jake reported that "Alex is full of himself. He has been doing an outstanding job and is well thought of by all and I saw many of his superiors." Graham was serving as an artillery officer in the 4th Armored Division and had seen steady action since Third Army broke out of Normandy. Jake closed his letter by telling Georgie, "I love you dearly and am glad you have Frances with you. Tell her that her Alex is as good a killer as I am only he does it better."[61]

There was also a change of command in VI Corps in late October. Lucian Truscott was promoted to lieutenant general and was in line to command the next army formed in France. In the end, Truscott took command of Fifth Army in Italy when Mark Clark was selected to command the Allied Fifteenth Army Group in that theater.[62] Truscott would be missed. In the words of the official history, Truscott "had in many ways dominated the Allied campaign in southern France from the Riviera beaches to the Vosges Mountains. For over two months he had feverishly kept his three American infantry divisions on the move, forever harassing the retreating Germans and allowing them little time to rest and reorganize."[63] Truscott's replacement was Major General Edward Brooks, who had successfully commanded the 2nd Armored Division in Normandy and during the drive across France. "Ted" Brooks, an artilleryman and combat veteran of the First World War, had served as Devers's chief of staff in the Armored Force in 1942. He arrived in VI Corps on 20 October to help plan the next attack, and he assumed command of the corps on 25 October. Devers was sorry to see Truscott leave but was pleased to have Brooks as a corps commander in Sixth Army Group.[64]

French First Army's main offensive efforts in October were in the high Vosges, north of Belfort. De Monsabert had convinced de Lattre that his II Corps could outflank the Belfort Gap from the north by seizing Le Tholy and Gerardmer and then advance over the Bussang and Oderen passes.[65] These efforts proved costly and produced only slight gains in the face of skillful German resistance, forcing de Lattre to order de Monsabert to cease offensive operations at the end of the month and rebuild his units.

The Allies' most critical effort across the Western Front in October was a logistical one. The French rail, canal, and road systems were put back into operation. American engineers continued to repair and improve the ports of Cherbourg and Marseille, and Lieutenant General J. C. H. Lee's Communications Zone personnel established and stocked a system of forward depots to support operations along the German border. In the south of France, Brigadier General Tom Larkin's SOS troops and engineers opened the French rail system and pushed a gasoline pipeline from the coast of Provence to Dijon. With increased logistical capacity in the forward areas, Twelfth and Sixth Army Groups were able to sustain more forces in the front lines and bring more divisions forward. Sixth Army Group reached a strength of eight American and seven French divisions by early November.

The arrival of the 44th, 100th, and 103rd Infantry Divisions in Seventh Army's forward areas allowed Patch to rotate divisions out of the line to rest, receive replacements, and retrain infantry units. Beginning on 24 October, Major General Ira Wyche's 79th Infantry Division of Haislip's XV Corps was withdrawn from the front and replaced by the 44th Division. The 79th was badly in need of rest and recuperation, having fought its way across France without a letup.[66]

The 79th Division was of special interest to Lieutenant General Patch, whose son, Captain Alexander "Mac" Patch, was a company commander in its 315th Infantry Regiment. General Patch wrote to his wife, Julia, on 24 September, telling her that he had learned through a small notice in *Stars and Stripes* that Mac had been "slightly wounded." The following day Patch visited the 79th Division's medical authorities to inquire about his son's condition and was told that "the wound was clean and not serious." Patch also told Julia that "an old Warrant Officer . . . made a special point of telling me that the boy's reputation in his regiment was very high," although "people in the regiment considered that he was too careless in taking sensible precautions." Patch noted in his letter that "I did not listen to this much because I was trying to conceal my pride in the information I was getting."[67]

Once he had located Mac in a hospital in England, Patch got permission for him to recuperate at Seventh Army headquarters. In a letter to Julia on 4 October, Patch told her the latest news of their son:

Jul Darling:
Seems to me it has been a long time since I've been able to write you. I know you will appreciate what an immense satisfaction

it is to have Mac with me for a short spell. Finally I learned the location of the hospital he had been sent to—it was in England— So I had John Warner fly over, get him out of that hospital (I got the aid of a high ranking medical officer) and spend his recuperation at my Hqtrs. He is having physical therapy treatments to restore the muscles of his right shoulder back to normal. He looks as well as ever and surely there is nothing wrong with his appetite or his morale.[68]

General Wyche informed Patch that Mac would receive the Silver Star for bravery and called him a "grand and courageous battlefield officer." Patch told Julia, "I had the greatest strain imaginable in trying to conceal my pride, pleasure, and satisfaction."[69]

Captain Patch was equally pleased to be with his father, as he related in a letter to his wife: "In the interval since my last letter the store of experiences that I have accumulated since I last saw you has been doubled. There will be so much to tell you my precious when we are together again. My past two days have been rich indeed. Seeing Dad again, of course, tops them all. Your father-in-law, beloved, is a very great man. I say that with prejudice, naturally, but it is none-the-less true. How great only a very few will ever know—not the public; only some of his close associates."[70]

Mac enjoyed the days spent with his father immensely, accompanying him on visits to Seventh Army units and talking with senior staff officers. He wrote in a letter to his mother and sister that it is "very elucidating" for "an anonymous company commander to travel abroad in the higher brackets and observe the machinations which shape his destiny." He found his father "the same as ever" and noted that they lived very comfortably in a villa that was the "former property of one of those unfortunate Frenchmen who bet on the wrong horse." Mac was "overcome with the smooth urbanity and art exhibited by our master in his relations with the French. . . . He out-flatters and out-compliments the French deputations and officials with the ease of an old campaigner. I can assure you that he makes firm friends for the U.S. in all his contacts." He found Lorraine a beautiful region, "but the weather is abominable. I fear your son and brother is in for a hard winter."[71]

All good times must come to an end, as they did for Mac when he wrote on 15 October, "I have at last been pronounced fit and ready for duty." He looked forward to being back with the "familiar faces and old friends" in his company and hoped "there have not been too many changes." He also expressed his feelings for his father:

> The opportunity of having had so long a visit with Dad I will always appreciate. I've enjoyed every minute of it. It has, I think, been grand for both of us. We are not readily given to compliments and expressions of emotions, your males, as you well know, yet father and son know and feel the mutual pride and respect that exist between us. What greater satisfaction can life hold than that? I have been able to face him squarely knowing that I stood the test, and in turn I know that there is no man of greater integrity and courage than my father, I know of no family more closely bonded together than we Patches. It will always be so.[72]

Captain Patch rejoined the 79th Infantry Division a week before it was scheduled to rotate out of the line, just as it launched an attack on 21 October.[73]

General Patch spent the night of 21 October at the division's headquarters. The next day he flew over the battlefield, "imagining I was seeing Mac leading his men." When he got back to Wyche's headquarters, he learned that Mac's company had been the first unit to reach its objective. As he told Julia, "you will know the pride I felt."[74] When he returned to Seventh Army headquarters that evening, Patch received the worst news possible. He shared his emotions in a letter to his wife:

> Had I not been to church this morning and remained afterwards to take communion, I doubt if I would have had the strength to write to you—for my heart is bleeding and my emotions . . . are close to breaking. Fate is unpredictable—How strange that our dear friend Lil Spragins should have been given the mission of notifying me that our beloved Mac had been killed. . . . Only three days ago I personally delivered our boy Mac back to his division. . . . I'm trying desperately, my darling Julia, to control my emotions tonight—I can only do so by writing you—I will not allow any other person to observe how I feel. He was such a magnificent boy. . . . Darling, I would so love to be able to be with you tonight, principally to try to add whatever strength I possess in comforting you.[75]

Seventh Army pulled the 79th Infantry Division out of the line on 24 October. Mac was buried the same day at the U.S. military cemetery in Epinal, France.[76]

Patch remained in command of Seventh Army, but he took four days off following the death of his son.[77] He had "recurring moments when it is hard for me to control my grief," but his response was "to think clearly and realize" that Mac's suffering was over.[78] On 28 October Patch returned to full duty, and his staff closed ranks around him.[79] Julia and his daughter Julia Ann encouraged him to go on and to rely on their love.[80] Devers wrote to tell him that Mac "was a fine soldier, a true son of his father and mother. Words cannot express what I want to say. I want you to know that you are a great soldier, a fine leader, an outstanding character in whom I repose all my confidence and affection."[81]

Patch was one of a number of senior officers whose sons or stepsons were killed in action. Major General "Iron Mike" O'Daniel's son was killed in Operation Market Garden in September. General Marshall's stepson was killed in Italy in May. Brigadier General Cuthbert Stearns's son was killed by a land mine on 19 October, while serving in Sixth Army Group. Major General Donald Stroh's son was killed in September. In their own way, each of these generals carried on. O'Daniel's response to sympathy for his loss was typical. He wrote in reply to a condolence letter: "I am more determined than ever to eliminate as many of the enemy as possible."[82]

The Germans' tough resistance along the western borders of the Reich in October ended the euphoria felt by so many Allied leaders in September. Field Marshal Montgomery blamed Eisenhower for the Allies' strategic reverse, and another series of meetings was held to clarify goals and objectives for the three army groups. Eisenhower's strategy had been consistent from the beginning of the campaign. The Allied armies were to advance on a broad front to the Rhine, with the main effort occurring in the north and carried out by Twenty-First and Twelfth Army Groups. Nonetheless, Montgomery argued doggedly against Ike's strategy, maintaining that his Twenty-First Army Group should make a powerful thrust through the German defenses, cross the Rhine north of Cologne, and push on to Berlin. Eisenhower repeatedly rejected a single thrust by Montgomery in the north, insisting on a continuous front and the participation of both army groups.[83]

In Eisenhower's mind, the seizure of crossings over the Rhine would be accomplished after the west bank of the Rhine, from Switzerland to the North Sea, had been cleared of German forces. But his guidance to his army group commanders did not make this clear. Devers believed that if his army group had an opportunity to cross the Rhine before the other groups reached the river, he should do so. Perhaps if Ike had spent more time discussing options with Devers, this misunderstanding would not have occurred. But after Sixth Army Group joined the crusade in Europe, Eisenhower failed to communicate effectively with Devers. For example, he did not give Devers prior warning of his 16 October visit to Sixth Army Group. Devers was at de Lattre's headquarters in Besançon when he was informed, during lunch, that Ike and Bradley would arrive at his headquarters in Vittel at 1600. Devers flew back to his headquarters, where he, Bradley, and Eisenhower discussed logistical issues but apparently not the forthcoming offensive.[84] On 17 October Devers and Eisenhower traveled by car to Epinal to visit Seventh Army headquarters, but we do not know what they discussed. Ike then spent an hour and a half with Patch before traveling on to Haislip's command post.[85] It is telling that on the few occasions when Eisenhower did go south, he spent more time at his friend Haislip's XV Corps' headquarters than he did at Devers's. Eisenhower also spent a great deal of time with Bradley and communicated often with Montgomery. This gave him plenty of opportunity to make his intentions clear to them. Ike and Bradley were also close friends; they talked often on the phone and spent considerable time together. Bradley had always been subordinate to the rising Eisenhower, whereas Devers had originally outranked Ike and never paid him the deference that might have made for a better relationship.

Although Devers sent a daily personal situation report to SHAEF, both Devers and Eisenhower were at fault for failing to meet face-to-face when critical matters were discussed. For instance, Eisenhower did not include Devers in an important meeting with Montgomery and Bradley on 18 October, when he outlined his vision for the November offensives. In these discussions, Sixth Army Group was cast in a supporting role.[86] Carlo D'Este has pointed out that Devers tried to stay out of Eisenhower's way, realizing the low regard the supreme commander had for him. According to D'Este, Eisenhower likewise avoided personal contact with Devers, often using Bedell Smith or Pinky Bull, his G-3, to convey orders to Devers.[87] Such poor personal relationships led to serious misunderstandings between the two men.

The 18 October meeting involving Eisenhower, Montgomery, and

Bradley led to the promulgation of Eisenhower's 28 October directive for a coordinated Allied offensive in November. Eisenhower specifically ordered Devers "to act aggressively with the object, initially, of overwhelming the enemy west of the Rhine and, later, in advancing into Germany." The southern group of armies was to advance in zone to the Rhine, secure crossings, and "deploy in strength across the Rhine." Eisenhower stressed that Sixth Army Group was to "protect the southern flank of the Central Group of Armies." Five days earlier, Eisenhower had informed Devers that the Allied forces "have had to shift the center of gravity of our forces further to the north" and stressed that the location of Seventh Army's main crossing of the Rhine would be in the vicinity of Mannheim and Karlsruhe. As noted by the authors of the official history, "Not surprisingly, given Eisenhower's indifference to the potential of the 6th Army Group," this directive did not specify a date for Devers to commence his attacks.[88]

Sixth Army Group Prepares for the November Offensive

As October came to an end, Devers, de Lattre, and Patch planned for their coordinated offensive. Seeking a better way to command an army group, Devers had authorized his G-3, Major General Reuben Jenkins, to create a Joint Planning Staff. The newly formed First Tactical Air Force (Provisional), commanded by Major General Ralph Royce, was represented on this planning staff, as were the intelligence and logistics sections of the army group's staff.[89] The Joint Planning Staff was to provide information "necessary to form an integrated plan and mold such information into feasible operational plans" for the two armies.[90]

Jenkins and his staff developed a plan that called for Seventh Army to be the main effort, while French First Army tied down German forces in its sector by launching a preliminary attack in the high Vosges, north of Belfort. The French attack, aimed at Colmar, would be supported by all available heavy artillery in the army group. Once it drew the German reserves to the French front, the artillery would shift to Seventh Army for the main attack. Jenkins believed that, "since we lacked the artillery and other resources to keep strong attacks by two armies going successfully, we should mass our means behind first one army and then the other in rapid succession in an effort to break the very obvious stalemate that was developing on our front."[91] Devers approved this preliminary plan on 15 October.

De Lattre, however, had a different vision of his army's role in the big offensive. He had concluded that it was nearly impossible to punch through the German defenses in the Vosges north of Belfort. Consequently, he completely reoriented his forces for the November drive. General Bethouart's I Corps, with four divisions, would attack south of the Belfort Gap, while de Monsabert feinted with two divisions in the mountains to the north. He also thought his army should attack at about the same time as Seventh Army launched its offensive. On 27 October de Lattre traveled to Vittel to submit this plan to Devers. De Lattre later wrote that, faced with the French "wish to effect a breach in the German lines on the Doubs and to break into the Belfort Gap," Devers "eagerly ratified my plan" and allocated several American battalions of heavy artillery to support it.[92]

As Sixth Army Group prepared for the offensive, Seventh Army continued local actions to obtain better jumping-off positions. It was rough going, as Devers noted in a letter to Georgie: "We are still moving in spite of the bad weather. . . . [I] was with Ham Haislip who is one of my top commanders. Towns are on fire everywhere. The Germans loot then set them on fire. However, many pay with their lives."[93] Devers was referring to Hitler's "scorched earth" policy. As the Germans fell back in the Vosges, they destroyed as many farms and villages as possible, leaving the civilian population destitute and without shelter for the winter.

While planning the offensive, Devers and de Lattre had to deal with a major threat to the French army's ability to carry out its ambitious plan. On 25 October Devers noted in his diary that the SHAEF G-3, Major General H. R. Bull, "arrived with some additional responsibilities for me. The trouble with the higher command is that they will not give you a directive, with what means you have at your disposal and a policy, and let you go ahead."[94] Sixth Army Group's additional responsibility was to send forces to western France and clear the Gironde estuary of German forces, thus opening Bordeaux, France's second largest port.[95] This mission was based on de Gaulle's initial request that two divisions from French First Army be sent to Paris and Toulouse to prevent communist-leaning FFI units from taking control.[96] That request morphed into one asking for regular forces to clear the Germans out of their enclaves in southwestern France. Devers and de Lattre were not consulted until after Eisenhower had already agreed to the request.[97] When Bull visited Devers on 25 October, he directed that a French corps headquarters and two French divisions be sent, with the first units departing Lorraine on 11 November. De Gaulle specifically asked for the French 1st DB and the French 1st Infantry Division, since these units were officered by men who were loyal to de Gaulle.[98]

When de Lattre received the order to send these forces west, he "rushed to Vittel, ready to plead, vehemently if necessary" against the operation. The French army commander demanded that the deployment be postponed until after his planned offensive, set to begin on 13 November, and he wanted to substitute the French 2nd DB from Seventh Army for the 1st DB. Devers agreed that the timing of this diversion of roughly 15 percent of the combat strength of Sixth Army Group and 25 percent of the French army was problematic. He refused to substitute Leclerc's 2nd DB for the 1st, but he postponed the departure of the first units to 16 November and eliminated the requirement to send a corps headquarters. Over the next three weeks, as the offensive unfolded, Devers repeatedly delayed the transfer of the French divisions, allowing events to change the plans SHAEF had imposed on Sixth Army Group with little thought for its operations.[99]

In all these discussions, Devers had to deal with the volatile French general. When de Lattre demanded that the mission be changed or canceled on 7 November, Devers refused to disobey the order from SHAEF. In response, de Lattre "went into a tirade," which Devers firmly curbed. De Lattre then became "a little more rational." As Devers noted in his diary, "He is a very difficult man to handle. . . . I have been very careful to use a good interpreter and to have people present in order that there be no misunderstanding due to his poor understanding of English and my lack of French."[100]

Beyond curbing de Lattre's tirade, Devers informed him that he considered French First Army and U.S. Seventh Army to have the same status and assured him, "I would certainly make sure that neither of them failed insofar as my powers permitted." Devers struck the right tone, knowing that although de Lattre was temperamental, he also craved "success and has great courage and I believe he will fight the 1st French Army realistically and effectively" in the upcoming offensive.[101] Again, Devers responded to this crisis in a productive manner and did not let superficial differences get in the way of effective communications and operations.

As preparations were under way for the November battles, Devers was finally replaced as the American Mediterranean theater commander and the deputy supreme Allied commander. Lieutenant General Joseph McNarney assumed those duties on 22 October and visited Devers on 1 November in Vittel. McNarney had already met with Clark in Italy, where he learned the Fifth Army commander loathed Devers. In Devers's view, Clark "felt he was abused; that we hadn't visited him enough; that troops had been taken away from him and that I was personally responsible. . . . Clark is a problem child, and childish, particularly when he is under pressure and not winning."[102] He had earlier shared his view of Clark with General Handy, the War Department's operations officer: "I do not recommend Clark either as Deputy Supreme Allied Commander or as Theater Commander. . . . He is very selfish and sees all his problems through himself and how it will affect him."[103] Devers was pleased to be finished with his multiple duties in the Mediterranean theater and to be clear of Clark.

The November Offensive

By 1 November, detailed plans for Seventh and French First Armies had been approved, and stocks of ammunition, food, and fuel had been accumulated for a sustained offensive. The question not yet answered was when to begin the attacks, since SHAEF had not specified a date for Sixth Army Group to start its major push.[104] Thus, it was up to Devers to determine when to launch his two armies against the German defenses. According to the final report of Sixth Army Group's G-3:

> Headquarters 6th Army Group, Seventh Army, and Third Army had studied the German habits [of defensive operations]. One of the enemy characteristics recalled was the habitual timing of his use of general reserves. Almost without fail, the German moved his general reserves on the evening of the second day or the morning of the third day of our attack. We decided to make this trait pay dividends. . . . 6th Army Group [would attack] not earlier than three days and not later than five days after Third Army's attack [began]. By this it was hoped that the second attack would catch the German general reserves on the move.[105]

Devers visited Bradley and Patton on 5 November to coordinate his plans with them. Patton hoped to begin his attack in the Metz area between 10 and 15 November, so Devers set Sixth Army Group's initial assaults for between 13 and 18 November. Seventh Army was to attack at least one day before the French kicked off their drive south of Belfort.[106]

Patch's objective was to push his two corps through the Vosges to Strasbourg. Initially, VI Corps was supposed to be the main effort, with Hais-lip's XV Corps supporting VI Corps' efforts to reach St. Die by driving toward the Saverne Gap. In the end, Patch was more flexible and allowed whichever corps was more successful to become the main effort. As planning progressed, the 100th and 103rd Infantry Divisions entered VI Corps' line, allowing Brooks to take the 3rd and 45th Divisions out to rest. By 10 November, XV Corps had two divisions in its front lines and two in reserve, while VI Corps had three divisions in its front lines and two in reserve. The additional divisions that had reached Sixth Army Group made it possible to begin the offensive with mostly rested units.[107]

As a preliminary operation with Seventh Army, de Monsabert's corps launched a diversionary attack on 3 November in the high Vosges to draw German attention and reserves from north and south of the army group's front. This effort reinforced German perceptions that the main Allied effort would come in the high Vosges.[108] De Lattre also carried out elaborate deceptions to convince the enemy that II Corps was the main effort. He even issued an order that would have allowed many troops to take leave and visit their homes in mid-November. Then he planned to launch Bethouart's I Corps in an attack between the Swiss border and Belfort, bypassing the industrial city of Montbeliard.[109]

On 8 November, without prior warning, Patton commenced his attack two days earlier than anticipated. Bradley and SHAEF also failed to tell Sixth Army Group that First and Ninth Armies were going to delay their jump-off until 16 November, hoping that the weather would improve and allow air support.[110] Caught off guard, Devers had to decide whether to move up the date for his armies' attacks to 13 November. Jenkins's Joint Planning Staff, "after a hurried conference and a review of G-4 [logistical] implications . . . agreed that the attack was feasible." Devers agreed and ordered Seventh and French First Armies to attack on 13 November. "As time for the attack approached, the weather on the 6th Army Group front grew progressively worse. Blinding rain or snowstorms raged through the whole area. In the Vosges area roads were already clogged by snow drifts and temperatures dropping below freezing. Streams and rivers through the lower areas had over-spilled their banks." Devers considered waiting for better flying weather, but late on 12 November he decided that the attacks must go ahead, since "the Germans will not expect us to attack in such weather. We will get surprise."[111]

After this decision, Devers visited the two corps expected to lead the

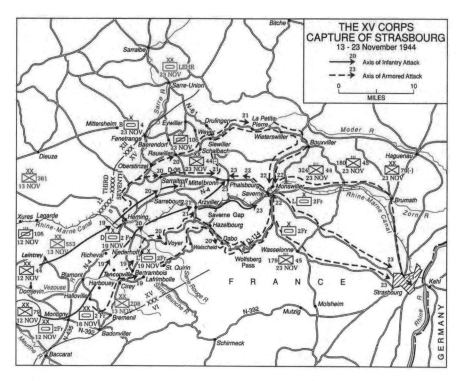

Figure 13.3. XV Corps' capture of Strasbourg, 13–23 November 1944

offensive. On 11 November he visited XV Corps and concluded, "I am confident that the XV Corps, under the able leadership of Haislip, will break
through into the Rhine Valley by the first of the month." The next day he
visited "General Bethouart at his command post [of French I Corps]" and
observed, "I am much impressed with his layout and his plan for attack. If
I can get this French army to attack, I am quite sure they too will end up in
the Rhine Valley by the first of the month, and probably sooner."[112]

At 0700 hours on 12 November, Seventh Army attacked. XV Corps,
aiming for Sarrebourg and Saverne, was initially given priority for artillery
support. Haislip had his two infantry divisions punch a hole through the
German front lines, which they found lightly occupied. Then the French
2nd DB passed through, following the numerous small roads to the east,
north, and south of the Saverne Gap. By 21 November, Leclerc's division
had outflanked the German defenses in the Saverne Gap and captured the
town of Saverne, on the edge of the Alsace plain.[113]

Meanwhile, on 12 November, de Lattre requested that his attack be postponed due to the weather. He also had an unexpected visit from de Gaulle and Churchill, who arrived that morning and spent most of the day at his headquarters. When they left, Churchill implored de Lattre not to attack in the atrocious weather.[114] Devers, who believed that a French attack on 13 November was essential, sent Lodge to plead with de Lattre to stick with the plan. Lodge arrived at de Lattre's headquarters just as de Gaulle and Churchill did, and he later recalled that he followed "them around all the time so that if the opportunity arose, I could get in and talk to General de Lattre." Only after Churchill left that afternoon was Lodge able to remind the Frenchman of "the importance we attached to his attacking and going through the Belfort Gap while Patch went through the Saverne Pass." De Lattre "didn't say anything," Lodge said, "he just listened to me."[115]

De Lattre had already decided to attack on 13 November, as planned. However, the snow was so bad the next morning that he was forced to postpone the offensive anyway. As it turned out, this delay reinforced his deception plan. When the French infantry divisions attacked at midday on 14 November, they took the Germans completely by surprise. The French artillery barrage caught the Germans out of their entrenchments and killed General Oschmann, commander of the 338th Volksgrenadier Division, which was covering the front. The French found a map on Oschmann's body detailing the German positions and minefields, greatly facilitating their advance. Over the next three days, the French broke the German defenses and drove north and then east toward the Rhine. By outflanking the German fortifications around Belfort, they were able to move swiftly. Their lead elements reached the Rhine River on the evening of 19 November, and Belfort fell on 20 November.[116]

On 22 and 23 November Haislip's infantry divisions followed the French 2nd Armored Division into Alsace and deployed to defend the left flank of XV Corps. VI Corps also began to make progress in the high Vosges, reaching St. Die on 22 November and St. Blaise-la-Roche the next day.[117] Seventh Army was firmly established on the Alsatian plain by these advances. But the most spectacular action of the day was Leclerc's armored columns' swift dash across the Alsatian plain and into Strasbourg, where they completely surprised the enemy.[118]

It was clear to Devers that the Seventh and French First Armies' offensives were achieving spectacular success. On 19 November he wrote to Georgie about the breakthroughs in the Saverne and Belfort Gaps. "This in spite

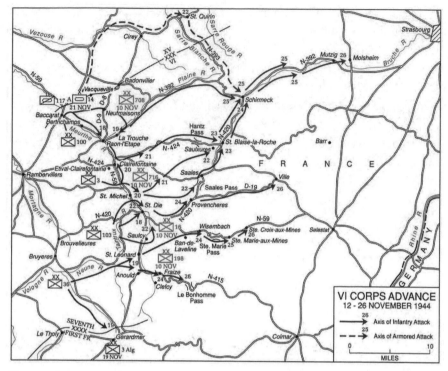

Figure 13.4. VI Corps' advance, 12–26 November 1944

of the great tacticians who have a fear of the Vosges and the weather and our ability to get the most out of our meager means for we are not the favored sons." He further observed, "The soldiers are well taken care of at the front and do not complain about anything and I question many of them."[119]

The next day Devers was on his way to visit Seventh Army and later noted in his diary, "I met Ted Brooks on the road and stopped to chat with him for a few minutes. He had just been up to needle the 100th Division to move a little faster. He is a great general and a great fellow, always three jumps ahead and driving on." When Devers caught up with Haislip, he learned that the 79th Infantry Division's assault had been a "masterpiece" and that XV Corps' units were moving forward, "even though bottlenecked by the mud, the rain and high water in the streams." He concluded, "This brilliant XV Corps is making tremendous progress."[120] Devers again demonstrated his understanding that a senior commander, even at the army group level, had to be well forward in an offensive to keep up the troops' morale and to keep his finger on the pulse of operations.

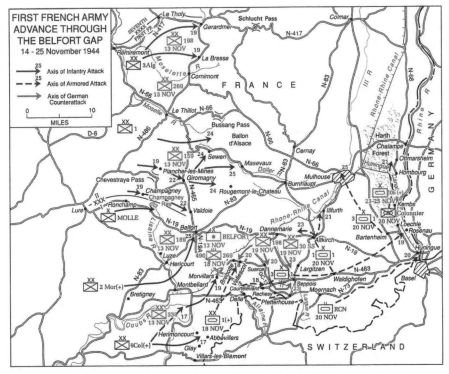

Figure 13.5. First French Army's advance through the Belfort Gap, 14–25 November 1944

During the army group's offensive, Devers sent daily reports to Eisenhower on the progress of his armies. He heard nothing back from Ike. On 23 November he vented some of his frustration to Major General Bull, the SHAEF G-3, and wrote in his diary: "Had a long talk with Bull in which I tried to impress him with the fact that we belong to SHAEF, that we are not just a piece on the end; that we are just as important as the 12th Army Group; and that we had not asked for any help except when we thought it vitally necessary; that we wanted him to understand that when we asked for something, we really needed it; and that we have just performed a brilliant maneuver in this Army Group which would have far reaching consequences for the future." He would have done better to hide his light under a bushel, but Devers could not pass up the opportunity to crow and stick a pin in Patton's reputation. "Patton is stopped on my left and I will have to do something to get him going again," he wrote in his diary. "This, in my opinion, was because he jumped off a little too early, and also because of the terrifically bad weather which dogged his footsteps."[121] Whether or not he actually said this to Bull, his exuberance was probably excessive.

The question now was what to do with the astounding victories of his two armies. Devers's orders were to clear the enemy from the west bank of the Rhine and seize a bridgehead over the river.

To Jump the Rhine?

Between 13 and 23 November 1944, Sixth Army Group's armies smashed through the German defenses in the Vosges Mountains and reached the Rhine in two places. Seventh Army broke through the Saverne Gap, seized Strasbourg, and prepared to cross the Rhine. French First Army broke through the Belfort Gap, unhinged German defenses in the high Vosges, and seized Mulhouse. These successes provided Devers's Sixth Army Group with several opportunities on the morning of 24 November.

With the collapse of German defenses in the Saverne and Belfort Gaps, Devers expected the French to clear all German forces from west of the Rhine in Alsace, and he expected Patch's Seventh Army to send forces across the Rhine north of Strasbourg. If Seventh Army could establish a bridgehead across the Rhine, it might unhinge the German defenses facing Patton's Third Army in Lorraine. A mood of euphoria permeated the headquarters of Sixth Army Group and Seventh Army as the staffs prepared orders for an assault across the Rhine.[122] It was clear to everyone that they would attempt to establish a bridgehead over the Rhine as soon as Strasbourg was cleared and a strong front had been established on the left flank of the army group facing north. On 20 November Sixth Army Group asked SHAEF for a minimum of two airborne regimental combat teams to seize critical terrain east of the Rhine sometime between 10 and 20 December.[123]

On 21 November Brigadier General Davidson, Seventh Army's engineer officer, ordered the 40th Combat Engineer Regiment to assemble river-crossing equipment for an assault on a two-regiment front and to have it ready to move by 23 November. The next day Devers conferred with Patch, and Seventh Army ordered XV Corps to protect the left flank and "reconnoiter the Rhine between Strasbourg and Munchhouse and take advantage of any opportunity for a quick crossing of the Rhine." The same day, Sixth Army Group asked SHAEF for two heavy pontoon battalions, in addition to the three already in the group's engineer depots.[124] SHAEF promptly refused to supply the airborne units or the extra bridging material.

With the capture of Strasbourg and the arrival of the French on the Rhine near Mulhouse, Sixth Army Group contemplated three courses of action, as described in the G-3's final report: "One was to hold on the north and divert forces to the south to assist the French in closing to the Rhine; Another was to follow exactly SHAEF's directive and launch an attack to the north in conjunction with Third Army to breach the Siegfried Line, while leaving the French to complete the job to the south. Seventh Army and planners of Headquarters 6th Army Group posed a third course of action. . . . Seventh Army wanted to cross the Rhine in stride."[125]

At this point, Generals Eisenhower and Bradley visited Sixth Army Group. As Devers wrote in his diary on 24 November, "Apparently Eisenhower came down to tell me that I was going to have to give some help to Patton and to change my mission. Instead of exploiting a crossing of the Rhine and then proceeding north, he wanted me to throw my forces directly to the north and west of the Rhine and break through the Siegfried Line in conjunction with Patton."[126] This climactic discussion took place in Vittel, after Eisenhower had visited Haislip's headquarters. While he was there, XV Corps successfully defeated a German counterattack north of Sarrebourg, but the Germans' attempt indicated that they still had plenty of fight left. The G-3's final report tersely noted that, "in a conference in Vittel, on 24 November, attended by General Eisenhower and General (then Lieutenant General) Bradley, the situation was discussed. Following the conference, Seventh Army was directed to swing the bulk of its forces northward in an attack to breach the Siegfried Line." French First Army was to clear the remaining Germans from the west bank of the Rhine.[127]

The next morning, Seventh Army ended all plans to jump the Rhine, and Patch began the time-consuming process of orienting the bulk of his forces north. The following day, Sixth Army Group ordered Seventh Army to drive north to help Twelfth Army Group, and it instructed the French to protect the right flank along the Rhine after eliminating German forces in a bridgehead around Colmar.[128]

David Colley, in his book *Decision at Strasbourg*, maintains that Eisenhower made a serious strategic mistake when he prevented Devers's Sixth Army Group from pushing across the Rhine in late November 1944. According to Colley, if the supreme commander had allowed Devers to send forces across the Rhine north of Strasbourg, "many young men's lives might have been spared," and "almost certainly the war would have been shortened." Instead, Colley concludes, "the Germans were given a free hand to continue their massive troop buildup in the Ardennes in preparation for the Battle of the Bulge."[129]

Seventh Army staff officers, including Brigadier General Gar Davidson, believed the army could have seized a bridgehead. When he learned of Eisenhower's decision, Davidson stated, "I [wish I] could have been in on the high level meeting for I doubt if anyone there really understood the extent of our engineering preparations and therefore the high probability of a swift crossing in force that could be sustained."[130] So perhaps Colley and others are right about the feasibility of the operation and the missed opportunity. But the problem with such "what if" scenarios is that we can never know how the alternative version would have played out. The authors of the army's official history agree that Eisenhower's decision had a profound effect on the campaign in the west in 1944. It also illustrated Eisenhower's unwillingness to exploit unexpected success and his poor relationship with Devers. Because Devers was one of his top two American ground force commanders, their dysfunctional relationship hindered decision making and the execution of Eisenhower's strategy for the defeat of Germany in 1944.

Devers was bitterly disappointed when he was ordered to end all preparations for a crossing of the Rhine near Strasbourg. He was shocked that the supreme commander chose to stick to his "broad front" strategy of advancing all Allied armies to the Rhine before establishing bridgeheads, rather than taking advantage of such a good opportunity in Alsace. Was Devers right to want to send forces across the Rhine in late November? And could he have done so while still accomplishing his assigned missions from Eisenhower?

Several other questions need to be considered to determine whether Eisenhower made a strategic blunder when he stopped Sixth Army Group from crossing the Rhine. First, how did Sixth Army Group fit into Eisenhower's strategy, and did a crossing of the Rhine in Alsace in late November conform to his vision? Second, was it possible for Seventh and French First Armies to cross the Rhine in late November with the forces at hand and maintain themselves there in the face of the logical German response?

In answer to the second question, Sixth Army Group's history, written in May 1945 by men who had come to respect the power and capabilities of the German army in the fall and winter of 1944–1945, concluded, "Neither army had a reasonable chance to seize a bridgehead." The French lacked the necessary amphibious and bridging equipment, and Seventh Army was not strong enough to both protect Patton's right flank and secure a bridge-head. Further, if Seventh Army had crossed, "The G-2 estimated that when a place of crossing was known to the enemy he could, with little delay bring three infantry and two armored divisions to attack the bridgehead." This action by the Germans would have required SHAEF to reinforce Sixth Army Group if it were to hold the bridgehead. Such a movement of forces would have compelled Eisenhower to change his main strategic effort from north of his front to south of it.[131]

The tactical situation was not favorable for an assault across the Rhine, given Seventh Army's condition and resources. When Patch ordered Hais-lip's XV Corps to prepare to cross the Rhine, he assumed the troops would come from the 44th and 79th Infantry Divisions. However, these divisions had been in action since 12 November and were spread across a thirty-mile front from Sarrebourg to Hagenau. The 45th Infantry Division was XV Corps' reserve, but it had been badly battered in the Vosges and was refit-ting. Haislip's other division, the French 2nd DB, encountered heavy fight-ing in Strasbourg from 23 through 25 November. At the same time, XV Corps was attacked by the Panzer Lehr Division near Rauwiller, north of Sarrebourg. Haislip's troops were badly stretched, and the 44th Infantry Division was able to turn back the Germans' Panzer Lehr only with help from the 4th Armored Division, borrowed from Third Army.[132] Meanwhile, Patch's VI Corps was still enmeshed in the high Vosges and was expected to send one division to relieve the French 2nd DB in Strasbourg.

It is hard to see how Patch could have both maintained his exposed northern flank and sent a force across the Rhine that was large enough to defend itself against the inevitable German counterattacks. In such a sce-nario, a great deal of artillery support would have been needed to stop the enemy's armor, especially since adverse weather prevented reliable air sup-port from the First Tactical Air Force. Further, there was a critical short-age of 105mm and 155mm artillery ammunition in Sixth Army Group after two weeks of offensive action by its armies. In fact, on 23 November Sixth Army Group reported to SHAEF that it had dramatically reduced its rate of artillery fire and, at the current allocation rates, could maintain only defen-sive operations.[133]

In answer to the question of whether a Rhine crossing in November would have conformed to the army group's mission, clearly, it would not. The offensive launched by Sixth Army Group was governed by a 28 Octo-ber 1944 directive that called for taking advantage of any opportunities to

368 JACOB L. DEVERS

"seize" bridgeheads east of the Rhine during the first phase of the action, while operations leading to their "capture" were reserved for the second phase. The term "seize" implied sudden action against little or no resistance. Yet the army group G-2's estimate of enemy reaction indicates that the element of surprise did not exist, and an assault over the Rhine would have encountered a strong German response. In SHAEF's 28 October order, Sixth Army Group's main mission was to protect the right flank of Twelfth Army Group. Spreading its forces across the Rhine would have jeopardized that mission. All along, Eisenhower had assumed that all his armies would advance to the Rhine before any of them crossed it. Unfortunately, he failed to make this clear to Devers in advance. At the end of the conference in Vittel, "the early success of Sixth Army Group caused but little change in General Eisenhower's plans. His apparent decision was to continue operations for decisive defeat of the enemy West of the Rhine and to await a more favorable opportunity for opening the SECOND PHASE involving the capture of bridgeheads over the RHINE and deployment on the East bank."[134]

Devers was sorely disappointed by Eisenhower's decision, but he loyally complied. He also characteristically gave credit where credit was due for his army group's dramatically successful operations:

> The First French Army, in a manner reflecting the highest credit on French Arms and traditions, has stormed and breached the main defenses of the Belfort Gap. . . . The Seventh U.S. Army, increasing the weight of its blows, has surged forward. It has freed many French towns . . . and is exploiting to the Northeast with strong forces. . . . The First Tactical Air Force, composed of American and French units . . . is supporting the attacks of the two armies in a decisive manner. The successful attacks of both armies have been ably supported by the Supply Services. . . . The noteworthy success of these operations has again revealed the superior leadership of our army commanders. The mettle of each officer, noncommissioned officer and soldier of the American and French forces . . . has been shown by these operations.[135]

In his diary, Devers revealed his personal feelings about Eisenhower's decision: "The decision not to cross the Rhine was a blow to both Patch and myself for we were really poised and keyed up to the effort, and I believe it would have been successful."[136]

The way ahead was unclear, and Devers had little time to reflect on the past. He had to concentrate on getting the French to accomplish the difficult task of eliminating what became known as the Colmar pocket while pushing Patch to the Siegfried Line. The German Nineteenth Army still had a bridgehead on the west bank of the Rhine; it had received significant reinforcements and was dug in for a long fight. Seventh Army was shifting forces north to aid Third Army, as Eisenhower had ordered, and it would have few reserves to spare to assist the French in an offensive against the Colmar pocket. In fact, the French army was nearing the point of exhaustion as de Lattre dealt with replacement and logistical problems and the planned diversion of forces to western France as ordered by de Gaulle.

14

Winter of Discontent

We will never know what would have happened if Eisenhower had agreed with Devers's plan to cross the Rhine in November 1944. We do know that their poor working relationship made it very difficult for Eisenhower to see virtue in any operational ideas put forth by Devers.

Eisenhower and Bradley's original purpose for visiting Sixth Army Group headquarters in Vittel on 24 November had nothing to do with the plan to jump the Rhine. Nor had they come to congratulate Devers and his troops for the spectacular successes they had achieved in the past twelve days.[1] Instead, their goal was to convince Devers to give two of his divisions to Third Army and provide more help in its quest to reach the Siegfried Line. Patton needed reinforcements because Third Army's offensive had bogged down in the soggy fields east of Metz, which it had captured after ten days of heavy fighting. Although Patton had originally planned to drive from his line of departure to the German frontier in two days, he had barely made it halfway due to strong resistance and miserable weather.[2] Farther north, Hodges's First Army had failed to achieve its goals in Operation Queen, which had included carpet bombing to try to blow a hole through the German defenses near Dueren, Germany. During the same period, the 28th Infantry Division suffered one of the worst tactical defeats of any American unit in the war. Learning nothing from that division's misery in the Huertgen Forest, Hodges and Bradley continued to throw infantry divisions into that killing zone east of Aachen for another month.[3]

After Eisenhower ordered a halt to preparations for a crossing of the Rhine, he, Devers, and Bradley had dinner and discussed various options. Devers wrote in his diary, "Apparently Eisenhower had come down to tell me that I was going to have to give some help to Patton and to change my mission. Instead of exploiting a crossing of the Rhine and then proceeding north, he wanted to throw my forces directly to the north to the west [bank] of the Rhine and break through the Siegfried Line in conjunction with Patton."[4] After drinks and dinner, the three men moved upstairs to Devers's suite to discuss Bradley's desire to take forces from Sixth Army

Group. Devers protested "vigorously, pointing out that the way Patton's front was to be shortened, all they had to do was to shift the boundary to the left and give me the mission of pushing north."[5] After a heated discussion about missed opportunities, force allocations, boundaries, and missions, Eisenhower agreed to move the army groups' boundary west, and Devers accepted his boss's order to swing Seventh Army north. The new boundary between Twelfth and Sixth Army Groups was not as far west as Devers thought it should be, but Seventh Army would not have to give up two divisions to Third Army, as Bradley had wanted.[6] When Bradley told Patton he was not getting reinforcements, the Third Army commander wrote in his diary, "Evidently Devers talked Eisenhower out of letting me have the XV Corps."[7]

Devers felt privately that "the Army Group boundary should be Patton's northern boundary, which is the Moselle, and Patton's army should come to the Sixth Army Group." With tongue in cheek, he wrote in his diary, "Why they do not do this, I do not know. Far be it from me to ask for more command."[8] Clearly, Devers was very disappointed by Eisenhower's decision about the crossing of the Rhine. He was also unhappy with the supreme commander's apparent lack of appreciation for the accomplishments of his army group. On 28 November he wrote to Georgie, "I have a lot of fine friends and a great fighting team, so all is well. I want the G.I.'s and the junior commanders to get the publicity for they are the boys who do the job in the final analysis."[9] Characteristically, he continued to praise his subordinates, telling Ted Brooks in a note, "You are a great leader. . . . I have every confidence in your ability."[10]

The acrimonious discussions between Devers and Eisenhower put another nail in the coffin of their relationship. Eisenhower came out of the meeting "as mad as hell over Devers' open criticism of his operational strategy."[11] Devers doubted seriously that he was on Ike's "team." Nonetheless, Devers had no recourse but to execute SHAEF's directive, and he did so swiftly.

Seventh Army's Drive to the German Frontier and the Occupation of Strasbourg

On 26 November Sixth Army Group ordered Seventh Army to turn north and attack alongside Third Army to breach the Siegfried Line. French First Army's objective was to destroy all remaining German forces west of the

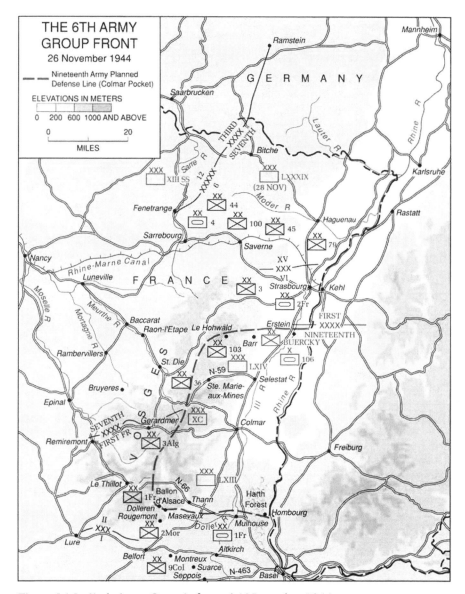

Figure 14.1. Sixth Army Group's front, 26 November 1944

Rhine, located in a bridgehead maintained by German Nineteenth Army with the remnants of eight divisions. This bridgehead included the Alsatian city of Colmar; hence it became known as the Colmar pocket. To help de Lattre eliminate this pocket, Sixth Army Group ordered Seventh Army to replace Leclerc's 2nd DB in Strasbourg with the 3rd Infantry Division

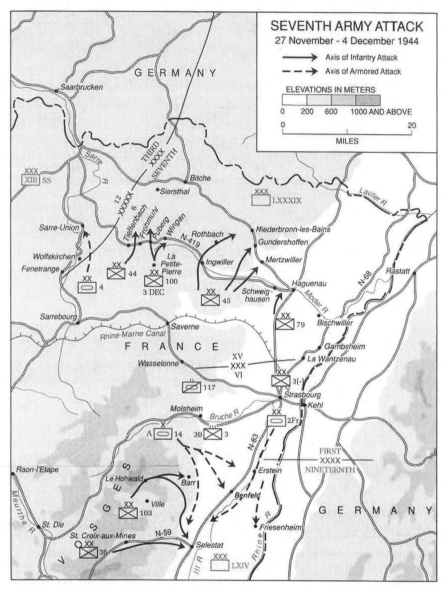

Figure 14.2. Seventh Army's attack, 27 November–4 December 1944

and to have the 2nd DB and the 36th and 103rd Infantry Divisions attack the Colmar pocket from the north.[12] Devers and Patch believed that with this help, the French would be able to eliminate the pocket west of the Rhine.[13]

Seventh Army reoriented its forces to the north over the next three

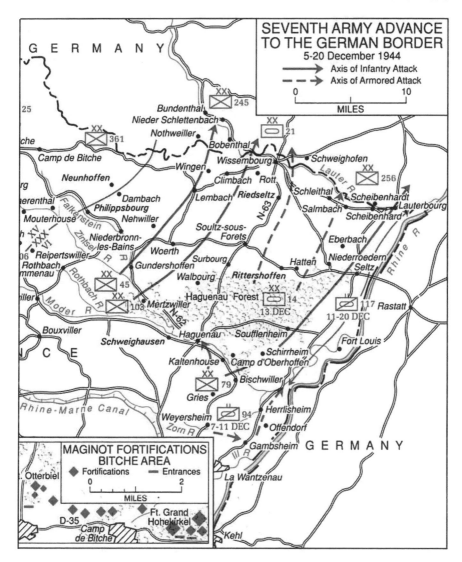

Figure 14.3. Seventh Army's advance, 5–20 December 1944

days. XV Corps was to advance on the west side of the low Vosges, connecting with and protecting Third Army's right flank. VI Corps' zone of operation was east of the Vosges, with its right flank on the Rhine.[14] During the next three weeks, Seventh Army fought its way to the Siegfried Line, liberating Hagenau and penetrating the German frontier north of Bitche.[15] Devers concluded that "Patch, with his usual foresight and keen judgment, had his troops in such a position that he could swiftly swing to the left in his drive to the north."[16]

Third and Seventh Armies worked well together in the drive toward the Siegfried Line. After a visit to Patton's headquarters on 5 December, Devers wrote in his diary: "George has the right idea and I believe that between us we can crack this front and get to the Rhine, probably faster than they can in the north. I wish he were under my command. Then I would be sure."[17] Devers and Patch also agreed to shift the 12th Armored Division into Third Army's sector on 7 December to relieve the exhausted 4th Armored Division and to help Patton's push north toward the Siegfried Line. The 12th Armored remained part of Seventh Army but worked with Third Army under the "tactical control" of Haislip's XV Corps for the first half of December.[18]

Meanwhile, O'Daniel's 3rd Infantry Division relieved Leclerc's 2nd DB in Strasbourg on 26 November and finished clearing the last German troops from the city. When the 3rd Infantry's troops entered Strasbourg, they found that Leclerc had issued an order that for every French soldier shot in the city by snipers, "five German hostages will be shot." The people shot would be selected at random, and any sniper captured would be summarily executed. Anyone who harbored snipers would also be shot.[19] When O'Daniel took over, he issued a statement to the population warning that "the regulations as issued by the Commander of the French Troops who liberated Strasbourg remain in force."[20] Word of Leclerc's proclamation got out through a news dispatch that was published in the Paris newspapers. SHAEF reacted immediately, asking on 5 December what action Sixth Army Group had taken to void the proclamation. By then, Devers had rescinded the order, and on 1 December he told de Lattre that Leclerc's proclamation was "completely at variance with the provisions of international law . . . which prohibit summary executions." He ordered de Lattre to inform all commanders of French First Army that the forces of Sixth Army Group would obey international law and that "no proclamations or notices at variance therewith will be published by such commanders."[21]

Seventh Army was also reminded to follow international law, and on 8 December its troops were instructed to treat all prisoners in strict accordance with the Geneva Convention on prisoners of war. Patch ordered the French governor of Strasbourg to put notices in the local newspaper rescinding Leclerc's proclamation, but the governor refused. On 10 December Major de Chizelle, a French army liaison officer, informed Seventh Army that the French-controlled newspaper would not publish the army group's order. Seventh Army's chief of staff then ordered the engineer section to reproduce posters with the new proclamation in French and German. But before this could be done, a compromise was reached, and the 3rd Infantry Division's commander issued a press release making it clear that the Geneva Convention would be followed by all Allied forces in the region.[22]

On a more positive note, when Seventh Army captured Strasbourg, a special team known as T Force was sent into the city to search the Germans' atomic bomb research facilities. T Force reached the main facility southeast of the city on 25 November and seized the papers of the German scientists working there. After the materials were reviewed, it was determined that the Germans' research on nuclear weapons was well behind that of the Manhattan Project. Lieutenant General Leslie Grove, director of the American atomic research program, informed SHAEF that the material captured at Strasbourg provided "the most complete, dependable and factual information we have obtained" about German efforts to build an atomic bomb.[23] The T Force commander also informed Seventh Army that "the Alsatians are so antagonistic toward the assumption of control by French new-comers that assassination of French officials has occurred," and he believed American troops instead of French should be kept in Strasbourg "until the violent feeling has subsided."[24] American forces remained in Strasbourg into early January 1945 to protect French officials.

The Colmar Pocket and French First Army

When the French broke through to the Rhine and defeated repeated German counterattacks to cut off their penetration, Lieutenant General Hermann Balck, commander of German Army Group G, assumed that Sixth Army Group would attempt to encircle German Nineteenth Army on the west side of the Rhine and destroy it. Consequently, he recommended to the German high command that Nineteenth Army be withdrawn to the east of the river. Hitler, however, vetoed any withdrawal from Alsace. Instead, the remaining forces west of the Rhine were reinforced and ordered to withdraw to more defensible terrain in a perimeter around Colmar and to hold the bridgehead at all costs.[25] Although de Lattre's effort to cut off the retreating Germans with a pincer attack east of Belfort succeeded in bagging 10,000 prisoners on 28 November, sufficient enemy units escaped to establish a new defensive perimeter west of the Rhine.

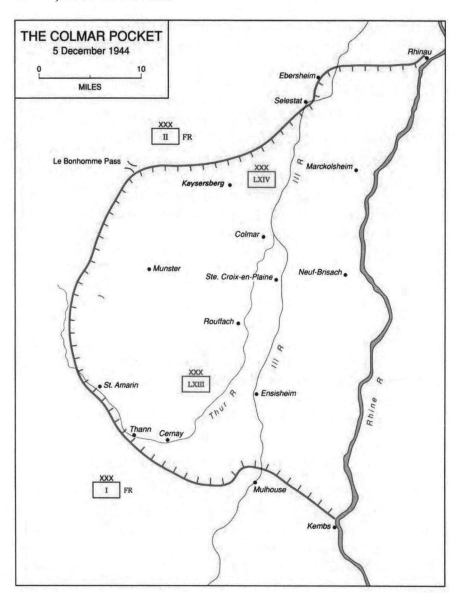

Figure 14.4. Colmar pocket, 5 December 1944

During the first two weeks of December, the French tried to break the German lines, to no avail. Horrible weather prevented air support; the terrain was soaked from heavy rains, preventing off-road maneuver; and the Germans proved once again to be masters of the defense. The French divisions suffered heavy losses during the offensive, including 5,800 men killed or wounded, 1,600 cases of frostbite, and 2,824 men sick. In de Lattre's words, by 12 December, French I Corps "was not unwilling, but just unable to do more."[26]

Eisenhower's decision to turn the bulk of Seventh Army north meant that there would be no pincer movement by Sixth Army Group's two armies to encircle the Colmar pocket.[27] Devers's assumption that the enemy would retreat across the Rhine when threatened with encirclement was a major miscalculation. He and Patch expected more from the French than they could deliver; consequently, Devers deployed too few forces against the northern flank of the Colmar pocket. These forces, fighting as part of French II Corps, made little progress against a stiffening German defense. After heavy fighting, the exhausted 36th and 103rd Infantry Divisions captured Selestat, well short of Colmar. Leclerc's 2nd DB and a combat command of the U.S. 14th Armored Division failed to make much progress across a battlefield laced with waterways and defended by German antitank guns.[28] When de Lattre told Sixth Army Group that his forces could not continue the offensive, Devers was disappointed and stated, "Your forces' exhaustion cannot . . . be notably different from that of other divisions at present engaged."[29]

Unfortunately, Devers was wrong. The French divisions had reached the end of their tether and were badly in need of rest, replacements, and reinforcements. The French army had suffered more than 27,000 battle casualties since 15 August, and another 18,000 French soldiers had been admitted to hospitals for injuries and illnesses.[30] In addition, Devers had ordered the French 1st Infantry Division to disengage and move to western France to take part in clearing the Garonne estuary, further weakening de Lattre's army along its 200-kilometer front. By early December, de Lattre's army had reached an important crossroad in its history: too many of the French cadre in the African divisions had become casualties, weakening the combat capability of those formations, and de Lattre had to rely on metropolitan Frenchmen as replacements, since North Africa could no longer fill the gaps in his ranks.[31]

The "Whitening" and "Amalgamation" of the French Army

As early as September, de Lattre had been planning how to solve these personnel problems. His army's situation was aggravated by the fact that the black troops from Senegal were unsuited (de Lattre believed) to fight in the winter weather of eastern France and needed to be pulled from the lines.

Therefore, de Lattre replaced more than 15,000 veteran Senegalese infantrymen from two of his divisions with recruits from partisan bands of the FFI.[32] These replacements were formed into units and then received the weapons, helmets, and often coats of the African soldiers they were replacing. Due to the urgency of this "whitening" of the ranks, the new men were not well trained, weakening their divisions just as German resistance stiffened in the Colmar pocket.[33]

The French also created twenty-four light infantry battalions from the FFI to attach to existing divisions. These units varied in capability and attitude. Many of them were used to the more casual discipline of the FFI and found it difficult to adjust to the stricter discipline of the regular French army. They also resented officers (like de Lattre) who had remained loyal to the Vichy regime until the German invasion in November 1942.[34] With a great deal of patience, de Lattre convinced most of these men to join his ranks and to serve loyally. Those battalions attached to armored divisions found the attitudes of their new units similar to those of the free-spirited partisan bands. The battalions attached to infantry divisions found it much harder to assimilate. Eventually, de Lattre assigned one regiment of FFI recruits to each infantry division.[35]

De Lattre felt that de Gaulle's government and the people of France were not supporting his efforts to maintain the French army; consequently, morale in his ranks was declining. He believed: "The profound cause of this malaise rests in the apparent non-participation of the country in the war. . . . The malaise is aggravated by the weariness of four uninterrupted months of campaigning, without any relief, and in particularly inclement weather conditions."[36] French First Army needed at least 8,000 replacements in December, in addition to the new FFI units, if it were to maintain its strength. It also needed additional divisions if it were to accomplish the missions assigned to it by SHAEF and Sixth Army Group.

De Lattre's challenges related to the integration, or "amalgamation," of men from metropolitan France into a professional colonial army were intensified by the shortage of arms, clothing, and equipment for the tens of thousands of new soldiers joining his army. Under the terms of the rearmament agreement reached between the French and the Anglo-American Allies in 1943, the Allies promised to provide arms, supplies, and equipment for no more than eight French divisions. With the influx of more than 70,000 recruits joining de Lattre by the end of November, new divisions had to be created and equipped.[37]

The manpower problems of French First Army were part of a bigger challenge faced by SHAEF in 1944–1945. De Gaulle's government estimated that there were roughly 400,000 FFI fighters in bands throughout the country in August 1944. De Gaulle and his staff believed that if these men were not employed in some fashion, they could become a major security concern. Consequently, the French offered to form security and labor units to assist the Allied forces, as long as the Allies provided arms, clothing, and logistical support for these units. They also requested help in reestablishing the French territorial recruitment system.[38]

SHAEF was willing to provide the support needed to form the security and labor units, as long as the French agreed to provide 100,000 of these men to aid the Anglo-American armies as rear-area security and support formations. By November, SHAEF and the French had reached an agreement to arm 120 security battalions.[39] De Gaulle's government also wanted to recruit eight additional French divisions, bringing the French army up to sixteen divisions. In September Eisenhower and Devers had opposed the creation of the new divisions, believing that the war would be over before they could be armed and trained.[40] By October, however, they both realized that the war was not going to end quickly. Eisenhower gave Devers permission to equip 52,000 FFI recruits in de Lattre's army, as long as Devers considered them necessary for military operations.[41] Eisenhower also recommended to Marshall, on 1 November, that additional French divisions be raised, concluding that the French contribution to the fighting in Italy and France "has saved thousands of American and British lives."[42]

The Combined Chiefs of Staff agreed to arm three new French divisions as the first phase of a program to expand the French army by eight divisions. These three divisions were formed by the end of November. One of them, the 27th Alpine Infantry Division, was assigned to guard the French-Swiss border in the Alps, freeing the veteran 4th Moroccan Mountain Division for service in Alsace. The other two divisions joined French First Army by January 1945. By the end of the war, five new divisions had joined the French army.[43]

Devers supported de Lattre during the whitening and amalgamation process as much as possible, although the critical decision to equip additional French forces rested with SHAEF and the CCS. De Lattre believed that Devers understood his challenges, and he also appreciated the "friendly understanding of Colonel Lodge, [who was] always so anxious to solve our difficulties."[44] Unfortunately, adding combat forces to the French army took time, and de Lattre had to work with what he had in December to eliminate the Colmar pocket. Another weakness of the French army was a shortage of logistics units; the 241,000-man French First Army was short 58,000 support troops in December.[45] In response to this shortage of French service units, Sixth Army Group agreed to shoulder more responsibility for the support of the French army.

To reinforce French efforts against the Colmar pocket, Devers ordered Seventh Army to transfer command of the 36th Infantry Division and the French 2nd DB to de Lattre on 4 December. Seventh Army would continue to support these divisions until the French were able to supply them. In a letter of instruction, Sixth Army Group ordered French First Army to "increase at once present efforts to destroy the enemy west of the Rhine."[46] De Lattre, in turn, instructed his troops to "surround and destroy the German forces in Alsace and the Vosges so that they would be unavailable for later use east of the Rhine."[47]

The 36th Infantry and 2nd DB were assigned to de Monsabert's II Corps, along the northern flank of the German bridgehead. The 36th Infantry Division hammered away at the German defenses during the first two weeks of December but made little progress beyond securing part of the Kaisersberg valley, "taking one small village after another while fending off almost continuous German counterattacks."[48] The 36th's commander, Major General Dahlquist, indicated in a letter to Devers that too much was being asked of his soldiers. Devers wrote in his diary:

> General Dahlquist said he is not going to offer a complaint with regards to orders he received from II French Corps, but that his troops are being subjected to the most continuous artillery fire that they have ever faced with small chance to strike back. He will carry out his orders, but in accomplishing the mission given him, his tired, depleted troops will be dissipated and in a short time cease to exist. General Dahlquist stated that the entire job of taking the large and strongly defended city of Colmar has been assigned to him, and the French troops have no intention of moving until the 36th Inf. Div. has taken the city.[49]

Devers ordered the 3rd Infantry Division to relieve the 36th on the day he received Dahlquist's letter.

During the same period, a major flap in French politics occurred as

Leclerc tried to get his 2nd DB reassigned from de Lattre's command to Seventh Army. The French commander was closely associated with the Free French organization that had been loyal to de Gaulle since the fall of France in 1940. Leclerc and a number of like-minded Frenchmen hated officers who had remained loyal to their nation's duly constituted government until the German invasion of Vichy France in November 1942. In particular, Leclerc had a deep personal loathing for de Monsabert and de Lattre. When Devers transferred Leclerc's division to French First Army, Leclerc went behind de Lattre's and Devers's backs and traveled to Paris to convince de Gaulle that his division should be withdrawn from French First Army and returned to Seventh Army.[50]

When he found out about Leclerc's shenanigans in Paris, Devers informed Eisenhower of Leclerc's request and explained why he had assigned additional forces to de Lattre. Devers noted, "The French Army . . . was making very little progress. As my main mission was to turn to the north and assist Third Army in its advance, and with the knowledge that I was not going to close the pocket rapidly, I passed the 36th Division and the 2nd DB to the 1st French Army. . . . These operations on the French Army front proceeded entirely too slowly."[51] The same day he wrote to Leclerc and refused his request for reassignment:

> I do not agree . . . that the sector and mission now assigned to you do not correspond to the capabilities of an armored division. It is noted that the enemy forces counterattack you with armor and a small group of infantry and anti-tank guns. Your organization is thoroughly capable of taking care of this situation. It is the only place on this front that we can use armor at present time with profit. I am sure that aggressive and energetic action on your part will enable your division to close the gap to the south and destroy the enemy west of the Rhine in that vicinity. Only when this is done will it be possible to give your division a rest.[52]

Unfortunately, Leclerc's division made little headway against the German defenses south of Strasbourg. Several weeks later Devers transferred the French 2nd DB to Seventh Army to help defeat the German Nordwind offensive, but he sent it south again in late January, to go against the Colmar pocket. Once again, Leclerc protested being assigned to French First Army, and Devers refused to change the assignment. In February, after the

Colmar battle was over, Devers sent Leclerc's command west for Operation Independence in place of the 1st DB, which had originally been slated for the assignment. In this way, Leclerc was removed from the front until May 1945.[53]

Holiday Season in France

In spite of Devers's belief that de Lattre had sufficient forces to clear the Germans from west of the Rhine, it was evident by mid-December that de Lattre would need additional resources to destroy the Colmar pocket. The French and American divisions in the line were exhausted, and shortages of artillery ammunition plagued efforts to make progress against the Germans. Devers, who was under pressure from Eisenhower to eliminate the Colmar situation, believed that de Lattre could have done more. In a stinging letter to the French general on 18 December, Devers vented his frustrations:

> It was with great confidence that I gave you the command of all the French Forces and certain American units . . . and assigned you the mission of rapidly reducing the German bridgehead. . . . The means put at your disposal for this intention were . . . sufficient for the reduction of this German force, if they had been employed with vigor and determination. I must avow that I am really dissatisfied with the results that you have obtained. . . . This situation will have, without doubt, considerable repercussions on the result obtained in the north since I am now deprived of the necessary means to exploit a breakthrough in the Siegfried Line which seems eminent [sic].[54]

De Lattre was not pleased by the contents of this letter, and he said so when he visited Devers on 22 December. In response, Devers told him that he had sensed a "defeatist attitude" in recent orders issued by French First Army. The two generals then discussed ways to reinforce the French forces with additional artillery and FFI replacements.[55]

The key point is that Devers and his subordinates candidly discussed major issues in an effort to solve problems—something Eisenhower had difficulty doing with Devers or Montgomery. The letter's tone reflects Devers's impatience, but also his willingness to deal plainly with subordinates. As his enlisted aide said of his boss in an interview, "There were some moments when quite a bit of things would be on his mind and he might not have been as gentle as sometimes."[56]

In this case, the root of the problem was that Devers and Eisenhower had misjudged the enemy's resolve to hold on to Alsace and overestimated French combat power. At the same time, Devers and Patch determined that Seventh Army needed another corps headquarters to provide command and control for the additional divisions that had already joined the army and for the six infantry regiments that were expected to arrive shortly.[57] Devers's request to SHAEF for an additional corps was granted, and on 25 December Major General Frank Milburn's XXI Corps was assigned to Sixth Army Group. In the meantime, SHAEF reminded Devers, "You should regard elimination of the bridgehead, which is now occupying eight of your divisions, of great importance."[58]

With Christmas coming and no end of the war in sight, Devers wrote to Georgie, "I shall miss you more this Christmas than ever before." He told her he had sent Major General O'Daniel home for a short leave in the United States. O'Daniel's "wife lives in Washington [and] is also home for Christmas. They have just lost their son. He is one of my great division commanders and I am very proud of him."[59] Devers continued to think about Frances, although he had received only one letter from her since his arrival in France. He asked Georgie to "tell Frances that the bedding roll was delivered to Alex yesterday, that he is in fine fettle and very happy indeed."[60] This letter was written less than a week after the 4th Armored Division had fought its way into Bastogne. Frances's husband, Colonel Alexander Graham, was the division's chief artillery officer.

While the French continued to struggle against the Colmar pocket, Seventh Army reached the German frontier, and on 16 December three divisions of VI Corps entered Germany. Devers believed that with three more divisions, Seventh Army could break through the Siegfried Line.[61] This was not to be, however, as Hitler demonstrated that the enemy always "gets a vote" in war.

The Battle of the Bulge and Nordwind

On 16 December three German armies struck First Army along a sixty-five-mile front in the Ardennes Forest of eastern Belgium and Luxembourg. Within hours, it was clear to Eisenhower that the aim of this offensive was to separate the Allied forces in the north from those in the south. Bradley, in contrast, saw it as a minor spoiling action by the enemy. When Bradley balked at moving forces to defeat the offensive, Eisenhower got directly involved in tactical decision making for the first time in the war: he ordered Bradley and Patton to send reserves into the Ardennes.[62] SHAEF became, in effect, an operational headquarters.

On 18 December SHAEF ordered Sixth Army Group to stop all offensive operations and prepare to take over a considerable part of Third Army's front so that Patton could turn his forces north to attack the German Bulge. Eisenhower also ordered Devers to contain enemy forces on Seventh Army's front with aggressive local action and to "eliminate the Colmar Pocket."[63]

On 19 December Devers joined Eisenhower, Bradley, and Patton in Verdun to discuss countermeasures to the German offensive. Following a brief review of the situation, Eisenhower decided that Sixth Army Group would take over the front-line positions of two corps of Third Army, allowing Patton to move most of his forces north. This adjustment in the boundary with Third Army added more than thirty miles to Seventh Army's front. Sixth Army Group (or the Southern Group of Armies, as it was known to SHAEF) was "to cease offensive operations, relieve Central Group of Armies westward to Saarlautern," and "be prepared to yield ground rather than to endanger the integrity of their forces."[64] According to Bedell Smith's biographer, D. K. R. Crosswell, "From the Verdun conference onward, SHAEF asserted greater direction over operations in Sixth Army Group, including movements down to division level."[65]

The situation in First Army's sector was critical by the time Eisenhower and his lieutenants met in Verdun. First Army commander Courtney Hodges had lost control of his army, and Bradley's headquarters in Luxembourg had no communications with First Army because the German advance had cut the telephone lines between them. Bradley refused to move his headquarters, in spite of encouragement from Ike to do so. "Bradley, who never ventured far from his headquarters in any case, became a virtual prisoner in Luxembourg."[66] Consequently, on 20 December Eisenhower gave Montgomery's Twenty-First Army Group control of all American forces north of the Bulge, leaving Bradley in charge of just Third Army and VIII Corps. This was appropriate, as Croswell notes, because "Hodges had lost the plot," and Bradley and Hodges "had let him [Eisenhower] down."[67]

In response to SHAEF's directives, Sixth Army Group ordered its two armies to assume the defensive and relieve elements of Third Army. However, it changed the phrasing of SHAEF's order to read: "Subject to securing essential lines of communication, Sixth Army Group will be prepared to yield ground rather than endanger the integrity of its forces."[68] In response, Seventh Army developed three successive defensive positions in its northeastern sector: the first just south of the German border, the second along the Maginot Line, and the third along the Moder River in northern Alsace. Patch planned to defend each line as strongly as possible. Devers endorsed this view, believing, as Patch did, that Seventh Army could hold its line even if the Germans attacked in strength.[69]

Shortly before Christmas, as the Battle of the Bulge raged, SHAEF learned from Ultra sources that the Germans were planning another offensive, code-named Nordwind, to strike Seventh Army on New Year's Eve. Eisenhower, who had been surprised once by the Germans, decided that once the Germans struck, Seventh Army should withdraw immediately from northern Alsace to a line along the eastern foothills of the Vosges. This would leave the city of Strasbourg and the 600,000 Frenchmen in the area at the mercy of the Germans. This decision was based in part on Eisenhower's desire to create a reserve to use in the north for Montgomery's operations and in part on his desire to avoid another Kasserine or Bulge surprise. Eisenhower personally picked Sixth Army Group's new "main position" and sent Major General Harold Bull, SHAEF's operations officer, to Seventh Army headquarters in Phalsburg to show Devers a draft of the plan on 26 December.[70]

Devers was shocked when he saw the extent of the withdrawal. In his diary he wrote, "The Germans will attack me now," and "the position I give up is much stronger than the one to which I go." Further, he realized that "giving up the town of Strasbourg is a political disaster to France."[71] Patch and Lodge also objected, with Lodge reiterating that such a move would be a political disaster.[72] Seventh Army's corps commanders, Haislip and Brooks, told Devers that they believed they could defend northern Alsace using Patch's carefully developed three-line defensive array. When Patton learned of Ike's decision to abandon Strasbourg without a fight, he told Bradley, "This is disgusting." It would, he believed, undermine the American people's confidence in their army and condemn the Alsatians to "death or slavery."[73]

After digesting SHAEF's draft plan, Devers set Patch and his staff to work on how to deploy their forces to meet the expected enemy offensive, knowing that "the Germans undoubtedly will attack me now down the gap west of the Vosges and I must stop them at the start."[74] The next morning Devers returned to Vittel to meet with de Lattre, but he did not share the extreme withdrawal envisioned by SHAEF. Instead, he directed de Lattre to move the 2nd DB back to reinforce Seventh Army and informed him that the French 1st Infantry Division was returning from western France to strengthen the French army.[75]

After meeting with de Lattre, Devers traveled to Versailles on 27 December to try to convince Eisenhower that such a deep withdrawal was not necessary to maintain the integrity of his forces. Devers made a strong pitch, telling his boss that Seventh Army's leaders were convinced they could defend their current positions. He also outlined Patch's plan to defend along three successive lines before falling back to the "main position" if the enemy threatened the army's integrity.[76] He pointed out that the major withdrawal Eisenhower had in mind would cause serious political problems with the French, and they probably would not obey orders to carry it out.[77]

That evening, Devers returned to his headquarters in Vittel and summarized in his diary the results of his talk with Eisenhower: "Eisenhower was very definite that I must move my troops back to the Vosges line and hang on, that I would get no replacements—in fact they were taking replacements away from me—and I would get no more ammunition and no more help; that I would undoubtedly be threatened down the Saar River Valley and that I would have to stop the drive."[78] Eisenhower believed he had made it clear to Devers that he was to withdraw all his forces back sixty kilometers to the "main position" along the edge of the Vosges. Devers, however, wrote in his diary, "I was impressed with the idea that Strasbourg and Mulhouse should be held if at all possible. . . . We are preparing [therefore] our positions in depth and will try to pull back slowly."[79]

Based on Devers's assumption that Strasbourg was to be defended as long as it did not risk Seventh Army's integrity, Sixth Army Group issued Letter of Instruction 7 on 28 December. It anticipated that Seventh Army would defend as long as possible along three lines, in succession, before withdrawing to the "main position." The last of these forward lines was hinged on the city of Strasbourg. The letter of instruction explicitly ordered that "efforts compatible with integrity of forces will be made to hold Strasbourg and Mulhouse."[80] Devers planned to withdraw from each defensive position only when ordered to do so by SHAEF, and each line would be prepared with minefields, fighting positions, and barbed wire.[81]

Hours after the letter of instruction was issued, the final order from SHAEF arrived. Sixth Army Group was to withdraw its forces rather than risk the "integrity" of their front. The order indicated that when Seventh Army was first attacked, it should withdraw all the way back to the SHAEF-directed "main position," rather than fighting along successive defensive positions.[82] Ike told the same thing to the Combined Chiefs of Staff on 31 December.[83] Clearly, Devers misunderstood Eisenhower's intention. Devers was hoping to contain the anticipated German offensive without having to sacrifice Alsace.

Meanwhile, the French chief of staff, Alphonse Juin, visited Bedell Smith at SHAEF headquarters on 28 December to ask about rumors that the Americans were preparing to abandon Alsace if attacked. Juin had learned of the plan from de Lattre. Smith acknowledged that such a move had been discussed, but he lied to Juin and told him it was only a staff study.[84] De Lattre, for his part, ordered his troops to defend their current positions. De Lattre, like Devers, did not plan to obey Eisenhower's order for an immediate withdrawal.[85]

On 31 December, as Ultra information confirmed the Germans' intention to launch Nordwind within twenty-four hours, Devers sent Eisenhower a summary of Sixth Army Group's plans and situation. After reviewing the forces available to his two armies and the strength of the anticipated German offensive, Devers updated his boss on the progress made to meet the enemy assault:

> Work of organizing the entire area for defense in great depth is progressing satisfactorily and every effort is being made to pinch out an Infantry Division as general reserve and place it west of the Vosges where it will be suitably disposed to meet an attack against XV Corps. I am convinced, after personally examining the problems confronting Patch, that it will take approximately 2 weeks to accomplish this if he is to prepare any semblance of defenses in the Alsace Plain. . . . In view of the very definite threat that has developed on the front of XV Corps, I must point out the necessity for leaving the Divisions currently earmarked for SHAEF Reserve in this area at least until this threat disappears, or until Patch is able to constitute a suitable general reserve.[86]

Devers's message described a "defense in great depth" rather than a with-drawal on first contact. He identified the main threat as being west of the Vosges, where the Germans, if successful, would cut Seventh Army's supply lines. His view that it would take two weeks to fully prepare a defense of the Alsatian plain indicated that he and Patch were planning to make a stand well forward of Eisenhower's "main position" and that Seventh Army was not planning an imminent withdrawal.

Devers sent another message to SHAEF on New Year's Eve, recom-mending that a corps of Third Army be transferred to Sixth Army Group and asserting that "all forces east of the Moselle must be under a single command." These actions, he believed, would best protect Third Army's current offensive against the southern flank of the Bulge. "No reply to this message was received."[87]

When he sent these messages, Devers had no way of knowing that Eisenhower's relationship with Montgomery had reached a low point by 30 December. All fall, Montgomery had barraged Eisenhower with a series of messages about the latter's failures as an Allied ground force commander. When Eisenhower gave Montgomery command of the American forces on the north shoulder of the Bulge, it went to Montgomery's head. When Eisenhower tried to get Monty to launch his part of a coordinated counter-attack against the flanks of the Bulge, the British prima donna refused until Eisenhower visited him in Hasselt, Belgium, on 28 December and agreed to delay the counteroffensive until 3 January.

The following day, 29 December, Montgomery sent a message to Eisenhower outlining his view of what needed to be done to achieve a successful campaign. He stated that the "failure" of the fall campaign was due to Ike's decision not to put Montgomery in charge of Bradley's army group in addition to his own Twenty-First Army Group. He went on to say that unless Eisenhower appointed a single land force commander now, the Allies would continue to "fail."[88] At the same time, British newspaper stories made it appear that Montgomery had saved the American army and implied it was only a matter of time before he would be appointed land force commander. Montgomery's message was the final straw for Eisen-hower, who also received a message from Marshall on 30 December. In it, the chief of staff made it clear that it would be unacceptable to the United States if Eisenhower gave up his position as land force commander to the field marshal.[89]

With this encouragement from Marshall, Eisenhower prepared a message to the Combined Chiefs of Staff, asking them to choose between Montgomery and himself. Given the massive preponderance of American forces in the European theater, the CCS would have had no choice but to support Eisenhower and replace Montgomery as Twenty-First Army Group commander. However, before Eisenhower could dispatch this message, Montgomery's loyal chief of staff, Freddie de Guingand, traveled to Versailles and "begged" Eisenhower to give him twenty-four hours to convince Montgomery of the trouble he was in. Ike relented, and the next day, 31 December, Montgomery wrote a letter of abject surrender to the supreme commander. Eisenhower accepted Montgomery's apology, averting a crisis in the alliance.[90]

Eisenhower also faced a serious altercation with the French government during this period because of his decision to abandon Strasbourg. After Juin's visit to SHAEF on 28 December, it became clear that Sixth Army Group had been ordered to withdraw from northeastern Alsace when Nordwind commenced. De Gaulle refused to accept this decision, and after Juin failed to get the order changed, the head of the French government wrote a New Year's Day letter to Eisenhower, setting forth his views. De Gaulle told the supreme commander that the French army would defend Strasbourg, turning it into another Stalingrad if necessary. De Gaulle also ordered de Lattre to prepare to move forces into Strasbourg, rather than to retreat.[91]

Consequently, Eisenhower could not have been in a worse mood. By the time Devers sent his New Year's Eve messages and tried to delay the withdrawal from Alsace, Eisenhower had no tolerance for any more disagreement from any subordinate, and certainly not from Devers. When the German offensive commenced late on New Year's Eve, Eisenhower expected Devers to order an immediate withdrawal to the main position in the Vosges. When this did not happen the next day, Eisenhower lost his temper and ordered Smith to call Devers, ask him why he had disobeyed orders to withdraw Seventh Army, and insist that Devers comply "at once."[92]

Devers capitulated in the face of another clear order and instructed his armies to withdraw to the main position along the Vosges by 5 January.[93] Smith also informed Devers that Eisenhower "thinks you've been disloyal." In the words of Rick Atkinson, "As for the supreme commander, he was now so vexed at a man whom he had long disliked that he considered sacking Devers and giving the command of his army group to Patch."[94] Devers, who was depressed about the situation and concerned about the ongoing battle, wrote to Georgie, "Perhaps tonight I have more on my mind than I have ever had before for the bad things catch up with you every now and then."[95]

Strasbourg Saved and Nordwind Defeated

Although SHAEF was willing to write off the people of Strasbourg, the French were not. On 1 January de Gaulle sent General du Vigier to talk with Devers in Vittel. When he arrived at Sixth Army Group headquarters, XV Corps had already stopped the German attack west of the low Vosges. Nonetheless, Devers had ordered Seventh Army to begin to pull back in Alsace and to be at Eisenhower's main position by the evening of 5 January. Upon learning this, du Vigier called the Americans cowards, and Devers, remarkably, did not take offense. He told du Vigier that orders were orders, but he admitted that "he had carried out his orders badly this time" by stretching the withdrawal out over five days. According to historian Frank Gurley, du Vigier realized "that his accusation of cowardice did not apply to this man."[96]

The next morning Devers sent Barr, his chief of staff, to SHAEF to convince Smith that Eisenhower should authorize Seventh Army to hold a line that included Strasbourg and that holding Strasbourg was the right thing to do militarily and politically. Devers reportedly told Barr "to sleep with Bedell Smith if necessary, but get those orders changed."[97] Du Vigier also returned to Paris and informed de Gaulle that Eisenhower had ordered Sixth Army Group to withdraw when attacked. De Gaulle was "incensed" that "Eisenhower had lacked the elementary courtesy of informing him of this inadmissible withdrawal of American troops from the sacred soil of Alsace-Lorraine." De Gaulle immediately wired appeals to Churchill and Roosevelt to get the order rescinded.[98] Roosevelt had the State Department notify the French government that it was a military matter and therefore he would not intervene.

On the afternoon of 2 January, Juin visited SHAEF again. Eisenhower was away visiting Bradley, and Smith told Juin that the decision was based purely on military necessity. That evening, when Ike returned, Smith briefed him about the latest appeal from the French, but the supreme commander remained adamant about not canceling his order. At 2200 hours Juin returned with a message from de Gaulle, threatening drastic action if

Strasbourg were abandoned without a fight. Barr again tried to talk sense to Smith, but to no avail.[99]

De Gaulle also sent an order to de Lattre to defend Alsace, thus putting him in a difficult position: should de Lattre be loyal to his American commander or to the French government? When he tried to explain this dilemma to de Gaulle and asked him to work through Devers, the imperious Frenchman lost his temper and reminded de Lattre that, above all, his loyalty was to France. De Lattre ordered the Algerian 3rd Infantry Division to prepare to move to Strasbourg to reinforce the French 10th Infantry Division, which was on its way from Paris.[100]

On the morning of 3 January, de Gaulle requested a meeting with Eisenhower. In addition, word reached SHAEF that Churchill and Field Marshal Alan Brooke would be arriving in Paris at midday to talk with Ike about Montgomery's situation. At the morning staff meeting, Eisenhower told Smith to call Devers and ask how far the Germans were from Strasbourg. Smith reached Devers at Patch's headquarters in Luneville, where the two were monitoring the successful defense of XV Corps and the more critical situation of VI Corps, where the Germans had penetrated Brooks's first line. Devers replied that the enemy was thirty miles from Strasbourg, and Smith advised him to hold them there until the afternoon meeting with de Gaulle, Churchill, and Brooke.[101]

That afternoon, de Gaulle and Juin returned to Trianon Palace to meet with Eisenhower and Smith. Churchill and Brooke were also present. De Gaulle opened by telling Eisenhower that "Alsace is sacred ground" and that allowing the Germans to regain Strasbourg could bring down the French government and cause anarchy in France. Ike retorted that if the French troops had fought harder to eradicate the Colmar pocket, there would have been no crisis. De Gaulle then threatened to pull French First Army out of the coalition, to which Eisenhower responded by threatening to cut off all supplies for the French. De Gaulle escalated this contest of dumb threats by stating that the French would deny the Allies the use of their railroads.[102]

At this juncture in the argument, Churchill left his seat and walked to the map spread before them. Pointing at the map, the prime minister said, "Strasbourg, this point." What he meant is unclear, but his calm interjection allowed time for Eisenhower to get his temper under control and to think about the political ramifications of his decision. With Anglo-American relations unstable, a rupture with the French could disrupt the military effort and the stability of the Western alliance.[103] Perhaps he realized that his intransigence was at least partly due to his distrust and dislike of Devers, who had advocated defending Alsace. After a short pause, Eisenhower relented and agreed to rescind his withdrawal order. De Gaulle, who knew from du Vigier that Devers could be trusted, "insisted that Bedell Smith and Alphonse Juin go to Vittel together to see Devers to make certain that there be no backsliding from the decision to defend Strasbourg."[104] Smith and du Vigier met with Devers the next day.

In a message to Marshall three days later, Eisenhower disingenuously claimed, "We studied the matter earnestly and decided that the original plan had to be modified to the extent of merely swinging the VI Corps back . . . with its right extending southward generally toward Strasbourg. . . . When de Gaulle came to see me [on 3 January] we had already put into effect the revised plan."[105]

SHAEF's order to defend northern Alsace was accompanied by permission for Sixth Army Group to use XXI Corps and its two divisions to meet the most dangerous German assaults in the area north of Strasbourg. Seventh Army's defense of the western portion of the line had been so successful by 5 January that the Germans realized they could not break XV Corps' lines. The first phase of Nordwind was over.

Once it was clear that the Germans had failed to breach XV Corps' front west of the Vosges, Hitler resolved to shift his offensive against VI Corps, hoping to capture Strasbourg with attacks from the north and south and from across the Rhine. The balance of forces in the region remained strongly in the Germans' favor, as fourteen German divisions faced Patch's seven infantry and two armored divisions. The horrible weather restricted Allied air support, and whenever the weather allowed air sorties, the new German jet fighters were as evident as the French and American aircraft.[106]

Thanks to Ultra, Devers and Patch knew the Germans were going to shift their main effort against Brooks's VI Corps. Eisenhower and Smith knew this as well, and Eisenhower sent Smith to Vittel to give Devers his new orders and to observe the situation firsthand. Smith arrived on 4 January and stayed for two days. On 5 January Devers noted in his diary, "[I] took Smith to see Patch at Luneville. Our situation seemed very sound to Bedell. I think he was impressed with the way we operate. There is no question about it—the Sixth Army Group is a team, with everyone working for each other."[107]

Sixth Army Group got help from SHAEF when Eisenhower allowed

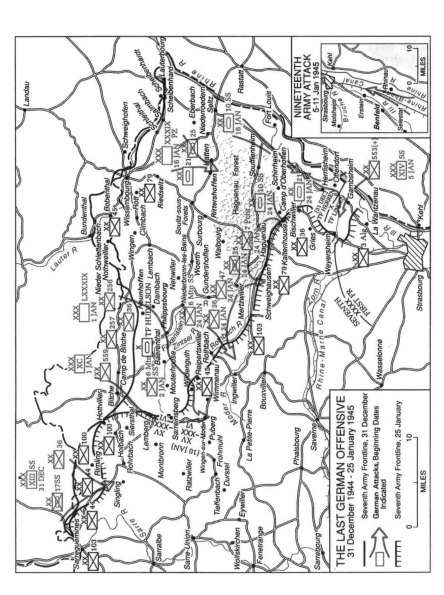

Figure 14.5. Last German offensive, 31 December 1944–25 January 1945

Devers to commit the SHAEF reserve of two divisions to the fight. Devers also moved the boundary between French First Army and Seventh Army north of Strasbourg, freeing American units to fight north of the city. In the words of the official history, "Even SHAEF had begun to pay some attention to the southern battlefield," with its promise to send Devers additional artillery and the battered 101st Airborne Division.[108]

Over the next two weeks, VI Corps needed all the help it could get. On its left flank, the Germans drove a wedge ten miles deep before being stopped. Patch moved forces from XV Corps to VI Corps to stem the enemy advance and to hold the passes in the Vosges. On Brooks's right, the Germans drove south into the Hagenau Forest and launched an assault across the Rhine at Gambshiem. Farther south, the Germans attacked the French from the northern edge of the Colmar pocket, hoping to get to Strasbourg from the rear. Patch and Brooks remained remarkably calm under the pressure of the enemy offensive, and Devers did all he could to find additional resources for his beleaguered forces.[109]

Devers shared his observations about the situation with his brother Frank, in a letter written at the height of the battle:

> We are in a terrible and hard battle at the moment against odds but have confidence in the result. . . . My French Command is doing a fine job. The French people are alright, they deserve more and I feel sure will come out of this war on a better and stronger foundation. Alsace is getting a going over, never live in a battle zone. . . . We have plenty of snow and freezing weather. The children are skating on the canals and rivers within sight of the Rhine and [of] our batteries which fire over their heads. . . . They seem dressed in warm clothing for they live in unheated houses or housing where only one room is heated. Washing is done at the village wash stands or through the broken ice in the canal or stream.[110]

He also told his brother, who lived in California: "The Japs of my Army who are Americans from the West Coast and Hawaii are real Americans and you westerners should know that they fight well and ask no favors. I am very fond of them."[111] He was referring to the men of the 442nd Infantry Regiment, who were typical of the soldiers who faced the German onslaught.

The toll on the men in the line was terrific, as was their fortitude. The constant strain of battle also took a toll on leaders, as Jake noted in a letter to Georgie: "Three of my division commanders have wormed out from old ailments, they did their best to carry on but finally were downed. Spragins 44th, Haffner 103rd, and Eagles 45th. The latter was dumped out of his jeep by running over a mine. [We] have younger men, very aggressive, replacing them."[112] General Haffner's replacement as commander of the 103rd Infantry Division was Brigadier General Tony McAuliffe, who would soon be promoted because of his leadership of the 101st Airborne Division during the siege of Bastogne. When McAuliffe reported to Devers at Sixth Army Group headquarters, he was running a high fever, but as he recalled later, "I wasn't letting anyone know. But as soon as I got in there General Devers and his people saw it. They made me stay a couple of days before I went down to the 103rd Division." Once in command of the 103rd, McAuliffe found that "Devers visited us rather frequently, although I was a long way from him. . . . I must say he didn't bother me much while I commanded the division."[113] McAuliffe ably commanded his division through the bitter fighting against the Nordwind offensive and then during the final drive into Germany.

Devers's habit of keeping a finger on the pulse of tactical operations aided him in his decision making. He and Patch committed every division available to stop the Germans, including four divisions that faced their first combat during one of the coldest Januarys on record. He told Georgie, "These are hectic days for me and the 6th Army Group. Ted [Brooks] is a fighting wizard and that helps as is Sandy [Patch] but we have a tough job ahead and time will tell."[114]

By 20 January, it looked as if the Germans were going to break the cohesion of VI Corps' front as Hitler committed his last reserves. That night, however, Devers ordered Patch to withdraw VI Corps under cover of darkness from its lines north of the Hagenau Forest to its third line of defense along the Moder and Rohrbach Rivers. This maneuver caught the enemy by surprise. When the Germans attacked on 21 January, they found the American positions empty. It took them two days to reset for an attack against Brooks's Moder line. By then, VI Corps had had a respite and was well dug in. On 25 January Seventh Army defeated the final attacks of the Nordwind offensive, and the next day Hitler ended his last offensive in the west.[115] Sixth Army Group's G-2 reported on 25 January that the enemy had committed every available unit in an attempt to break Brooks's defenses. "In sum, the enemy has lost the initiative. . . . From the Moselle to the Rhine, he [can] only attempt to stabilize the front."[116]

Seventh Army stopped the Germans because of the tenacity and hard fighting of the American soldiers who held the lines. Their sacrifice was made worthwhile by the sound leadership and tactical judgment of Patch, Brooks, Haislip, and many other officers. Brooks handled his corps in a superb manner, prompting Devers to comment in his diary, "Ted Brooks has fought one of the greatest defensive battles of all time with very little. He has been able to inspire his men to fight."[117]

The costs of defending northern Alsace and Strasbourg were high. The Germans lost an estimated 23,000 men killed, wounded, or captured.[118] Seventh Army and French First Army lost 25,924 soldiers killed, wounded, or missing in January. Another 47,688 soldiers in Sixth Army Group were "non-battle casualties." During the same period, 26,050 soldiers returned to their units from the medical system.[119] The total strength of Sixth Army Group at the end of January was 614,821 soldiers, with 318,722 in Seventh Army and 296,099 in French First Army.

Given these casualties, was it wise for Devers, de Lattre, and Patch to hold Alsace? From an operational perspective, the German army could not afford such losses on top of those suffered in the Battle of the Bulge. Tactically, it was probably less costly to hold on to the ground south of the Moder-Rohrbach line than it would have been to retake all of northern Alsace. As a result of the battle, the German army lost the initiative in the west. Politically, it was critical for continued good relations with the French army and the French people, who would never have forgiven the betrayal of the people of Alsace.

Seventh Army and French First Army had succeeded in holding on to Alsace, but each was desperately short of replacements—especially infantrymen. The French army was short 9,193 infantrymen, and Seventh Army's divisions were short 17,455. All Allied divisions in the European theater were in a similar situation. With too few replacements, or reinforcements, coming from the United States, SHAEF combed its support units for combat-fit men, but the shortages persisted.

In December Devers noted that Lieutenant General Johnny Lee, commander of the Communications Zone, "is trying to involve us in the colored question again, and apparently has. However we will solve that too."[120] Devers was referring to Lee's message of 4 January 1945 inviting soldiers in service units to volunteer for reclassification as infantrymen. With Eisenhower's concurrence, Lee wrote, "This opportunity to volunteer will be extended to all soldiers without regard to color or race."[121] Allowing blacks to volunteer as infantry replacements in units assigned to all-white divisions violated the War Department's segregation policy, but Eisenhower assured Marshall that if more African Americans volunteered than were needed in black combat units, he would create segregated battalions.[122] Eventually, more than 4,000 black soldiers volunteered to serve as infantrymen. They were organized in platoon-size units, given basic infantry training, and assigned to infantry divisions in March 1945.[123] It was a step forward for racial integration, but it had little more than symbolic effect in 1945.

In the meantime, Devers and Sixth Army Group still had to deal with the German-held Colmar pocket in the south and the resumption of offensive operations against the Siegfried Line in the north. Fortunately, the German army had committed all available reserves in its winter offensives and was now facing a Russian winter offensive in the east and Eisenhower's strengthened forces in the west.

15

Victory in Europe

While Seventh Army was defending northern Alsace and Strasbourg, Sixth Army Group prepared to eliminate the Colmar pocket. The existence of the pocket was a major irritant to Eisenhower, and it did nothing to improve his opinion of Devers. On 12 January Eisenhower explained to Marshall how he believed the pocket had developed:

> At the moment our most worrisome area is the south. . . . When Devers turned his complete Seventh Army northward, he was badly mistaken in the ability of the French Army to finish off the Colmar pocket. At that time he had been directed to turn part of the 15th Corps northward, west of the Vosges, in order to support Patton's right but it was expected that his first concern east of the mountains would be to clean up his rear. I must say that he can scarcely be blamed for making a miscalculation with respect to the French. . . . Nevertheless, it is a very bad thorn in our side today.[1]

Eisenhower did not write a similar letter assessing Bradley's role in the Battle of the Bulge; in fact, back in December he had recommended that Bradley be promoted.[2]

In January Marshall asked Eisenhower to evaluate Bradley, Patton, Devers, and other three-star generals and solicited his advice on their promotions. Eisenhower responded "that only Spaatz and Bradley should be promoted on the first list," and "with respect to Devers . . . I am not yet ready to make a recommendation. . . . I probably will recommend Patton at a later date, possibly ahead of Devers."[3] When it came to Devers, the continued existence of the Colmar pocket may have been the last straw for Eisenhower. In any case, its reduction was critical to Sixth Army Group.

Elimination of the Colmar Pocket

The German bridgehead covered 850 square miles west of the Rhine. Its circular shape gave the Germans the advantage of interior lines. The eight enemy divisions in the pocket were supported by an armor brigade and had prepared elaborate defensive works. In the words of Colonel Jonathan Seaman, a Sixth Army Group staff officer, "The short, interior lines of communications permitted the Germans to mass their forces with great rapidity to meet any attacks attempted by the French First Army."[4]

De Lattre understood the need to eliminate the German forces west of the Rhine as soon as the crisis in the north ended. In early January he visited Sixth Army Group headquarters to brief Devers on his tentative plan to crush the Colmar pocket. Devers and his joint planning staff appreciated the French general's concept of a pincer attack by forces north and south of the pocket, but they did not believe the French were strong enough to execute the plan alone.[5]

By 14 January, Sixth Army Group had prepared a plan, code-named Operation Cheer, for the final assaults against the German bridgehead. The plan called for an initial attack by French I Corps against the southern flank, followed two days later by an assault by French II Corps in the north. The planners believed that II Corps needed to be reinforced by three American divisions. Consequently, when the SHAEF chief of staff visited Sixth Army Group on 14 January, Devers asked Smith for two divisions from the SHAEF reserve. Smith agreed and arranged to transfer the 28th Infantry and 10th Armored Divisions to Sixth Army Group, with the proviso that the badly battered 28th be used in a defensive role. These divisions and the 3rd Infantry Division were assigned to French II Corps. Smith also arranged for the 101st Airborne Division to be assigned to Devers's command.[6]

Operation Cheer opened on 20 January when French I Corps attacked the southern shoulder of the Colmar pocket.[7] After initial gains made during a blizzard, French progress slowed, but the pressure in the south drew German reserves from the north. On 22 January de Monsabert's II Corps launched its assault. The U.S. 3rd and French 1st Infantry Divisions slogged their way across the Ill River over the next eight days. By 31 January, in spite of a serious counterattack against the 3rd Division, II Corps had crossed the Colmar Canal near Holtzwihr. The Germans, however, rallied and stopped further advances by the exhausted French and Americans. At that point, Devers realized that the "situation on the front does not look good," and additional forces would be needed to finish the operation.[8]

During a short visit to Vittel on 27 January, Eisenhower emphasized that the Colmar pocket "was the one sore in the whole front." He left

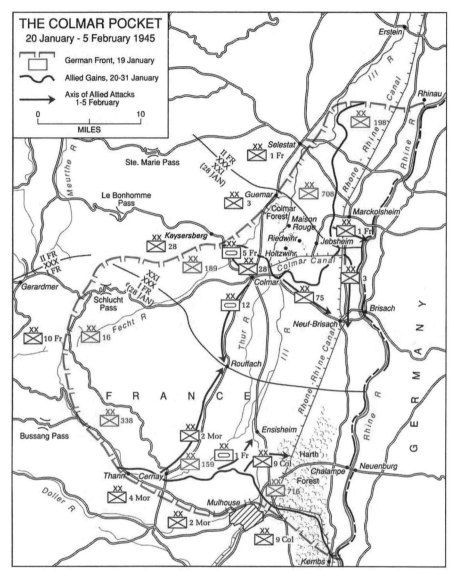

Figure 15.1. Colmar pocket, 20 January–5 February 1945

Devers with the feeling that "it was an obsession with him to get it out." Devers offered no excuses, but he did explain that he could not "lick the weather" and assured Eisenhower, "I realized that it was my responsibility and that he could count on me."[9]

On 29 January the German high command got permission to pull divisions out of the northern extension of the pocket around the town of Erstein, although Hitler ordered Nineteenth Army to continue to defend most of the bridgehead. Meanwhile, Devers assigned Frank Milburn's XXI Corps to French First Army to strengthen the push against the northern front. SHAEF transferred the 75th Infantry and 12th Armored Divisions to Sixth Army Group, and Devers and de Lattre agreed to resume the two-pronged pincer movement to cut off the German forces by seizing Neuf Brisach on the Rhine. Devers was on hand at de Monsabert's headquarters to watch the final drive commence on 31 January.[10]

With the additional forces of U.S. XXI Corps, French First Army renewed its assaults. Progress on I Corps' front remained slow, but XXI and II Corps made significant progress in the north. By 3 February, the U.S. 3rd Infantry Division was near Neuf Brisach, and the 28th Infantry and 5th French Armored Divisions had taken Colmar. These gains unhinged the German defenses and threatened their last bridges over the Rhine. On 5 February the 12th Armored Division passed through the 28th Infantry Division and drove south from Colmar toward Rufach, while the 3rd Infantry Division captured Neuf Brisach. In the south, French I Corps broke through the German lines and drove north toward the 3rd Infantry Division. Two days later, all German troops who had not escaped across the Rhine were encircled. French forces then cleared the pocket while XXI Corps moved north to rejoin Seventh Army. The Colmar pocket was finally eliminated.[11]

With clear relief, Devers wrote to Georgie: "The Colmar Pocket is no more and about 80% of the German 19th Army who held it are prisoners or dead. This is a headache which is cured." He also sent her a copy of his family tree, "as dug from the records of Strasbourg. This should please Kits. I have sent her the original letters Lodge got for me. . . . If the Field Marshal [Montgomery] can get going for he has all the help and the Russians keep going we may get it over in a hurry. If he fails, and I have not much confidence in him, then we will have to pinch hit and fight on. Maybe the Russians can clean up the job, they certainly are doing a great job."[12]

Sixth Army Group suffered heavy losses during the winter battles in Alsace. Seventh Army had 7,168 battle and 16,224 nonbattle casualties in February. The French suffered 4,316 battle and 36,540 nonbattle casualties. The medical system returned 31,968 sick and wounded to the units during the month.[13] The German Nineteenth Army listed its losses at 22,000 men killed, wounded, or captured, and fewer than 10,000 German troops escaped across the Rhine.[14]

During the final battle of the Colmar pocket, Devers visited and evaluated French leaders and staff below the corps level "in an endeavor to appraise their capabilities and learn their problems first hand." He shared his observations with his army group staff on 2 February. "Devers charged his staff not to criticize the French for their difficulties but to help in correcting them." He also noted that after the Colmar offensive, the French army would need a period of "refitting and retraining before it would be ready for major offensive action."[15] This approach showed growth on Devers's part as a coalition leader, and ultimately, it was the best way to get the most from de Lattre's army.

Devers gave credit to his subordinates for their handling of the winter battles, and he wrote many letters of commendation to them and their units.[16] He also shared his thoughts about some of his key leaders with Georgie: "We decorated Ted Brooks today. . . . Ham Haislip I see once in a while. He is heavy as is his chief of staff Menoher, but doing an excellent job. Likes to be praised, needs it for his peace of mind but when the heat is on, measures up. . . . Sandy Patch is in wonderful form and beloved by all. . . . Very fond of Larkin, he is a real soldier and made my line of supply perfect."[17]

Eisenhower, in contrast, offered little praise for the tremendous efforts of the American and French forces. Bradley was miffed at the transfer of reinforcements to Devers for Operation Cheer and claimed that Devers was "using up" Twelfth Army Group's rested divisions; in addition, he charged "that the defensive efforts of the Seventh Army had been 'poorly handled.'"[18] In December Eisenhower had asked Bradley to evaluate the senior officers in the theater and list them in order of preference for promotion, based on their contributions to the war effort. Not surprisingly, Bradley listed Smith, Spaatz, and Hodges as the top three and ranked Devers as twenty-third out of thirty-two men.[19] This assessment jibed with Eisenhower's.

When Marshall was considering general officer promotions on 12 January, he told Eisenhower that he agreed that Spaatz and Bradley should be promoted, but he specifically asked about Patton and Devers.[20] On 1 February, as the battle of the Colmar pocket raged, Eisenhower dictated a memorandum ranking the value of thirty-eight generals. Bradley, Spaatz, and Smith were his top three, in spite of Bradley's performance in the early stages of the Battle of the Bulge. He listed Devers at number twenty-four, well behind Hodges, at number eleven. About Devers he wrote, "The proper position of this officer is not yet fully determined in my own mind. The over-all results he and his organization produce are generally good, sometimes outstanding. But he has not, so far, produced among the seniors of the American organization here the feeling of trust and confidence that is so necessary to continued success."[21] To Eisenhower, the fact that Sixth Army Group had never suffered a setback like the Battle of the Bulge did not seem to matter.

It is fair to say that Devers harbored resentment toward Eisenhower and that he occasionally expressed his frustration in front of other officers. For example, Colonel John Guthrie, Seventh Army's G-3, claimed in 1988 that Devers had expressed criticism "in large matters and small of Eisenhower, often in open briefings or meetings." Guthrie believed "it smacked of jealousy and disloyalty," and he was surprised that Eisenhower had rated Devers as high as twenty-fourth out of thirty-eight officers. In the same letter to the author of the army's official history, Guthrie admitted that Devers and his staff were "always in the middle when taking Seventh Army resources for the support of the First French Army, plus fending off the efforts of Eisenhower's HQ to reduce 6th Army Group (and thus Seventh Army) to the most minimal role possible."[22] However, there seem to be no other critiques of Devers by senior officers who served in Seventh Army or Sixth Army Group.

The discussion of promotions continued. On 1 March Marshall asked Eisenhower "whom he had in mind, besides Bradley and Spaatz," for promotion to full general: Patton or Devers? The chief of staff then asked, if Patton were promoted ahead of Devers, "would you not have to relieve Devers? Otherwise he would be discredited."[23] Eisenhower responded that if only two were to be promoted in the European theater, they should be Bradley and Spaatz. However, if more than two were promoted, "then by force of circumstances and present organization Devers will have to be [the] third nomination."[24]

Marshall then recommended a number of generals for promotion to the president. Devers was promoted on 8 March, Spaatz on 11 March, Bradley on 12 March, and Patton on 14 April. On 14 March Eisenhower sent a message to Devers noting that *Stars and Stripes* had carried a notice of his nomination for a fourth star. He told Devers, "I not only send my warm congratulations, but look upon your promotion as a token of the War Department's tribute to the great work performed by the Sixth Army Group during the past six months. All your friends here join me in sending best wishes and good luck."[25] The same day, Eisenhower wrote to Bradley:

"As you know, I have long felt that such action [as your promotion] was overdue and it is almost needless for me to say 'Congratulations.' I am truly happy."[26] Hodges was promoted on 15 April, but Patch and Simpson, both army commanders, were not promoted until 1954 (Patch posthumously, having died in 1945). They both resented the fact that their contributions and accomplishments had not been recognized at the time.[27]

Meanwhile, Georgie faced her own challenges at home, as she coped with the losses suffered by many friends. She did not share her feelings with Jake, but in a letter to her sister-in-law, her pain was clear: "The Stearns' boy, the O'Hara son-in-law, the Aleshire son-in-law, and so many little fellows who grew up at West Point are gone, or blind, or lame. Allan McBride dead—Lesley McNair and his boy—the Patch boy, the O'Daniel boy—too many to write [about]. I have scarcely a day that does not take me to see one of my sad friends, or calls for a note of sympathy."[28]

Georgie, like the rest of the nation, hoped the war would end soon. Her thoughts were with her husband, and she wrote to his sister: "I am busy and interested, but it's darn lonely. The time grows no pleasanter the longer Jamie stays away. He is weary too." She also shared some news about her son-in-law: "Had a chance to send Alex some eagles for a promotion present. . . . Poor fellow. He seems little fitted by temperament and disposition for the cold and mud and filth and indecencies of the battlefront."[29]

After his army group defeated the last German offensive in the west and destroyed the Colmar pocket, Devers sensed that the war was coming to an end. In a letter to Georgie he commented about his uncertain future in the army: "Since I am not in the union, anything can happen to me when the Germans are snowed under. . . . Of course I want to go to China after coming home but that is too much to hope."[30]

Eisenhower and his other senior commanders felt the same way about the impending end of the European war. By February, it was clear that victory was assured, although no one knew how quickly it would come. The Allied forces in western Europe had grown to 3.7 million men organized in three army groups, nine armies, twenty corps, and seventy-three divisions. The Germans nominally had eighty divisions facing Eisenhower's forces, but they were badly understrength. The Allied air forces dominated the sky and made German movement on the ground extremely difficult. Additionally, the Germans could not reinforce their western front due to the Russian winter offensive that carried the Red Army to the Oder River in February.[31]

On 20 January Eisenhower described his strategic concept to the Com-

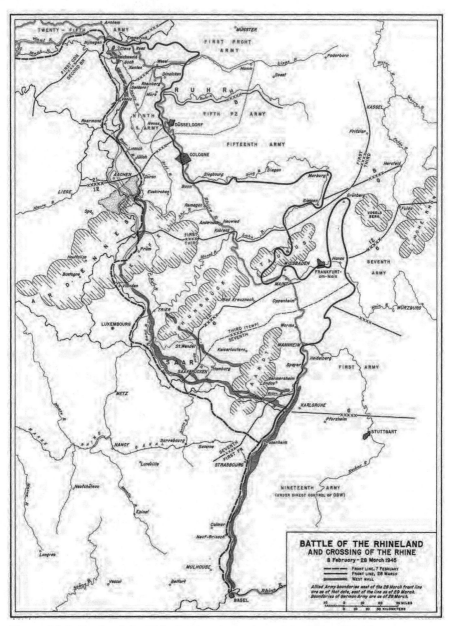

Figure 15.2. Battle of the Rhineland and crossing of the Rhine, 1945

bined Chiefs of Staff.[32] He planned to launch his final offensive in three phases. The main effort in the first phase was to be carried out by Montgomery's army group north of the Ruhr, with the objective of getting to the Rhine. Twelfth Army Group was to protect Montgomery's right flank and then advance to the Rhine in the second phase. Sixth Army Group was to remain on the defensive until the third phase, when Third and Seventh Armies were to breach the Siegfried Line and capture the German industrial area known as the Saar. Each army group was instructed to prepare plans to execute this strategy.[33]

For Sixth Army Group, the elimination of the Colmar pocket changed the tactical situation significantly. French First Army was able to take over the defense of the Rhine from Switzerland to the German border, freeing American divisions for the coming offensive. The French army's shortened front allowed de Lattre to rotate his divisions out of the line for rest and retraining and to send two divisions to western France for Operation Independence. Seventh and French First Armies established a series of rest centers throughout Alsace, providing their combat troops with the opportunity to get out of the line, take shelter from the weather, and enjoy warm showers and food. For the first time since landing in France, Sixth Army Group had enough American divisions to rotate them out of the line periodically. This addressed what Devers and the army group's G-1 thought was "the main problem of morale and welfare," which was "maintaining units almost constantly in combat."[34]

While the troops rotated through the rest centers, Sixth Army Group prepared for the upcoming offensive. It was scheduled to start in mid-March, allowing time for the weather to improve, units to shift, and supplies to be accumulated. Eisenhower planned for Montgomery's army group, reinforced by U.S. Ninth Army, to attack first. When it reached the Rhine, First Army (in Twelfth Army Group) would begin its offensive to get to the Rhine from Cologne to Bonn, followed by an attack by Third Army to force crossings over the Moselle near Koblenz and drive southeast toward Mainz. Seventh Army would then launch its assault against the Siegfried Line along the southern border of the Rhineland.[35]

Montgomery launched his offensive on 23 February, and within a week, his armies were nearing the Rhine.[36] Eisenhower notified Bradley and Devers that the offensive in the north was progressing well and that Twelfth and Sixth Army Groups should be prepared to attack within a matter of days. First Army attacked toward Cologne and Bonn on 27 February and reached the Rhine on 5 March. German resistance along the entire front was far weaker than expected, and on 9 March First Army captured an intact bridge over the Rhine at Remagen.[37]

Since Sixth Army Group's offensive was to be carried out by Seventh
Army, Patch and his staff prepared the final plan, which Devers approved
on 5 March. Seventh Army's main effort was an attack up the Blies River
valley on the axis of Sarreguemines-Kaiserlautern-Worms. XV Corps would
lead the attack, and Patch ordered preparations to seize crossings over the
Rhine near Worms.[38] An intelligence estimate on 10 February indicated
that all known enemy reserves in the area between the Moselle and the
Rhine, known to the Americans as the "Saar-Palatinate," had been withdrawn. German options were to defend in place or retreat, first into the
Siegfried Line and then across the Rhine.[39]

Patton's offensive against the western flank of the Saar-Palatinate commenced on 5 March and quickly breached the German defenses along the
Moselle. On 15 March, after two days of heavy air attacks by XII Tactical
Air Command, Seventh Army attacked with its three corps abreast. In the
center, XV Corps made rapid progress, capturing many prisoners on the first
day. Patch's troops found the German defenses lightly manned, and they
penetrated the Siegfried Line with little resistance. Due to the rapid success
of Third and Seventh Armies, Patton, Eisenhower, Devers, and Patch met
at Patton's headquarters in Luneville on 17 March and agreed that Patton's
army could continue its drive toward objectives in Seventh Army's assigned
sector. When asked if he minded, Patch replied, "We are all in the same
army and . . . the objective was to destroy the German army."[40]

Devers agreed, but he worried about the possibility of fratricide if the
armies were not properly coordinated. He and Bradley authorized Seventh
and Third Armies, respectively, to deal with each other along the boundary,
and each army allowed its corps to coordinate directly with its neighbor.
Devers believed that Patton might be "up to his old tricks," but he assured
Eisenhower that Sixth Army Group "would cooperate thoroughly with the
Third Army."[41]

The Allied offensives were going well across the front, and "hardly any
semblance of organization remained in German ranks. . . . Highways were
littered with wrecked and burning vehicles and the corpses of men and animals."[42] On 18 March Devers wrote to Georgie, "The Germans are definitely defeated. . . . I of course shall be glad and hope they will send me on
to the Pacific."[43] SHAEF was so certain of success that it issued plans for
the occupation of Germany, code-named Operation Eclipse. Sixth Army
Group began planning for Eclipse in early February, noting that "Operation Eclipse is considered to be a continuation of present military opera-

tions" and that the "exact conditions and situations that will exist at the time the operation becomes effective cannot be foretold."[44]

The offensive picked up steam as Third and Seventh Armies caught the German Seventh and First Armies in the Saar-Palatinate in a hammer-and-anvil operation.[45] Devers was thrilled, and he wrote to Georgie on 21 March, "We have broken the Siegfried Line in several places. . . . Saw Bradley and George and Sandy yesterday. We are working very closely together and in great harmony for we in the 6th A.G. believe only in defeating the Germans and my French Command plays along. . . . Our operations are moving so fast it is hard to keep up even with airplanes as transportation."[46]

The French contribution to the offensive was twofold: they protected the army group's long right flank along the Rhine, and de Lattre provided two divisions commanded by de Monsabert to operate under Seventh Army's control along the west bank of the river. As Seventh Army advanced, the French assumed more defensive frontage along the Rhine.[47] From the French perspective, the French forces moving north with Seventh Army provided access to crossing points over the Rhine. This was fortunate, because de Gaulle expected de Lattre to force a crossing as soon as possible so that France would have some say in the occupation of Germany when the war ended.

French forces also carried out two other missions assigned to Sixth Army Group by SHAEF. The French "Army Detachment of the Alps" was responsible for defending the French borders with Switzerland and Italy, and the "Army Detachment of the Atlantic" was responsible for eliminating the German pocket around the Gironde estuary in western France. The Alpine front was a static defensive mission, but operations in western France were designed to destroy the German garrisons around Bordeaux. The campaign against the German garrisons on the coast had originally been known as Operation Independence and had been planned for December. Operation Independence, however, was postponed repeatedly during the heavy fighting of November, December, and January. Once the Colmar pocket was eliminated, French forces could be sent west to reinforce the Army Detachment of the Atlantic.[48]

In late March Sixth Army Group's G-3, Reuben Jenkins, worked with French general de Larminat to plan the offensive against the German-held pockets on the Atlantic coast. General Leclerc's 2nd DB joined de Larminat to assist in the campaign, while the First Tactical Air Force provided close air support.[49] Operation Independence was carried out from 15 April through

2 May. FFI forces, which had been formed into brigades, and the 2nd DB were responsible for the brunt of the fighting, with support from American artillery and aviation units. Sixth Army Group's history notes, "Detachment of the Atlantic carried out Operation Independence on schedule as planned, and was completely successful. . . . The innumerable problems of organization, coordination and supply for its varied elements were solved not without difficulty and with much skill and intelligence."[50]

De Larminat's offensive was a good example of how well Sixth Army Group worked with the French. In addition to artillery and air support, American units provided the bulk of the logistical support for the FFI forces, which accounted for the majority of the army detachment's soldiers. These French soldiers deserved the credit bestowed on them by Sixth Army Group's history: "The relatively inexperienced FFI troops of the command, after a miserable winter of inactivity under fire, carried out their parts of the operation successfully. They derived much benefit from the opportunity to take part in a full-scale operation."[51] Devers, Jenkins, and the army group staff deserved credit as well.

Crossing the Rhine

German resistance west of the Rhine ended on the night of 22 March, when the Germans destroyed the last bridge over the river. Seventh and Third Armies captured more than 90,000 Germans and killed thousands more in the week of 15–22 March. The coordination of two army groups by Eisenhower and his subordinates "provided a remarkable example of offensive maneuver."[52] Eisenhower's personal participation in discussions with his army group commanders was a welcome relief from his method of running operations during the fall and winter.

On the night of 22 March, Third Army crossed the Rhine near Oppenheim and established a solid bridgehead against light opposition. Seventh Army cleared the remaining enemy from pockets of resistance west of the Rhine and began moving boat and bridge units toward the river along congested roads. Patch ordered Haislip's veteran XV Corps to launch a two-division assault across the river near Worms on 26 March. The 3rd and 45th Infantry Divisions, supported by intense artillery and air attacks and duplex-drive swimming tanks, launched their assaults at 0230 and quickly broke the thin German defenses along the east bank in two places. By nightfall, the 45th Division had advanced eight miles, cutting the auto-

Figure 15.3. Drive to the Elbe, 4 April–7 May 1945

bahn running from Darmstadt to Mannheim. Seventh Army engineers rapidly installed a 1,040-foot-long heavy pontoon bridge and a 948-foot-long treadway bridge over the Rhine, allowing the 12th Armored Division to cross and exploit the breach in German defenses.[53]

In twelve days, Seventh Army had broken through the Siegfried Line,

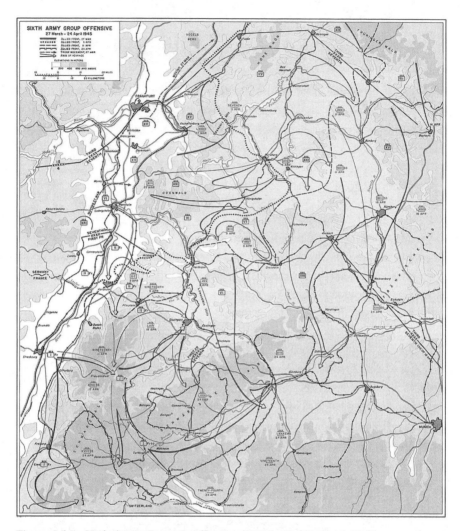

Figure 15.4. Sixth Army Group's offensive, 27 March–24 April 1945

cleared the west bank of the Rhine, and established a large bridgehead on the east bank. On 27 March the 45th Infantry Division made contact with Third Army units near Aschaffenburg, thirty miles east of the Rhine, and the Twenty-First and Twelfth Army Groups closed the ring around the Ruhr pocket. By the end of March, the German Seventh and First Armies had ceased to be effective combat formations, leaving only scattered resistance in front of U.S. Third and Seventh Armies.[54]

Devers was present for Seventh Army's assault across the Rhine, and he wrote to Georgie the same day, "Just returned from a reconnaissance of my area and we are on the move in a big way. The Rhine is behind us." As he traveled through the Palatinate, he found that "the roads are full of people, generally young and middle age returning to their homes in Germany or France. Many of these people were forced to labor for Germany, so many of them are Poles, Russians, Czechs. All look badly [nourished] and our problems of getting them placed and fed is exceedingly large. . . . In spite of this element I get a great elation in seeing the destruction which we have caused to the German cities."[55]

American military government teams followed on the heels of Seventh Army's combat units. As they entered German cities, they were faced with daunting tasks. Conditions in the Palatinate were "chaotic." "In Zweibrucken . . . the entire business district was razed." Water and sewer services were cut, there was no civil government, and thousands of newly liberated slave laborers and prisoners were streaming into the city. In Homburg, "dead horses and human corpses were common throughout the business district," and fires raged out of control.[56]

Military government teams operating at army and corps levels were responsible for establishing order, feeding survivors, and screening German civilian officials for those who had not been thoroughly tainted by Nazi activities. Antiaircraft troops, with little to shoot at, were brought in to establish security and to stop looting. The government teams established camps to feed displaced persons and organized civilian work parties to clear debris and bodies from the streets of towns and villages. "German civilians in general were found to be subdued and in a state of terror."[57]

For the remainder of the war, civil affairs were a major concern for Allied commanders. As their armies pushed into Germany, Devers reminded Patch and de Lattre that the establishment of a military government was a "command responsibility." Caring for the tens of thousands of displaced persons and concentration camp victims was also a priority, "simultaneous with the destruction of the enemy in the field." They were instructed to use all the resources at their disposal, "insofar as the military situation permits," to establish law and order.[58] Devers also "received numerous complaints from French authorities concerning looting and destruction of civilian property" by American troops in France. In response, he ordered his senior American commanders to stop such actions immediately and to see that all French property was returned to its rightful owners.[59]

On 27 March Sixth Army Group issued orders for a continuation of the offensive. Seventh Army was instructed to encourage aggressive independent action by its corps and to be ready to advance in several directions, depending on the situation. French First Army was directed to regroup, cross the Rhine in the Germersheim area on order, and then seize Karlsruhe and Pforzheim. Three days later, Devers ordered de Lattre to speed up preparations for a crossing of the Rhine near Speyer. Anticipating this order, de Lattre had already set his forces in motion for a crossing the next morning.[60] This came as a surprise to Sixth Army Group, but it was possible because de Lattre took advantage of the German disarray caused by Seventh Army's advances farther north. The French crossings took the Germans completely by surprise, although the enemy fought stubbornly to defeat them.[61]

De Lattre's decision to accelerate his assault over the Rhine came in response to de Gaulle's order to cross, "even if the Americans are not agreeable and even if you have to cross it in boats."[62] De Gaulle feared that France would not get into Germany before the end of the war and therefore would not be assigned an occupation zone. By having French First Army advance at least as far as Stuttgart, he believed he would be in a stronger position with the Anglo-American Allies over the issue of a French zone. De Gaulle's desire to use French First Army to achieve strategic political goals would badly complicate Devers and de Lattre's relationship in the final weeks of the war.

The French assault on Easter morning, 31 March, succeeded in spite of a severe shortage of bridging and assault boats and fierce German resistance. Brooks helped de Monsabert with bridging and boats and allowed French armor and artillery units to cross on bridges in VI Corps' sector.[63] Devers and the other American leaders of Sixth Army Group were more than willing to let the French take part in the heavy fighting inside Germany. Over the next five days, the French expanded their bridgehead and pushed south to capture Karlsruhe. More than 130,000 French troops in four divisions had joined Seventh Army in southern Germany.[64]

Just as his army succeeded in crossing the Rhine, de Lattre created unnecessary friction when he issued a notice "requiring all German military personnel within the zone" occupied by his army to surrender by a certain date or face draconian measures. Devers took exception to the notice because it stated that every German soldier who did not surrender "would be held responsible as a partisan . . . without regard to his clothing, open carriage of arms or other circumstances." He also found it unacceptable that "every German soldier in civilian clothes will be considered a spy and shot." Devers ordered de Lattre to amend his notice to fit the rules of land warfare and to conform to Sixth Army Group's "Directive for Military Government of Germany," dated 2 December 1944.[65] De Lattre did so grudgingly.

The Final Offensive into Germany

On 1 April Brigadier General Reuben Jenkins, Sixth Army Group's operations officer, visited headquarters to "determine what SHAEF was thinking" about future actions. The army group's planning staff had concluded that Sixth Army Group should swing to the southeast, into southern Germany, and that French First Army should join Seventh Army in this maneuver. The SHAEF planners generally agreed with this concept.[66] Jenkins estimated that the remnants of the three German armies facing Sixth Army Group numbered roughly 22,000 combat infantrymen, while the two armies in Devers's army group totaled more than 600,000 men and twenty full-strength divisions.[67]

On 2 April, as the Ruhr pocket was eliminated by Twenty-First and Twelfth Army Groups, SHAEF issued orders for further operations. Eisenhower's directive ignited the last major Allied dispute over strategy in the European theater. Montgomery had assumed that his Twenty-First Army Group would cross the Rhine and then drive to Berlin with the help of Ninth Army. But when Ninth and First Armies encircled the Ruhr and most of German Army Group B, Eisenhower decided to move Ninth Army back to Twelfth Army Group's command and to direct Montgomery to advance northeast, toward Bremen and Jutland. The supreme commander made it clear that the British army group's task was to protect the northern flank of Bradley's army group, not to drive beyond the Elbe River toward Berlin. Bradley was to eliminate the German forces in the Ruhr pocket and then launch the main effort of the Western armies across central Germany toward Leipzig and the upper Elbe. Sixth Army Group was to protect Bradley's right flank, clear German forces from the Black Forest, and advance southeast on a Nuremberg-Regensburg-Lenz axis.[68]

After a flurry of ineffectual efforts to change Eisenhower's main effort to a thrust toward Berlin, British leaders concluded that his operational plan would stand. Montgomery, who finally got the message, agreed to execute his portion of the plan and wrote to Eisenhower, "It is quite clear to me what you want."[69]

Sixth Army Group issued instructions on 3 April for its armies' roles in the drive across Germany. Seventh Army's left flank corps was to protect Twelfth Army Group's right flank along a line from Ludwigsburg to Bayreuth. Its center corps was to capture Nuremberg and continue south toward Linz, while its right-hand corps was to drive south along the Neckar River from Heidelberg and cut off German forces in the Stuttgart area. One French corps was supposed to clear the Black Forest and the east bank of the Rhine to the Swiss border, while the other captured Karlsruhe and Pforzheim and prepared to move east toward Stuttgart.[70] Both armies continued to advance in their zones for the next week, but they waited to launch the final offensive until the Ruhr pocket was cleared and Twelfth Army Group was ready to move toward the Elbe in strength.

From his forward headquarters in Heidelberg, Devers gave Georgie a picture of the situation in early April:

> Here I am living in one of the most livable homes of one of the most successful and wealthy Germans. . . . The people are miserable and scared and they have a right to be so for they know what they did to others and those Russians, Poles, French are numerous and free, having dropped their work the day our Armies passed by them. Results, fields well prepared for spring harvest but no one to work them at present. We have a real problem, to get the people back to work on the farms and to get the displaced millions back to their homes and to feed those that need it. . . . How will we ever put this Europe on the right track?[71]

In a message to Marshall, Devers described some of the horrors American troops were witnessing in Germany:

> Recently we overran a hospital at Heppenheim which contained 288 of our American wounded, along with many French, Russian, Polish and Italian prisoners. I found that the men had literally starved for lack of food and that this had been deliberate. . . . I removed our wounded immediately by air to our hospitals in the Paris area. . . . The roads are crowded with displaced persons working their way toward the Rhine. . . . Our advance is so rapid that this makes a terrific problem for us. In a remarkably short time, nevertheless, we seem to be able to get some semblance of order, on the surface at

least. . . . The destruction of the larger German cities by air is complete. There is literally nothing left in those cities.[72]

A week later, Devers let Georgie know that their son-in-law had been shot by a German sniper. Fortunately, "the bullet went through his wrist and did hardly any damage. He kept right on with his job and his fingers and wrist are OK though he says he has a time getting dressed."[73] Alex's wounding was a reminder that Germans were still resisting the Allies' advances. Another 10,677 American soldiers were killed in battle in April, including 1,710 soldiers of Sixth Army Group.[74] These losses became more personal for Devers when he learned on 14 April that Major General Willis Crittenberger's son had been killed. He lamented to Georgie, "All our Army sons are going it seems."[75]

Most of Seventh Army's forces still were encountering organized resistance in the first two weeks of April. XV Corps had to overcome strong defenses in Aschaffenburg and was forced to commit a regiment from the 45th Infantry Division to a three-day, house-to-house fight to clear the city. Milburn's XXI Corps had to fight for two days to get into Wurzburg, which finally fell on 7 April. Farther south, VI Corps ran into strong resistance near Heilbronn on 4 April, which it took eight days to overcome.[76] By midmonth, however, it was evident that the German army's command system had been shattered, leaving its various units fighting a series of disjointed and hopeless defensive battles.[77]

Sixth Army Group's G-2 noted on 7 April, "The enemy is completely restricted to a single capability: To delay his defeat. . . . The existence of strategic reserves within Germany is now certainly no longer credible." The three German armies facing Sixth Army Group totaled fewer than 30,000 combat troops on a front of more than 200 kilometers. For the remainder of the war, the only serious opposition came from scattered garrisons in some of the major cities. On 18 April the last German forces in the Ruhr pocket surrendered. Bradley's forces captured 317,000 Germans; thousands more had died in the fighting.[78]

On 15 April, when it was clear that the battle against the Ruhr pocket was coming to a successful conclusion, Eisenhower modified his plans. The British army group was to continue its drive northeastward to the Elbe, seize Hamburg, and be prepared to liberate Denmark. Bradley's armies were to defend a line along the Elbe and Mulde Rivers while launching "a powerful thrust to join hands with the Russians in the Danube valley and seize Salzburg." Sixth Army Group was to shift its left boundary to the south and concentrate Seventh Army in a drive southeastward to overrun eastern Bavaria, seize the Brenner Pass, and occupy western Austria. Sixth Army Group's objective was to prevent the retreating Germans from establishing a "national redoubt" in the Alps for a last stand.[79]

Devers learned of the change in plans on 14 April, while he and Jenkins were at Twelfth Army Group discussing future operations with Bradley. Bradley had been alerted by SHAEF about the change in his army group's direction, and he shared this information with Devers. The next day Devers returned to Heidelberg and set his and Patch's staffs to work preparing to move Seventh Army into a narrower zone facing in a new direction. He then flew to SHAEF to discuss the new plan with Eisenhower. Eisenhower agreed with Devers that Sixth Army Group should undertake the operation against the German Nineteenth Army's rear as soon as possible. The supreme commander also reinforced Devers with two divisions and made it clear that he wanted Seventh Army moved out of Third Army's new zone of advance as quickly as practicable. Devers departed "immediately" for Bradley's headquarters to arrange details for the shift in forces that involved all of XV Corps and half of XXI Corps.[80]

When Devers and Jenkins reached Twelfth Army Group, they found Bradley, Patton, and Hodges discussing the shift of forces. "Within about 30 minutes the two Army Group commanders had completed their arrangements," and Bradley issued oral instructions to Patton for his shift to the southeast. Devers returned by airplane to Heidelberg by 1700 hours and met with Patch and his G-3. During a short conference with Patch, Devers stressed the need for Seventh Army to cut off German Nineteenth Army as quickly as possible while shifting its two left-hand corps to the south. With these oral instructions, Patch set his forces in motion in the new direction before receiving Letter of Instruction 14 the next day.[81]

The manner in which Devers handled this situation represented a major step forward in his relationships with his boss and his neighboring army group commander. By flying from Heidelberg to visit Bradley, then back to his own headquarters to alert his staff, then on to SHAEF to meet Eisenhower, and then back to confer with Bradley before returning to meet Patch in Heidelberg, all within twenty-four hours, Devers enabled Sixth Army Group to react swiftly before receiving written orders. He also minimized the chance of confusion or misunderstanding in a very fluid tactical situation.

To continue Seventh Army's drive, Haislip swung XV Corps to the southeast and headed to Bamberg and Nuremberg. Haislip's forces overran Bamberg with little resistance, but when they approached Nuremberg, they found that the Germans had reinforced the garrison with the 2nd Mountain Division and remnants of the 17th SS Panzer Grenadier Division.[82] On 16 April the 3rd and 45th Infantry Divisions encircled Nuremberg and began to probe its defenses. In the words of the official history, "It was a grueling fight for Nuremberg, made all the more difficult by deadly anti-aircraft fire directed against the men on the ground. Once the ring of flak guns was broken, the fight developed into the slow, often costly, business of clearing one crumbling building after another." It took two days for the 3rd Infantry Division to reach and breach the medieval walls of the inner city. On 20 April, Hitler's birthday, the "Rock of the Marne" Division defeated the last German counterattack and cleared the city.[83]

Meanwhile, on the army's right flank, Brooks's VI Corps pushed south along the Neckar to cut off Stuttgart. Sixth Army Group's plan called for the French to finish clearing the Black Forest and, once VI Corps had cut off the German retreat from Stuttgart, to attack Stuttgart from the west and southwest.[84] With these maneuvers, Devers hoped to encircle the remnants of German Nineteenth Army in the Stuttgart area and the southern Black Forest.[85] Jenkins summarized the intent of the plan and the anticipated role of the French: "The original concept of this operation was that the initial effort by First French Army would be more in the nature of a holding effort which would indicate weakness and encourage the German to stay in his position until VI US Corps was in proper position. . . . [This] was explained in considerable detail to General de Lattre personally at a conference in his office on the afternoon of 17 April."[86]

But de Lattre had other ideas. Believing that such a plan "destroyed all benefits of the maneuver of the last ten days," he ordered de Monsabert to begin his attack against the Stuttgart area from the west and southwest on 18 April.[87] In Jenkins's words, "General de Lattre's premature action to the west of Stuttgart carried his troops across the Neckar into the zone of action of the VI Corps." The French general took this action in spite of several cables from Devers ordering him to stop. "As a result a goodly portion of the German *Nineteenth Army* escaped to the southeast."[88] Without the help of VI Corps, it took the French three days to clear the Germans out of Stuttgart. When Devers ordered de Lattre to turn the city over to VI Corps, the French general refused, based on orders from de Gaulle.[89]

Nonetheless, Allied advances continued across the front against diminishing resistance. Back home, however, Georgie felt that "V-E Day seems like a mirage—retreating in time as the armies advance in space." She shared her hopes for the end of the war, as well as Jake's view of the Germans, with her sister-in-law Kitts: "Now that we are in Germany we find it's not the Nazis who are monsters, but the German people—all of them—who are criminals and bestial things we hate to think of as men. . . . Jamie writes that their doctors are cruel, sadistic monsters—He has investigated their hospitals and prisons. . . . The sights he has seen in the prison camps have made him free of any consideration of the enemy—soldier or civilian."[90]

In war, depravity and bestiality affect both sides. After the French seized Stuttgart, they initially failed to establish order among the 800,000 residents and the tens of thousands of newly liberated slave laborers in the city. Reports soon reached Devers that French troops had committed more than 30,000 rapes, and the city was out of control. Devers sent the 100th Infantry Division into Stuttgart to establish order and a military government, and he ordered de Lattre to withdraw the French troops. De Lattre protested the establishment of a U.S. military government and informed Devers that de Gaulle had ordered him to hold Stuttgart as part of a de facto French occupation zone.[91]

After learning of the situation in Stuttgart, Devers "sent a stern cable to General de Lattre" and called Smith to explain the situation.[92] He then traveled to Stuttgart to investigate. He recorded in his diary: "Upon arriving in Stuttgart on April 27th I immediately contacted General Patch and General Burress [commander of the 100th Infantry Division]. . . . I had with me Colonel Lodge. I verified facts and found them to be substantially as stated . . . but greatly exaggerated." There had been 1,500 to 2,000 rapes and much looting. Devers and Lodge visited the French headquarters, and Devers told the French commander, "I desired very much in the interest of the French nation that he take immediate steps to correct these conditions."[93] The French executed a few rapists but continued to ignore Devers's and Eisenhower's orders to evacuate the city.[94] Devers was forced to accept the situation, and he changed the boundary between the French and Seventh Army, giving Stuttgart to the French. He left Lodge in Stuttgart for several days to ensure that the French restored order.[95]

The French occupation of Stuttgart undermined Allied cohesion. Eisenhower made this clear in a letter to de Gaulle on 28 April:

As you are aware, orders were issued by General Devers to General de Lattre de Tassigny to evacuate Stuttgart. . . . I regret to learn that because of instructions received direct from you General de Lattre has declined to obey the orders of his Army Group Commander. . . . Under the circumstances, I must of course accept the situation, as I myself am unwilling to take action which would reduce the effectiveness of the military effort against Germany. . . . I can do nothing else than fully inform the Combined Chiefs of Staff of this development, and to point out that I can no longer count with certainty upon the operational use of any French forces they may contemplate equipping in the future.[96]

De Gaulle responded by telling Eisenhower that the military use of the city and its administration were not the same thing, and no one was denying Devers the use of Stuttgart for logistical and administrative purposes.[97] The French leader also took Eisenhower's letter as acceptance, "with regret," of a French garrison in the city.[98]

De Lattre later excused his disobedience by reasoning that "since all fighting in that region had ceased, we were no longer in the operational circumstances in which I was subordinated to the Allied Command." Instead, he deemed it a political issue and felt obligated to follow the orders of the French government and de Gaulle, who instructed him "to keep a French garrison in Stuttgart and to establish a military government there."[99]

While the Stuttgart incident was unfolding, Seventh Army continued south with VI Corps, headed toward Ulm to seize crossings over the Danube. On 23 April, however, Seventh Army notified Sixth Army Group that French armor units were driving east toward Ulm, well inside VI Corps' sector. Devers again ordered de Lattre to halt his advance into the American zone so that VI Corps could continue south. De Lattre again ignored Devers's order. Fortunately, when French troops encountered outposts of the 10th Armored Division near Ehingen on 23 April, the American troops recognized the intruders as French and did not open fire. On 24 April the American 44th Infantry and 10th Armored Divisions and several French platoons seized Ulm. Brooks allowed the French to fly their national colors over the city's old fort, as Napoleon had done in 1805 after defeating the Austrians. With honor satisfied, de Lattre withdrew his troops into his own sector.[100]

Franco-American relations were further harmed by de Lattre's decision to send forces to Ulm in spite of the boundary between his and Patch's armies. However, de Gaulle's insistence on seizing territory in Germany to force his Western Allies to give France a zone of occupation achieved the desired result. In June the French received a zone of occupation in the Rhineland, west of the Rhine. But in the words of Rick Atkinson, "France and the United States . . . would emerge from the war as wary allies, their mutual distrust destined to shape postwar geopolitics for decades."[101]

In spite of these political setbacks, the campaign continued to its inevitable end. Sixth Army Group's G-2 intelligence estimate for 28 April noted that German Army Group G, "opposite 6th Army Group failed to receive sufficient reinforcements during the week to aid in either the establishment of a front line or even to replace the approximately 78,600 odd troops lost as prisoners of war during the period."[102] After crossing the Danube in a number of places, Seventh Army advanced across terrain lacking "any cross corridors of strong natural defensive positions" from which the Germans could reestablish defensive lines. Although rumors flew that the enemy might strongly defend Munich, there was growing evidence that the "hold of the Nazi overlords upon the *Wehrmacht* and the people is definitely weakening, particularly in Bavaria."[103]

There was plenty of evidence to support the G-2's optimistic estimate. During the month of April, Seventh Army captured 265,556 enemy soldiers, and the French captured another 109,393.[104] German civilians saw the writing on the wall. In the cities of Augsburg and Munich, they organized resistance groups to force the garrisons to surrender rather than allow the remnants of their cities to be destroyed in house-to-house fighting. In Munich a series of unconnected revolts took place beginning on the evening of 27 April. Although the Waffen SS units in the city fought back, the insurgents succeeded in preventing the die-hard Nazis from destroying the city's bridges. American troops arrived on 29 April, and by the end of the next day, they had eliminated German resistance.[105]

As the 42nd and 45th Infantry Divisions approached Munich, they overran a Nazi death camp near Dachau, where more than 30,000 emaciated inmates were still alive. Devers visited Dachau and described it to Georgie:

> The camp is located at the intersection of a big fine woods. It is on a railroad. On the sidings were 41 cars—along the track here and there were dead bodies of starved people. Twenty-one of the

cars had been unloaded but 20 still had some 100 dead women, children, men, young and old, some naked, all poorly and lightly clothed if at all. . . . Inside the walled camp were indescribable sights. . . . Kennels where the dogs were left who guarded or attacked the poor wretches who were confined in the camp. Gas chambers, with a prisoner who operated them telling you what he did without reason to really know what he was doing. Clothes taken from the dead bodies in great piles being fumigated to be given to other prisoners—a horrible mess. Two large rooms about 20 feet square full of dead bodies—all had died of starvation or the result of poor care.[106]

Such scenes were encountered by Allied armies throughout Germany and central Europe. American and British commanders quickly concluded that the German atrocities had to be documented. As Jake told Georgie, "We are showing this camp to all soldiers, Germans, Congressmen, Senators of all nations. . . . For the German people to say that—first they are not Nazi— Second that they did not know of these things cannot be accepted. You can smell these camps for miles and there are about 10 of them in my area alone. Dachau is the worst."[107]

When Dachau was liberated, the surviving inmates hacked to death as many of the camp guards as they could seize. Rabbi David Eichhorn, an American army chaplain who arrived at Dachau on the day of its liberation, wrote, "We stood aside and watched while those guards were beaten to death."[108] When the camp guards surrendered to the 45th Infantry Division, American soldiers, in a blind rage, lined them up along a wall and murdered many of them in cold blood. According to Seventh Army's history, when the 157th Infantry Regiment approached the camp, "a stiff fire fight developed between the Americans and the SS guards, some 300 of whom were killed."[109] The reality is that the troops took justice into their own hands. They had seen too much, and the thin veneer of discipline broke down. Even American doctors refused to treat wounded SS guards.[110]

When Patch heard of the American atrocities, he sent the Seventh Army's inspector general to investigate. The inspector general concluded that at least twenty-eight camp guards had been gunned down in cold blood. However, even though a judge advocate officer confirmed that "a violation of the letter of international law" had occurred, not a single American soldier was charged with a crime. General Haislip stated, "The unbalancing effects of the horrors and shock of Dachau on combat troops already fatigued by more than thirty days' of continuous action" accounted for the breakdown of discipline and the ensuing murders.[111]

As XV Corps liberated Dachau and captured Munich, Brooks's VI Corps drove into Austria and opened the Alpine passes to Italy. Initially, the Allies had planned for the British and American armies in Italy to fight their way into Austria. However, due to the German forces' disintegration in southern Germany and their continued resistance in northern Italy, SHAEF gave Sixth Army Group the mission of occupying Austria. This, the SHAEF planners concluded, would be the quickest way to overrun the Alpine regions, where they thought the Germans might attempt a last-ditch defense in a "national redoubt."[112]

As VI Corps advanced, more than 30,000 German soldiers surrendered each day. Brooks's advance confirmed that the Germans had not prepared a final national redoubt. The fight had gone out of the German army and the German people. The mess left behind by the "thousand-year Reich" is still hard to imagine. Devers, who was with Brooks in the Alps on 29 April, had seen the evidence of German barbarity firsthand, and he wrote to Georgie, "The horrors and brutality of the Nazi people is everything the papers say. . . . All Germans are responsible and all who fought with them. . . . Again, I say the news reports are not exaggerated."[113]

Across Seventh Army's front, the only major delays in the advance were blown bridges, an occasional antitank ambush, and clogged mountain roads. "Unseasonable cold and heavy rain, often mixed with snow," slowed the advance more than the enemy did. The roads were crowded with German troops and civilians fleeing from the advancing Russians, forcing Seventh Army to deal with an increasing torrent of displaced persons and prisoners of war.[114]

The final week of the war in Europe saw Seventh Army driving south to the Alpine passes, with its left-hand forces aiming for Salzburg, the center heading toward Innsbruck, and the right-hand corps moving toward Landeck and the pass into northern Italy. De Lattre, hoping to garner additional glory for the French and to occupy more enemy territory, tried to send an armored division toward the Alpine pass into Italy near Landeck. This time, however, "in an ill-disguised artifice not lost on General de Lattre, the 6th Army Group directed a change in the map coordinates" of the boundary between Seventh and French First Armies. This move denied the French access to the passes into western Austria.[115]

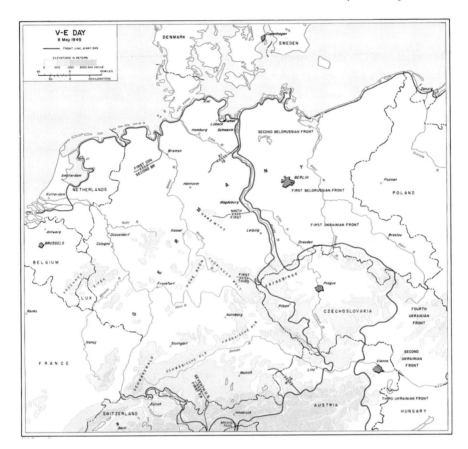

Figure 15.5. V-E Day, 8 May 1945

At the same time, Seventh Army units controlled the road networks to Austria, forcing the French to continue south to the German-Swiss border. On 2 May the German forces in Italy officially surrendered, and a civilian resistance movement took control of Innsbruck, saving it from house-to-house combat.[116] De Lattre then made a last, desperate attempt to get forces across the Alps by sending a ski-equipped French platoon over snow-blocked back roads toward Landeck. The effort was futile, as American forces reached Landeck and then linked up with Fifth Army troops coming from Italy on 3 May. To the east, Salzburg and Oberammergau surrendered, and troops from XV and XXI Corps converged on Hitler's mountain retreat in Berchtesgaden. "It was congestion, not resistance that slowed entry into Berchtesgaden."[117]

The German Surrender

During the last week of April, Allied armies advanced into Germany from the west and east. On 25 April American and Russian soldiers met southeast of Torgau, Germany. First Army units stopped along the Elbe River, in compliance with orders from Eisenhower, who had notified the Russians that the Elbe would be the eastern edge of the advance in central Germany. Farther north, Montgomery's Twenty-First Army Group drove to the Baltic Sea, east of Denmark, preventing a Soviet advance into that country. In the south, Third Army drove into Czechoslovakia, while Sixth Army Group overran western Austria.[118]

On 3 May SHAEF informed Devers that the Germans had asked to whom they should surrender their forces in Austria. At that point, the Allies had agreed that each army group would accept the surrender of the enemy forces in its sector. Therefore, Devers's chief of staff, Major General Barr, notified the Germans that they should arrange for the surrender of Army Group G to Sixth Army Group.[119] Barr and Jenkins drew up the terms of surrender on the night of 3–4 May. At the same time, the Germans were advised to travel to XV Corps headquarters in Harr, near Munich, to meet Devers for the surrender. During the afternoon of 4 May, Devers flew to Harr and sent Jenkins to give Brooks a copy of the surrender terms, which he would use in his negotiations for the surrender of the German Nineteenth Army.[120] The terms called for an immediate cessation of hostilities and the unconditional surrender of all forces under the command of the German army group.

On the afternoon of 5 May, Generals Devers, Patch, Haislip, and Jenkins, along with several other senior officers, met the German delegation at a small factory near Harr. The Germans were handed a copy of the terms of surrender, and the head of the German delegation, General Herman Foertsch, requested and was given thirty minutes to study the document in an adjoining room. At the end of the allotted time, Foertsch and his staff returned and sat down at a long table opposite Devers and his senior officers.[121] "Looking steadily at Foertsch, General Devers asked him if he had read and understood the terms of surrender." Foertsch replied that he had and then suggested several changes that would benefit both sides. Foertsch explained that because his forces were so scattered and his communications so disrupted, it would take more than a few hours to get the news of the cessation of hostilities and the surrender to them. He also asked that German officers and military police be allowed to keep their pistols and that armed German guards be placed at the sites where the Germans were to turn over their arms, ammunition, and equipment. This was intended to prevent those materials from falling into the wrong hands and thereby threatening law and order. Devers accepted these modifications.[122] Then, looking coldly at Foertsch, Devers said, "There must be no misunderstanding of this point. This is no armistice—this is unconditional surrender. Do you understand?" Foertsch stiffened, his facial muscles worked, and he flushed. After nearly a minute, he got himself under control and said, "I can assure you, Sir, that no power is left at my disposal to prevent it."[123] With this exchange complete, Devers, Patch, and Haislip signed the draft document for the Allies, and Foertsch did so for the Germans. After lunch, final copies of the terms of surrender, with Foertsch's suggestions incorporated, were signed by both parties.[124]

De Lattre was perhaps the only person unhappy with the way the Germans had surrendered in Austria and southern Germany. He believed German Twenty-Fourth Army should have surrendered to French First Army, since de Lattre's forces had been opposite that army in the line. The Germans refused, saying that Twenty-Fourth Army no longer existed; its forces were part of Nineteenth Army, which surrendered to Brooks's VI Corps on 5 May. It was clear to Devers that Foertsch's surrender in Harr applied to all the forces in Army Group G, including Nineteenth Army. Consequently, Devers refused to surrender the former commander of German Twenty-Fourth Army to de Lattre.

Over the next twenty-four hours, word of the surrender was passed to the German and Allied forces in Sixth Army Group's sector. "The war was over for hundreds of thousands of soldiers. It ended soon thereafter for all the soldiers in Europe."[125] On 7 May Eisenhower accepted the overall surrender of the German forces at his headquarters in Reims in a ceremony with Russian and British representatives but no French participants. The next day, another surrender ceremony was held in Berlin, presided over by the Russians, with German, American, British, and French representatives. Fittingly, de Lattre represented the French army and nation.[126]

The official "Victory in Europe" day was 8 May. Eisenhower's order of the day to every member of the Allied Expeditionary Forces accurately summed up the campaign in western Europe:

The crusade on which we embarked in the early summer of 1944 has reached its glorious conclusion. It is my especial privilege . . .

to commend each of you for valiant performance of duty. . . . Your accomplishments at sea, in the air, on the ground and in the field of supply have astonished the world. . . . You have confused, defeated and destroyed your savagely fighting foe. On the road to victory you have endured every discomfort and privation and have surmounted every obstacle. . . . Full victory in EUROPE has been attained.[127]

With a sense of relief, millions of American, Russian, British, and French soldiers awoke to a world without shell fire. The war was over in Europe, but the challenges of reestablishing peace and rebuilding Europe were profound. The immediate task was to deal with the millions of displaced people wandering around Germany and central Europe. During the final months of the war, more than 6 million German soldiers and airmen surrendered to the Western Allies. The Russians captured another 2 million. British, American, and French armies had to deal with at least 6 million non-Germans liberated from forced labor throughout Germany. They also liberated about 2 million Allied prisoners of war and had to deal with another 2 million German civilians who had fled the Russian advance.[128] The miracle is that they dealt with such a massive situation with efficiency and a fair amount of order.

The German surrenders brought the fighting to a sudden end. Devers was certainly glad that the European war was over. However, he was "in a letdown mood because after seeing Dachau, Munich and the hundreds of thousands of prisoners we have captured, our own Allied prisoners released, and the thousands of displaced persons in this part of Germany, I am convinced that . . . Europe has been set back a hundred years." Typically, he reacted by helping to get as many German soldiers as possible back to work on the railroads and farms, and he "strongly recommended that the miners and useful citizens get back to their occupations in order that food may be provided for this part of the world."[129]

Fortunately, SHAEF and the Combined Chiefs of Staff had done a great deal of preparation for the end of the war. Operation Eclipse was SHAEF's plan for the occupation of Germany. Originally prepared in November 1944, it included steps for the initial disarmament of the German forces, the establishment of law and order, the return of Allied forces into the zones of occupation already agreed on, and the eventual complete disarmament of Germany.[130] After the initial occupation of southern Germany and the disarming of German forces there, Devers and Sixth Army Group headquarters prepared to carry out new assignments in Europe. But the situation in Europe and the world changed rapidly, and events overtook the well-laid plans of the War Department for the redeployment and disbandment of forces.

16

Postwar Challenges

The top priority for the U.S. Army in May 1945 was to withdraw most of its forces from Europe in an orderly but rapid fashion. Many units, such as First Army's headquarters and staff, were headed to the Pacific, where they would take part in the invasion of Japan. Hundreds of thousands of men in Europe were slated to return to the United States for demobilization. In the meantime, they experienced an inevitable emotional letdown after spending weeks, months, or years fighting the Germans and struggling to survive in harsh conditions. Since these men would have little to do while waiting for redeployment or demobilization, Devers alerted his commanders about the potential for serious morale problems, and he reminded them that leaders in the chain of command must avoid "loose talk and criticism" of the situation. Devers directed his subordinates to stress "the appearance, discipline, and attitude of the soldiers" as standards changed "from the present battle standard to one more nearly resembling that of peace time." Sensing that there would be a "natural tendency for a letdown in discipline," Devers advised Patch to organize rest camps as soon as possible and to provide forty-eight-hour passes to Paris. He also authorized the liberal use of motor transportation for groups of soldiers to visit their former battlefields in France or to travel to the Army Recreation Center at Garmisch-Partenkirchen.[1]

As Devers issued these instructions, the army thought it had time to implement an orderly redeployment schedule. Political factors in the United States immediately got in the way, however, as Congress and the American people demanded a far more rapid demobilization program. As Marshall wrote to Eisenhower, "I fear the weight of public opinion in the U.S. will be such that unless the task is handled properly we may be forced to take measures that will interfere with redeployment and result in the prolongation of the Japanese war."[2] Eisenhower had hoped to have a month after the end of hostilities before moving the first units to the Pacific and sending home those soldiers who had served overseas the longest. But the War Department ordered him to begin demobilization on 12 May. At least

17,500 men were sent home in May, and another 35,000 returned to the United States in June. The War Department also established a quota and a timetable: 240,000 men were to be redeployed to the Pacific theater in June, and the entire process was to be completed within twelve months.[3]

Occupation and Redeployment

According to SHAEF's plan for postwar operations in Europe, Sixth Army Group's mission was to organize and direct redeployment training for the units that would be transferred to the Pacific. Twelfth Army Group was charged with the tasks of occupying Germany and redeploying units to the United States for demobilization.[4]

Sixth Army Group had commenced preparations for its postwar mission well before the end of hostilities. In April a planning staff had been organized and sent to Paris to coordinate with the SHAEF staff. By 10 May, this planning group had presented its plan to SHAEF for approval, and Sixth Army Group's Training Memorandum 1 had been published. On 18 May, however, SHAEF realized that due to the accelerated redeployment and demobilization schedules, the army group would have only 723 units to train instead of the 3,360 initially planned for, and most of those were small service units. As a result, Eisenhower decided it was not necessary for Sixth Army Group to oversee the program. Instead, each major command would be responsible for training its own units being redeployed.[5]

Meanwhile, in preparation for its training mission, Sixth Army Group transferred control of Seventh Army to Twelfth Army Group. French First Army and the French Alpine Army Detachment reverted to French national control by the end of May.[6] With the departure of Seventh Army, Devers had to bid farewell to Alexander Patch, his most senior American subordinate and a very close friend. Patch received orders on 23 May to return to Washington, D.C., where he was to join the army staff. In a farewell letter, Devers praised Patch for being a "magnificent team player" who was always willing to try anything, "even though the forces at your command were on the thin side." Devers closed by telling Patch, "You are one of the great leaders of this war."[7] Patch responded, "I shall ever remain grateful to you for the opportunity which you gave me to command the Seventh Army." He also told Devers, "No Army commander could ever hope to have more courageous, unselfish, energetic, and enthusiastic backing and support than you rendered me during the exercise of my command."[8]

The two men never saw each other again. Patch died of pneumonia in San Antonio in November 1945. Weakened by dysentery and malaria contracted while commanding XIV Corps in the final conquest of Guadalcanal in 1943, and probably depressed by the death of his only son, Patch never received the accolades and the fourth star given to others such as Courtney Hodges and Mark Clark. Nonetheless, Patch died knowing that his forces had never been surprised or defeated by the enemy. His untimely death spared him from seeing his only grandson die the following year. Congress posthumously promoted Patch to full general in 1954.

With the cancellation of its training mission, the transfer of Seventh Army to Twelfth Army Group, and the return of de Lattre's forces to French national control, there was no reason to maintain Sixth Army Group. For a few weeks in June, Devers commanded both Sixth and Twelfth Army Groups while Bradley was away. As the senior American general in Europe after Eisenhower, he also commanded SHAEF in his boss's absence in mid-June. However, these were caretaker positions that ended with the demobilization of the army groups.

One of Devers's last official acts involving the French First Army was his attendance at a gala celebration at Lake Constance put on by de Lattre. He also received an honorary doctorate from Nancy University. Devers parted on good terms with his prickly French subordinate and was justifiably proud of how well he had handled the French army, with Lodge's able service. In a letter to de Lattre on 10 May, Devers commended the French for "the brilliant feats they have performed." He reminded de Lattre that his French soldiers had suffered through a brutal fall campaign in the Vosges before they "smashed forth with such vigor that the Belfort Gap was breached and the Rhine reached with a burst of power and speed that left the enemy bewildered." He closed by telling de Lattre:

> I have considered it a singular honor to have the First French Army as part of my command. Never before has so large a force of French fighting men operated under the command of one other than a Frenchman. . . . And so we have come to the end of a long struggle. My fervent hope is for a lasting peace—a peace in which every man will have the right to live his life in freedom. I wish for France a speedy return to the greatness in which the world has for so many centuries known her. With God's help, we will achieve these aims.[9]

This letter highlights one of Devers's most important contributions to the victory in Europe: his ability to get the most out of de Lattre's army, while avoiding the kind of mistakes made by Eisenhower in his handling of the French. For their part, the French had every reason to believe they had fought well in Italy and in France and that their First Army had made a significant contribution to victory.

After leaving Devers's command, de Lattre continued to serve France. In 1948 he became commander of the land forces of the Western European Union, an organization of nations whose goal was to deter Russian aggression in central Europe. In 1950 de Lattre assumed command of the French forces in Indochina, where he did much to restore French morale and inflicted several tactical defeats on the Vietminh. His chief opponent, General Vo Nguyen Giap, later remarked "that de Lattre was the only French general whom he feared."[10] Sadly, de Lattre's only son was killed in action in Vietnam in 1951, and "like Patch before him, he bore his grievous loss with dignity and no apparent loss of control" over his forces. The same year, de Lattre was diagnosed with cancer and returned to Paris, where he died on 11 January 1952.[11]

As he said farewell to his soldiers and commanders, Devers could not help but wonder what his next assignment would be. All he could do was await word from Marshall, who remained chief of staff until 3 December.[12] Even though Devers had many duties to attend to as he concluded his European service, he also took time to help a friend he had known at West Point in the 1920s. On 20 May 1945 Colonel Russell "Red" Reeder wrote to Devers from Walter Reed Hospital, asking for his assistance in getting assigned to the Military Academy. Reeder had landed on Utah Beach on D-day as commander of the 12th Infantry Regiment. That same day, he was severely wounded by shrapnel. His leg was amputated, and he spent the next ten months recovering. Reeder earned the Distinguish Service Cross for his action on 6 June 1944. He now asked for Devers's help in getting a permanent assignment in the Athletic Department at the Military Academy. He advised Devers, "All Regular Army officers who have been wounded like I have, and who cannot pass the physical exam at the end of the war with Japan . . . will be returned to civilian life." Reeder, who graduated from the Academy in 1926, had a solid record as a football and baseball player and as a coach, and he believed he could continue to serve the army well in the Athletic Department.[13] Devers responded a week later, telling Reeder that nothing "would give me greater pleasure than to write the letter to the Superintendent of the Military Academy which you request." He enclosed a copy of that letter and told Reeder that he knew "of no finer place to live, nor a greater mission in life than training cadets, and I know of no better man to do it. . . . You will be a real inspiration."[14] Reeder was given a temporary job as a regimental commander at the Academy in 1946, and upon his disability retirement in 1947, he was appointed assistant athletic director at West Point, where he ably served until 1967.

During his last month with Sixth Army Group, Devers visited various units to say good-bye to the soldiers who had served with him, and he took time to remember those who had died. On 30 May 1945, during a Memorial Day service in Heidelberg, he asked his listeners to remember the service of two soldiers as exemplars of the thousands of men killed during the liberation of Europe. The first was Technician Fifth Grade Eugene F. Patenaude of the Special Service Force, who had led the evacuation of several wounded comrades from a minefield in the Vosges. "Patenaude's leadership was abruptly ended when another mine exploded. The wounded men were saved; the man who saved them sacrificed his life." The second man was Captain Alexander Patch III, killed while leading his company in an attack in October 1944. Patch "was painfully wounded, but refused to be evacuated for medical aid. Weakened by pain and loss of blood, for more than two hours he remained at the head of his" men until they reached their objective. By then, it was too late for medics to save him, and "a gallant captain gave his life in the cause of his men and country."[15]

Devers went on to tell his audience that when he looked at the American military cemeteries, "I cannot think, today, of row upon row of nameless crosses" as merely statistics. "Nor can you. Each of you will remember some individual friend or comrade who gave the last true measure of devotion. It is for him that you are here. It is his particular memory you honor." In closing, Devers reminded his audience that 23,303 American soldiers of Sixth Army Group had been killed in action. Another 107,583 soldiers were wounded, and 15,266 remained missing. Each one was "someone's comrade—someone's son, or husband, or father. In each of their homes today there is mourning and memoriam." He continued, "Our tribute to these men cannot be paid here. It must be paid in our preservation of the freedom and of the ideals they died to save. The rights of the individual; the sanctity of the home; the preservation of the family; freedom of religion, of speech, of assembly, and of the press; eternal vigilance on behalf of the oppressed and the under-privileged; racial and religious toleration; freedom from fear and from want—these are the treasures our comrades gave to us today, to treasure and preserve that their deaths be not in vain."[16]

There are few things harder for a commander to do than to say good-bye to his soldiers and to remember those who died while under his command. These duties and the psychological letdown accompanying the end of the war must have taken an emotional toll on Devers. Yet the memories of his soldiers inspired Devers to continue to perform to the best of his ability in whatever job the army assigned him. In June he learned that he would assume command of the Army Ground Forces. In this position, Devers would help transition the army from war to peace and identify and apply the lessons of World War II to the future force.

The Road Home

The details of transferring or demobilizing the roughly 3.5 million American soldiers and airmen in Europe were daunting. Before the end of the war, Marshall had spent a great deal of time and effort developing plans for a smooth transition from war to peace for the army and the American people. One aspect of this plan was how soldiers and units would return home. Marshall wanted to honor the various organizations that had served in Europe, and he explained his concerns in a letter to Eisenhower on 7 May 1945:

> The cessation of hostilities brings up the question of what procedure to follow in the return of senior officers to this country. . . . The question of handling reception and publicity for officers returning to this country . . . is one which requires some consideration. . . . If one is honored more than another the adverse reaction extends right down to the newest replacement that has joined the latter's organization. It is surprising how much men in one organization, like an army or an air force, resent the acclaim and publicity that the commander of another army or air force may receive.[17]

Marshall was concerned that the first men home would receive large celebratory receptions, while those who returned later might be met "by tired reception committees and bored publics." To avoid this situation, his staff developed plans to bring home four or five groups of both senior officers and soldiers representing units from many different commands. Marshall suggested that the first group include Hodges and Hoyt Vandenberg, representing the air force, along with selected corps and division commanders, company-grade combat officers, and enlisted soldiers who were slated to participate in the Pacific war against Japan. A week or two later, a second group that might include Bradley, Clark, Cannon, some corps commanders, and young company officers and enlisted men would come home. Several similarly representative groups would follow at short intervals, allowing each group to savor the welcome of the American people. In Marshall's plan, Eisenhower and Smith would return last, since "following you any reception would be anticlimax."[18] Eisenhower agreed with the underlying principles of the plan and suggested that the groups have itineraries taking them to different parts of the country, allowing more of the nation to celebrate. Marshall agreed with this suggestion.[19] In general, this phased return of representative groups was followed.

On 20 June Devers was ordered to travel home with a group that included Simpson (Ninth Army), Major General Leroy Irwin (XII Corps), Major General Edwin Parker (78th Infantry Division), Major General William Kepner (Eighth Air Force), Colonel Creighton Abrams (4th Armored Division), Captain Woodward Altgelt (102nd Infantry Division), and Lieutenant Harry Horner (Ninth Air Troop Carrier Command). All were granted two weeks' leave in the States. Some would be returning to duty in Europe; others, like Devers, would be moving on to new jobs.[20]

By the time he left Europe on 23 June, Devers knew that Marshall had selected him to command the Army Ground Forces. His final efficiency report as Sixth Army Group commander indicated where Devers stood in Eisenhower's eyes. Eisenhower described him as "an enthusiastic, energetic officer; loyal and devoted to duty. . . . His command contained a French Army and General Devers performed valuable service in securing the cooperation, often under difficult conditions, of those forces." Then, after these words of praise, Eisenhower ranked Devers as the third most valuable officer on a list of three officers in his grade, after Spaatz and Bradley. He closed by writing, "While my list contains only three officers of the rank of General, Patton and Hodges also served under me. General Devers is, however, number 5 on [my] whole Theater list, and should be listed immediately after General Hodges."[21]

It is unclear whether Devers saw this report before he went home. In any case, he and his group flew to New York for an initial welcome and then split up to visit their respective hometowns for celebrations. On his way home, Devers took part in ceremonies in Pittsburgh honoring all Pennsylvania veterans before flying to Harrisburg airport on 26 June. Georgie, Frances, and Kitts met him there and accompanied him to York for victory celebrations that included a buffet luncheon in the Yorktowne Hotel and a parade through the city. The parade ended at the York County Fairgrounds, where 15,000 people had gathered to honor the most senior soldier among the 7,000 men York had sent to war.[22]

In preparation for Devers's homecoming, a York newspaper published a story by his boyhood friend Bill Eckenrode about Jake's upbringing in York. Eckenrode opened his account by discussing Devers's name. "We have been informed that the late President Roosevelt, important members of the cabinet, brother army officers, and just plain G.I.'s always called him or referred to him as 'Jakie' Devers. However he has always been 'Jake' to us, who had the privilege of knowing him in York." Eckenrode ended by pointing out that Devers was coming back "as the unassuming, friendly, likeable, unaffected Jake" he was when he left York for a career in the army.[23] Following these celebrations, Devers took two weeks' leave, as he and Georgie made the somewhat difficult transition to being together again and adjusting to a new tempo of life.

Devers had been overseas since May 1943, serving in high-pressure jobs with responsibilities that affected the lives of hundreds of thousands of soldiers and civilians. He had taken no extended time off. His hectic schedule had included visiting front-line units; dealing with the British, the French, the U.S. Navy, and the Army Air Force; and commanding two American theaters of operations and Sixth Army Group. His rocky personal relations with men like Mark Clark, Bedell Smith, Harold Alexander, and Dwight Eisenhower added stress that is impossible to gauge. Remarkably, he was seldom ill.[24] He remained focused on supporting and encouraging subordinates such as Eaker, Patch, and de Lattre. But by June 1945, Devers was exhausted and homesick, and he needed a rest before assuming his new responsibilities.

Fortunately, the army had a program designed to help soldiers "decompress." On 3 July Devers was ordered to report to the Army Ground Forces Redistribution Center in Miami, Florida, where he was expected to relax, recreate, and get reacquainted with his wife.[25] The Deverses arrived in Miami on 7 July, and after about a week there, Georgie sent Kitts a progress report: "Jamie seems to be relaxing and regaining his place in a war-less community. He was very difficult for a while—was tired—impatient—very full of the tone of command to everyone, and then unhappy when he saw the surprise and resentment he caused. If I can make him last out the two weeks here he will be more like his old self, and much happier in his new duties."[26] They stayed at the center until 21 July, enjoying their "huge apartment . . . with our own chef and kitchen . . . and friends we hadn't seen in years." It seemed to help Devers return to his role as a husband and ease his transition from war to peace. For Georgie, it was also a welcome return to a world with "no ration points to consider, and all the fruit, fish, vegetables and beef one could use."[27]

Although the nation could not afford to send every returning combat veteran to such centers, it provided this service to many of them. As Georgie noted, the center was "a treat Uncle Sam had for men returning from long periods overseas. . . . Each man could have his wife with him, and there were 2,000 enlisted men and 2,000 officers there all the time." The army nurses who had been captured on Bataan were there at the same time as the Deverses, along with "lots of men from the prison camps of Germany."[28]

Army Ground Forces Command

By the end of their stay in Florida, Devers had begun to think about his next assignment as commander of the Army Ground Forces (AGF). The AGF had been created in 1942 to assume responsibility for the organization, command, and training of all army ground forces in the United States. Its first commander, Lesley McNair, was Devers's old friend from the 4th Field Artillery and his most important mentor. The Army Air Forces, under Hap Arnold, and the Army Services of Supply, under Brehon Somervell, had been organized at the same time as the AGF.[29]

During the war, the AGF, the Army Air Forces, and the Army Services of Supply (renamed the Army Service Forces in March 1943) were the three most important organizations that reported directly to the chief of staff.[30] General Marshall used these organizations to consolidate, respectively, ground force matters, air force matters, and logistical tasks. This tripartite arrangement allowed Marshall to reduce the number of agencies and officers reporting directly to him, enabling him to focus on strategic and policy matters at the highest levels. The independent offices of the chiefs of the combat arms, such as the chiefs of cavalry, infantry, and field artillery, were abolished at the same time, and their functions were shifted to the AGF.[31] This system allowed Marshall to direct a global war while McNair, Arnold, and Somervell dealt with the details.

Marshall's selection of Devers to head the AGF indicates his continued high regard for Jake in 1945. There was a great deal to be done to reorganize the army, and Devers was highly qualified to do so, given his experiences with the Armored Force, two overseas theaters of operations, and Sixth Army Group. Devers was fortunate that his appointment was made before Eisenhower became chief of staff in December 1945, although it is possible that Ike would have selected him as well.

Georgie and Jake Devers returned to Washington, D.C., in late July, residing for a short time in their "Yellow House" before moving in August to government quarters on the Army War College campus (soon renamed Fort McNair). Georgie was pleased with her new surroundings, noting in a letter to Kitts, "Here we are in another set of Army Quarters, and about the loveliest post in the Army. The [Potomac] river is right at the back door." They had rented the Yellow House, fully furnished, to the head of Trans World Airlines, since the army provided all the furnishings for their new quarters.[32]

Georgie also looked forward to having Colonel Alexander Graham return home so that he and Frances could be reunited and get on with their life. Many old army friends were coming home as well, and once the atomic bombs were dropped on Japan, it was clear that the war was nearly over. During this period of transition, Georgie monitored Jake's health, telling Kitts in late August, "Jamie looks fine, and feels like himself this week. Up to now he has been tired and sleepy." Devers's love of baseball and football also returned, and he was looking forward to the Military Academy's football season.[33]

The AGF command was an immense job in 1945. Georgie described Devers's new assignment in another letter to Kitts: "It is a big job and full of many unpleasant duties."[34] Personnel issues were just one area of concern as the army rapidly demobilized. Many officers would be reverting to lower ranks, if they were lucky enough to stay on active duty, as the army shrank from 8 million men in June 1945 to a little over 1 million by July 1947 (including the Army Air Forces).[35] Informing men of their demotion was one of the more difficult aspects of Devers's new job. As Georgie said, "It's easier to promote men in action . . . than to demote them after they have had a try and failed to keep up with success—or being promoted to some place too big for them."[36]

Though he immediately immersed himself in his job, Devers also looked "forward to seeing people he had not seen in years, and to having the pressure let up." However, he and Georgie soon found that "this official kind of life into which his success has thrust him, with me . . . is wearing." In addition to his long days working to reorganize and demobilize the army, Devers was expected to play an active role in the social scene in the capital. For example, after a full day of work on 7 November, Jake and Georgie attended a dinner at the British embassy that lasted well past midnight. The next day they took part in a celebration at the Russian embassy in honor of the Bolshevik Revolution of October–November 1917 and attended an awards ceremony at the British embassy. They learned the importance of "watching what one says," which was a constant strain. Devers was often the senior army officer present at a social event, making it difficult to leave early. By the end of November, Georgie and Jake were looking forward to a family Christmas in York with Kitts.[37]

When Devers took over the AGF, it controlled all the ground forces in the United States. This included the army schools, the Armored Force, the training centers, all ground force units returning from overseas, and the army branch schools (armor, cavalry, infantry, and so on). Devers reported directly to the army chief of staff, and his headquarters maintained liaison offices with staff in the Pentagon. The army staff had no authority over the ground forces in the United States except through Devers's command. The AGF was also in charge of the boards established to evaluate the lessons learned during the war and make recommendations for doctrinal and organizational changes to prepare the ground forces for future combat service.[38]

Devers brought a number of key staff officers from Sixth Army Group to the AGF, including Major General Dave Barr, his chief of staff; Colonel Eugene Harrison, his G-2; and Brigadier General Reuben Jenkins, his G-3. They each served for a brief period in the same positions with the AGF. Harrison recalled that Devers began his assignment "with his usual enthusiasm" and "organized the job to make it a training command which would inspect and supervise the training of all the units in the continental United States."[39] When these men moved on to other assignments, Devers brought in experienced combat leaders such as J. Lawton Collins and Charles Bolte to help direct the AGF.

Bolte was a critical member of Devers's organization, serving as chief of staff. Since Devers traveled a great deal, visiting units and installations across the United States, Bolte handled most matters that came up at headquarters. He recalled that he and Devers had a routine. When Devers returned from a trip, Bolte would brief him on the issues that had arisen in his absence and the decisions Bolte had made. Bolte remembered, "He didn't always agree with or accept our solutions but I will say he did in most part and I would get action." Bolte stated he had never served with or for "a more satisfying commander" than Devers, "in the sense of the relationship of a chief of staff, of a No. 2 executive, to his chief." He especially liked Devers's "forthrightness" and "simplicity in [taking a] direct approach to problems and relationships."[40]

When Devers arrived at the AGF in Washington, he asked for a civilian, rather than a warrant officer, to serve as his personal secretary. Mrs. Dorothy Benn (later Ham), then working in the War Department Secretariat, was selected for the position and joined Devers's staff in July 1945. Dorothy, a widow whose husband had been killed in 1943, and her daughter Bonnie became close friends of Jake and Georgie Devers. Dorothy served as Devers's secretary until his retirement from the army in 1949 and continued to work with him in the private sector. She remembered that his major concerns revolved around "the things that were of importance to the foot soldier—his moral well-being, his physical well-being, his equipment, his housing, his training, and his transportation."[41]

During the fall of 1945, boards of senior officers studied how the armed forces should be organized in the future. During a November interview with the Simpson Board, Devers endorsed a tripartite organization of the army into air, ground, and service forces. He believed that these organizations should have a great deal of autonomy and that the army staff should do less "operating" and more "policy making." He also advocated keeping the army's combat and service branches under the control of the AGF, rather than re-creating the "chiefs of arms"—positions that had been eliminated in Marshall's reorganization of 1942.[42]

Based on wartime lessons learned, especially about manpower, Devers and the AGF staff identified questions and issues that required guidance from the War Department. For example, in a letter to General Thomas Handy, the army's deputy chief of staff, the AGF asked about the racial mix of the ground forces—specifically, "What number of Negro troops will Army Ground Forces be required to absorb as of July, 1946?" and "What will the War Department policy be on segregation of Negro troops and officers?" Devers also asked Handy whether responsibility for the Organized Reserve Corps, the Reserve Officer Training Corps, and the National Guard would be transferred to the AGF prior to the final decision on the permanent structure of the War Department. These questions and others, about policies regarding women in the armed forces, the establishment of a "National Intelligence Agency," and the continuation of the selective service, were, to a large extent, dependent on decisions by the president and Congress.[43] It would be at least three years before some of these questions were answered, as U.S. military policies underwent significant changes.

Army Reorganization, 1946–1947

When Eisenhower replaced Marshall as chief of staff in December 1945, the thinking about the organization of the army quickly changed directions. Based on recommendations of the Simpson Board, the War Department issued Circular 138 on 14 May 1946, revising much of Marshall's 1942 organizational framework. "Under Circular 138 the Army Ground Forces and the Army Air Forces continued as separate commands," with the AGF serving "as the headquarters through which the General Staff would command the ground troops in the continental United States."[44] The Army Service Forces headquarters was eliminated, and most of the independent administrative and technical agencies that Marshall had abolished or subordinated were reinstated as separate divisions of the War Department.[45] Devers had testified before the Simpson Board in November that "the only way to do things is to have the technical service chiefs [such as chief of ordnance] under a CG, ASF."[46] His advice was ignored.

The General Staff was reorganized in such a way as to give each of the six G sections more autonomy and to weaken the wartime supremacy of the Operations Division. These staff sections and the newly independent agencies all reported to the chief of staff, undoing Marshall's efforts to ease the burdens of the person in that position. The assistant chiefs of staff were designated "directors," and the G staffs were renamed directorates. For example, the assistant chief of staff for personnel, formerly the G-1, became the director of the Directorate of Personnel and Administration. The new setup weakened the power of the AGF command and increased that of the army staff.[47] Six numbered armies were created under the AGF to operate the posts and installations within the United States. This created another layer of authority, further obfuscating lines of authority, responsibility, and command. The commanders of these armies included senior officers such as Courtney Hodges, Manton Eddy, Jonathan Wainwright, Bill Simpson, and Mark Clark.[48]

The official history concludes that due to the reorganization of 1946,

"The War Department again became a 'loose federation of warring tribes' with 'little armies within the Army.'" Thanks to the abolition of the Army Service Forces, the War Department "could not avoid the management problems which General Somervell and General Marshall had solved by establishing firm executive control at the top." Eisenhower's hope that "teamwork, cooperation, and persuasion" among the many fiefdoms he created would replace "tight executive control" was misplaced.[49] Nonetheless, the 1946 reorganization left the AGF and its commanding general with a great deal of responsibility, power, and autonomy.

Manpower: Shortages and Utilization

One of the most difficult challenges facing the armed forces and the AGF in 1945–1947 was related to personnel. For example, one of Eisenhower's first messages to the army's air, ground, and service forces concerned manpower shortages and the need to release as many men possible, as quickly as possible, from active duty. Because of the acceleration of discharges, Eisenhower noted that the army was not going to have enough personnel to meet its requirements. Nonetheless, he noted, "The most serious aspect of the problem in the immediate future is the enormous public and legislative pressure to demobilize the forces." The War Department was "partially committed in public" to discharge all individuals with more than two years' service as rapidly as possible in 1946.[50]

Eisenhower felt that "drastic efforts" by all commands were needed to reduce personnel requirements and expedite the return of men to the United States. At the same time, the occupation forces overseas were the highest priority for manpower, making it essential that the AGF and Army Service Forces examine and justify "the essentiality of every man in uniform in the U.S." As a result, units in the United States would have to be manned at "a much reduced strength." The chief of staff ordered Devers and other commanders to conduct a thorough analysis of personnel needs "on the basis of the most drastic economy" and to provide the War Department with an estimate of their "rock-bottom" troop requirements for the coming year by 20 December 1945.[51]

During 1946, as the army wrestled with organizational and personnel challenges, Devers found ways to work effectively within the new War Department framework. He directed his staff to develop "The Army Ground Forces Plan," which was published in October 1946 and reflected ongoing changes in the international situation. Hopes that "lasting peace" with the Soviet Union could be maintained through "compromise, discussion, and an earnest desire to arrive at mutually acceptable conditions" had been dashed by communist aggression in Greece and China. The plan noted, "It is clear that there is now a definite lining up of the East and of the West." Although the emerging alignments did not "necessarily presage war," they were strong indicators of how the powers would align in the event of war. Therefore, the AGF and the United States had to be prepared.[52]

In 1946 army strength was limited by presidential order to 1,070,000 soldiers and airmen. In October the total strength was 1,009,000, with 254,100 servicemen overseas in occupation forces comprising three and two-thirds divisions and twenty-eight air groups. This included troops in Hawaii, Alaska, Panama, and the Philippines. Servicemen in the continental United States totaled 620,900 men in the air, ground, and service units, organized in seven and two-thirds divisions and forty-two air groups. Of these personnel, 298,900 were in the replacement system or in War Department intelligence organizations. An additional 134,000 men were preparing to conduct universal military training if Congress approved that program.[53]

Assuming that the next war would be total war, "with no restrictions on weapons or targets," the AGF plan asked, what "will be the role of the Army Ground Forces in such a future war?" The answer was that, initially, the AGF would assist the civil powers and repel any invaders from the homeland. Subsequently, ground forces would be transported overseas to take part in an attack on the enemy as "one part of the Land, Sea, and Air team." Therefore, it was critical that the naval, ground, and air services act as coequal members of a unified team.[54]

The plan noted, "The Commanding General, Army Ground Forces, commands the six armies within the continental United States." One of his principal duties was to prepare for and, on order, execute operations for the defense of the nation. To prepare for possible war, the AGF plan listed a number of actions it needed to take. One was a reduction of "branch consciousness" by establishing artillery and armor as branches and assigning them the functions of field artillery, coast artillery, and cavalry. Further, "the establishment of new branches to serve new weapons" should be avoided to enhance close-knit ground forces.[55]

The AGF plan also called for improvements in the training and handling of replacements, the development of realistic mobilization plans, and the consolidation of AGF schools into "centers" for infantry, armor, and artillery. Other schools, such as the Intelligence School at Fort Riley, Kansas, the Mountain and Winter Warfare School at Camp Carson, Colorado, and the Physical Training School at Camp Lee, Virginia, were to be maintained. Plans for a single "Officers' Basic Course" were under consideration to provide all officers with a common foundation and understanding of matters such as intelligence, political awareness, aid to civil powers, and air defense.[56]

The AGF plan included policy proposals about officer strength, assignments, promotions, and elimination and the recruitment and retention of soldiers. It emphasized the AGF's role in the training and readiness of the Organized Reserve Corps and the National Guard, which were important to the army's ability to fight in any future conflict. Consequently, throughout his tenure as AGF commanding general, Devers paid special attention to the National Guard and reserve components.[57]

Devers's plan to consolidate ground combat officers into three branches—armor, infantry, and artillery—was intended to decrease branch parochialism and train well-rounded officers. Common basic training would prepare combat arms officers to serve in branches other than their own. Then, it was hoped, "the assignment of an officer can be determined more by his capabilities than by the branch in which he was originally commissioned."[58] In answer to a question asked during a talk he gave at the Command and General Staff School in 1946, Devers stressed, "We are trying to produce a rounded combat officer." His goal was to give every officer "training of a varied nature in order that he might be familiar with all the various phases of combat arms." As a result, "the Regular Army officer . . . will no longer be essentially a specialist." To achieve this goal, "training must, and according to our present plans, will be broadened out to cover the entire field [of the combat arms]."[59]

Although he succeeded in getting the branches consolidated, Devers did not achieve his goal of having combat arms officers assigned to branches other than their own before they became lieutenant colonels. He did, however, make some progress that the army could later build on. He selected highly successful combat veterans to reorganize and energize the armor, infantry, and artillery centers where the combat arms basic courses were taught. For example, he sent Brigadier General Bruce Clarke, the hero of the Battle of St. Vith, to the armor center at Fort Knox. There, Clarke put combat veterans such as Colonel Creighton Abrams in charge of instruction and curriculum development.[60]

In the midst of the army's reorganization, the secretary of war decided that AGF headquarters should vacate its offices in the Pentagon and at Fort McNair, opening space for the expansion of the army staff and the War College, respectively. This decision was made in the spring of 1946, but evidently, the AGF was slow to respond. AGF chief of staff Bolte recalled that "some of my friends in the Chief of Staff's Secretariat" asked "when are you going to obey your orders?" Bolte relayed this conversation to Devers and told him, "I think we ought to begin to carry out our instructions . . . to go down to Fort Monroe and reduce the staff."[61] By 3 July 1946 the move was under way, and Devers officially assumed command of Fort Monroe, Virginia, on 1 October 1946.[62]

The move to Fort Monroe meant that Georgie would have to leave her home on "the loveliest post in the army" and reestablish her household.[63] Georgie wrote to Kitts, "By the time I get to Monroe, I'll have lived in 7 houses in 6 years."[64] She moved on 24–25 September, her eighteenth move in thirty-five years, and she found "it harder each time."[65] However, she soon wrote to Kitts from her quarters at 33 Fenwick Road, Fort Monroe, "I like Monroe the best of all my homes. The water is entrancing—and the busy harbor life enthralling to me." It was fortunate that she loved her new surroundings, since her husband was "seldom here for two days at a time, but is not often away for more than three."[66]

Dorothy Benn and her daughter Bonnie moved to Fort Monroe as well. Bonnie, who never knew her father, noted in an interview, "The General was the man who was in my life the longest of any man." She described him as a "good, kind, honorable, and reasonable man" who was always "above board." Bonnie said, "There was no façade about him." She remembered him as "an optimistic man who fixed problems rather than wringing his hands."[67]

In May 1947 the furniture from the Yellow House was moved to the Deverses' new quarters at Fort Monroe. They continued to rent out the Yellow House. Georgie was "so glad to have my own things around me again. . . . I feel I am a 'person' and 'living' again."[68] But not everything was rosy for Georgie, who continued to worry about Frances's inability to manage money or a household. For example, she told Kitts, "I take it that Alex has taken charge of their lives to a greater extent and Frances has some adjusting to do, or else. More power to him."[69] The Grahams visited the Deverses several times in 1948 as they moved from one post to another. Georgie told Kitts how things went during one visit:

I am coming up for air after a week of the Grahams. It's always exciting and exhilarating, but strenuous. They know twice as many people as I do, and the phone calls from N.Y., Columbia, S.C., Chicago, Boston, Fort Sill, Washington all day and all night, would keep a secretary busy. One night, when they were dancing at the club, I had four numbers for them to call when they got home. About 3 AM, from other states and cities. You know they left here for KY by way of Washington for 48 hours, then NY for 24![70]

Devers was largely absent during the Grahams' visits to Fort Monroe. He was busy setting up camps for the newly instituted draft and the training of inductees.

Relations with the National Guard and Reserve Forces

The military policy of the United States in 1945–1946 rested firmly on the conclusion that the National Guard and the reserve organizations would provide a significant number of forces if a major conflict occurred. The National Guard had provided twenty-seven infantry divisions in the military buildup of 1940–1942. These divisions and the Guardsmen who served in them proved their combat worthiness in all theaters of the war. During the late 1940s the War Department worked to reorganize twenty-seven National Guard infantry divisions and two armored divisions and to find volunteers to fill them. In response to a 1947 letter from Eisenhower that stressed the importance of supporting the "civilian components," Devers told the chief of staff, "I am thoroughly in accord with your view that the National Guard and Organized Reserve Corps are just as much a part of the Army of the United States as is the Regular Army."[71]

By the summer of 1947, the National Guard had activated 2,000 units of various sizes and recruited 80,000 men. The AGF had established about 81 percent of the component parts of the Organized Reserve Corps, but shortages of money for training, supplies, equipment, and facilities delayed the achievement of the goals set by the War Department. In an enclosure to his letter to Eisenhower, Devers noted, "Legislation is needed" to pay reservists for their periods of training and to equip the forces.[72]

Devers visited National Guard and reserve training facilities regularly. Such visits helped bridge the gap between the regular army and the civilian components, as the adjutant general of the Tennessee National Guard indicated in a letter to Devers: "Your interest in the Tennessee National Guard which was so well demonstrated by your visit to our school . . . was an inspiration to all personnel and will contribute materially to the successful completion of organization of the National Guard of this state."[73] Devers's understanding of the personal touch, honed over the past four decades, was evident in his dealings with National Guard and reserve leaders and soldiers.

At times, however, Devers had to prod some of the army commanders to deal with the civilian components in a fair and reasonable manner. In May 1947, for example, he heard from Senator Lodge that General Courtney Hodges, commander of First Army, was not giving sufficient responsibility and authority to the Massachusetts National Guard's adjutant and commander. Devers traveled to Boston to meet with Lodge, the governor, and the National Guard commander. After listening to their complaints, Devers wrote to Hodges to remind him, "My method of command and leadership is to decentralize to commanders in the field as much as possible, and of course anything that can be done to accomplish that all along the chain of command would, in my opinion, be most beneficial." Devers understood the importance of the interaction between regular army officers and guardsmen and reservists. He told Hodges, "We must convince them that we are sincere in making every effort possible to assist them." He observed, "[our] problems [with the civilian components] are difficult, but not unsolvable" if faced head-on. He closed by saying, "I am sure you understand what we are driving at."[74]

Devers praised other army commanders, such as Lieutenant General Manton Eddy, who "were outstanding in the promotion of civilian component organization and training." However, the more he dealt with the civilian components, the more he believed that "drastic modification in policies and thinking" was required to solve the problems involved.[75] In the end, Devers was unable to fix all the problems between the active forces and the civilian components, but he helped improve the National Guard and the Organized Reserve Corps.

Devers's approach to the complaint involving Hodges was typical of how he dealt with difficult situations throughout his career. He identified the problem, talked with the appropriate people, and developed a solution to ameliorate if not totally solve it. The importance of the National Guard and reserve components was becoming increasingly obvious as the active-duty armed forces shrank. The world situation was changing, and the demands on the military were increasing, without a concomitant increase in funding for the ground forces.

Combat Readiness, 1947–1948

While the armed forces were demobilizing and reorganizing, they remained responsible for carrying out missions assigned by the president. By early 1947, communist actions in eastern Europe and China increased the likelihood that the army might be called on to provide ground forces for overseas operations. The army, however, was in no shape to carry out any serious expeditionary missions. As historian Russell Weigley notes, the postwar army, "under the shadow of atomic power," seemed to be irrelevant to future wars. Weigley describes a grim situation: "The combat strength of the Army resided in ten divisions, a division-size European Constabulary, and nine separate regimental combat teams. . . . Except for the 1st Infantry Division in Germany, however, economies had caused the Army to skeletonize its divisions. The infantry regiments had two rather than three battalions, and the artillery battalions had two rather than three batteries. . . . The active infantry battalions were short one rifle company. No division had its wartime complement of weapons."[76]

Inadequate defense appropriations by Congress and the Truman administration were part of the problem. In addition, recruiting efforts had failed to fill the authorized ranks, and Congress had allowed the Selective Service Act to lapse. This left units underfunded and undermanned. Devers brought this situation to Eisenhower's attention in September 1947: "I am seriously concerned over the inability of Army Ground Forces under current War Department directives and policies, to perform that portion of its assigned mission which requires it to have plans for the movement overseas of a corps consisting of an Infantry and an Airborne Division, and an Armored Combat Command." He pointed out that the AGF General Reserve, which had been authorized 71,000 men in one armored, one airborne, and two infantry divisions, had been reduced in September 1946 "to 47,575 soldiers assigned to one infantry and one airborne division and just one armored combat command." These units were authorized just 80 percent of their required strength. "Effective 1 July 1947, this figure was further reduced to the present authorized strength of 45,356," and the six U.S.-based armies were allowed to use General Reserve units to carry out missions that were formerly assigned to civilian employees on the various bases and posts.[77]

The situation was even worse than Devers described. Of the 45,356 authorized soldiers, only 37,160 were assigned to the AGF's General Reserve. Of these, more than 14,000 men were being diverted to carry out administrative tasks, leaving only 18,797 men available to train for overseas deployment and combat. This last number included personnel "who are sick in hospital, AWOL, on guard, furlough, post fatigue, and performing normal unit overhead." This meant, Devers noted, that fewer than 15,000 men of the General Reserve were available for training. Devers told Eisenhower, "These conditions are and have been known to the War Department Staff, but I wish to be sure that you are personally acquainted with them."[78] The bottom line was that the AGF General Reserve could deploy no more than a composite division of one regiment from the 82nd Airborne Division, Combat Command A of the 2nd Armored Division, and one regiment from the 2nd Infantry Division.

To remedy this situation, Devers believed, the War Department had to take several steps: fill and maintain the units at authorized strength with soldiers who had at least nine months of service remaining, give priority to the General Reserve units for training and equipment, and place the General Reserve units directly under AGF control for training, rather than under the regional army commands. Devers had his doubts that the War Department would do much, especially in the absence of conscription. Nonetheless, he reminded Eisenhower that, given "the disparity between possible requirements and our present capabilities I feel it necessary that the situation be brought to your personal attention, with a view to such modification of existing directives as you may feel desirable and practical."[79]

The immediate impetus for Devers's letter to Eisenhower had been a War Department staff study on how to dispatch an Army–Air Force Task Force to Greece to help defeat a communist insurrection there.[80] Devers responded to the staff study with a "determined non-concurrence" with the list of ground units proposed for the task force. The list had been prepared by Lieutenant General Lauris Norstad, the army G-3, "after the receipt of recommendations from the Army Ground Forces, which were not accepted."[81] According to Devers, the army staff did not have a clear picture of the readiness status of the units selected. In the end, Norstad accepted most of Devers's recommendations for building a task force around the 82nd Airborne Division, and he promised to relieve some General Reserve units from administrative tasks in the United States.[82] Nonetheless, the shortage of personnel and money continued to plague the army and could be remedied only by congressional action.

A major cause of the shortage of soldiers was that the Selective Service Act had lapsed in 1947, and too few men were enlisting in the armed forces. At the end of World War II, Congress and a majority of the American people had been in favor of retaining some sort of universal military training (UMT), but the details of such a program were vague. As a stopgap to keep the armed forces manned, Congress continued conscription while it debated UMT. However, by 1947, no consensus had been reached on the nature of UMT or on continuing the draft.[83] In fairness to Congress, during the first three years after the war, there seemed to be no external threat to the United States, and it was thought that the air force and the navy provided ample protection from invasion. In this environment, the Truman administration and Congress cut the military budget, with the army as the biggest "bill-payer." This situation continued until 1950.[84]

"Foot in Mouth" Disease

Senior military officers were frustrated by Congress's reluctance to address the dire manpower and financial state of the armed forces. Devers was no exception, and in 1946 it got him into trouble. A reporter from the *Atlanta Constitution* wrote that Devers had "lambasted Congress here yesterday as a group of cowardly men afraid of touching the controversial draft bill." This description did not sit well with congressmen or with Eisenhower. Ike directed his chief deputy, General Thomas Handy, to ask Devers whether he had actually made such an inappropriate statement. Devers contacted Josh Skinner, the managing editor of the *Atlanta Constitution,* who admitted that Devers had not used the words "cowardly men." According to Skinner, the reporter had put the phrase in quotation marks "to give his impression of the General's remarks. The General himself did not use the word."[85] Whether or not Devers had called Congress cowardly, the damage had been done, and he was to blame for even implying such a thing to a reporter.

Devers's directness got him in trouble again the next year as the navy, air force, and army vied for their shares of the limited appropriations for defense. The navy and air force had a number of advantages that frustrated army leaders in the late 1940s, just as they had frustrated Marshall in the two years before the Second World War. Marshall had shown great patience and political skill in the prewar period; similarly, Eisenhower exhibited solid political instincts in his years as chief of staff. Unfortunately, Devers did not tread as carefully when it came to making public statements about military budgets and the other services. In an editorial in the *Washington Post* on 5 October 1947, reporter John Norris asked, "Are national defense costs too high" and "can the armed services . . . be trimmed?" Norris wrote, "Many Army leaders answer these questions in the affirmative." He continued:

> General Jacob Devers, commander of the Army Ground Forces, believes that substantial savings can be made in airplane and air base building costs. [According to Devers,] "Military planes don't need all the refinements they carry today." . . . The building of airfields for heavy bombers can be simplified. B-36 type bombers require very long runways of especially reinforced concrete. Devers suggested that the Air Force economize by "beefing up" only a strip at each end of the runway instead of the entire length. . . . The Army Ground Forces chief also believes that some of the special tailoring which goes into warplanes is not strictly necessary.

Norris went on to note that air force major general Emmett O'Donnell, who flew B-29 bombers over Japan during the war, disagreed with Devers. O'Donnell was quoted as saying, "With the tremendous destruction made possible by the atomic bomb, we feel that we should put the best we got into the airplanes, instruments and equipment to get it to its target."[86]

It took less than twenty-four hours for the secretary of the army to bring Devers's inappropriate remarks to Eisenhower's attention. Ike reacted swiftly, sending a personal letter to Devers that opened with this statement: "Every officer is of course entitled to his own convictions." However, it is "his duty to submit these to the proper authority" before airing them in public. The chief of staff stressed that when such suggestions or comments apply "to organizations other than the Department of the Army," they should be brought to the attention of the appropriate office responsible. Eisenhower noted, "Only damage to the Army can result from public criticism by Army personnel of any sister service." Regardless of the merits of his comments, Devers had made a major public relations mistake. Eisenhower handled the situation politely, but clearly. He closed his missive by reminding Devers of "the implications of giving this type of opinion and comment to the press."[87] This seemed to end the matter, but it might have had some bearing on Devers's future.

Devers as Chief of Staff?

At the end of World War II, George Marshall looked forward to retirement, and it was clear to him and most people in the government that General Dwight D. Eisenhower was the logical choice to replace him. Marshall wrote to Eisenhower in early September 1945, "I do not think there is a shadow of a doubt regarding your appointment to succeed me."[88] Therefore, he kept Ike informed of personnel matters, demobilization, and reorganization plans.

Eisenhower, however, wanted to retire in 1945, and General Omar Bradley wanted to be chief of staff. But the president had other plans: he wanted Bradley to take over and fix the Veterans Administration and for Eisenhower to replace Marshall.[89] Thus, a compromise was struck. Eisenhower agreed to serve as chief of staff for two years, and Bradley agreed to head the Veterans Administration until Ike retired; Bradley would then become chief of staff. Truman reluctantly accepted Marshall's resignation and nominated Eisenhower for chief of staff in November 1945.[90]

Few people outside of Truman, Marshall, Eisenhower, and Bradley knew about the deal that had been made. However, it was common knowledge by mid-1947 that Eisenhower planned to leave the army in 1948 and become president of a university. Did Devers hope that he would be selected to replace Ike as chief of staff? There is no direct evidence that he did, although it would have been out of character if he did not. His sister Kitts told an interviewer in 1974 that she never "heard him talk about it but my opinion is—now this is purely my opinion—but every man who gets near the top as he did would have wanted to finish his career as Chief of Staff."[91]

There were some who actively lobbied President Truman to choose Devers. On 28 June 1947 the Fayetteville, North Carolina, Chamber of Commerce wrote to Truman and recommended Devers for the post. The members had watched Devers command Fort Bragg in 1940–1941 and believed that "General Devers would be a most fit successor to General Eisenhower."[92] The Business and Professional Women's Club of Fayetteville also wrote to Truman to "recommend to you for your consideration a man that we all here in Fayetteville love and admire. A man that did, and is, still doing a wonderful job for his country."[93] There is no evidence that Devers encouraged the citizens of Fayetteville to lobby on his behalf.

Given his cool relationship with Eisenhower, it is doubtful that Devers entertained any real hope of being selected for the job. In addition, his mandatory retirement date was September 1949, leaving insufficient time to serve a full two-year term as chief. In early 1948 Bradley became chief of staff, and Eisenhower became president of Columbia University.

During Eisenhower's tenure as chief of staff, he wrote three officer efficiency reports on Devers. For the period 1 July to 31 December 1946, Ike wrote that the nature of Devers's duties "is such as to preclude observation and supervision of his work to the degree" envisioned by the regulations governing efficiency reports. Nonetheless, he wrote, "I have conferred during the past year with him and have determined that he is performing his duties in a manner eminently satisfactory to the War Department and in such a manner as to be classed superior."[94]

In Devers's efficiency report for the first half of 1947, Eisenhower rated him fifth out of eight full generals and noted, "He renders willing and generous support of the plans of his superiors regardless of his personal views in the matter." He ended the report by describing Devers as "an alert, impulsive and energetic officer of complete loyalty and devotion to duty."[95] In his final report on Devers, for the period ending 6 February 1948, Eisenhower admitted that much of his opinion of Devers was based on "wartime contacts," although he was "acquainted" with his work as AGF commander. He characterized Devers as "a positive, confident type, bordering on the impulsive. . . . I would prefer to use him in command positions rather than in one demanding long, patient, and exhaustive study and analysis."[96]

Eisenhower's assessment of Devers as energetic and bordering on the impulsive was an accurate portrayal of a man who spent his career getting things done. From his days as a lieutenant through his service as AGF commander, Devers always looked for ways to work the system, cut red tape, and expedite problem solving. The results were often outstanding, such as his efforts to facilitate the development of the DUKW and the self-propelled 105mm howitzer. He looked for opportunities to "push the ball downfield," such as when he planned to jump the Rhine. He seldom "took council of his fears," as Eisenhower had done during the Nordwind crisis of December 1944. He was also open to new ideas and technologies. For example, as AGF commanding general, he encouraged the army to look into the use of helicopters. He served as a member of the Joint Research and Development Committee with General Spaatz in 1946, and he encouraged the efforts of Larry Bell, president of Bell Aircraft Corporation, to sell the military on the idea of employing helicopters.[97]

General Bruce C. Clarke, who served as AGF G-3 in 1947, remembered years later how Devers encouraged the army to buy Bell helicopters. Bell had called Clarke and asked for a meeting with him and Devers. Clarke arranged it, and during lunch, Bell pointed out that his Buffalo factory had finished its wartime orders and was idle. "He went on to say that he had developed a helicopter which he felt had a future with the Army," but he needed an order for fifty helicopters to make production worthwhile. After the meeting, Devers sent a letter to Eisenhower recommending the purchase of Bell helicopters. Ike replied that although "he was favorably inclined," the army did not have the funds; however, "he would approve the use of Army Ground Forces funds if General Devers could spare any." Devers directed Clarke to search for the necessary funds, and by canceling some other activities, the AGF found the funds to pay for the helicopters. Clarke recalled that when he was a corps commander in Korea in 1953, he and Bell flew around visiting troops in Bell helicopters. He ended his reminiscence by noting, "The great use and value of helicopters in Vietnam stems in good part to the forward looking actions of Generals Devers and Eisenhower."[98]

As AGF commander, Devers continued to cultivate personal relationships with industrialists, as he had done with Detroit executives in 1941–1943, when he was with the Armored Force. During the war, these relationships had helped get manufacturers and the Ordnance Office working together to develop tank engines, tracks, and guns. After the war, he visited Bell's factory in Buffalo and introduced Bell to several important air force officers. Bell later thanked him for talking with Lieutenant General Pete Quesada, "as he will be of great help in pioneering the helicopter program as will General Eaker."[99] Devers also visited various business conferences, including that of the aircraft industry.

Devers helped revive joint army-navy amphibious training and encouraged the secretary of war to stay abreast of such developments. In November 1947 the two services carried out their first joint amphibious training operation since the end of World War II. The exercise, conducted near Panama City, Florida, involved elements of the 2nd Armored Division and naval and air units. The AGF provided an "aggressor force" that had been trained at Fort Riley to simulate potential enemy forces. Preparations for this exercise took more than a year. Air force, navy, and army units worked together to iron out issues related to communications, intelligence, and doctrine.[100] Senator Lodge, in a report to Senator Arthur Vandenberg, characterized the joint exercise as one of "the most encouraging of recent developments I have seen in the defense of America because it was evidence of real teamwork between our services."[101]

Whether it involved the development or exploitation of new technologies or the revival of joint training, Devers continued his energetic and optimistic efforts to improve training and prepare forces for future conflicts. As he did so, the U.S. military underwent yet another major reorganization—one that would dramatically affect both the AGF and Devers.

Further Army Reorganization, 1947–1949

The Eisenhower reorganization of 1946 had eliminated the Army Service Forces and many of Marshall's streamlining reforms implemented during the war. During Eisenhower's tenure as chief of staff, the various parts of the War Department continued to jockey for resources and influence. At the same time, the Truman administration began the process of creating a Department of Defense to unify the armed services.

After years of study and quite a bit of debate among the services, Congress passed the National Security Act of 26 July 1947. The act created a single military department directed by a civilian secretary of defense. The secretary of defense was more a coordinator than a director of defense matters, with limited effective control over the secretaries of the army, navy, and air force (now officially separated from the army), who continued to have direct access to the president. Under the provisions of the act, the War Department was renamed the Department of the Army, and a new Department of the Air Force was created as a coequal to the Departments of the Army and Navy.[102] The act also created a National Security Council to advise the president on national security policy and renamed the Office of Strategic Services the Central Intelligence Agency. The 1947 act officially recognized the Joint Chiefs of Staff (JCS) and limited it to 100 staff officers. The chairman of the JCS was designated an adviser to the secretary of defense but had little authority over the uniformed service chiefs.[103]

The National Security Act failed to unite the armed services in a Department of Defense in any real sense. In a statement to Congress in 1958, President Eisenhower characterized the national defense establishment created in 1947 as "little more than a weak confederacy of sovereign military units . . . a loose aggregation that was unmanageable."[104] In 1949 Congress amended the act to strengthen the authority of the secretary of defense and to remove the three service secretaries from the National Security Council. The changes in the 1947 act, in the words of Millett and Maslowski, "started a trend to centralize defense planning in the office of the Secretary of Defense."[105]

While the consolidation of the armed forces in a Department of Defense was under way, a study by the army staff recommended that the AGF's control over army units and installations in the United States be ended. This study, known as the Cook Report, recommended in late 1947 that the AGF be turned into a special staff agency and renamed the Army Field Forces (AFF); the title of its commanding general would be changed to chief of the Army Field Forces. The Cook Report also advocated separating the six regional armies in the United States from the newly named Army Field Forces; these armies would report directly to the army chief of staff. The AFF would retain responsibility for the army schools, the combat arms boards, the training of individuals and units, and the development of combat doctrine.[106] The impetus for these changes was the confusion caused by the Eisenhower reorganization. The army staff, the AGF, the technical and administrative services, and the field armies had engaged in numerous "petty local disputes" over budgets, base operations, and relations with the civilian components, and these issues were regularly referred to the chief of staff for resolution. Confusion was also caused by the divided loyalty of the six army commanders, who reported on administrative matters to the Department of the Army and on tactics and training to AGF headquarters.[107]

Devers recommended an alternative solution to this confusion in September 1947. In Devers's view, the armies should remain under AGF control, and they should have command authority over most installations in their areas.[108] Eisenhower's successor, Bradley, rejected this course of action and ordered that the Cook Report's recommendations be implemented. Army Circular 64, issued on 10 March 1948, stripped the AGF of its command functions and renamed it the AFF, which was designated the operating agency for the Department of the Army within the United States. Its functions were restricted to "the general supervision, co-ordination, and inspection of all matters pertaining to the training of all individuals utilized in a field army."[109]

The Army Field Forces

Bradley's decision changed Devers's situation significantly. He was effectively demoted to the head of a staff agency that reported to the army staff.

The changes in the structure of the army did not, however, eliminate the confused lines of authority. Although the AFF was charged with supervising training in all army schools, the technical branches also controlled branch-specific curricula in their schools. This situation created the potential for disputes between the AFF and the technical branches over what was to be taught and how training was to be supervised.

Devers dealt with this situation in a personal manner, discussing it with the chiefs of the various technical branches. For example, in June 1948 Devers wrote to Major General Edward Witsell, the adjutant general of the army, to determine how the AFF could carry out its training supervision functions while avoiding conflict with the adjutant general's school at Camp Lee, Virginia. He wrote, "I have been giving considerable thought as to how I can best discharge the responsibilities assigned my office. . . . I have thus far been able to work out highly suitable arrangements with the several Army commanders whereby some administrative and command entanglements . . . have been foreseen and obviated even before they had a chance to arise. I have every confidence that your Office and mine will continue to exercise the closest and most sympathetic collaboration in pursuit of our common goal." Devers went on to say, "I am convinced that through exercising a close supervisory interest in the curricula and teaching processes of the Army Schools . . . I will be using the most effective means open to me to carry out the responsibilities laid upon my office" by Army Circular 64. He added that in the adjutant general's school, there was little overlap or chance of disagreement over programming, doctrine, or instructional method, and "fiscal, logistic, and administrative matters are beyond the province of my office." Devers assured Witsell that the AFF would work only through the adjutant general's office, unless they both agreed that, in specific matters, direct communication between the schools and the AFF was acceptable. He closed his letter by saying he had not yet given guidance to his staff on these matters because he wanted to get Witsell's thoughts first.[110]

Major General Witsell responded positively to Devers's letter, assuring him, "I concur completely in the principles and ideas you have expressed." Witsell was "satisfied that no problems of overlapping responsibility or jurisdiction will arise that we cannot solve immediately." Witsell also welcomed AFF staff members to visit his school and to make suggestions that would improve its academic functions.[111]

To ensure that all the schools were working toward the same training objectives, the AFF issued instructions to them and to the Command and General Staff College prescribing the level of training and the appropriate curricula. Devers believed that if these instructions were followed, he could "assure the Chief of Staff that approved and effective instructional methods are employed" and that no harmful gaps or overlap existed in the schools.[112] By working patiently and civilly with the various branch chiefs, Devers did everything he could to minimize doctrinal or pedagogical conflicts.

During his last year at the AGF-AFF, Devers continued to work to improve training, develop new technologies, and prepare the army for future conflicts. He was probably disappointed when he lost command authority over the armies in the United States, and he could not have been pleased when he was demoted to chief of an organization reporting to the army staff. Nonetheless, in one of the longest assignments of his career, he had played an important role in the army's transition from war to peace and its efforts to prepare for threats from communist aggression.

Devers consistently picked the best men he could find for critical command and staff positions in the AGF and in the army schools. He remained open to new ideas and technologies. And he worked hard to rebuild the National Guard and the reserves. Bradley noted in Devers's officer efficiency report for the first half of 1948 that he was "a fine executive who possesses a high degree of mental and physical energy."[113] In his August 1949 report, Bradley wrote that Devers was "conscientious and energetic" and "does not hesitate to assume responsibility." Further, "he is in better physical condition than many officers who are much younger." Devers finished his army career on a high note, with Bradley noting, "He has a pleasing personality and makes friends easily."[114] This is not the description of a man who had become bitter.

17

Retirement and Beyond

Jacob Devers was in his fortieth year of army service in 1949. Under existing rules, his mandatory retirement date was the end of the month of his sixty-second birthday: 30 September 1949. He and Georgie had started making concrete plans for their retirement in mid-1948. In September 1948 Georgie wrote to Kitts, "We are going to build on the farm at Leesburg, VA." Georgie's father had decided to "give Jamie the farm and me the house," and she was pleased that Jake was interested in the 130-acre farm, which could support a small herd of cattle.[1] They also decided to keep the "Yellow House" in Georgetown, where Georgie had lived during the war.[2]

Georgie anticipated having a view of the Blue Ridge Mountains "instead of blue water." She sensed she would miss Fort Monroe but felt the move was "right and it's wise."[3] Although Devers knew next to nothing about raising cattle or farming, the prospect intrigued him. He and Georgie planned to build a modern one-story, five-room house on the property. Georgie looked forward to a scaled-down lifestyle and the end of her official responsibilities for entertaining. She told Kitts: "I was either making beds or getting out the blankets or putting them away, fighting moths and mildew. The house [at Fort Monroe] is so big and there are so many meals to plan and buy for. Heaven will consist of a two room cottage for me!"[4]

As Georgie looked forward to a simpler life, Jake continued to work long hours as commander of the Army Field Forces. Georgie sensed that he would have difficulty adjusting to retirement after such an eventful career. Their plans for the Lyon farm were part of Georgie's efforts to help her husband adapt to being retired. "The house," she told Kitts, "will be ready and waiting for him, so he'll have no time to wonder what he'll do the day after he is retired as so many men have done."[5]

Devers had few hobbies to pursue after retirement.[6] He had participated in his last polo game in 1939. He occasionally played golf but had not done so very often, due to his hectic schedule during his last eight years of service. Eisenhower, Marshall, Smith, and Bradley faced similar challenges after retiring from the army. However, unlike Devers, they continued in government service. Marshall served as Truman's representative to China in 1946, secretary of state in 1947, and secretary of defense in 1949. Smith served as ambassador to Russia and then head of the newly established Central Intelligence Agency. Bradley became head of the Veterans Administration before taking over as chief of staff of the army in 1948, and Eisenhower became president of Columbia University after his tour of duty as chief of staff.

Eisenhower and Bradley also wrote books about their exploits in the war. Eisenhower received the Pulitzer Prize for *Crusade in Europe,* and the book set the tone for postwar views of his role in the conflict. He avoided open criticism of Devers and made the following observation about Sixth Army Group's invasion of southern France: "There was no development of that period which added more decisively to our advantages or aided us more in accomplishing the final and complete defeat of Germany than did this secondary attack coming up the Rhône Valley."[7] When Bradley published his autobiography in 1951, he sent a copy to Devers.[8] Jake responded with a thank-you note but could not help pointing out to Bradley, "Of course I cannot agree with you about the command set-up in Europe. You almost lost the battle because of it. . . . I am sure that you would not have had your logistic troubles if you had used my command system. We didn't have trouble coming into Southern France—and I used exactly that command set-up."[9]

Marshall refrained from writing an account of the war beyond the documents he presented to Congress and the president. Perhaps he chose not to write a postwar book because he had witnessed firsthand the battle of the books in the 1920s among the leading generals of World War I.[10] Devers never thought about writing a war memoir. For one thing, he was too busy as AGF commander to devote time to such a project. Also, like Marshall, he did not feel comfortable as a writer. Further, from 1945 to his retirement, Eisenhower and Bradley were his superior officers, and much of what he had to say might have been critical of their wartime decisions.

Retirement

On 3 August 1949, with Devers's retirement a little more than a month away, Senator Henry Cabot Lodge Jr. addressed the Senate concerning the general's lifetime of service to the nation. After briefly listing Devers's major commands during the war and noting the "innumerable ways" he had "left his mark" on the army, Lodge told the senators that what he really wanted to discuss were Devers's "personal qualities":

> General Devers was 100 percent the military professional in the very finest sense of the term. His time was spent, except for a few brief hours of sleep at irregular intervals, in doing the job of a general. A man of boundless energy, he demanded much of others, and drove everyone hard, but no harder than he drove himself. He had no favorites, no stable companion or crony to relieve the loneliness of high command. Like the captain of a ship, he had no sociability of any kind. His entire life throughout the war was the life of a soldier, and everyone was treated alike and according to his utility in the scheme of things.

Lodge further noted that Devers drew on the experience of a lifetime when the war came. And because he took a genuine interest in others, he was able to choose "the best subordinates he could find. . . . He gave his whole trust to the people in whom he once expressed his faith."[11]

Lodge had worked for Devers during the most important year of the general's wartime service (1944–1945). He had had Devers's full confidence in his dealings with de Lattre and the French. He knew that Devers did not harass his subordinates; instead, he empowered them so that each man felt, in Lodge's words, as if he were "in business for himself." Devers had the "knack of taking men who had not always been successful" and letting them know that he expected the very best from them. Devers took responsibility for his decisions and actions. He had "imagination and a rare ability to understand the factors which are important in war." Devers was, according to Lodge, "the very archetype of the man on whom the Nation completely and utterly depends when its life hangs in the balance. Yet, with all these honors and achievements, it can truthfully be said that he is not, in the words of St. Paul, puffed up."[12]

During his final summer on active duty, Devers underwent his end-of-service physical examination, which revealed "no incapacitating defect warranting appearance before an Army retirement board," meaning that he had no need for disability payments.[13] He received his retirement orders on 2 September 1949, and his retirement date was set for 30 September. He was also promoted to full general on the army retirement list as of 1 October.[14]

The Deverses moved to the Lyon farm on Seneca Road near Herndon,

Virginia, in late September. The farm, which they called York Hill, was about thirty-five miles south of Sugarloaf, Maryland, with views of the Blue Ridge Mountains to the north. The brick house was about half a mile from their gate on the county road. Georgie described her new home to Kitts in glowing terms: "The house has a large living room . . . glass to the mountains and to the court, [with a] fireplace for cord logs at the right end. A tiny pie shaped study, a 12 × 12 ft. octagonal dining room for my round table. A big kitchen, dressing room, bath and our big bedroom 22 x 15 at the left. Two bedrooms and bath between on the right. . . . Heat in the floor . . . wood paneling stained and waxed, nothing to paint or paper, no upkeep." She also had a dishwasher, garbage disposal, washer and dryer, and a new Frigidaire "ice box" with a deep freezer compartment.[15] Georgie and Jake employed a Mexican couple to work as a cook and a handyman, and Dorothy Benn Ham remembered that there were "constant complications" concerning the couple's immigration status. Jake "went far beyond the call of ordinary kindness to unravel their troubles."[16] The couple moved away in the summer of 1950, after their immigration issues were settled.

Devers jumped right into the life of a gentleman farmer and raised cattle for a while. In addition to learning how to care for the animals, he kept busy mowing the grass around the house and planting trees and shrubs. He and Georgie frequently entertained army friends and people from York. One guest from York described her impressions in a letter to Kitts: "Their house is so light and sunny—I love the round dining room with the four big closets filled with beautiful Dresden china. . . . Their house is so compact, and complete in every detail."[17]

Georgie seemed to be very happy at the farm. She told Kitts, "I like the country best in the winter. I love the open fires, the long lamp-lit evenings and the wide winter skies, and the cool air." She and Jake planted shade trees around the house and planned a garden, although she realized a garden is "always so much nicer in thought than in fact." She liked the pictures of the vegetables on the seed packages "as much as I do the things themselves."[18]

With so much work on the farm, the Deverses needed some help, so in September 1950 they hired an African American couple to take over the duties of cook and handyman. Curtis and Beatrix Murphy had been working in Washington and were recommended to the Deverses by a friend named Mrs. Adele Murphy. Beatrix and Curtis "had just gotten married and had lost [their] first child." The young couple moved into a small house on the farm, and as Beatrix remembered, the Deverses "let us fix [it] up . . . they gave us a whole house all to ourselves."[19]

After the Murphys had been on the farm for about a month, General Devers invited them into his study to talk about their "situation." It turned out that the young couple owed a hospital bill of about $2,000. "Well," Beatrix recalled, "he paid my hospital bill" and "said we could pay it back as we went along." However, Devers never let them repay him. "From then he went on and made our life much better. I mean we began to understand how to give and how to take, and how to live, and how to understand people."[20] Devers allowed Curtis to order all the tools he needed from Sears to fix up their house. Curtis noted that even though Jake was "set in his ways," he usually allowed Curtis to do things his way. Curtis considered Devers "more than just a boss to me—and to my family—he's been, to me, a father; to my children and my family."[21] Curtis later became Jake's driver.

When Beatrix had another child, Georgie took an active part in helping the young mother with her son. "I mean," Curtis recalled, "she practically raised James. She washed him, she bathed him, she clothed him." The Murphys considered Georgie "part of the family," and since Beatrix "didn't know anything about babies," Georgie taught her how to care for an infant. "She was excellent with children. And she taught him [James] beautiful things and she would always give him something lovely—so did the General—my son adored both of them."[22] Dorothy Benn Ham recalled Georgie dancing around the living room with James when he was two years old, "singing a gay little song."[23] The Murphy children became like grandchildren to Jake and Georgie, whose daughter Frances had no children.

Not surprisingly, Curtis found Jake to be a "rather impatient person"; initially, he would say "you have all the time on the world" to get a task done, but later he would "want it finished right now."[24] Nonetheless, Curtis and Beatrix were devoted to the Deverses and were an important part of their lives. For a brief period in the 1950s, when Jake and Georgie moved in with her newly widowed mother, the Murphys worked in Fredericksburg. When the Deverses moved back to their Yellow House in Georgetown, the Murphys moved to Alexandria and resumed their roles as housekeeper and handyman-driver. When the Murphys bought a house in Alexandria, Devers loaned them the money for the down payment.[25] They worked for Devers until his death in 1979.

The Murphys provided several insights into Devers's personality and character. Curtis remembered, for instance, the time "a colored soldier" came by and asked the general for a $200 loan. Devers loaned him $100, not expecting repayment. As it turned out, "He paid every cent of it back." Curtis also remembered the time Jake and Georgie helped a young doctor establish a clinic in nearby Chantilly, Virginia. Some years later, when Curtis drove the general out there, the doctor was glad to see him and told Jake that "he will always be indebted to him because otherwise he wouldn't have gotten his clinic" started because he was a "foreigner" and new to the area. In Curtis's view, Devers "has always helped somebody! He helped everybody."[26]

The American Automobile Association

Although Jake enjoyed living on the farm, he found that raising cattle and doing his chores in the yard did not fully absorb his energy or hold his interest. Therefore, when Major General L. D. Gasser (Ret.) asked him to join the American Automobile Association (AAA) as managing director of the AAA Foundation for Traffic Safety, Devers accepted.[27] He planned to commute from the farm to Washington and work in AAA headquarters.

Characteristically, before he retired, Devers had helped find jobs for many of his personal staff. For example, he had found his secretary, Dorothy Benn, a job with the U.S. Diplomatic Mission in Japan. She later described what happened: "On the very day I was leaving my home in Pennsylvania . . . I had a telegram from General Devers asking me to stop to see him at his home." Once she arrived at the farm, Georgie said, "Jamie, you'd better get us a drink before we start talking." After they were settled in the living room, Devers told Dorothy that he wanted her to stay in the Washington, D.C., area and serve as his executive assistant at AAA. Although her household possessions were in storage and some of her luggage was already on its way to Japan, Dorothy accepted the offer. Georgie then suggested that Dorothy "should move into one of the guest rooms . . . and stay there until [she] could find a place to live in the Washington area." Dorothy accepted and lived at the farm for about three months.[28]

Dorothy's daughter Bonnie lived with her close friend "Linkey" during this period, but she visited the farm often. Bonnie has fond memories of her time with the Deverses. She talked to and chased the cattle, much to Jake's chagrin. She played with his boxer, Sambo, admired the peacocks that roamed the property, and rode an old workhorse named Lily. She recalled that Georgie loved her mother Dorothy and treated her "perhaps like a daughter." Years later, when Bonnie had two sons, Jake saw "them as the sons he did not have."[29]

Bonnie's mother, Dorothy Benn, was an incredibly talented woman. She was a graduate of Temple University and had earned a master's degree in English before the war. Her first husband, William Benn, was an air force bomber pilot who had been listed as missing in 1943 and was presumed dead. She and their daughter Bonnie moved from California to Washington, where she worked in the War Department as a secretary. She remarried in 1960, three years after her husband's remains were found in New Guinea. Her second husband was Dr. William T. Ham, a Harvard professor who had moved to Washington to work in the Roosevelt administration. Professor Ham died in 1973.[30]

While Dorothy lived at the farm, Georgie treated her like a family member. As Dorothy commented later, "No hostess could have been kinder. Often when I returned after an evening spent in the city . . . I would find the latest copy of an interesting magazine on my bedside stand, together with an inviting bit of fresh fruit . . . and I knew that Mrs. Devers had herself come to the guest wing of the house [and] turned down my bed." She felt like a welcome guest in the house. Dorothy recalled about Jake, "Those were the days when the General came to breakfast every morning (particularly on weekends) with the day's agenda (long lists of things to be accomplished) all mapped out . . . not only for himself but for everyone on the premises." And although he was generous to family and friends, he retained "many of the marks of a frugal Pennsylvania Dutchman." For example, Dorothy revealed that he was careful to instruct his aides to turn off all the lights when he left his hotel room, and he regularly reused envelopes. He never liked to waste time either.[31]

Dorothy bought a house in Falls Church, Virginia, in early 1950. When her first husband's remains were found in New Guinea in 1957, Devers arranged for a small plane to carry Dorothy and Bonnie to Kentucky, where Benn would be buried; he accompanied them to the service at the cemetery. Dorothy noted, "The kindness, consideration, and generosity extended by the General to his relatives and the relatives of Mrs. Devers [were] unbounded." She also remembered that Jake did not forget the faithful service of his wartime orderlies James Johnson and Sergeant Turnipseed or his driver George Williams. She said, "All of the persons whom I have met or know who have worked for and with General Devers have utter and lasting devotion for him—persons like Generals Bolte, Bruce Clarke, David Barr, [and] Ambassador Henry Cabot Lodge."[32]

Devers began his new job with the AAA Foundation for Traffic Safety in January 1950. He had accepted the position because he was "intrigued by the concept presented as a challenge and a much-needed constructive effort to combat the growing problem of traffic accidents and fatalities."[33] He and Dorothy Benn were the entire staff of the foundation, which had offices in the Mills Building at the corner of Pennsylvania Avenue and Seventeenth Street in Washington, near Blair House. Devers's primary task was to raise money for the foundation from individuals and businesses "with vested or social interests in prevention of . . . accidents."[34]

Devers worked to develop communication and cooperation with the local AAA chapters throughout the United States. He took a special interest in the School Safety Patrol program and in safety films produced for use in schools. In these efforts, he was guided by the safety measures developed by the AAA's Traffic Safety Department under the direction of Burton Marsh. Marsh and other AAA executives felt that "Devers' name and personality would be of immense value because of the contacts he had or could have with prominent persons" who could make substantial financial contributions to the foundation.[35] Devers did not travel much or give many speeches, and most of his efforts were directed toward making personal contact with executives in major American companies such as General Motors and the American Trucking Association. He also visited several of the larger AAA chapters, such as the one in Chicago, to enlist their active support and cooperation. But he often found that "the clubs seemed resistant" to involvement with the national organization. Although he was glad to be busy and to have an opportunity to meet interesting and active people, he did not enjoy fund-raising or approaching people with the "ulterior motive of asking them to contribute money."[36]

Devers worked for AAA for just one year, largely because of his dislike of fund-raising. Near the end of 1950, when another opportunity arose, he tendered his resignation. He left on good terms with AAA and moved on to work for the Fairchild Engine and Airplane Corporation.

Fairchild Engine and Airplane Corporation

Devers's title at Fairchild was technical assistant to the president, and Dorothy Benn continued to serve as his executive assistant. His office was on the tenth floor of the Cafritiz Building at 1625 I Street, Washington, D.C. Fairchild produced the "Flying Boxcar" (C-119) transport aircraft for the air force from 1947 to 1955. More than a thousand of these planes were built and saw extensive service in the Korean War, the French war in Indochina (1950–1955), and the Vietnam War (1962–1973). Devers had been very interested in the development of this aircraft while at Army Field Forces, and according to Dorothy, he offered "valuable suggestions concerning the requirements of a transport that had to do with the mobility of troops and equipment."[37]

Devers was primarily a part-time adviser to the president of Fairchild.[38] In 1959, in a report mandated by Congress from retired military officers who worked for private companies that sold services or goods to the military, Devers described his role with Fairchild: "My sole endeavors, working with the designers and technical people, have been to secure a fighting organization which is air-transportable, which has light weight equipment, including rifles and, in many instances, changing the shape of equipment so that it can be airborne. The emphasis being on surveillance, and a balance between mobility and firepower."[39]

One of his early projects was to advise designers working on the aircraft being developed to replace the Flying Boxcar.[40] He also tried to get the military interested in that aircraft. For example, in a letter to Lieutenant General John Leonard, the commanding general of Fort Bragg and XVIII Airborne Corps, Devers explained, "I am intensely interested in air transportability and airborne operations." He believed that too many agencies were involved in the development of the new plane and that "specifications for a proper plane [have gotten] way out of hand." Devers emphasized to Leonard that "industry wants to give the Field Forces the airplane they need to carry their soldiers where they want them to go and then to supply them." In closing, he assured Leonard that "this is a problem that needs the advice of industry," and "I believe I know some of the answers."[41]

He wrote a similar letter to Brigadier General Bruce Clarke, commander of the 1st Armored Division, urging Clarke to reduce the weight of any new tank designs: "If we are going to go into air transportability, we have to have lighter weights and cargo planes that can land in short, rough fields." He closed by offering to take Clarke to lunch the next time he was in Washington and invited him to "stay with me out in the country."[42]

Devers also wrote to Dr. Vannevar Bush on behalf of the Fairchild Corporation. Bush had been the wartime head of the Office of Research and Development and led the Carnegie Institution in 1953. Bush oversaw the work of eight government research facilities that helped develop military equipment. Devers told Bush that Fairchild was building a prototype of a light cargo plane that would be able to land on "almost any kind of field in a very short distance," and it was trying to develop a cargo plane that could carry a 30,000-pound payload. It was also building a prototype of a "Transair Tractor," designed to replace the army's two-and-a-half-ton truck. He closed the letter by saying, "Sometime I would like to have Albert E. Blomquist, of Blomquist and Associates, brief you."[43] Fairchild failed to get contracts for any of this equipment.

Many "high-ranking air force officers came and went" through the office of Fairchild's president Richard Boutelle, and as his technical assistant, Devers contributed his military perspective to the development of the Armalite AR14 rifle.[44] Fairchild had acquired the Armalite Company in 1954 and established an Armalite Division. Armalite had been experimenting with plastics and metal alloys in an attempt to develop a lighter rifle to replace the army's M-1 Garand rifle, and Boutelle thought a lighter rifle might interest the army.[45] Devers believed the weapon had the potential to increase the firepower of infantrymen while reducing the weight of their rifles.

In a 1958 letter to Lieutenant General Bruce Clarke, now the commanding general of the Continental Army Command, Devers mentioned that Fairchild was "intensely interested in the drone program, which we think is well on the way to a break-through in . . . battlefield surveillance." He also noted that Fairchild's AR10 and AR15 rifles "meet the requirement of lightness—a requirement not met by any other rifle known to us—and which are far superior to anything that the Ordnance has produced." In closing, he told Clarke, "If we are properly supported I am sure we can equip the . . . Army so that it will have the hardware necessary to do the job."[46]

In the end, the army did not fund the drone program, and the Armalite rifle lost out to the M-14, which had greater long-range accuracy. In another letter to Clarke in 1959, Devers stood by his belief that the AR15 was a better weapon than the M-14, which he characterized as "obsolescent." He emphasized that his "only interest in this whole matter . . . is to see that the Army gets what it wants and needs, and that is light-weight, air transportable equipment to meet the conditions of the modern battlefield."[47]

When Fairchild had financial difficulties in 1959, it sold the license for the Armalite AR15 to the Colt Company. In the 1960s Colt sold 5 million M-16 rifles to the military to replace the M-14. The M-16 was based on the Armalite AR15 and remained the standard army rifle for decades.[48]

It is unclear what sort of impact Devers had during his years with Fairchild. He was not very good at small talk or cocktail parties, and Dorothy believed that "when it came to the lighter side of life as it was lived by some corporate executives—the trips, the parties, the drinks, the stories—the General was the proverbial fish out of water—and this quickly became apparent." Evidently, however, the Fairchild executives understood and "respected" this aspect of Devers's personality.[49]

Devers worked for Fairchild until 1959. During the Eisenhower administration, there was growing criticism of former senior military officers who represented companies that sold equipment or services to the Pentagon. Devers was one of those officers, but there is absolutely no evidence that he did anything illegal or unethical in his work with Fairchild. Dorothy was convinced that his motive for accepting the position was "his continuing interest in the good of the military services and the equipment being produced by industry for them." She was troubled that other retired officers working for the private sector did not have "the kind of basic integrity that was the foundation of the activities of JLD."[50]

During Devers's tenure at Fairchild, the corporation failed to secure the contract to build the replacement for the Flying Boxcar, and it failed to win some other key contracts as well. By 1959, the company was losing money and had closed its offices in downtown Washington and concentrated its staff and military advisers in Alexandria, Virginia. Dorothy remembered her last days with Fairchild as "unpleasant." "Business had fallen off and personnel changes created an entirely different atmosphere." When Fairchild closed its Virginia office and moved its activities to Long Island, Devers and Dorothy resigned.[51]

Meanwhile, in early 1952, Georgie's father died. After some deliberation, Georgie and Jake decided to move from the Herndon farm to the Lyon home in Washington, so they could help look after Georgie's mother. Jake was not cut out to be a farmer, and his work with the AAA and then with Fairchild made living at the farm impractical. Eventually, the Deverses moved back to the Yellow House in Georgetown. They sold the farm in 1957.[52]

The United Nations Commission to Kashmir

During the 1950s, Devers found several ways to serve his country outside of his work with Fairchild (which was only part time). In 1951 he was appointed military adviser to the United Nations commission that was facilitating negotiations between India and Pakistan over Kashmir, the disputed border area between those two newly independent nations. Secretary of State George Marshall had recommended Devers for the position, indicating Marshall's continued faith and trust in him. The commission's head agreed that Devers could sit in on deliberations between the two countries, "with the understanding that I would have no comments to make unless questions were directed to me."[53]

Devers arrived in Karachi, Pakistan, on 1 July 1951. He reported to Georgie that the "tough, pleasant, strenuous trip" had required three changes of planes and three nights of travel. The last leg was on a heavily loaded Air France Constellation, where the "service was perfect and as I am a good traveler I really enjoyed the trip." Before leaving New York, he had visited General Douglas MacArthur. During a layover in Paris, Devers had dinner with Eisenhower; they were joined by Jake's friends Ira and Ruth Eaker, "Tooey" and Ruth Spaatz, and Mrs. Curtis LeMay. "Ike was in fine form, told me a lot of things and verified some other things. He did most of the talking as did Mac in New York." Devers also mentioned to Georgie that both MacArthur and Eisenhower seemed interested in becoming president. He then wrote, "Life is funny. I really enjoyed my position and am glad I am sitting where I am. If you were here it would be perfect."[54]

During the Kashmir commission's shuttle diplomacy between Karachi and Delhi, Devers found both the Indians and the Pakistanis basically likable. "Many lack know-how, knowledge and skills for the work they are responsible for but they are all trying hard."[55] The commission worked for three months to find a peaceful resolution to the territorial dispute over Kashmir. In Devers's view, a solution could have been found if all parties had acted in good faith. Unfortunately, the Indian leader Nehru rejected an agreement the commission had worked out with the Pakistanis. "This," he noted years later, "immediately set up the problem which made everything difficult from there on and became Nehru's policy."[56]

Georgie felt the Kashmir mission pushed Jake's "personal horizons—perhaps a little wider." However, the negotiations stretched on through the fall, and by the end of October, Georgie told Kitts that Jake was "tired, mentally and physically," and wanted nothing more than to sit in his easy chair and have "time to meditate and think about the questions of the day."[57] In late 1951 Devers traveled to Paris to advise the United Nations about the ongoing attempts to broker a compromise between India and Pakistan. Georgie and her niece accompanied him, and they spent Christmas together in the French capital. Devers "had a very hectic time" but believed he had clarified the situation for the Security Council.[58]

Georgie kept busy at the farm during Jake's long absences with the UN mission. Although she had accompanied him on several trips to Europe, she told Kitts that "with family, cows, dogs, cats, fowls, servants, taxes, etc.," she was doubtful she could get away to visit York while he was away. She also mentioned that Jake was pessimistic about the chances of avoiding war between India and Pakistan, but at least the UN efforts "staved off war for a few more months."[59] In the end, no compromise could be reached, and to this day, Kashmir remains a major point of contention between the two countries. Nevertheless, Devers played an important part in the deliberations of the Kashmir commission and provided it with sound military advice.

Devers, like many others, found it difficult to get results through the United Nations. In a letter to his friend Lou Holland, he noted that the "United Nations is truly a debating society. It is a place where the Russians have a chance to call us all kinds of names." He was sure, however, that "we are not going to have a war, at least in '52, for I am convinced the Russians know they could not win. And I firmly believe they are afraid of war." As he told Holland, "One thing is sure—practically every nation in this world, outside of the Russian orbit, depends on the United States. They talk big, but when you get tough they immediately come to terms."[60] Devers, like many Americans in 1951, believed the United States needed a change in leadership. He felt the nation needed a leader who could stand up to Russian threats and lead the free world. During 1951, Dwight D. Eisenhower emerged as the logical choice for president of the United States.

I Like Ike

Eisenhower definitely wanted to be president, but as an active-duty officer, he was precluded by law from "directly" seeking the nomination.[61] In the fall of 1951 many internationally minded Republicans feared that the isolationist senator Robert Taft would get the Republican nomination. In September Thomas E. Dewey approached retired general Lucius Clay, who was a very close friend of Eisenhower's, and asked him to persuade Ike to throw his hat in the ring. Over the next three months Clay convinced Eisenhower to accept the Republican nomination if it were offered, as long as he did not have to actively campaign during the presidential primaries. Clay and

Dewey also agreed that Senator Henry Cabot Lodge Jr. should be the official head of the "draft Eisenhower" group, since Dewey was anathema to
many Republicans after his failed bids for president in 1944 and 1948. President Truman had a hand in getting Ike to commit, telling Eisenhower that
if he got the GOP nomination, Truman would retire to Missouri.[62] On 6
January 1952 Lodge announced that Eisenhower's name would be on the
New Hampshire primary ballot.[63]

During his visit to Paris in July 1951, Devers had sensed that Eisenhower was thinking of running. Once Lodge made the official announcement, Devers openly supported his former boss. In February 1952 Georgie
told Kitts, "Jamie says to make up your mind and vote for Ike." In Georgie's view, sixteen years of Democratic administrations had made politics
"more sordid, more extravagant, and less responsive to the electorate."[64]
Devers told his good friend in York, Philip Glatfelter, that he was "more
convinced than ever that Ike is the only man worth trying to elect in order
to improve this terrible situation that exists in the world today."[65] In April
Devers contributed $25 to Eisenhower's campaign.[66]

Eisenhower accepted the Republican nomination, and Lodge and others did a good job of running his campaign. Ike won in November; Lodge,
however, who had devoted too little time and energy to his own reelection, lost his Senate seat to John F. Kennedy. Devers continued to corre-
spond with Lodge and often shared his thoughts about international issues.
For example, in 1953 Devers forwarded a "Memorandum on China" from
General Ying H. Wen. Wen believed the Chinese "have had enough of the
Communists," but the "masses of the Chinese people will not join up or
follow Chiang Kai-Shek." Devers told Lodge that he generally agreed with
Wen, "if" the right leader for China could be found. Devers believed that
Eisenhower had handled the Chinese issue well "up to this point" and had
"shown wonderful patience and . . . great leadership."[67]

Devers was pleased with the Eisenhower administration's foreign policy
in its first three years. He told the president in a letter, "I would like to take
this opportunity to congratulate you on the magnificent work you have
done. . . . You have stopped creeping socialism and started the trend in the
correct direction." He also credited the administration with "rais[ing] the
standards of morality as practiced in government," and he felt that Ike had
demonstrated "true leadership" in the nation and the world.[68]

By 1956, his views toward Eisenhower's performance during the European campaign of 1944–1945 had mellowed, as he indicated to a historian

who was writing about Allied leaders in World War II: "I was never one of his men. However, he had a most difficult position—and for my book did an outstanding job. He made mistakes, as all good men do. He had dislikes, but when he was in trouble such as the Bulge, he always rose to the occasion and made the correct decisions. . . . Since he has been President he has lived up to my standards of integrity and morality and what is best for the country."[69]

During the Eisenhower administration, Devers represented the president at a number of important ceremonial events. In 1954 he attended the tenth anniversary celebrations of the invasion of southern France, and in 1956 he and Georgie assisted the Battlefield Monuments Commission in dedicating the military cemeteries at Epinal and Draguignan, France, and at Nettuno, Italy.[70] He also answered the call of the governor of Pennsylvania in 1952 when he was asked to serve on a commission set up to investigate conditions in the state's penal system. Devers served as spokesman for the commission's members as they visited nearly every prison in the state. After exhaustive study and careful deliberation, the commission produced a report in 1954 that made a number of recommendations for improvements in the penal system.[71] As Devers's relationship with Fairchild came to an end, President Eisenhower tapped him to replace George Marshall as chairman of the American Battlefield Monuments Commission. Devers accepted and served in that role until 1969.[72]

The 1960s

The American Battlefield Monuments Commission (ABMC) operates American military monuments and cemeteries around the world. First established in 1923 to manage the American cemeteries on the European battlefields of World War I, the commission's responsibilities grew significantly after the Second World War. When Devers became its chairman, the commission was responsible for twenty-four overseas cemeteries that held the remains of 125,000 Americans who had died overseas. Those cemeteries also contain "Tablets of the Missing," listing the names of another 94,000 Americans whose remains were never recovered. The ABMC is also responsible for twenty-six major memorials, such as the Saint-Mihiel monument from World War I and the Pointe du Hoc memorial from World War II.

The ABMC is not responsible for the daily operation and maintenance of the cemeteries and monuments. It serves more like a corporate board of directors, setting general policy and representing the commission's interests to Congress and the White House. The day-to-day operations of the ABMC are carried out by retired American officers and noncommissioned officers who direct and oversee the work done by locals in France, Italy, the United Kingdom, and elsewhere to maintain the cemeteries and monuments. When Devers became ABMC chairman, the overseas staff of the ABMC included 41 Americans and 392 foreign nationals.[73]

In July 1960 Jake and Georgie sailed to France, where they planned to combine his inspection tour of ABMC sites with a sightseeing trip. When they landed in Brest, Georgie was experiencing extreme discomfort from a lung infection, so she was unable to accompany him to the cemeteries of Normandy, southern France, and Tunisia or any of the local tourist attractions. She later reported to Kitts, "Jamie, entirely disinterested, saw every place I had hoped to . . . and brought pictures and descriptions to me on the ship or sitting forlornly on the shore . . . waiting for the crowd to climb up or down the cliffs." As they traveled along the African coast, Georgie found it "unbelievably hot and dusty and dirty . . . but Oh, so beautiful—blue and gold, all shades of both, and I was so sick and so stupid not to take a plane straight home."[74]

When they arrived in Paris in August, Georgie reported to Kitts that her "right lung was filled up with fluid . . . that kept my heart under strain till it gave out in Paris (heart failure is the term) on August 14th."[75] After Georgie spent several weeks in a Paris hospital, they flew home to Washington, where she was admitted to Walter Reed Hospital. By that time, her weight had fallen to 115 pounds, and she was diagnosed with pneumonia. She remained hospitalized until 10 September, when she returned home to the Yellow House.

Georgie's illness was a wake-up call, and she realized she had to take better care of herself. As she told her sister-in-law, she "had never given a thought to 'me,' but had kept such a watchful eye on mother." Her bout with pneumonia had taught her "how better to use what's left of me." The Deverses curtailed their entertainment schedule, in part to allow Georgie to recover, but she admitted that her desire for an active social life was "much curtailed by ambition and desire anyway."[76]

During their European trip and Georgie's illness, Mrs. Lyon's housekeeper, Elnora, had taken care of Georgie's mother and maintained their home. Curtis Murphy continued to serve as Devers's driver and handyman, but his wife Beatrix worked only part time, as she was busy raising their two children. While Georgie was recovering, she told Kitts, "Jamie as usual has shouldered all the responsibilities that I dropped . . . with such tact and delicacy—that I am almost reluctant to tell mother that I am coming home." Mrs. Lyon had enjoyed being "his girl," and Jake had made her feel "so important to his well-being and comfort that he has kept her mind off of my troubles. . . . He is the greatest man that I have ever known."[77]

Although the Deverses entertained less frequently after Georgie's recovery, Jake remained committed to his role as chairman of the ABMC. In that capacity, he returned to Europe on several occasions and stayed informed about French politics, since so many of the commission's sites were in France. The 1950s were a difficult period for France domestically, and Devers had personal insight into that nation's recent history and its leaders. For the first half of the decade, France fought a costly and unsuccessful war against Vietnamese nationalists and communists in Vietnam. At home, the French Communist Party was one of the largest political parties in the nation, and it opposed French participation in the North Atlantic Treaty Organization (NATO) and in the Indochina war. By 1958, the Fourth French Republic was on the brink of collapse when French settlers in French-controlled Algeria launched a coup against the Paris government. The settlers feared that the government was going to allow the Algerian majority to gain political equality. Rebel paratroopers seized Corsica and were contemplating a descent on Paris with airborne forces when Charles de Gaulle agreed to come out of retirement and assume executive authority in France. During the next few months, the French wrote and ratified a new constitution creating the Fifth Republic.

In January 1959 de Gaulle became the first president of the Fifth Republic, and for the next ten years, he led France. Not surprisingly, the strong-willed leader steered a new course in international relations. For example, he refused to allow his country to rely on its Anglo-American allies for security and insisted that France develop an independent nuclear weapons capability. In 1966, after foreign policy disagreements with the Johnson administration over the Vietnam War and other NATO issues, de Gaulle pulled the French armed forces out of the NATO military command. Americans generally condemned de Gaulle's actions, but Devers, who had dealt extensively with the French during the war, understood de Gaulle's views and the fragility of French domestic politics. In a letter to a friend in 1962, Devers noted, "I am a De Gaulle-ist. I have just been to France and I am for de Gaulle more than ever. . . . The man is far-sighted."[78]

Devers also had strong views about President Kennedy's response to the Russians' attempt to establish nuclear missile bases in Cuba in 1962. In a letter to a friend he noted, "The President did the only thing he could do. He should have done it earlier." He felt that Kennedy was right to call the Soviets' bluff and did not believe the Russians were willing to go to war with the United States over Cuba. Devers was also a supporter of the American policy of "containment" in Europe and believed that "through some means like the Common Market or the Atlantic Union or the Atlantic Council, we can find a way to turn European problems back to the Europeans and solve our domestic problems on a high plane of integrity."[79]

As chairman of the ABMC, Devers had several opportunities to meet President Kennedy, and he told a friend, "[the] President is pretty sharp. He has to be. I don't agree with a good many of his ideas, but as a fellow he is certainly likeable, helpful, and alert."[80] In 1965 the Association of the United States Army awarded Devers the George Catlett Marshall Medal for his "selfless and outstanding service to the United States of America" as head of the ABMC. In 1969, feeling that he should make way for a younger chairman, Devers resigned from the commission.[81]

Devers's work with the ABMC did not absorb all his energy, and he continued to make himself available as a consultant to the secretary of the army and the chief of staff. As a result, in May 1964 Devers and several other prominent retired generals were asked to take part in a large military exercise known as Joint Exercise Desert Strike. This "war game," held during the summer of 1964 near Needles, California, was the largest military training exercise conducted since World War II. More than 100,000 air force and army personnel took part, and the simulated combat involved more than 8,000 tanks and other vehicles and 800 aircraft.[82]

The scenario was as follows: Two countries, "Colonia" and "Nezona," shared a border along the Colorado River between California and Nevada, and they went to war over rights to the river's water. Devers was the leader of the Nezona government, and his war cabinet included his friend Ira Eaker and political scientist Raymond L. Garthoff, an expert in Soviet nuclear war strategy. Colonia was led by retired lieutenant general Clyde Eddleman, a former army vice chief of staff. He was assisted by retired Marine Corps general Merrill B. Twining and nuclear physicist Norman F. Ramsey, who had been NATO's first science adviser in the 1950s. These two "cabinets" simulated the political process through which a conflict over territory or water might escalate into an armed conflict.[83]

Desert Strike was also a training exercise for the military units involved and a test for many pieces of new equipment. Devers and the other senior role players steered the operation through its phases, allowing the active-duty military leaders to conduct tactical maneuvers in response to the changing situation. Devers told Georgie, "We eat well, work hard, but have a lot of fun. The experience is rich. . . . We even use Telestar, sending messages 6,000 miles in a matter of minutes." Despite advances in military technology, he remained convinced that the quality of personnel was the critical factor.[84] On 20 May Devers reported to Georgie, "We are really in a war. I have a cabinet of strong characters and I am in the middle."[85] The Nezonians launched a surprise attack across the Colorado River (simulating a Soviet-type attack in Europe) and initially drove the outnumbered Colonians (playing the role of NATO forces) back using conventional weapons. The Colonians then turned the tables on the aggressors by using modern military systems and superior airpower to stop the Nezonians; they then launched a flanking attack across the river with army airborne forces and marine assault units. The two nations got to the brink of nuclear war before they found a political solution to end the conflict.

The exercise went on for over a month. On 25 June Devers wrote, "The old men are getting tired and rather short in their relations with each other." The desert, "with its heat and dust and sand," was wearing on everyone involved.[86] When it ended, Desert Strike was considered a successful display of joint operations and a proving ground for new equipment and military procedures. Although he had enjoyed participating in the exercise, it was a physically demanding experience for the seventy-seven-year-old Devers. Nevertheless, later that summer he and Georgie vacationed in Spain, and when they returned, they met President Johnson.

Georgie, however, was beginning to show signs of failing health. Over the next three years, Georgie's heart disease forced her to spend time in Walter Reed Hospital. After an extended stay there in late 1966, Georgie insisted on going home to the Yellow House. She told her housekeeper "she had come home to die with her friends" and "couldn't think of any better place."[87] Jake was certainly concerned about Georgie, but he did his best not to let her or others see his worry. Beatrix Murphy recalled that Devers said little about the situation, but one could "see it in his expressions . . . if you knew him very well."[88]

Georgie's health declined rapidly in December 1966, causing the Deverses' close friends Bill and Dorothy Ham to forgo a Christmas Day visit to the Yellow House. Dorothy, who was devoted to both Georgie and Jake, wrote them a few days later, "It was only a real concern that we might disturb you that kept Bill and me from stopping at 1430 Thirty-third Street on Christmas afternoon on our way home from a short visit to Bonnie's." She thanked them for the gifts of cheese, fruit, and money and shared her hope that Georgie would get better. Dorothy then took the opportunity to review her thoughts about her family's relationship with the Deverses over the past twenty-one years:

> How often I have tried to convey to you how profoundly grateful I am that that path of mine . . . led me to the office of the Army Ground Forces . . . as Secretary to the Commanding General—and from there to Fort Monroe where I really learned to know Mrs. Devers too. I won't ever forget, either, the months I spent in your home on Seneca Road [near Herndon] and the warmth I felt there in your home—the Christmas Bonnie and I spent with you when her doll had his own place set at your table. [There are] myriads of reasons why "the Devers" mean more to me than I could ever express to anyone.[89]

A little more than a month later, Georgie returned to Walter Reed for the last time. She refused to leave her home on a stretcher and insisted that Curtis Murphy carry her down the stairs and put her in the ambulance. During her last few days at home, Georgie was characteristically thinking of others. For example, she took Beatrix Murphy aside and assured her there was "nothing wrong" with her children James and Ann, so "for heaven's sake stop fussing with them." She ended this counseling session by saying, "If I don't see you again, I want you to take care of the General for me."[90]

Georgie Lyon Devers died on 8 February 1967 in her seventy-sixth year. She was buried in Arlington Cemetery in a plot reserved for her and her husband.

Final Years

Jacob Devers turned eighty in September 1967. After Georgie's death, many friends and relatives encouraged him to move from the large, three-story Yellow House into an apartment somewhere in northwest Washington, where many of his friends lived. Jake refused. For the next decade, he remained in the Yellow House and continued to use his third-floor office. He walked up the two flights of stairs rather than use the elevator he had installed after Georgie's heart attack in 1965.[91]

General Devers chose to live a "normal" life. He personally answered the many condolence letters and cards he received "as soon as it was possible to do so."[92] He also took time to write a letter to the surgeon general thanking him for the fine care Georgie had received at Walter Reed.[93] Dorothy Ham continued to work as his part-time assistant, helping him deal with his voluminous correspondence. She generally went to his house twice a week, unless she and her husband were out of town. Dorothy maintained his files, typed his letters, and helped Devers prepare the speeches he gave to various groups.[94]

Catherine "Kitts" Devers also helped her brother adjust to his new life. As Dorothy said in 1972, Kitts "did all she could do, and still does all she can to help the General in those places and situations where a woman's touch is needed."[95] For the most part, however, Jake took charge of his own household affairs, even picking out wedding gifts for the children of friends who were getting married.

Curtis and Beatrix Murphy continued to work for the general at the Yellow House. Curtis served as chauffeur, although Devers kept his driver's license current until age ninety and occasionally drove himself. Beatrix cooked and cleaned, although by her own admission, she was not a great cook. But regardless of what she cooked, Jake would tell her, "You're doing a fine job." Devers also sent her to a cooking course at the Smithsonian Institution, where she was "the only Negro woman . . . taking the Julia Childs Course." He continued to take a personal interest in the Murphy children, Ann and James. He regularly provided them with tickets to symphonies, sports events, and lectures and even paid for Ann's school trip to Europe.[96]

Well into the mid-1970s Devers pursued an active life. He was regularly out of bed by 7:30. He played golf in the summer at the Army-Navy Country Club, although, according to Curtis Murphy, he didn't care much for the game but played for the exercise.[97] He was a member of the Cosmos Club, the Smithsonian Institution, the National Geographic Society, the Army-Navy Club, and the National Zoological Society. He regularly attended lectures at these organizations and took a keen interest in the news. Dorothy Ham recalled that he maintained an "amazing philatelic collection" and "started ten or twelve young people on stamp collections." His photography collection was arranged chronologically in seventy large albums that provided a pictorial record of his career and included photos of many prominent world leaders. Until at least age ninety, Devers studied investment publications and managed his own financial affairs. When his investments did well, he called it "good luck," but Dorothy called it "good management." He kept detailed records of his contributions, subscriptions, and all matters relating to his personal affairs.[98]

In 1973 Dorothy's husband Bill died. She continued to work for Devers, and little changed in their longtime professional relationship. But a year after her husband's death, Jake surprised Dorothy by asking if he could "court her." She said yes. After a year of courtship, the eighty-eight-year-old Devers asked Dorothy to marry him. She thought it over for several weeks before accepting his proposal.[99] Devers was twenty-three years older than Dorothy and had several medical problems, including shortness of breath caused by "organic heart disease," but for his age, he was in remarkably good shape.[100]

Jake and Dorothy were married on 28 May 1975 and had four happy years together. They had been associates for thirty years and were devoted to each other. Dorothy's daughter Bonnie had two sons that Jake treated like grandsons, and their decisions to attend the U.S. Military Academy may have been inspired by Jake's lifetime of service to the nation.[101]

Frances and Alex Graham lived in the Washington area and saw Jake and Dorothy periodically. They also attended Army-Navy football games with the Deverses in Philadelphia whenever they could. The day after the Army-Navy game of 26 November 1977, Alex died of a massive heart attack. Frances was distraught, and there was little Jake or Dorothy could do to help her through her grief.

Devers's physical examination records from 10 November 1975 indicate that he was in remarkably good health, with some minor hearing loss and small cataracts. The doctor noted that his pulmonary system was only "slightly worse since November 1973" and that Devers had a "mild" level of "organic heart disease . . . manifested by mitral insufficiency and 1st degree heart block."[102] His doctor prescribed Oretic and potassium chloride and directed him to return in one month for a follow-up visit.[103] Over the next six months, Devers's symptoms improved, and his blood pressure remained in the normal range (120/80).[104] Devers continued to play nine holes of golf four to five times a week, weather permitting, and his health remained stable for the next year before major problems developed.[105]

In May 1977 Devers returned to Walter Reed Hospital with complaints of shortness of breath and "decreased energy." Dorothy had also observed an abnormal breathing pattern known as Cheyne-Stokes, in which "progressively deeper and sometimes faster breathing [is] followed by a gradual decrease that results in a temporary stop in breathing called apnea." The underlying cause in Devers's case was probably congestive heart failure.[106] Because of his age, Devers was hospitalized for further treatment that included "left heart unloading with nitrates." Remarkably, when he was discharged on 13 June, Devers's pulse was 70 and his blood pressure 104/74. The doctor noted, "this is a well-developed, well-nourished white male in no acute distress," and Devers reported that "he once again had his equilibrium back."[107]

Dorothy and Jake continued to play golf after this hospitalization, but they monitored his health carefully. By the end of 1977, they noticed increased symptoms of heart disease. On 3 January 1978 Devers was admitted to Walter Reed, his chief complaints being chest pain and shortness of breath. The doctor diagnosed his condition as "congestive heart failure." Devers remained in the hospital for two weeks, during which time he was treated for various symptoms. When he was discharged on 18 January he weighed 157 pounds and was ambulatory and "feeling well," although still short of breath. He was suffering from mitral insufficiency, chronic congestive heart failure, and atrial fibrillation.[108]

Back home, Devers's condition slowly deteriorated, in spite of regular follow-up hospital visits. For most of the last year of his life, Devers was basically bedridden, although his mental faculties appeared to be unimpaired. Things took a turn for the worse on 3 October 1979, when he was readmitted to Walter Reed. Jacob Devers died of respiratory arrest on 15 October 1979. He was ninety-two years old. A long journey had come to an end. His wife Dorothy lived until 2007, when she died in Florida. His daughter Frances died in 1986.

General Jacob L. Devers is buried in Arlington National Cemetery, next to his first wife, Georgie Lyon Devers. His son-in-law Colonel Alexander Graham and his daughter Frances Graham are buried nearby. Devers donated his official and personal papers and most of his personal memorabilia to the York County Historical Society in York, Pennsylvania, where these items are carefully preserved and open to researchers.

Last Thoughts

This biography has described the personality, career, and service of a great American soldier and his family. He was a good person in every way. He did all he could to make the lives of those around him as pleasant and productive as possible. Above all, he gave a lifetime of service to his nation. Equally important are the things he did not do. Jacob Devers did not forget his boyhood friends or community. He did not cheat on his wife. He did not blame his subordinates for his own mistakes or failures. He was not overtly or covertly disloyal to his superior officers. He did not forget to take care of those who served him. He did not publicly castigate the character of others.

Devers's contributions to Allied victory in the Second World War were many and significant. He built Fort Bragg, trained the 9th Infantry Division, organized the Armored Force, commanded the European theater as Eighth Air Force came to maturity, served as deputy commanding general of the Mediterranean theater, and led Sixth Army Group in its incredibly successful invasion of southern France and its drive across the Rhine. He dealt with the French, showing empathy for their problems. He accepted whatever missions Generals Marshall and McNair gave him and accomplished them efficiently. In every assignment, he cared deeply for the well-being of his soldiers and loyally supported his superiors. Jacob Loucks Devers is a man who should never be forgotten by a grateful nation.

Acknowledgments

I owe thanks to many people for their help with this biography of Jacob Devers. First, as always, I thank my wife Jane, who worked diligently with me during our research trips to various archives and proofread every chapter. The impetus for this work came from Hal Nelson, Layne Van Arsdale, Andy Morris, Bill Stofft, and Rick Atkinson, who first suggested that I write a biography of Devers during a staff ride in Alsace. Hal, Layne, and Andy read every chapter and provided suggestions and insights.

Hal and Janet Nelson helped immensely during our research trips to the Military History Institute in Carlisle, Pennsylvania. General Nelson served as my research assistant at the MHI and at the York County Heritage Trust archive in York, Pennsylvania. The MHI staff, including Dr. Con Crane, Colonel Matt Dawson, and Richard Baker, made my many trips there very productive. Marty Andresen deserves special recognition for his volunteer work. Harry and Lynne Dolton facilitated our research trips to the National Archives in Washington, and Harry gave me the benefit of his clear understanding of strategy.

The staff and volunteers at the York County Heritage Trust, especially director Lila Fourham-Shaull, were of tremendous help. The Devers and Griess Papers are housed in that archive, giving researchers access to hundreds of boxes of material from Jacob Devers's life. Tim Nenninger, of the National Archives in College Park, Maryland, provided access to World War II documents and gave me sound advice and encouragement. Frank Shirer, chief archivist at the army's Center for Military History, and Robert Dalessandro, its director, gave me access to Devers's personnel file at the National Archives facility in St. Louis, Missouri. Eric Voelz copied the 3.75-inch-thick file and sent it to me.

The staff of the U.S. Military Academy library, special collections, and archive guided me through the Patch and Devers Papers and Devers's cadet records. Al Aimone, Suzanne Christoff, and Susan Lintelman were of special help. Lance Betros, former head of the Department of History, shared his insights into the history of the Academy during Devers's years there as a cadet and a member of the staff and faculty. Jim and Lois Johnson facilitated our research trips to West Point, and Jim provided sage advice as always.

I especially want to thank Roger Cirillo, director of publications for the Association of the United States Army, for arranging support for some of my research and providing a number of useful books and sources. Roger was instrumental in getting this book to publication.

I also owe special thanks to Bonnie Benn Stratton Hamstreet and her husband Roger for their insights into the lives of Jacob, Georgie, and Dorothy Devers. Bonnie first met Devers in 1945, when her mother Dorothy went to work for him. Dorothy was a close friend of both Georgie and Jake Devers and became Devers's second wife.

This biography has been greatly improved by the work of copyeditor Linda Lotz. I am incredibly appreciative of her thorough and well-informed review and her suggestions for corrections. Allison Webster, the acquisitions editor at the University Press of Kentucky, skillfully guided me through the sometimes daunting process of getting a book published. Her patience, clarity, and professionalism made this a pleasant experience.

Finally, thanks to Brigadier General Thomas Griess, researchers like me have access to transcripts of the interviews he conducted with General Devers, his family, and many of the people who knew him. Without these oral histories and documents, I could not have written this comprehensive biography. Tom Griess, then a colonel, was working on the Devers project when I met him in 1977. He was head of the History Department at the Military Academy when I arrived to teach European history. Griess conducted extensive research into Devers's life and service at the National Archives, the Center for Military History, and other archives. He worked closely with the York County Heritage Trust and deposited most of his research materials there. In the end, Griess completed just one chapter of his own planned biography of Devers before serious matters at the Academy absorbed his full attention. Griess also made it possible for me to complete my doctorate in history and always encouraged my interest in research and writing. I and hundreds of other army officers owe him so much.

All these people helped me with this work, and I deeply appreciate it. Any mistakes in the book, however, are mine.

Notes

Abbreviations

AGF	Army Ground Forces
CCS	Combined Chiefs of Staff
CG	commanding general
CMH	Center for Military History
DDE	Dwight D. Eisenhower
DP	Jacob Devers Papers, York County Heritage Trust
ETOUSA	European Theater of Operations, U.S. Army
GP	Thomas Griess Papers, York County Heritage Trust
MHI	Military History Institute, Carlisle, Pennsylvania
NA	National Archives
NATOUSA	North African Theater of Operations, U.S. Army
OPD	Operations Plans Division, U.S. Army staff
PRO	Public Records Office, U.K.
RG	Record Group
USMA	United States Military Academy, West Point, New York
YCHT	York County Heritage Trust, York, Pennsylvania

Introduction

1. Jeffrey J. Clarke and Robert R. Smith, *Riviera to the Rhine* (Washington, DC: CMH, 1993); Gordon Harrison, *Cross-Channel Attack* (Washington, DC: CMH, 1951); Forrest C. Pogue, *The Supreme Command* (1954; repr., Washington, DC: CMH, 1989); Charles MacDonald, *The Siegfried Line Campaign* (1963; repr., Washington, DC: CMH, 1990); Hugh Cole, *The Ardennes: The Battle of the Bulge* (Washington, DC: CMH, 1965).

2. Eisenhower memorandum, 1 February 1945, in *The Papers of Dwight David Eisenhower: The War Years*, 5 vols., ed. Alfred Chandler (Baltimore: Johns Hopkins University Press, 1970), vol. 4, message 2271; hereafter cited as *Eisenhower Papers*.

3. Martin Blumenson, ed., *The Patton Papers, 1940–1945* (New York: Houghton Mifflin, 1974), 414.

4. Ibid.; John A. English, *Patton's Peers: The Forgotten Allied Field Army Commanders of the Western Front, 1944–1945* (Mechanicsville, PA: Stackpole Books, 2009), 165.

5. Blumenson, *Patton Papers, 1940–1945,* 558.

6. Ibid., 636.

7. Omar Bradley and Clay Blair, *A General's Life: An Autobiography by General of the Army Omar Bradley* (New York: Simon and Schuster, 1983), 210.

8. Ibid.

9. Carlo D'Este, *Eisenhower: A Soldier's Life* (New York: Henry Holt, 2002), 483, 368, 670.

10. Rick Atkinson, *The Guns at Last Light: The War in Western Europe, 1944–1945* (New York: Henry Holt, 2013); Douglas Porch, *The Path to Victory: The Mediterranean Theater in World War II* (New York: Farrar, Straus and Giroux, 2004); Stephen R. Taaffe, *Marshall and His Generals: U.S. Army Commanders in World War II* (Lawrence: University Press of Kansas, 2011).

11. David Colley, *Decision at Strasbourg: Ike's Strategic Mistake to Halt Sixth Army Group at the Rhine in 1944* (Annapolis, MD: Naval Institute Press, 2008).

1. From York to West Point

1. *The 1909 Howitzer* (New York: Charles Willard, 1909).

2. Ibid.

3. Officer Efficiency Reports by Omar Bradley, 7 June 1948 and 22 August 1949, Devers Personnel File, NA, St. Louis, MO.

4. Michael A. Markey, *Jake: The General from West York Avenue* (York, PA: Historical Society of York County, 1998), 10–12.

5. Catherine Sophia Devers to her nephew James Devers, 6 February 1961, 1, box 2, DP; Markey, *Jake*, 10–15; Griess-Devers interview, tape 12, 14, box 3, DP.

6. Devers interview, tape 2, 10, box 23, GP.

7. Devers interview, tape 12, 7, box 3, DP.

8. Catherine Devers to James Devers, 6 February 1961, 1.

9. Markey, *Jake*, 15–16.

10. Ibid., 16.

11. Catherine Devers to James Devers, 6 February 1961, 2.

12. Markey, *Jake*, 17.

13. William Eckenrode, "Story of Gen. Devers' Early Life in York," *York Dispatch*, 26 June 1945, box 35056, Frank Devers Papers, YCHT.

14. Catherine Devers to James Devers, 6 February 1961, 2.

15. Markey, *Jake*, 14; Thomas Griess, "Prologue," 17, box 23, GP.

16. Devers interview, tape 12, 9, box 3, DP.

17. Ibid., 13.

18. Griess, "Prologue," 13.

19. Ibid., 14.

20. Catherine Devers to James Devers, 6 February 1961, 2.

21. Ibid.

22. Devers interview, tape 2, 9, box 23, GP.

23. Ibid.; Catherine Devers to James Devers, 6 September 1961, 2, box 2, DP.

24. Devers interview, tape 2, 7, box 23, GP.

25. Catherine Devers to James Devers, 6 February 1961, 2.

26. Markey, *Jake*, 17.

27. Devers interview, tape 2, 9, box 23, GP.

28. Eckenrode, "Story of Devers' Early Life," 1.

29. Ibid.

30. Catherine Devers interview, 11 February 1974, tape 61, 6, box 8, GP.

31. Markey, *Jake*, 18.

32. Eckenrode, "Story of Devers' Early Life."

33. Devers interview, tape 2, 6, box 23, GP.

34. Griess, "Prologue," 22.

35. Ibid., 9.

36. Markey, *Jake*, 19; Ira Weiser, "Reminiscences of Jake" (handwritten notes from sometime before 1956, when Weiser died).

37. Eckenrode, "Story of Devers' Early Life."

38. Devers interview, tape 2, 6, box 23, GP.

39. Ibid., 7.

40. Catherine Devers to James Devers, 6 February 1961, 2.

41. Devers interview, tape 2, 7, box 23, GP; Devers interview, tape 2, 7, box 3, DP.

42. Catherine Devers interview, tape 61, 10–14, box 8, GP.

43. Markey, *Jake*, 19.

44. A. Wanner, *Annual Report of the Public Schools of York* (York, PA: 1905), 26. I am grateful to the wonderful librarian-archivists Lila Fourhman-Shaull and Victoria Miller of the York County Heritage Trust for providing this information.

45. Walter Bond interview, 8 September 1965, box 2, DP; Griess, "Prologue," 24.

46. Devers interview, tape 12, 10, and tape 30, 59, box 3, DP; Markey, *Jake*, 20–21; Griess, "Prologue," 26; Devers interview with Professor Mac Coffman, 3 August 1971, 3 (copy in author's possession, courtesy of Coffman; hereafter cited as Coffman interview).

47. Devers interview, tape 12, 10, box 3, DP.

48. Markey, *Jake*, 21; Devers interview, tape 12, 10, box 3, DP.

49. Bond interview, 8 September 1965; Griess, "Prologue," 26.

50. Griess, "Prologue," 12; Markey, *Jake*, 20.

51. Griess, "Prologue," 25–26.

52. Eckenrode, "Story of Devers' Early Life."

53. Devers interview, tape 12, 11, box 3, DP.

54. Ibid.

55. Markey, *Jake*, 18–19; Devers interview, tape 12, 11, box 3, DP.

56. Devers interview, tape 12, 11, box 3, DP.

57. Eckenrode, "Story of Devers' Early Life."

58. Ibid.

59. Ibid.

60. Ibid.

61. Griess, "Prologue," 25; Devers interview, tape 12, 11, box 3, DP.

62. Devers interview, tape 12, 11, box 3, DP.

63. Ibid.

64. Devers interview, tape 2, 8, box 23, GP.

65. Quoted in Markey, *Jake,* 21.

66. Ibid.; Devers interview, tape 12, 12, and tape 30, 57, box 3, DP.

67. Devers interview, tape 2, 8, box 23, GP.

68. Devers interview, tape 30, 59, box 3, DP.

69. Ibid., 57–58.

70. Ibid., 58.

71. Ibid.; Eckenrode, "Story of Devers' Early Life"; Markey, *Jake,* 22; Coffman interview, 4.

72. Lance Betros, *Carved from Granite: West Point since 1902* (College Station: Texas A&M University Press, 2012), 80–82.

73. Markey, *Jake,* 22; Devers interview, tape 30, 59, box 3, DP.

74. Griess, "Prologue," 25.

75. Catherine Devers to James Devers, 6 February 1961, 2.

76. Ibid.

77. Coffman interview, 1.

78. Markey, *Jake,* 23; Devers interview, tape 14, 19, box 3, DP.

79. Edward M. Coffman, *The Regulars: The American Army 1898–1941* (Cambridge, MA: Belknap Press of Harvard University Press, 2004), 144–48; Devers interview, tape 12, 21, box 3, DP.

80. Devers interview, tape 14, 19, box 3, DP.

81. Betros, *Carved from Granite,* 22.

82. Ibid.

83. Ibid., 22–23.

84. Devers interview, tape 14, 20, box 3, DP.

85. Betros, *Carved from Granite,* 23.

86. Devers to Ira Weiser, 23 July 1905, box 3, DP.

87. Ibid.

88. Ibid.

89. Ibid.

90. "Abstract of Delinquencies," 10 July 1905, in *Description and School History of Cadets,* USMA Archives.

91. Devers to Weiser, 23 July 1905.

92. Martin Blumenson, *Patton: The Man behind the Legend, 1885–1945* (New York: William Morrow, 1985), 48–49.

93. Devers interview, tape 32, 11, box 3, DP.

94. Devers to Weiser, 23 July 1905.

95. Catherine Devers interview, tape 61, 17, box 8, GP.

96. "Abstract of Delinquencies," 25 and 29 July 1905.

97. Devers interview, tape 14, 32, box 3, DP.

98. Devers to Weiser, 15 August 1905, box 3, DP.

99. Ibid., 25 August 1905.

100. Quoted in Betros, *Carved from Granite,* 242.

101. Ibid.

102. Devers interview, tape 14, 30–31, and tape 15, 7, box 3, DP.

103. Ibid., tape 14, 32.

104. Devers to Weiser, 2 September 1905, box 3, DP.

105. "Abstract of Delinquencies," 2 and 4 September 1905.

106. Betros, *Carved from Granite,* 113.

107. Ibid.

108. Devers to Weiser, 11 October 1905, box 3, DP.

109. Ibid., 30 September 1905.

110. Ibid., 18 November 1905.

111. Ibid., 17 December 1905.

112. Ibid., 22 December 1905.

113. Ibid.

114. Ibid., 6 January 1906, 1.

115. Devers interview, tape 15, 6, box 4, DP.

116. Devers to Weiser, 6 January 1906, 1, box 3, DP.

117. Ibid., 12 September 1905.

118. Ibid., 20 September 1905.

119. Ibid., 20 January 1906.

120. Ibid., 22 March 1906.

121. Ibid., 11 March 1906.

122. Ibid., 18 June 1906.

123. Ibid., 2 July 1906; Betros, *Carved from Granite,* 217.

124. Devers to Weiser, 29 July 1906, box 3, DP.

125. Ibid., 30 September 1906.

126. See Betros, *Carved from Granite,* 113, for the curriculum; Markey, *Jake,* 24.

127. Devers to Weiser, 16 October 1906, box 3, DP.

128. Ibid., 31 October 1906.

129. Ibid., 13 December 1906.

130. Markey, *Jake,* 25. See also Timothy Nenninger, ed., *The Way of Duty, Honor, Country: The Memoir of General Charles Pelot Summerall* (Lexington: University Press of Kentucky, 2010), xi, 83. Summerall was the senior instructor of artillery tactics at the Academy from 1905 to 1911.

131. Nenninger, *Way of Duty,* 82–83.

132. Ibid., 82–84.

133. Ibid., 84.

134. Devers interview, tape 15, 13, box 4, DP.

135. Coffman interview, 10.

136. Barbara Tuchman, *Stilwell and the American Experience in China, 1911–1945* (New York: Macmillan, 1970), 20–21.

137. Ibid., 21.

138. Coffman interview, 10.

139. Ibid.

140. Ibid.

141. Devers to Weiser, 17 February 1907, 5 March 1907, and 28 April 1907, box 3, DP.

142. Ibid., 24 May 1907.
143. Ibid.
144. Catherine Devers interview, tape 61, 17, box 8, GP.
145. Ibid.
146. Betros, *Carved from Granite,* 113.
147. Devers to Weiser, 23 September 1907, box 3, DP.
148. "Abstract of Deficiencies," September 1907–June 1909.
149. Devers to Weiser, 1 December 1907, box 3, DP.
150. Ibid., 9 February 1908.
151. Ibid., 8 March 1908.
152. Ibid., 7 June 1908.
153. Betros, *Carved from Granite,* 213.
154. Devers to Weiser, 23 August 1908, box 3, DP.
155. Ibid., 4 October 1908.
156. Ibid., 8 November 1908.
157. Ibid.
158. Ibid., 25 April 1909.
159. Devers interview, tape 26, 16–18, box 4, DP.
160. Ibid., 17.
161. Betros, *Carved from Granite,* 113.
162. Coffman, *The Regulars,* 149.
163. Devers to Weiser, 25 May 1909, box 3, DP.
164. Coffman, *The Regulars,* 150; Devers interview, tape 15, 12, box 4, DP.
165. Devers interview, tape 15, 12–13, box 4, DP.

2. Apprenticeship

1. Devers interview, tape 15, 14, box 4, DP.
2. Ibid.
3. Ibid., 15.
4. Ibid., 17.
5. Ibid., 18.
6. Ibid., 19.
7. Ibid., tape 17, 26–27.
8. Coffman, *The Regulars,* 79.
9. Ibid., 79–80.
10. Devers interview, tape 15, 17, and tape 31, 86, box 4, DP.
11. Coffman, *The Regulars,* 154; Devers interview, tape 17, 27, box 4, DP.
12. Russell Weigley, *History of the United States Army* (New York: Macmillan, 1967), 325–26; Forrest C. Pogue, *George C. Marshall: Education of a General, 1880–1939* (New York: Viking Press, 1963), 97, 84–85.
13. Devers interview, tape 15, 20–21, box 4, DP.
14. Ibid., tape 18, 12–14.
15. Efficiency Record, 1909–1916, Devers Personnel File, NA, St. Louis, MO.

16. Ibid., "Evaluation for 21 January to 30 June 1910."

17. Devers interview, tape 15, 18, box 4, DP.

18. Weigley, *History of the United States Army,* 334–35.

19. Devers interview, tape 17, 23–24, box 4, DP.

20. Ibid., 23.

21. Ibid., 24.

22. Ibid., 26.

23. Ibid., 30–31.

24. Ibid.

25. Ibid., tape 18, 1.

26. Ibid., 1–3.

27. Coffman, *The Regulars,* 114–16; Inspector General Reports, Fort Hamilton, New York, 1926–1934, RG 159, NA, College Park, MD.

28. Devers interview, tape 18, 2–4, box 4, DP.

29. Ibid., 3.

30. Ibid.

31. Ibid., 2, 4–7.

32. Ibid., 5–6.

33. Ibid., 9.

34. Efficiency Report for 1 July 1910–31 December 1911, Devers Personnel File, NA, St. Louis, MO.

35. Devers interview, tape 33, 88, box 4, DP.

36. Ibid., tape 31, 87–90.

37. Ibid., 89–90.

38. Ibid., 90.

39. Ibid., 90–91.

40. Ibid., 92–95.

41. Ibid., 94–95.

42. Ibid., tape 20, 30.

43. Ibid., tape 31, 95–96.

44. Ibid.

45. Ibid., tape 17, 42–43.

46. Ibid., 43.

47. Ibid., 44–45.

48. Ibid., 46–47.

49. Ibid., 47.

50. Ibid., 44.

51. Noce interview, tape 47, 1, box 4, DP.

52. Summary of Efficiency Reports, 1 January 1913–20 August 1916, Devers Personnel File, NA, St. Louis, MO.

53. Devers interview, tape 36, 43, box 4, DP.

54. Ibid., tape 18, 25.

55. Devers to Mrs. Frank Lyon, 28 October 1916, box 4, DP.

56. Devers interview, tape 18, 16, box 4, DP.

57. Ibid., 19.

58. Devers to Mrs. Frank Lyon, 28 October 1916, box 4, DP.

59. Devers interview, tape 18, 21–22, box 4, DP.

60. *Field Artillery,* comp. Janice McKenney, Army Lineage Series, 9th Field Artillery, 388–89.

61. Devers interview, tape 18, 17, box 4, DP.

62. Ibid., 18–19.

63. Ibid., tape 36, 10.

64. Ibid., 10–11.

65. Ibid.

66. Ibid., 12.

67. Summary of Efficiency Reports, 1916–1917, Devers Personnel File, NA, St. Louis, MO.

68. Devers interview, tape 36, 43–44, box 4, DP.

69. Ibid., tape 18, 23–24.

70. Ibid., 25.

71. Ibid., 26.

3. World War I and the Roaring Twenties

1. Weigley, *History of the United States Army,* 352–59; Edward Coffman, *The War to End All Wars: The American Experience in World War I* (Lexington: University Press of Kentucky, 1998), 18–19; James Scott Wheeler, *The Big Red One: America's Legendary 1st Infantry Division from World War I to Desert Storm* (Lawrence: University Press of Kansas, 2007), 9–12. Michael Doubler, *I Am the Guard: A History of the Army National Guard, 1636–2000* (Washington, DC: Department of the Army, 2001), 169–72.

2. Coffman, *The Regulars,* 142–201; Allan Millett and Peter Maslowski, *For the Common Defense: A Military History of the United States of America* (New York: Free Press, 1994), chap. 10.

3. Millett and Maslowski, *For the Common Defense,* 327, 331–34.

4. Ibid., 284–305, 318–19, 326.

5. Ibid., 339–42; Coffman, *War to End All Wars,* 11–19.

6. Coffman, *War to End All Wars,* 24–31; Weigley, *History of the United States Army,* 354–60; Wheeler, *Big Red One,* chap. 1.

7. Devers interview, tape 18, 26, box 4, DP.

8. Boyd Dastrup, *King of Battle: A Branch History of the U.S. Army's Field Artillery* (Fort Monroe, VA: U.S. Army Training and Doctrine Command, 1992), 148–50.

9. Morris Sweet, *Fort Sill: A History* (Fort Sill, OK: n.p., 1921).

10. Ibid.; Dastrup, *King of Battle,* 154–55.

11. Dastrup, *King of Battle,* 154, 158.

12. Devers interview, tape 19, 38–39, box 4, DP.

13. Colonel H. C. Jackson to Devers, 16 November 1949, box 48, DP.

14. Devers to Jackson, 29 November 1949, ibid.

15. Devers interview, tape 18, 27, box 4, DP.

16. Ibid.

17. Ibid., 27–28.

18. Center for Military History (CMH), *Order of Battle of the United States Land Forces in the World War,* vol. 3, pt. 2, *Zone of the Interior* (Washington, DC: CMH, 1988), 928–29.

19. Ibid., vol. 3, pt. 1, 198–99; Dastrup, *King of Battle,* 163.

20. CMH, *Order of Battle,* vol. 3, pt. 1, 202–3; Dastrup, *King of Battle,* 163.

21. Devers interview, tape 18, 28–29, box 4, DP.

22. Ibid., tape 27, 56.

23. Alexander and Frances Devers Graham interview, March 1975, tape 71, 24, box 54, DP.

24. Devers interview, tape 19, 35, box 4, DP.

25. Ibid., 35–36.

26. Dastrup, *King of Battle,* 71–75.

27. Devers interview, tape 19, 37, box 4, DP.

28. Special Efficiency Report, 2 September 1919, Devers Personnel File, NA, St. Louis, MO.

29. Coffman, *War to End All Wars,* 70, 231; Gary Mead, *The Doughboys: America and the First World War* (New York: Overlook Press, 2002), 252.

30. Coffman, *War to End All Wars,* 69–70, 73, 231–33; Donald Smythe, *Pershing: General of the Armies* (Bloomington: Indiana University Press, 1986), 72, 142.

31. Devers interview, tape 1, box 4, DP.

32. Coffman, *War to End All Wars,* 317–18.

33. Ibid., 69, 71–72, 231.

34. Ibid., 70; Coffman, *The Regulars,* 216–18.

35. Coffman, *War to End All Wars,* 72, 314–18.

36. Quoted in Mead, *Doughboys,* 345–46.

37. Devers interview, tape 19, 35, box 4, DP.

38. Ibid., 39.

39. For example, the army produced a record of the tactical actions in France for use by officers on staff rides. This book, *American Armies and Battlefields in Europe* (Washington, DC: CMH, 1938), was reprinted in 1995 and is still used by officers for instructional purposes. The seventeen-volume *United States Army in the World War, 1917–1919* (Washington, DC: CMH, 1948), provides a very detailed history of the American Expeditionary Forces. The army published L. Hunt's *American Military Government of Occupied Germany, 1918–1920* (Washington, DC: Government Printing Office, 1943), a history of the occupation of Koblenz, Germany, for the instruction of future military governors.

40. Devers interview, tape 19, 41, box 4, DP.

41. Ibid., 42–43.

42. Ibid., 43–44.

43. Peter Schifferle, *America's School for War: Fort Leavenworth, Officer Edu-*

cation, and Victory in World War II (Lawrence: University Press of Kansas, 2010), 14–17.

44. Millett and Maslowski, *For the Common Defense,* 380–85; Weigley, *History of the United States Army,* 398–403; Wheeler, *Big Red One,* 117–23.

45. CSA Statistical Reports, boxes 4, 6, and 14 for the period 1920–1939, RG 165, NA, College Park, MD.

46. Special Report 192, 20 October 1925, box 6, RG 165, NA, College Park, MD; J. Votaw, "The Interwar Period: 1920–1941," in *Reference Guide to United States Military History, 1919–1945,* ed. R. Schrader (New York: Facts on File, 1994), 24–42.

47. Devers interview, tape 19, 48, box 4, DP.

48. Ibid., 45–46.

49. Ibid., 49.

50. William Ganoe, *MacArthur Close-up* (New York: Vantage Press, 1962), 13.

51. Ibid., 20.

52. Devers interview, tape 19, 39–40, box 4, DP.

53. J. Devers, "The Mark of the Man on USMA," Spring 1964, 16–19.

54. Lance Betros, ed., *West Point: Two Centuries and Beyond* (Abilene, TX: McWhiney Foundation Press, 2004), 599; D. Clayton James, *The Years of MacArthur,* vol. 1, *1880–1941* (Boston: Houghton Mifflin, 1970), chap. 10.

55. Devers interview, tape 19, 66–67, box 4, DP.

56. Ibid., 52, 58–59.

57. Alexander and Frances Devers Graham interview, tape 71, 24–25, box 54, DP.

58. Devers interview, tape 19, 56–57, box 4, DP.

59. Ibid., 63.

60. Ibid., 53. For Bryden, see D. K. R. Crosswell, *Beetle: The Life of General Walter Bedell Smith* (Lexington: University Press of Kentucky, 2010), 220, 224–26.

61. Crittenberger interview, tape 56, 2, YCHT.

62. Ibid.

63. See Devers to Lodge, 12 December 1941, Military Records, 1944, and Devers to Crittenberger, 29 July 1944, carton 7, Correspondence, Henry Cabot Lodge Jr. Papers, Massachusetts Historical Society.

64. Bradley and Blair, *A General's Life,* 49–52.

65. Griess interview with General Williston Palmer, tape 53, 1, box 6, GP.

66. Griess interview with Brigadier General Eugene L. Harrison, tape 69, 1, box 8, GP.

67. Devers interview, tape 19, 53–55, box 4, DP.

68. Ibid., 55.

69. Ibid.

70. Memorandum from the Assistant to the Commandant, Robert S. Donaldson, 17 October 1922, box 4, DP.

71. Efficiency Reports, 1919–1924, Devers Personnel File, NA, St. Louis, MO.

72. Devers interview, tape 19, 61–62, box 4, DP.

73. Ibid., 60.

74. Ibid., 59.

75. Ibid., 61.

76. Betros, *Carved from Granite*, 120–22.

77. James, *Years of MacArthur*, 1:267–68. See also Ganoe, *MacArthur Close-up*, 23–24.

78. James, *Years of MacArthur*, 1:270–71.

79. Ibid., 276–77.

80. Devers interview, tape 19, 65–66, box 4, DP.

4. Professional Growth

1. Coffman, *War to End All Wars*, 11–12, 125–26; Crosswell, *Beetle*, 164–65; D'Este, *Eisenhower*, 178–79.

2. Schifferle, *America's School for War*, 31.

3. Ibid., 31–32, 34–35.

4. Ibid., 79–80.

5. D'Este, *Eisenhower*, 178–79.

6. Devers interview, tape 26, 9–12, box 6, DP.

7. Ibid., tape 37, 7, box 4.

8. Ibid., 8–9.

9. Pogue, *Marshall: Education of a General*, 101.

10. Coffman, *War to End All Wars*, 264.

11. Ibid., 264–65. For more examples of the importance of Leavenworth graduates in the AEF, see James Cooke, *Pershing and His Generals* (Westport, CT: Praeger, 1997).

12. Schifferle, *America's School for War*, 48.

13. Devers interview, tape 37, 8, box 6, DP.

14. Ibid.

15. Ibid., tape 26, 11–12, box 4.

16. Ibid., 16–18.

17. Ibid., 26, 9.

18. Report from the General Staff School, 19 June 1925, Devers Personnel File, NA, St. Louis, MO.

19. Schifferle, *America's School for War*, 63, 100–101.

20. Devers interview, tape 26, 12–13, box 4, DP.

21. Ibid., tape 32, 108–9.

22. Dastrup, *King of Battle*, 197.

23. Ibid., 197–98.

24. Devers interview, tape 26, 22, box 4, DP.

25. Ibid., 28–29.

26. Ibid., 26.

27. Efficiency Reports for 30 June 1928 and 17 June 1929, Devers Personnel File, NA, St. Louis, MO.

28. Devers interview, tape 26, 23–24, box 4, DP.

29. Ibid., tape 27, 27.

30. Ibid., 24.

31. Ibid., 24–25.

32. Ibid., 36.

33. Millett and Maslowski, *For the Common Defense*, 399.

34. Dastrup, *King of Battle*, 180–82; Devers interview, tape 27, 32, box 4, DP.

35. Devers interview, tape 27, 39–40, box 4, DP.

36. Ibid., 40–41.

37. Griess interview with Georgie Hays Craig McClerkin, tape 22, 5, box 6, GP.

38. Ibid.

39. Alexander and Frances Devers Graham interview, tape 71, 26–27, box 54, DP.

40. Ibid., 27–28.

41. Devers interview, tape 27, 39–40, box 4, DP.

42. Ibid., 41–43.

43. Ibid., 41–42.

44. Major General Fred T. Austin to Devers, 13 December 1928, box 4, DP.

45. Devers interview, tape 27, 43–44, box 4, DP.

46. Coffman, *The Regulars*, 315.

47. Ibid., 231.

48. MHI, *Annual Report of the Chief of Field Artillery*, vols. 20–21 (1930–1932), 103.

49. Devers interview, tape 27, 32–33, box 4, DP.

50. Martin Blumenson, ed., *The Patton Papers, 1885–1940* (Boston: Houghton Mifflin, 1972), 973–74.

51. Ibid., 913–34.

52. Dastrup, *King of Battle*, 180–82.

53. Ibid., 182–83.

54. Ibid., 180–88.

55. Ibid., 190.

56. Ibid., 185–201.

57. General Anthony McAuliffe interview, tape 53, 1, box 4, DP.

58. Efficiency Reports for 16 February 1930–30 June 1931, Devers Personnel File, NA, St. Louis, MO.

59. G4 #13, Committee 6, file 394-6, and G3, Committee 6, file 398-3B, Army War College Curricular Archives, 1932–1933, MHI.

60. G3 Course, report of Committee 6, "Expeditionary Force," 29 September 1932, file 393-6, ibid.

61. Ibid.

62. Weigley, *History of the United States Army*, 406–7; G3 Course, file 396-6, 2, Army War College Curricular Archives, 1932–1933, MHI. The latter noted that roughly 40,000 regular army soldiers were stationed overseas, not including 6,433 Philippine Scouts.

63. "Psychological Appraisal of the British People," supplement 2 to the report

of G2, Committee 8, "A Strategic Study of the British Empire," 22 December 1932, file 392-8, Army War College Curricular Archives, MHI.

64. David M. Kennedy, *Freedom from Fear: The American People in Depression and War, 1929–1945* (New York: Oxford University Press, 1999), 92; Weigley, *History of the United States Army*, 402.

65. Graham interview, tape 71, 7, box 54, DP.

66. Devers interview, tape 26, 17–18, box 4, DP.

67. Ibid., tape 38, 3–4; *Biographical Register of the Officers and Graduates of the United States Military Academy*, vol. 8 (Chicago: Lakeside Press, 1940), 217.

68. Devers interview, tape 38, 1, and tape 21, 69, box 4, DP.

69. Ibid., tape 21, 69–70.

70. Ibid., 70. See also ibid., tape 38, 1–2.

71. Graham interview, tape 71, 32–33, box 54, DP.

72. Ibid., 6–7.

73. Devers interview, tape 38, 4, box 4, DP.

74. Graham interview, tape 71, 11, box 54, DP.

75. Ibid., 10.

76. Ibid., 11–12.

77. Ibid., 8–9; Weigley, *History of the United States Army*, 402.

78. Pogue, *Marshall: Education of a General*, 273–80.

79. Larry Bland and Sharon Ritenour Stevens, eds., *The Papers of George Catlett Marshall*, 5 vols. (Baltimore: Johns Hopkins University Press, 1981–2003), 1:657–58.

80. Graham interview, tape 71, 18–19, box 54, DP.

81. Ibid., 11.

82. Ibid., 14.

83. Erskine interview, August 1971, tape 46, 2–3, box 4, DP.

84. Ibid.

85. Graham interview, tape 71, 19–20, box 54, DP.

86. Ibid., 11.

87. Ibid., 4–5.

88. Ibid., 3–4.

5. The Approach of War

1. He served in the 4th, 9th, 6th, and 16th Field Artillery Regiments and with the artillery detachment at West Point. He also briefly commanded the 1st and 14th Field Artillery Regiments at Fort Sill in 1918.

2. Kennedy, *Freedom from Fear*, 384–86.

3. Ibid., 393–95.

4. Alexander and Frances Devers Graham interview, tape 71, 31–32, box 54, DP.

5. Thurston Hughes to Devers, 11 November 1935, box 4, DP.

6. Ibid.; Devers interview, tape 38, 22, box 4, DP.

7. Betros, *Carved from Granite*, 175.

8. Ibid., chap. 5; Devers interview, tape 38, 23–25, box 4, GP.

9. "Memorandum of the Board to the Superintendent," 1 February 1936, Athletic Board proceedings, 1936–1939, USMA Archives.

10. Devers interview, 8 July 1968, tape 2, 11, box 23, GP.

11. Efficiency Report for 1 July 1935–30 April 1936, Devers Personnel File, NA, St. Louis, MO.

12. Board minutes, 15 May, 5 June, and 19 June 1936, Athletic Board proceedings, 1936–1939.

13. Graham interview, tape 71, 30, box 54, GP.

14. "Memorandum of the Board to the Superintendent," 1 February 1936, Athletic Board proceedings, 1936–1939.

15. Devers interview, tape 38, 23, box 4, GP.

16. Ibid., 50.

17. Army Athletic Association memorandum, "Accomplishments of General J. Devers While G.M.A.," 5 March 1965, 1, Devers file, USMA Library.

18. Ibid., 1–2; Devers interview, tape 38, 24–26, box 4, GP; Erskine interview, tape 46, 7, box 4, GP.

19. Board minutes, 30 June 1936, Athletic Board proceedings, 1936–1939.

20. Army Athletic Association memorandum, "Accomplishments of General J. Devers," 2; Devers interview, tape 38, 25–26, box 4, GP.

21. Devers interview, tape 38, 27–28, box 4, GP.

22. Betros, *Carved from Granite*, 179–80; Devers interview, tape 38, 24, box 4, GP.

23. Betros, *Carved from Granite*, 176; Athletic Board proceedings, 1936–1939. Gar Davidson left the Academy for a field assignment in early 1938 and was replaced as head football coach by Captain William H. Wood.

24. Board minutes, 20 December 1937, Athletic Board proceedings, 1936–1939. The three-year eligibility rule was scheduled to begin with the class of 1940, which had entered the Academy in 1936.

25. Devers interview, tape 38, 31–34, box 4, GP.

26. Ibid., 33.

27. Ibid., 35.

28. Ibid., 35–37.

29. Board minutes, 19 December 1936 and 29 January 1938, Athletic Board proceedings, 1936–1939.

30. Ibid., 31 August 1938.

31. Griess-Harrison interview, tape 69, 9–10, box 8, GP.

32. USMA, *Official Register of Officers and Cadets, USMA, 1937* (West Point, NY: Academy Printing Office, 1937), 8.

33. U.S. Military Academy, *Annual Report, 1938* (West Point, NY: USMA Publishing Office, 1939), 1.

34. USMA, *Annual Report, 1939* (West Point, NY: USMA Publishing Office, 1939); *Official Register of Officers and Cadets* (West Point, NY: USMA Publishing Office, 1909).

35. Devers interview, tape 38, 43–44, box 4, GP.

36. Ibid., 45–46.

37. George J. Richards, "Outline of Status and History of Stewart Field," 13 November 1944, Stewart Airfield file, USMA Special Collections; Devers interview, box 4, tape 38, 46–47, GP; USMA, *Official Register of the Officers and Cadets* (West Point, NY: USMA Publishing Office, 1938), 19.

38. Devers interview, tape 38, 48–50, box 4, GP.

39. Georgie to Kitts Devers, 3 April 1939, box 4, DP. The Deverses saved few letters written before 1939.

40. Devers interview, tape 31, 97, box 4, DP.

41. President Roosevelt to Brigadier General Jay Benedict, 26 June 1939, box 4, DP.

42. Georgie to Kitts, 3 April 1939, box 4, DP.

43. Ibid.

44. Georgie to Kitts, [circa April 1939], box 4, DP. There is no date on the letter, but it was written after the 3 April letter.

45. Brigadier General Jay Benedict to Devers, 26 June 1939, box 4, DP.

46. Ed Cray, *General of the Army: George C. Marshall, Soldier and Statesman* (1990; repr., New York: Cooper Square Press, 2000), 139–40.

47. Weigley, *History of the United States Army,* 423.

48. Forrest C. Pogue, *George C. Marshall: Ordeal and Hope, 1939–1942* (1965; repr., New York: Viking Press, 1966), 82–83.

49. Weigley, *History of the United States Army,* 419.

50. Bland and Stevens, *Marshall Papers,* 2:48–49.

51. Weigley, *History of the United States Army,* 424.

52. Bland and Stevens, *Marshall Papers,* 2:48–49.

53. Georgie to Kitts, 5 August 1939, box 5, DP.

54. Devers to Colonel Frank Scowden, 17 August 1939, and Devers to Brigadier General Jay Benedict, 18 August 1939, box 5, DP.

55. Devers to Brigadier General J. Cummins, 27 September 1939, box 5, DP.

56. Devers to Major John Gilman, 13 September 1939, box 5, DP.

57. Georgie to Kitts, 14 September 1939, box 5, DP.

58. Georgie to Mrs. Ella Devers, 24 September 1939, box 5, DP.

59. Georgie to Mrs. Devers and Kitts, 11 October 1939, box 5, DP.

60. Ibid.

61. Georgie to Kitts, 24 September 1939, box 5, DP.

62. Ibid.

63. Devers to Kitts and Mrs. Devers, 3 June 1940, box 5, DP.

64. Marshall to Major General David L. Stone, 3 October 1939, in Bland and Stevens, *Marshall Papers,* 2:69–70.

65. Devers to Kitts, 30 November 1939, box 5, DP; Georgie to Mrs. Devers, 23 December 1939, ibid.

66. Marshall to Van Voorhis, 2 April 1940, in Bland and Stevens, *Marshall Papers,* 2:186–88.

67. Devers's summation to Lieutenant Colonel Robert Crawford, 11 October 1939, box 12, GP.

68. Colonel Russell "Red" Reeder to Griess, 30 March 1983, box 4, GP.

69. Van Voorhis to Marshall, 23 March 1940, in Bland and Stevens, *Marshall Papers,* 2:186–88, fn. 2, 5.

70. Ibid., 209, fn. 1.

71. Efficiency Report for 8 January–30 June 1940, Devers Personnel File, NA, St. Louis, MO.

72. Marshall to Van Voorhis, 14 February 1940, in Bland and Stevens, *Marshall Papers,* 2:158–59.

73. Georgie to Mrs. Devers, 29 April 1940, box 5, DP.

74. Bradley to Devers, 24 April 1940, box 5, DP.

75. Devers to Alexander Graham, 15 June 1940, box 5, DP; Georgie to Mrs. Devers, 6 July 1940, ibid.

6. Marshall's Fireman and Division Command

1. Weigley, *History of the United States Army,* 425–27; Bland and Stevens, *Marshall Papers,* 2:217–18.

2. Weigley, *History of the United States Army,* 426.

3. Pogue, *Marshall: Ordeal and Hope,* 19–21, 39–40.

4. Ibid.; Bland and Stevens, *Marshall Papers,* 2:251; Kennedy, *Freedom from Fear,* 457–59.

5. Devers to Colonel Thurston Hughes, 15 July 1940, box 6, DP.

6. Marshall memorandum, 4 August 1939, in Bland and Stevens, *Marshall Papers,* 2:27–28.

7. Marshall memorandum to General Watson, 23 April 1941, ibid., 484–85.

8. Devers to Van Voorhis, 2 August 1940, box 6, DP.

9. Ibid.

10. Weigley, *History of the United States Army,* 426–27; Kennedy, *Freedom from Fear,* 458–59.

11. Weigley, *History of the United States Army,* 428–30.

12. Devers to Van Voorhis, 10 August 1940, box 6, DP.

13. Griess-Harrison interview, tape 69, 1, box 8, GP.

14. For Churchill's 4 July 1940 speech, see Martin Gilbert, ed., *The Churchill War Papers: May 1940–December 1940* (New York: W. W. Norton, 1995), 469–70.

15. Quoted in Kennedy, *Freedom from Fear,* 452.

16. Churchill to Roosevelt, 15 August 1940, in Winston Churchill, *The History of the Second World War: Their Finest Hour* (New York: Bantam Books, 1962), 349; Kennedy, *Freedom from Fear,* 452–54, 460–61.

17. Churchill, *History of the Second World War,* 347.

18. Marshall to Brigadier General Edmund Daly, 13 September 1940, in Bland and Stevens, *Marshall Papers,* 2:304–5.

19. Devers interview, tape 1, 7–8, box 1, DP.

20. Ibid., 8–9.

21. Ibid., 9–10.

22. Adjutant of the Army to Devers, 28 September 1940, box 6, DP; Devers to Patton, Simpson, and Lee (congratulating them on their promotions), 27 September 1940, ibid.

23. Devers to Brigadier General Sanderford Jarman, 29 September 1940, ibid.

24. Georgie to Kitts, 4 October 1940, ibid.

25. McAuliffe interview, July 1972, box 12, GP. For Smith, see Crosswell, *Beetle*.

26. Devers interview, tape 3, 1, box 6, DP.

27. Devers to Brigadier General DeRussy Hoyle, 28 October 1940, box 6, DP.

28. Devers interview, tape 3, 2, box 6, DP.

29. Ibid., 2–3.

30. Griess-Harrison interview, tape 69, 13–14, box 8, GP.

31. Georgie to Kitts, 21 January 1941, box 6, DP.

32. Devers interview, tape 3, 3, box 6, DP; Georgie to Catherine Devers, 21 January 1941, ibid.

33. Marshall to Van Voorhis, 24 January 1941, in Bland and Stevens, *Marshall Papers,* 2:397.

34. NBC Radio Address on the Progress of National Defense, 29 November 1940, ibid., 355–57.

35. Devers interview, tape 3, 3–4, box 6, DP.

36. Ibid., tape 20, 42–43.

37. Ibid., tape 3, 3–4.

38. Ibid., tape 20, 44.

39. Ibid., tape 3, 5; Marshall to Devers, 19 March 1941, in Bland and Stevens, *Marshall Papers,* 2:452.

40. Devers interview, tape 3, 7, box 6, DP.

41. Ibid.

42. Morris J. MacGregor Jr., *Integration of the Armed Forces, 1940–1965* (Washington, DC: CMH, 2001), 3–7.

43. Public Law 783, 76th Congress, 16 September 1940, cited in Ulysses Lee, *The Employment of Negro Troops* (Washington, DC: CMH, 2000), 73–74.

44. Bland and Stevens, *Marshall Papers,* 2:336.

45. Devers interview, tape 3, 8–10, box 6, DP.

46. Colonel R. C. Moore, Deputy Chief of Staff, to Devers, 13 February 1941, RG 165, Records of the War Department, General and Special Staffs, NA, College Park, MD.

47. Memorandum for the Chief of Staff, 15 July 1941, ibid.

48. Georgie to Kitts, 26 February 1941, box 6, DP.

49. Graham interview, tape 71, 49, box 54, DP.

50. Georgie to Kitts, 15 January 1940, box 5, DP.

51. Georgie to Mrs. Ella Devers, 23 May 1940, box 5, DP.

52. Graham interview, tape 71, 50, box 54, DP.

53. Georgie to Kitts, 21 January 1941, box 6, DP.

54. *York Dispatch*, 17 March 1941.

55. Georgie to Kitts, 7 June 1941, box 6, DP.

56. Colonel Carlos Brewer to Devers, 25 October 1940, box 6, DP.

57. Weigley, *History of the United States Army*, 428.

58. Joseph B. Mittelman, *Eight Stars to Victory: A History of the Veteran Ninth U.S. Infantry Division* (Columbus, OH: Heer and Terry, 1948), 30.

59. Ibid., 31.

60. Weigley, *History of the United States Army*, 431.

61. Ibid.; Mittelman, *Eight Stars to Victory*, 31.

62. Weigley, *History of the United States Army*, 429–30; Kent Greenfield, Robert R. Palmer, and Bell I. Wiley, *The Army Ground Forces: The Organization of Ground Combat Troops* (Washington, DC: CMH, 1987), 34–43.

63. Greenfield et al., *Army Ground Forces*, 36–41; Mittelman, *Eight Stars to Victory*, 32–33.

64. Quoted in Mittelman, *Eight Stars to Victory*, 33.

65. Ibid., 32.

66. *Raleigh News and Observer*, 15 March 1941, box 12, GP.

67. Ibid.

68. *Washington Post*, 20 July 1941, box 7, DP.

69. Christopher Gabel, *The U.S. Army GHQ Maneuvers of 1941* (1991; repr., Washington, DC: CMH, 1992), chaps. 8, 9; Mittelman, *Eight Stars to Victory*, 33.

70. Mittelman, *Eight Stars to Victory*, 34.

7. Forging the Thunderbolt

1. Devers interview, tape 4, 1, box 4, DP.

2. Russell Weigley, *The American Way of War* (New York: Macmillan, 1973), 216–18.

3. Army Ground Forces Historical Section, *The History of the Armored Force, Command and Center*, study no. 27, 1946, 1.

4. Geoffrey Perret, *There's a War to Be Won: The United States Army in World War II* (New York: Ivy Books, 1991), 39–40; Millett and Maslowski, *For the Common Defense*, 400.

5. Blumenson, *Patton Papers, 1885–1940*, 780–83.

6. Army Ground Forces, *History of the Armored Force*, 2–3.

7. Ibid., 5.

8. Weigley, *History of the United States Army*, 410.

9. Army Ground Forces, *History of the Armored Force*, 3.

10. Weigley, *History of the United States Army*, 410–12.

11. Army Ground Forces, *History of the Armored Force*, 4.

12. Robert Doughty, *The Breaking Point: Sedan and the Fall of France, 1940* (Hamden, CT: Archon Books, 1990); Karl-Heinz Frieser, *The Blitzkrieg Legend: The 1940 Campaign in the West* (Annapolis, MD: Naval Institute Press, 2005).

13. Greenfield et al., *Army Ground Forces*, 56–57.

14. Army Ground Forces, *History of the Armored Force,* 7–8.

15. Ibid., 16.

16. Greenfield et al., *Army Ground Forces,* 57–58.

17. Ibid., 59.

18. Army Ground Forces, *History of the Armored Force,* 18.

19. Blumenson, *Patton Papers, 1940–1945,* 21, 29, 36.

20. Ibid., 18.

21. Devers interview, tape 38, 13, box 8, DP.

22. Ibid., tape 4, 1–2.

23. Ibid., 2.

24. Ibid., 1.

25. Ibid., 13, 25.

26. Ibid., 4–5.

27. Ibid., 5–6.

28. Army Ground Forces, *History of the Armored Force,* 89–90.

29. Blumenson, *Patton Papers, 1940–1945,* 7–8.

30. Graham interview, tape 71, 16–18, box 54, DP.

31. Devers interview, tape 38, 7, box 4, DP.

32. Devers was promoted to brigadier general on 1 May 1940 and got his second star on 1 October 1940. Patton got his first star on 1 October 1940 and was promoted to major general on 4 April 1941.

33. Blumenson, *Patton Papers, 1940–1945,* 21, 29–36.

34. Patton to Beatrice, 9 August 1941, ibid., 41–42.

35. Gabel, *U.S. Army GHQ Maneuvers of 1941,* 120–21.

36. Ibid., 105–11.

37. Ibid., 122–23.

38. Devers to McNair, 18 December 1941, box 9, RG 337, 58A, NA, College Park, MD.

39. Gabel, *U.S. Army GHQ Maneuvers of 1941,* 124.

40. Ibid., 121.

41. Hanson W. Baldwin, "War Games Bare Laxity in Discipline," *Washington Post,* 1 October 1941, copy in box 8, DP.

42. Devers to Marshall, 4 October 1941, box 8, DP.

43. Gabel, *U.S. Army GHQ Maneuvers of 1941,* 187.

44. Devers to Marshall, 8 December 1941, box 8, DP.

45. Georgie to Kitts, 18 August 1941, ibid.

46. Devers to Kitts, 2 September 1941, ibid.

47. Crittenberger interview, tape 56, 2, box 8, DP.

48. Taaffe, *Marshall and His Generals,* 123–24. This book will say a great deal more about Devers's relationships with Eisenhower and Bradley.

49. Devers interview, tape 4, 13–14, box 8, DP.

50. Ibid., 14.

51. Marshall to Devers, 24 September 1941, in Bland and Stevens, *Marshall Papers,* 2:617–18.

52. Devers to Marshall, 1 October 1941, box 8, DP.

53. Ibid.

54. Army Ground Forces, *History of the Armored Force*, 87.

55. Memorandum for General Wesson, 1 December 1941, box 4, GP. This memorandum included the minutes of the 25 November 1941 meeting.

56. Ibid.

57. Devers interview, tape 4, 7, box 8, DP.

58. Ibid., 9.

59. Ibid., 10.

60. Army Ground Forces, *History of the Armored Force*, 95.

61. Ibid.; Devers to McNair, 30 June 1942, box 4, GP; 2nd Endorsement from CG Services of Supply to CG AGF, 18 July 1942, RG 337, HQ, AGF files, NA, College Park, MD.

62. Devers interview, tape 1, 5, and tape 38, 17–18, box 8, DP.

63. Ibid., 18–19.

64. Blumenson, *Patton Papers, 1940–1945,* 58–59; Bland and Stevens, *Marshall Papers,* 3:170.

65. Devers interview, tape 4, 16, box 8, DP.

66. Ibid.

67. Ibid., tape 38, 20.

68. Blumenson, *Patton Papers, 1940–1945,* 58–60.

69. Ibid., 56–57.

70. McNair to Devers, 8 September 1942, box 1234, RG 337, 55A, NA, College Park, MD; Greenfield et al., *Army Ground Forces,* 68–72. I Armored Corps became Seventh Army in 1943. III Armored Corps became XIX Corps.

71. McNair to Devers, 9 May 1942, box 9, RG 337, 58A, NA, College Park, MD.

72. Georgie to Kitts, 6 October 1941, box 8, DP.

73. Georgie to Kitts, 24 April 1942, box 9, DP.

74. Ibid., 29 July 1942.

75. Ibid.

76. Ibid., 6 October 1942.

77. Ibid., 12 October 1942.

78. Ibid., 1 September 1942.

79. Ibid., 11 September 1942.

80. Lee, *Employment of Negro Troops,* 121–22.

81. Ibid., 119–21.

82. Copy of a 27 January 1942 memorandum for the Adjutant General, box 4, GP.

83. MacGregor, *Integration of the Armed Forces,* 24–25.

84. Devers interview, tape 36, 33–34, box 8, DP.

85. Ibid., 33.

86. Lee, *Employment of Negro Troops,* 350–56.

87. Devers interview, tape 36, 35, box 8, DP.

88. Major General Peterson to General Marshall, 22 September 1942, box 333, RG 165, Records of the War Department, General and Special Staffs, NA, College Park, MD.

89. Major General A. D. Bruce to Devers, 25 September 1942, box 9, DP.

90. Efficiency Report for 9 March–31 December 1942, signed on 16 January 1943, Devers Personnel File, NA, St. Louis, MO.

91. Marshall to Devers, December 1942, box 9, DP.

8. On to the War

1. George Howe, *Northwest Africa: Seizing the Initiative in the West* (Washington, DC: CMH, 2002), 7–10.

2. Ibid., 9–14.

3. Ibid., 13–15; Rick Atkinson, *An Army at Dawn: The War in North Africa, 1942–1943* (New York: Henry Holt, 2002), 17–18; D'Este, *Eisenhower,* 336–37.

4. Omar Bradley, *A Soldier's Story* (New York: Henry Holt, 1951), 172–73; Bradley and Blair, *A General's Life,* 210. In *Eisenhower in War and Peace* (New York: Random House, 2012), 29, Jean Edward Smith claims that Devers and Eisenhower were both in the 19th Infantry Regiment in 1915. However, there is no evidence in Devers's personnel file that supports Smith's claim. Devers was a math instructor at the Military Academy in 1915.

5. Atkinson, *Army at Dawn,* 170.

6. Howe, *Northwest Africa,* 253–54.

7. Atkinson, *Army at Dawn,* 207–10.

8. Ibid., 218.

9. D'Este, *Eisenhower,* 364, 375–77.

10. Quoted in Atkinson, *Army at Dawn,* 200.

11. Quoted in D'Este, *Eisenhower,* 363–64.

12. Atkinson, *Army at Dawn,* 199; D'Este, *Eisenhower,* 357.

13. Marshall to Eisenhower, 22 December 1942, in Bland and Stevens, *Marshall Papers,* 3:488.

14. Marshall to Eisenhower, 30 December 1942, ibid., 497.

15. D'Este, *Eisenhower,* 366.

16. Ibid., 417. See ibid., 31–32, 34–35, 87, 92, and 293 for discussions of Ike's temper.

17. Devers to Georgie, 21 December 1942, box 9, DP.

18. D'Este, *Eisenhower,* 305–6.

19. Taaffe, *Marshall and His Generals,* 30.

20. "Report of the Mission Headed by Lieutenant General Jacob L. Devers to Examine the Problems of the Armored Forces in the European Theater of Operations," tabs A through E, Army Ground Forces Project File, entry 55a, box 1234, RG 337, NA, College Park, MD.

21. Ibid., tab J.

22. Ibid., tab I.

23. Howe, *Northwest Africa*, 330–34.

24. "Ordnance Annex" to "Report of the Mission," 18 January 1943, 1–3.

25. Ibid., 3–4.

26. Ibid., 5–6.

27. "Report of the Mission," tab M.

28. Ibid., tab N.

29. "Ordnance Annex," 4, 7–9, 21.

30. Harry C. Butcher, *My Three Years with Eisenhower: The Personal Diary of Captain Harry C. Butcher, USNR, Naval Aide to General Eisenhower, 1942–1945* (New York: Simon and Schuster, 1946), 229, 233, 234.

31. Ibid., 234.

32. Griess-Harrison interview, tape 70, 43, box 8, GP.

33. Ibid.

34. "Report of the Mission."

35. Ibid., tab P.

36. Wheeler, *Big Red One*, 155–62.

37. "Report of the Mission," tab P.

38. Devers to Ward, 17 September 1942, box 2, 1st Armored Division, 1942–1943, correspondence folder, Orlando Ward Papers, MHI. These letters were provided to the author by Brigadier General Harold Nelson (Ret.), who found them in the Ward Papers.

39. Ward to Devers, 5 November 1942, ibid.

40. Ibid., 11 December 1942.

41. "Report of the Mission," tab Q, 1–2.

42. Blumenson, *Patton Papers, 1940–1945*, 149.

43. George Patton to Beatrice, 9 January 1943, ibid.

44. Patton to Devers, 22 August 1942, ibid., 84.

45. Patton to Devers, 14 October 1942, ibid., 89.

46. "Report of the Mission," tabs R and P.

47. Ibid., tab S.

48. Ibid., tab T.

49. Maurice Matloff and Edwin Snell, *Strategic Planning for Coalition Warfare, 1943–1944* (Washington, DC: CMH, 1994), 10–12.

50. Ibid., 13.

51. Ibid., 13–14.

52. Ibid., 18–24.

53. Ibid., 24–26.

54. Ibid., 26–29.

55. "Report of the Mission," tab V.

56. "Air Force Annex" to "Report of the Mission," 1–2.

57. "Report of the Mission," tab W.

58. Ibid., "Conclusions."

59. Ibid.

60. Ibid., "Recommendations."

61. Greenfield et al., *Army Ground Forces,* 329.

62. Note attached to "Recommendations" of "Report of the Mission."

63. Greenfield et al., *Army Ground Forces,* 296.

64. Ibid., 329.

65. Marshall to McNair, 14 February 1943, RG 337, HQ, AGF, General Correspondence 1940–44, box 9, NA, College Park, MD.

66. Greenfield et al., *Army Ground Forces,* 296.

67. McNair to Major General A. D. Bruce, 19 February 1943, RG 337, 58A, box 9, NA, College Park, MD.

68. AGF memorandum for General Marshall, 2 February 1943, RG 165, CSA Correspondence, 1942–43, box 60, NA, College Park, MD.

69. Ibid.

70. Ibid.

71. Memorandum for the Deputy Chief of Staff, 9 April 1943, RG 165, entry 13, box 44, NA, College Park, MD.

72. Army Ground Forces, *History of the Armored Force,* 15–16.

73. Gabel, *U.S. Army GHQ Maneuvers of 1941,* 121.

74. Greenfield et al., *Army Ground Forces,* 319–22.

75. Ibid., 320–21.

76. Devers interview, tape 4, 13–23, box 8, DP.

77. Albert Garland and Howard McGraw Smyth, *Sicily and the Surrender of Italy* (Washington, DC: CMH, 2002), 89, 160, 170.

78. Marshall to Devers, 9 August 1943, box 12, DP.

79. Devers interview, tape 3, 12, box 11, DP.

80. Efficiency Report for 1 January–8 May 1943, signed by Lieutenant General McNair, 21 May 1943, Devers Personnel File, NA, St. Louis, MO.

9. European Theater Commander

1. H. H. Arnold, *Global Mission* (New York: Harper and Brothers, 1949), 404.

2. Georgie to Kitts, 10 May 1943, box 10, DP.

3. War Department [WD] Confirmatory Orders, 7 May 1943, and WD message to ETOUSA and Iceland Base Command, 8 May 1943, RG 165, entry 418, box 1713, NA, College Park, MD.

4. Maurice Matloff and Edwin Snell, *Strategic Planning for Coalition Warfare, 1941–1942* (Washington, DC: CMH, 1999), 183–87; Arnold, *Global Mission,* 303–5.

5. Roland G. Ruppenthal, *Logistical Support of the Armies,* 2 vols. (Washington, DC: CMH, 1995), 1:26–29.

6. Matloff and Snell, *Strategic Planning for Coalition Warfare, 1941–1942,* 187–90; Albert C. Wedemeyer, *Wedemeyer Reports!* (New York: Henry Holt, 1958), 103–10.

7. Wesley Craven and James Cate, eds., *The Army Air Forces in World War II: Europe: Torch to Pointblank, August 1942 to December 1943* (Chicago: Univer-

sity of Chicago Press, 1949), 210–11; Ruppenthal, *Logistical Support of the Armies,* 1:29–30.

8. Ruppenthal, *Logistical Support of the Armies,* 1:26.

9. Ibid., 37.

10. Arnold, *Global Mission,* 315–16.

11. D'Este, *Eisenhower,* 303–6; Wedemeyer, *Wedemeyer Reports!* 131–32.

12. Quoted in Ruppenthal, *Logistical Support of the Armies,* 1:39–40.

13. Wedemeyer, *Wedemeyer Reports!* 139, 160–61, 163.

14. Arnold, *Global Mission,* 321.

15. Ruppenthal, *Logistical Support of the Armies,* 1:53–76.

16. MHI, "History of Allied Force Headquarters and Headquarters, NATOUSA," 183–87.

17. Ibid., 90–92.

18. Craven and Cate, *Army Air Forces: Torch to Pointblank,* 287.

19. Ibid., 300, 305; Matloff and Snell, *Strategic Planning for Coalition Warfare, 1943–1944,* 27–29.

20. Craven and Cate, *Army Air Forces: Torch to Pointblank,* 300.

21. Arnold, *Global Mission,* 484–85.

22. Ruppenthal, *Logistical Support of the Armies,* 1:100–104.

23. Craven and Cate, *Army Air Forces: Torch to Pointblank,* 308–9.

24. Ibid., 309.

25. Ibid., 309–10.

26. Ruppenthal, *Logistical Support of the Armies,* 1:121–23.

27. Memorandum from Marshall to Arnold, 30 April 1943, RG 165, E442, box 43, NA, College Park, MD.

28. Press release of HQ, ETOUSA, May 1943, box 10, DP.

29. Devers to Georgie, 8 May 1943, box 11, DP. Devers wrote, "My head is full of a number of things."

30. Georgie to Kitts, 31 May 1943, ibid.

31. Devers to Georgie, 22 September 1943, ibid.

32. Devers to Georgie, 30 September 1943, ibid.

33. Devers to Mrs. Lyon, 4 October 1943, ibid.

34. Devers's Command Guidance on Assuming Command, May 1944, box 12, GP; Lynne Olson, *Citizens of London: The Americans Who Stood with Britain in Its Darkest, Finest Hour* (New York: Random House, 2010), 157–60. Olson thoroughly examines American and British attitudes toward each other in 1940–1942.

35. Devers letter, 24 October 1943, box 11, DP.

36. Williston Palmer interview, tape 53, 14, box 11, DP.

37. Report on "Morals and Conduct," 2, box 32, GP.

38. Ibid., 2–3.

39. Ibid.

40. Ibid., 3.

41. MacGregor, *Integration of the Armed Forces,* 17–25.

42. Rick Atkinson, *The Day of Battle: The War in Sicily and Italy, 1943–1944* (New York: Henry Holt, 2007), 381–83.

43. Report on "Morals and Conduct," 9–10.

44. MacGregor, *Integration of the Armed Forces,* 38.

45. Devers to Georgie, 2 November 1943, box 11, DP.

46. Ibid., 7 November 1943.

47. Anthony Eden to John Dill, 24 August 1943, 1, box 59, DP.

48. Memorandum from General Marshall to Field Marshal Sir John Dill, 6 September 1943, box 59, DP.

49. Ibid., 1–3.

50. Griess-Harrison interview, tape 69, 21, box 8, GP.

51. Ibid., 22.

52. Palmer interview, tape 53, 13, box 11, DP.

53. Memorandum from Marshall to FDR, Subject: Message from Ambassador Winant regarding General Devers, 21 June 1943, RG 165, Records of the Office of Chief of Staff, box 44, NA, College Park, MD.

54. Ibid.

55. Ibid.

56. Griess's conclusions based on Devers's interviews on the subject of Churchill, box 12, GP.

57. Devers interview, tape 3, 14, box 11, DP; Alan Brooke, *War Diaries of Alan Brooke, 1939–1945,* ed. Alex Danchev and Daniel Todman (Berkeley: University of California Press, 2001), 422–23, 432–35; Olson, *Citizens of London.* Olson's book is a thorough study of the roles played by Harriman, Edward Morrow, and Ambassador Winant in Britain during the war.

58. Devers interview, tape 3, 14, box 11, DP.

59. Devers to Marshall, 18 May 1943, box 11, DP. Colonel Tristram Tupper served as the public affairs officer of the Armored Force and was Marshall's brother-in-law. He was a talented screenwriter and well suited to public relations and press relations.

60. Devers to Marshall, 1 June 1943, box 59, DP.

61. Craven and Cate, *Army Air Forces: Torch to Pointblank,* 376, 600, 635–36.

62. Ibid., 639–40.

63. Arnold to Devers, for Eaker, 2 June 1943, RG 498, ETO Historian Administration File, box 88, NA, College Park, MD.

64. Eaker memorandum to Devers, 4 June 1943, ibid.

65. Ibid.

66. Arnold to Devers, 16 June 1943, box 11, DP.

67. Devers to Arnold, 23 June 1943, ibid.

68. Ibid.

69. Ibid.

70. Robert Lovett to Eaker, 18 June 1943, 1, RG 107, box 19, NA, College Park, MD.

71. Arnold to Devers, 7 July 1943 (assuring him that the air force would provide two crews for each bomber), box 59, DP; Lovett to Eaker, 18 June 1943, 2.

72. Lovett to Eaker, 18 June 1943, 2, 5.

73. Arnold to Devers, 20 June 1943, RG 498, ETO Historian Administration File, box 88, NA, College Park, MD.

74. Devers to Arnold, 23 June 1943, ibid.

75. Eaker to Arnold, 8 June 1943, ibid.

76. Arnold to Marshall, 1 May 1943, 2, RG 165, E442, box 43, NA, College Park, MD.

77. Eaker to Arnold, 8 June 1943, RG 498, ETO Historian Administration File, box 88, NA, College Park, MD.

78. DDE to CCS, 28 July 1943, in *Eisenhower Papers,* vol. 2, message 1145.

79. DDE to Marshall, 30 July 1943, ibid., 1154.

80. Alan Brooke's Diary, entry for 30 July 1943, Liddell Hart Library, King's College; Brooke, *War Diaries,* 434.

81. Memorandum to Marshall and Arnold, 1 August 1943, Subject: Additional Bomber Groups for Avalanche, RG 165, box 44, NA, College Park, MD; Craven and Cate, *Army Air Forces: Torch to Pointblank,* 493–95.

82. Butcher, *My Three Years with Eisenhower,* 379–80.

83. DDE to CCS, 12 August 1943, in *Eisenhower Papers,* vol. 2, message 1180 (see n. 1 for Devers's response).

84. DDE to Marshall, 3 August 1943, ibid., 1161.

85. Taaffe, *Marshall and His Generals,* 107–8.

86. Bradley and Blair, *A General's Life,* 210.

87. Blumenson, *Patton Papers, 1940–1945,* 414.

88. DDE to the CCS, 15 September 1943, in *Eisenhower Papers,* vol. 3, message 1257.

89. Craven and Cate, *Army Air Forces: Torch to Pointblank,* 511, 536; Matloff and Snell, *Strategic Planning for Coalition Warfare, 1943–1944,* 392–93, table 4.

90. Devers to Marshall, 8 August 1943, RG 165, box 44, NA, College Park, MD; emphasis in the original.

91. Devers to Arnold, 17 August 1943, RG 498, ETO Historian Administration File, box 88, NA, College Park, MD.

92. Arnold, *Global Mission,* 449–50.

93. Ibid., 485–87.

94. Matloff and Snell, *Strategic Planning for Coalition Warfare, 1943–1944,* 26n, 132; Harrison, *Cross-Channel Attack,* 49.

95. Harrison, *Cross-Channel Attack,* 48.

96. Ibid., 49–52.

97. Matloff and Snell, *Strategic Planning for Coalition Warfare, 1943–1944,* 168–69.

98. Ibid., 168–70; General Board, U.S. Forces European Theater, *Strategy of the Campaign in Western Europe, 1944–1945* (U.S. European Command: 1946), 3.

99. Memorandum from Lieutenant General Morgan to principal COSSAC staff officers, 5 August 1943, RG 331, Records of Allied Operational Headquarters, NA, College Park, MD, copy in box12, GP.

100. Harrison, *Cross-Channel Attack,* 53.

101. Devers to Marshall, 18 May 1943, box 11, DP.

102. Ibid., 19 May 1943.

103. Colonel P. W. Edwards, War Department Staff, to Major General I. H. Edwards, Chief of Staff, ETOUSA, 5 September 1943, 1–2, box 59, DP.

104. Ibid., 1.

105. Undated memorandum, box 4, GP, from RG 165, Records of the War Department General and Special Staff, Office of Director of Plans and Operations, OPD Book 12, NA, College Park, MD.

106. Pogue, *Supreme Command,* 43, 44n17.

107. Ibid., 44–45.

108. Griess's account of the Pogue-Devers interview, 12 August 1958, box 12, GP. Devers told Pogue that he witnessed a discussion between Churchill and Stimson on 20 July in which the prime minister told the secretary of war that he did not intend to execute Overlord.

109. Henry L. Stimson and McGeorge Bundy, *On Active Service in Peace and War* (New York: Harper and Brothers, 1947), 429, 436–38.

110. Ibid., 438–39; Martin Gilbert, *Winston S. Churchill: Road to Victory, 1941–1945* (London: Heinemann, 1986), 470.

111. Devers to Marshall, 6 July 1943, box 11, DP.

112. Major General Raymond Barker to Devers, 24 August 1943, 1, box 12, DP.

113. Ibid., 30 August 1943, 1.

114. Morgan to Devers, 6 July 1943, RG 498, ETO Historian Administration File, box 88, NA, College Park, MD.

115. Devers's message W-4421 to Marshall, 13 September 1943, box 1, Raymond Moses Papers, MHI.

116. Marshall's message R-3267 to Devers, ibid.; the same message is in box 12, DP.

117. Devers's message W-4763 to Marshall, 21 September 1943, box 1, Moses Papers.

118. Major General Handy memorandum for Marshall, 22 September 1943, RG 165, box 44, NA, College Park, MD.

119. Marshall to Devers, 24 September 1943, 1–2, box 1, Moses Papers.

120. Devers to Morgan, 7 October 1943, box 59, DP.

121. Palmer interview, tape 53, 12–13, box 11, DP.

122. Devers interview, tape 8, 140, box 11, DP.

123. Devers to Georgie, 9 and 24 October 1943, box 11, DP.

124. Larry Bland, ed., *George C. Marshall: Interviews and Reminiscences for Forrest C. Pogue* (Lexington, VA: George C. Marshall Foundation, 1996), 627.

125. Summary of Service and Assignments, Devers Personnel File, NA, St. Louis, MO.

126. Devers to Marshall, 13 December 1943, 1–2, box 11, DP.

127. Ibid., 2.

10. Mediterranean Theater of Operations

1. Forrest C. Pogue, *George C. Marshall: Organizer of Victory, 1943–1945* (New York: Viking Press, 1973), 264–74; Kennedy, *Freedom from Fear*, 686–91.

2. Pogue, *Marshall: Organizer of Victory*, 276–77.

3. Ibid., 272.

4. Ibid., 273.

5. Ibid., 319–21.

6. Matloff and Snell, *Strategic Planning for Coalition Warfare, 1943–1944*, 347, 352–56.

7. Bland and Stevens, *Marshall Papers*, 4:193–94; Matloff and Snell, *Strategic Planning for Coalition Warfare, 1943–1944*, 361–63.

8. Matloff and Snell, *Strategic Planning for Coalition Warfare, 1943–1944*, 365–66.

9. Ibid., 378.

10. Ibid., 381; Brooke, *War Diaries*, 490–91.

11. Bland and Stevens, *Marshall Papers*, 4:197.

12. Eisenhower to Devers, 13 December 1943, in *Eisenhower Papers*, vol. 3, message 1411.

13. Devers to Georgie, 18 December 1943, box 12, DP.

14. Eisenhower to Marshall, 17 December 1943, 1–2, in *Eisenhower Papers*, vol. 3, message 1423.

15. Butcher Diary, 12 December 1943, DDE Library, Abilene, KS.

16. Marshall to Eisenhower, 23 December 1943, in Bland and Stevens, *Marshall Papers*, 4:202.

17. Marshall to Eisenhower, 21 December 1943, in *Eisenhower Papers*, vol. 3, message 1440, fn. 1.

18. Eisenhower to Marshall, 25 December 1943, in Bland and Stevens, *Marshall Papers*, 4:204, fn. 6; see also *Eisenhower Papers*, vol. 3, message 1428.

19. Eisenhower to Marshall, 27 December 1943, in *Eisenhower Papers*, vol. 3, message 1440.

20. Devers to Eisenhower, 27 December 1943, box 12, DP.

21. Devers to Georgie, 27 and 29 December 1943, box 11, DP; Devers interview, tape 3, 17, ibid.

22. Memoranda for Admirals King and Leahy and for the British Joint Staff Mission, 27 December 1943, box 4, GP.

23. Marshall to Devers, 28 December 1943, box 12, DP.

24. Devers's memorandum for Colonel W. A. Ganoe, 1 January 1944, box 12, DP.

25. D'Este, *Eisenhower*, 483, 567–68.

26. Taaffe, *Marshall and His Generals*, 109.

27. Devers to Georgie, 1 January 1944, box 12, DP.

28. Crosswell, *Beetle*, 538.

29. Devers to Georgie, 1 January 1944, box 12, DP.

30. Ibid.

31. Eisenhower to Marshall, 18 January 1944, in *Eisenhower Papers,* vol. 3, message 1486.

32. Devers to Georgie, 9 January 1944, box 16, DP.

33. Brooke, *War Diaries,* 504–5.

34. Butcher, *My Three Years with Eisenhower,* 472.

35. Eisenhower to Devers, 16 and 19 January 1944, in *Eisenhower Papers,* vol. 3, messages 1482 and 1488.

36. Crosswell, *Beetle,* 560–61.

37. Devers to Georgie, 11 January 1944, box 16, DP.

38. Eisenhower to Marshall, 29 January 1944, RG 165, OPD Executive File, box 45, NA, College Park, MD.

39. Eisenhower to Devers, 1 and 7 February 1944, in *Eisenhower Papers,* vol. 3, messages 1527 and 1533.

40. Devers to Georgie, 11 January 1944, box 16, DP. He wrote: "Well I am slipping. A bad cold caught up with me and to bed I went."

41. Brooke, *War Diaries,* xliii.

42. Devers Diary, 8 January 1944, MHI.

43. Brooke, *War Diaries,* xxxix.

44. Ibid., 499, entry for 14 December 1943.

45. Ibid., 519, entry for 8 February 1944.

46. See Marcel Vigneras, *Rearming the French* (1957; repr., Washington, DC: CMH, 1989), 33–44, for the decision to rearm the French forces in North Africa.

47. Devers to Georgie, 9 January 1944, box 16, DP.

48. Porch, *Path to Victory,* 507.

49. Martin Blumenson, *Salerno to Cassino* (Washington, DC: CMH, 2002), 244–45.

50. Porch, *Path to Victory,* 510.

51. Atkinson, *Day of Battle,* 324–25.

52. Blumenson, *Salerno to Cassino,* 293–94.

53. Ibid., 296–97.

54. Ibid., 297–98.

55. Ibid., 302.

56. Ibid., 302–4.

57. Churchill to Roosevelt, 8 January 1944, in Gilbert, *Churchill: Road to Victory,* 640, fn. 1 (also in RG 165, OPD-PM File, NA, College Park, MD); Devers Diary, 8 January 1944.

58. Blumenson, *Salerno to Cassino,* 303.

59. Devers Diary, 7 January 1944.

60. Atkinson, *Day of Battle,* 325–26.

61. Quoted in ibid., 325.

62. Gilbert, *Churchill: Road to Victory,* 640; Churchill to Roosevelt, 8 January 1944, in Winston Churchill, *Closing the Ring* (New York: Bantam Books, 1962), 383.

63. Atkinson, *Day of Battle,* 323.

64. Ibid., 324.

65. Blumenson, *Salerno to Cassino*, 305–10.

66. Ibid., 308–12.

67. Atkinson, *Day of Battle*, 330.

68. C. J. C. Molony, *History of the Second World War: The Mediterranean and Middle East*, vol. 5, pt. 2, *The Campaign in Sicily 1943 and the Campaign in Italy, 3rd September 1943 to 31st March 1944* (Uckfield, UK: Naval and Military Press, 2004), 606–13; Blumenson, *Salerno to Cassino*, 314–15; Porch, *Path to Victory*, 532–34.

69. Blumenson, *Salerno to Cassino*, 319; Atkinson, *Day of Battle*, 364.

70. Atkinson, *Day of Battle*, 343; Blumenson, *Salerno to Cassino*, 321.

71. Porch, *Path to Victory*, 531.

72. Blumenson, *Salerno to Cassino*, 322–26.

73. Ibid., 322–28; Porch, *Path to Victory*, 521–23; Atkinson, *Day of Battle*, 332–33.

74. Atkinson, *Day of Battle*, 331.

75. Ibid.

76. Blumenson, *Salerno to Cassino*, 322–34; Porch, *Path to Victory*, 531–32; Atkinson, *Day of Battle*, 339–45.

77. Atkinson, *Day of Battle*, 343.

78. Ibid., 343–47; Blumenson, *Salerno to Cassino*, 340–46.

79. Blumenson, *Salerno to Cassino*, 341–46; Atkinson, *Day of Battle*, 347–49.

80. Blumenson, *Salerno to Cassino*, 350–51.

81. Marshall to Devers, 6 January 1944, box 16, DP. Marshall sent the identical message to Eisenhower, Stilwell, and MacArthur.

82. Devers to Marshall, 14 January 1944, box 16, DP.

83. Ibid.

84. Peter Mansoor, *The GI Offensive: The Triumph of American Infantry Divisions, 1941–1945* (Lawrence: University Press of Kansas, 1999), 31–34.

85. Ibid., 10–11.

86. Ibid., 11.

87. Devers to Georgie, 18 January 1944, box 16, DP.

88. Devers Diary, entries for 19 and 22 January 1944.

89. Ibid., 19 February 1944.

90. Devers to Edwin Sibert, 20 January 1944, box 16, DP.

91. Devers to Georgie, 3 February 1944, ibid.

92. Devers to Georgie, 22 January 1944, ibid.

93. Devers to Thomas Handy, 2 February 1944, ibid.

94. Ibid.

95. Devers to McNair, 4 February 1944, ibid.

96. Devers to Marshall, 5 February 1944, ibid.

97. Blumenson, *Salerno to Cassino*, 252.

98. Devers to Georgie, 27 January 1944, box 16, DP.

99. Memorandum to the President, War Department Manpower Board

(WDMB), "Advance Information Re Theater of Operations Section, WDMB, Report on General Survey of NATO Bases," 20 March 1944, 1, box 59, DP.

100. Major General Thomas Larkin to President, WDMB, 4 April 1944, 1, RG 165, OPD Executive Files 8 and 9, box 46, NA, College Park, MD.

101. Marshall to Devers, 13 April 1944, box 16, DP.

102. Devers to Marshall, 15 April 1944, 2, ibid.

103. Ibid., 1.

104. Devers to Marshall, 14 February 1944, RG 165, OPD Executive Files 8 and 9, box 45, NA, College Park, MD.

105. Molony, *History of the Second World War,* 645–46; Blumenson, *Salerno to Cassino,* 353.

106. Molony, *History of the Second World War,* 646.

107. Ibid.; Blumenson, *Salerno to Cassino,* 354.

108. Blumenson, *Salerno to Cassino,* 355, referring to Lucas's diary entry for 10 January 1944.

109. Ibid., 356.

110. Ibid., 357–61; Molony, *History of the Second World War,* 660–68.

111. Devers to Georgie, 22 January 1944, box 16, DP.

112. Blumenson, *Salerno to Cassino,* 386; Porch, *Path to Victory,* 535–36.

113. Devers interview, tape 8, 141, box 11, DP.

114. Blumenson, *Salerno to Cassino,* 361–65; Molony, *History of the Second World War,* 660–66.

115. Devers to Georgie, 27 January 1944, box 16, DP.

116. Blumenson, *Salerno to Cassino,* 389–91.

117. Molony, *History of the Second World War,* 672–78, 723–47; Blumenson, *Salerno to Cassino,* 392–96.

118. Gilbert, *Churchill: Road to Victory,* 667.

119. Brooke, *War Diaries,* 517.

120. Blumenson, *Salerno to Cassino,* 424–25.

121. Ibid., 425–26, quoting Lucas's diary, 16 February 1944.

122. Ibid., 427.

11. Stalemate in Italy and the Invasion of Southern France

1. Eaker to Robert A. Lovett, 23 January 1944, 3, RG 107, box 19, NA, College Park, MD.

2. Ibid., 2.

3. Ibid., 4.

4. Ibid.

5. Ibid., 5.

6. Ibid.

7. Ibid.

8. Ibid., 5–6.

9. Georgie to Kitts Devers, January 1944, box 16, DP.

10. Ibid.

11. Devers to Georgie, 3 February 1944, box 16, DP.

12. Devers to Georgie, 7 February 1944, ibid.

13. Mary Alice Jaqua to Georgie, 2 May 1944, ibid.

14. Georgie to Kitts, 12 February 1944, ibid.

15. Devers to Marshall, 14 February 1944, RG 165, OPD Executive Files 8 and 9, box 45, NA, College Park, MD.

16. Clarke and Smith, *Riviera to the Rhine,* 5–7.

17. Porch, *Path to Victory,* 456.

18. Ibid., 456–57.

19. Matloff and Snell, *Strategic Planning for Coalition Warfare, 1943–1944,* 365, 369–70.

20. Ibid., 378–79, 383.

21. Ibid., 413; Eisenhower to Marshall, 17 January 1944, in *Eisenhower Papers,* vol. 3, message 1483.

22. Eisenhower to Marshall, 17 January 1944.

23. Anvil-Dragoon Index, December 1943–October 1944, 1, WO 204/27, PRO; Blumenson, *Salerno to Cassino,* 449–50.

24. Devers to Patton, 2 February 1944, box 16, DP.

25. Eisenhower to Marshall, 12 February 1944, RG 165, War Department General and Special Staff, NA, College Park, MD; copy in box 5, GP.

26. Marshall to Devers, 13 February 1944, box 5, GP.

27. Patton to Beatrice Patton, 26 February 1944, in Blumenson, *Patton Papers, 1940–1945,* 418.

28. Patton to Beatrice Patton, 20 February 1944, ibid.

29. Clarke and Smith, *Riviera to the Rhine,* 31; *Seventh Army War Diaries,* vol. 1, entries for 10 January, 14 August, and 29 February 1944, Alexander Patch Papers, USMA Special Collections.

30. *Seventh United States Army Report of Operations: Seventh Army 1944–1945,* 3 vols. (Heidelberg, Germany: Aloys Graf, 1946), 1:3–5.

31. Handy to Devers, 21 February 1944, box 5, GP.

32. Ibid., 28 February 1944.

33. Anvil-Dragoon Index, 2, entry for 2 March 1944.

34. *Seventh Army War Diaries,* 1:45, 48, entries for 5 and 8 March 1944.

35. Pogue, *Marshall: Organizer of Victory,* 377; Truman Strobridge and Bernard Nalty, "From the South Pacific to the Brenner Pass: General Alexander M. Patch," *Military Review* 61 (June 1981): 41–48.

36. Taaffe, *Marshall and His Generals,* 38–40.

37. Devers to Patch, 18 August 1941; Devers to Patch, n.d. [early 1942], box 1, Patch Papers.

38. Taaffe, *Marshall and His Generals,* 204; Handy to Devers, 21 February 1944, box 5, GP.

39. J. E. Hull to Devers, 10 March 1944, box 16, DP.

40. Devers to Georgie, 22 February 1944, ibid.

41. Atkinson, *Day of Battle*, 400–410.

42. Blumenson, *Salerno to Cassino*, 401–3.

43. Ibid., 404.

44. Ibid., 408; Atkinson, *Day of Battle*, 432–33.

45. Atkinson, *Day of Battle*, 437.

46. Quoted in Blumenson, *Salerno to Cassino*, 413.

47. Ibid., 416–17.

48. Devers to Georgie, 18 March 1944, box 16, DP.

49. Blumenson, *Salerno to Cassino*, 433–34.

50. Ibid., 434.

51. Ibid., 435.

52. Quoted in ibid., 436.

53. Ibid., 436–37. Blumenson is quoting Eaker to Arnold, 6 March 1944, Mathews File, CMH.

54. Ibid., 439–42.

55. Ibid., 442–44.

56. Quoted in ibid., 444.

57. Devers to Marshall, 22 March 1944, box 16, DP.

58. Ibid., 1.

59. Blumenson, *Salerno to Cassino*, 444–48.

60. Devers to Marshall, 22 March 1944, 2.

61. Blumenson, *Salerno to Cassino*, 448.

62. Devers to Marshall, 22 March 1944, 1.

63. Devers to Major General Barr, 23 May 1944, box 16, DP.

64. Major General Daniel Noce, G-3 AFHQ, to the Chief of Staff, NATOUSA, 20 May 1944, ibid.

65. Devers to McNair, 4 February 1944, ibid.

66. E. N. Harmon to Devers, 26 February 1944, 3, 1, ibid.

67. Devers to Harmon, 3 March 1944, ibid.

68. Harmon to Devers, 28 March 1944, ibid.

69. Crittenberger to Devers, 31 March 1944, ibid.

70. Matloff and Snell, *Strategic Planning for Coalition Warfare, 1943–1944*, 420–22; Pogue, *Supreme Command*, 114–15.

71. Matloff and Snell, *Strategic Planning for Coalition Warfare, 1943–1944*, 422–24; Pogue, *Supreme Command*, 116–17.

72. Matloff and Snell, *Strategic Planning for Coalition Warfare, 1943–1944*, 424.

73. Marshall to Eisenhower, 16 March 1944, in Bland and Stevens, *Marshall Papers,* 4:348–50.

74. Wilson to Alexander, 5 March 1944, WO 204/27, PRO.

75. Devers to Wilson, 21 March 1944, ibid.

76. *Seventh Army War Diaries*, 1:89–90, entry for 30 April 1944.

77. Major General J. E. Hull to Marshall, 14 March 1944, 1–2, box 16, DP.

78. Marshall to General Thomas Handy, 14 March 1944, in Bland and Stevens, *Marshall Papers,* 4:341–42, fn. 1.

79. Marshall to Eisenhower, 16 March 1944, ibid., 348–50.

80. Marshall to Eisenhower, 25 March 1944, ibid., 374–76.

81. Vigneras, *Rearming the French,* 7–8.

82. Ibid., 16, 28.

83. Ibid., 17–19, 24–27.

84. Ibid., 30–33, 35.

85. Ibid., 35–36, 38.

86. Porch, *Path to Victory,* 526.

87. Vigneras, *Rearming the French,* 101, 111, 117.

88. Jean de Lattre de Tassigny, *The History of the French First Army,* trans. Malcolm Barnes (London: George Allen and Unwin, 1952), 23.

89. Ibid., 24.

90. Ibid., 24–25.

91. Memorandum from Colonel L. Higgins to Devers, 16 January 1944, box 13, DP; Olson, *Citizens of London,* 218–19.

92. Marshall to Devers, 31 January 1944, box 16, DP.

93. Memorandum: State of Franco-American Military Relations in North Africa, 21 January 1944, 1, 2, ibid.

94. Devers to Georgie, 7 February 1944, ibid.

95. Devers to Marshall, 13 February 1944, 1, 2, RG 165, OPD Executive Files 8 and 9, box 45, NA, College Park, MD.

96. Vigneras, *Rearming the French,* 155.

97. Devers to Marshall, 13 February 1944, 2.

98. Ibid.

99. *Seventh Army War Diaries,* 1:74, 87, 89–90, entries for 13, 28, 30 April and 1 June 1944.

100. Devers to Marshall, 13 February 1944, 2.

101. Ibid., 3.

102. Devers to Georgie, 20 March 1944, box 16, DP.

103. Ernest Fisher, *Cassino to the Alps* (Washington, DC: CMH, 2002), 19–20; Pogue, *Supreme Command,* 117.

104. Devers to Georgie, 24 March 1944, box 16, DP.

105. Devers to McNair, 12 April 1944, ibid.

106. Devers to Marshall, 15 April 1944, ibid.

107. Devers to Georgie, 14 May 1944, ibid.

108. Devers to Thomas Handy, 30 April 1944, RG 165, OPD Executive Files 8 and 9, box 46, NA, College Park, MD.

109. Atkinson, *Day of Battle,* 511.

110. Fisher, *Cassino to the Alps,* 33–34; Atkinson, *Day of Battle,* 512.

111. Devers to Georgie, 14 May 1944, box 16, DP.

112. Fisher, *Cassino to the Alps,* 60–62.

113. Atkinson, *Day of Battle,* 531.

114. Fisher, *Cassino to the Alps,* 66.

115. Atkinson, *Day of Battle,* 541–44.

116. Fisher, *Cassino to the Alps,* 122–58.

117. Atkinson, *Day of Battle,* 552.

118. Ibid., 548.

119. Devers to Marshall, 25 May 1944, box 16, DP.

120. Devers to Georgie, 4 June 1944, box 17, DP.

121. Devers to Arnold, 4 June 1944, box 4, GP. This letter is from the Arnold Papers, box 50, folder 241, Library of Congress Manuscript Division.

122. Memorandum for the President from Marshall, Subject General Devers, 6 June 1944, RG 165, box 58, NA, College Park, MD.

123. Devers to Marshall, 13 June 1944, 2, box 17, DP.

124. Wilson to Alexander, 22 May 1944; Fifteenth Army Group to CG, Fifth Army, 24 May 1944, WO 204/27, PRO.

125. Wilson to Alexander, 7 June 1944, ibid.

126. Churchill to Wilson, 7 March 1944, Italian Campaign Communications, WO 214/15, PRO.

127. Devers to Handy, 30 April 1944, RG 165, OPD Executive Files 8 and 9, box 46, NA, College Park, MD.

128. Churchill to Alexander, 31 May 1944, WO 214/15, PRO.

129. Pogue, *Supreme Command,* 219–21.

130. Alexander to Brooke, 8 June 1944, WO 214/15, PRO.

131. Wilson to Alexander, 8 June 1944, ibid.

132. Pogue, *Supreme Command,* 223; Eisenhower to Wilson, 6 July 1944, in *Eisenhower Papers,* vol. 3, message 1802.

133. *Seventh Army War Diaries,* 1:112, entry for 1 June 1944.

134. Devers to Marshall, 1 July 1944, 1, box 17, DP.

135. Marshall to Devers, 16 July 1944, in Bland and Stevens, *Marshall Papers,* 4:523–24, fn. 1.

136. Eisenhower to Marshall, 8 July 1944, in *Eisenhower Papers,* vol. 3, message 1811; fn. 2 describes Marshall's reply to this message.

137. Eisenhower to Marshall, 12 July 1944, ibid., message 1822.

138. Marshall to Devers, 16 July 1944, 1–2, box 17, DP.

12. Sixth Army Group

1. Pogue, *Supreme Command,* 220–21; Fisher, *Cassino to the Alps,* 257–58.

2. Butcher, *My Three Years with Eisenhower,* 633–34.

3. Eisenhower to Marshall, 5 August 1944, in *Eisenhower Papers,* vol. 4, message 1883.

4. Clarke and Smith, *Riviera to the Rhine,* 75–79, 203.

5. Patch to Truscott, 25 June 1944, box 17, DP.

6. Clarke and Smith, *Riviera to the Rhine,* 78.

7. Truscott to Patch, 27 June 1944, 1, box 17, DP.

8. Clarke and Smith, *Riviera to the Rhine,* 42–43, 45.

9. De Lattre, *History of French First Army,* 53.

10. Clarke and Smith, *Riviera to the Rhine*, 46–49.

11. Ibid., 49.

12. Major General W. D. Styer, Chief of Staff, ASF, to Lieutenant General Somervell, 15 July 1944, 2–3, box 59, DP. Styer was on an inspection tour of the Mediterranean theater.

13. Vigneras, *Rearming the French*, 130–38.

14. Ibid., 165–67, 188; *Seventh Army Report of Operations*, 1:66–67.

15. Vigneras, *Rearming the French*, 167–68.

16. Ibid., 169.

17. Clarke and Smith, *Riviera to the Rhine*, 47–48, 51.

18. Ibid., 92.

19. Atkinson, *Guns at Last Light*, 192–94; *Seventh Army War Diaries*, 1:199, entry for 13 August 1944.

20. Devers to Marshall, 9 August 1944, box 17, DP.

21. Clarke and Smith, *Riviera to the Rhine*, 65–67.

22. Ibid., 82–83, 97–98.

23. Ibid., 95–97.

24. Ibid., 78–79.

25. Ibid., 101–4.

26. Ibid., 108–13; Samuel Elliot Morrison, *The Invasion of France and Germany, 1944–1945* (Boston: Little, Brown, 1957), 258–67.

27. Clarke and Smith, *Riviera to the Rhine*, 115–16.

28. Atkinson, *Guns at Last Light*, 191; Morrison, *Invasion of France and Germany*, 241–42.

29. Atkinson, *Guns at Last Light*, 191.

30. Quoted in ibid.

31. Clarke and Smith, *Riviera to the Rhine*, 115–17.

32. Morrison, *Invasion of France and Germany*, 272.

33. Ibid., 272–74; Clarke and Smith, *Riviera to the Rhine*, 121–22.

34. Clarke and Smith, *Riviera to the Rhine*, 133–34.

35. Devers to Marshall, 21 August 1944, 1, box 17, DP; *Seventh Army War Diaries*, 2:204, entries for 18 and 19 August 1944.

36. Clarke and Smith, *Riviera to the Rhine*, 200–207.

37. De Lattre, *History of French First Army*, 75.

38. Ibid., 107.

39. Ibid., 114.

40. Ibid., 115–16; Atkinson, *Guns at Last Light*, 203–5.

41. Devers to Lodge, 12 December 1941, Henry Cabot Lodge Jr. Papers, carton 7, Correspondence and Military Papers, 1924–1981, Massachusetts Historical Society.

42. Crittenberger to Lodge, June 1942, ibid.

43. Stimson to Lodge, 7 July 1942, ibid.

44. Devers to Crittenberger, 29 July 1944, carton 7, Military Records, 1944, Lodge Papers.

45. Memorandum, Sixth Army Group French Liaison Officer, 14 August 1944, ibid.

46. Clarke and Smith, *Riviera to the Rhine,* 137; Atkinson, *Guns at Last Light,* 206–7.

47. Clarke and Smith, *Riviera to the Rhine,* 166–68.

48. Atkinson, *Guns at Last Light,* 212.

49. *Seventh Army War Diaries,* 2:220–21, entry for 30 August 1944. Atkinson gives a slightly higher number of German prisoners.

50. Lodge interview, tape 60, 3, box 4, GP.

51. De Lattre, *History of French First Army,* 127–33; Anthony Clayton, *Three Marshals of France: Leadership after Trauma* (London: Brassey's, 1992), 106–7.

52. Lodge to Devers, 26 August 1944, carton 7, Military Records, 1944, Lodge Papers; Lodge interview, tape 60, 3, box 4, GP.

53. Devers Diary, 27 August 1944, MHI.

54. Lodge interview, tape 60, 4, box 4, GP.

55. Clarke and Smith, *Riviera to the Rhine,* 173–81, map 10.

56. Ibid., 180–81.

57. Ibid., 182.

58. Ibid., 189.

59. Ibid., 192–93.

60. Devers to Marshall, 21 August 1944, 1–2, box 17, DP.

61. Atkinson, *Guns at Last Light,* 194.

62. Devers to Marshall, 21 August 1944, 1, 3.

63. Devers Diary, 21 August 1944.

64. Devers to Georgie, 22 August 1944, box 17, DP.

65. Devers Diary, 20 August 1944.

66. Devers to Major General Lowell Rooks, Deputy Chief of Staff, AFHQ, 16 September 1944, box 20, DP.

67. Devers to Wilson, 19 October 1944, ibid.

68. Devers Diary, 19 September 1944.

69. Devers to Georgie, 29 August 1944, box 17, DP.

70. Devers Diary, 20 August 1944.

71. *Seventh Army Report of Operations,* 1:250–51; Devers Diary, 30 August 1944.

72. Eisenhower to Marshall, 30 August 1944, in *Eisenhower Papers,* vol. 4, message 1924. Patch was technically in operational command. Devers was comfortable playing a somewhat indirect role.

73. Ibid., fn. 5.

74. Eisenhower to Bradley, 15 September 1944, in *Eisenhower Papers,* vol. 4, message 1956.

75. Marshall to Eisenhower, 6 September 1944, in Bland and Stevens, *Marshall Papers,* 4:574–75.

76. Devers Diary, 5 September 1944.

77. Devers to Georgie, 9 September 1944, box 17, DP.

78. Butcher, *My Three Years with Eisenhower*, 643.

79. Eisenhower to Marshall, 31 August 1944, in *Eisenhower Papers*, vol. 4, message 1925.

80. Memorandum, 5 September 1944, ibid., message 1936.

81. Devers to Major General L. W. Rooks, AFHQ, 22 August 1944, box 17, DP.

82. Marshall to Eisenhower, 6 September 1944, in Bland and Stevens, *Marshall Papers*, 4:575, fn. 2. The French 1st Infantry Division, under Seventh Army's control, met the 6th Armored Division on 11 September.

83. Bagration was the Soviet offensive from 22 June to 19 August 1944 in western Russia. German losses were somewhere between 400,000 and 550,000 men killed or captured. German losses in Normandy topped 200,000 men killed, wounded, or missing. Another 200,000 German troops were encircled in French ports along the Atlantic coast.

84. "A History of the Headquarters Sixth Army Group," 1:2–3, RG 331, Sixth Army Group Adjutant General's Records, UD242A, Decimal Files, box 157, NA, College Park, MD.

85. Ibid., 3.

86. Ibid., 26.

87. *Seventh Army War Diaries*, 2:249, 251; *Seventh Army Report of Operations*, 1:286.

88. Devers Diary, 18 September 1944.

89. Lodge memorandum, 8 September 1944, Lodge Papers.

90. Ibid.

91. Devers to Georgie, 18 September 1944, box 20, DP.

92. Devers to Eisenhower, 20 September 1944, ibid.

93. Ibid.

94. Eisenhower to Marshall, 14 September 1944, in *Eisenhower Papers*, vol. 4, message 1953.

95. Ibid.

96. Eisenhower to Montgomery, 15 September 1944, ibid., message 1957. The same message was sent to Bradley and Devers.

97. "History of Headquarters Sixth Army Group," 1:5.

98. Devers Diary, 22 September 1944.

99. Clarke and Smith, *Riviera to the Rhine*, 229–30.

100. Devers Diary, 5 October 1944.

101. D'Este, *Eisenhower*, 594.

102. Clarke and Smith, *Riviera to the Rhine*, 230; Eisenhower to the CCS, 29 September 1944, in *Eisenhower Papers*, vol. 4, message 2010.

13. The Vosges and Alsace Campaigns

1. Clarke and Smith, *Riviera to the Rhine*, 196–97.

2. "History of Headquarters Sixth Army Group," 1:1.

3. Ibid., 4–5.

4. Ibid., 6.

5. Final Report, G-3 Section, Sixth Army Group, 1 July 1945, 11, RG 407, entry 427, box 1308, NA, College Park, MD.

6. Ibid., 11.

7. Ibid., 11–12.

8. Taaffe, *Marshall and His Generals,* 193.

9. *Seventh Army War Diaries,* 2:261–62, entry for 23 September 1944.

10. Devers to Georgie, 23 September 1944, box 20, DP.

11. Blumenson, *Patton Papers, 1940–1945,* 553.

12. Ibid., 557–58.

13. Devers to Georgie, 23 September 1944.

14. D'Este, *Eisenhower,* 580.

15. Devers to Georgie, 23 September 1944.

16. Devers Diary, 21 September 1944, MHI.

17. Final Report, G-3 Section, Sixth Army Group, 13; Clarke and Smith, *Riviera to the Rhine,* 233, 238–51.

18. Devers Diary, 22 September 1944.

19. "History of Headquarters Sixth Army Group," 1:15.

20. Ibid., 16; *Seventh Army War Diaries,* 2:268–69, entry for 27 September 1944.

21. *Seventh Army War Diaries,* 2:272, entry for 29 September 1944.

22. Garrison H. Davidson, *Grandpa Gar: The Saga of One Soldier as Told to His Grandchildren* (n.p.: 1974), 93, MHI.

23. "History of Headquarters Sixth Army Group," 1:14.

24. Davidson, *Grandpa Gar,* 93.

25. *Seventh Army War Diaries,* 2:273, entry for 30 September 1944.

26. Ibid., 287, entry for 4 October 1944.

27. "History of Headquarters Sixth Army Group," 1:17.

28. Clarke and Smith, *Riviera to the Rhine,* 207–8.

29. *Seventh Army Report of Operations,* 2:319–20.

30. "History of Headquarters Sixth Army Group," 1:18–19.

31. Devers to de Lattre, 26 September 1944, box 20, DP.

32. Devers Diary, 28 September 1944.

33. *Seventh Army War Diaries,* 2:275, entry for 30 September 1944.

34. Ibid.

35. Ibid.

36. De Lattre, *History of French First Army,* 194.

37. Devers Diary, 1 October 1944.

38. *Seventh Army War Diaries,* 2:279, entry for 1 October 1944.

39. Devers Diary, 2 October 1944.

40. Devers to Georgie, 3 October 1944, box 20, DP.

41. Ibid.

42. *Seventh Army War Diaries,* 2:300; Devers Diary, 4 and 5 October 1944.

43. Devers Diary, 5 October 1944.

44. Eisenhower to Bradley, 4 October 1944, in *Eisenhower Papers,* vol. 4, message 2025, fn. 1.

45. Bland and Stevens, *Marshall Papers,* 4:624.

46. Ibid. The source for Marshall's reaction is Bland, *Marshall: Interviews and Reminiscences,* 345.

47. Devers Diary, 8 October 1944.

48. De Lattre, *History of French First Army,* 194–95.

49. Bland, *Marshall: Interviews and Reminiscences,* 333.

50. Pogue, *Marshall: Organizer of Victory,* 476.

51. "History of Headquarters Sixth Army Group," 1:22.

52. Marshall to Devers, 9 October 1944, box 20, DP.

53. Major General Barr to Henry Cabot Lodge, 10 October 1944, ibid.

54. "History of Headquarters Sixth Army Group," 25–26.

55. Devers Diary, 8 October 1944.

56. Ibid.

57. Ibid., 11 October 1944; "History of Headquarters Sixth Army Group," 1:25.

58. Devers to Georgie, 14 October 1944, box 20, DP.

59. Russell Weigley, *Eisenhower's Lieutenants: The Campaigns of France and Germany, 1944–1945* (Bloomington: Indiana University Press, 1990), 347–69.

60. Clarke and Smith, *Riviera to the Rhine,* 252–96; Weigley, *Eisenhower's Lieutenants,* 345–46.

61. Devers to Georgie, 20 October 1944, box 20, DP.

62. Atkinson, *Guns at Last Light,* 364.

63. Clarke and Smith, *Riviera to the Rhine,* 322.

64. Ibid., 276–91, 322–23.

65. Ibid., 297–310.

66. Ibid., 255–56; "History of Headquarters Sixth Army Group," 1:27.

67. Patch to Julia Patch, 24 September 1944, 1, box 1, Patch Papers, USMA.

68. Patch to Julia Patch, 4 October 1944, 1–2, box 2, Patch Papers.

69. Ibid.

70. Captain Patch to his wife, 30 September 1944, box 1, Patch Papers.

71. Captain Patch to Mom and Sis, 6 October 1944, box 2, Patch Papers.

72. Captain Patch to Mom and Sis, 15 October 1944, 1–2, ibid.

73. Clarke and Smith, *Riviera to the Rhine,* 270–71.

74. Patch to Julia, 22 October 1944, 1, box 1, Patch Papers.

75. Ibid., 2–4.

76. *Seventh Army War Diaries,* 2:330–31, entry for 24 October 1944.

77. Ibid., 338, entry for 28 October 1944.

78. Patch to Julia, 24 October 1944, 2, box 1, Patch Papers.

79. *Seventh Army War Diaries,* 2:338, entry for 28 October 1944.

80. Julia Patch to Patch, 25 October 1944, 1, box 1, Patch Papers. Patch responded, "I cannot over emphasize my love and admiration for you both for that message—It shall be an example to me."

81. Devers to Patch, 23 October 1944, box 1, Patch Papers.

82. Major General John W. O'Daniel to Colonel W. T. Sexton, 9 November 1944, box 2, John W. O'Daniel Papers, MHI.

83. Pogue, *Supreme Command*, 293–96.

84. Devers Diary, 16 October 1944.

85. Ibid., 17 October 1944; *Seventh Army War Diaries*, 2:314–15, entry for 17 October 1944.

86. Pogue, *Supreme Command*, 310.

87. D'Este, *Eisenhower*, 659.

88. Clarke and Smith, *Riviera to the Rhine*, 353.

89. "History of Headquarters Sixth Army Group," 1:24, 26.

90. Final Report, G-3 Section, Sixth Army Group, 18.

91. Ibid., 15.

92. De Lattre, *History of French First Army*, 216–17.

93. Devers to Georgie, 1 November 1944, box 20, DP.

94. Devers Diary, 25 October 1944.

95. "History of Headquarters Sixth Army Group," 1:36, copy of the order from SHAEF, 3 November 1944.

96. De Lattre, *History of French First Army*, 219. De Gaulle made the original request to de Lattre on 7 October. On 28 October the French Committee of National Liberation reached an agreement with SHAEF, after several weeks of negotiations.

97. Clarke and Smith, *Riviera to the Rhine*, 359–60.

98. Ibid., 220; "History of Headquarters Sixth Army Group," 1:36.

99. De Lattre, *History of French First Army*, 220–22; Clarke and Smith, *Riviera to the Rhine*, 360, 415, 419.

100. Devers Diary, 7 November 1944.

101. Ibid.

102. Ibid., 1 November 1944.

103. Devers to Major General Thomas Handy, 9 September 1944, box 10, GP.

104. Clarke and Smith, *Riviera to the Rhine*, 353.

105. Final Report, G-3 Section, Sixth Army Group, 19.

106. Devers Diary, 5 November 1944; Final Report, G-3 Section, Sixth Army Group, 19.

107. Clarke and Smith, *Riviera to the Rhine*, 342–44.

108. De Lattre, *History of French First Army*, 206–7.

109. Ibid., 217–19.

110. Clarke and Smith, *Riviera to the Rhine*, 363.

111. Final Report, G-3 Section, Sixth Army Group, 20–21.

112. Devers Diary, 11 and 12 November 1944.

113. Final Report, G-3 Section, Sixth Army Group, 21–22; Clarke and Smith, *Riviera to the Rhine*, 368–79.

114. De Lattre, *History of French First Army*, 228.

115. Lodge interview, tape 60, 7–8, box 4, GP.

116. De Lattre, *History of French First Army,* 229–49.

117. Clarke and Smith, *Riviera to the Rhine,* 387–405.

118. Ibid., 379–83.

119. Devers to Georgie, 19 November 1944, box 20, DP.

120. Devers Diary, 20 November 1944.

121. Ibid., 23 November 1944.

122. Clarke and Smith, *Riviera to the Rhine,* 433–37; Davidson, *Grandpa Gar,* 94–95.

123. *Seventh Army War Diaries,* 2:387, entry for 20 November 1944.

124. Ibid., 390–92, entries for 21 and 22 November 1944.

125. Final Report, G-3 Section, Sixth Army Group, 23.

126. Devers Diary, 24 November 1944. See also Bradley's memorandum to his G-3 (box 4, GP), stating that the purpose of the visit was to try to get XV Corps transferred back to Twelfth Army Group.

127. Final Report, G-3 Section, Sixth Army Group, 23.

128. *Seventh Army War Diaries,* 2:401, entry for 26 November 1944.

129. Colley, *Decision at Strasbourg,* xi–xiii. See ibid., 134–44, for details of the decision and the discussions between Devers and Eisenhower.

130. Davidson, *Grandpa Gar,* 94.

131. "History of Headquarters Sixth Army Group," 1:54–55.

132. Clarke and Smith, *Riviera to the Rhine,* 373–86.

133. See Ruppenthal, *Logistical Support of the Armies,* 2:266–67, fn. 74, for the memo and chap. 11 for the shortage of artillery ammunition in the European theater from October through December 1944.

134. "History of Headquarters Sixth Army Group," 1:54.

135. Ibid., 52.

136. Devers Diary, 26 November 1944.

14. Winter of Discontent

1. Atkinson, *Guns at Last Light,* 373.

2. See Hugh Cole, *The Lorraine Campaign* (Washington, DC: CMH, 1984), 300, for Patton's boast, 319–449 for the Third Army offensive; Weigley, *Eisenhower's Lieutenants,* 381–401; Clarke and Smith, *Riviera to the Rhine,* 438–39.

3. Weigley, *Eisenhower's Lieutenants,* 364–69. See MacDonald, *Siegfried Line Campaign,* 341–74, for the disaster of the 28th Division, and 399–463 for First Army attacks in the Huertgen Forest.

4. Devers Diary, 24 November 1944, MHI.

5. Ibid.

6. Clarke and Smith, *Rhine to the Riviera,* 439–43.

7. Blumenson, *Patton Papers, 1940–1945,* 582.

8. Devers Diary, 24 November 1944.

9. Devers to Georgie, 28 November 1944, box 20, DP.

10. Devers to Major General Ted Brooks, 27 November 1944, ibid.

11. Clarke and Smith, *Riviera to the Rhine,* 440.

12. Sixth Army Group Letter of Instruction 3, 26 November 1944, in "History of Headquarters Sixth Army Group," 1:57–59.

13. Clarke and Smith, *Riviera to the Rhine,* 442, 454.

14. *Seventh Army War Diaries,* 2:401–2, entry for 26 November 1944.

15. Final Report, G-3 Section, Sixth Army Group, 24–26; Clarke and Smith, *Riviera to the Rhine,* 449–84.

16. Devers Diary, 26 November 1944.

17. Ibid., 5 December 1944.

18. Clarke and Smith, *Riviera to the Rhine,* 465–66.

19. Devers to de Lattre, 1 December 1944, incl. 1, RG 331, box 96, NA, College Park, MD.

20. Ibid., 2 December 1944, incl. 2; *Seventh Army War Diaries,* 3:415, 427, entries for 1 and 7 December 1944.

21. Devers to de Lattre, 1 December 1944.

22. *Seventh Army War Diaries,* 3:435, entry for 10 December 1944.

23. Ibid., 2:401, entry for 26 November 1944; Grove quoted in Atkinson, *Guns at Last Light,* 371–72.

24. *Seventh Army War Diaries,* 2:410, entry for 29 November 1944.

25. Clarke and Smith, *Riviera to the Rhine,* 435–36.

26. De Lattre, *History of French First Army,* 262–90.

27. Ibid., 271–72.

28. Clarke and Smith, *Riviera to the Rhine,* 455–59.

29. De Lattre, *History of French First Army,* 295.

30. Papers of Sixth Army Group Medical Branch, file 1, RG 331, NA, College Park, MD.

31. *Seventh Army Report of Operations,* 2:509.

32. De Lattre, *History of French First Army,* 177.

33. Ibid., 171, 177.

34. Ibid., 170.

35. Ibid., 176.

36. Ibid., 294.

37. Ibid., 173.

38. Vigneras, *Rearming the French,* 319–21.

39. Ibid., 320–21, 330–31.

40. Ibid., 321–23, 330–31.

41. Ibid., 324.

42. Eisenhower to Marshall, 1 November 1944, in *Eisenhower Papers,* vol. 4, message 2088.

43. Vigneras, *Rearming the French,* 332–57.

44. De Lattre, *History of French First Army,* 173–75.

45. Vigneras, *Rearming the French,* 337.

46. Sixth Army Group Letter of Instruction 4, 2 December 1944, in "History of Headquarters Sixth Army Group," 1:65–66.

47. Ibid., 68.

48. Clarke and Smith, *Riviera to the Rhine*, 488.

49. Devers Diary, 17 December 1944.

50. Clarke and Smith, *Riviera to the Rhine*, 488–89.

51. Devers to Eisenhower, 18 December 1944, box 21, DP.

52. Devers to General Jacques Leclerc, 18 December 1944, ibid.

53. Devers Diary, 31 January, 1 and 11 February 1945; Clarke and Smith, *Riviera to the Rhine*, 489, fn. 25.

54. Devers to de Lattre, 18 December 1944, carton 7, Lodge Papers. This is the English copy of a letter Lodge translated into French and delivered to de Lattre.

55. Devers Diary, 22 December 1944.

56. Turnipseed interview, tape 46, 5, box 20, DP.

57. Devers Diary, 14 December 1944.

58. *Seventh Army Report of Operations,* 2:509, from a message sent on 10 December 1944; SHAEF message to Sixth Army Group, 13 December 1944, in "History of Headquarters Sixth Army Group," 1:73.

59. Devers to Georgie, 7 December 1944, box 20, DP.

60. Ibid., 31 December 1944.

61. Message from Sixth Army Group to SHAEF, 14 December 1944, in "History of Headquarters Sixth Army Group," 1:72–73.

62. D'Este, *Eisenhower,* 641–49; Atkinson, *Guns at Last Light,* 439–41.

63. Eisenhower to Bradley and Devers, 18 December 1944, in *Eisenhower Papers,* vol. 4, message 2178.

64. SHAEF to Sixth Army Group, 20 December 1944, in "History of Headquarters Sixth Army Group," 1:75–77.

65. Crosswell, *Beetle,* 832.

66. Ibid., 811.

67. Ibid., 812, 816–17.

68. Sixth Army Group Letter of Instruction 5, 21 December 1944, in "History of Headquarters Sixth Army Group," 1:78–79.

69. *Seventh Army War Diaries,* 3:469–74, entries for 28–31 December 1944.

70. Franklin L. Gurley, "Policy vs. Strategy: The Defense of Strasbourg in Winter 1944–1945," *Journal of Military History* 58 (July 1994): 486–87; "History of Headquarters Sixth Army Group," 1:87; Atkinson, *Guns at Last Light,* 474.

71. Devers Diary, 26, 28, 29 December 1944.

72. Gurley, "Policy vs. Strategy," 486–88.

73. Ibid., 488, quoting from Blumenson, *Patton Papers, 1940–1945,* 2:599.

74. Devers Diary, 26 December 1944.

75. "History of Headquarters Sixth Army Group," 1:88.

76. Gurley, "Policy vs. Strategy," 489–90.

77. Ibid., 489.

78. Devers Diary, 27 December 1944.

79. Ibid.

80. "History of Headquarters Sixth Army Group," 1:89–93. A sketch map of

these three lines is in Sixth Army Group's Letter of Instruction 7, prepared on 20 December 1944. It was the basis for Seventh Army's defense plans, as described in ibid., 90.

81. Gurley, "Policy vs. Strategy," 490.

82. Ibid., 490–91.

83. Eisenhower to the CCS, 31 December 1944, in *Eisenhower Papers*, vol. 4, message 2209.

84. Gurley, "Policy vs. Strategy," 491.

85. Ibid., 492.

86. Devers, Sixth Army Group, to Eisenhower, SHAEF, 31 December 1944, in "History of Headquarters Sixth Army Group," 1:99–100.

87. Ibid., 101.

88. Weigley, *Eisenhower's Lieutenants*, 542–43; D'Este, *Eisenhower*, 654–56.

89. D'Este, *Eisenhower*, 655–56.

90. Ibid., 656–58; Weigley, *Eisenhower's Lieutenants*, 542–44.

91. Gurley, "Policy vs. Strategy," 493–94.

92. Crosswell, *Beetle*, 830–31; Atkinson, *Guns at Last Light*, 476.

93. Gurley, "Policy vs. Strategy," 494. For Devers's synopsis of discussions with SHAEF, 1–5 January 1945, see "Summary of Directions in Chronological Order Concerning Holding Strasbourg or Not Holding Strasbourg," Devers file, box 1, MHI.

94. Atkinson, *Guns at Last Light*, 476.

95. Devers to Georgie, 2 January 1945, box 22, DP; Wayne M. Dzwonchyk, "General Jacob L. Devers and the First French Army" (MA thesis, University of Maryland, 1975), 72.

96. Gurley, "Policy vs. Strategy," 495.

97. Dzwonchyk, "Devers and First French Army," 75; Coffman interview, 3 August 1971, 29.

98. Gurley, "Policy vs. Strategy," 497, 498.

99. Ibid., 500.

100. Ibid., 501–2; Crosswell, *Beetle,* 831 .

101. Gurley, "Policy vs. Strategy," 504–5; Crosswell, *Beetle*, 831–32.

102. Atkinson, *Guns at Last Light*, 480; Gurley, "Policy vs. Strategy," 505–6.

103. Gurley, "Policy vs. Strategy," 506–7.

104. Ibid., 507.

105. Eisenhower to Marshall, 6 January 1945, in *Eisenhower Papers*, vol. 4, message 2224.

106. Clarke and Smith, *Riviera to the Rhine*, 513–16. See map 14.5 for the divisions involved.

107. Devers Diary, 5 January 1945.

108. Clarke and Smith, *Riviera to the Rhine*, 522–23.

109. Ibid., 513–22; Final Report, G-3 Section, Sixth Army Group, 33–36.

110. Devers to Frank Devers, 6 January 1945, box 35056, Frank Devers Papers, YCHT.

111. Ibid.

112. Devers to Georgie, 8 January 1945, box 22, DP.

113. Major General Anthony McAuliffe oral history, tape 53, 10, box 20, DP.

114. Devers to Georgie, 18 January 1945, box 22, DP.

115. Final Report, G-3 Section, Sixth Army Group, 35; Clarke and Smith, *Riviera to the Rhine*, 526–27.

116. Final Report, G-3 Section, Sixth Army Group, 15.

117. Devers Diary, 17 January 1945.

118. Clarke and Smith, *Riviera to the Rhine*, 527.

119. G-1 After Action Report, January 1945, in "History of Headquarters Sixth Army Group," 1:157.

120. Devers Diary, 6 January 1945.

121. Draft letter of Lieutenant General Lee, 4 January 1945, in *Eisenhower Papers*, vol. 4, message 2218.

122. Eisenhower to Marshall, 7 January 1945, ibid., message 2227.

123. Lieutenant General Ben Lear, Deputy Theater Commander, to Devers, 10 February 1945, box 22, DP.

15. Victory in Europe

1. Eisenhower to Marshall, 12 January 1945, in *Eisenhower Papers*, vol. 4, message 2237.

2. Eisenhower to Marshall, 21 December 1944, ibid., message 2191.

3. Eisenhower to Marshall, 14 January 1945, ibid., message 2238; see fn. 1 for Marshall's message to Eisenhower.

4. Jonathan Seaman, "The Reduction of the Colmar Pocket: A 6th Army Group Operation," *Military Review* 31 (October 1951): 44; Clarke and Smith, *Riviera to the Rhine*, 537–38; Sixth Army Group's G-2 Weekly Intelligence Summary, week ending 13 January 1945, in "History of Headquarters Sixth Army Group," 1:130–31.

5. Final Report, G-3 Section, Sixth Army Group, 37.

6. Ibid.; Sixth Army Group Letter of Instruction 9, 18 January 1945, in "History of Headquarters Sixth Army Group," 1:134, 136–38.

7. Seaman, "Reduction of the Colmar Pocket," 46.

8. Ibid., 47; Devers Diary, 26 January 1945, MHI; Clarke and Smith, *Riviera to the Rhine*, 541–48.

9. Devers Diary, 27 January 1945. This was Eisenhower's only visit.

10. "History of Headquarters Sixth Army Group," 1:146. Devers was on the north flank of the pocket, while his chief of staff, Barr, was on the south flank.

11. Final Report, G-3 Section, Sixth Army Group, 37–40; Clarke and Smith, *Riviera to the Rhine*, 550–51.

12. Devers to Georgie, 9 February 1945, box 22, DP.

13. Extract of G-1 After Action Report for February 1945, in "History of Headquarters Sixth Army Group," 2:213.

14. Clarke and Smith, *Riviera to the Rhine*, 557.

15. "History of Headquarters Sixth Army Group," 2:159.

16. Devers to de Lattre, 9 February 1945; Devers to Brigadier General Gordon Saville, 21 February 1945; Devers to Brooks, 27 March 1945; Devers to Patch, 27 March 1945; Devers to Major General Frank Milburn, 27 March 1945, all in box 69, DP.

17. Devers to Georgie, 2 March 1945, box 22, DP.

18. Clarke and Smith, *Riviera to the Rhine*, 556.

19. Bradley memorandum for Eisenhower, 1 December 1944, box 4, GP.

20. Marshall to Eisenhower, 12 January 1945, box 22, DP.

21. Eisenhower memorandum, 1 February 1945, in *Eisenhower Papers*, vol. 4, message 2271.

22. John S. Guthrie to Jeffrey Clarke, 22 October 1988, box 4, GP.

23. Eisenhower to Marshall, 2 March 1945, in *Eisenhower Papers*, vol. 4, message 2307, fn. 1.

24. Eisenhower to Marshall, 2 March 1945, ibid., message 2307.

25. See footnotes to message 2238, ibid., for the order of promotions; Eisenhower to Devers, 14 March 1945, ibid., message 2337.

26. Eisenhower to Bradley, 14 March 1945, ibid., message 2336.

27. General William Simpson to Devers, 18 December 1954, box 61, DP. Simpson noted in his letter, "I don't believe I shall ever get over the disappointment I had over not receiving this promotion during or shortly after the war. . . . I talked to Sandy Patch several times in 1945 before he passed on about this and he felt rather keenly about it that he also had not been promoted."

28. Georgie to Kitts, 12 February 1945, box 22, DP.

29. Georgie to Kitts, 2 March 1945, ibid.

30. Devers to Georgie, 10 March 1945, ibid.

31. Charles MacDonald, *The Last Offensive* (Washington, DC: CMH, 1993), 5–6.

32. Eisenhower to the CCS, 20 January 1945, in *Eisenhower Papers*, vol. 4, message 2254.

33. Eisenhower to Bradley, 20 February 1945, ibid., message 2291.

34. Major General Sawbridge, G-1 Sixth Army Group, to Lieutenant General Ben Lear, 30 January 1945, 1–3, box 22, DP.

35. Eisenhower to Bradley, 20 February 1945, in *Eisenhower Papers*, vol. 4, message 2291.

36. MacDonald, *Last Offensive*, 136–83. By 9 March, Twenty-First Army Group was on the Rhine and preparing to cross.

37. Ibid., 185–210.

38. Final Report, G-3 Section, Sixth Army Group, 43.

39. "History of Headquarters Sixth Army Group," 2:168–70.

40. *Seventh Army Report of Operations*, 3:720; MacDonald, *Last Offensive*, 257–58.

41. Devers Diary, 17 March 1945.

42. MacDonald, *Last Offensive,* 259.

43. Devers to Georgie, 18 March 1945, box 22, DP.

44. "History of Headquarters Sixth Army Group," 2:163–64.

45. MacDonald, *Last Offensive,* 241–43.

46. Devers to Georgie, 21 March 1945, box 22, DP; "History of Headquarters Sixth Army Group," 2:225.

47. MacDonald, *Last Offensive,* 238.

48. "History of Headquarters Sixth Army Group," 3:290–317, provides a detailed narrative of the operation from inception to completion.

49. Ibid., 257.

50. Ibid., 317.

51. Ibid.

52. MacDonald, *Last Offensive,* 264–65.

53. Ibid., 266–89; John Turner and Robert Jackson, *Destination Berchtesgaden: The Story of the United States Seventh Army in World War II* (London: Ian Allan, 1975), 152–55.

54. *Seventh Army Report of Operations,* 3:738.

55. Devers to Georgie, 26 March 1945, box 22, DP.

56. *Seventh Army Report of Operations,* 3:735–36.

57. Ibid., 736–38.

58. Devers to Patch and de Lattre, 31 March 1945, box 22, DP.

59. Devers to the Commanders of Seventh Army, First Tactical Air Force, and Sixth Army Group Special Troops, 22 March 1945, ibid.

60. Final Report, G-3 Section, Sixth Army Group, 50–51; De Lattre, *History of French First Army,* 420–23.

61. For Sixth Army Group's Letter of Instruction 11 and the French crossing, see "History of Headquarters Sixth Army Group," 2:235–36, 238; Final Report, G-3 Section, Sixth Army Group, 50.

62. De Lattre, *History of French First Army,* 421.

63. Ibid., 423, 428.

64. Ibid., 430–37; Clayton, *Three Marshals of France,* 114–16.

65. Devers to de Lattre, 13 April 1945, box 23, DP.

66. "History of Headquarters Sixth Army Group," 2:246–47.

67. Ibid., 254.

68. SHAEF Order 261, 2 April 1945, in "History of Headquarters Sixth Army Group," 3:247–48; Eisenhower to his senior leaders, 2 April 1945, in *Eisenhower Papers,* vol. 4, message 2385.

69. Atkinson, *Guns at Last Light,* 576–80; Eisenhower to Montgomery, 8 April 1945, in *Eisenhower Papers,* vol. 4, message 2402.

70. Sixth Army Group Letter of Instruction 13, 3 April 1945, in "History of Headquarters Sixth Army Group," 3:248–50.

71. Devers to Georgie, 7 April 1945, box 23, DP.

72. Devers to Marshall, 3 April 1945, ibid.

73. Devers to Georgie, 12 April 1945, ibid.

74. Atkinson, *Guns at Last Light,* 596; G-1 Report for April 1945, in "History of Headquarters Sixth Army Group," 3:289. The French lost 2,135 soldiers as well.

75. Devers to Georgie, 14 April 1945, box 23, DP.

76. MacDonald, *Last Offensive,* 410–18; Turner and Jackson, *Destination Berchtesgaden,* 154–61.

77. Turner and Jackson, *Destination Berchtesgaden,* 166.

78. MacDonald, *Last Offensive,* 371–72.

79. Eisenhower to Senior Commanders, 15 April 1945, in *Eisenhower Papers,* vol. 4, message 2415.

80. "History of Headquarters Sixth Army Group," 3:264–65.

81. Ibid., 265–66.

82. MacDonald, *Last Offensive,* 422–24.

83. Ibid., 424–25; Turner and Jackson, *Destination Berchtesgaden,* 162–64.

84. "History of Headquarters Sixth Army Group," 3:265–66; Sixth Army Group Letter of Instruction 14, 16 April 1945, ibid., 266–69.

85. Ibid.

86. "History of Headquarters Sixth Army Group," 3:273.

87. De Lattre, *History of French First Army,* 458.

88. "History of Headquarters Sixth Army Group," 3:273.

89. Translation of a letter from de Lattre to Devers, 26 April 1945, box 23, DP.

90. Georgie to Kitts, 19 April 1945, ibid.

91. Translation of a letter from de Lattre to Devers, 26 April 1945.

92. Remarks dictated by General Devers on the morning of 27 April 1945, RG 331, box 38, NA, College Park, MD.

93. Devers Diary, 27 April 1945.

94. Atkinson, *Guns at Last Light,* 611.

95. "History of Headquarters Sixth Army Group," 3:281.

96. Eisenhower to de Gaulle, 28 April 1945, box 23, DP.

97. Eisenhower to de Gaulle, 28 April 1945, in *Eisenhower Papers,* vol. 4, message 2457, fn. 2.

98. De Lattre, *History of French First Army,* 491.

99. Ibid., 490.

100. Final Report, G-3 Section, Sixth Army Group, 57; MacDonald, *Last Offensive,* 431–32.

101. Atkinson, *Guns at Last Light,* 611.

102. G-2 Estimate of the Enemy Situation, 28 April 1945, in "History of Headquarters Sixth Army Group," 3:283.

103. Ibid., 284.

104. Sixth Army Group, G-1 After Action Report for April 1945, ibid., 289.

105. MacDonald, *Last Offensive,* 436–37.

106. Devers to Georgie, 4 May 1945, box 23, DP.

107. Ibid.

108. Quoted in Atkinson, *Guns at Last Light,* 612.

109. Turner and Jackson, *Destination Berchtesgaden,* 174. There is a photo

showing German soldiers lined up along a wall, with many Germans "feigning death after the Americans had fired a volley after a fleeing SS man" (ibid., 172).

110. Atkinson, *Guns at Last Light*, 612–13.

111. Quoted in ibid., 613.

112. Final Report, G-3 Section, Sixth Army Group, 61–63; MacDonald, *Last Offensive*, 440–42.

113. Devers to Georgie, 29 April 1945, box 23, DP.

114. MacDonald, *Last Offensive*, 440–41.

115. Ibid., 438–39.

116. *Seventh Army Report of Operations*, 3:840, 845.

117. MacDonald, *Last Offensive*, 442.

118. "History of Headquarters Sixth Army Group," 3:318–20.

119. Ibid., 320.

120. Ibid., 320–21.

121. Ibid., 322.

122. Ibid., 322–23.

123. Ibid., 323.

124. Ibid.

125. Ibid., 324.

126. MacDonald, *Last Offensive*, 474–75.

127. "Order of the Day by the Supreme Commander," in "History of Headquarters Sixth Army Group," 3:329.

128. H. Potter and staff, eds., *The First Year of the Occupation*, 3 vols. (Frankfurt, Germany: U.S. Army History, 1947), 1:62–69; Earl Ziemke, *The U.S. Army in the Occupation of Germany, 1944–1946* (Washington, DC: CMH, 1990), 239–42, 249–50, 284, 291; MacDonald, *Last Offensive*, 478, fn. 8.

129. Devers Diary, 5 May 1945.

130. Ziemke, *U.S. Army in the Occupation of Germany*, 163–65.

16. Postwar Challenges

1. Devers to Patch, 12 May 1945, 1, box 23, DP.

2. Quoted in Ziemke, *U.S. Army in the Occupation of Germany*, 328; Weigley, *History of the United States Army*, 485–86.

3. Ziemke, *U.S. Army in the Occupation of Germany*, 329–30.

4. "History of Headquarters Sixth Army Group," 3:345–46; Sixth Army Group press release, 22 May 1945, box 23, DP.

5. "History of Headquarters Sixth Army Group," 3:347–48.

6. Ibid., 345–47.

7. Devers to Patch, 1 June 1945, box 23, DP.

8. Patch to Devers, 1 June 1945, ibid.

9. Devers to de Lattre, 10 May 1945, 1–2, ibid.

10. English, *Patton's Peers*, 241–42.

11. Ibid., 242.

12. Smith, *Eisenhower in War and Peace,* 455–58. Eisenhower became chief of staff on 3 December 1945. Marshall retired briefly before Truman convinced him to become secretary of state.

13. Colonel Russell Reeder to Devers, 20 May 1945, box 19, DP.

14. Devers to Colonel Russell Reeder, 31 May 1945, ibid.

15. Devers's Memorial Day address, 30 May 1945, in "History of Headquarters Sixth Army Group," 3:362.

16. Ibid., 363. *Seventh Army Report of Operations,* 3:1029, lists 15,271 killed in action or died of wounds and 9,837 missing in action.

17. Marshall to Eisenhower, 7 May 1945, in Bland and Stevens, *Marshall Papers,* 5:169–70.

18. Ibid., 170.

19. Ibid., 177–78.

20. ETOUSA order, 20 June 1945.

21. Efficiency Report, n.d. (but signed before the end of June 1945), 1, 2, Devers Personnel File, NA, St. Louis, MO.

22. Markey, *Jake,* 92–94.

23. Eckenrode, "Story of Devers' Early Life," 12.

24. Medical Records for 1943–1945, Devers Personnel File, NA, St. Louis, MO.

25. War Department Order for Temporary Duty, 3 July 1945, to General Jacob L. Devers, ibid.

26. Georgie to Kitts, 12 July 1945, 2, box 35, DP.

27. Georgie to Kitts, 27 August 1945, 2, ibid.

28. Ibid., 3.

29. Weigley, *History of the United States Army,* 442–43; Perret, *There's a War to Be Won,* 66.

30. Ruppenthal, *Logistical Support of the Armies,* 1:131.

31. James Hewes, *From Root to McNamara: Army Organization and Administration, 1900–1963* (Washington, DC: CMH, 1975), 126–28; Weigley, *History of the United States Army,* 442–43.

32. Georgie to Kitts, 28 August 1945, 1, box 35, DP.

33. Ibid., 2.

34. Georgie to Kitts, 12 July 1945, box 35, DP.

35. Weigley, *History of the United States Army,* 485–86.

36. Georgie to Kitts, 12 July 1945.

37. Georgie to Kitts, 8 November 1945, box 35, DP.

38. Weigley, *History of the United States Army,* 485–88.

39. Griess-Harrison interview, tape 70, 41, box 8, GP.

40. Griess interview with Charles Bolte, tape 52, 11, box 10, GP.

41. Dorothy C. Ham, response to questions by Griess, circa 1964, 3, box 70, GP.

42. Interview with General Devers by the Simpson Board, 10 December 1945, 1–2, box 5, GP.

43. Devers to General Thomas Handy, 28 December 1945, box 10, DP.

44. Weigley, *History of the United States Army*, 487–88.

45. Ibid., 488; Hewes, *From Root to McNamara*, 137–58.

46. Interview with General Devers by the Simpson Board, 2.

47. Weigley, *History of the United States Army*, 486–87.

48. Ibid., 488–89; Hewes, *From Root to McNamara*, 158–62.

49. Hewes, *From Root to McNamara*, 162.

50. Eisenhower to Devers, 8 December 1945, 1, box 35, DP.

51. Ibid., 1–2.

52. "The Army Ground Forces Plan," 4 October 1946, 1, box 10, GP.

53. Ibid., 2.

54. Ibid., 3.

55. Ibid., 3–4.

56. Ibid., 4–5.

57. Ibid., 6–7.

58. Attachment to ibid. The attachment was prepared on 3 September 1946 to explain the details and rationale for branch consolidation.

59. J. L. Devers, "Discussion at Command and General Staff College, 2nd Command Class," 3 April 1946, 1, 2 MHI.

60. Oral history interview typescript, 92–94, box 3, Bruce C. Clarke Papers, MHI.

61. Bolte interview, July 1972, tape 52, 8, box 10, GP.

62. War Department Special Order 187, 27 August 1946, and Fort Monroe General Order 17, 1 October 1946, Devers Personnel File, NA, St. Louis, MO.

63. Georgie to Kitts, 27 August 1945, box 35, DP.

64. Georgie to Kitts, 13 August 1946, ibid.

65. Georgie to Kitts, 27 August 1946, ibid.

66. Georgie to Kitts, 14 October 1946, ibid.

67. Bonnie Hamstreet (nee Benn), telephone interview with the author, 9 August 2012.

68. Georgie to Kitts, 5 May 1947, box 35, DP.

69. Georgie to Kitts, 13 August 1946, ibid.

70. Georgie to Kitts, 20 July 1948, ibid.

71. Eisenhower to Devers, 28 April 1947; Devers to Eisenhower, 7 May 1947, box 10, GP.

72. Enclosure to Devers to Eisenhower, 7 May 1947, ibid.

73. Brigadier General George Butler to Devers, 25 August 1947, Devers Personnel File, NA, St. Louis, MO.

74. Devers to General Courtney Hodges, 20 May 1947, box 29, DP.

75. Devers to Lieutenant General J. Lawton Collins, 4 November 1947, box 10, GP.

76. Weigley, *History of the United States Army*, 502–3.

77. Devers to Eisenhower, 20 September 1947, 1, box 10, GP.

78. Ibid., 1–2.

79. Ibid., 3.

80. War Department study, "Dispatch of an Army–Air Force Task Force to Greece," 15 September 1947, box 10, GP.

81. War Department Plans and Operations Division memorandum, "Subject: Dispatch an Army–Air Force Task Force to Greece," 22 September 1947, ibid.

82. Norstad to Devers, "Subject: Dispatch of an Army–Air Force Task Force to Greece," 13 October 1947, 1–2, ibid.

83. Weigley, *History of the United States Army,* 498–500.

84. Ibid., 502.

85. Memorandum for General Handy from Devers, 11 May 1946, RG 165, entry 13, box 285, NA, College Park, MD.

86. John Norris, "Defense Experts Disagree on Economy—and on Atomic Weapons," *Washington Post,* 5 October 1947, sec. II, RG 165, entry 13, box 355, NA, College Park, MD.

87. Eisenhower to Devers, 6 October 1947, box 29, DP.

88. Marshall to Eisenhower, 4 September 1945, in Bland and Stevens, *Marshall Papers,* 5:192–93.

89. Marshall to Eisenhower, 16 May 1945, ibid.

90. Smith, *Eisenhower in War and Peace,* 455–56; Bradley and Blair, *A General's Life,* 439–40.

91. Catherine Devers interview, 11 February 1974, tape 61, 20, box 8, GP.

92. Fayetteville Chamber of Commerce to President Truman, 28 June 1947, Devers Personnel File, NA, St. Louis, MO.

93. Business and Professional Women's Club of Fayetteville, NC, to Truman, 1 July 1947, ibid.

94. Efficiency Report for 1 July to 31 December 1946, ibid.

95. Efficiency Report for 1 January to 30 June 1947, ibid.

96. Efficiency Report for 1 July 1947 to 6 February 1948, ibid.

97. Orders dated 3 July 1946 for the Joint Research and Development Committee, ibid.; Larry Bell to Devers, 16 July 1946, box 29, DP.

98. Bruce C. Clarke, "Yesterday," *Army Aviation Magazine,* February 1970, 23, box 35, DP.

99. Bell to Devers, 16 July 1946.

100. Devers to the Secretary of War, 18 September 1947, box 29, DP.

101. Senator Lodge to Senator Vandenberg, 11 November 1947, 3, ibid.

102. Hewes, *From Root to McNamara,* 166–67.

103. Millett and Maslowski, *For the Common Defense,* 503–4; Hewes, *From Root to McNamara,* 165.

104. Eisenhower quoted from a message to Congress, 5 April 1958, in Hewes, *From Root to McNamara,* 166.

105. Millett and Maslowski, *For the Common Defense,* 505.

106. Hewes, *From Root to McNamara,* 170–71.

107. Ibid., 168–69.

108. Ibid., 170, fn. 11, citing Devers to Eisenhower, 12 September 1947; ibid., 169, for Devers's recommendations.

109. Ibid., 168–71.

110. Devers to Major General Edward Witsell, 30 June 1948, 1, 2, Devers Personnel File, NA, St. Louis, MO.

111. Major General Edward Witsell to Devers, 14 July 1948, ibid.

112. Devers to Witsell, 30 June 1948, 2, ibid.

113. Officer Efficiency Report, 7 June 1948, ibid.

114. Officer Efficiency Report, 22 August 1949, ibid.

17. Retirement and Beyond

1. Georgie to Kitts, 7 September 1948, box 35, DP.

2. Dorothy Benn Ham interview, 7, box 70, DP; the interview was conducted in 1972 by Colonel Griess. The address of the Yellow House is 1430 Thirty-Third Street NW, Georgetown, Washington, DC.

3. Georgie to Kitts, 7 August 1948, box 35, DP.

4. Ibid., 5 June 1948.

5. Ibid., 12 November 1948.

6. Catherine Devers interview, tape 61, 21, box 8, GP.

7. Dwight D. Eisenhower, *Crusade in Europe* (New York: Doubleday, 1948), 394.

8. Bradley, *A Soldier's Story.*

9. Devers to Omar Bradley, 1 June 1951, box 32, DP.

10. Most notably, J. J. Pershing's *My Experiences in the World War,* Peyton March's *The Nation at War,* and Robert Lee Bullard's *Personalities and Reminiscences of the War.*

11. "Retirement of Gen. Jacob L. Devers," remarks of Hon. Henry Cabot Lodge Jr. of Massachusetts in the Senate of the United States, 3 August 1949, 2, Devers Personnel File, NA, St. Louis, MO.

12. Ibid., 2–3.

13. Physical Examination Report, 25–26 August 1949, Devers Personnel File.

14. Retirement, 2 September 1949, and Extract to Special Order 171, 1 September 1949, ibid.

15. Georgie to Kitts, 12 November 1948, 2, box 35, DP.

16. Dorothy Benn Ham interview, 10.

17. Mrs. Purdon Whitely to Kitts, 14 November 1949, box 48, DP.

18. Georgie to Kitts, 6 February 1952, 2, box 35, DP.

19. Griess-Murphy interview, 12 February 1974, 1–2, box 8, GP.

20. Ibid., 2–3.

21. Ibid, 4.

22. Ibid., 5.

23. Dorothy Benn Ham interview, 13.

24. Griess-Murphy interview, 9.

25. Ibid., 8.

26. Ibid., 13–14.

27. Major General L. D. Gasser (Ret.) to Devers, 29 October 1949, offering the position, box 48, DP; Mr. H. L. Bemis to Devers, 20 December 1949, thanking him for accepting the position, ibid.

28. Dorothy Benn Ham interview, 7.

29. Author's phone conversations with Bonnie Benn Hamstreet, 19 March 2014, 9 August 2012.

30. Ibid., 9 August 2012.

31. Dorothy Benn Ham interview, 12, 7, 11.

32. Ibid., 10.

33. Dorothy Benn Ham interview, 8, box 32, DP; this same interview is transcribed in box 70 as well.

34. Ibid.

35. Dorothy Benn Ham interview, 5, box 70, DP.

36. Ibid., 6.

37. Ibid., 8; Dorothy Benn Ham interview, 15, box 32.

38. R. S. Boutelle, President of the Fairchild Corporation, to All Divisional Managers, 18 March 1953, box 65, DP.

39. Devers's Employment Report to Congress for the Years 1951–1959, box 30, GP.

40. Devers to Colonel Jules Gonseth, 17 October 1955, box 61, DP. Devers discussed the new transport aircraft designated the C-123B by Fairchild, and he reported its "remarkable success" in landing and getting off of "soft fields."

41. Devers to Lieutenant General John Leonard, 12 February 1951, box 46, DP.

42. Devers to Brigadier General Bruce Clarke, 18 May 1951, ibid.

43. Devers to Dr. Vannevar Bush, 22 September 1953, box 65, DP.

44. Dorothy Benn Ham interview, 8, box 70; ibid., 15, box 32.

45. Armalite Inc., *A Historical Review of Armalite* (Geneseo, IL: Armalite, 2010), 1–3.

46. Devers to Lieutenant General Bruce Clarke, 18 August 1958, box 65, DP.

47. Ibid., 6 July 1959.

48. Armalite, *Historical Review of Armalite,* 3–4.

49. Dorothy Benn Ham interview, 8, box 70.

50. Ibid., 9.

51. Ibid.

52. Devers to L. C. Herkness, 1956, 1, box 65, DP.

53. Devers interview, tape 13, 8, box 32, DP.

54. Devers to Georgie, 1 July 1951, 1–2, box 40, DP.

55. Ibid., 2.

56. Devers interview, tape 13, 8, box 32, DP.

57. Georgie to Kitts, 31 October 1951, box 35, DP.

58. Devers to Lou Holland, 3 January 1952, box 69, DP; Georgie to Kitts, 19 November 1951, box 35, DP.

59. Georgie to Kitts, 16 August 1951, box 35, DP.

60. Devers to Holland, 3 January 1952.

61. Smith, *Eisenhower in War and Peace,* 508.

62. Ibid., 503–8.

63. Ibid., 509.

64. Georgie to Kitts, 6 February 1952, box 35, DP.

65. Devers to Philip Glatfelter, 23 January 1952, box 46, DP.

66. Robert McLaughlin to Devers, 25 April 1952, ibid. McLaughlin thanked Devers for the contribution.

67. Devers to Lodge, 12 June 1953, box 65, DP.

68. Devers to Eisenhower, 11 October 1955, box 61, DP.

69. Devers to Mr. L. C. Herkness, 18 September 1956, 2, box 65, DP.

70. Ibid.

71. Markey, *Jake,* 103–5.

72. Major General C. K. Gailey to Devers, 23 December 1959, box 49, DP. Gailey congratulated Devers on his appointment.

73. Record of Proceedings of the American Battlefield Monuments Commission, 7 June 1968, box 69, DP.

74. Georgie to Kitts, 6 September 1960, 2, box 35, DP.

75. Ibid.

76. Ibid.

77. Ibid., 1.

78. Devers to L. C. Herkness, 6 August 1962, box 49, DP.

79. Ibid., 30 October 1962.

80. Ibid., 13 June 1963.

81. Markey, *Jake,* 105–6.

82. *Joint Exercise Desert Strike,* Big Picture TV series, 1964.

83. Devers to Georgie, 17 May 1964, box 35, DP.

84. Ibid.

85. Ibid., 20 May 1964.

86. Ibid., 25 June 1964.

87. Griess-Murphy interview, tape 62, 10, box 8, GP.

88. Ibid.

89. Dorothy Benn Ham to the Deverses, the Fifth Day of Christmas, 1966, box 35, DP.

90. Griess-Murphy interview, tape 63, 11, box 8, GP.

91. Dorothy Benn Ham interview, 13–14, box 70.

92. Ibid.

93. Lieutenant General Leonard Heaton, Surgeon General, to Devers, 2 March 1967, Devers Personnel File.

94. Dorothy Benn Ham to Devers, 26 September 1970, box 35, DP.

95. Dorothy Benn Ham interview, 14, box 70.

96. Griess-Murphy interview, tape 63, 12–13, 14–15.

97. Ibid., 17–19.

98. Dorothy Benn Ham interview, 15–16, box 70.

99. Author's phone conversation with Bonnie Hamstreet, 10 April 2014; obituary for Dorothy Catherine Cardwell Benn Ham Devers, October 2007.

100. Annual Physical Examination, 10 November 1975, Devers Personnel File.

101. Markey, *Jake,* 112.

102. Medical Record, 10 November 1975, Devers Personnel File.

103. Dr. Robert W. Enquist, Major Medical Corps, to Devers, 4 December 1975, ibid.

104. Medical Records for January–May 1976, ibid.

105. Medical Record for 26 May 1977, ibid.

106. Medical Record for 19 May 1977, ibid.; Wikipedia entry for "Cheyne-Stokes"; author's telephonic discussion with Dr. J. J. H. Schwarz, Battle Creek, MI, 13 April 2014.

107. Medical Records for 19 May and 13 June 1977, Devers Personnel File.

108. Medical Record for 3–18 January 1978, ibid.

Selected Bibliography

Books and Articles

Alexander, Field Marshal, and John North, eds. *The Alexander Memoirs, 1940–1945*. New York: McGraw-Hill, 1962.

Ambrose, Stephen. *The Supreme Commander: The War Years of General Dwight D. Eisenhower*. Garden City, NY: Doubleday, 1970.

Anderschat, Richard W. *Factors Affecting Success in Coalition Command*. Carlisle, PA: U.S. Army War College, 1986.

Army Ground Forces Historical Section. *The History of the Armored Force, Command and Center*. Study no. 27, 1946.

Arnold, H. H. *Global Mission*. New York: Harper and Brothers, 1949.

Atkinson, Rick. *An Army at Dawn: The War in North Africa, 1942–1943*. New York: Henry Holt, 2002.

———. *The Day of Battle: The War in Sicily and Italy, 1943–1944*. New York: Henry Holt, 2007.

———. *The Guns at Last Light: The War in Western Europe, 1944–1945*. New York: Henry Holt, 2013.

Axelrod, Alan. *Bradley: A Biography*. New York: Palgrave Macmillan, 2008.

Badsey, Stephen. *Into the Reich: Battles on Germany's Western Front, 1944–1945*. 1993. Reprint, London: Osprey, 2002.

Betros, Lance. *Carved from Granite: West Point since 1902*. College Station: Texas A&M University Press, 2012.

———, ed. *West Point: Two Centuries and Beyond*. Abilene, TX: McWhiney Foundation Press, 2004.

Biographical Register of the Officers and Graduates of the United States Military Academy. Vol. 8. Chicago: Lakeside Press, 1940.

Bishop, Harry G. "The Trend of Field Artillery." *Field Artillery Journal*, March–April 1931, 116–38.

Bland, Larry, ed. *George C. Marshall: Interviews and Reminiscences for Forrest C. Pogue*. Lexington, VA: George C. Marshall Foundation, 1996.

Bland, Larry, and Sharon Ritenour Stevens, eds. *The Papers of George Catlett Marshall*. 5 vols. Baltimore: Johns Hopkins University Press, 1981–2003.

Blumenson, Martin. *Patton: The Man behind the Legend, 1885–1945*. New York: William Morrow, 1985.

———. *Salerno to Cassino*. Washington, DC: CMH, 2002.

———, ed. *The Patton Papers, 1885–1940*. Boston: Houghton Mifflin, 1972.

———. *The Patton Papers, 1940–1945*. New York: Houghton Mifflin, 1974.

Bonn, Keith. *When the Odds Were Even*. New York: Ballantine Books, 2006.

Bradley, Omar. *A Soldier's Story*. New York: Henry Holt, 1951.

Bradley, Omar, and Clay Blair. *A General's Life: An Autobiography by General of the Army Omar Bradley.* New York: Simon and Schuster, 1983.

Brooke, Alan. *War Diaries of Alan Brooke, 1939–1945.* Edited by Alex Danchev and Daniel Todman. Berkeley: University of California Press, 2001.

Brown, Matthew. *Strategic Leadership Assessment of General Jacob L. Devers.* USAWC Strategy Research, 2001.

Butcher, Harry C. *My Three Years with Eisenhower: The Personal Diary of Captain Harry C. Butcher, USNR, Naval Aide to General Eisenhower, 1942–1945.* New York: Simon and Schuster, 1946.

Chandler, Alfred, ed. *The Papers of Dwight David Eisenhower: The War Years.* 5 vols. Baltimore: Johns Hopkins University Press, 1970.

Churchill, Winston. *The History of the Second World War: Their Finest Hour.* New York: Bantam Books, 1962.

Clarke, Jeffrey J., and Robert R. Smith. *Riviera to the Rhine.* Washington, DC: CMH, 1993.

Clayton, Anthony. *Three Marshals of France: Leadership after Trauma.* London: Brassey's, 1992.

Coakley, Robert, and Richard Leighton. *Global Logistics and Strategy, 1943–1945.* Washington, DC: CMH, 1968.

Coffin, Robert E., and David D. Scott. "Operation Dragoon: A Forging of Allies." *Army* 44, no. 8 (1994): 40–50.

Coffman, Edward M. *The Regulars: The American Army, 1898–1941.* Cambridge, MA: Belknap Press of Harvard University Press, 2004.

———. *The War to End All Wars: The American Experience in World War I.* Lexington: University Press of Kentucky, 1998.

Cole, Hugh. *The Ardennes: The Battle of the Bulge.* Washington, DC: CMH, 1965.

———. *The Lorraine Campaign.* Washington, DC: CMH, 1984.

Colley, David. *Decision at Strasbourg: Ike's Strategic Mistake to Halt Sixth Army Group at the Rhine in 1944.* Annapolis, MD: Naval Institute Press, 2008.

Cooke, James. *Pershing and His Generals.* Westport, CT: Praeger, 1997.

Crackle, Theodore. *West Point: A Bicentennial History.* Lawrence: University Press of Kansas, 2002.

Craven, Wesley, and James Cate, eds. *The Army Air Forces in World War II: Europe: Argument to V-E Day, January 1944 to May 1945.* Chicago: University of Chicago Press, 1951.

———. *The Army Air Forces in World War II: Europe: Torch to Pointblank, August 1942 to December 1943.* Chicago: University of Chicago Press, 1949.

Cray, Ed. *General of the Army: George C. Marshall, Soldier and Statesman.* 1990. Reprint, New York: Cooper Square Press, 2000.

Crosswell, D. K. R. *Beetle: The Life of Walter Bedell Smith.* Lexington: University Press of Kentucky, 2010.

Dastrup, Boyd. *King of Battle: A Branch History of the U.S. Army's Field Artillery.* Fort Monroe, VA: U.S. Army Training and Doctrine Command, 1992.

DeFelice, Jim. *Omar Bradley: General at War.* Washington, DC: Regnery, 2001.

De Lattre de Tassigny, Jean. *The History of the French First Army.* Trans. Malcolm Barnes. London: George Allen and Unwin, 1952.

D'Este, Carlo. *Eisenhower: A Soldier's Life.* New York: Henry Holt, 2002.

Devers, Jacob L. "Airtransportability of the Infantry Division." *Military Review* 29, no. 1 (April 1949): 14–18.

———. "Artillery Integration." *Field Artillery Journal,* September–October 1947, 303.

———. "Devers's Remarks to the Armor Association." *Armor,* March–April 1953, 16–21.

———. Introduction to Hanson Baldwin, *Tiger Jack: Major General John S. Wood.* Fort Collins, CO: Old Army Press, 1979.

———. "Major Problems of a Theater Commander in Combined Operations." *Military Review* 27 (October 1947): 3–15.

———. "The Mark of the Man on USMA." *Assembly* 23 (Spring 1964).

———. "Operation Dragoon: The Invasion of Southern France." *Military Affairs* 10, no. 2 (1946): 3–41.

———. "Tactical Notes from the Italian Campaign." *Military Review* 24, no. 7 (October 1944): 3–8.

Doubler, Michael. *I Am the Guard: A History of the Army National Guard, 1636–2000.* Washington, DC: Department of the Army, 2001.

Doughty, Robert. *The Breaking Point: Sedan and the Fall of France, 1940.* Hamden, CT: Archon Books, 1990.

Dzwonchyk, Wayne M. "General Jacob L. Devers and the First French Army." MA thesis, University of Maryland, 1975.

Eisenhower, David. *Eisenhower at War, 1943–1945.* New York: Random House, 1986.

Eisenhower, Dwight D. *Crusade in Europe.* New York: Doubleday, 1948.

Eisenhower, S. D. *Yanks: The Epic Story of the American Army in World War I.* New York: Free Press, 2001.

English, John A. *Patton's Peers: The Forgotten Allied Field Army Commanders of the Western Front, 1944–1945.* Mechanicsburg, PA: Stackpole Books, 2009.

Fisher, Ernest. *Cassino to the Alps.* Washington, DC: CMH, 2002.

Frieser, Karl-Heinz. *The Blitzkrieg Legend: The 1940 Campaign in the West.* Annapolis, MD: Naval Institute Press, 2005.

Gabel, Christopher. *The U.S. Army GHQ Maneuvers of 1941.* 1991. Reprint, Washington, DC: CMH, 1992.

Ganoe, William. *MacArthur: Close-up.* New York: Vantage Press, 1962.

Garland, Albert, and Howard McGraw Smyth. *Sicily and the Surrender of Italy.* Washington, DC: CMH, 2002.

Gilbert, Martin. *Winston S. Churchill: Road to Victory, 1941–1945.* London: Heinemann, 1986.

Greenfield, Kent, Robert R. Palmer, and Bell I. Wiley. *The Army Ground Forces: The Organization of Ground Combat Troops.* Washington, DC: CMH, 1987.

Gurley, Franklin L. "Policy vs. Strategy: The Defense of Strasbourg in Winter 1944–1945." *Journal of Military History* 58 (July 1994): 481–514.

Hamilton, Nigel. *Monty, Master of the Battlefield*. London: Hamish Hamilton, 1983.

Harrison, Gordon. *Cross-Channel Attack*. Washington, DC: CMH, 1951.

Hastings, Max. *Armageddon: The Battle for Germany, 1944–1945*. New York: Random House, 2005.

———. *Winston's War: Churchill, 1940–1945*. New York: Alfred A. Knopf, 2010.

Heefner, Wilson. *Dogface Soldier: The Life of General Lucian K. Truscott, Jr.* Columbia: University of Missouri Press, 2010.

Hewes, James. *From Root to McNamara: Army Organization and Administration, 1900–1963*. Washington, DC: CMH, 1975.

Hobbs, Joseph P., ed. *Dear General: Eisenhower's Wartime Letters to Marshall*. 1971. Reprint, Baltimore: Johns Hopkins University Press, 1999.

Howe, George. *Northwest Africa: Seizing the Initiative in the West*. Washington, DC: CMH, 2002.

James, D. Clayton. *The Years of MacArthur*. Vol. 1, *1880–1941*. Boston: Houghton Mifflin, 1970.

Jenkins, Reuben. *Report to the General Board, European Theater of Operations: Operation of 6th Army Group Headquarters*. October 1946.

Kennedy, David M. *Freedom from Fear: The American People in Depression and War, 1929–1945*. New York: Oxford University Press, 1999.

Langford, James R. "Jacob Devers and the American Thunderbolt." *Army History* (Winter 2011): 34–41.

Lee, Ulysses. *The Employment of Negro Troops*. Washington, DC: CMH, 2000.

Linn, Brian M. *Guardians of Empire: The U.S. Army and the Pacific, 1902–1940*. Chapel Hill: University of North Carolina Press, 1997.

MacDonald, Charles. *The Last Offensive*. Washington, DC: CMH, 1993.

———. *The Siegfried Line Campaign*. 1963. Reprint, Washington, DC: CMH, 1990.

MacGregor, Morris J., Jr. *Integration of the Armed Forces, 1940–1965*. Washington, DC: CMH, 2001.

Markey, Michael. *Jake: The General from West York Avenue*. York, PA: Historical Society of York County, 1998.

———. "Quartermaster to Victory." *Army* 44, no. 8 (1994): 51–52.

Matloff, Maurice, and Edwin Snell. *Strategic Planning for Coalition Warfare, 1941–1942*. Washington, DC: CMH, 1999.

———. *Strategic Planning for Coalition Warfare, 1943–1944*. Washington, DC: CMH, 1994.

Mead, Gary. *The Doughboys: America and the First World War*. New York: Overlook Press, 2002.

Millett, Allan, and Peter Maslowski. *For the Common Defense: A Military History of the United States of America*. New York: Free Press, 1994.

Mittelman, Joseph B. *Eight Stars to Victory: A History of the Veteran Ninth U.S. Infantry Division*. Columbus, OH: Heer and Terry, 1948.

Molony, C. J. C. *History of the Second World War: The Mediterranean and Middle East*.

Vol. 5, pt. 2, *The Campaign in Sicily 1943 and the Campaign in Italy, 3rd September 1943 to 31st March 1944.* Uckfield, UK: Naval and Military Press, 2004.

Morrison, Samuel Elliot. *The Invasion of France and Germany, 1944–1945.* Boston: Little, Brown, 1957.

Nenninger, Timothy, ed. *The Way of Duty, Honor, Country: The Memoir of General Charles Pelot Summerall.* Lexington: University Press of Kentucky, 2010.

Official Register of the Officers and Cadets of the U.S.M.A., June 1906. West Point, NY: USMA Press, 1906.

Olson, Lynne. *Citizens of London: The Americans Who Stood with Britain in Its Darkest, Finest Hour.* New York: Random House, 2010.

Perret, Geoffrey. *There's a War to Be Won: The United States Army in World War II.* New York: Ivy Books, 1991.

Pogue, Forrest C. *George C. Marshall: Education of a General, 1880–1939.* New York: Viking Press, 1963.

———. *George C. Marshall: Ordeal and Hope, 1939–1942.* 1965. Reprint, New York: Viking Press, 1966.

———. *George C. Marshall: Organizer of Victory, 1943–1945.* New York: Viking Press, 1973.

———. *The Supreme Command.* 1954. Reprint, Washington, DC: CMH, 1989.

Porch, Douglas. *The Path to Victory: The Mediterranean Theater in World War II.* New York: Farrar, Straus and Giroux, 2004.

Potter, H., and staff, eds. *The First Year of the Occupation.* 3 vols. Frankfurt, Germany: U.S. Army History, 1947.

Rawson, Andrew. *Eyes Only: The Top Secret Correspondence between Marshall and Eisenhower.* Stroud, UK: Spellmount, 2012.

Ruppenthal, Roland G. *Logistical Support of the Armies.* 2 vols. Washington, DC: CMH, 1995.

Rusiecki, Stephen. *In Final Defense of the Reich: The Destruction of the 6th SS Mountain Division "Nord."* Annapolis, MD: Naval Institute Press, 2010.

Schifferle, Peter. *America's School for War: Fort Leavenworth, Officer Education, and Victory in World War II.* Lawrence: University Press of Kansas, 2010.

Seaman, Jonathan. "The Reduction of the Colmar Pocket: A 6th Army Group Operation." *Military Review* 31 (October 1951): 37–50.

Seventh United States Army Report of Operations: Seventh Army 1944–1945. 3 vols. Heidelberg, Germany: Aloys Graf, 1946.

Smith, Jean Edward. *Eisenhower in War and Peace.* New York: Random House, 2012.

Smith, Walter Bedell. *Eisenhower's Six Great Decisions.* New York: Longmans, 1956.

Smythe, Donald. *Pershing: General of the Armies.* Bloomington: Indiana University Press, 1986.

Stimson, Henry L., and McGeorge Bundy. *On Active Service in Peace and War.* New York: Harper and Brothers, 1947.

Stoller, Mark. *George C. Marshall: Soldier-Statesman of the American Century.* New York: Simon and Schuster, 1989.

Summerall, Charles P. "Field Artillery Progress." *Field Artillery Journal* (November–December 1930): 604–8.

Sunderland, Riley. *History of the Field Artillery School, 1911–1942.* Fort Sill, OK, n.d.

Sweet, Morris. *Fort Sill: A History.* Fort Sill, OK: n.p., 1921.

Taaffe, Stephen R. *Marshall and His Generals: U.S. Army Commanders in World War II.* Lawrence: University Press of Kansas, 2011.

Truscott, Lucian. *Command Missions: A Personal Story.* New York: Dutton, 1954.

Tuchman, Barbara. *Stilwell and the American Experience in China, 1911–1945.* New York: Macmillan, 1970.

Turner, John, and Robert Jackson. *Destination Berchtesgaden: The Story of the United States Seventh Army in World War II.* London: Ian Allen, 1975.

Vigneras, Marcel. *Rearming the French.* 1957. Reprint, Washington, DC: CMH, 1989.

Wedemeyer, Albert C. *Wedemeyer Reports!* New York: Henry Holt, 1958.

Weigley, Russell. *The American Way of War.* New York: Macmillan, 1973.

———. *Eisenhower's Lieutenants: The Campaigns of France and Germany, 1944–1945.* 1974. Reprint, Bloomington: Indiana University Press, 1990.

———. *History of the United States Army.* New York: Macmillan, 1967.

Wheeler, James Scott. *The Big Red One: America's Legendary 1st Infantry Division from World War I to Desert Storm.* Lawrence: University Press of Kansas, 2007.

Whiting, Charles. *America's Forgotten Army: The Story of the U.S. Seventh.* Rockville Centre, NY: Sarpedon, 1999.

Wittels, David. *These Are the Generals.* New York: Alfred A. Knopf, 1941.

Wyant, William K. *Sandy Patch: A Biography of Lt. Gen. Alexander M. Patch.* New York: Praeger, 1991.

Yiede, Harry, and Mark Stout. *First to the Rhine: The Sixth Army Group in World War II.* St. Paul, MN: Zenith Press, 2007.

Archival Sources

British National Archives, London
War Office Files
WO 32/10858: Wilson's dispatches, 16 February 1943–8 January 1944.

WO 204/27: Operation Anvil papers, including an index of correspondence related to it.

WO 204/315: AFHQ—Ground defense, organization of command, and movement of French forces in the Mediterranean and Africa, 10 February–26 July 1943.

WO 204/1047: AFHQ, July 1943–June 1944, training of French forces.

WO 214/15 and 214/16: correspondence between Alexander, Wilson, and Churchill, 1944.

Eisenhower Library, Abilene, Kansas
Robb, Air Marshal J. M. Notes from meetings of supreme commander, 1944–1945.

Library of Congress, Washington, DC
Patton, George S., Papers.

Massachusetts Historical Society
Lodge, Henry Cabot, Jr., Papers

Military History Institute, Carlisle, Pennsylvania
Davidson, Garrison H. *Grandpa Gar: The Saga of One Soldier as Told to His Grand-children.* 1974.
Devers, Jacob. Diary, 1943–1945.
———. "Discussion at Command and General Staff College, 2nd Command Class." 3 April 1946.
———. "Major Problems Confronting a Theater Commander in Combined Operations." 1947.
———. "Problems of Combined Planning." Presentation to U.S. Forces Staff College, Norfolk, VA, 10 May 1948.
Haislip, Wade, Papers.
Hanson, Chester B. "War Diaries, 20 February–1 October 1944." Chester B. Hanson Collection, box 4.
Jenkins, Reuben, Papers.
Lee, J. C. H. *Service Reminiscences of Lt. Gen. John C. H. Lee, U.S. Army Retired.* Mimeographed typescript with handwritten corrections.
Lucas, John P. "From Algiers to Anzio," 28 October 1948. John P. Lucas Papers.
Moses, Raymond, Collection.
OCMH interviews by Forrest Pogue:
Interview with Albert Kenner, surgeon for the Armored Force, Fort Knox, 1941–1942.
Interview with Major General Ray W. Barker, COSSAC planner, 1943–1944.
Interview with Alphonse Juin, 6 December 1946.
Interview with Walter Bedell Smith, 13 May 1947.
Interview with Colonel Ford Tremble, SGS SHAEF, 17 December 1947.
Interview with Major General Robert W. Crawford, G-4, SHAEF, 5 May 1948.
O'Daniel, John W., Papers.
"Preparation for the Defense of the Town of Strasbourg in the Year 1944 and the Battle for Strasbourg (23–25 November 1944)." Ms. B-545.
Quinn, William, Papers.
Reschke, Kurt. "The LXXXIX Corps in Operation Nordwind, 14–23 January 1945." Ms. B-826.
Sixth Army Group Record of Progress, 02–6, 1945/3.
"Summary of Directions in Chronological Order Concerning Holding Strasbourg or Not Holding Strasbourg," 3 January 1945. CMH Papers.
Ward, Orlando, Papers.

National Archives, College Park, Maryland
RG 107
RG 159
RG 165
RG 319
RG 331
RG 337
RG 407
RG 492
RG 498

National Archives, St. Louis, Missouri
Personnel file of General Jacob L. Devers.

U.S. Military Academy, West Point, New York
"Abstract of Delinquencies," 1905–1909.
Athletic Board proceedings, 1934–1939.
Orders and memos, U.S. Corps of Cadets, 1920–1924.
Patch, Alexander, Papers.

York County Heritage Trust, York, Pennsylvania
Devers, Jacob, Papers.
Griess, Thomas, Papers.

Index

Numbered military units are listed in alphabetical order, as if spelled out. For example, *14th Infantry Regiment* appears before *4th Armored Division*.

reading completed 1/15/15 BFf